Soldiers of Florida

in the

Seminole Indian-Civil

and

Spanish-American Wars.

Prepared and published under the supervision of the

Board of State Institutions,

As authorized by Chapter 2203 Laws
of Florida, approved May 14, 1903.

This volume was reproduced
from a personal copy located in
the Publishers private library

Please direct all correspondence and book orders to:
SOUTHERN HISTORICAL PRESS, Inc.
PO Box 1267
Greenville, SC   29602-1267

Preface.

For a number of years it has been evident that steps should be taken to put in permanent form the rolls of Florida's soldiers, if the names of these men were to be recorded in history and the memory of their honorable service preserved to future generations. Attempts by camps of Confederate Veterans to secure and preserve the rolls known to be in existence met with indifferent success. R. E. Lee Camp No. 59, of Jacksonville, was one of the most successful to gather up any appreciable number of rolls, but unfortunately these, with all the other archives and relics of the War Between the States, were destroyed in the great fire of 1901. This irreparable loss seemingly impressed on the minds of the Legislature the importance of gathering up and putting into shape such records as still remained. The result was the passage in 1903 of the following act, introduced by Mr. Long of Bradford, and known as Chapter 5203, Laws of Florida.

CHAPTER 5203

An Act to compile a History of the Soldiers of Florida serving in the Indian, Mexican, Spanish-American and War Between the States, Containing a Roster of the Soldiers Engaged in the Several Wars, with all Records Appertaining Thereto.

Be it Enacted by the Legislature of the State of Florida:

Sec. 1. That the Governor of the State of Florida be and he is hereby authorized to secure the publication of one thousand copies in book form of the complete roster of each company by name and name of all the regiments furnished by Florida in the Indian, Mexican, Spanish-American and the late War between the States, to contain a complete roster of what regiment each company served in, with the regimental officers and staff, with dates of service, what brigade, and battles said regiments took part in, with casualties, name, rank and date of same. Also with what army each regiment served.

Sec. 2. That the said compilation shall be as near as possible a complete history of service as can be obtained from the rolls now in the possession of the State, in the War Department at Washington and elsewhere. The said compilation to be begun as soon as practicable and be continued until such history is complete; the printing and binding to be done under the direction of the Board of State Institutions. And the publication when completed shall be under control of the Governor, who in his discretion shall furnish free of cost to the colleges, seminaries, schools and public libraries of the State, each a copy; and to exchange for similar publications from other

States; and be authorized to sell copies to those wanting them at a sufficient sum to cover the cost of publication.

Sec. 3. That there shall be appropriated the sum of five thousand dollars ($5,000) out of any money in the Treasury not otherwise appropriated, to meet the expense of compiling the roster, and the Comptroller be, and he is required to draw his warrant on the State Treasurer for the above amount for the above purpose; provided, however, that no appointment shall be made by the Governor nor any action whatever taken hereunder until the Governor shall have ascertained and reported in writing to the Board of State Institutions that the work contemplated by this Act can be properly done for the sum of five thousand dollars or less.

Sec. 4. This Act to take effect upon its passage and approval by the Governor.

Approved May 14, 1903.

The proviso in Section 3 caused me to hesitate some time before taking any steps to have the work done. I fully realized the task set before me and the responsibility attached thereto. The difficulties in the way of making a complete record were almost insurmountable, but neglect to put the law into execution was to lose the one opportunity ever presented to preserve the names and records of many gallant men to whom the State owed at least the inscription of their names and service on her rolls in such shape that posterity might know the men who willingly offered at her command all they had to give.

Every day's delay added to the difficulties already thickly gathered around the subject. Old age was dulling the minds and weakening the memory of the men who half century ago answered so blithely the State's call for service. Fire, mold, insects and vermin with the ravages of time were rapidly destroying the written records and death in his relentless march was daily removing the actors in the great tragedy If the work so necessary, was to be done at all, it must be done at once.

The number of years that had elapsed since the close of the war, the fact that for several years immediately following its close the State had been in the hands of men hostile to the South, anxious to break down its traditions and blot out its story, added immensely to the difficulties that must be surmounted. No one connected with this compilation anticipated for a moment an approach to perfection; on the contrary errors and inaccuracies were looked forward to as inevitable, but the surest way to correct an error and reach the truth is to publish to the world the evidence at hand, then, those in possession of the information will come forward and correct the errors that may exist. If the imperfect record is not published the errors may never be discovered and justice not be done.

Taking this, the only reasonable vi w of the matter, the Board of State Institutions ordered the work published.

It has been a matter of surprise that after all these years so many documents have escaped destruction, and when the mind runs back and the burned rolls of three years ago and the books and documents, known to have existed in other parts of the State, but now lost, are recalled, it is equally a matter of great regret that the work has been so long delayed.

In the progress of the compilation several thousand letters have been written to survivors asking for certain information, later printed forms were sent out requiring only a few minutes time to fill out. Many answered fully all the questions asked and gave in detail the information required, taking considerable trouble to substantiate all the statements made. Great effort has been put forth to get at the true record in every instance and where has been failure, it is owing to inability to find those possessing the desired knowledge.

All the names and dates published are taken from old muster rolls, official documents or are derived from sources deemed reliable. Advantage has been taken of every available source of information to ensure as far as possible the correctness of these records, but in spite of every effort errors have crept in and for lack of proper evidence much that should be incorporated in the compilation has been of necessity omitted.

This compilation puts in compact, permanent form all the records now held by the State and the information that has been gathered during the progress of the work. In this shape existing errors can readily be detected and corrected and omissions supplied; something hitherto impossible because the errors and omissions could not be known to exist. Out of these corrections of the published rolls will grow the perfect work that must supply one of the most interesting chapters in the history of Florida.

W. S. JENNINGS,
Governor.

Soldiers of the Seminole Indian War 1835-1843, and the Mexican War.

Owing to the rules of the War Department in Washington, it is impossible to get the names of the men who served in the Seminole Wars of 1835-43, and the War with Mexico, and the survivors of these wars who still live in Florida are unable to furnish the information needed for the purpose of this work. The reason given by the Department for issuing the order that stands in the way of procuring these names is as follows: "The muster rolls and other records of individual officers and enlisted men and organizations which are on file in the Record and Pension Office of this Department, and which pertain to the War of the Rebellion, the Mexican War, the various Indian Wars, the War of 1812, and the War of the Revolution, have become so delapidated through years of constant handling or other causes, that it has been found necessary to adopt stringent measures for their preservation, and to restrict reference to them to cases to which such reference is absolutely necessary." This order bears date of 1897.

The records show that in the Seminole Wars of 1835-43, the force employed is reported as 10,169 regulars and 29,953 volunteers. The casualties reported were 18 regular officers and 310 men killed, 20 regular officers and 270 men wounded; of the volunteers 5 officers and 50 men were killed, and 24 officers and 234 men were wounded. What proportion of the volunteers were enlisted from Florida cannot be stated for the reasons given above.

In the Mexican War Florida had about three companies.

Florida in the Indian War.

The depredation of the Indians upon the stock of the people of South Florida and persistent violation of all their agreements on the part of certain members of the Seminole Tribe created such a great degree of distrust of their intention that Governor Brown was compelled early in 1852 to take cognizance of the existing situation.

A. Jernigan reported on the 19th of January, 1852, that he had seen abundance of Indian sign on the St. Johns River below Lake Poinsett. That he had found fresh beef bones near their camp and that the Mail-rider from Tampa reported that he saw the light of their fires on each side of the road on the previous night. Captain Jernigan further reported that he had raised a company in obedience to the instructions of the Governor, and that he would thoroughly examine the whole country, protect the frontier and assist in moving the Indians. On February 29th, 1852, Governor Brown wrote to

General B. Hopkins at Mellonville, Fla., as follows: " I find from the letters I have received, that there is great alarm and excitement among the people on the frontier on account of the movement of the Indians; if you think there is good cause for alarm and that the situation of the people on the frontier is insecure, you will organize, as provided by the general Militia Law by this State, a sufficient force for their protection, and take command of it, and such steps as may be required for its assistance, and appoint such Staff Officers as the necessity of the case may demand." General Hopkins made a personal investigation and organized on March the 2nd, the company with Aaron Jernigan, Captain. As soon as the organization was completed General Hopkins began active operation, and soon discovered the Indians in the neighborhood of Lake Harney and other points nearly one hundred and fifty miles north of where the Indians should have been. Soon after taking the field he captured several ndians, some of which were sent West. From developments it was evident that the prompt action of Governor Brown awed the Indians into pursuing at least a quiet policy. The operation of this company extended through the summer and into the winter of 1852. While there was comparatively little danger in the service it was extremely arduous and very disagreeable, much of the country in which they operated being under water several inches during the whole summer months and they frequently found themselves without supplies for either men or horses. On the 13th of December, 1852, the operations of General Hopkins had so much allayed the apprehensions of the people of the frontier that they felt comparatively safe and the company for the time was disbanded, or to use the language of General Hopkins, "furloughed without rations."

Muster Roll of Captain Aaron Jernigan's Company, General Hopkin's Division Florida Troops.

NAMES.	MUSTERED IN.	MUSTERED OUT.	REMARKS.
OFFICERS.			
Major Gen. commanding—			
Benjamin Hopkins	March 2, '52		
Colonel and Adj. Gen.—			
Oscar Hart	May 3, '52		
Lt. Col. and Q. M. Gen.—			
Arthur Ginn	April 23, '52		
Lt. Col. and Aid de Camp—			
Thomas W. Jones	March 2, '52		Killed at Fort Mellon June 1, '52.
John L. Hopkins	June 2, '52		
Surgeon—			
Algernon S. Spear	March 2, '52		
1st Lt. and Asst. Commissary—			
John R. Hogans	March 2, '52		Resigned Nov. 16, at Fort Mellon.
Captain—			
Aaron Jernigan	March 2, '52		
1st Lieutenant—			
Isaac Jernigan	March 2, '52		
2nd Lieutenant—			
Needham Yates	March 2, '52		
ENLISTED MEN.			
Andrews, William	Aug. 15, '52	July 26, '52	
Ashley, Hiram A	May 3, '52	June '52	
Butler, Thomas H	May 3, '52	June 2, '52	
Byrd, Jesse	June 27, '52	Dec. 13, '52	
Byrant, Demsey	July 4, '52		
Byrd, Wiley	Sept. 12, '52		
Cooper, Isham	July 4, '52	March 28, '52	
Crews, B. M.	March 2, '52	March 28, '52	
Curry, Jones	May 3, '52		
Darling, John	April 20, '52	July 26, '52	
Davis, William J	April 26, '52	Sept. 5, '52	
Dupree, Erastus	July 4, '52		Promoted to 3rd Sergeant May 16, '52.

Muster Roll of Captain Aaron Jernigan's Company, General Hopkin's Division Florida Troops.
(CONTINUED,)

NAMES.	MUSTERED IN	MUSTERED OUT.	REMARKS.
Dupree, Jesse	July 4, '52		Promoted 2nd Sergeant.
Faulkner, Benjamin	Nov. 6, '52		
Freeman, Wilson	May 3, '52	Sept. 6, '52	
Gardiner, John H	April 18, '52	Sept. 5, '52	
Goode, Henry B	May 3, '52	Aug. 2, '52	2nd Sergeant.
Goodbread, James	March 2, '52	March 28, '52	
Gore, Daniel L	Oct. 20, '52		
Greene, James E	March 2, '52	March 28, '52	
Grouard, George M	March 2, '52	June 2, '52	
Harvey, James A	March 2, '52	Sept. 30, '52	
Higginbotham, Caleb	March 2, '52	Sept. 6, '52	Promoted 1st Sergeant, vice Towle, discharged.
Higginbotham, Joseph	March 2, '52	Sept. 21, '52	
Hogans, George W	March 2, '52	Sept. 5, '52	
Houston, John C	May 6, '52		
Hudson, Samuel	July 4, '52		
Hughey, George	March 2, '52		
Hughey, John	Nov. 1, '52		
Hunter, William	April 27, '52	May 22, '52	
Jernigan, Aaron, Jr	March 2, '52		
Jernigan, Elias	March 2, '52		
Johns, William W	May 3, '52	Sept. 5, '52	
Kain, Dempsey, Jr	May 3, '52	Sept. 6, '52	
Kersh, Joseph	May 3, '52	Aug. 2, '52	
King, George	July 4, '52		
Lee, David B	March 2, '52		
Manuel, Asa	Sept. 19, '52	Dec. 12, '52	
Marsh, Reuben	May 26, '52	Oct. 6, '52	
Moody, David	May 3, '52		
Murphy, Thomas	March 2, '52	July 26, '52	
Nevin, Patrick	June 7, '52	Nov. 30, '52	
Nix, James P	July 4, '52		
Norton, Louis	June 5, '52	July 26, '52	
O'Berry, Wesley	Sept. 5, '52		
O'Steen, H. E	June 1, '52	July 26, '52	
Patrick, John B	March 2, '52		
Penton, Thomas	May 3, '52	Sept. 5, '52	
Potter, Constant	June 5, '52	Nov. 16, '52	
Rialls, Aaron	May 3, '52	July 26, '52	
Rowe, William	April 18, '52	Nov. 30, '52	
Scott, Thomas	April 27, '52		Died at Fort Mellon Sept. 22, '52.
Silcox, David	April 18, '52	May 26, '52	
Smart, James M	April 18, '52		
Sparkman, Daniel G	Aug. 25, '52	Dec. 13, '52	
Sparkman, Alfred	Aug. 25, '52		
Thompson, David	March 2, '52		Accidentally killed March 18, '52.
Towle, Patrick H	March 2, '52	Sept. 16, '52	1st Sergeant.
Turner, David	April 18, '52		
Turner, Joseph	March 2, '52		
Williams, Dock	May 3, '52	May 10, '52	
Williams Randall	Nov. 17, '52		
Winegord, Isaac	April 17, '52		

Indian War of 1854-55.

During the years 1853 and a part of 1854 the Indians had been comparatively quiet, so quiet in fact that no apprehension was felt by either the military or citizens. Lieutenant Hartseff, under orders from Colonel Harvey
Brown, left Ft. Myers on the 9th of December, 1855, to examine the country
southeast of Lake Okeechebee and near the Big Cypress. He had visited
Forts Simon Drum and Shackelford, both of which he found burned but saw
no signs of hostilities; meeting in fact, only one Indian and a boy driving
hogs from Fort Drum. He went one day's march toward Billystown and,
camping on a pine island covered with saw palmetto and about three miles
from Billystown, employed two days (18-19) examining the country; visiting
Billystown and several villages, but seeing no Indians and not the slightest
evidence that any during the summer had been there. All the paths even
were overgrown. He ordered his party to prepare for an early start for Fort
Myers Thursday, Dec. 20, 1855. The Lieutenant and his escort, two non-

commissioned officers, eight mounted privates and two footmen with two six-mule teams, were almost ready to take up the line of march at daybreak, when they were attacked by a body of Indians, estimated from 25 to 40, distanced only from fifteen to twenty yards and concealed behind the trees. The result of this fight was 4 killed, 4 wounded and 3 escaped; Lieutenant Hartseff was himself desperately wounded and did not reach Fort Simon Drum, a distance of only one day's march, until Sunday afternoon. Shortly after this the Indians attacked the residence of Doctor Bradden on Manatee River. Immediately upon receipt of information of the attack on Lieutenant Hartseff, Governor Broome ordered Captain William B. Hooker to the front, and in quick succession followed the companies of F. M. Durrance, W. H. Kendrick, Abner D. Johnson, Leroy C. Lesley, A. J. T. Wright, Asa Stewart, Robert Youngblood, Enoch Daniel, W. B. Hardee, Alexander Bell, Thomas Hewett, Edward T. Kendrick, John Addison, John Parker, John McNeill, S. L. Sparkman, R. B. Sullivan, Hansfords D. Dyches, Aaron Jernigan, James O. Devall. No rolls were furnished to the companies of Dyches, Jernigan or Devall. These companies rendered excellent service and, if left to their own devices and unhampered by instructions from Washington, would undoubtedly have moved the Indians from Florida.

Roll Field and Staff Officers Indian War 1855.

NAMES.	MUSTERED IN.	MUSTERED OUT.	REMARKS.
OFFICERS.			
Colonel—			
M. Whit Smith	Dec. '55	Jan. 13, '58	
First Lieutenant and Surgeon—			
Gilbert L. Key	Dec. '55	Jan. 13, '58	
John B. Eichelberger	Dec. '55		
John H. Peck	Dec. '55		
Elisha Carter	Dec. '55		
George W. Price	Dec. '55		
Franklin Branch	Dec. '55		
Columbus R. Alexander	Dec. '55		
Robert L. Kendrick	Dec. '55		
1st Lieut., A. Q. M. and Com'y.—			
Samuel E. Hope	Dec. '55	Jan. 13, '58	
2nd Lieut., A. Q. M., and Com'y—			
Joseph M. Taylor	Dec. '55	Jan. 13, '58	
Asst. Quartermaster—			
Edward R. Ives	Dec. '55	Jan. 13, '58	
Sergt., Co. Q. M., and Com'y.—			
Francis B. Hagan			
Quartermaster's Clerk—			
Rich rd N. Jeffereys	Dec. '55	Jan. 13, '58	
Wagon Master—			
Perry G. Wall	Dec. '55	Jan. 13, '58	

William B. Hooker's Company, Seminole War of 1856.

NAMES.	MUSTERED IN.	MUSTERED OUT.	REMARKS.
Captain—			
William B. Hooker	Jan. 3, '56		This Company was mustered out of the State service and into the service of the United States Feb. 21, 1856, at Fort Meade, Fla.
1st Lieutenant—			
John Parker	Jan. 3, '56		
2nd Lieutenant—			
Joseph M. Pearce	Jan. 3, '56		
ENLISTED MEN.			
Alderman, Jesse	Jan. 3, '56		
Alderman, Mathew	Jan. 3, '56		

William B. Hooker's Company, Seminole War of 1856.
(CONTINUED.)

NAMES.	MUSTERED IN.	MUSTERED OUT.	REMARKS.
Alderman, Michael	Jan. 3, '56		Corporal.
Alderman, Mitchel	Jan. 3, '56		
Alderman, William	Jan. 3, '56		
Braning, David	Jan. 3, '56		
Barber, William W	Jan. 3, '56		
Burnett, Matthew	Jan. 3, '56		
Brown, Henry	Jan. 3, '56		
Canova, Andrew	Jan. 3, '56		
Cathron, Aaron C	Jan. 3, '56		
Campbell, William L	Jan. 3, '56		
Carlton, Isaac	Jan. 3, '56		
Collins, William A	Jan. 3, '56		
Driggers, Mathew	Jan. 3, '56		Farrier and blacksmith.
Driggers, Jacob	Jan. 3, '56		
English, Eli	Jan. 3, '56		
Gillet, Daniel	Jan. 3, '56		
Gillet, Daniel K	Jan. 3, 56		
Gillet, David W	Jan. 3, '56		
Greene, Jas. D	Jan. 3, '56		
Guilley, William	Jan. 3, '56		
Guilley, Nathan	Jan. 3, '56		
Guy, Benjamin	Jan. 3, '56		
Guy, William B	Jan. 3, '56		
Hall, William	Jan. 3, '56		Sergeant.
Hendry, George W	Jan. 3, '56		Sergeant.
Hendry, George W, Jr	Jan. 3, '56		
Hendry, Albert J	Jan. 3, '56		
Henderson, Robert	Jan. 3, '56		
Hilliard, Benjamin	Jan. 3, '56		Bugler.
Hilliard, Benjamin, Jr	Jan. 3, '56		
Hooker, John J	Jan. 3, '56		
Hooker. William J	Jan. 3, '56		
Hooker, Stephen P	Jan. 3, '56		
Hollingsworth, William R	Jan. 3, '56		
Hollingsworth, John H	Jan. 3, '56		Wounded at the Filles place, June 14, 1856.
Howard, Seth	Jan. 3, '56		
Ivey, Francis A	Jan. 3, '56		Sergeant.
Ivey, William I	Jan. 3, '56		
Jones, Lucertes	Jan. 3, '56		
Langford, Henry	Jan. 3, '56		
Lanier, Lewis	Jan. 3, '56		
McLeod, Daniel J	Jan. 3, '56		
McLeod, John	Jan. 3, '56		
McLeod, William	Jan. 3, '56		
McCullough, William	Jan. 3, '56		
McDonald, John	Jan. 3, '56		
McMullen, James P	Jan. 3, '56		
Moore, Joseph	Jan. 3, '56		
Main, David	Jan. 3, '56		
Moody, Benjamin	Jan. 3, '56		
Moody, James A	Jan. 3, '56		
Moody, William B	Jan. 3, '56		
O'Neill, John	Jan. 3, '56		
Orr, Henry B	Jan. 3, '56		
Parker, William	Jan. 3, '56		Killed at Tille's place, June 14, '56.
Pelham, Richard	Jan. 3, '56		
Platt, John	Jan. 3, '56		
Platt, Lewis B	Jan. 3, '56		
Platt, William C	Jan. 3, '56		
Raulerson, Jacob R	Jan. 3, '56		
Riggs, John W	Jan. 3, '56		Corporal.
Riggs, Joshua D, C	Jan. 3, '56		
Russell, David	Jan. 3, '56		Corporal.
Simmons, William	Jan. 3, '56		
Singletary, Simpson	Jan. 3, '56		
Skipper, John L	Jan. 3, '56		Wounded at Peace River, June 14, '56.
Sloan, Daniel	Jan. 3, '56		
Sloan, Alford	Jan. 3, '56		
Sloan, Joseph	Jan. 3, '56		
Sloan, Owen	Jan. 3, '56		
Smith, Renney J	Jan. 3, '56		
Stallings, William W	Jan. 3, '56		
Summerall, Thomas	Jan. 3, '56		
Thomas, James H	Jan. 3, '56		Bugler,
Tyson, George	Jan. 3, '56		
Underhill, John	Jan. 3, '56		Corporal,
Underhill, William	Jan. 3, '56		
Waters, Isaac	Jan. 3, '56		
Weeks, John	Jan. 3, '56		
Wilson, James T	Jan. 3, '56		
Whiddon, Bennett	Jan. 3, '56		
Whidden, James. Jr	Jan. 3, '56		
Whidden, John	Jan. 3, '56		

William B. Hooker's Company, Seminole War of 1856.
(CONTINUED.)

NAMES.	MUSTERED IN.	MUSTERED OUT.	REMARKS.
Whidden, Edward	Jan. 3, '56		
Whidden, Jesse	Jan. 3, '56		
Whidden, Maxfield, Sr	Jan. 3, '56		
Whidden, Maxfield, Jr.	Jan. 3, '56		
Whidden, William	Jan. 3, '56		
Whidden, Willoughby	Jan. 3, '56		
Whidden, William J.	Jan. 3, '56		
Whidden, James, Sr	Jan. 3, '56		Wounded at Peace River. June 16. '56,
Weeks, Levi	Jan. 3, '56		
Crane, Henry A.	Jan. 3, '56		

Durrance's Company, Seminole War of 1856.

NAMES.	MUSTERED IN.	MUSTERED OUT.	REMARKS.
OFFICERS.			
Captain—			
F. M. Durrance	Dec. 29, '55	'57	
1st Lieutenant—			
Edward T. Kendrick	Dec. 29, '55		Edward F. Kendrick raised a company and was
Willoughby Tillis	Aug. 27, '56	'57	mustered service Aug. 29, '56.
2nd Lieutenant—			
Alderman Carlton	Dec. 29, '55	'56	Killed at the Tillis Place, June 14, 1856.
Joseph Howell		'57	
ENLISTED MEN.			
Attman, James R.	Dec. 29, '55	Dec. '57	
Attman, William	Dec. 29, '55	Dec. '57	
Attman, John	Aug. 27, '56	Dec. '57	4th Sergeant.
Attman, Lewis	Aug. 27, '56	Dec. '57	
Baxley, Samuel	Aug. 27, '56	Dec. '57	
Baxley, Willis	Aug. 27, '56	Dec. '57	
Blount, John	Aug. 27, '56	Dec. '57	
Blount, Redding	Dec. 29, '55	Dec. '57	
Bogges, F. C. M.	Dec. 29, '55	Dec. '57	1st Sergeant.
Boney, David J. W.	Aug. 27, '55	Dec. '57	
Branen, Joseph S.	Aug. 27, '55		
Branen, Millage	Dec. 29, '55	Dec. '57	
Brocker, Stephen	Dec. 29, '55	Aug. '56	
Brooker, William P.	Dec. 29, '55	Aug. '56	Wounded at Peace River, June 16, 1856.
Brown, Raigdon	Dec. 29, '55	Aug. '56	
Brown, Reigdon H.	Dec. 29, '55	Aug. '56	
Brown, William H.	Dec. 29, '55	Dec. '57	
Canady, Henry	Aug. 27, '55	Dec. '57	
Canady, James H.	Aug. 27, '56	Dec. '57	
Carlton, Daniel H.	Dec. 29, '55	Aug. '56	Wounded at the Tillis Place, June 14, 1856.
Crews, Isham	Dec. 29, '55	Aug. '56	
Davis, Stafford	Dec. 29, '55	Aug. '56	
Downing, Charles W.	Dec. 29, '55	Dec. '57	
Durrance, George T.	Dec. 29, '55	Aug. '56	
Durrance, Jesse H.	Dec. 29, '55	Dec. '57	
Durrance, John R.	Dec. 29, '55	Dec. '57	
Durrance, Joseph L.	Dec. 29, '55	Dec. '57	2nd Sergeant.
Durrance, William H.	Dec. 29, '55	Dec. '57	Bugler.
Dyning, Jeremiah	Dec. 29, '55	Dec. '57	
Eason, M. H.	Dec. 29, '55	Dec. '57	
Edwards, Marvin H.	Dec. 29, '55	Aug. '56	1st Sergeant.
Ellis, Thomas	Dec. 29, '55	Aug. '56	Corporal.
Ellis, Thomas B.	Dec. 29, '55	Dec. '57	
Evans, John	Dec. 29, '55	Dec. '57	Corporal.
Filmore, Martin	Aug. 27, '56	Dec. '57	
Garrison, Green	Dec. 29, '55	Dec. '57	
Green, Israel	Dec. 29, '55	Dec. '57	
Green, John	Dec. 29, '55	Dec. '57	
Godwin, Jacob	Dec. 29, '55	Dec. '57	
Godwin, John	Dec. 29, '55	Aug. '56	
Godwin, Samuel S.	Dec. 29, '55	Aug. '56	
Haywood, John	Dec. 29, '55	Dec. '57	
Harrell, James M.	Dec. 29, '55	Aug. '56	Corporal.
Hendry, Charles W.	Aug. 27, '56	Dec. '57	
Hall, William	Aug. 27, '56	Dec. '57	
Hague, Gideon	Aug. 27, '56	Dec. '57	
Hearn, James	Aug. 27, '56	Dec. '57	
Hickey, Dennis	Dec. 29, '55	Aug. '56	
Hill, Thomas W.	Dec. 29, '55	Dec. '57	
Hinson, Alfred G.	Dec. 29, 55	Aug. '56	
Hogan, A. S.	Aug. 27, '56	Dec. '57	
Hogan, Daniel	Dec. 29, '55	Dec. '57	

Durrance's Company, Seminole War of 1856.
(Continued.)

NAMES.	MUSTERED IN.	MUSTERED OUT.	REMARKS.
Howell, George			Killed at Peace River, June 16, 1856.
Howell, John	Dec. 29, '55	Aug. '56	Promoted 2nd Lieutenant.
Howell, Joseph	Dec. 29, '55	Aug. '56	
Kenady, James H	Dec. 29, '55	Aug. '56	Corporal.
McClelland, Jesse	Dec. 29, '55	Dec. '57	
McClelland, Erastus W	Dec. 29, '55	Aug. '56	
McClelland, Maxfield	Dec. 29, 55	Dec. '57	
McClelland, Moses A	Dec. 29, '55	Aug. '56	
McClelland, Silas, Sr	Dec. 29 '55	Dec '57	Corporal.
McClelland, William	Dec. 29, '55	Dec. '57	
McClelland, William E	Aug. 27, '56	Dec. '57	
McDonald, Nelson			
Mansfield, George	Dec. 29, '55	Dec. '57	
Mansfield, William H	Dec. 29, '55	Dec. '57	Corporal.
McCormick, Thomas	Dec. 29, '55	Aug. '56	
Payne, Cyrus D	Dec. 29, '55	Dec. '57	2nd Corporal.
Platt, Berrien	Dec. 29, '55	Dec. '57	
Platt, Peter	Dec. 29, '55	Dec. '57	
Prine, Robert F. F	Dec. 29, '55	Aug. '56	Killed at Peace River, June 16, 1856.
Pollard, Wyley D. K	Dec. 29, '55		Farrier.
Rauls, Christopher C	Dec. 29, '55	Aug. '56	
Raulerson, Jackson	Dec. 29, '55	Dec. '57	
Raulerson, John	Dec. 29, '55	Dec. '57	1st Corporal.
Raulerson, John B	Dec. 29, '55	Dec. '57	
Raulerson, Raburn	Dec. 29, '55	Dec. '57	
Roberts, James	Dec. 29, '55	Aug. '56	
Scott, Charles H	Dec. 29, '55	Dec. '57	
Seward, Felix J	Aug. 27, '56	Dec. '57	
Seward, Henry S	Aug. 27, '56	Dec. '57	
Seward, Walter B	Dec. 29, '55	Dec. '57	
Seward, Zachariah	Aug. 27, '56	Dec. '57	
Shepard, Isaac	Dec. 29, '55	Dec. '57	
Shepard, William W	Dec. 29, '55	Dec. '57	
Sistrunk, Henry	Dec. 29, '55	Dec. '57	
Starling, Levi	Dec. 29, '55	Aug. '56	
Stephens, James A	Dec. 29, '55	Aug. '56	Corporal, promoted Sergeant.
Summerall, Joseph	Dec. 29, '55	Aug. '56	
Thomas, John	Dec. 29, '55	Dec. '57	
Thomas, Lewis	Aug. 27, '56	Dec. '57	
Tillis, Dempsey	Dec. 29, '55	Dec. '57	4th Corporal.
Tillis James L	Dec. 29, '55	Aug. '56	
Tillis, Willoughby	Dec. 29, '55	Aug. '56	
Townsend, Lorenzo D	Dec. 29, '55	Aug. '56	Bugler.
Tyre, Jacob H	Dec. 29, '55	Dec. '57	3rd Sergeant.
Tyre, John	Dec. 29, '55	Dec. '57	Farrier.
Tyre, Thomas L	Dec. 29, '55	Aug. '56	2nd Sergeant.....
Tucker, John E	Dec. 29, '55	Aug. '56	
Underhill, Joseph	Dec. 29, '55	Aug. '56	
Underhill, Thomas	Dec. 29, '55	Dec. '57	3rd Sergeant.
Varnes, Federick	Dec. 29, '55	Dec. '56	
Varn, Josiah	Aug. 27, 56	Dec. '57	
Varn, William	Aug. 27, '56	Dec. '57	
Waring, Francis H	Dec. 29, '55	Dec. '57	
Watters, Isaac	Aug. 27, '56	Dec. '57	Bugler.
Weissboad, Herman	Dec. 29, '55	Dec. '57	
Whidden, Bennett, Jr	Dec. 29, '55	Aug. '56	
Whidden, Eli P	Dec. 29, '55	Dec. '57	
Whidden, James L	Dec. 29, '55	Dec. '57	Wounded at Peace River, June 16, 1856.
Whidden, John	Dec. 29, '55	Aug. '56	
Whidden, Lott	Dec. 29, '55	Aug. '56	Killed at the Tillis Place, June 14, 1856.
Whitehurst, George W	Dec. 29, '55	Dec. '57	
Wiggens, John R	Dec. 29, '55	Dec. '57	
Wiggins, William	Aug. 27, '56	Dec. '57	
Williams, James	Dec. 29, '55	Dec. '57	
Williams, Randall B	Dec. 29, '55	Aug. '56	

Kendrick's Company, Seminole War of 1856.

NAMES.	MUSTERED IN.	MUSTERED OUT.	REMARKS.
OFFICERS.			
Captain—			
William H. Kendrick	Jan. 1, '56	Dec. '57	
1st Lieutenant—			
Francis M. Durrance	Jan. 1, '56	Aug. '56	
Nathaniel M. Moody	Jan. 1, '56	Dec. '57	Farrier, promoted 1st Lieutenant.
2nd Lieutenant—			
John Knight	Jan. 1, '56	Aug. '56	

Kendrick's Company, Seminole War of 1856.
(CONTINUED.)

NAMES.	MUSTERED IN.			MUSTERED OUT.		REMARKS.
Morgan, Mizell	Jan.	1,	'56	Dec.	'57	Sergeant, promoted 2nd Lieutenant.
ENLISTED MEN						
Allen, William E.	Aug.	27,	'56	Dec.	'57	Sergeant.
Barco, Thomas	Aug.	27,	'56	Dec.	'57	Corporal.
Barnes, Caleb	Jan.	1,	'56	Aug.	'56	
Barnes, James F	Jan.	1,	'56	Dec.	'57	
Bates, George W	Jan.	1,	'56	Dec.	'57	
Bates, James M	Jan.	1,	'56	Dec.	'57	Farrier.
Bates, John M	Jan.	1,	'56	Dec.	'57	
Bates, Robert J	Jan.	1,	'56	Dec.	'57	
Bird, Jackson	Jan.	1,	'56	Aug.	'56	
Bissett, George	Jan.	1,	'56	Dec.	'57	
Boyett, Anderson	Jan.	1,	'56	Aug.	'56	
Boyett, Edward	Aug.	27,	'56	Dec.	'57	Bugler.
Boyett, James A	Jan.	1,	'56	Aug.	'56	
Boyett, John	Jan.	1,	'56	Dec.	'57	Corporal.
Boyett, John G. B.	Aug.	27,	'56	Dec.	'57	
Boyett, Nathan—	Jan.	1,	'56	Dec.	'57	Sergeant.
Bradford, James I	Jan.	1,	'56	Aug.	'56	
Branch, Charles L	Jan.	1,	'56	Aug.	'55	
Branch, Samuel E. I	Jan.	1,	'56	Aug.	53	
Branch, William T	Jan.	1,	'56	Dec.	'57	
Brown, James L	Jan.	1,	'56	Aug.	'56	
Buek, Richard W	Aug.	27,	'56	Dec.	'57	
Carter, Jesse W	Jan.	1	'56	Dec.	'57	
Chapman, Nathaniel T	Aug.	27,	'56	Dec.	'57	
Coleman, John	Aug.	27,	'56	Dec.	'57	
Davis, William H	Jan.	1,	'56	Dec.	'57	
Douglass, Daniel R	Aug.	27,	'56	Dec.	'57	
Dugger, James J	Aug.	27,	'56	Dec.	'57	
Garrison, William M	Aug.	27,	'56	Dec.	'57	
Gobrick, Peter	Jan.	1,	'56	Dec.	'57	
Godwin, Jacob	Jan.	1,	'56	Dec.	'57	
Green, John C.	Aug.	27,	'56	Dec.	'57	
Hagan, Francis B	Jan.	1.	'56	Dec.	'57	
Hall, Stephen D	Aug.	27,	'56	Dec.	'57	Sergeant.
Halliday, Edward E	Aug.	27,	'56	Dec.	'57	
Ham, Alonzo	Jan.	1,	'56	Dec.	'57	
Hammock, Samuel	Jan.	1,	'56	Dec.	'57	
Harrell, Edward E	Aug.	27,	'56	Dec.	'57	
Harrell, John W	Jan.	1,	'56	Dec.	'57	
Hand, James H	Jan.	1,	'56	Dec.	'57	
Harris, Joseph	Aug.	27,	'56	Dec.	'57	
Harn, Henry J	Jan.	1,	'56	Dec.	'57	
Harn, Henry, Jr	Aug.	27,	'56	Dec.	'57	
Hawthorn, Kedar	Jan.	1,	'56	Aug.	'56	
Hawthorn, Washington L	Jan.	1,	'56	Aug.	'56	
Hutchinson, James E	Aug.	27,	'56	Dec.	'57	
Jackson, James W	Jan.	1,	'56	Dec.	'57	
Jackson, Thomas B	Jan.	1,	'56	Dec.	'57	
Jackson, William S.	Aug.	27,	'56	Dec.	'57	
Jones, Mathew E.	Jan.	1,	'56	Dec.	'57	
Kersey, Libourn	Jan.	1,	'56	Dec.	'57	
Kyle, Christopher H	Aug.	27,	'56	Dec.	'57	
Lanier, Isaac	Jan.	1,	'56	Dec.	'57	
Leggett, Benjamin	Jan.	1,	'56	Aug.	'56	
McMinn, Charles I	Jan.	1,	'56	Aug.	'56	
Marsh, James I	Jan.	1,	'56	Aug.	'56	
Mathews, William H	Jan.	1,	'56	Dec.	'57	
Mobley, Ramson	Aug.	27,	'56	Dec.	'57	
Moody, Enoch M	Aug.	27,	'56	Dec.	'57	
Morris, James E.	Jan.	1,	'56	Dec.	'57	
Nettles, Isaac	Aug.	27,	'56	Dec.	'57	
O'Neill, Seaborn C	Jan.	1,	'56	Aug.	'56	
O'Neill, William D	Jan.	1,	'56	Dec.	'57	Corporal.
Osborn, David	Jan.	1,	'56	Dec.	'57	
Overstreet, William R	Jan.	1,	'56	Dec.	'57	
Phelps, Enoch B	Jan.	1,	'56	Dec.	'57	Sergeant.
Phelps, Joseph I	Jan.	1,	'56	Aug.	'56	
Platt, John B.	Jan.	1,	'56	Dec.	'57	
Platt, Joshua A	Aug.	27,	'56	Dec.	'57	Corporal.
Pinkston, Daniel W	Jan.	1,	'56	Aug.	'56	Corporal.
Powell, George M.	Jan.	1,	'56	Dec.	'57	
Prevatt, Seth S.	Aug.	27,	'56	Dec.	'57	Corporal.
Rivers, Sylvester	Jan.	1,	'56	Aug.	'56	
Ryols, Daniel C.	Aug.	27,	'56	Dec.	'57	
Sharp, Charles W	Jan.	1,—	'56	Aug.	'56	
Smith, Andrew J	Aug.	27,	'56	Dec.	'57	
Smith, John	Aug.	27,	'56	Dec.	'57	
Smith, William	Jan.	1,	'56	Dec.	'57	
Stafford, George	Jan.	1,	'56	Dec.	'57	Corporal.
Stafford, William	Jan.	1,	'56	Dec.	'57	
Sylvester, Augustine	Jan.	1,	'56	Aug.	'56	
Sylvester, Eli	Aug.	27,	'56	Dec.	'57	

Kendrick's Company, Seminole War of 1856.
(CONTINUED.)

NAMES.	MUSTERED IN.	MUSTERED OUT.	REMARKS.
Sumner, Jesse C.	Jan. 1, '56	Dec. '57	
Thigpen, William H.	Jan. 1, '56	Dec. '57	
Thomas, James M.	Jan. 1, '56	Dec. '57	
Thomas, William	Jan. 1, '56	Dec. '57	
Tucker, Alonzo	Jan. 1, '56	Dec. '57	
Tucker, Edward D.	Jan. 1, '56	Dec. '57	
Tucker, Lewis M.	Jan. 1, '56	Dec. '57	
Tucker, Pleasant	Jan. 1, '56	Dec. '57	
Tucker, Thomas R.	Jan. 1, '56	Dec. '57	
Tucker, William W.	Jan. 1, '56	Aug. '56	
Tyner, Jackson	Jan. 1, '56	Dec. '57	
Tyner, Jordan	Jan. 1, '56	Dec. '57	
Tyner, Wilson	Jan. 1, '56	Dec. '57	
Thompson, William I.	Jan. 1, '56	Aug. '56	Corporal.
Tucker, Jesse H.	Jan. 1, '56	Aug. '56	Sergeant.
Tucker, Joseph M.	Jan. 1, '56	Aug. '56	Sergeant.
Wamsley, Lewis W.	Jan. 1, '56	Dec. '57	
Watson, William I.	Jan. 1, '56	Aug. '56	
Weeks, Andrew J.	Jan. 1, '56	Aug. '56	
Weeks, George W.	Jan. 1, '56	Dec. '57	Sergeant.
Weeks, Silas	Aug. 27, '56	Dec. '57	
Wells, Jacob	Aug. 27, '56	Dec. '57	
Wills, Israel I.	Aug. 27, '56	Dec. '57	
Williams, Abraham F.	Jan. 1, '56	Aug. '56	
Williams, Irwin I.	Jan. 1, '56	Aug. '56	
Williams, James M.	Aug. 27, '56	Dec. '57	
Williams, Judge E.	Jan. 1, '55	Aug. '56	
Williams, Robert H.	Jan. 1, '56	Aug. '56	
Wilkinson, Malcolm H.	Jan. 1, '56	Aug. '56	
Wilson, John	Jan. 1, '56	Dec. '57	
Wingate, Richard	Jan. 1, '56	Dec. '57	

Johnston's Company, Seminole War of 1856.

NAMES.	MUSTERED IN.	MUSTERED OUT.	—	REMARKS.
OFFICERS.				
Captain—				
Abner D. Johnston				
1st Lieutenant—				
Bee. W. Crews	Dec. 29, '55	Aug. '56		
James P. F. Johnston	Dec. 29, '55	Dec. '57		
2nd Lieutenant—				
James Weeks	Dec. 29, '55	Dec. '57		
ENLISTED MEN.				
Aiken, John	Dec. 29, '55	Dec. '57		Sergeant.
Aiken, Preston	Dec. 29, '55	Dec. '57		
Barrington, John S.	Dec. 29, '55	Aug. '56		Sergeant.
Badger, Edward N.	Aug. 27, '56	Dec. '57		
Beckham, Alex C.	Dec. 29, '55	Aug. '56		
Beckham, Hiram	Aug. 27, '56	Dec. '57		
Beckham, Jerome M.	Aug. 27, '56	Dec. '57		
Beckham, Marion J.	Dec. 29, '55	Aug. '56		
Beckham, Robert I.	Aug. 27, '56	Dec. '57		Bugler.
Bennett, Charles	Dec. 29, '55	Aug. '56		
Berill, Granville	Dec. 29, '55	Aug. '56		
Black, George W.	Aug. 27, '56	Dec. '57		
Bradshaw, Dixon G. H.	Dec. 29, '55	Dec. '57		
Bradshaw, James B.	Dec. 29, '55	Aug. '56		
Brown, Nathaniel L.	Dec. 29, '55	Aug. '56		
Brown, William C.	Dec. 29, '55	Aug. '56		
Calson, William H.	Aug. 27, '56	Dec. '57		Corporal.
Carter, Hardee	Aug. 27, '56	Dec. '57		
Caruthers, Augustus L.	Dec. 29, '55	Aug. '56		Corporal.
Chiver, Daniel B.	Dec. 29, '55	Aug. '56		
Clay, Shadrach H.	Aug. 27, '56	Dec. '57		
Cochron, Edward	Aug. 27, '56	Dec. '57		
Cook, James H.	Aug. 27, '56	Dec. '57		
Colding, James B.	Aug. 27, '56	Dec. '57		
Colding, Samuel	Aug. 27, '56	Dec. '57		
Colding, Thomas C.	Aug. 27, '56	Dec. '57		
Colson, Abraham	Aug. 27, '56	Dec. '57		
Collins, David	Aug. 27, '56	Dec. '57		
Collins, George W.	Dec. 29, '55	Dec. '57		
Collins, James A.	Dec. 29, '55	Dec. '57		
Colson, Thomas K.	Aug. 27, '56	Dec. '57		
Condy, James A.	Dec. 29, '55	Aug. '56		

Johnston's Company, Seminole War of 1856.
(CONTINUED.)

NAMES.	MUSTERED IN.	MUSTERED OUT.	REMARKS.
Crawford, Emanuel	Dec. 29, '55	Aug. '56	
Crews, Edward F	Dec. 29, '55	Aug. '56	
Crum, Harmon	Dec. 29, '55	Aug. '56	Corporal.
Crum, James B	Dec. 29, '55	Aug. '56	
Daniel, Moses	Aug. 27, '56	Dec. '57	Sergeant.
Dickson, John S	Aug. 27, '56	Dec. '57	
Duncan, Daniel			
Evans, Charles	Dec. 29, '55	Dec. '57	
Fassie, James C	Aug. 27, '56	Dec. '57	
Fussell, Arnold B	Dec. 29, '55	Aug. '56	
Fussell, Jesse C	Dec. 29, '55	Aug. '56	
Fussell, William	Dec. 29, '55	Aug. '56	
Gant, Jason	Dec. 29, '55	Dec. '57	Corporal.
Gant, John B	Dec. 29, '55	Dec. '57	
Golden, Darling	Aug. 27, '56	Dec. '57	
Griffin, Francis	Aug. 27, '56	Dec. '56	
Godwin, Seaborn	Dec. 29, '55	Dec. '57	
Hanley, Well	Dec. 29, '55	Aug. '56	
Harchey, Wells	Aug. 27, '56	Dec. '57	
Hart, Christopher C	Dec. 29, '55	Aug. '56	
Hart, William B	Dec. 29, '55	Aug. '56	
Hays, George F	Dec. 29, '55	Aug. '56	
Hays, Robert	Dec. 29, '55	Aug. '56	
Hays, William J	Dec. 29, '55	Aug. '56	
Hutchinson, David	Dec. 29, '55	Dec. '57	
Hutchinson, Lewis	Aug. 27, '56	Dec. '57	
Jernigan, Aaron, Jr	Aug. 27, '56	Dec. '57	
Jernigan, Moses	Aug. 27, '56	Dec. '57	
Johnston, John W	Dec. 29, '55	Dec. '57	
Jones, David	Aug. 27, '56	Dec. '57	
Jones, James	Aug. 27, '56	Aug. '56	
Jones, James W	Dec. 29, '55	Aug. '56	
Jones, Watkins	Aug. 27, '56	Dec. '57	
Key, William	Aug. 27, '56	Dec. '57	
Lamar, John H	Aug. 27, '56	Dec. '57	
Lea, Calvin J	Dec. 29, '55	Aug. '57	
Lewis, Charles W	Dec. 29, '55	Aug. '57	
Lewis, Littleton R	Aug. 27, '56	Dec. '57	
Lockerly, Irvin	Dec. 29, '55	Aug. '56	
Logan, Thomas L	Dec. 29, '55	Aug. '56	
Logan, William	Dec. 29, '55	Aug. '56	
McCought, Austin	Dec. 29, '55	Aug. '56	
McNair, James S	Dec. 29, '55	Dec. '57	
McNair John E	Aug. 27, '56	Dec. '57	
Marsay, John J	Aug. 27, '56	Dec. '57	
Massey, John	Dec. 29, '55	Aug. '56	
Matchett, Jacob	Dec. 29, '55	Aug. '56	
Matchett, John W	Dec. 29, '55	Dec. '57	Sergeant.
Meritt, Josiah	Dec. 29, '55	Aug. '56	
Meritt, Paton	Dec. 29, '55	Aug. '56	
Mills, George	Dec. 29, '55	Aug. '56	
Mims, John L	Dec. 29, '55	Dec. '57	Bugler.
Mobley, George R	Dec. 29, '55	Aug. '56	
Mobley, John	Dec. 29, '55	Dec. '57	
Morgan, John A	Aug. 27, '56	Dec. '57	
Murchey, James H	Dec. 29, '55	Aug. '56	Bugler.
Newberry, David J. W	Dec. 29, '55	Aug. '56	
Newberry, Hezekiah	Dec. 29, '55	Aug. '56	
Odom, James P	Dec. 29, '55	Dec. '57	
Pagett, William W	Aug. 27, '56	Dec. '57	
Parker, William	Aug. 27, '56	Dec. '57	
Parrish, Hiram	Dec. 29, '55	Dec. '57	Sergeant.
Phelps, Joseph T	Aug. 27, '56	Dec. '57	
Rains, Mathew	Aug. 27, '56	Dec. '57	
Ross, Lorenzo D	Dec. 29, '55	Aug. '56	
Rutherford, Austin G	Dec. 29, '55	Aug. '56	
Shiver, Daniel	Aug. 27, '56	Dec. '57	
Sims, Benjamin F	Aug. 27, '56	Dec. '57	
Sims, John S	Aug. 27, '56	Dec. '57	
Sinclair, Alexander	Aug. 27, '56	Dec. '57	
Skipper, John F	Aug. 27, '56	Dec. '57	
Sloan, Alexander L	Dec. 29, '55	Aug. '56	
Sloan, William W	Dec. 29, '55	Aug. '56	
Stafford, William H	Aug. 27, '56	Dec. '57	
Stanley, James W	Dec. 29, '55	Dec. '57	Farrier.
Stanley, Millard	Aug. 27, '56	Dec. '57	Sergeant.
Stanley, Miller	Dec. 29, '56	Aug. '56	
Stewman, Thomas H	Aug. 27, '56	Dec. '57	Corporal.
Swicord, Benjamin F	Aug. 27, '56	Dec. '57	
Swicord, Joseph	Dec. 29, '56	Aug. '56	
Swicord, Michael	Dec. 29, '56	Dec. '57	
Swicord, William	Aug 27, '56	Dec. '57	
Swicord, William F	Dec. 29, '55	Aug. '56	
Thompson, Abner J	Dec. 29, '55	Dec. '57	Sergeant.

Johnston's Company, Seminole War of 1856.
(CONTINUED.)

NAMES.	MUSTERED IN.	MUSTERED OUT.	REMARKS.
Tillman, John B.	Dec. 29, '55	Dec. '57	
Tucker, Elijah H. H.	Aug. 27, '56	Dec. '57	
Wall, James G.	Dec. 29, '55	Aug. '56	
Wall, James S.	Aug. 27, '56	Dec. '57	
Weeks, Richard B. C.	Aug. 27, '56	Dec. '57	
Weeks, Stephen	Dec. 29, '55	Dec. '57	
Weeks, Richard A. K. C.	Dec. 29, '56	Aug. '56	
Wells, Simeon H.	Aug. 27, '56	Dec. '57	
Whitman, Bryant	Dec. 29, '55	Aug. '56	
Whitman, Jacob	Dec. 29, '55	Aug. '56	
Whitman, Michael	Dec. 29, '55	Dec. '57	
Williams, Alexander R.	Aug. 27, '56	Dec. '57	
Williams, Benjamin B.	Aug. 27, '56	Dec. '57	
Williams, Blaney	Dec. 29, '56	Aug. '56	
Williams, William H.	Aug. 27, '56	Dec. '57	
Williams, Wilson C.	Aug. 27, '56	Dec. '57	
Wilson, Simeon	Aug. 27, '56	Dec. '57	
Williamson, Crawford	Dec. 29, '55	Aug. '56	Corporal.
Wooley, Aaron	Dec. 29, '55	Aug. '56	Bugler.
Sylvester, William H.	Aug. 27, '56	Dec. '57	

Lesley's Company, Seminole War of 1856.

NAMES.	MUSTERED IN.	MUSTERED OUT.	REMARKS.
OFFICERS.			
Captain—			
Leroy G. Lesley			
1st Lieutenant—			
Streaty Parker			
2nd Lieutenants—			
F. A. Hendry			
Henry A. Crane			Promoted to 1st Lieutenant and Quartermaster.
ENLISTED MEN			
Altman, Lewis			
Alderman, James			
Booth, Richard			
Blount, Redding			
Blount, Redding R.			
Blount, Nathan			
Blount, Jacob J.			
Blount Owen			Sergeant.
Barton, John W.			
Boney, David J. W.			
Ballard, William C.			
Clark, Elias D.			
Clark, John J.			
Campbell, William N.			
Campbell, William L.			
Caruthers, Freeman			Farrier.
Carney, John			
Davidson, John			Corporal.
Drew, Octavius			
Dyches, Wilson			
Eady, Joseph			
Fuel, John E.			
Ferguson, Francis			
Gunthers, John B.			
Gay, James L.			
Hague, Gideon			
Handcock, James F.			
Handcock, Martin J.			
Handcock, Jordan			
Halliday, Edward B.			
Haygood, James D.			Bugler.
Hill, Henry R.			
Hickey, John E.			
Hutchinson, Joseph			
Hogan, James B.			
Hambleton, George			
Johnson, John			Corporal.
Lesley, John T.			Corporal.
Lesley, Emory L.			Bugler.
Long, Levi			
Long, Nathaniel			
Long, James T.			
Lockhart, Joel L.			
Lang, Oswald			

Lesley's Company, Seminole War of 1856.
(CONTINUED.)

NAMES.	MUSTERED IN.	MUSTERED OUT.	REMAR
Main, David			
Mizell, Joseph			
Mizell, Enoch			
Manley, James M.			
McGuire, Sherod B.			Sergeant.
Nob es, Alfred			
Newberry, Hiram			
Oats, John C.			
Ormond, Alexander W.			
Paget, William W.			
Price, George W.			Sergeant.
Rogers, William P.			
Rawls, James W.			
Sherley, Thomas			
Seward, Henry S.			
Seward, Zachariah, Sr.			
Seward, Zachariah.			
Seward, Felix			
Seals, Cornelius			
Shepherd, Robert R.			Sergeant.
Summerall, David			
Vickers, John			
Varn, William B.			
Varn, Josiah			
Wordehoff, Antoine			Corporal.
Whidden, James			
Whidden, Noah			
Whidden, Willoughby, Jr.		✪	
Willingham, William H.			
Willingham, William J.			
Wiggins, Andrew			
Wiggins, James R.			
Williams, William H.			
White, David			
Whitehurst, David S.			
Whitehurst, John			
Whitehurst, Robert T.			
Mitchell, Thomas			
Harris, Samuel S.			

Wright's Company, Seminole War 1856.

NAMES.	MUSTERED IN.	MUSTERED OUT.	REMARKS.
OFFICERS.			
Captain—			
A. J. T. Wright			
1st Lieutenants—			
F. Raulerson			
A. B. Bexley			
2nd Lieutenant—			
W. J. Mickler			
ENLISTED MEN.			
Alford, J. B. L.			
Blackshear, C. S.			
Biglow, R. J.			Corporal.
Bryan, John M.			
Brown, B. I.			
Beasley, Isaiah			
Brown, J. L.			
Bryan, William P.			
Brannin, Alvin			
Benton, David			
Bigelow, Robert J.			Corporal.
Bryant, William			Farrier.
Blackshear, Cicero S.			
Charles, R. H.			Sergeant.
Cannon, James			
Crews, John			
Curry, James			
Durrance, George			
Fraser, John C.			
Fraser, William			Corpora,l
Goodbred, William S.			
Garrett, Chamel			
Griffis, William H.			
Greene Thomas J.			Corporal.
Herbert, George S.			

Wright's Company, Seminole War 1856.
(CONTINUED.)

NAMES.	MUSTERED IN.	MUSTERED OUT.	REMARKS.
Harriett, Joseph			
Hunter, Henry			
Hunter, Archibald			
Hardee, William B			
Hargroves, Clayton			
Hamilton, John G			
Herrington, Henry			Bugler.
Hall, Augustus			Corporal.
Ivey, James L			
Jeffreys, Joseph A			
Johns, James B			
Jarrard, David, Jr			
Keene, John			
Keene, Noah			
Keene, Thomas			
Keene, Harris			
Keene, Humphrey			
Keene, Randall			
Lemack, James H			
Miller, John			
Mickler, John H., Jr			
Morgan, Daniel A			
Martin, A. H			Sergeant.
Miller, John			
Mickler, Peter S			
Mickler, John H., Sr			
McClure, John C			
Oglesby, Josiah			
Howell, Lewis			
Roberts R. L			
Rewis, R. D			
Rewis, Obadiah			
Ravels, William			
Smith, George W			
Stanand, Dempsey			
Stuggs, Lorenzo D			
Smith, Henry T			Promoted to Captain
Slaughter, C. L			
Slaughter, Moses H			
Stapleton, Francis			
Summerall, Henry			
Slaughter, William H			
Smith, James W. W			
Smith, John			
Turner, James S			
Turner, C. C			
Tucker, Elijah R			
Tompkins, I. W. M			1st Sergeant. Promoted 1st Lieutenant.
Tompkins, Donald			Corporal.
Tison, Simeon			Corporal. Promoted to Sergeant.
Tison, William O			
Wright, Levi			
Wilkerson, Robert			
Wilkerson, D. P			
Walker, James R			
Warner, Francis			
Yearty, William			
Simons, John			
Tompkins, J. W. M			
Tyre, Benjamin			
Parker, Benjamin			
Sweeney, Thomas			Sergeant.
Wright, L. M. G			Bugler.

McNeil's Detachment, Seminole War of 1856.

NAMES.	MUSTERED IN	MUSTERED OUT.	REMARKS.
OFFICERS			
Lieutenant—			
John McNeil			
ENLISTED MEN			
Alexander, Albert I			
Alexander, James A			
Bayet, Edward			
Bassett, Josiah B			
Bassett, John F			
Bassett, John			

McNeil's Detachment, Seminole War of 1856.
(CONTINUED.)

NAMES.	MUSTERED IN.	MUSTERED OUT.	REMARKS.
Bankwright, Hilliard P.			
Bankwright, Wade E.			
Brown, William			Corporal.
Colding, Samuel B.			
Colding, James			
Cray, Scott W.			
Enicks, Andrew S.			
Garrison, William M.			Sergeant.
Hart, William			Sergeant.
Hancock, Henry			
Hancock, James M. J.			
Hope, Samuel E.			
Hope, David			
Johnson, Charles N.			
Johnson, William M.			
Johnson, Washington			
Johnson, Jesse M.			
McNeil, John, Jr.			
Mizel, Joshua, Jr.			
McNatt John B.			
McGeachy, Alex. P.			
Osborn, Robert E.			Corporal.
Pearce, Samuel I.			
Scott, Alexander			
Wiggins, Richard C.			
Wells, Jacob			
Whitehurst John A.			
Whitehurst, Levi S.			

Stewart's Company, Seminole War of 1856.

NAMES.	MUSTERED IN.	MUSTERED OUT.	REMARKS.
OFFICERS.			
Captain—			
Asa Stewart			
1st Lieutenant—			
Franklin Raulerson			
2nd Lieutenant—			
N. Raulerson			
ENLISTED MEN			
Alexander, John			
Arnold, F. D.			
Atkinson, M.			
Altman, David			
Baker, A. A.			
Baker, William J.			
Baker, John F.			
Bennett, William			
Byrd, William			
Bynum, C. F.			Corporal.
Brannin, H. M.			
Brown, John C.			
Brown, Jeremiah			
Brooks, Thomas			
Bush, William			
Chesser, Thomas			
Curry, Jones			Corporal.
Chesser, William H.			
Compton Thomas			
Crews, John			
Curry, Joel			
Cobb, N. S.			
Davis, Thomas			
Dean, Thadeus R.			
Duke, D. L.			Sergeant.
Duke, G. F.			Corporal.
Ellis, Thomas C.			
Emanuel, I. S.			Sergeant.
Fountain, James J.			
Fryerson, J. J.			
Gillet, Anderson			
Gillet, J. J.			
Giddens, Patrick			
Hires, D. O.			
Hires, George A.			
Hagens, M. D.			
Hagens, William H.			

Stewart's Company, Seminole War of 1856.
(Continued.)

NAMES.	MUSTERED IN.	MUSTERED OUT.	REMARKS.
Harrington, Jasper			
Hunter, Elijah			
Humphreys, J. P.			Corporal.
Ivey, M. J.			
Ivey, Robert			
Johnston, John			
Kite, Benjamin			
Law, Thomas D.			
Law, Josiah B.			
Lea, G. W.			
Merrit' William			Musician.
Morgan, D. A.			
Morgan, Levin			
Martin, Hiram			
Medlin, W. R.			
Medlin, John			
Munroe, Neil			
McGowen, Joseph			
McCaskell, P. H.			
McCoy, Church			Farrier.
Nichols, R. G.			
Nobles, Saunders			
Patrick, Thomas			
Peacock, Isam			
Phelps, I. P.			
Peterson, John L.			
Peterson, Timothy			
Raulerson, Moses			
Raulerson, Hardee			
Raulerson, John G.			
Raulerson, William			Sergeant.
Roberts, William			
Rogers, Julian D.			
Sistrunk, H. K.			
Sistrunk, James S.			
Sistrunk, Gasper			
Sistrunk, Thomas W.			
Sistrunk, D. M.			
Strange, Peter			
Sutton, John A.			
Snellgrone, George M.			
Summerall, Allen			
Shirley, Jonathan			
Shirley, Jackson			
Smith, James H.			
Smith, Milton			
Smith, Hamilton			
Shepherd, Miles			
Tooke, James T.			
Thomas, James			1st Sergeant.
Tucker, E. R.			Bugler.
Tucker, William J.			
Willis, Joseph J.			
West, Elijah			
Walker, Isham			
Wood, Burr			
Wilkerson, Joseph			
Wall, William W.			
Wall, David H.			
Whitehurst, D. S.			
Whitehurst, Levi S.			
Whitehurst, Mabury			
Wood, John			

Robert Youngblood's Detachment, Seminole War of 1856.

NAMES.	MUSTERED IN.	MUSTERED OUT.	REMARKS.
OFFICERS.			
1st Lieutenant—			
Robert Youngblood			
2nd Lieutenant—			
Asa Clark, Jr.			
ENLISTED MEN			
Adkins, John W.			
Adams, John			
Buck, Richard			Sergeant.
Byrd, Berry			

Robert Youngblood's Detachment, Seminole War of 1856.
(CONTINUED.)

NAMES.	MUSTERED IN.	MUSTERED OUT.	REMARKS.
Benton, Henry			
Barry, W. F.			
Bridges, S. M.			
Cason, Ransom			
Carlton, Lewis			
Clark, John E.			
Dyess, George			Corporal.
Dennison, W. P.			
Denison, J. W.			
Gilbert, Jackson			Sergeant.
Harrison, A. H.			Sergeant.
Holbrook, William			
Hazle, John			
Jones, Jerome M.			Sergeant.
Jones, John.			
Johns, Jerry			
Johns, Levi M. C.			
Johns, Cornelius			
Johns, Burt			
Kelly, William			
Kilbrew, J. C.			
Kirtlin, James			
Lewis, George			
Merre, James			
Martin, James H.			
Morrison, R.			
Page, James L.			
Parker, Richard W.			
Sharp, George			Corporal.
Sanchez, Francis			
Shepherd, F.			
Schlaird, Henry			
Stokes, Binkey			
Tyner, A. I.			
Turner, James			
Thomas, Isaiah			
Thomas, Ezekiel			
Thomas, James M.			
Weeks, James T.			
Williamson, William R.			Corporal.
Wimble, James			Corporal.

Enoch Daniel's Detachment, Seminole War of 1856.

NAMES.	MUSTERED IN.	MUSTERED OUT.	REMARKS.
OFFICERS.			
Lieutenant—			
Enoch Daniels			
ENLISTED MEN			
Brown, Jeremiah			
Cowden, S.			
Daniels, James G.			
Daniels, James W.			
Daniels, Lewis			
Gore, William			
Hudson, Hamilton			
Hudson, Samuel, Jr.			
Hudson, Samuel, Sr.			
Hudson, Garrett			
Hudson, James			
Hogans, E. D.			
Hogans, Jessup			
Hogans, Stephens			
Hill, William A.			
Hatcher, John R.			
Kirkland, O. P. H.			
Lane, Benjamin			
Mooney, Alfred			
Morrison, Hugh			
Newsom, Jasper			
Nobles, Saunders			
Ostein, Isaac			
Starlin, James			
Smith, Benjamin			
Smith, Aaron			
Smith, Hamilton			
Smith, James H.			

Enoch Daniel's Detachment, Seminole War of 185
(CONTINUED.)

NAMES.	MUSTERED IN.	MUSTERED OUT.	REMARKS.
Smith, William P.			
Smith, W. F.			
Stapleton, F.			
Walker, L. F.			
Walker, L. A.			
Wilkerson, Lewis			
Wilkinson, Joseph			
Wilkinson, Willis			
Worthington, G.			
Worthington, S.			
Watterson, Robert			

Hardee's Detachment, Seminole War of 1856.

NAMES.	MUSTERED IN.	MUSTERED OUT.	REMARKS.
OFFICERS.			
William B. Hardee			Sergeant.
ENLISTED MEN.			
Baron, R.			
Cason, W.			
Cason, N.			
Crooms, G.			
Hall, N.			
Lemaeks, W.			
Lemacks, J.			
Locker, J.			
Most, J.			
Moore, A. J.			
Suggs, Lorenzo			
Thomas, W.			

Bell's Company, 'Seminole War of 1856.

NAMES.	MUSTERED IN.	MUSTERED OUT.	REMARKS.
OFFICERS.			
Captain—			
Alexander Bell			
1st Lieutenant—			
John V. Stewart			
2nd Lieutenant—			
A. W. Miller			
ENLISTED MEN.			
Allen, M. P.			
Blaek, Alfred			1st Sergeant
Callahan, William			
Callahan, James P.			
Callahan, Samuel			
Cason, Noah			
Cason, William			
Crooms, George P.			
Carter, Jacob			
Cason, William			
Cooper, James H.			
Doliff, Abner			
Davis, Jacob			
Ellis, Sevin J.			
Foster, W. N.			
Foster, James D.			Sergeant.
Forbes, R. B.			
Ferguson, Thomas			
Frierson, J. D.			
Gill, Francis H.			
Hatch, William			
Hatch, Silas			
Hatch, Isaac			Corporal.
Hatch, Paul			
Hasbrouch, D. C.			Corporal.
Hamilton, J. C.			
Henderson, H. F.			
Hurst, Archibald			

SOLDIERS OF FLORIDA.

Bell's Company, Seminole War of 1856.
(CONTINUED.)

NAMES.	MUSTERED IN.	MUSTERED OUT.	REMARKS.
Hagan, Patrick.			
Howell, William.			
Hines, Rufus.			
Keith, James H.			
Kelly, H. G. W.			
Kelly, Willey.			
Lamb, Theodore.			Corporal.
Lamb, Mitchell.			
Lemacks, William.			
Lee, J. T.			
Lee, Jesse.			
Mannin, Israel.			
Morrow, David.			
Miller, M.			
Poucher, Simeon.			
Register, Mitchell.			
Rooks, James.			
Ross, Francis B.			Sergeant.
Suggs, Noah P.			
Suggs, Thomas.			
Threete, James A.			
Tillman, George W.			
Tillman, Mathew D.			
Watts, Richard.			Sergeant.
Walker, Benjamin.			Corporal.
Wilson, Robert.			
Whitefield, J. J.			
Whitehurst, B.			

Hughey's Company, Seminole War of 1856.

NAMES.	MUSTERED IN.	MUSTERED OUT.	REMARKS.
OFFICERS.			
Captain—.			
Thomas Hughey.			
1st Lieutenant—			
Eben F. Tucker.			
2nd Lieutenant—			
Jackson Poole.			
ENLISTED MEN			
Allen, Richard.			
Allison, William.			
Brown, James M.			Corporal.
Brannen, Wiley J.			Corporal.
Brownlee, A. H.			
Barnes, J. W.			
Cosgrove, Edward.			
Corsey, G. W.			
Clyde, E. W.			
Curry, Jones.			
Curry, Russell.			
Duke, N. B.			
Ellis, John P.			Corporal.
Edwards, John.			
Hughes, H. C.			1st Sergeant.
Hull, B. F.			Sergeant.
Hull, Thomas.			
Hayes, James H.			
House, William G.			
House, Edward.			
Hughey, B. H.			
Lynch, Charles.			
Lundy, Edward.			
McKeever, Neil.			
Mason, J. W.			Sergeant.
Poindexter, J. B.			Sergeant.
Randolph, R. E.			
Shaw, Tillman.			
Scarborough, A.			
White, W. A.			Corporal.
Wright, Thomas C.			

Edward T. Kendrick's Company, Seminole War of 1856.

NAMES.	MUSTERED IN.	MUSTERED OUT.	REMARKS.
OFFICERS.			
Captain—			
Edward T. Kendrick		Jan. 13, '58	
1st Lieutenant—			
John Q. Stewart		Jan. 13, '58	
2nd Lieutenant—			
Thomas B. Law		Jan. 13, '58	
ENLISTED MEN			
Allen, William		Jan. 13, '58	
Alcox, Jesse H		Jan. 13, '58	
Brookes, William T		Jan. 13, '58	
Brown, Bryant		Jan. 13, '58	
Brown, Francis M		Jan. 13, '58	
Bassett, John F		Jan. 13, '58	
Brown, Jeremiah		Jan. 13, '58	Bugler.
Brown, William		Jan. 13, '58	Bugler.
Brewton, James W		Jan. 13, '58	Corporal.
Dudley, James V. R		Jan. 13, '58	
Davis, Thomas S		Jan. 13, '58	
Godwin, Merida M		Jan. 13, '58	
Haskins James B. T		Jan. 13, '58	
Howard, Seth			
Hicks, Richard T		Jan. 13, '58	
Hall, Jesse		Jan. 13, '58	
Hagan, John		Jan. 13, '58	
Hargrove, Clayton		Jan. 13, '58	
Herndon, U. C		Jan. 13, '58	2nd Sergeant.
Hogans, Tency		Jan. 13, '58	
Ivey, James I		Jan. 13, '58	
Johns, James R		Jan. 13, '58	
Jones, Mitchell		Jan. 13, '58	
Jones, Harrison		Jan. 13, '58	Sergeant.
Kersh, Stephen		Jan. 13, '58	
Lenier, Lewis		Jan. 13, '58	
Lockhart, Joel L		Jan. 13, '58	
Lloyd, Isham		Jan. 13, '58	
Mansell, Addison		Jan. 13, '58	
McGeachy, Evan C		Jan. 13, '58	Corporal.
McLeod, William		Jan. 13, '58	
Moore, Reiley		Jan. 13	
Peterson, John L		Jan. 13 '58	1st Sergeant.
Raulerson, Hardee		Jan. 13, '58	Sergeant.
Richardson, William S		Jan. 13, '58	Corporal.
Snowden, Edward		Jan. 13, '58	
Summerall, Henry		Jan. 13, '58	
Stephens, Isham		Jan. 13, '58	
Stephens, Green		Jan. 13, '58	
Tillis, Lafayette		Jan. 13, '58	Sergeant.
Thompson, Erasmus M		Jan. 13, '58	
Whitehurst, Mayberry		Jan. 13, '58	
Webb, George		Jan. 13, '58	
Wemple, James		Jan. 13, '58	
Walker, Ezekiel		Jan. 13, '58	
Weeden, Frederick		Jan. 13, '58	
Woodman, Ambrose		Jan. 13, '58	Farrier.

NAMES.	MUSTERED IN.	MUSTERED OUT.	REMARKS.
OFFICERS.			
1st Lieutenant—			
John Addison			
2nd Lieutenant—			
John Conliff			
ENLISTED MEN.			
Addison, John A			Corporal.
Addison, William H			Bugler.
Addison, David J			Farrier.
Addison, Joel I			
Atgroth, Joseph			
Allen, William Quin			
Beggs, John			
Braden, Joseph			
Branch, Franklin			
Barrow, Reuben T. B			
Barrow, John B. W			
Chairs, Furman			
Clark, Henry A			

(CONTINUED.)

NAMES.	MUSTERED IN.	MUSTERED OUT.	REMARKS.
Cole, Richard B			
Collins, George W			
Conliff, James			
Crawford, Christopher Q			
Craig, John			
Dugger, Isaac L			
G (name illegible)			
Gawero, Michael			
Gibson, Jesse G			
Gilley William T			
Glazier Ezekiel			
Glazier James A			
Goddard, Isa A			
Garpet Rodolphus			
Harrison, William H			
Hawkins Daniel L			
Hunter, Nathaniel P			
Johnston, William H			
Johnston, Levin P			
Kennedy, George R			
Johnston, Joshua M			
Lee, Edmund			
Marr, Edmund			
McLean, John			
McNeil, Archibald			
Mirick, John C			
McMillan, Daniel			
Matsker, George			
Oglesby, Benjamin			
Oglesby, George W			
Peterson, Christian			
Peterson, Henry			
Rawles, Colten B			Sergeant.
Rawles, William A. L			
Snell, Hampton V			
Smith, Isaiah			
Redd, Isaac A			
Redd, David D			
Townsend, Darien N			1st Sergeant.
Vanderipe, James			
Vanderipe, William H			Corporal.
Weaver, Albert			
Williams, James G			
Woodruff, Joseph			
Wyatt, William H			
Wyall, German H			Sergeant.
Whitaker, William H			Corporal.

Parker's Company, Seminole War of 1856.

NAMES.	MUSTERED IN.	MUSTERED OUT.	REMARKS.
OFFICERS.			
Captain—			
John Parker	Oct. 8, '56	Dec. 15, '56	
1st Lieutenant—			
William H. Whitaker	Oct. 8, '56	Dec. 15, '56	
2nd Lieutenant—			
German H. Wyatt	Oct. 8, '56	Dec. 15, '56	
ENLISTED MEN			
Addison, John A	Oct. 8, '56	Dec. 15, '56	
Addison, John	Oct. 8, '56	Dec. 15, '56	Bugler.
Addison, Joel J	Oct. 8, '56	Dec. 15, '56	
Addison, William N	Oct. 8, '56	Dec. 15, '56	
Barrow, Reuben T	Oct. 8, '56	Dec. 15, '56	
Beggs, John A	Oct. 8, '56	Dec. 15, '56	
Beasley, Isaiah	Oct. 8, '56	Dec. 15, '56	
Brinkley Reuben G	Oct. 8, '56	Dec. 15, '56	
Boyet, Henry	Oct. 8, '56	Oec. 15, '56	
Campbell, James R	Oct. 8, '56	Dec. 15, '56	
Carliff, James	Oct. 8, '56	Dec. 15, '56	Farrier
Collins, George W	Oct. 8, '56	Dec. 15, '56	
Cockran, Aaron C	Oct. 8, '56	Dec. 15, '56	
Craig, John	Oct. 8, '56	Dec. 15, '56	
Driggers, Mathew W	Oct. 8, '56	Dec. 15, '56	
Driggers Henry W	Oct 8, '56	Dec. 15, '56	
Gates, Josiah	Oct. 8, '56	Dec. 15, '56	
Gaeero, Michael	Oct. 8, '56	Dec. 15, '56	

Parker's Company, Seminole War of 1856.
(CONTINUED.)

NAMES.	MUSTERED IN.	MUSTERED OUT.	REMARKS.
Gilley, William T.	Oct. 8, '56	Dec. 15, '56	
Gibson, Jesse	Oct. 8, '56	Dec. 15, '56	
Garbet, Rodolph	Oct. 8, '56	Dec. 15, '56	
Goddard, Asa	Oct. 8, '36	Dec. 15, '56	
Green, James B	Oct. 8, '56	Dec. 15, '56	
Glazier, Ezekiel	Oct. 8, '56	Dec. 15, '56	Corporal.
Glazier, James	Oct. 8, '56	Dec. 15, '56	
Hawkins, Daniel	Oct. 8, '56	Dec. 15, '56	
Harrison, William H	Oct. 8, '56	Dec. 15, '56	
Hewit, Edward G	Oct. 8, '56	Dec. 15, '56	
Hooker, Stephen	Oct. 8, '56	Dec. 15, '56	
Johnson, William H	Oct. 8, '56	Dec. 15, '56	
Johnson, Levin P	Oct. 8, '56	Dec. 15, '56	
Lee, Edmund	Oct. 8, '56	Dec. 15, '56	
Marr, Edward	Oct. 8, '56	Oct. 15, '56	
Mink, John C.	Oct. 8, '56	Dec. 15, '56	
McLean, John L	Oct. 8, '56	Dec. 15, '56	
Oglesby, Benjamin	Oct. 8, '56	Dec. 15, '56	
Oglesby, George	Oct. 8, '56	Dec. 15, '56	
Platt, William C	Oct. 8, '56	Dec. 15, '56	
Platt, Lewis B	Oct. 8, '56	Dec. 15, '56	
Platt, John	Oct. 8, '56	Dec. 15, '56	
Porter, James A.	Oct. 8, '56	Dec. 15, '56	
Rawls, William A. L	Oct. 8, '56	Dec. 15, '56	Corporal.
Raulerson, William	Oct. 8, '56	Dec. 15, '56	Sergeant.
Red, David D	Oct. 8, '56	Dec. 15, '56	
Smith, Isaih	Oct. 8, '56	Dec. 15, '56	
Tison, George	Oct. 8, '56	Dec. 15, '56	
Townsend, David	Oct. 8, '56	Dec. 15, '56	1st Sergeant.
Tucker, George	Oct. 8, '56	Dec. 15, '56	
Vanderipe, James	Oct. 8, '56	Dec. 15, '56	
Vanderipe, William	Oct. 8, '56	Dec. 15, '56	Corporal.
Williams, Joseph H	Oct. 8, '56	Dec. 15, '56	
Williams, James D	Oct. 8, '56	Dec. 15, '56	
Willingham, William	Oct. 8, '56	Dec. 15, '56	
Willingham, William H	Oct. 8, '56	Dec. 15 '56	
Wilkinson, Neil T.	Oct. 8, '56	Dec. 15, '56	
Woodruff, Joseph	Oct. 8, '56	Dec. 15, '56	Sergeant.
Wyatt, William H	Oct. 8, '56	Dec. 15, '56	

Roll of Captain R. B. Sullivant, Indian War of 1855.

NAMES.	MUSTERED IN.	MUSTERED OUT.	REMARKS.
OFFICERS			
Captain—			
R. B. Sullivant	Sept. 6, '56	'57	
1st Lieutenant—			
William R. Gibbons	Sept. 6, '56	'57	
2nd Lieutenant—			
Joseph Underhill	Sept. 6, '56	'57	
ENLISTED MEN.			
Johnson, James A	Sept. 6, '56	'57	1st Sergeant.
Philips, H. S.	Sept. 6, '56	'57	Sergeant.
Sullivant, Henry	Sept. 6, '56	'57	Sergeant.
Rials, Aaron	Sept. 6, '56	'57	1st Corporal.
Sullivant, Jackson	Sept. 6, '56	'57	Corporal.
Billingsley, E. F.	Sept. 6, '56	'57	Corporal.
Bird, William	Sept. 6, '56	'57	Corporal.
Underhill, Jeremiah.	Sept. 6, '56	'57	
Booth, William	Sept. 6, '56	'57	
Deklo, D. F.	Sept. 6, '56	'57	
Bearden, S. R.	Sept. 6, '56	'57	
Green, Louis	Sept. 6, '56	'57	
Jones, John.	Sept. 6, '56	'57	
Smith, David	Sept. 6, '56	'57	
Glessen, Louis W	Sept. 6, '56	'57	
Sweet, Henry M.	Sept. 6, '56	'57	
Sweat, Edmond	Sept. 6, '56	'57	
Register, James	Sept. 6, '56	'57	
Lee, Benjamin	Sept. 6, '56	'57	
Sullivant, John	Sept. 6, '56	'57	
Wood, Benjamin	Sept. 6, '56	'57	
Brooker, Joseph	Sept. 6, '56	'57	
Davis, E. J.	Sept. 6, '56	'57	
Drigors, Jacob	Sept. 6, '56	'57	
Burns, Jacob	Sept. 6, '56	'57	
Passmore, Alexander	Sept. 6, '56	'57	

Roll of Captain R. B. Sullivant, Indian War of 1855.

(CONTINUED.)

NAMES	MUSTERED IN.	MUSTERED OUT.	REMARKS.
Sears, John	Sept. 6, '56	'57	
Noles, Jackson	Sept. 6, '56	'57	
Youngblood, Isaiah	Sept. 6, '56	'57	
Nobles, I. T.	Sept. 6, '56	'57	
Cain, Dempsey	Sept. 6, '56	'57	
Sehan, S. E.	Sept. 6, '56	'57	
Oberry, W. C.	Sept. 6, '56	'57	
Ashley, Edward W.	Sept. 6, '66	'57	
McCrancy, Nathan	Sept. 6, '56	'57	
Booth, James	Sept. 6, '56	'57	
Branning, William H.	Sept. 6, '56	'57	
Chancey, Samuel	Sept. 6, '56	'57	
Johnson, W. W.	Sept. 6, '56	'57	
Sullivant, B. W.	Sept. 6, '56	'57	
Billingsley, James	Sept. 6, '56	'57	
Clark, John	Sept. 6, '56	'57	
Hagans, David	Sept. 6, '56	'57	
Brookersen, Joseph	Sept. 6, '56	'57	
Stanley, William	Sept. 6, '56	'57	
Gibbons, James S.	Sept. 6, '56	'57	
Tawls, George	Sept. 6, '56	'57	
Jones, James	Sept. 6, '56	'57	
Roberts, R. B.	Sept. 6, '56	'57	
Shedd, W. W.	Sept. 6, '56	'57	
Curry, Z. J.	Sept. 6, '56	'57	
Taylor, Alfred	Sept. 6, '56	'57	
Bennett, Hiram	Sept. 6, '56	'57	
Bennett, Willie	Sept. 6, '56	'57	
Philips, A. J.	Sept. 6, '56	'57	
Wilkerson, Bryant	Sept. 6, '56	'57	
Polk, Zackariah	Sept. 6, '56	'57	
Green, James A.	Sept. 6, '56	'57	
Varns, Jacob H.	Sept. 6, '56	'57	
Mercer, John	Sept. 6, '56	'57	
Davis, Andrew	Sept. 6, '56	'57	
Philips, John	Sept. 6, '56	'57	
McColanhan, Henry	Sept. 6, '56	'57	
Hampton, Robert	Sept. 6, '56	'57	
Sparkman, Lewellin	Sept. 6, '56	'57	

Roll of Captain S. L. Sparkman's Company, 1855.

NAMES.	MUSTERED IN.	MUSTERED OUT.	REMARKS.
OFFICERS.			
Captain—			
S. L. Sparkman	Dec. 1, '55	Jan. 1, '60	
ENLISTED MEN			
Majors, O. P.	Dec. 1, '55	Jan. 1, '60	
McKinney, A. J.	Dec. 1, '55	Jan. 1, '60	
Gainey, Richard	Dec. 1, '55	Jan. 1, '60	
Simmes, Abram	Dec. 1, '55	Jan. 1, '60	
Carney, William	Dec. 1, '55	Jan. 1, '60	
Flint, Martin	Dec. 1, '55	Jan. 1, '60	
Rowe, A. J.	Dec. 1, '55	Jan. 1, '60	
Mather	Dec. 1, '55	Jan. 1, '60	
Harris, Joseph M.	Dec. 1, '55	Jan. 1, '60	
Sparkman, M. K.	Dec. 1, '55	Jan. 1, '60	
Ruching, W. W.	Dec. 1, '55	Jan. 1, '60	
Neeley, W. L.	Dec. 1, '55	Jan. 1, '60	
Smith, W. W.	Dec. 1, '55	Jan. 1, '60	
Simmons, George	Dec. 1, '55	Jan. 1, '60	
Platt, Peter	Dec. 1, '55	Jan. 1, '60	
McClelland, G.	Dec. 1, '55	Jan. 1, '60	
Hawkins, John W.	Dec. 1, '55	Jan. 1, '60	
Fritch, John M.	Dec. 1, '55	Jan. 1, '60	
Simmons, Marshall	Dec. 1, '55	Jan. 1, '60	
Franklin, George	Dec. 1, '55	Jan. 1, '60	
Dees, Henry	Dec. 1, '55	Jan. 1, '60	
Collins, John	Dec. 1, '55	Jan. 1, '60	
Campbell, W. J.	Dec. 1, '55	Jan. 1, '60	
Bryant, J. C.	Dec. 1, '55	Jan. 1, '60	
Bryant, F. M.	Dec. 1, '55	Jan. 1, '60	
Smith, George W.	Dec. 1, '55	Jan. 1, '60	
Lanier, H. M.	Dec. 1, '55	Jan. 1, '60	
Blocker, William M.	Dec. 1, '55	Jan. 1, 60	
Frier, Henry	Dec. 1, '55	Jan. 1, '60	
Well, Samuel A.	Dec. 1, '55	Jan. 1, 60	

Roll of Captain S. L. Sparkman's Company, 1855.

(CONTINUED.)

NAMES.	MUSTERED IN.	MUSTERED OUT.	—	REMARKS.
Sylvester, Henry	Dec. 1, '55	Jan. 1, '60		
Robertson, A. B.	Dec. 1, '55	Jan. 1, '60		
Peirce, T. C.	Dec. 1, '55	Jan. 1 '60		
Hollingsworth, S. T.	Dec. 1, '55	Jan. 1, '60		
Buffum, R. V.	Dec. 1, '55	Jan. 1, '60		
Hollingsworth, Stephen	Dec. 1, '55	Jan. 1, '60		
Hollingsworth, Timothy	Dec. 1, '55	Jan. 1, '60		
Zebenden, C.	Dec. 1, '55	Jan. 1, '60		
Rogers, Samuel J.	Dec. 1, '55	Jan. 1, '60		
Collins, Hardy	Dec. 1, '55	Jan. 1, '60		
Lanier. R. H.	Dec. 1 '55	Jan. 1, '60		
Rushing, W. T.	Dec. 1, '55	Jan. 1, '60		

PART II

*Florida in the War
Between the States*

1861-1865

Florida in the War Between the States.

With the causes that led up to the war and the convention that took Florida out of the Union, this record has nothing to do, but it may with propriety mention some facts precedent to the organization of the various companies and regiments that served during the War Between the States.

In January 1861, the United States occupied, on the Appalachicola river the arsenal at Chattachoochee, where a small quantity of arms and munitions of war were stored; on Pensacola Bay, the Navy Yard, Fort Barrancas with forty pieces of artillery, the Fort Barrancas barracks, where there was a battery of field artillery; Fort McRae with 125 pieces of artillery; Fort Pickens with 201 heavy guns; on Amelia Island, the uncompleted work, Fort Clinch; at St. Augustine, Fort Marion with 6 field batteries, and at the extreme south Fort Taylor and the barracks at Key West and on Garden Key, one of the Dry Tortugas, the stupendous but uncompleted work, Fort Jefferson, covering thirteen and one-half acres, and designed to mount 300 guns, which it had been the special ambition of Jefferson Davis, as Secretary of War and Senator, to make the commanding fortress of the Gulf.

On January 5, 1861, Senator Yulee wrote from Washington to Joseph Finnegan, "The immediate important thing to be do e is the occupation of the forts and arsenals in Florida . . . the "naval station and forts at Pensacola being first in importance." This was the policy pursued in all the Southern States on the ground that the works had been constructed by the public money of the United States for the defense of each State, so that the State, when leaving the Union, had a better title to the property than any one else. Self defense was a further justification. In every case promises were offered to account for the property taken, in the final and general settlement with the United States.

Pensacola at once became the point in Florida upon which the attention of both North and South were most anxiously concentrated. At the forts near this city was apparently to be decided the question whether the National Government would or would not submit peacefully to the secession of Florida. In this uncertain condition the commanding officer, fearing a clash of arms, abandoned the main and the Navy Yard and took refuge in Fort Pickens.

Lieut. Adam J. Slemmer, in the absence of his captain, John H. Winder, who afterward became a general in the Confederate army, had command of the company of United States artillery stationed at Pensacola Bay. The Navy Yard and the vessels in the bay, the war steamer Wyandotte and the store-ship Supply were under the orders of Commodore Armstrong, Commander Ebenezer Farrand, afterward an officer in the Confederate navy, being second in command. The 70 ordinary sailors and 48 marines at the Navy

Yard were under command of Capt. Joseph Watson. Old Fort Barrancas and Fort McRae, each powerful works as against attacks from water, were not designed to resist an assault from the rear, and any attempt to defend them or the Navy Yard from such an assault would have been futile and inviting the immediate destruction of the Navy Yard. On January 8, 1861, Lieutenant Slemmer began the removal of powder from the Spanish fort to Fort Barrancas; that night a party of citizens who were reconnoitering were warned off by a shot from Fort Barrancas. On January 10 Slemmer abandoned the mainland, spiked the guns at Fort Barrancas, destroyed over 20,000 pounds of powder at Fort McRae and transferred his men to Fort Pickens on Santa Rosa Island, where he h d a secure stronghold, though his force was inadequate to properly garrison it.

Military companies from Alabama were already arriving at Pensacola to assist Florida in taking possession of the Navy Yard and defensive works. These Alabama volunteers were under the command of Colonel Tennant C. Lomax, a Mexican War veteran. Chief in command at Pensacola was the appointee of the Florida State Convention, Major-General William H. Chase, a native of Massachusetts, and officer of the United States army from 1819 to 1856, who during his official connection with the United States army had superintended the construction of Fort Taylor and the defenses of Pensacola Bay. After his resignation from the rmy in 1856 he became a resident of Pensacola and President of Alabama & Florida Railroad Company.

Among the Florida troops on duty at that time were the Pensacola Rifle Rangers, commanded by Capt. E. A. Perry, an officer destined to serve with distinctio both in the military and civil history of Florida, and the Santa Rosa Guards, organized at Milton, Fla., under command of Capt. William Harrison. The Rifle Rangers became Company A of the 2nd Florida Infantry, and served in the Army of Northern Virginia. The Santa Rosa Guards were disbanded after about three months' service and its members joined other commands. On January 12, 1861, Colonel Lomax, with the Florida and Alabama troops, seven companies, numbering 700 men, marched to the Navy Yard, and halted at the East Gate. Leaving his men he, with Gene al Chase's aides, Col. R. L. Campbell, Captain Randolph, late of the United States army, Captain Farrand, la e of the United States Navy, and two Alabama officers, Marks and Burroughs, proceeded to the office of Commodore Armstrong, where in the name of Governor M. S. Perry he dem ded the surrender of the Navy Yard and stores. To this demand Armstrong announced that he would relinquis his authority to the representative of the sovereignty of Florida.

The flag of the United States was immediately hauled down and the flag of the State raised in its place. The marines remaining in the barracks were at onc paroled and allowed to go North on the store-ship Supply.

Lieutenant Slemmer determined to hold Fort Pickens and decl ned to admit that the Governors of Florida and Alabama had any authority to demand his surrender. General Chase made the second demand, which was refused; later on a third attempt was made to induce the Lieutenant to abandon his position, but without success. On the mainland was assembled a force of volunteers ample to make the assault, and had not the Florida Senators and other leaders in Washington, including Senator Jefferson Davis, telegraphed advice that no blood be shed, the first battle of the war would have been fought on Santa Rosa Island in January 1861.

While these events were transpiring at Pensacola two companies of volunteer infantry, one under A. Perry Amaker of Leon county, and the other under James Patton Anderson of Jefferson county, had marched from Tallahassee to St. Marks, to take passage for Pensacola to engage in the proposed attack on Fort Pickens. When that attack was abandoned these troops returned to their respective stations to be called within three months to the arsenal at Chattahoochee, where they became a part of the 1st Florida Regiment.

At the same time that the Navy Yard was occupied the Florida militia, under orders of Gove nor Perry, occupied Fort Clinch on Amelia Island, and on January 7, 1861, Old Fort Marion and the arsenal at St. Augustine were seized by the same authority, and Fort Marion soon put in condition for defense by an artillery company under Captain Gibbs, another volunteer organization. At the time these seizures of the United States fortifications and arsenals were made, it was not known that war would result from the act of secession. In all the posts surrendered, there was only a nominal guard and no attempts at resistance were made. On the St. Johns river defensive works were begun, and batteries erected to command and protect the bar; this work was done by the Jacksonville Light Infantry, under command of Capt. Holmes Steele and by the citizens of the section.

About January 20, Fort Jefferson on Garden Key was re-enforced by the United States authority. While their troops were disembarking, the steamer Galveston, of New Orleans, approached with a Confederate force on board, evidently intending to take possession, but seeing it was too late put about and disappeared.

Forts Taylor, Jefferson and Pickens with the islands commanded by them, and Fortress Monroe in Virginia, were the only places in the South that continued under the stars and stripes during the entire period of the war. From Key West re-enforcements were sent to Fort Pickens in the later part of January, but through the interposition of Senator Mallory, and upon the pledge of General Chase that hostilities would be commenced, the artillery-men were not landed. Mallory yet hoped that amicable adjustment might be made by which the South would be permitted to leave the Union peacefully. A cannon shot would rouse the people to arms from the Lakes to the Gulf and defeat the efforts to compromise the differences between the sections.

A state of war actually existed in Florida three months before the fall of Fort Sumter; the truce of Pensacola Bay was an armed and watchful one. On March 11, 1861, General Braxton Bragg arrived in Pensacola and assumed command of all the Confederate forces; by his direction the construction of land batteries was immediately resumed.

It is unfortunate that so little remains in the custody of the State of the records of the early organization of troops by the State authority. It is supposed that most of these records were destroyed by some one at the Capitol before it was occupied by the Federals in 1865 to prevent any incriminating evidence falling into their hands that might be used in case of prosecution for "treason," of which there was much talk; this however is merely supposition. From what was left it would appear that these records were lost or destroyed during the re-construction period.

It is known that the militia organization of the State was soon broken up, the men belonging to it volunteering for Confederate State service and the message of Governor Milton, after he went into office in the year 1861, shows that he viewed this proceeding with sincere regret. It was his ambition to create an army for "the independent nation of Florida," and while assisting the Confederacy to the limit of his ability, reserved the right of Florida to maintain an army of her own. Said the Governor in his special message in November 1861, "volunteering has broken up the militia," and "the service was disorganized by individuals organizing volunteers under the authority of the Secretary of War, a power inconsistent with the rights of a free, sovereign and independent State." The men who enlisted, however, were anxious only about the probability of receiving orders to go to the front, and whenever this appeared unlikely they resigned or broke up their companies and enlisted in those most likely to receive orders to go immediately to the front.

The first regiment organized was known as the 1st Florida Infantry. It was composed of two companies from Leon, two companies from Alachua and one each from Franklin, Jackson, Madison, Gadsden, Jefferson and Escambia counties. These companies, with the exception of Company K (Pensacola Guards), which was from Escambia county, rendezvoused at Chattahoochee arsenal where they went into Camp of Instruction. There, on April 5, 1861, the regiment was mustered into the military service of the Confederate States for twelve months, and was organized by the election of Capt. James Patton Anderson, of Jefferson county, Colonel; William K. Beard, of Leon county, as Lieutenant-Colonel, and Thadeus MacDonell, of Alachua county, as Major. Upon the completion of the organization of the regiment it was ordered to Pensacola where it arrived April 12, 1861, and was there joined by Company K. Like all regiments mustered in in the early days of 1861, it enlisted for twelve months and served almost its entire term in Pensacola and in that vicinity.

On October 8, 1861. General Bragg planned an attack on the Federal camps on Santa Rosa Island. The immediate command of this expedition was entrusted to Gen. Richard Henry Anderson, of South Carolina, an old army officer. Anderson's subordinate commanders were: James R. Chalmers with 350 Mississipians and Alabamians; Col. James Patton Anderson, with 400 men, and John K. Jackson with 250 Georgians. In addition to these there was one independent company from Georgia and one arti.lery company. The troops landed on Santa Rosa Island at 2 o'clock on the morning of October 9, 1861; surprised the camp of New York Zouaves, who were quickly driven out at the point of the bayonet and their camp and buildings adjacent thereto set on fire. Finding it impossible to inflict further damage on the Federals General Anderson ordered a retreat. Twenty prisoners were taken by the Confederates, among them was Maj. Israel Bodges. The Federal loss was 14 killed and 36 wounded. Confederate loss 28 killed, 39 wounded and 30 captured. Of this number the 1st Regiment lost 6 killed, 8 wounded and 12 captured. Killed, Capt. Richard Bradford, of Company F; Sergt. W. R. Routh; Privates Henry A. Tillinghast and John Hale, of Company A; Privates Lewis F. Thompson and Smith, of Company B; wounded, Corporal Lanier and Privates James Eeles, of Company B; William McCorckle, Philip L. Simms and William Denham, of Company A; James Hicks and Amos Sharitt, of Company B; Peter O'Neal, of Company C. Captured, Lieuts. F. M. Farley, of Company E; S. Y. Finley, of Company C, and Parker.

In March 1862, the 1st Regiment was ordered to Corinth, Miss., to join General Bragg's army. The regiment got as far as Montgomery when their term of enlistment expired and they were mustered out April 6, 1862. But four companies were formed immediately from the ranks of the 1st as follows: Company A, Capt. W. G. Poole (Poole was 2nd Lieutenant in Company D, 1st Florida); Company D, Capt. A. Denham (Denham was 1st Lieutenant in Company I); Company E, 1st Lieut. John E. Miller, commanding (formerly a 3rd Lieutenant in Company K, 1st Florida). These four companies were formed into a battalion, of which Maj. T. A. MacDonnell took command. The battalion did gallant service at Shiloh, receiving complimentary mention in general orders and were accorded the right to inscribe the name of the battle on their flag. An old battle flag of the Western Army, now preserved at the Capitol at Tallahassee, bears the inscription: "First and Third Florida, Shiloh and Perryville." Major MacDonnell was wounded and disabled in the opening of the battle. Capt. T. Sumter Means was wounded, captured and later resigned. Capt. W. C. Bird was also wounded in this battle, and Laurie Anderson, battalion adjutant, was killed. Lieut.-Col. W. K. Beard, on General Bragg's staff, was wounded in the arm. After the battle of Shiloh, in which the Floridians lost 2 officers and 14 men killed, 7 officers and 51 men wounded, two companies from Louisiana, known as B and C, were added to the battalion making a battalion of six companies and Maj. Franklin H. Clarke assigned to the command with the following Field and Staff: 2nd Lieut. A. Robert Pollard, Adjutant; —. —. Frome, Assistant Surgeon; 1st Lieut. Monheimer, Assistant Quartermaster; J. P. Butler, Sergeant Major; F. M. Rowe, Quartermaster-Sergeant; Louis Hyer, Commissary Sergeant; —. —. Austin, Ordinance Sergeant, and Daniel R. Monroe, Hospital Steward. In May 1862, Clarke was promoted Lieutenant-Colonel; W. G. Poole, promoted Major; Pollard, 1st Lieutenant and Adjutant; Forme, Surgeon; Monheimer, Assistant Quartermaster, was dropped from the roll by order of the War Department; Thomas D. Wolfe, appointed Sergeant-Major (John P. Butler, Sergeant-Major, appointed April 23, 1862, returned to his company (C) May 31, 1862); F. M. Rowe, Quartermaster-Sergeant; Daniel R. Monroe, Hospital Steward; Louis M. Brisbin and John Snider, Company C; Felix Segiane and Samuel McGill, Company B; and John Callen, Company A, Musicians. On July 5th Major MacDonnell returned to his command, reported for duty and by order of General Bragg relieved Lieutenant Clarke. In July 1862, Major Miller reached Chattanooga with six companies from Florida, and the Florida and Confederate Guards Response Battalion was dissolved, the two companies from Louisiana going to the Crescent Regiment and the 5th Company of Washington Artillery. The four Florida companies were joined by the six companies under Major Miller and the 1st Florida was re-formed under command of William Miller, who was promoted Colonel; T. A. MacDonnell promoted Lieutenant-Colonel, and G. A. Ball, Major. In August, 1862, the 3rd Florida Regiment reached Chattanooga and with the 1st Florida, 3rd Louisian , and the 41st Mississippi were formed into a brigade and placed under command o: Brig.-Gen. John C. Brown, Maj.-Gen. Patton Anderson's Division. In this brigade the 1st took part in the Kentucky campaign. On their return to Chattanooga on December 13, 1862, the 1st and 3rd was so decimated that they were united, and were afterward known as the 1st and 3rd Regiments consolidated. The 3rd, forming the right wing, and the 1st, the left wing of the regiment. The consolidated regiment was under the command of Col. William Miller, who was shortly promoted to Brigadier-General and ordered to Florida. The 1st and 3rd Regiment consolidated participated in all the great battles of the Western Army and in every engagement won honors for the State whose colors it carried.

It is seriously to be regretted that a more detailed account of the career of this Regiment cannot be given at this time. In the revised addition which it is hoped will follow this work an effort will be made to tell the whole story of the gallant men who fought under the flags of the 1st and 3rd Florida Regiments.

Old Guards, Mounted Rangers—Captain James H. Breaker.

The Old Guards were mustered into the service of the State by Captain Joseph M. Taylor March 29th 1862. After three months service they were mustered out under General Order No. IX, by Captain Joseph M. Taylor at Brookville, Florida.

NAMES.	MUSTERED IN.	MUSTERED OUT.	REMARKS.
OFFICERS.			
Captain—			
James H. Breaker	March 29, '62	May 17, '62	
1st Lieutenant—			
M. C. Peterson	March 29, '62	May 17, '62	
ENLISTED MEN.			
Allen, Darlin	March 29, '62	May 17, '62	
Allen, John B	March 29, '62	May 17, '62	2nd Sergeant.
Andreas, Jackson L	March 29, '62	May 17, '62	
Baker, John F	March 29, '62	May 17, '62	
Baker, Thadeus L	March 29, '62	May 17, '62	
Bassett, John	March 29, '62	May 17, '62	
Bayer, Nathan	March 29, '62	May 17, '62	
Boyet, John	March 29, '62	May 17, '62	
Burnham, A. G	March 29, '62	May 17, '62	
Cray, William R	March 29, '62	May 17, '62	2nd Corporal.
Crughton, John P	March 29, '62	May 17, '62	
Ederington, Francis H	March 29, '62	May 17, '62	
Ellis, Thomas E	March 29, '62	May 17, '62	
Elverton, Goodman P	March 29, '62	May 17, '62	
Frierson, Aaron T	March 29, '62	May 17, '62	
Frierson, William L	March 29, '62	May 17, '62	
Gerard, Jacob A	March 29, '62	May 17, '62	
Harrell, Edward M	March 29, '62	May 17, '62	
Harrell, John E	March 29, '62	May 17, '62	
Hayman, James	March 29, '62	May 17, '62	
Hill, Chesly D	March 29, '62	May 17, '62	
Hope, Henry	March 29, '62	May 17	
Hope, William	March 29, '62	May 17, '62	
Hunt, William J	March 29, '62	May 17, '62	
Jackson, Thomas B	March 29, '62	May 17, '62	
Junp, Thomas J	March 29, '62	May 17, '62	

Old Guards, Mounted Rangers—Captain James H. Breaker.
(Continued.)

NAMES.	MUSTERED IN.	MUSTERED OUT.	REMARKS.
Kersy, Liborn	March 29, '62	May 17, '62	
Law, Joshua B	March 29, '62	May 17, '62	
McNeil, John	March 29, '62	May 17, '62	
Mayo, Anderson	March 29, '62	May 17, '62	
Mayo, Washington T	March 29, '62	May 17, '62	1st Sergeant.
Mein, William H	March 29, '62	May 17, '62	
Mickler, Jacob B	March 29, '62	May 17, '62	
Mizell, Joshua	March 29, '62	M y 17, '62	
Mizell, Morgan	March 29, '62	May 17, '62	
Mundon, Allen B	March 29, '62	May 17, '62	
O'Neil, Cotton B	March 29, '62	May 17, '62	1st Corporal.
Osman, Robert C	March 29, '62	May 17, '62	
Parnell, Gillis	March 29, '62	May 17, '62	
Pearce, Samuel I	March 29, '62	May 17, '62	
Pinkston, James T	March 29, '62	May 17, '62	
Pinkston, Thomas G. B	March 29, '62	May 17, '62	
Seals, Cornelius	March 29, '62	May 17, '62	
Smith, William S	March 29, '62	May 17, '62	
Strange, Peter	March 29, '62	May 17, '62	
Sykes, Frederick	March 29, '62	May 17, '62	
Thomas, Spencer T	March 29, '62	May 17, '62	
Thompson, J	March 29, '62	May 17, '62	
Townsend, John	March 29, '62	May 17, '62	
Tucker, Elijah H	March 29, '62	May 17, '62	
Wall Perry G	March 29, '62	M y 17, '62	

Milton Artillery—Captain George C. Acosta.

A roll of artillery company, recorded as the Milton Artillery, organized for the defense of the St. Johns River and Jacksonville. There is nothing to show when this Company entered the service, how long it remained in service or where or what that service was. The names of a few of the members of this Company are to be found in the 11th Regiment. Evidently the Company was organized early in the War and was dissolved. after possibly a few weeks organization, and its members enlisted in other commands.

NAMES.	MUSTERED IN.	MUSTERED OUT.	REMARKS.
OFFICERS.			
Captain—			
George C. Acosta			
1st Lieutenant—			
John Thomas			
2nd Lieutenant—			
John Price			Re-enlisted, Co. D, 11th Regiment.
3rd Lieutenant—			
John Price, Jr			Re-enlisted, Co. D, 11th Regiment.
ENLISTED MEN.			
Adams, George W			Re-enlisted, Co. D, 11th Regiment.
Allen, William S			
Andrew, John C			
Bigelow, E			
Bigelow, L. B			
Calwell, George			
Campbell, Wesley			
Capella, Laurence			
Cole, William			
Cottle, Reuben			
Firnhendorf, Bernch			
Games, Joseph			
Gilchrist, George			
Gillen, William J			
Grisham, Ephriam			
Grotley, John			
Hammon, Elias			Re-enlisted, Co. D, 11th Regiment.
Hammon, Semore			
Hammon, William			
Hammon, William B			
Hartley, Gabriel			
Hartley, Joseph			
Hartley, William			

Milton Artillery—Captain George C. Acosta.
(CONTINUED.)

NAMES.	MUSTERED IN.	MUSTERED OUT.	REMARKS.
Hopkins, G. W.			
Jerika, Henry.			
Joiner, Elbert S.			
Jones, Mitchell.			
Lag, James.			
Low, Archibald.			
Mason, Charles J.			
McDowell, John C.			
McGregor, Patrick.			
McIntire, R. W.			
O'Neal, Henry.			
Ortegas, Ignedis.			
Ortegas, John.			
Petty, George.			
Petty, George, Jr.			
Phillips, Robert.			
Pickett, H.			Re-enlisted Co. D, 11th Regiment.
Roberts, Andrew J.			Re-enlisted, Co. D, 11th Regiment.
Roberts, F. M.			
Roberts, Isaih.			
Roberts, Josiah, Jr.			
Roberts, J. M.			
Roberts, Washington.			
Songer, Henry C.			
Santo, Joseph.			
Scott, Edward.			
Serdy, Julius.			
Sittlebery, John.			
Stone, Charles.			
Sutty, John C.			
Tanner, Joseph.			
Thebaut, Bartolo.			
Turner, C. T.			
Vinson, James.			
Whitaker, James.			
Wilford, Lewis.			
Wingett, Joel B.			
Wingett, John D.			
Worley, George.			

Taylor Eagles—Captain John M. Hendry.

This Company was called into the service of the State by the Governor on the 28th day of October, 1861, but the record does not show who mustered, to what command it was attached or where it served. The ages given show that the men were all within the military age except five, who were sixteen and seventeen years of age.

NAMES.	MUSTERED IN.	MUSTERED OUT.	REMARKS.
OFFICERS.			
Captain—			
J. M. Hendry	Oct. 22, '61		
1st Lieutenant—			
William H. Sevor	Oct. 22, '61		
2nd Lieutenant—.			
J. H. Baker	Oct. 22, '61		
3rd Lieutenant—			
William J. Smart	Oct. 22, '61		
ENLISTED MEN.			
Anderson, Jerry W.	Oct. 22, '61		
Arnold, Francis M.	Oct. 22, '61		
Blanton, A.	Oct. 22, '61		
Blanton, J. B.	Oct. 22, '61		
Boyett, James	Oct. 22, '61		
Brantley, A.	Oct. 22, '61		
Carlton, T. A.	Oct. 22, '61		
Devane, G. I.	Oct. 22, '61		
Duncan, A. J.	Oct. 22, '61		
English, J. C.	Oct. 22, '61		
Flinn, S. B.	Oct. 22, '61		
Harrell, W. H.	Oct. 22, '61		
Henderson, W.	Oct. 22, '61		

Taylor Eagles—Captain John M. Hendry.
(CONTINUED.)

NAMES	MUSTERED IN.	MUSTERED OUT.	REMARKS.
Hendry, J. W.	Oct. 22, '61		
Hendry, R. W.	Oct. 22, '61		
Howren, A. C.	Oct. 22, '61		
Howren, J. B.	Oct. 22, '61		
Jackson, James O.	Oct. 22, '61		
Lanier, Bird.	Oct. 22, '61		
Lewis, John.	Oct. 22, '61		
McCall, B. F.	Oct. 22, '61		
McMullen, D. J.	Oct. 22, '61		
McMullen, E. H.	Oct. 22, '61		
Morgan, J. N.	Oct. 22, '61		
Newborne, William	Oct. 22, '61		
O'Neal, C. C.	Oct. 22, '61		
O'Quinn, J. R.	Oct. 22, '61		
Robertson, W. E.	Oct. 22, '61		
Rowell, David.	Oct. 22, '61		
Sharpe, C. W.	Oct. 22, '61		
Sloane, Malachi.	Oct. 22, '61		
Sloane, W. R.	Oct. 22, '61		
Starling, Alfred.	Oct. 22, '61		
Taylor, William B.	Oct. 22, '61		
White, S. R.	Oct. 22, '61		
Woods, F. M.	Oct. 22, '61		
Woods, John.	Oct. 22, '61		
Woods, T. J., Jr.	Oct. 22, '61		
Zipperor, J. A.	Oct. 22, '61		
Zipperor, S. G.	Oct. 22, '61		
Zipperor, T. E.	Oct. 22, '61		

Bartow Cavalry—Captain John W. Brady.

This Company was raised under an order from Governor John Milton, dated October 11th, 1861, and was ordered attached to the 1st Cavalry Regiment, Florida State Troops, Colonel John Bradford commanding. The mustering was done by John W. Brady and James L. Winter, at Jacksonville, Fla., October 14th, 1861, but there is nothing to show where the Company served or when it was mustered out of service.

NAMES.	MUSTERED IN.	MUSTERED OUT.	REMARKS.
OFFICERS.			
Captain—			
John W. Brady	Oct. 11, '61		
1st Lieutenant—			
James L. Winter.	Oct. 11, '61		
2nd Lieutenant—			
Charles C. Hanford	Oct. 11, '61		
3rd Lieutenant—			
S. I. Robinson.	Oct. 11, '61		
ENLISTED MEN			
Atkinson, William	Oct. 11, '61		
Bacon, John G.	Oct. 11, '61		
Bacon, Sylvesta.	Oct. 11, '61		
Barbee, Joseph A.	Oct. 11, '61		
Bigelow, E.	Oct. 11, '61		
Bigelow, Lucius.	Oct. 11, '61		
Brown, E.	Oct. 11, '61		
Brown, Hen.	Oct. 11, '61		
Burney, M.	Oct. 11, '61		
Burnham, William.	Oct. 11, '61		
Byrne, John.	Oct. 11, '61		
Dacosta, John B.	Oct. 11, '61		
Cannon, David M.	Oct. 11, '61		
Carmichael, J.	Oct. 11, '61		
Cox, Hatch.	Oct. 11, '61		
Fawcett, J.	Oct. 11, '61		
Flynn, Charles M.	Oct. 11, '61		
Gardner, George.	Oct. 11, '61		
Gardner, Isaac.	Oct. 11, '61		
Gardner, John.	Oct. 11, '61		
Geiger, John.	Oct. 11, '61		
Goodspead, C.	Oct. 11, '61		

Bartow Cavalry—Captain John W. Brady.

(CONTINUED.)

NAMES.	MUSTERED IN.	MUSTERED OUT.	REMARKS.
Gordon, William M	Oct. 11, '61		
Grace, Major C	Oct. 11, '61		
Gunn, S. W	Oct. 11, '61		
Hagin, John	Oct. 11, '61		
Hagins, Joseph R	Oct. 11, '61		
Hall, William J	Oct. 11, '61		
Hartley, Benjamin	Oct. 11, '61		
Hartley, Frank	Oct. 11, '61		
Hartley, George	Oct. 11, '61		
Hartley, Redwick	Oct. 11, '61		
Hirsch, G	Oct. 11, '61		
Hogan, Reuben	Oct. 11, '61		
Holmes. Alexander	Oct. 11, '61		
Houston, L	Oct. 11, '61		
Hudnall, James	Oct. 11, '61		
Hudnall, Samuel	Oct. 11, '61		
Hudwell, Francis, Jr	Oct. 11, '61		
Hughes, Reuben	Oct. 11, '61		
Hurlburt, James	Oct. 11, '61		
Jaudon, Elias, Jr	Oct. 11, '61		
Jaudon, Henry	Oct. 11, '61		
Jaudon, William	Oct. 11, '61		
Kernan, Thomas	Oct. 11, '61		
LaCourse, Joseph	Oct. 11, '61		
Lorricy, John	Oct. 11, '61		
Low, Columbia	Oct. 11, '61		
McFall, Charles	Oct. 11, '61		
McGraw, Robert	Oct. 11, '61		
Matess, Theodore	Oct. 11, '61		
Mills, J. L	Oct. 11, '61		
Miller, Nathaniel W	Oct. 11, '61		
Miranda, Thomas	Oct. 11, '61		
Peterson, Archibald	Oct. 11, '61		
Plunk, Michael	Oct. 11, '61		
Puty, George, Jr	Oct. 11, '61		
Richardson, James	Oct. 11, '61		
Roberts, Joseph	Oct. 11, '61		
Rouse, Ansel	Oct. 11, '61		
Shadd, John D	Oct. 11, '61		
Sidberg, John D	Oct. 11, '61		
Silcox, Wade	Oct. 11, '61		
Silcox, Isaac	Oct. 11, '61		
Sparkman, Alfred	Oct. 11, '61		
Sparkman, Luke	Oct. 11, '61		
Sparkman, William	Oct. 11, '61		
Spiers, William	Oct. 11, '61		
Sweat, Alfred J	Oct. 11, '61		
Turknett, James	Oct. 11, '61		
Turknett, Lawrence	Oct. 11, '61		
Waldon, Robert	Oct. 11, '61		
Weedman, Bernard	Oct. 11, '61		
Weedman, Phillip	Oct. 11, '61		
Wheaton, T. J	Oct. 11, '61		
Whitaker, Jacob	Oct. 11, '61		
Wilden, John D	Oct. 11, '61		
Wilford, Lewis	Oct. 11, '61		

Florida Cavalry—Captain M. F. Irvin.

Under orders of Brigadier General W. E. Anderson, commanding Western Brigade of Florida Militia, issued October 2nd, 1862, this Company was mustered into service on the 3rd day of October, and remained in service until the 11th, when they were regularly mustered out by the Captain commanding. The Captain reported that his company was not uniformed, that he and his officers were duly commissioned by the State; he also reported as a part of his company equipment two teamsters, two wagons, four mules and one servant.

Florida Cavalry—Captain M. F. Irvin.
(CONTINUED.)

NAMES.	MUSTERED IN.	MUSTERED OUT.	REMARKS
OFFICERS.			
Captain—			
John M. F. Irwin	Oct. 3, '62	Oct. 11, '62	
1st Lieutenant—			
H. K. Garrett	Oct. 3, '62	Oct. 11, '62	
2nd Lieutenant—			
Elijah A. Martin	Oct. 3, '62	Oct. 11, '62	
3rd Lieutenant—			
ENLISTED MEN.			
Anderson, John B.	Oct. 3, '62	Oct. 11, '62	1st Corporal.
Anthony, L. M.	Oct. 3, '62	Oct. 11, '62	Surgeon.
Bellamy, B. A.	Oct. 3, '62	Oct. 11, '62	
Bryan, Ham G.	Oct. 3, '62	Oct. 11, '62	2nd Corporal.
Burke, C. C.	Oct. 3, '62	Oct. 11, '62	Sergeant.
Butler, M. A.	Oct. 3, '62	Oct. 11, '62	
Coker, James P.	Oct. 3, '62	Oct. 11, '62	
Dekle, T. G. H.	Oct. 3, '62	Oct. 11, '62	
Dickson, James W.	Oct. 3, '62	Oct. 11, '61	
Dickson, William F.	Oct. 3, '62	Oct. 11, '62	
Edwards, John W.	Oct. 3, '62	Oct. 11, '62	
Gannon, John W.	Oct. 3, '62	Oct. 11, '62	
Glover, Ben P.	Oct. 3, '62	Oct. 11, '62	2nd Sergeant.
Godwin, Thomas A.	Oct. 3, '62	Oct. 11, '62	
Harvey, Charles E.	Oct. 3, '62	Oct. 11, '62	1st Sergeant
Harvey, John L.	Oct. 3, '62	Oct. 11, '62	
Harvey, William H.	Oct. 3, '62	Oct. 11, '62	
Hinson, Joseph B.	Oct. 3, '62	Oct. 11, '62	
Irwin, Sam S.	Oct 3, '62	Oct. 11, '62	
Killgore, A. W.	Oct. 3, '62	Oct. 11, '62	
Land, James C.	Oct. 3, '62	Oct. 11, '62	Corporal.
Logan, William H.	Oct. 3, '62	Oct. 11, '62	Corporal.
Minchin, N. S.	Oct. 3, '62	Oct. 11, '62	
Morgan, N. M. A.	Oct. 3, '62	Oct. 11, '62	
Nichol, Joseph J.	Oct. 3, '62	Oct. 11, '62	Sergeant.
Prather, Thomas F.	Oct. 3, '62	Oct. 11, '62	Cornet.
Scott, Andrew	Oct. 3, '62	Oct. 11, '62	

Jackson Black Hawk Cavalry—Captain A. B. Hamilton.

This Company formed a part of the 1st Regiment, 1st Brigade, Florida Volunteer Militia, commanded by Lieutenant Colonel Thomas C. James, was called into the service of the State by Governor Milton on the 19th day of October, 1861, for a term of six months unless sooner discharged. The Mustering Officer, C. M. Harris, certified to the correctness of the roll, the condition of their horses and equipments and their acceptance into the service of the State for the term specified.

NAMES.	MUSTERED IN.	MUSTERED OUT.	REMARKS.
OFFICERS.			
Captain—			
A. B. Hamilton	Oct. 19, '61		
1st Lieutenant—			
Z. S. Fenn	Oct. 19, '61		
2nd Lieutenant—			
H. M. Pace	Oct. 19, '61		
3rd Lieutenant—			
Phelix Grimsley	Oct. 19, '61		
ENLISTED MEN			
Armstead, George	Oct. 19, '61		
Bazzett, Charles E.	Oct. 19, '61		
Carpenter, Henry	Oct. 19, '81		
Carpenter, William	Oct. 19, '61		
Corbit, Nicholas	Oct. 19, '61		
Cowan, James	Oct. 19, '61		
Daniels, William	Oct. 19, '61		
Davis, Martin	Oct. 19, '61		
Dickson, Columbus	Oct. 19, '61		
Dykes, J. H.	Oct. 19, '61		

Jackson Black Hawk Cavalry—Captain A. B. Hamilton.
(CONTINUED.)

NAMES.	MUSTERED IN.	MUSTERED OUT.	REMARKS.
Dykes, Moses	Oct. 19, '61		
Edwards, John G.	Oct. 19, '61		
Hare, Harrison	Oct. 19, '61		
Hatcher, James	Oct. 19, '61		
Homistead, George	Oct. 19, '61		
Jackson, L. Berry	Oct. 19, '61		
Johnson, Gasaway	Oct. 19, '61		
Jones, James T.	Oct. 19, '61		
Jones, Pittman	Oct. 19, '61		
Jones, W. M.	Oct. 19, '61		
Kemp, Calhoun	Oct. 19, '61		
Kidd, Robert	Oct. 19, '61		
Kittleband, John	Oct. 19, '61		
Lander, Charles D.	Oct. 19, '61		
Lanier, Anthony	Oct. 19, '61		
Lapo, Giles	Oct. 19, '61		1st Sergeant.
Lupo, James	Oct. 19, '61		
Lupo, John	Oct. 19, '61		
McDaniel, Eramus	Oct. 19, '61		
McDonald, William	Oct. 19, '61		2nd Sergeant.
Malloy, S. P.	Oct. 19, '61		
Masburn, L. Q.	Oct. 19, '61		3rd Sergeant
Mayo, Jasper	Oct. 19, '61		
Mercer, W. T.	Oct. 19, '61		
Perkins, William	Oct. 19, '61		
Phillips, William A.	Oct. 19, '61		
Sexton, Ambrose	Oct. 19, '61		
Sexton, James W.	Oct. 19, '61		
Sexton, Seth R.	Oct. 19, '61		
Shelfer, Levi	Oct. 19, '61		
Simpson, Augustus	Nov. 1, '61		
Simpson, William D.	Nov. 1, '61		
Sneed, Anderson	Oct. 19, '61		
Webster, James	Oct. 19, '61		
Williams, James B.	Oct. 19, '61		Sergeant.
Williams, Newton J.	Oct. 19, '61		1st Corporal.
Wilson, James	Oct. 19, '61		
Witherspoon, Robert H.	Oct. 19, '61		Sergeant.
Wood, R.	Oct. 19, '61		4th Sergeant.
Wood, Warren L.	Oct. 19, '61		
Wright, W.	Oct. 19, '61		3rd Corporal. Promoted Sergeant.
Yon, Martin	Oct. 19, '61		

Dixie Blues—Captain R. M. Scarborough.

The Dixie Blues were mustered into the State's service in 1861. There is nothing to show how long they served or where their services were rendered. It is evident that the duration of service was not very long, because members of this Company were found enrolled in regiments formed early in 1862.

NAMES.	MUSTERED IN.	MUSTERED OUT.	—	REMARKS.
OFFICERS.				
Captain—				
R. M. Scarborough				
1st Lieutenant—				
John Rogers				
2nd Lieutenant—				
Cornelius Rogers				
ENLISTED MEN.				
Atkinson, R. J.				
Bagget, J. W.				
Barr, James A.				
Borven, James				
Bryant, George W.				4th Corporal.
Bryant, James				
Butler, M. G.				
Campbell, M. M.				
Clark, William				
Collins, Benjamin				
Coonrod, P. T.				
Edenfield, C. W.				
Edenfield, Elias J.				Re-enlisted, Co. A, 6th Regiment, March '62.

Dixie Blues—Captain R. M. Scarborough.

(Continued.)

NAMES.	MUSTERED IN.	MUSTERED OUT.	REMARKS.
Edgerton, William C.			1st Corporal.
Edwards, Hill.			Musician.
Evans, Julius.			
Everitt, Henry.			Re-enlisted, Co. I, 6th Regiment, March, '62.
Farr, Titus.			
Faircloth, M.			
Fletcher, Joseph C.			Re-enlisted, Co. A, 6th Regiment, March, '62.
Garner, R.			
Glenn, O. S.			
Goodson, J.			
Goodson, L.			
Goodson, M.			
Grice, H.			
Hawkins, J.			
Hitcher, Joseph.			
Johnson, Neil.			4th Sergeant.
Junkins, J.			
Keen, Thomas.			
Keen, W. R.			
Kenedy, J. T. H.			Re-enlisted, Co. A, 6th Regiment, March, '62.
Kirkland, S. H.			
Kirkland, W. J.			Re-enlisted, Co. A, 6th Regiment, March, '62.
McAliley, Samuel.			
McCoy, John.			
McDonald, Daniel.			Clerk; Re-enlisted, Co. E, 6th Regiment March, '62.
McDonald, James A.			1st Sergeant.
McDougald, J.			
McJunkin, J.			
McMillan, Archibald.			3rd Corporal.
McPhaul, Archie.			Re-enlisted, Co. B, 6th Regiment, March, '62.
McPhaul, C. C.			
McPhaul, Hamilton.			Re-enlisted, Co. A, 6th Regiment, March, '62.
McPhaul, John.			
McVicker, Alexander.			
Miller, James M.			Musician.
Morgan, R. A.			
Morgan, W. W.			Re-enlisted, Co. H, 5th Regiment, March, '62.
Nixon, James M.			2nd Sergeant.
Padgett, J. W.			
Richards, John.			
Richards, W. N.			
Rowan, James.			
Sadler, James.			
Sadler, John.			Re-enlisted, Co. A, 6th Regiment, March, '62.
Sanders, John D.			
Sealey, J.			
Shepard, W. H.			
Silas, John.			
Simpson, John.			
Smith, James.			
Spear, Thomas B.			2nd Corporal.
Strange, B. F.			
Strange, Samuel.			
Strange, Wiggins.			
Suber, L. P.			Re-enlisted, Co. A, 6th Regiment, March, '62.
Thomas, P. F. M.			Re-enlisted, Co. A, 6th Regiment, March, '62.
Toler, B. S.			
Toler, J. W.			
Tomberlin, James.			
Tomberlin, J. W.			
Vanlandingham, John.			3rd Sergeant.
Watford, M.			

Aucilla Guards—Captain William Bailey, Jr.

The Aucilla Guards were mustered into service November 28, 1861, by Captain William J. Bailey, Jr., commanding the Post of St. Marks. Upon the formation of the 5th Regiment, in March 1862, this Company was dissolved and most of its members joined the 5th Regiment.

Aucilla Guards—Captain William Bailey, Jr.
(CONTINUED.)

NAMES.	MUSTERED IN.	MUSTERED OUT.	REMARKS.
OFFICERS.			
Captain—			
William Bailey, Jr.	Nov. 28, '61		Became Captain Co. G, 5th Regiment, March, '61.
1st Lieutenant—			
Joseph McCants	Nov. 28, '61		
2nd Lieutenant—			
J. S. Walker	Nov. 28, '61		
3rd Lieutenant—			
William S. Harris	Nov. 28, '61		
ENLISTED MEN.			
Atkinson, Craven	Nov. 28, '61		Corporal.
Atkinson, Jesse	Nov. 28, '61		
Ayers, Ira	Nov. 28, '61		Re-enlisted, Co. G, 5th Regiment, March, '62.
Bazemore, Stephen	Nov. 28, '61		
Bishop, Elijah	Nov. 28, '61		Re-enlisted, Co. G, 5th Regiment, March, '62.
Bishop, Ely	Nov. 28, '61		Re-enlisted, Co. G, 5th Regiment, March, '62.
Bishop, Hilary	Nov. 28, '61		Re-enlisted, Co. G, 5th Regiment, March, '62.
Brown, W. H.	Nov. 28, '61		Re-enlisted, Co. G, 5th Regiment, March, '62.
Carroll, William J.	Nov. 28, '61		
Chestnut, John	Nov. 28, '61		
Crosby, Paul	Nov. 28, '61		Corporal.
Crosby, Thomas	Nov. 28, '61		
Gill, B. L.	Nov. 28, '61		Re-enlisted, Co. G, 5th Regiment, March, '62; Promoted 2nd Lieutenant.
Gray, Asa	Nov. 28, '61		
Grubbs, S. G.	Nov. 28, '61		
Holton, George	Nov. 28, '61		
Huggins, Thomas	Nov. 28, '61		Re-enlisted, Co. G, 5th Regiment, March, '62.
Jenkins, Samuel	Nov. 28, '61		Re-enlisted, Co. C, 5th Regiment, March, '62.
Johns, J. M.	Nov. 28, '61		Re-enlisted, Co. G, 5th Regiment, March, '62.
Johnson, S. W.	Nov. 28, '61		Re-enlisted, Co. G, 5th Regiment, March, '62.
Jones, Joseph W.	Nov. 28, '61		Re-enlisted, Co. G, 5th Regiment, March, '62.
Kinsey, John	Nov. 28, '61		
Kinsey, Joseph	Nov. 28, '61		
Kinsey, William N	Nov. 28, '61		
Lynn, J. B.	Nov. 28, '61		
Norris, William S.	Nov. 28, '61		Re-enlisted, Co. A, 5th Regiment, March, '62.
Poppell, John	Nov. 28, '61		Re-enlisted, Co. G, 5th Regiment, March, '62.
Raysor, Alfred, Jr.	Nov. 28, '61		
Raysor, E. H.	Nov. 28, '61		1st Corporal.
Raysor, George	Nov. 28, '61		2nd Sergeant; Re-enlisted, Co. G, 5th Regiment; Promoted 1st Lieutenant, March, '62.
Roosor, G. D.	Nov. 28, '61		Re-enlisted, Co. G, 5th Regiment, March, '62.
Raysor, J. M.	Nov. 28, '61		Sergeant.
Richardson, William M.	Nov. 28, '61		Re-enlisted, Co. G, 5th Regiment, March, '62.
Scott, Samuel	Nov. 28, '61		
Simmons, James	Nov. 28, '61		
Strickland, William	Nov. 28, '61		Re-enlisted, Co. G, 5th Regiment. March, '62.
Tuten, James	Nov. 28, '61		
Walker, Berry	Nov. 28, '61		Re-enlisted, Co. G, 5th Regiment, March, '62'
Walker, G. R.	Nov. 28, '61		1st Sergeant; Re-enlisted, Co. G, 5th Regiment, Promoted 1st Lieutenant, March, '62.
Walker, James	Nov. 28, '61		Re-enlisted, Co. G, 5th Regiment. March, '62.
Walker, J. A.	Nov. 28, '61		Sergeant; re-enlisted, Co. G, 5th Reg't March '62
Walker, John S.	Nov. 28, '61		
Walker, Stephen J.	Nov. 28, '61		
Wheeler, J. C.	Nov. 28, '61		Re-enlisted, Co. G, 5th Regiment, March, '62.
Wheeler, J. H.	Nov. 28, '61		Re-enlisted, Co. G, 5th Regiment, March, '62.
Whidden, W. R.	Nov. 28, '61		2nd Corporal.
Whitehurst, Burrel	Nov. 28, '61		
Whitehurst, M. S.	Nov. 28, '61		
Whitehurst, Perry	Nov. 28, '61		
Williams, Arons	Nov. 28, '61		

Florida Volunteer Coast Guards—Captain Henry Mulrenan.

This Company was organized and called into the State of Florida by Special Order No. 2, issued from the Adjutant General's office, Tallahassee, November 27th, 1861. They were mustered by Henry Mulrenan, Captain commanding, no station or term of service is stated.

NAMES.	MUSTERED IN.	MUSTERED OUT.	REMARKS.
OFFICERS.			
Captain—			
Henry Mulrenan	Nov. 27, '61		
1st Lieutenant—			
Walter C. Maloney	Nov. 27, '61		

Florida Voluntere Coast Guards—Captain Henry Mulrenan.
(CONTINUED,)

NAMES.	MUSTERED IN	MUSTERED OUT.	REMARKS.
2nd Lieutenant—			
Robert B. Smith	Dec. 1 , '61		
3rd Lieutenant—			
Samuel B. Ashley	Nov. 27, '61		
ENLISTED MEN.			
Alberry, Benjamin	Nov. 27, '61		Seaman.
Allison, John	Dec. 1, '61		Mate.
Anderson, Charles	Nov. 27, '61		Seaman.
Baker, John	Jan. 1, '62		Seaman.
Barnett, James	Dec. 1, '61		Seaman.
Berry, Charles H	Nov. 27, '61		Mate.
Bethel, John	Dec. 1, '61		Coxswain.
Buckley, Timothy	Jan. 1, '62		Mate.
Burns, Thomas	Nov. 27, '61		Seaman.
Butler, Thomas	Dec. 15, '61		Seaman.
Chapman, Charles	Nov. 27, '61		Seaman.
Cole, Charles I	Nov. 27, '61		Coxswain.
Collins, James C	Dec. 15, '61		Seaman.
Combs, Charles	Dec. 15, '61		Seaman.
Crusoe, Peter	Dec. 1, '61		Seaman.
Diar, Francisco	Jan. 25, '62		Seaman.
Dorsey, Edward	Nov. 27, '61		Seaman.
Edward, George W	Dec. 1, '61		Seaman.
Fagan, Joseph	Jan. 1, '62		Seaman.
Feliz, Rouplina	Dec. 1, '61		Seaman.
Felkrob, Ordrof	Jan. 25, '62		Seaman.
Franklin, William	Nov. 27, '61		Seaman.
Herrymand, William	Jan. 1, '61		Seaman.
Josslyn, William A	Jan. 1, '61		Seaman.
Lovett, James	Dec. 20, '61		Seaman.
Low, Alfred	Dec. 1, '61		Seaman.
Martin, Antonio	Jan. 25, '62		Seaman.
Mason, John	Jan. 25, '62		Seaman.
Marrilar, Augustus	Nov. 27, '61		Seaman.
Miller, Charles	Dec. 15, '61		Seaman.
Miller, Moody	Jan. 25, '61		Seaman.
Morgan, Samuel	Nov. 27, '61		Coxswain.
Morrison, John B	Dec. 15, '61		Seaman.
Moss, Josephus	Nov. 27, '61		Seaman.
Olivera, Marquis	Dec. 1, '61		Seaman.
Richards, George	Dec. 24, '61		Seaman.
Rogers, Julius D	Jan. 1, '62		Seaman.
Russell, John	Jan. 1, '62		Seaman.
Sands, John B	Nov. 27, '61		Seaman.
Sawyer, William	Dec. 1, '61		Seaman.
Sherbert, Julion	Nov. 27, '61		Coxswain.
Simpson, Johnston	Jan. 25, '62		Seaman.
Smith, George W	Jan. 1, '62		Seaman.
Sullivan, James	Jan. 25, '62		Seaman.
Swain, Byaman C	Dec. 15, '61		Seaman.
Tolbert, James W	Jan. 27, '62		Seaman.
Watson, Robert	Dec. 1, '61		Mate.
Whitehurst, Daniel	Feb. 1, '62		Seaman.
Williams, Peter	Dec. 1, '61		Seaman.

Infantry Company—Captain James P. McMullen.

Mustered into the service of the State of Florida on July 20th, 1861, to October 20th, 1861, by order of Brigadier General J. M. Taylor. This Company was stationed at Clearwater Harbor, and at the expiration of their three months' service was mustered out and the men composing it joined other commands.

NAMES.	MUSTERED IN.	MUSTERED OUT.	REMARKS.
OFFICERS.			
Captain—			
James McMullen	July 20, '61	Oct. 20, '61	
1st Lieutenant—			
G. W. Whitehurst	July 20, '61	Oct. 20, '61	
2nd Lieutenant—			
Levi S. Wh tehurst	July 20, '61	Oct. 20, '61	
3rd Lieutenant—			
A. J Youngblood	July 20, '61	Oct. 20 't'1	

Infantry Company—Captain James P. McMullen.
(CONTINUED.)

NAMES.	MUSTERED IN.	MUSTERED OUT.	REMARKS.
ENLISTED MEN.			
Arnold, H. G.	July 20, '61	Oct. 20 '61	
Arnold, M. E.	July 20, '61	Oct. 20, '61	
Boothe, R.	July 20, '61	Oct. 20, '61	2nd Sergeant.
Bowden, B. I.	July 20, '61	Oct. 20, '61	1st Corporal.
Branch, John.	July 20, '61	Oct. 20, '61	
Branch, J. L.	July 20, '61	Oct. 20, '61	
Brownlow, B. E.	July 20, '61	Oct. 20, '61	Sergeant.
Brownlow, J. P.	July 20, '61	Oct. 20, '61	
Campbell, W. N.	July 20, '61	Oct. 20, '61	
Carlisle, J. S.	July 20, '61	Oct. 20, '61	
Clay, Adam.	July 20, '61	Oct. 20, '61	
Clay, W. S.	July 20, '61	Oct. 20, '61	
Collier W T.	July 20, '61	Oct. 20, '61	Sergeant.
Crawford, Jesse.	July 20, '61	Oct. 20, '61	
Crum, D. B.	July 20, '61	Oct. 20, '61	
Garrison, G. A.	July 20, '61	Oct. 20, '61	
Garrison, J. N.	July 20, '61	Oct. 20, '61	
Garrison, S. D.	July 20, '61	Oct. 20, '61	Corporal.
Gaskins, Lewis.	July 20, '61	Oct. 20, '61	
Gaward, Frank R.	July 20, '61	Oct. 20, '61	
Griner, David.	July 20, '61	Oct. 20, '61	Corporal.
Griner, M. P.	July 20, '61	Oct. 20, '61	
Hay, Abram.	July 20, '61	Oct. 20, '61	
Hay, J. R.	July 20, '61	Oct. 20, '61	
Hern, H. B.	July 20, '61	Oct. 20, '61	
Hill, R. Robert.	July 20, '61	Oct. 20, '61	
Holland, G. W.	July 20, '61	Oct. 20, '61	
Kittles, Lawrence.	July 20, '61	Oct. 20, '61	
Leavett, James.	July 20, '61	Oct. 20, '61	
McLead, Ferinand.	July 20, '61	Oct. 20, '61	
Marsh, M.	July 20, '61	Oct. 20, '61	
Mobley, W. L.	July 20, '61	Oct. 20, '61	
Moody, J. M.	July 20, '61	Oct. 20, '61	
Moody, N. M.	July 20, '61	Oct. 20, '61	
Papy, Charles.	July 20, '61	Oct. 20, '61	
Parker, W. P.	July 20, '61	Oct. 20, '61	
Patterson, Martin.	July 20, '61	Oct. 20, '61	
Rogers, J. D.	July 20, '61	Oct. 20, '61	1st Sergeant.
Ross, T. D.	July 20, '61	Oct. 20 '61	
Smith, G. W.	July 20, '61	Oct. 20, '61	
Stevens, John.	July 20, '61	Oct. 20, '61	
Stephenson, S. H.	July 20, '61	Oct. 20, '61	
Swain, B. C.	July 20, '61	Oct. 20, '61	
Tillman, J. W.	July 20, '61	Oct. 20, '61	
Townsend, Elijah.	July 20, '61	Oct. 20, '61	
Tullis, J. A.	July 20, '61	Oct. 20, '61	
Turner, A. C.	July 20, '61	Oct. 20, '61	
Turner, D. B.	July 20, '61	Oct. 20, '61	
Washington, G. P.	July 20, '61	Oct. 20, '61	2nd Corporal.
White, W. B.	July 20, '61	Oct. 20, '61	
Whitehurst, B. D.	July 20, '61	Oct. 20, '61	
Whitehurst, J. S.	July 20, '61	Oct. 20, '61	
Whitehurst, M. E.	July 20, '61	Oct. 20, '61	
Whitehurst, Walton.	July 20, '61	Oct. 20, '61	
Youngblood, D. N.	July 20, '61	Oct. 20, '61	
Youngblood, S. S.	July 20, '61	Oct. 20, '61	

Shellpoint Rangers—Captain A. C. Lang.

There is nothing in the record to indicate when or where this Company was mustered in or by whom. Presumably it was sometime in 1861. A total absence of any record of the Company subsequent to its recorded roll would indicate that it was one of the companies that was dissolved after a short service and whose members re-enlisted in other commands. This supposition is rather sustained by the fact of several names appearing on this roll appear latter on the roll of companies in Scott's battalion of cavalry.

NAMES.	MUSTERED IN.	MUSTERED OUT.	REMARKS.
OFFICERS.			
Captain—			
A. C. Lang.			

Shellpoint Rangers—Captain A. C. Lang.

(CONTINUED.)

NAMES.	MUSTERED IN.	MUSTERED OUT.	REMARKS.
1st Lieutenant—			
William A. Giles			
2nd Lieutenant—			
Johnathan Watson			
3rd Lieutenant—			
John Eubanks			
ENLISTED MEN.			
Ange, Oden			
Andrews, Elijah			
Baker, Jacob			
Baker, John M.			Corporal.
Baker, Marhew			Sergeant.
Bell, James			
Bell, W. K.			
Bracker, Andrew			
Bracker, John			
Braswell, Henry			Corporal.
Braswell, Marida			Drummer.
Coleman, John M.			1st Sergeant.
Coleman, W. K.			
Cone, D. W.			
Danilson, James			
Eubanks, Hardee			
Fountain, Green			
Fountain, W. E.			
Giles, James M.			Fifer.
Giles, William W.			
Gwaltny, James F.			
Hemby, J. T.			2nd Corporal.
Johnston, I. W.			
Johnston, L. T.			
Johnston, William			
Johnston, Wylie			
Mathews, John			
Mathew, Steven W.			2nd Sergeant.
Maxwain, Charles			
Ogletree, Wylie			
Pelt, Durant			
Pervis, John N.			
Porter, William R.			
Richardson, A.			
Roddenberry, Allen			
Roddenberry, George			
Roddenberry, Richard			
Smith, R. B.			
Spears, William			
Spears, Zinmanon			
Stokely, J. B.			
Stokely, John			
Tulley, A. P.			
Tulley, G. W.			
Tulley, William C.			1st Corporal.
Vickers, Stephen			
Watson, Henry			
Watson, James			Sergeant.
White, T. W.			

Coast Guards—Captain A. B. Noyes.

This Company was mustered into Confederate service October 9, 1861, for a period of three months unless sooner discharged, and were to be stationed at St. Marks. There is no record as to who the mustering officer was; presumably it was Captain Noyes. From the mustering note it would appear that they were not at once assigned to duty, because the note says "when called into Confederate service of the Confederate States." On the 10th of October, 1861, this Company was called into the service of the State. There is no record that it ever entered into the Confederate service as a company, nor is there any record of its discharge from service.

Coast Guards—Captain A. B. Noyes.
(Continued.)

NAMES.	MUSTERED IN.	MUSTERED OUT.	REMARKS.
OFFICERS.			
Captain—			
A. B. Noyes	Oct. 9, '61		
1st Lieutenant—			
Charles W. Johnson	Oct. 9, '61		
2nd Lieutenant—			
Thomas W. Anderson	Oct. 18, '61		
ENLISTED MEN.			
Anderson, Henry	Oct. 10, '61		Seaman.
Anderson, Rufus			
Anderson, William H	Oct. 10, '61		Seaman.
Ashley, J. Benjamin			Seaman.
Barr, James M	Oct. 15, '61		Seaman.
Balliste, John			
Benton, William N	Oct. 9, '61		
Blackwell, William	Oct. 10, '61		Seaman.
Blitchington, William			
Blythe, Thomas S	Oct. 14, '61		Seaman.
Blythe, William	Oct. 9, '61		Coxswain.
Brantley, H. A	Oct. 15, '61		Coxswain.
Brown, William C	Oct. 20, '61		Seaman.
Buford, J. N. C			
Butler, E. A	Nov. 8, '61		
Calahan, Charles	Oct. 13, '61		Seaman.
Calahan, Thomas	Oct. 13, '61		Seaman.
Cannon, L. S			Seaman.
Castillo, James	Oct. 9, '61		Pilot.
Comporet, John B	Oct. 13, '61		Seaman.
Condellary, William			Seaman.
Cox, James	Oct. 10, '61		Seaman.
Curry, Joseph	Oct. 14, '61		Seaman.
Davis, A. P			Seaman.
Davis, Genis	Oct. 10, '61		
Davis, George A			Seaman.
Davis, John			Seaman.
Davis, Levi	Oct. 16, '61		Seaman.
Day, Thomas W			
Dudley, James	Oct. 20, '61		Seaman.
Dudley, Milton	Oct. '61		
Ellis, Nicholas A	Oct. 13, '61		Seaman.
Ellis, William R. L	Nov. 11, '61		
Faircloth, Allen D	Oct. 9, '61		Seaman.
Faircloth, John	Oct. 9, '61		Seaman.
Faircloth, Richard			Seaman.
Ferguson, George W	Oct. 9, '61		Seaman.
Franklin, Joseph			
Fuguay, Cornelius	Nov. 11, '61		
Fuguay, G. W			
Freet, Nicholas			Gunner.
Ghano, Abram	Oct. 18, '61		
Hall, H. P			
Hall, Oscar C	Nov. 6, '61		
Hamlin, George W	Oct. 21, '61		Carpenter.
Hance, John	Oct. 9, '61		
Haros, Sam	Oct. 13, '61		
Henderson, James M	Oct. 10, '61		Seaman.
House, John			Seaman.
Hughes, Henry	Oct. 14, '61		Seaman.
Hutchinson, John L. T	Oct. 15, '61		Seaman.
Kennedy, D. M			Coxswain.
Kinlock, James S	Oct. 15, '61		
Langston, Jesse	Oct. 10, '61		
Lavco, John			
Lavill, Patrick T	Oct. 13, '61		
Lee, E	Oct. 9, '61		
Lee, W. C. H	Oct. 9, '61		Boatswain's Mate.
McKinnon, John			
McLain, John C	Oct. 9, '61		
McLaren, John M			Coxswain.
Mariano, Joseph			
Miller, Frank	Oct. 13, '61		
Minhard, Andrew	Oct. 15, '61		
Moore, Lewis C	Oct. 13, '61		
Neil, J. Q			Seaman.
Nicholas, Fred	Oct. 10, '61		
Norton, William	Oct. 15, '61		
Parkinson, William	Oct. 10, '61		
Perkins, John H			
Ponse, Anthony			Seaman.
Powell, William	Oct. 20, '61		
Preston, Thomas	Oct. 13, '61		
Purefy, Thomas	Oct. 10, '61		
Rawlins, J. T			
Remington, A. H			Seaman.

Coast Guards—Captain A. B. Noyes.
(CONTINUED.)

NAMES.	MUSTERED IN.	MUSTERED OUT.	REMARKS.
Roath, C. D.			Seaman.
Romano, Emanuel	Oct. 10 '61		Seaman.
Seeley, Jesse			
Seeley, William	Oct. 20, '61		
Seiver, William			
Shinks, T. H.	Oct. 10, '61		
Shipke, John			Seaman.
Shuler, David R.	Oct. 20, '61		
Silva, Emanuel	Oct. 10, '61		Seaman.
Smith, Patrick	Oct. 20, '61		
Stewart, Clarence			
Sweat, James G.	Oct. 18, '61		Seaman.
Thomas, John C	Oct. 20, '61		Seaman.
Ward, Harvey	Oct. 13, '61		
West, G. O.	Oct. 9, '61		Coxswain.
West, Isaac	Oct. 9, '61		Seaman.
Whitaker, William S	Oct. 20, '61		Sergeant of Marines.
Whitaker, W. W.	Oct. 23, '61		
Williamson, James	Oct. 9, '61		Boatswain.
Wood, William F.	Oct. 20, '61		Seaman.
Wright, Robert	Oct. 9, '61		Seaman.
Warner, William			

Calhoun Rangers—Captain Angus McAllister.

The Calhoun Rangers were reported for duty at Camp Milton, Apalachicola, Florida, December 9th, 1861, in accordance with Special Order No. 83. There is nothing about the roll to indicate the length of time this Company served, but the names of a large number of the members are found on the rolls of Company H, 5th Infantry, and a few on the 6th, and several were members of Dunham's Artillery; thus showing conclusively that it could not have been in service more than three months.

NAMES.	MUSTERED IN.	MUSTERED OUT.	REMARKS.
OFFICERS.			
Captain—			
Angus McAllister	Dec. 9, '61		
1st Lieutenant—			
Joel P. Atkinson	Dec. 9, '61		
2nd Lieutenant—			
J. V. B. McClendon	Dec. 9, '61		
ENLISTED MEN.			
Alfred, Jasper	Dec. 9, '61		
Ayers, David	Dec. 9, '61		Re-enlisted, Co. H, 5th Regiment, '62.
Ayers, John	Dec. 9, '61		Re-enlisted, Co. H, 5th Regiment, '62.
Ayers, Solomon	Dec. 9, '61		Re-enlisted, Co. H, 5th Regiment, '62.
Ayers, Thomas	Dec. 9, '61		Re-enlisted, Co. H, 5th Regiment, '62.
Ayers, William	Dec. 9, '61		
Burges, G. W.	Dec. 9, '61		
Burges, Samuel	Dec. 9, '61		Re-enlisted, Co. H, 5th Regiment, '62.
Caraway, John D.	Dec. 9, '61		2nd Corporal; Re-enlisted, Co, H, 5th Regiment '62.
Clarke, William B	Dec. 9, '61		
Cowan, Thomas J	Dec. 9, '61		2nd Sergeant.
Dillard, John	Dec. 9, '61		Re-enlisted, Co. H, 5th Regiment, '62.
Dudley, A. C.	Dec. 9, '61		1st Sergeant; Re-enlisted, Co. H, 5th Regiment, '62.
Evans, W. L.	Dec. 9, '61		Re-enlisted, Co. H, 5th Regiment, '62.
Foster, G. W.	Dec. 9, '61		
Gasque, Benjamin F	Dec. 9, '61		1st Corporal; Re-enlisted, Co. H, 5th Regiment, '62.
Greene, Franklin	Dec. 9, '61		
Hagan, George W. B	Dec. 9, '61		Re-enlisted, Co. H, 5th Regiment, '62.
Hagan, Henry D.	Dec. 9, '61		Re-enlisted, Co. H, 5th Regiment, '62.
Ham, Jesse	Dec. 9, '61		
Hill, Francis A	Dec. 9, '61		
Johns, Richard	Dec. 9, '61		
Johns, William	Dec. 9, '61		
Keen, James	Dec. 9, '61		
Killer, John	Dec. 9, '61		

Calhoun Rangers—Captain Angus McAlister.
(CONTINUED.)

NAMES.	MUSTERED IN.	MUSTERED OUT.	REMARKS.
Licett, Lemuel B.	Dec. 9, '61		Re-enlisted, Co. H, 5th Regiment, '62.
McClelland, John P.	Dec. 9, '61		
McDonald, George LaFayette	Dec. 9, '61		Re-enlisted, Co. H, 5th Regiment, '62.
Messer, Joel	Dec. 9, '61		
Messer, Peter	Dec. 9, '61		
Nall, James	Dec. 9, '61		Re-enlisted, Co. F, 6th Regiment, '62.
Nixon, Daniel G.	Dec. 9, '61		Sergeant.
Parker, John	Dec. 9, '61		Re-enlisted, Co. G, 6th Regiment, '62.
Richards, Daniel U.	Dec. 9, '61		Sergeant; Re-enlisted, Co. A, 2nd Cavalry, '62.
Richards, G. W.	Dec. 9, '61		
Richards, Raleigh	Dec. 9, '61		Re-enlisted, Dunham's Artillery.
Register, James	Dec. 9, '61		Corporal.
Riles, Ralph	Dec. 9, '61		
Snyder, Silas	Dec. 9, '61		
Spears, John	Dec. 9, '61		Re-enlisted, Co. H, 5th Regiment, '62.
Spears, William	Dec. 9, '61		Re-enlisted, Co. H, 5th Regiment, '62.
Stanfield, Jasper	Dec. 9, '61		Re-enlisted, Dunham's Artillery.
Ulrich, John	Dec. 9, '61		Re-enlisted, Dunham's Artillery.
Varner, Elijah	Dec. 9, '61		Re-enlisted, Co. F, 6th Regiment, '62.
Varner, Joel T.	Dec. 9, '61		
Varner, Jonah	Dec. 9, '61		
Ward, A. Jackson	Dec. 9, '61		Re-enlisted, Co. H, 5th Regiment, '62.
Ward, William	Dec. 9, '61		
Whittington, Ferinand	Dec. 9, '61		
Yon, Newton	Dec. 9, '61		Corporal; Re-enlisted, Co. H, 5th Regiment, '62.
York, Martin	Dec. 9, '61		

Columbia Trapiers—Captain J. R. Francis.

The Columbia Trapiers, Captain J. R. Francis, were called into the State service by Governor John Milton, January 1st, 1862. There is nothing anywhere to show where this Company was organized, where stationed or what service it rendered.

NAMES.	MUSTERED IN.	MUSTERED OUT.	REMARKS.
OFFICERS.			
Captain—			
J. R. Francis	Jan. 1, '62		
1st Lieutenant—			
G. M. Cline	Jan. 1, '62		
2nd Lieutenant—			
A. G. Keene			
3rd Lieutenant—			
W. S. Horrington	Jan. 1, '62		
ENLISTED MEN.			
Adams, J. W.	Jan. 1, '62		
Amerson, S. T.	Jan. 1, '62		
Barnes, James A.	Jan. 1, '62		
Bloome, Watson W.	Jan. 1, '62		
Brannen, James S.	Jan. 1, '62		
Brock, Eli	Jan. 1, '62		
Buford, Daniel	Jan. 1, '62		
Buford, Washington	Jan. 1, '62		
Curry, J. M.	Jan. 1, '62		
Curry, John W.	Jan. 1, '62		
Dalrymple, G. D.	Jan. 1, '62		
Danill, G. W.	Jan. 1, '62		
Davis, I. C.	Jan. 1, '62		
Daugherty, William H.	Jan. 1, '62		
Dupree, W. H.	Jan. 1, '62		
Forsom, John S.	Jan. 1, '62		
Grisham, Columbus	Jan. 1, '62		
Gure, John	Jan. 1, '62		
Haster, W. J.	Jan. 1, '62		
Herrol, William	Jan. 1, '62		
Hewett, J. W.	Jan. 1, '62		
Moore, Jacob T.	Jan. 1, '62		
Moore, P. G.	Jan. 1, '62		
Mosely, R. M.	Jan. 1, '62		
Owens, W. J.	Jan. 1, '62		
Pratt, G. W.	Jan. 1, '62		
Price, J. D.	Jan. 1, '62		

Columbia Trapiers—Captain J. R. Francis.
(CONTINUED.)

NAMES.	MUSTERED IN.	MUSTERED OUT.	REMARKS.
Reeve, Berry	Jan. 1, '62		
Reeve, G. S.	Jan. 1, '62		
Reeve, G. W.	Jan. 1, '62		1st Sergeant.
Reeves, James N.	Jan. 1, '62		
Reeve, John J.	Jan. 1, '62		
Reeve, Wiley	Jan. 1, '62		
Reeves, W. R.	Jan. 1, '62		
Rodney Henry H.	Jan. 1, '62		
Rorolerson, Jackson	Jan. 1, '62		
Rorolerson, N.	Jan. 1, '62		
Russell, James W.	Jan. 1, '62		
Smith, Bryant W.	Jan. 1, '62		
Somers, Michael	Jan. 1, '62		
Sowell, I. W.	Jan. 1, '62		
Sure, William J.	Jan. 1, '62		
Thomas, Jesse	Jan. 1, '62		
Thompson, William	Jan. 1, '62		
Tison, John	Jan. 1, '62		
Tison, William	Jan. 1, '62		
Tucker, Eliza	Jan. 1, '62		
Wandle, John E.	Jan. 1, '62		
Williams, John	Jan. 1, '62		

Concordia Infantry—Captain Wilk. Call.

The Concordia Infantry was mustered into the service of the State by Francis L. Darcy Adjutant and Inspector General, for the term of twelve months, from the 4th day of September, 1861, unless sooner discharged. The names and number of these men are to be found in the 6th Regiment in the 1st Cavalry and in Scott's 5th Cavalry Battalion; as the 6th Regiment was organized in March, 1862, it is manifest that this Company must have been dissolved. after six months' service in the State.

NAMES.	MUSTERED IN.	MUSTERED OUT.	REMARKS.
OFFICERS.			
Captain—			
Wilk. Call	Sept. 4, '62		
1st Lieutenant—			
Hugh Black	Sept. 11, '62		Re-enlisted, Co. A, 6th Regiment as 3rd Lieutenant.
2nd Lieutenant—			
W. H. Shelfer	Sept. 4 '62		Re-enlisted, Co. D, Scott's Battalion.
3rd Lieutenant—			
L. B. Timmons	Sept. 4, '62		Re-enlisted, Co. B 6th Regiment as Corporal.
ENLISTED MEN			
Autman, James R.	Sept. 4, '62		
Ball, Hart	Sept. 4, '62		
Benton, James	Sept. 4, '62		
Bunnells, G. W.			
Burns, B. B.	Sept. 17, '62		
Burns, Mack	Sept. 4, '62		
Burns, Seaborn	Sept. 17, '62		
Butler, Green B.	Sept. 14, '62		
Butler, Jesse B.	Sept. 14, '62		Re-enlisted, Co. A, 6th Regiment.
Brady, Solomon			
Cannon, John	Sept. 7, '62		Re-enlisted, Co. C, 6th Regiment.
Cannon, Thomas W.	Sept. 7, '62		Re-enlisted, Co. A, 6th Regiment.
Causseaux, Peter B.	Sept. 7, '62		
Chasen, Thomas B.	Sept. 14, '62		
Chester, F. I.	Oct. 9, '62		
Chester, S. W.	Oct. 9, '62		
Crosby, Henry A.	Oct. 17, '62		
Darcy, Joseph A.			
Elkins, Joseph W.			
Ellenor, J. D.			Re-enlisted, Co. F, 1st Cavalry.
Fain, F. W.			Re-enlisted, Co. C, 6th Regiment.
Ferrell, W. D.			Re-enlisted, Co. C, 6th Regiment.
Flowers, H. A.			Re-enlisted, Co. A, 6th Regiment.
Goza, William W.			
Gray, George			

Concordia Infantry—Captain Wilk Call.
(Continued.)

NAMES	MUSTERED IN.	MUSTERED OUT.	REMARKS.
Griffin, J. E.			Re-enlisted, Co. E, 6th Regiment.
Hand, A. F.			
Harrison, Benjamin	Sept. 4, '62		
Harrison, Thomas	Sept. 4, '62		
Harrison, W. S.	Sept. 4, '62		1st Corporal, Re-enlisted, Co. B, 6th Regiment.
Herring, C. S.	Sept. 16, '62		Sergeant; Re-enlisted, Co. G, 6th Regiment.
Herndon, William L.			
Houck, Joseph.			
Johnson, John B.			Re-enlisted, Co. I, 2nd Cavalry.
Johnson, John H.			
Joyner, B. H.	Sept. 4, '62		1st Sergeant; Re-enlisted, Co. D, Scott's Batt.
Joyner, Lawrence R.			Re-enlisted, Co. B, 6th Regiment.
Kemp, B. A.	Sept. 4, '62		2nd Corporal; Re-enlisted, Co. C. 6th Regiment.
Lang, Thomas F.			
Langston, Irvin			
Langston, John R.			Re-enlisted, Co. A, 6th Regiment.
Langston, Morgan			
Langston, William			
Laslie, John C.			
Lott, Z. Madison	Sept. 4, '62		Corporal; Re-enlisted, Co. B, 6th Regiment.
Lynn. John.			Re-enlisted, Co. F, 1st Cavalry.
Lynn, William N.			Re-enlisted, Co. F, 1st Cavalry.
Mashburn, W.			
Mobley, B.			
Moore, Charles E.			Re-enlisted, Co. D, Scott's Battalion.
Parrot, Wilson M.			
Reeves, Raburn			Re-enlisted, Co. B, 6th Regiment as 2nd Lieut.
Revell, Stephen.			Re-enlisted, Co. A, 6th Regiment.
Rich, G. W.			
Roberts, Richard.			
Rogers, J. M.	Oct. 9, '62		Corporal.
Sanders, J. C.	Sept. 7, '62		Sergeant; Re-enlisted, Co. A, 6th Regiment.
Scott, David W.			Re-enlisted, Co. F, 1st Cavalry.
Shelfer, J. J.			Re-enlisted, Co. D, Scott's Battalion.
Speer, H. L., Jr.			Re-enlisted, Co. C, 6th Regiment.
Spinks, William W.			
Stokes, J. D.			
Truluck, David			Re-enlisted, Co. B, 6th Regiment.
Truluck, Arter.			
Ulmore, S. B.			
Wammock, Henry M.,	Sept. 4, '62		2nd Sergeant.
Wammock, Miles M.			
Wammock, William M.			

Coast Guards—Captain James L. Miller's Company.

Captain James L. Miller's Company of Coast Guards, at Crystal River, Fla., from the 27th of May, 1861, to August 21, 1861.

NAMES.	MUSTERED IN.	MUSTERED OUT.	REMARKS.
OFFICERS.			
Captain—			
James L. Miller.			
1st Lieutenant—			
Obediah E. Edwards.			
2nd Lieutenants—			
Jacob A. Ganard.			
Jesse W. Allen.			1st Sergeant.
Charles N. Buford.			2nd Sergeant.
Jesse E. Clarady.			3rd Sergeant.
Henry D. Edwards.			4th Sergeant.
Early A. Allen.			1st Corporal.
John J. Allen.			2nd Corporal.
Antonio A. Everett.			3rd Corporal.
James W. Johns.			4th Corporal.
ENLISTED MEN.			
Allen, John E.			
Allen, Jeremiah A.			
Allen, Zachariah E.			
Allen, William E.			
Allen, James E.			
Bertiere, William.			
Cryster, Henry.			
Decatur, A. J.			

Coast Guards—Captain James L. Miller's Company.
(CONTINUED.)

NAMES.	MUSTERED IN.	MUSTERED OUT.	REMARKS.
Edwards, Daniel			
Everett, Joseph A			
Garland, M. W.			
Garrison, Isaac N			
Hodges, Joel			
Hill, Robert M.			
Hodges, Andrew E.			
Hahn, Asher B.			
Johns, Jehu P.			
Johns, Lewis J.			
Kelly, Henry			
Morton, Joel W.			
Morton, William D.			
Mason, Calvin H.			
Peterson, Peter			
Parsons, John			
Peterson, Henry			
Peterson, William			
Patselago, Antonio			
Paul, William H.			
Peterson, Charles			
Riley, James O.			
Willis, Richard			
Winn, Thomas S.			
Johns, Henry M.			

Mounted Volunteers—Lieutenant J. R. Durrance's Detachment.

First Lieutenant J. R. Durrance's Detachment of Florida Mounted Volunteers; at Fort Meade, Florida, 14th of July, 1861, to August 27, 1861.

NAMES.	MUSTERED IN.	MUSTERED OUT.	REMARKS.
OFFICERS.			
1st Lieutenants—			
John R. Durrance			
William H. Mansfield			Sergeant.
Berrien Platt			Corporal.
ENLISTED MEN.			
Altman, John			
Altman, Jesse			
Brown, William			
Durrance, William H.			
Durrance, Jesse H.			
Durrance, Joseph L.			
Durrance, George S.			
Durrance, F. M.			
Ellis, Andrew J.			
Kendrick, E. T.			
Hodgess, William P.			
Hollingsworth, T.			
Scott, Charles H.			
Williams, Lewellen			
Smith, James D.			

Coast Guards—Lieutenant Michael L. Shannahan's Detachment.

First Lieutenant Michael. L. Shannahan's Detachment, Coast Guards, called into service by Brigadier General Jos. M. Taylor, the 13th of July, 1861, to September 13, 1861.

NAMES.	MUSTERED IN.	MUSTERED OUT.	REMARKS.
OFFICERS.			
1st Lieutenant—			
Michael L. Shannahan			
SEAMEN.			
Bishop, Samuel			

Coast Guards—Lieutenant Michael L. Shannahan's Detachment.
(CONTINUED.)

NAMES.	MUSTERED IN.	MUSTERED OUT.	REMARKS.
Jamerson, Daniel			
Kelly, Thomas			
Guillion, Joseph			
Morrison, John			
Smith, James			
Taylor, John A			
Turner, Richard B			

Coast Guards—Lieutenant Able Merander's Detachment.

Second Lieutenant Able Merander's Detachment, Coast Guards, called into service by Brigadier General Jos. M. Taylor, July 14, 1861, to September 5, 1861

NAMES.	MUSTERED IN.	MUSTERED OUT.	REMARKS.
OFFICERS.			
2nd Lieutenant—			
Able Merander			
SEAMEN. }			
Allison, John			
Buckley, Timothy			
Barnett, James			
Bethel, John			
Sanches, Poncho			
Woods, Anderson			
William, James			

Roll, Field and Staff—1st Florida Infantry.

NAMES.	MUSTERED IN.	MUSTERED OUT.	REMARKS.
Colonels—			
J. Patton Anderson	April 5, '61	April 26, '65	Promoted Brigadier-General and Major-General.
William Miller	April 5, '61	April 26, '65	Promoted Brigadier-General August 2, '64.
Lieutenant-Colonels—			
William K. Beard	April 5, '61	April 26, '65	Transferred to staff of General Hardee; wounded at Shiloh, April 6, '62.
Thadeus A. McDonald	April 5, '61	April 26, '65	Promoted Lt.-Col.; wounded at Shiloh, April 6, '62.
Majors—			
Thadeus A. McDonald	April 5, '61		Promoted Lieutenant-Colonel.
W. G. Poole	April 5, '61		Wounded and disabled at Perryville.
Glover A. Ball	April 5, '61	April 26, '65	
Surgeons—			
C. B. Gamble	April 5, '61		Promoted Chief Surgeon, 1st Brigade (Anderson).
P. W. B. Hodges	April 5, '61		
Assistant Surgeons—			
Adjutants—			
W. M. Davidson	April 5, '61		Returned to his Company, G, of which he took command; Promoted Captain, transferred to Staff Patton Anderson.
Laurence Anderson	April 5, '61		Killed at Shiloh, April 6, '62.
James H. Nicholson	April 5, '61	April 26, '61	Promoted Major.
Sergeant Majors—			
G. A. Ball	April 5, '61	April 26, '65	
Quartermaster—			
Commissary—			
Quartermaster Sergeants—			
Commissary Sergeants—			
Robert R. Shepard			
Chaplains—			
Hospital Steward—			

Roll Company A—1st Florida Infantry.

NAMES.	MUSTERED IN.	MUSTERED OUT.	REMARKS.
OFFICERS.			
Captain—			
A. Perry Amaker	April 5, '61	April 4, '62	
W. G. Poole			Promoted Captain.
1st Lieutenants—			
Lawrence M. Anderson			Killed at Shiloh April 6, '62 as 1st Lieut. of Co. A.
Hugh Archer	April 5, '61	April 4, '62	Florida C. R. Battalion.
W. B. Runyan			Resigned November 3, '64.
2nd Lieutenants—			
Theodore Ball	April 5, '61	April 4, '62	
W. H. Collier	April 5, '61		
James B. Galbrath	April 5, '61	April 4, '62	
ENLISTED MEN.			
Ashley, Ludwick			Shot at Shiloh, Tenn., April 6, '62; Re-enlisted at end of term in Capers Bird's Company.
Beech, M. A.	April 5, '61	April 4, '62	
Bond, Thomas H.	April 5, '61	April 4, '62	1st Sergeant.
Bradford, Edward, Jr.	April 5, '61	April 4, '62	
Britten, J. W.	April 5, '61	April 4, '62	2nd Sergeant.
Bull, M. A.	April 5, '61	April 4, '62	Musician.
Callin, John	April 5, '61	April 4, '62	
Campbell, William C.	April 5, '61	April 4, '62	
Comparet, John	April 5, '61	April 4, '62	Musician.
Coleman, Crittendon J.	April 5, '61	April 4, '62	
Cooper, William P.	June 1, '61		
Corbitt, George C.	June 1, '61	April 4, '62	
Demilly, L. L.	June 1, '61	April 4, '62	Corporal.
Denham, A. J.	June 1, '61	April 4, '62	Shot at Santa Rosa Island Fla., '61; imprisoned last nine months of the war.
Denham, William G.	Jan. , '61	April 4, '62	Re-enlisted in Gamble's Battery.
Eccles, James	Jan. , '61	April 4, '62	
Elles, Frank	Jan. , '61	April 4, '62	
Elles, William	Jan. , '61	April 4, '62	Killed at Perryville October 8, '62.
Grant, Samuel W	Jan. , '61	April 4, '62	Killed at Santa Rosa Island, October 9, '61.
Hale, John			Corporal.
Hall, William H.	April 5, '61	April 4, '62	Wounded Sept. 20, '63, at Chickamauga.
Hatcher, Henry			
Henderson, H. J.	April 6, '61	April 4, '62	Mentioned for gallantry at Chickmauga.
Hernandez, Randolph			
Herring, N. W.	April 5, '61	April 4, '62	
Hogue, John H.	April 5, '61	April 4, '62	
Hogue, William S.	April 5, '61	April 4, '62	
Killen, Hugh	April 5, '61	April 4, '62	
Lloyd, Thomas	April 5, '61	April 4, '62	
McCorkle, William	April 5, '61	April 4, '62	
McDonald, Bryant	April , '61	April 4, '62	
McElroy, D. E.	April 5, '61	April 4, '62	
Mason, Arthur			Wounded at Chickmauga September 20, '63.
Meeks, H. L.		April , '65	
Meredith, W. E.	April 5, '61	April 4, '62	
Messer, William	April 5, '61	April 4, '62	
Morgan, John	April 5, '61	April 4, '62	
Muir, Alexander	April 5, '61	April 4, '62	
Paley, C. W.		April , '65	
Paul, J.			Died in hospital April 2, '62.
Paul, P. P.			
Petus, Handy	April 5, '61	April 4, '62	3rd Sergeant.
Potter, Daniel	April 5, '61		4th Sergeant; killed on Santa Rosa Island Oct. 9 '61
Routh, William R.	April 5, '61		
Roark, John		April 4, '62	
Rawls, S. E.		April 4, '62	
Sellier, Charles F.	April 5, '61	April 4, '62	Re-enlisted in Gambles Battery, '62.
Scott, E. T.	April 5, '61	April 4, '62	
Shine, Thomas W	April 5, '61	April 4, '62	Re-enlisted, April '62, Co. K, 5th Florida.
Simms, B. P.		June 18, '62	
Simms, Philip L.	April 5, '61	April 4, '62	
Simmons, W. A. W.		April 4, '62	
Stephens, Allen A.	April 5, '61	April 4, '62	
Taylor, John L.	April 5, '61	April 4, '62	Corporal.
Taylor, Evan	April 5, '61	April 4, '62	
Thompson, Barry			Killed by railroad car February '62.
Tillinghast, Henry A.	April 5, '61	April 4, '62	Company Clerk; Killed at Santa Rosa Island, October 9, '61.
Wall, R. G.	April 5, '61	April 4, '62	
Walker, A. B.	April 5, '61	April 4, '62	
Watson, Robert	April 5, '61	April 4, '62	
Watkins, Alex	April 5, '61	April 4, '62	
Weeks, Levy	April 5, '61	April 4, '62	
West, Charles M	April 5, '61	April 4, '62	Died at Corinth April 20, '62.
West, J.			
Willis, Alex	April 5, '61	April 4, '62	
Williams, Robert	April 2, '61		Sergeant; died in hospital May, '62 of disease.
Wilson, J. H	April 5, '61	April 4, '62	
Winslett, Samuel	April 5, '61	April 4, '62	

Roll Company B—1st Florida Infantry.

NAMES.	MUSTERED IN.	MUSTERED OUT.	REMARKS.
OFFICERS.			
Captain—			
William E. Cropp	April 5, '61	April 4, '62	Killed in Virginia; a member of Stewart's Cavalry.
John T. Miller	April 5, '61	April 26, '65	Promoted Captain; Wounded at Shiloh, April 6, '62.
1st Lieutenant—			
W. T. Orman	April 5, '61	April 4, '62	Re-enlisted.
2nd Lieutenant—			
C. F. Bubcock	April 5, '61	April 4, '62	Re-enlisted '62.
3rd Lieutenants—			
N. W. Hunter	April 5, '61	April 4, '62	
E. C. Stevens	April , '61	April 4, '62	Re-enlisted, '62; shot at Shiloh, April 6, '62 a Lieutenant Co. A, Florida G. R. Battalion; promoted Lieutenant, this Company
ENLISTED MEN.			
Abbott, T. J.	April 5, '61	April 4, '62	1st Sergeant.
Ammerson, Hugh	April 5, '61	April 4, '62	
Armstrong, J. T.	April 5, '61	April 4, '62	
Ashrands, Sid	April 5, '61	April 4, '62	
Austin, C. B.	April 5, '61	April 4, '62	4th Sergeant
Bahl, William	April 5, '61	April 4, '62	
Barefoot, Thomas	April 5, '61	April 4, '62	Re-enlisted in Co. B; died of disease in hospital on the Mississippi River.
Bates, F. I.			Died at Perryville, Ky., October 8, '62
Beach, A.			
Bell, George W.			
Betha, William F.	Jan. , '62	April 26, '65	
Brockenbrough, George	April 5, '61		
Broer, George W.	Jan. 15, '62		Promoted Sergeant; shot at Shiloh, Tenn., April 6, '62.
Brogan, Thomas L.	Jan. 15, '62	April 4, '62	
Brown, Benjamin F.			Died at Shiloh April 6, '62.
Brown, John			Sergeant; died at Opalusus.
Bull, S. K.	April 5, '61	April 4, '62	
Carlton, John	April 5, '61	April 4, '62	
Carter, John			Corporal; died at Ringgold, Ga., February, '63.
Clark, B. L.	April 5, '61	April 4, '62	
Cleveland, S. T. B.	April 5, '61	April 4, '62	
Clinsbower, L.	April 5, '61	April 4, '62	
Coppadge, James T.	April 5, '61	April 4, '62	
Congree, James L.	April 5, '61	April 4, '62	
Coups, James T.	April 5, '61	April 4, '62	
Coyle, B.	April 5, '61	April 4, '62	
Coyle, C.	April 5, '61	April 4, '62	
Flanders, W. E.		April 4, '62	
French, John		April 4, '62	
Freeman, J.			
Gibson, Hiram	April 5, '61	April 4, '62	
Gibson, T. D.	April 5, '61	April 4, '62	
Gorrie, John M	April 5, '61	April 4, '62	Re-enlisted; promoted 1st Sergeant.
Grady, Henry	April 5, '61	April 4, '62	2nd Sergeant.
Grogan, Alexander	April 5, '61	April 4, '62	
Gunter, Decater			Died in hospital at Pollard, Ala
Hale, J. L.			Missing at Shiloh.
Hancock, William A	April 5, '61	April 4, '62	2nd Corporal.
Harris, John	April 5, '61	April 4, '62	
Harrison, John R	April 5, '61	April 4, '62	Re-enlisted and served to close of war.
Harrison, T. E.	April 5. '61	April 4, '62	3rd Sergeant.
Hicks, Joseph	April 5, '61	April 4, '62	
Hill, R. L.	April 5, '61	April 4, '62	Re-enlisted and served to close of war.
Hockstrapper, Charles	April 5, '61	April 4, '62	
Holden, Robert	April 5, '61	April 4, '62	
Horne, Lewis	April 5, '61	April 4, '62	
Howell, W. E.			Sergeant; killed at Shiloh April 6, '62.
Jackson, J. B.			
Jackson, R.			
Johnson, Jasper A.	April 5, '61	April 4, '62	
Johnson, William	April 5, '61	April 4, '62	
King, John W			Sergeant; wounded at Perryville October 8, '62, and died.
Lassiter, Henry J.			Died at Chattanooga November 8, '63.
Lewis, David			Killed at Shiloh April 6, '62.
Lloyde, J. W.			
Lovitt, James	April 5, '61	April 4, '62	
Lucas, John A.	April , '61	April 4, '62	Re-enlisted and served to end of war.
Lynn, Joseph	April 5, '61	April 4, '62	
Lyon, C. B.			Missing in Kentucky September 15, '62.
Lyons, James	April 5, '61	April 4, '62	
McCardle, Isaac	April 5, '61	April 4, '62	
McCardle, W. W.			Died November 24, '63.
McDonald, James	April 5, '61	April 4, '62	
McGowan, John	April 5, '61	April 4, '62	
McKay, Robert	April 5, '61	April 4, '62	Shot in right lung September 20, '63.
McKenzie, Andrew W	April 5, '61	April 4, '62	
McLeod, J.			
Mahoney, John	April 5, '61	April 4, '62	
Neally, Andrew J			Died during the war.
Nichols, L.	April 5, '61	April 4, '62	

Roll Company B—1st Florida Infantry.
(CONTINUED.)

NAMES.	MUSTERED IN.	MUSTERED OUT.	REMARKS.
Pascal, George W			Died in hospital.
Parker, J			
Petry, William, Jr	April 5, '61	April 4, '62	1st Corporal.
Pooser, George E	April 5, '61	April 4, '62	3rd Corporal.
Potts, T. J	April 5, '61	April 4, '62	
Powell, E	April 5, '61	April 4, '62	
Powers, A. F	April 5, '61	April 4, '62	
Raney, D. G	April 5, '61	April 26, '65	
Reynolds, Richard	April 5, '61	April 4, '62	
Robinson, John A			Corporal; died at Gainsville, Ala., '62.
Rodgers, Henry J			Killed at Shiloh April 6, '62.
Rodgers, James			Killed at Shiloh April 6, '62.
Roloph, William	April 5, '61	April 4, '62	
Scott, E. F			Died at Chattanooga.
Sharitt, Amos R	June 5, '61	April 4, '62	Wounded at Santa Rosa Island September, '61.
Sharitt, J. L	April 5, '61	April 4, '62	Re-enlisted.
Smith, John			Killed at Murfreesborough January 23, '63.
Smith, T. R	April 5, '61	April 4, '62	
Smith, William E	April 5, '61	April 4, '62	Killed at Santa Rosa Island October 9, '61.
Stanford, T		—	
Stevens, B. H			Corporal.
Stevens, E. C	April 5, '61	April 4, '62	Shot at Shiloh April 6, '62; Re-enlisted.
Stockwell, William		April 26, '65	
Stoper, A. T	April 5, '61	April 4, '62	Corporal.
Taylor, Henry			Mentioned for gallantry at Chickmauga.
Thompson, John J	April 5, '61	April 4, '62	
Thompson, Lewis F		April 26, '65	Killed on Santa Rosa Island October 9, '61.
Trimmer, W. H	March 27, '61	April 4, '62	Re-enlisted November, '62; transferred from Richmond, Va., to Dunham's Artillery at Lake City; promoted to Quartermaster-Sergeant of Battery.
Tuten, C. D			1st Sergeant.
Vaughn, James			
Walker, A. B			Wounded at Perryville October 8, '62.
Watson, R. H			Wounded at Perryville October 8, '62.
Williams, J. R			
Wilson, J			
Wilson, J. H			Wounded at Perryville October 8. '62.
Williams, Sam			Dead.
Williamson, W. H			
Wood, B. B			
Wood, William	April 5, '61	April 4, '62	
Wynn, Charles E			Died at Ringgold, Ga., '63.

Roll Company C—1st Florida Infantry.

NAMES.	MUSTERED IN.	MUSTERED OUT.	REMARKS.
OFFICERS.			
Captains—			
B. W. Powell	April 5, '61	April 4, '62	Expiration of term.
T. Sumter Menans	April 5, '61	April 4, '62	1st Lieut.; promoted Capt.; wounded and captured at Shiloh April 6, '62; Capt. Co. E, Florida and C. G. R. Battalion.
J. D. Turner			Promoted Captain.
1st Lieutenant—			
Oliver P. Hull	April 5, '61		Promoted 1st Lieutenant from 2nd Lieutenant; killed at Shiloh April 6, '62.
2nd Lieutenants—			
John A. Emmerson	April 5, '61	April 4, '62	
R. Y. H. Law	April 5, '61	April 4, '62	Re-enlisted, Co. C, 7th Infantry.
W. W. Tucker	April 5, '61	April 4, '62	2nd Sergeant; promoted 2nd Lieutenant, Jan. 23, '62; wounded at Shiloh April 6, '62; also wounded September 20, '63.
3rd Lieutenant—			
J. A. Woodburn	April 5, '61	April 4, '62	Promoted 3rd Lieutenant.
ENLISTED MEN.			
Arnow, Porter R	April 5, '61	April 4, '62	
Ashurst, Watson	April 5, '61	April 4, '62	
Baker, E			Died in Tupelo, Miss., July 15, '62, of disease.
Baker, John			Died at Lagrange, Tenn., June 17, '62.
Bauknight, S. J	April 5, '61	April 4, '62	
Bender, John	April 5, '61	April 4, 62	Re-enlisted Co. C; killed at Perryville Oct. 8, '62.
Bennett, E. R	April 5, '61	April 4, '62	Promoted Corporal.
Branch, John	April 5, '61	April 4, '62	
Bremer, George A	April 5, '61	April 4, '62	
Bridgeman, George	March , '62		Killed at Dallas, Ga., June 27, '64.
Brickle, Morgan			Died at Lagrange April 10, '62.
Broome, R. W	April 5, '61	April 4, '62	1st Sergeant.
Brown, F. M	April 5, '61	April 4, '62	
Cameron, A. S	April 5, '61	April 4, '62	

Roll Company C—1st Florida Infantry.

(CONTINUED.)

NAMES.	MUSTERED IN.	MUSTERED OUT.	REMARKS.
Cames, J. B.		April 4, '62	
Carter, Jesse	April 5, '61	April 4, '62	
Clark, Abner			Died at Vaden, Miss., June 2, '62.
Coker, Silas	Feb. '62		Wounded at Perryville, Ky., '62.
Colmer, W. D.	April 5, '61	April 4, '62	
Cooper, W. H.			Killed at Perryville October 8, '62.
Crosby, John	April 5, '61	April 4, '62	4th Sergeant.
Cotheran, A. J.	April 5, '61	April 4, '62	
Crosby, J. O.	April 19, '61	April 4, '62	Promoted Color Sergeant; Re-enlisted.
Davis, J. M.	April 5, '61	April 4, '62	
Davis, R. H.	April 5, '61	April 4, '62	
Demaker, James L.	April 5, '61	April 4, '62	1st Corporal.
Dickinson, William			
Dixon, Josiah	April 5, '61		
Devine, J. T.	April 5, '61		
Dodson, W. H.			Wounded at Perryville October 8, '62.
Edwards, J. G. A.	April 5, '61	April 4, '62	
Fleming, J. E.	April 5, '61	April 4, '62	
Forrest, James	April 5, '61	April 4, '62	
Foster, Thadeus	April 5, '61	April 4, '62	
Gaston, William L.			Corporal; killed at Missionary Ridge Nov. 25, '63.
Geiger, W. H.	April 5, '61	April 4, '62	2nd Sergeant.
Hale, Pir.kney			Died at Grenada, Miss.
Harris, Thomas E.	April 5, '61	April 4, '62	
Hoose: F. M.	April 5, '61	April 4, '62	2nd Corporal.
Howard, Harrison	April 5, '61	April 4, '62	
James, Joseph G.	April 5, '61	April 4, '62	
Johnson, J. J.			
Jones, Thomas W.			
Jordan, E. P.	April 5, '61	April 4, '62	
Kennedy, Thomas S.	April 5, '61	April 4, '62	
Kennedy, Wilson N.	April 5, '61	April 4, '62	
Kittrel, Stanley			Killed at Missionary Ridge November 25, '63.
Kyle, C. H.			Killed at Shiloh April 6, '62.
Lamb, J. D.			Killed at Chickamauga September 20, '63.
Leland, George A.	April 5, '61	April 4, '62	
Lloyd, J. W.	April 5, '61	April 4, '62	
Loeb, Maurice			
Lynn, H.			Deserted.
Martin, Samuel	Feb. 15, '62	April 26, '65	Transferred July 4, '62, to Capt. Denham's Co.
Miller, M. E.	April 5, '61	April 4, '62	
Miller, Samuel T.	April 5, '61	April 4, '62	Sergeant.
Mixon, E. M.	April 5, '61	April 4, '62	
Morris, John			Died at Knoxville November 29, '62.
Morrison, Nathaniel	April 5, '61	April 4, '62	Re-enlisted in Co. C; killed at Shiloh April 6, '62.
Muir, Alexander J.	April 5, '61	April 4, '62	Promoted Sergeant.
Neal, A. J.	April 5, '61	April 4, '62	Promoted Sergeant; wounded September 20, '63.
Neely, James	April 5, '61	April 4, '62	Transferred to Co. C; wounded September 20, '63; mentioned for gallantry at Chickamauga.
Neely, Samuel	April 5, '61	April 4, '62	
O'Neal, Peter	April 5, '61	May 28, '62	
Parker, James	April 5, '61	April 4, '62	
Pearson, John W.	April 5, '61	April 4, '62	
Pinkney, James			Died at Corinth, Miss., April 21, '62.
Price, George L.	April 5, '61	April 4, '62	
Roddenberry, Mathew			Died May 15, '62, in service.
Rawles, Samuel B.	April 5, '61	April 4, '62	
Sharp, R. B.			Died at Monticello October, '62
Shears, J. W.	April 5, '61	April 4, '62	
Shepard, F. M.			
Simenten, J. H.	April 5, '61	April 4, '62	
Simmons, W. A. W.			
Smith, C. P.	April 5, '61	April 4, '62	Promoted Corporal.
Smith, Jacob			Died at Lagrange, Tenn., April 10, '62.
Smith, Thomas	April 5, '61	April 1, '62	
Smith, W. M.	April 5, '61	April 4, '62	
Stafford, E. C.	April 5, '61	April 4, '62	
Stanford, Thomas	April 5, '61	April 4, 62	
Starling, Levi	April 5, '61	April 26, '65	Shot near Murfreesborough, Tenn., Dec. 4, '64. also at Shiloh, Tenn., April 6, '62.
Stephens, E. C.	April 5, '61	April 4, '62	3rd Corporal; Re-enlisted in Co. B; shot at Shiloh April 6, '62.
Strickland, Johnathan	April 5, '61	April 4, '62	Promoted Corporal.
Surles, Robert	April 5, '61		Promoted Corporal; died at Tullahoma Jan. 25, '62
Tate, T. M.	April 5, '61	April 4, '62	4th Corporal.
Taylor	April 5, '61		Sergeant.
Thomel, A. A.	April 5, '61	April 4, '62	
Thompson, A. L.	April 5, '61	April 4, '62	
Thompson, Henry			Died at Montgomery, Ala., March, '62 of pneumonia.
Thompson, L. F.	April 5, '61	April 1, '62	
Timons, L. E.	April 5, '61	April 4, '62	
Turner, George W.			Wounded at Chickamauga September 20, '63.
Turner, J. C.			
Turner, N. J.	April 5, '61		Killed at Shiloh April 6, '62.
Walker, J. A.			

Roll Company C—1st Florida Infantry.
(CONTINUED.)

NAMES.	MUSTERED IN.	MUSTERED OUT.	REMARKS.
Walker, Joel E.	Feb. '62	April 26, '65	Shot at Dallas, Ga., May 28, '64.
Wall, S. J.	Feb. '62	April 4, 62	
Watts, R. B.			Killed at Shiloh April 6, '62.
White, George W.			Killed at Perryville October 8, '62.
Whitehurst, Perry			Deceased at Monticello hospital July 5, '63.
Williams, George			Wounded at Chickamauga September 20, '63; mentioned for gallantry.
Williams, W. A.			Died at Shiloh April 6, '62.
Williamson			Sergeant.
Wood, Benjamin	April 5, '61	April 4, '62	

Roll Company D—1st Florida Infantry.

NAMES.	MUSTERED IN.	MUSTERED OUT.	REMARKS.
OFFICERS.			
Captains—			
R. B. Hilton	April 5, '61	April 4, '62	
C. L. McKinnon		April 26, '65	Wounded at Dallas Ga., May 28, '64.
1st Lieutenants—			
Walter Gwynn	April 5, '61	April 4, '62	
Neil J. McKinnon		May , '62	Re-enlisted Capt. C. L. McKinnon's Co; was in prison when paroled, June 18, '65.
John L. McKinnon		April 26, '65	Promoted 1st Lieutenant.
C. Alonzo Landrum			Promoted 2nd Lieutenant; then 1st Lieutenant.
2nd Lieutenants—			
William D. Evans			Resigned March 21, '63.
Robert W. McCollum			Promoted 2nd Lieutenant; resigned April 22, '63.
W. G. Poole	April 5, '61	April 4, '62	Seriously wounded at Perryville; promoted Capt., Co. A, 1st Battalion; Major of Florida and C. G. R. Battalion.
C. E. Hayward	April 5, '61		Appointed 2nd Lieutenant April 15, '62; Co. A, Florida and C. G. R. Battalion.
3rd Lieutenants—			
John W. Nash	April 5, '61	April 4, '62	Re-enlisted, '62, in R. N. Gardner's Co. K, 5th Florida, and served to close of war.
W. B. Runyan			Appointed 3rd Lieutenant May 27, '62; Florida and C. G. R. Battalion.
ENLISTED MEN.			
Alford, James			
Alsobrook, R.			
Anderson, Alex L.	April 5, '61		Shot at Murfreesborough Jan. 1, '63; Sept. 20, '63.
Anderson, Duncan			
Anderson, J. L.			Died, Chattanooga September 2, '62
Anderson, J. S.	April 5, '61	April 4, '62	
Anderson, L. M.	April 5, '61	April 4, '62	Sergeant; promoted 1st Lieut. and Capt. of 1st Battalion; killed at Shiloh April 6, '62.
Anderson, Walker	April 5, '61	April 4, '62	Promoted 1st Lieutenant, then Captain May 27, '62 of Co. A, Florida and C. G. R. Battalion.
Ansell, W. W.	April 5, '61	April 4, '62	
Ard, William D.			Died in Florida November 10, '62, of fever.
Armstrong, John	April 5, '61	April 4, '62	
Bachelor, J. J.	April 5, '61	April 4, '62	Re-enlisted in Co. K.
Baker, B. J.	April 5, '61	April 4, '62	
Baker, C. B.			Died in hospital at Grenada, Miss.
Baker, F. W.	April 5, '61	April 4, '62	2nd Sergeant.
Barefoot, Thomas	April 5, '61	April 6, '62	
Barnett, J. E.			Killed, Perryville, October 8, '62.
Barnett, Jackson F.			
Barnhill, A.			
Beale, Jasper			
Blocker, John R.	April 5, '61	April 4, '62	Re-enlisted in 2nd Cavalry.
Blount, Benjamin A.			Died at Sparta, Tenn., Sept. 6, '62, from fever.
Bloxham, W. D.	April 5, '61	April 4, '62	Re-enlisted, '62; promoted Captain Co. C, 5th Infantry and transferred to Quartermaster Department at Madison.
Brevard, E.	April 5, '61	April 4, '62	
Brickle, Richard	April 5, '61	April 4, '62	
Brown, John E.			Killed at Perryville, Ky., October 8, '62.
Brown, H. S.	April 5, '61	April 4, '62	
Brown, S. J.	April 5, '61	April 4, '62	
Brown, W. J.	April 5, '61	April 4, '62	
Brown, William L.			Wounded at Chickamauga, Ga., September 20, '63.
Bullard, James W.			
Campbell, H.			Died at Sparta, Tenn., December 15, '62.
Caswell, G.			
Caswell, Michael V.	May 15, '62		
Christie, A. C.			
Collaway, Jesse	April 5, '61	April 4, 62	
Coxkroft, William A.			Died at Sparta, Tenn., June 25, of pneumonia.
Crafford, John L.			Died in Georgia August 29, '63.
Croom, A. Church	April 5, '61	April 4, '62	Re-enlisted again in Co. C, 2nd Cavalry; transferred to Scott's Battalion Cavalry and promoted Sergeant.

Roll Company D—1st Florida Infantry.

(CONTINUED.)

NAMES.	MUSTERED IN.	MUSTERED OUT.	REMARKS.
Croom, H. C.	April 5, '61	April 4, '62	Transferred to Co. F, 2nd Regiment Cavalry; promoted to 3rd Lieutenant.
Denham		June 27, '61	Disability; Corporal.
Dodgen			Corporal.
Donald, Charles M.			Wounded Septemper 20, '63, at Chickamauga.
Duval, Phillip	Aprl 5, '61	Aprl 4, '62	Promoted Sergeant.
Edgar, George M.	April 5, '61	April 4, '62	
Evans, Henry R.			
Faulk, T.			
Fener, Thomas			Died in Montgomery, Ala., August, '63, of typhoid fever.
Freeman, John	April 5, '61	April 4, '62	
Gallaher, E. Y.	April 5, '61	April 4, '62	2nd Corporal.
Gillett, Thomas M.	April 5, '61	April 4, '62	
Gray, A.			
Grice, W. J.	June 20, '61		Shot at New Hope Church, Ga., June, '64.
Gurley, M. P.	April 5, '61	April 4, '62	
Hart, J. J.	April 5, '61	April 4, '62	Wounded at Shiloh April 6, '62.
Hart, Laurie			Wounded at Shiloh April 6, '62.
Herron, F. M.	April 5, '61	April 4, '62	
Hartwell, George			Died June 12, '62, of measles.
Holly, Robert H.			
Horten, Berry	April 5, '61	April 4, '62	
Houck, W. F.	April 5, '61	April 4, '62	
Howard, George W	April 5, '61	April 4, '62	
Hudnall, T. W	April 5, '61	April 4, '62	Re-enlisted in Gamble's Artillery.
Infinger, Charles.			
Infinger, Thomas			Wounded at Chickamauga September 20, '63.
Johnson, Alexander	April 5, '61	April 4, '62	Wounded at Shiloh April 6, '62; New Hope Church March 28, '63; also at Missionary Ridge December 27. '63.
Joiner, James			
Jones, G. L.			
Kemp, Henry			
Kemp, Joshua F.			
Kemp, William H.			Died May 29, '62 of measles at Walton county, Fla.
King, J.			
King, W. J.	April 5, '61	April 4, '62	Corporal.
Kinden, William	April 5, '61	April 4, '62	
Kirkland, James J.			
Leaman, C. E.	April 5, '61	April 4, '62	
Lester, E.			
Lindley, H. L.	April 5, '61	April 4, '62	
Lyles, Richard	April 5, '61	April 4, '62	Missing at Shiloh.
McCollum, Archibald L.			Died October 23, '63, of fever.
McDonald, Charles L.			Died December 18, in Georgia, from wounds.
McDonald, Daniel M.			Died of pneumonia July 29, '62.
McDonald, Norman M.	Feb, 28, '62	April 26, '65	Shot at Dallas, Ga., July 25, '64.
McDonald, O.			
McIver, Angus C.			
McIver, Colin C.	July 19, '61	June 12, '65	From Camp Chase.
McIver, D. C.			Died at Chattanooga Sept. 9, '62 of typhoid.
McIver, John C.			
McKinnon, Alexander D		June 12, '65	
McKinnon, Daniel L.			
McLean, Calvin			Died at Chattanooga Dec. 10, '62, of pneumonia.
McLean, Daniel G.			
McLean, Daniel K.			Died at Dunlap September, '62, of typhoid.
McLean, John L.		April 26, '65	
McLean, J. Love			
McLean, Lauchlin D			Promoted Corporal.
McLean, Malcolm P.	July , '61		Corporal; promoted Sergeant; captured at Nashville Dec. 16, '64; carried to Camp Chase and through exposure and neglect lost an eye.
McLeod, John	April 5, '61	April 4, '62	Corporal; promoted Sergeant; shot at Chickmauga Sept. 20, '63; died at Madison, Fla., Sept. 21, '64.
Macon, Arthur	April 5, '61	April 4, '62	
Marcheal, Edward D			Died at Dunlap, Tenn., Sept. 19, '62, of pneumonia.
Maxwell, G. Troup	April 5, '61	April 4, '62	
Meagher, R. A.	April 4, '61	April 5, '62	1st Sergeant.
Miller, Elias B			
Milton, S.			
Mimmes, H.	April 5, '61	April 4, '62	
Modlin, F. M.	April 5, '61	April 4, '62	
Moore, G. J.	April 5, '61	April 4, '62	
Morris, William	April 5, '61	April 4, '62	
Morrison, A. P.			Died at Sulphur Springs, Tenn., December 20, '63, of pneumonia.
Moorison, Malcolm P			
Moseley, B. F.		April 26, '65	
Nelson, G.			
Norris, Allen	April 5, '61	April 4, '62	
Norris, G.			
Norris, Henry	April 5, '61	April 4, '62	
Paddison, W	April 5, '61	April 4, '62	
Page, Allen			Died in Alabama July 20, '63, of puenmonia.
Pastell, George W	April 5, '61	April 4, '62	
Patten, R. B.	April 5, '61	April 4, '62	1st Corporal.

Roll Company D—1st Florida Infantry.
(CONTINUED.)

NAMES.	MUSTERED IN	MUSTERED OUT.	REMARKS.
Patterson, Joseph			
Porter, Levi			Killed at Chickmauga September 20, '63.
Puller, A. J	April 5, '61	April 4, '62	
Race, W. T.	April 5, '61	April 4, '62	
Raborn, J. W			Died June 6, '62, of brain fever.
Randolph, Eston	April 5, '61	April 4, '62	
Randolph, William	April 5, '61	April 4, '62	
Rooks, Jesse W			Died in Florida of measles June 19, '62.
Rooks, Thomas F.			
Rooks, William W			Died May 12, '62, of sunstroke.
Sanders, J. G.			Died in Alabama August 8, '62, of fever.
Scott, Alford	April 5, '61	April 4, '62	
Sessions, T.			
Shean, Erastus B			Died of brain fever September 4, at Dunlap.
Silcox, Benjamin			Died at Chattanooga September 9, '63.
Silcox, David			Died at Sulphur Springs, Tenn., March 23, '63, of
Silcox, Jesse			pneumonia.
Silcox, William H			Reported as a deserter.
Singleton, W. H.			
Stafford, J. E.	April 5, '61	April 4, '62	
Steele, J.			
Surles			Corporal.
Taurence, Benjamin F			Wounded at Chickamauga September 20, '63.
Taylor, James			
Taylor, Latson L			Died in Alabama August 5, '62, of fever.
Thomas, J. G.	April 5, '61	April 4, '62	
Tiner, T.			
Tiner, William A. J			
Tipton, I.	April 5, '61	April 4, '62	
Walker, L. B.	April 5, '61	April 4, '62	
Ward, Asa			
Ward, B. F.		April 26, '65	Deserted
Ward, Isaac			
Wescott, J. D., Jr	April 5, '61	April 4, '62	
Willie, W. A.	April 5, '61	April 4, '62	
Wilson, Benjamin	April 5, '61	April 4, '62	
Williamson, Elbert	April 5, '61	April 4, '62	
Woodberry, Samuel C.	April 5, '61	April 4, '62	
Worthington, William			Died June 29, '62, of brain fever.
Wright, Elias			Died in Florida, October 6, '62.
Wright, George			
Wright, Hamilton			Died July 15, '62, of measles.
Wright, James			Died at Chattanooga October 30, of fever.
Write, James			Died in Florida October, '63, of fever.

Roll Company E—1st Florida Infantry.

NAMES.	MUSTERED IN.	MUSTERED OUT.	REMARKS.
OFFICERS.			
Captains—			
Hyer H. Baker	April 5, '61	April 4, '62	
A. B. McLeod		April 26, '65	Wounded by fall during battle of Rocky Face Mountain, Ga., May 1, '64.
1st Lieutenants—			
mThomas E. Clark	April 5, '61	April 4, '62	Re-enlisted; promoted Capt. Co. E, 8th Infantry.
William McPherson			Promoted Captain.
Henry W. Reddick	March 20, '62		
2nd Lieutenants—			
F. M. Farley	April 5, '61	April 4, '62	Re-enlisted; Co. E, May, '62, Resigned Nov. 2, '63
W. H. DuBose	April 5, '61	April 4, '62	
3rd Lieutenants—			
Murdock C. McKee	March 20, '62		Died, Chattanooga, Tenn., October, '62.
Henry T. Wright			
ENLISTED MEN.			
Alexander, George L	April 5, '61	April 4, '62	Sergeant.
Anderson, Daniel L	July 1, '61		Discharged, January, '62, for disability.
Armistead, Anthony	April 5, '61	April 4, '62	Corporal.
Armistead, Lawrence T	April 5, '61	April 4, '62	
Appleton, W. L.	April 5, '61	April 4, '62	
Ayres, Jesse W	April 5, '61	April 4, '62	
Bailey, Thomas J	April 5, '61	April 4, '62	
Baker, Beverly	April 5, '61	April 4, '62	
Balcolm, A. L.	March 20, '62		
Barbaree, Henry	April 5, '61	April 4, '62	Re-enlisted.
Barron, Green	March 20 '62		
Beauchamp, John C	April 5, '61	April 4, '62	
Bonds, W H	March 2, '62		Lost sense of hearing by explosion of shell at Atlanta, Ga., August 15, '64.

Roll Company E—1st Florida Infantry.

(CONTINUED.)

NAMES.	MUSTERED IN.	MUSTERED OUT.	REMARKS.
Bowers, Addison	April 5, '61	April 4, '62	2nd Corporal.
Brantley, H. M.	April 5, '61	April 4, '62	
Brantley, John D.	April 5, '61	April 4, '62	
Bray, William	April 5, '61		Deserted March 14, '64.
Bright, Henry A.	April 5, '61	April 4, '62	
Brown, Benjamin F.		April 26, '65	
Brown, Felix	April 5, '61	April 4, '62	
Bush, E. B.	April 5, '61	April 4, '62	
Cadle, William G.	April 5, '61	April 4, '62	
Campbell, W. L.			
Corley, Robert J.	April 5, '61	April 4, '62	
Cotton, James			1st Sergeant.
Cotton, Jesse-N	March 11, '62		Captured; imprisoned at Chicago till June, '65.
Cotton, John A.	March 11, '62		Corporal.
Cotton, Shadrack	March 11, '62		Died at Ringgold, Ga., September, '62, of disease.
Davis, Marius M.	April , '61	April 4, '62	Re-enlisted, August, '62.
Davis, William	March 11, '62		
Dockries, J. A.	July 21, '61		Discharged, '62, for disability; re-enlisted 29th Alabama and served to close of war
Donald, John W.	April 5, '61	April 4, '62	
Donalson, Benjamin F.	March 11, '62		
Drummonds, Eugene E.	April 5, '61	April 4, '62	
Eldridge, Daniel-D.	March 11, '62		
Eldridge, James K. P.	April 5, '61	April 4, '62	Re-enlisted.
Eldridge, Jeremiah M.	April , '61		Died in Florida of brain fever, '62.
Evans, H. R.		April 26, '65	
Evans, William D.	July , '61	April 26, '65	
Faulks, James W.	March , '62		
Ferguson, William G.	April 5, '61	April 4, '62	
Finley, Sam Y.	April 5, '61	April 4, '62	Re-enlisted; promoted Capt. Co. I, 6th Infantry. Died of disease February 13, '63, at Walton, Fla.
Glissen, Joe			
Glissen, Mathew			
Glisson, Philip			Died at Harrodsburg, Ky., Oct., '62, of pneumonia.
Godwin, Marion C.			
Gomillion, Elijah			Died in Kentucky September, '62, of disease.
Gomillion, William			Died August 2, '62, at Montgomery.
Gonsales, James E.			
Grimes, Jesse-F.			
Gulbedge James			
Harrison, Benjamin J.			Died at Chattanooga January 6, '62.
Hawel, William G.	March 11, '62		
High, James C.	April 5, '61	April 4, '62	
Holland, William M.			Transferred to 29th Alabama.
Houck, Josiah	April 5, '61	April 4, '62	
Jackson, John B.	April 5, '61	April 4, '62	
Jones, John C.	April 5, '61	April 4, '62	
Jones, Uzzell A.	April 5, '61	April 4, '62	
Kelly, William	April 5, '61	April 4, '62	
Kennedy, John	April 5, '61	April 4, '62	
Kilbee, John C.	April 5, '61	April 4, '62	
Kilgore, A. J.	April 5, '61	April 4, '62	
Land, Henry			Died at Chattanooga of disease September, '62.
Langford, Benjamin	March 11, '62		Wounded near Atlanta, Ga., August, '64.
Lassiter, Ephriam	March 11, '62		
Lassiter, Henry	April 5, '61	April 4, '62	
Lassiter, H. L.	April 5, '61	April 4, '62	
Lassiter, James			Died in Kentucky, September, '62.
Lassiter, Joseph M.			Died of erysipelas, September, '62.
Lassiter, Wiley B.	March , '62		Captured at Atlanta, Ga., July 22, '64; imprisoned at Camp Chase, Ohio, where he died Jan. 7, '65.
Lewis, Alfred			Deserted March 14, '64.
Lewis, Calvin	April , '61		Died of congestive chill at Bluff Springs, Florida, June 5, '62.
Lewis, Wiley			
Lillaram, Lewis	March 11, '62		Corporal.
Lowry, William	Dec. , '61		Discharged August, '64, for disability.
McClung, LaFayette	April 5, '61	April 4, '62	1st Sergeant.
McCullough, Edward M.	April 5, '61		Corporal; died in service.
McCullum, Gaines	March 11, '62		
McDonald, Allen	March 2, '62	April 26, '65	Wounded at New Hope Church, Atlanta, July 22, '64, and at Franklin, Tenn., November 30, '64.
McDonald, John A.	March , '62		Sergeant; died in Florida June 7, '62.
McDonald, Peter P.	July , '61		Transferred to Co. H, 6th Florida; wounded at Dallas, Ga., '64.
McIntosh, John C.	April 5, '61	April 4, '62	
McKay, William			Died at Dunlap, Tenn., September, '62.
McKenzie, Randal	March 11, '62		
McKenniss, William H.	April 5, '61	April 4, '62	
McKinnon, A. D.			1st Sergeant.
McKinnon, J. L.			Promoted 2nd Lieutenant Co. D, 1st Regiment.
McLeod, John P.			Sergeant.
McLeod, Norman	March 11, '62		
McLeod, W. B.	March 2, '62		Sergeant; discharged Sept. 20, '64, for disability; lost arm near Atlanta, Ga., August 24, '64.
McNealy, J. W.	April 5, '61	April 4, '62	
McNealy, Sidney	April 5, '61	April 4, '62	
McRae, Daniel R.	March , '62		
Mathis, J. L.			Transferred to 29th Alabama.

Roll Company E—1st Florida Infantry.
(CONTINUED.)

NAMES.	MUSTERED IN.	MUSTERED OUT.	REMARKS.
Michemex Moses	March , '62		Died at Chattanooga, Tenn., September, '62.
Moates, Francis			
Moates, James M		April 26, '65	
Moates, Johnathan	March , '62		Died in Kentucky, November 10, '62.
Moore, Daniel D			Corporal.
Morriss, J. E. D	April 5, '61	April 4, '62	
Nelson, Josiah			Died at Harrodsburg, Ky., February 28, '63.
Norris, John			Killed at Perryville October 8, '62.
Norwood, William			Died at Atlanta, Ga., November 27, '63.
Parker, Benjamin F	April 5, '61	April 4, '62	
Paulk, Jonathan	April 5, '61	April 4, '62	
Pitts, Isaac			Bugler.
Rabon, Asa	April 5, '61	April 4, '62	
Rayner, Elijah			
Redd, William G	April 5, '61	April 4, '62	
Reddick, James W	May , '61		Discharged for broken leg.
Reddick, Madison M			Sergeant.
Register, John	April 5, '61	April 4, '62	Sergeant.
Rodgers, Henry T	April 5, '61	April 4, '62	
Rogers, J. M			Shot at Chattanooga November 23, '63.
Rogers, Jesse	Aug. , '61	April 4, '62	Re-enlisted August, '62, in Alex McLeod's Co.; captured, '63; imprisoned at Rock Island, Ill., and remained there till the close of the war.
Rogers, Neverson	Aug. , '61		Discharged, '62, for disability.
Ryals, James M	April 5, '61	April 4, '62	
Sands, Robert			Wounded September 20, '63.
Sansom, B. F	April 5, '61	April 4, '62	
Sasser, Josiah	April 5, '61	April 4, '62	
Slater, Charles	April 5, '61	April 4, '62	Musician.
Saunders, William A	April 5, '61	April 4, '62	
Sims, Henry G	April 5, '61	April 4, '62	
Smith, J. W	March 2, '62	April 26, '65	Shot at Atlanta, Ga., Aug. 24, '64; promoted Corp.
Spence, Isaac	March 2, '62	April 26, '65	Wounded at Murfreesborough, Tenn., Dec. 31, '62
Spence, Richard			
Strabry, A. E	April 5, '61	April 4, '62	
Stephens, Benjamin	April 5, '61	April 4, '62	Corporal.
Stephens, B. H	March , '61	April 26, '65	
Stephens, James	April 5, '61	April 4, '62	
Thompson, Benjamin			
Thompson, Jesse			
Thompson, William			Promoted Sergeant; died at Chattanooga Sept. '62
Thornton, William			Sergeant.
Truett, Cass			Died at Ringgold, Georgia.
Truett, James			
Truett, John			Killed at Perryville, October 8, '62.
Truett, Noel R			Died at Marietta, Ga., November 20, '62.
Walker, Berry A	June , '61	April 26, '65	Prisoner at Elmira, N. Y., when war closed.
Watford, William T	April 5, '61	April 4, '62	
Watson, Benton H			
Watson, George W			Killed at Perryville October 8, '62.
Watson, William A			Bugler.
Ward, Michael			
West, Mathew	April 5, '61	April 4, '62	
Welch, Isaac			
Wheeler, John			Honorable mention at Chickamauga.
Whidden, Burnett	April 5, '61	April 4, '62	1st Corporal.
White, John			Killed at Atlanta, Ga., July 25, '64.
Williams, John		April 26, '65	
Williams, J. V		April 26, '65	

Roll Company F—1st Florida Infantry.

NAMES.	MUSTERED IN.	MUSTERED OUT.	REMARKS.
OFFICERS.			
Captains—			
Richard Bradford	April 5, '61		Killed on Santa Rosa Island October 9, '61.
Vans Randell	April 5, '61	April 4, '62	Promoted Captain October, '61.
John Walston	June '62		
1st Lieutenants—			
D. F. Livingston		April 4, '62	
Isaiah Cobb			Promoted Captain, of Co. I, '64.
2nd Lieutenants—			
Thomas Moseley		April 4, '62	
William H. Whitner	April 5, '61		
James F. Hart			
3rd Lieutenant—			
John McDavid			

Roll Company F—1st Florida Infantry.

(CONTINUED.)

NAMES.	MUSTERED IN.	MUSTERED OUT.	REMARKS.
ENLISTED MEN.			
Allen, R. J.			
Ard, Daniel	June '62	April 26, '65	
Ard, George			
Ard, Jesse		April 26, '65	
Baggett, Edward	June '62		Died, Harrodsburg, Ky., October 13, '62.
Baker, John	April 5, '61	April 4, '62	
Barker, Emanuel	April 5, '61	April 4, '62	
Berry, James	June '62	April 26, '65	
Bishop, J. W.	April 5, '61	April 26, '65	Re-enlisted, May, '62.
Blackman, J. P.			
Botts, W. F.		April 26, '65	Lost leg in war.
Boyette, John A.	April 5, '61	April 4, '62	
Boyan, Edward H.	April 5, '61	April 4, '62	Promoted Corporal.
Burch, George C.	April 5, '61		Re-enlisted, '62; imprisoned at Fort Delaware.
Butler, A. K.	April 5, '61	April 4, '62	
Carlsile, James	April 5, '61		Died Pollard, Ala., October 1, '62.
Cauley, A. J.			
Cauley, Henry			
Chestnut, Jacob	April 5, '61		Died, Bluff Springs, January 6, '62.
Clemens, Jasper	April 5, '61	April 4, '62	
Cobb, B. N.			Corporal; killed at Perryville October 2, '62.
Cobb, O.			Wounded, September 20, '63.
Collier, William H.	April 5, '61	April 26, '65	Promoted 1st Leutenant Co. D; Co. A of F. and C. G. R. Battalion.
Crane, William			
Daniel, James			
Davis, Ephriam W.	Mch. 20, '62	April 26, '65	Wounded in left arm.
Davis, M. D.			
DeLaughter, Pickens	April 5, '61	April 4, '62	Promoted 1st Corporal.
Dixon, Josiah B.	April 5, '61		
Dozier, A. J.	April 5, '61	April 4, '62	Re-enlisted, '62.
Drew, James E.	April 5, '61	April 26, '65	Re-enlisted, March, '62.
Edwards, John E.	April 5, '61	April 4, '62	
Exum, William	April 5, '61	April 4, '62	
Ezell, Jesse B.	April 5, '61		
Faulk, Asa	June '62		
Faulk, John M.	June '62		Died, Kingston, Ga., January 18, '64.
Fisher, L. C.			Sergeant.
Franklin, James H.	Mch. '62	April 26, '65	
Frater, Louis			
Gaston, William L.	April 5, '61	April 4, '62	
Gatlin, G. W.			Died July 9, '62, at Bluff Springs.
Gideon, Benjamin	June '62		
Godlie, John E.	April 5, '61	April 4, '62	
Grimes, G. W.			Transferred September 20, '63.
Grimes, James T.	Mch. 20, '62		
Grimes, John W.	Mch. 20, '62	April 26, '65	
Grimes, Thomas			
Grimes, W. J.			
Guest, Mathew	Mch. 20, '62	April 26, '65	
Hamilton, John	April 5, '61	April 4, '62	
Hammock, Samuel	April 5, '61	April 4, '62	Re-enlisted and served to close of war.
Harris, Britton	Mch. 20, '62		
Harris, Luke	Mch. 20, '62		
Harrold, E. M.	April 5, '61	April 4, '62	
Harvis, S. H.	April 5, '61		
Hays, E. J.	April 5, '61	April 4, '62	
Hines, William G.	April 5, '61	April 4, '62	Promoted Corporal.
Hinton, J. S.	April 5, '61	April 4, '62	
Hollyman, C. F.	April 5, '61	April 4, '62	
Howell, William E.	April 5, '61	April 4, '62	
Jarvis, William, Jr.	April 5, '61	April 4, '62	
Jernigan, Blake	April 5, '61		Died at Montgomery, Ala., September, '62.
Jernigan, J. W.	Mch. 20, '62		
Johnson, John A.	April 5, '61	April 4, '62	
Jones, Curtis	April 5, '61	April 4, '62	
Jordan, W. Harrison	Mch. 20, '62		Died, Tullahoma, Tenn., January 30, '63.
Jordan, W. J.	Mch. 20, '62		
Kelly, W. H.	Mch. 20, '62		
Kennedy, A. J.	Mch. 20, '62		
Kilk, Robert	Mch. 20, '62		Died, Knoxville, November 10, '62.
Kilpatrick, William B.	April 5, '61	April 4, '62	
Lansdon, B. L.	Mch. 20, '62		Died at Travers, Tenn., November 20, '63.
Livingston, C. S.	April 5, '61	April 4, '62	2nd Sergeant.
Livingston, J. F.	April 5, '61	April 4, '62	1st Sergeant; re-enlisted and served to close of war.
Long, Joseph	Mch. 20, '62		
Lemmox, Frank M.	April 5, '61	April 4, '62	
Lundy, Andrew J.	Mch. 20, '62		Killed at Dallas, Ga., '64.
Lundy, R.		April 26, '65	Captured and imprisoned.
Lynch, James	April 5, '61	April 4, '62	
McCaskill, E. F.	Mch. 20, '62		Corporal.
McCaskill, E. V.	Mch. 20, '62		Killed, Missionary Ridge, November 25, '63; honorable mention at Chickamauga.
McDonald, E. M.	April 5, '61	April 4, '62	
McDavid, D. M.	Mch. 20, '62		Corporal.

Roll Company F—1st Florida Infantry.
(CONTINUED.)

NAMES.	MUSTERED IN.	MUSTERED OUT.	REMARKS.
McLellan, Duncan	Mch. 20, '62		
McMillan, A. M.	Mch. 20, '62		Sergeant.
Madox, William	Mch. 20, '62		
Martin, S. P.	April 5, '61		Killed, Perryville October 8, '62.
Mathis, John W.	April 5, '61	April 4, '62	
Mays, Richard	April 5, '61	April 4, '62	Re-enlisted and served to close of war.
Mims, Jesse	Mch. 20, '62		Sergeant.
Mobley, James A.	April 5, '61	April 4, '62	
Morris, Burett	Mch. 20, '62		
Morris, John	Mch. 20, '62		
Morrison, Robert	Mch. 20, '62		
Moseley, Malcomb J.	April 5, '61	April 4, '62	
Nelson, T. J.			Died, May 20, at Chattanooga.
Nichols, J. L.	Mch. 20, '62		Died, Bluff Springs, Fla., '62.
Norris, Wiley	Mch. 20, '62		
Odum, George L.	April 5, '61	April 4, '62	
Oneal, John W.	April 5, 61	April 4, '62	
Overstreet, George W.	April 5, '61	April 4, '62	
Patterson, D. R.	April 5, '61	April 4, '62	
Patterson, J. J. H.	April 5, '61	April 4, '62	
Patterson, John W.	April 5, '61	April 4, '62	
Peacock, A. E.	April 5, '61	April 4, '62	
Peacock, John	Mch. 20, '62		
Phillips, Robert A.		April 4, '62	Re-enlisted and served to close of war.
Pittman, Manley	April 5, '61	April 4, '62	
Poige, E. E.	April 5, '61	April 4, '62	
Polk, Napoleon	Mch. 20, '62		
Polk, Robert	Mch. 20, '62		
Polk, William	Mch. 20, '62		
Pope, B. C.	April 5, '61	April 4, '62	
Pope, Redmond	Mch. 20, '62		
Pogers, James T.	April 5, '61	April 4, '62	
Salles, A. N.	April 5, '61	April 4, '62	
Salles, John	April 5, '61	April 4, '62	
Sappington, Joseph H.	April 5, '61	April 4, '62	
Sauls, Wilson	April 5, '61	April 4, '62	
Seely, J. H.	Mch. 20, '62		Wounded September 20, '63.
Seely, J. O.	April , '61	April 26, '65	
Sherer, William	Mch. 20, '62		
Shepard, R. R.	Mch. 20, '62		Sergeant.
Skipper, Thomas	April 5, '61	April 4, '62	
Snellgrove, S. W.	Mch. 20, '62		Died, Knoxville, Tenn., November 25, '62.
Sparrow, P. S.	Mch. 20, '62		
Starling, Levi	April 5, '61	April 4, '62	
Sunday, A. J.	Mch. 20, '62		
Sunday, J. R.	Mch. 20, '62		
Sunday, Richard	Mch. 20, '62		
Sutton, James T.	April 5, '61	April 4, '62	
Sutton, Rufus	April 5, '61	April 4, '62	
Thomas, J. A.	April 5, '61	April 4, '62	
Tucker, Jordan	April 5, '61	April 4, '62	Re-enlisted, Smith's Co., 2nd Cavalry.
Tuten, Charles D.		April 26, '65	Wounded; captured at Nashville, '64; imprisoned at Camp Douglass, Ill.
Varn, Thomas J.		April 4, '62	
Walfrip, William H.	April 5, '61	April 4, '62	
Walston, H. C.	Mch. 20, '62		Corporal; died, Bluff Springs, Fla., July 18, '62.
Waring, M. Howell	April 5, '61	April 26, '65	1st Sergeant; re-enlisted and served to close of war.
Watts, Richard	April 5, '61	April 4, '62	
Webb, William S.	April 5, '61	April 4, '62	
Wheeler, Isaac	Mch. 20, '62		
Whitlock, Charles S.	April 5, '61	April 4, '62	
Whitner, Benjamin F.	April 5, '61	April 4, '62	Re-enlisted, Co. C, 8th Infantry; promoted Captain, and served to close of war.
Whittle, Emanuel	April 5, '61	April 4, '62	
Whitty, Edward	April 5, '61	April 4, '62	
Wiggins, J. L.	Mch. 4, '62		
Williams, A. B.	Mch. 4, '62		Killed at Perryville, Ky., October 8, '62.
Williams, John J.	April 5, '61	April 4, '62	
Williams, John R.	April 5, '61	April 4, '62	
Williams, R. G.	April 5, '61	April 4, '62	
Williams, Thomas W.	April 5, '61	April 4, '62	
Wilson, Joseph W.	Mch. 20, '62		1st Sergeant.
Worrell, R. T.	April 5, '61	April 4, '62	
Young, William	April 5, '61	April 4, '62	

Roll Company G (Young Guards)—1st Florida Infantry.

NAMES.	MUSTERED IN.	MUSTERED OUT	REMARKS.
OFFICERS.			
Captain—			
John H. Gee	April 5, '61	April 6, '62	

Roll Company G (Young Guards)—1st Florida Infantry.

(Continued.)

NAMES.	MUSTERED IN.	MUSTERED OUT.	REMARKS.
1st Lieutenants—			
William M. Davidson	April 5, '61	April 6, '62	Transferred to Staff Gen. Patten Anderson and promoted to Captain.
F. G. Howard			2nd Lieutenant; promoted 1st Lieutenant.
2nd Lieutenants—			
William W. Wilson	April 5, '61	April 6, '62	Re-enlisted in Co. B, 8th Regiment, as private.
J. L. West			Promoted 2nd Lieutenant in '62.
3rd Lieutenants—			
A. W. Smith	April 5, '61	April 4, '62	Re-enlisted, Co. B, 8th Regiment, as private.
William J. Gaines			Promoted Lieutenant.
ENLISTED MEN.			
Apple, J.			Deserted.
Atwell, John			
Austin, G. W.	April 5, '61	April 6, '62	
Baggett, Nicholas			Wounded at Chickamauga September 20, '63.
Baggett, Thomas			Died, Sept. 10, '62, at Chattanooga, of fever.
Barrow, J. J.			Corporal; Wounded at Chickamauga, September 20, '63; and deserted.
Black, Wesley	April 5, '61	April 6, '62	Prisoner of war.
Blackshear, Abram			Died in Conechu county, Ala., Nov. 25, '62, of disease.
Blow, H. S.			Prisoner of war.
Blow, John W.			
Booth, Jesse C.	April 5, '61	April 6, '62	Re-enlisted May, '62, in Co. K, 2nd Florida Cavalry and promoted 2nd Lieutenant.
Booth, R. C.	April 5, '61	April 6, '62	Promoted Surgeon.
Botts, M. F.			Deserted.
Botts, S. B.			Deserted.
Bower, John M.			
Bracewell, J. P.	April 5, '61	April 6, '62	Re-enlisted May, '62, Co. B, 8th Regiment.
Bray, Alfred			Wounded at Chickamauga, Sept. 20, '63; died Jan. 1, '64, of wounds at Newman, Ga.; honorable mention.
Bray, G.			
Brown, G.			Sergeant; left in charge of wounded at Perryville.
Brown, W. J.	April 5, '61	April 6, '62	
Bruce, Hector	April 5, '61	April 6, '62	Re-enlisted, Co. B, 8th Regiment; wounded, Gettysberg.
Burghard, John	April 5, '61	April 6, '62	
Butts, James			Died at Dalton April 9, '63, of pneumonia.
Ceausseaux, S. K.	April 5, '61	April 6, '62	Re-enlisted, Co. B, 8th Regiment.
Cobb, S. J.			
Cook, William	April 5, '61	April 6, '62	
Corbitt, C. C.	April 5, '61	April 6, '62	
Dearborn, Jackson	April 5, '61	April 6, '62	
Dickson, Jesse	April 5, '61	April 6, '62	
Dickson, J. L.	Apr l 5, '61	April 6, '62	
Dismukes, E. P.	April 5, '61	April 6, '62	Re-enlisted, Co. B, 8th Regiment; promoted 2nd Sergeant.
DuPont, C. H.	April 5, '61	April 6, '62	
DuPont, J. H.	April 5, '61	April 6, '62	
Elliott, Isaac J.			Died at Tullahoma February 25, '63, of pneumonia
Elliott, N.xon	Apr l 5, '61	April 6, '62	
Emmitt, J. A.			Disabled and detailed on Quartermaster Dept.
Emmitt, Robert A.			
Floyd, Charles J.			
Folk, Jordan			Died in service.
Freeman, J. W.			Captured at Perryville.
Flowers, J. C.			Deserted.
Foster, J. M.			Captured at Glasgow.
Garrett, John			
Gee, R. C.	April 5, '61	April 6, '62	
George, Moses A.			Deserted at Bruton July 31, '62.
Goodfellow, J. S.			Corporal; died in service.
Griffin, Jackson			
Gunn, C. C.	April 5, '61	April 6, '62	
Gunn, William J	April 5, '61	April 6, '62	
Harris, B. A.			Died January, '63, at Chattanooga, Tenn.
Harris, S. H.	April 5, '61	April 6, '62	
Hawkins, N.			Deserted.
Hinote, Elijah			Died, Sept, 15. '62, at Chattanooga of fever.
Holloman, John	April 5, '61	April 6, '62	
Howell, J. O.			Sergeant.
Johnson, A. J.			Deserted.
Kennedy, John A.			Corporal; died November 10, '62.
Keoppen, C. H.	April 5, '61	April 6, '62	
Killer			
Leonard, S. S.			
Love, Archibald B.	April 5, '61	April 6, '62	Re-enlisted, Co. B, 8th Florida Regiment.
Love, A. D.	April 5, '61	April 6, '62	1st Corporal; Re-enlisted. Co. B, 8th Regiment.
Love, Henry H.	April 5, '61	April 6, '62	Re-enlisted Co. B, 8th Regiment.
Love, J. J. R.	April 5, '61	April 6, '62	Re-enlisted Co. B, 8th Regiment; promoted Corp.
Love, T. R.	April 5, '61	April 6, '62	Re-enlisted Co. B, 8th Regiment; promoted 1st Lieutenant.
McCall, Chalmers	April 5, '61	April 6, '62	Re-enlisted Co. B, 8th Regiment.
McElroy, W. S.	April 5, '61	April 6, '62	
McIver, A. N.	April 5, '61	April 6, '62	

Roll Company G (Young Guards)—1st Florida Infantry.
(CONTINUED.)

NAMES.	MUSTERED IN.	MUSTERED OUT.	REMARKS.
McGinn, Thomas			
McPherson, Colin	April 5, '61	April 6, '62	Re-enlisted Co. B, 8th Regiment; promoted Sergt.
McRae, Philip	April 5, '61	April 6, '62	
Malone, John W	April 5, '61	April 6, '62	Re-enlisted Co. B, 8th Regiment; promoted Sergt.
Martin, A. J			Deserted.
Mauper, D. R			Died December 23, '63, in Conechu county, Ala.
Mitchell, W. A	April 5, '61	April 6, '62	2nd Sergeant.
Moore, J. F. C			
Moore, R. C	'62	May 1, '65	
Monroe, B. H	April 5, '61	Apr l 6, 62	
Muse, C. M	April 5, '61	April 6, '62	
Nathans, A. M	April 5, '61	April 6, '62	
Newton, B	April 5, '61	April 6, '62	
Owens, Edward	April 5, '61	April 6, '62	
Peavy, Allen			Died at Atlanta of pneumonia.
Pellam, W. J			Mortally wounded at Perryville October 8, '62.
Penton, John			Wounded at Chickamauga September 20, '63.
Pintham, John			Captured at Perryville October 8, '62.
Raibon, N			Died in service.
Randolph, R. H	Apr l 5, '61	April 6, '62	Re-enlisted, Co. B, 8th Florida Regiment.
Rivenbark, George			Died on Santa Rosa Island June 1, '64, of fever.
Rivenbark, Robert N			Died in service and buried in Lexington Cemetery
Roberts, J. O. A	April 5, '61	April 6, '62	Re-enlisted, Co. B, 8th Regiment.
Roddenberry, William A			Died in Knoxville, Jan. 1, '63, of pneumonia.
Rollo, Lawrence			Sergeant; captured and paroled at Glascow, Ky.
Russ, Jacob			Deserted at Bruton July 31, '62.
Rushing, A			Died in service.
Sera, C. P			
Shaw, D. A	April 5, '61	April 6, '62	Re-enlisted, Co. B, 8th Regiment.
Shaw, R. G	April 5, '61	April 6, '62	
Simmons, H			Corporal; deserted August 1, '62, at Milton, Fla
Smith, A			
Smith, Gabriel	April 5, '61	April 6, '62	
Smith, T. E	April 5, '61	April 6, '62	
Smith, T. Y	April 5, '61	April 6, '62	
Smith, William			
Sowell, C. C			
Sowell, C. L			
Stathem, William A			
Stego, R			Corporal; died in service.
Stewart, R. F			
Stockton, William T., Jr	April 5, '61	April 6, '62	
Subers, J. J	April 5, '61	April 6, '62	
Sylvester, James	April 5, '61	April 6, '62	Re-enlisted, Co. B, 8th Regiment.
Sweat, John W			Died in service.
Thomas, T. G	April 5, '61	April 6, '62	
Thompson, J. O			Sergeant; died in service.
Towers, Charles D	April 5, '61	April 6, '62	Corporal; promoted Sergeant; re-enlisted Co. E
Tuten, Artemus	April 5, '61	April 6, '62	2nd Cavalry, May, '62.
Wade, W. H	April 5, '61	April 6, '65	
Waters, Moses			
West, Benjamin			
West, J. C	April 5, '61	April 6, '65	
Westcott, L. R	April 5, '61	April 6, '65	Re-enlisted Co. B, 8th Regiment; promoted 1st
Whittle, Ambros W	April 5, '61	April 6, '65	Sergeant.
Zeigler, G. B	April 5, '61	April 6, '65	
Zeigler, N. H	April 5, '61	April 6, '65	Corporal.

Roll Company H (Gainesville Minute Men)—1st Florida Infantry.

NAMES.	MUSTERED IN.	MUSTERED OUT.	REMARKS.
OFFICERS.			
Captains—			
T. J. Myers	April 6, '61	April 6, '62	
C. Gonzalez			Promoted Captain.
H. H. Malone			Promoted Captain; resigned, March 21, '63.
John D. Leigh			Promoted Captain; wounded at Chickamauga September 20, '62.
1st Lieutenant—			
John D. Young	April 5, '61	April 4, '62	
2nd Lieutenants—			
Oliver P. Hull	April 5, '61	April 4, '62	Re-enlisted Co. C; promoted 1st Lieutenant, and killed at Shiloh.
J. Austin McCreight	April 5, '61	April 4, '62	
A. C. Tippin	May 13, '62		Wounded seven times in different places.
3rd Lieutenant—			
G. R. Mayo			
ENLISTED MEN.			
Allen, Franklin	April 5, '61	April 4, '62	Transferred to Co. K; died at Columbus, Ga,, '63.

Roll Company H (Gainesville Minute Men)—1st Florida Infantry.
(CONTINUED.)

NAMES.	MUSTERED IN.	MUSTERED OUT.	REMARKS.
Archellers G. M.			Died, Jan. 1, '62, of wounds at Murfreesborough
Baggett, G. M.			Died, September, '62, at Chattanooga.
Baggett, William			Died, September 20, '63.
Bass, Jackson	April 6, '61	April 4, '62	
Baskin, Robert	April 5, '61	April 4, '62	
Bishop, George W	May 8, '62		
Blake, Thomas H	May 8, '62	April 4, '62	
Bond, J. E. F.	Oct. '62		Wounded at New Hope Church, Ga., May 28, '64, captured and paroled at close of war.
Bray, Jarrett	April '62		Shot at Bentonville, N. C., March 19, '65.
Brock, Meredith E.	April 5, '61	April 4, '62	
Broome, Charles M	April 5, '61	April 4, '62	Re-enlisted and served to close of war.
Broome, George K	April 5, '61	April 4, '62	
Brewton, E. W			Deserted.
Burman, J. A			Deserted.
Burnett, John G	April 5, '61	April 4, '62	
Cain, Thomas Y	April 5, '61	April 4, '62	
Caruth, W. L	April 5, '61	April 4, '62	
Carmicheal, James A	April 5, '61	April 4, 62	
Casselberry, S.			
Cauthron, Lewis M	April 5, '61	April 4, '62	
Chamberlain, Garrett V	April 5, '61	April 4, '62	
Clarke, H. E.			
Clark, John E	April 5, '61	April 4 '62	
Clark, Lewis			Died in service.
Clowney, Robert C	April 5, '61	April 4, '62	2nd Corporal.
Coleman, William J			1st Sergeant.
Crowder, John G	April 5, '61	April 4, '62	
Culp, G. M. D	April 5, '61	April 4, '62	
Daniel, James E	April 5, '61	April 4, '62	
Daniel, William S	April 5, '61	April 4, '62	Corporal.
Denton, John D	April 5, '61	April 4, '62	
Denton, Robert J	April 5, '61	April 4, '62	
Dickison, John			Honorable mention at Chickamauga.
Diching, Philip	April 5, '61	April 4, '62	
Dixon, E. A.			Deserted.
Dollahite, W. H.			
Downing, A. F.			Deserted.
Downing, Bryan			Sergeant.
Downing, Deolyhite			
Downing, Elishua			
Downing, William			
Egan, James M	April 5, '61	April 4, '62	
Ellis, E. R.			Died at Ringgold, Ga., '62, of disease.
Ellis, P. G.			Died January, '63, of pneumonia.
Emmons, E.			Died in Hoganville, Ky., September 22, '62.
Faulk, J. A			Died in service.
Fewell, Samuel A	April 5, '61	April 4, '62	Re-enlisted, January 29, '62, Capt. Poole's Co.; served to close of war.
Finley, J. M.			
Fitzgerald, Robert	April 5, '61	April 4, '62	
Gates, Louis			Died at Chattanooga November, '62, of disease.
Gay, L. C.			
Godwin, E. C.			...
Godwin, Jonathan			
Godwin, L. J			Died at Ringgold, Ga., '62, of disease.
Godwin, Thomas			
Godwin, William			
Goff, William E	April 5, '61	April 4, '62	
Greeen, Charls H	April 5, '61	April 4, '62	
Haires, Shadrack W	April 5, '61	April 4, '62	
Hammock, Jesse			Died at Lookout Mountain, August 3, '62, of fever
Hammock, Willie			Killed at Perryville, Ky.
Hardee, James	April 5, '61	April 4, '62	
Harris, George W	April 5, '61	April 4, '62	Missing at battle of Perryville.
Hart, Joel F			Died November 26, '62.
Hathcox, John W	April 5, '61	April 4, '62	
Hicks, Abner M	April 5, '61	April 4, '62	
Highsmith, J. F. M	April 5, '61	April 4, '62	
Hilburn, Ben			Prisoner of war.
Holland, Ray			Died at Chattanooga February, '63, of pneumonia.
Howard, C. A.			Corporal; died in service.
Hull, Henry R	April 5, '61	April 4, '62	
Jackson, Robert	April 5, '61	April 4, '62	
James, Lloyd	April 5, '61	April 4, '62	
Jern gan, Jesse			Died at Chattanooga Sept. 30, '62, of disease.
Jernigan, M.			
Jernigan, S. H.			Corporal; died at Chattanooga September 25, '62, of disease.
Johnston, James J	April 5, '61	April 4, '61	
Johnston, M.			Prisoner of war.
Johnson, Noel			
Jones, Jerome N	April 5, '61	April 4, '62	
Jones, Seaborn			Deserted.
Jones, W ll am H			
Kent, W. A.			Prisoner of war.
King, J. W. T.			Corporal; prisoner of war.

Roll Company H (Gainesville Minute Men)—1st Florida Infantry.

(CONTINUED.)

NAMES.	MUSTERED IN.	MUSTERED OUT.	REMARKS.
King, Thomas H.	April 5, '61	April 4, '62	
Kittrell, Isham W.	April 5, '61	April 4, '62	
Lamb, J. D.	Apr l 5, '61	Apr l 4, '62	
Lamb, Marshall	April 5, '62	April 4, '62	
Lane, Lev n A.	April 5, '61	April 4, '62	
Lang, David	April 5, '61	April 4, '62	2nd Sergeant; re-enlisted as Capt., Co. C, 8th Regiment; promoted to Major; Lieutenant-Colonel; Colonel; commanded Brigade '63-4-5.
Laritern, E. J.	Apr l 5, '61	Apr l 4, '62	
Lassiter, Craven	April 5, '61	April 4, '62	Re-enlisted, Co. C, 8th Infantry.
Lassiter, Craven	May '62		Corporal; deserted.
Leigh, James	April 5, '61	April 4, '62	
Lewis, David H.	April 5, 61	April 4, '62	
Lewis, Thomas B.	Apr l 5, '61	Apr l 4, '62	
Lew s, W lbar G.			
Lovelace, W. B.			Prisoner of war.
Lynch, J. Q. A.			
McCaulker, J. A.	April 5, '61	April 4, '62	
McCall, Willie L.	April 5, '61	April 4, '62	Re-enlisted, April, '62, Co.K; wounded at Perryville, October 8, '62; promoted April, '62, to 2nd Lieutenant; 1st Lieutenant '62, and promoted Captain Co. K.
McDonnell, Augustus O.	April 5, '61	April 4, '62	
MacDonnell, William M.	April 5, '61	April 4, '62	
McFarland, D. B.			
Mantle, John	April 5, '61	April 4, '62	
Massey, Thomas D.			
Mayo, G. R.			
Mayo, M. B.			Sergeant.
Mayo, Warren			Killed at Chattanooga September 20, '63
Mays, J. R.			
Miller, John	April 5, '61	April 4, '62	Corporal.
Morgan, James P.			Died in service.
Morris, J. A.	April 5, '61	April 4, '62	
Nappier, H. A.	April 5, '61	April 4, '62	Promoted Sergeant; re-enlisted Co. K, 1st Infantry
Nipper, Andrew F.			
Nobles, James	April 5. '61	April 4, '62	
Oats, Young P.	April 5, '61	April 4, '62	
Owens, James	April 5, '61	April 4, '62	
Pardue, James L.	April 5, '61	April 4, '62	
Parker, A. J.			Died in service.
Parker, S. R.			
Peavy, M. V.	April 5, '61	April 4, '62	
Pooser, F. D.			Killed at Perryville, Ky., October 8, '63.
Powell, James			
Purvis, Thomas	April 5, '61	April 4, '62	
Richardson, John G.	April 5, '61	April 4, '62	
Richwood, G. C.			Deserted August 11, at Montgomery, Ala.
Roach, Nicholas	April 5, '61	April 4, '62	
Rosseau, R. R.			Died in service.
Russell, Isaac	April 5, '61	April 4, '62	
Smith, John C.			Served to the close of the war.
Smith, L. B.			
Smith, Robert			Prisoner of war.
Snell, C. H.	April 5, '61	April 4, '62	Prisoner of war.
Sparkman, John L.			
Stanton, J. A.	April 5, '61	April 4, '62	
Stewart, DeWitt L.	Apr l 5, '61	April 4, '62	
Swanson, F. M.	April 5, '61	April 4, '62	
Tahlon, Henry	April 5, '61	April 4, '62	
Tedder, B. A.			Killed at Perryville, Ky., October 8, '63.
Thomas, John			Died at Tallahassee, January '63, of pneumonia.
Thompson, William			
T ppin, D. J.			
Tippin, G. W.			Corporal; died at Bardstown, Tenn., September 26, '62, of fever.
Tippin, J. E.			
Tippin, R. H. M.	April 5, '61	April 4, '62	
Todd, J. J.	April 5, '61	April 4, '62	
Tooten, Robert	April 5, '61	April 4, '62	
Turner, Thomas O.		April 4, '62	3rd Sergeant; promoted 1st Sergeant; re-enlisted in Williams' Co.
Vaughn, John J.			Killed at Shiloh, April 6, '62.
Vincent, Willis H.	Apr l 5, '61		Killed at Perryville October 8, '63.
Walker, J. A.	April 5, '61	April 4, '62	
Weaver, Andrew J.			Died at Chattanooga, September, '62, of fever.
Weaver, L. C.	April 5, '61	April 4, 62	
Weeks, S. S.			Died, Conechu, January, '63, of smallpox.
White, J. D.			
White, W. H.			
Wilson, Henry	April 5, '61	April 4, '62	
Wilson, Joel	April 5, '61	April 4, '62	
Woodrae, James			Promoted Lieutenant Co. D, 1st Florida Infantry.
Wright, H. T.	April 5, '61	April 4, '62	
Yarborough, Millet S.			

Roll Company I—1st Florida Infantry.

NAMES.	MUSTERED IN.	MUSTERED OUT.	REMARKS.
OFFICERS.			
Captains—			
J. Patton Anderson	April 5, '61		Promoted Col.; Brig.-Gen.; Maj.-Gen.
Thompson B. Lamar	April 5, '61		Promoted Colonel; killed, Petersburg, Va., '64.
W. Capers Bird	April 5, '61	April 4, '62	1st Lieutenant; promoted Captain of Co. C, Fla. and C. G. R. Battalion on reorganization; wounded, Shiloh, April 6, '62.
D. B. Coleman	Mch. 25, '62		Promoted Captain; died, Bluff Springs Jan. 15, '62
Andrew Denham			Promoted Captain, Co. D, Fla. and C. G. R. Bat.
Isaiah Cobb			Promoted Captain.
1st Lieutenants—			
Richard Turnbull	April 5, '61	April 4, '62	2nd Lieutenant; promoted 1st Lieutenant; resigned September, '61, on account of ill health.
C. Satter			Promoted 1st Lieutenant; resigned March 25, '62.
2nd Lieutenants—			
William Scott	April 5, '61	April 4, '62	
W. L. Dennis	April 5, '61	April 4, '62	3rd Sergeant; promoted 2nd Lieutenant
Thomas Morgan			
3rd Lieutenants—			
W. W. Blackburn	April 5, '61	April 4, '62	Re-enlisted; promoted Sergeant; 3rd Lieutenant May 27, '62.
Charles H. Ellis			Promoted 3rd Lieutenant Dec., '62; 1st Lieut.,'63
W. F. Brown			Killed, Perryville, October 8, '62.
ENLISTED MEN.			
Allen, Moses			Died at Catusus Spr ngs, '63.
Baggett, E. E			Honorable mention at Chickamauga.
Barrow, John G			Died, Perryville, October 17 '62, from wounds.
Bassemore, William	April 5, '61	April 4, '62	
Baxter, John J			
Bellamy, William D	May '61	April 4, '62	Re-enlisted, '62; wounded at Olustee, Feb. 10, '64.
Bender, John	April 5, '61	April 4, '62	
Bonington, Wash			Died, Chattanooga, March 20, '63, of wounds.
Braddy, Charles B			
Brickle, Morgan F			Died in service May 20, '62.
Brown, V. S			Corporal.
Brown, D. A	April 5, '61	April 4, '62	
Buelow, D. B			Died of wounds, Oct. 13, '62, at Chattanooga.
Carter, J. D	April 5, '61	April 4, '62	
Cannon, H. C	April 5. '61	April 4, '62	
Carr, W. M			Died May 3, '62, at Montgomery.
Clark, Abner			Died in service, January 2, '62.
Clayton, A. B	April 5, '61	April 4, '62	Re-enlisted, Gamble's artillery; transferred to Co.
Clayton, C. S	April 5, '61	April 4, '62	E, Dyke's Battery.
Clem, T. Vann	Apr 1	April 4, '62	Corporal.
Coaker, Silas	April 5, '61	April 4, '62	
Cooper, J. B	April 5, '61	April 4, '62	
Cooper, W. H	April 5, '61	April 4, '62	
Copeland, J. E	April 5 '61	April 4, '62	
Coburn, J. L			Died at Chicago, Ill., Feb. 13, '63, of wounds.
Cuthbert, Thomas S	April 5, '61	April 4, '62	
Daggin, Wilson	April 5 '61	April 4 62	
Davis, G. W		June 12, '65	From prison at Camp Chase.
DeLaughter, J	April 5, '61	June 12, '65	
Devine, John T	April 5, '61	April 26, '65	
Diamond, James			Died at Tullahoma April 10, 63.
Ellenwood, A. A	April 5, '61	April 4, '62	
Ellenwood, C	April 5, '61		Corporal.
Ellis, David			Died at Chattanooga April 25, '63.
Faulk, William			Died at Knoxville February 4, '63.
Fennell, Alexander	April 5, '61	April 4, '62	
Flowers, Jesse	April 5, '61	April 4, '62	
Fuller, J. P			Died at Chattanooga October 20, '62.
Gill, John J	April 5, '61	April 4, '62	
Gillett, Thomas M	April 5, '61	April 4, '62	
Graham, Daniel	April 5, '61	April 4, '62	
Graham, T. J	April 5, '61	April 4, '62	
Hall, J. G			Died at Jackson, Miss., July 21, '62.
Hall, W. H			Died at Chattanooga, October 20, '63.
Hale, D. Pinkney			Died in service May 20, '62.
Hammock, George W			Died at Chattanooga August 29, '62.
Hart, John			
Hill, J. G	April 5, '61	April 4, '62	
Holder, D. P			Died August 8, '62, at Chattanooga.
Holly, James	April 5, '61	April 4, '62	
Horten, B	April 5, '61	April 4, '62	
Houck, James	April 5, '61	April 4, '62	
Jacobs, William	April 5, '61	April 4, '62	
Jenkins, Thomas	April 5, '61	April 4, '62	
Jernigan, A. W			Sergeant; killed September 20, '62.
Jernigan, George			Died at Chattanooga October 20, '62.
Jones, A. J			Sergeant.
Kittrell, S	April 5, '61	April 4, '62	
Kyle, C. H	April 5, '61	April 4, '62	

Roll Company I—1st Florida Infantry.

(CONTINUED.)

NAMES.	MUSTERED IN.	MUSTERED OUT.	REMARKS.
Kyle, J. M.		May 13, '62	For disability; wounded three times.
Levines, R.			Sergeant; died at Ringgold, Ga., November 21, '62
Lord, William R.	April 5, 61	April 4, '62	
Lynn, Charles.	April 5, '61	April 4, '62	
McDuffie, D.	April 5, '61	April 4, '62	
McClelland, C. E.	April 5, '61	April 4, '62	
McRae, Dan.			Sergeant; wounded at Chickamauga Sept. 20, '63.
Martin, J. A.	April 5, '61	April 4, '62	
Martin, J. T.			Died, February 21, '62.
Martin, J. Y.			Died at Ringgold, Ga., May 15, '63.
Mason, B. F.			Corporal; wounded at Chickamauga Sept. 20, '63.
May, A. N.	April 5, '61	April 4, '62	
Mitchell, W. G.			Died at Pollard, Ala., April 5, '63.
Mixon, B. L.			Corporal; promoted 2nd Sergeant.
Moore, W. J.	April 5, '61	April 4, '62	
Morr s, John.	Apr l 5, '61	April 4, '62	
Neely, James.	April 5, '61	April 4, '62	
Neely, Sam.	Apr l 5, '61	April 4, '62	
Patterson, B. T.			Died at Laurel Hill Springs February 10, '62.
Patterson, S. F.			Died in Tennessee January 29, '63.
Pickeran, Evans.			Died May 20, '62, in service.
Porter, B. J.	April 5, '61	April 4, '62	
Porter, Columbus.	April 5, '61	April 4, '62	
Pringle, F. D.			
Pringle, Thomas D.			Died at Bluff Springs May 1, '62.
Prosser, Samuel.	April 5, '61	April 4, '62	
Rogers, George F.	Apr l 5, '61	April 4, '62	
Russell, William B.	April 5, '61	April 4, '62	
Sharp, Robert.	April 5, '61	April 4 '62	
Sheppard, M. T.	April 5, '61	April 4, '62	
Sheppard, R. R.		April 26, '65	
Shilling, John.	April 5, '61	April 4, '62	
Simmons, W. A. W.	April 5, '61	April 4, '62	Re-enlisted and served to close of war.
Smith, Jacob C.	April 5, '61	April 4, '62	Re-enlisted; died May 15, '62.
Soueter, George.			
Staley, J. B.	April 5, '61	April 4, '62	
Standley, H.	April 5, '61	April 4, '62	
Stephens, Ben H.		April 26, '65	
Stewart, John.	April 5, '61	April 4, '62	
Surls, Robert.	April 5, '61	April 4, '62	
Summerlin, J. C.	April 5, '61	April 4, '62	
Thanas, J. L.			Killed at Missionary Ridge November 25, '63.
Thompson, H.	April 5, '61	April 4, '62	
Tucker, W. W.	April 5, '61	April 4, '62	2nd Sergeant; 1st Lieutenant January 23, '62; 1st Florida Battalion.
Turnbull, Theo.	April 5, '61	April 4, '62	
Turner, J. D.	April 5, '61	April 4, '62	4th Sergeant; promoted 1st Lieutenant and Captain of Co. C, 1st Florida Regiment.
Turner, J. M.	Apr l 5, '61	April 4, '62	1st Corporal; promoted 1st Sergeant.
Turner, N. E.	Ap'il 5, '61	April 4, '62	Promoted Corporal; 4th Sergeant.
Walker, Jesse.	April 5, '61	Apri, 4, '62	Killed at Murfreesborough March 25, '6 .
Walker, Joel E.	April 5, '61	April 4, '62	
Walker, L. B.			
Walker, M. W.	April 5, '61	April 4, '62	
Walker, W. J.	April 5, '61	April 4, '62	
Warren, H. F.	April 5, '61	April 4, '62	
Washington, J. M.	April 5, '61	April 4, '62	
White, George.	April 5, '61	April 4. '62	
Whittey, E.		April 29, '62	Corporal; discharged for disability.
Whitehurst, Hillary W.	Mch. 1, '61	April 26, '65	
Whitehurst, Perry.			
Williams, D.	April 5, '61	April 4, '62	
Williams, John K.	April 5, '61	April 4, '62	
Wynn, W. W.	April 5, '61	April 4, '62	Re-enlisted and served to close of war.

Roll Company K (Pensacola Guards)—1st Florida Infantry.

NAMES.	MUSTERED IN.	MUSTERED OUT.	REMARKS.
OFFICERS.			
Captains—			
A. H. Bright.	June 11, '61		Re-enlisted April 1, '62'
Augustus O. MacDonell.			Elected 2nd Lt. Co. K, 1862; promoted 1st Lt.; promoted Captain, 1863; severely wounded at Perryville.
Daniel Williams.			3rd Lieutenant; promoted Captain; resigned January 2, '64.
1st Lieutenant—			
William McR. Jordan.	June 11, '61	April 4, '62	
2nd Lieutenants—			
Robert Abercrombie.	April 5, '61	April 4, '62	
J. J. Vaughen.			

Roll Company K (Pensacola Guards)—1st Florida Infantry.
(Continued.)

NAMES.	MUSTERED IN.	MUSTERED OUT.	REMARKS.
3rd Lieutenant—			
Benj. F. Overman	April 5, '61		Private; promoted 3rd Lieutenant,
ENLISTED MEN.			
Allen, Loning G.			
Anderson, John			Killed at Perryville October 8, '62.
Andrew, William	June 11, '61	April 4, '62	
Amos, E. W.	June 11, '61	April 4, '62	
Anthony, H.			Died May 20 '62.
Armstrong, A.			Died in hospital May, '62.
Austin, C. B.			Sergeant.
Bachelor J. J.	June 11, '61	April 4, '62	Re-enlisted from Co. D; killed at Shiloh April 6,
Bell, William T	June 11, '61	April 4, '62	'62.
Bhutrun, William	June 11, '61	April 4, '62	
Binnicker, James L.	April 2, '62	April 26, '65	Wounded at Missionary Ridge November 15, '63.
Blaylock, Albert B.	June 11, '61	April 4, '62	
Brent, Daniel G.	June 11, '61	April 4, 62	Corporal; promoted Sergeant; transferred to Ordnance Office at Pollard, Ala.
Bonifay, Eugene C.	June 11, '61	April 4, '62	Re-enlisted and served to close of war.
Bonifay, Francis C.	June 11, '61	April 4, '62	Re-enlisted and served to close of war.
Bonifay, Henry	June 11, '61	April 4, '62	Re-enlisted; killed at Shiloh April 6, '62.
Bridges, James		April 4, '62	Re-enlisted; died of pneumonia at Tullahoma in hospital.
Brown, H. S.			Died May 15, '62, of pneumonia at Holly Springs, Miss.
Buckner, William			Died at Shiloh April 7, '62.
Caro, James W.	June 11, '61	April 4, '62	
Chamberlain, G. V.			Corporal; promoted Sergeant; killed at Murfrees
Christian, August.	June 11, '61	April 4, '62	borough January 21, '62.
Clark, John			Corporal.
Collier, William Holme			Promoted 1st Lieutenant Fla. and C. G. R. Battalion; killed at Murfreesborough.
Commyns, Joseph	June 11, '61	April 4, '62	
Commyns, Thomas	June 11, '61	April 4, '62	
Coson, J.			
Cradock, J. Hindon	June 11, '61	June 17, '62	
Crawford, James	June 11, '61	April 4, '62	
Crosby, Richard.	June 11, '61	April 4, '62	
Dallas, T. B	June 11, '61	April 4, '62	Corporal.
Davis, George W	June 11, '61	April 4, '62	
Davis, Oliver	June 11, '61	April 4, '62	Died at Corinth, May ,'62, of disease.
Defu, Andrew J.	June 11, '61	April 4, '62	
Duffu, J.			Corporal.
Dukes, David H.	June 11, '61	April 4, 62	
Duncan, W. D.			Died at Tullahoma April 6, '62.
Gatlin, S.			Died at Tullahoma, Tenn., in hospital.
Gonzales, Jasper G.	June 11, '61	April 4, '62	
Gonzales, Manuel F.	June 11, '61	April 4, '62	
Gunter, Decater.	June 11, '61	April 4, '62	Re-enlisted.
Goodwyn, Iverson	June 11, '61	April 4, '62	
Hale, J. L.	June 11, '61	April 4, '62	
Hall, Albert			Killed at Shiloh April 6, '62.
Hall.			Died at Pensacola August, '63.
Hawks, W.			Died June 22, '62, in hospital.
Hart, James.			Head shot off April 6, '62, at Shiloh.
Hardee, Robert J.	June 11, '61	April 4, '62	
Hatch, Henry	June 11, '61	April 4, '62	
Hernandez, M.			
Hernandez, Randolph.	June 11, '61	April 4, '62	Sergeant.
Hernandez, Robert.			Sergeant; died at Cassels, Ga., December, '61.
Hinton, Josh			Died at Shiloh April 6, '62.
Horten, Neil H.	June 11, '61	April 4, '62	
Hunter, Edward	June 11, '61	April 4, '62	
Hyer, Albert	June 11, '61	April 4, '62	Severely wounded at Shiloh; promoted Lieutenant and transferred to staff of General Stanton.
Hyer, Louis.	June 11, '61	April 4, '62	
Jackson, Bolling H.	June 11, '61	April 4, '62	
Johnson, Daniel.			Died at Corinth.
Jordan, George.	June 11, '61	April 4, '62	
Kelly, Barnard.	June 11, '61	April 4, '62	
Kelly, Pat.	June 11, '61	April 26, '65	
Kilpatrick, William			Died at Madison, Fla., Sept., '63, of pneumonia.
King, W. J.			Died at Harrodsberg December 11, '62, from wounds received at Perryville.
Kirkland, William B.	June 11, '61	April 4, '62	Re-enlisted; died at Chattanooga March, '63.
Kirwin, John W	June 11, '61	April 4, '62	Killed at Murfreesborough January 28, '62.
Laird, Louis.			
Laird, W.			
Lent, Charles.			Died at Laurel Hill, Miss., of disease.
Leminox, F. M.			
Lindsey, H.			Killed at Shiloh April 6, '62.
McCardle, Isaac.			Killed at Shiloh April 6,'62; mentioned for gallantry.
McCarty, Charles.			Killed at Missionary Ridge Novemper 25, '62.
McCoy, Robert.			
McDonald, William M.			Sergeant.
Mier, William	June 11, '61	April 4, '62	
Mitchell, George N. J.	June 11, '61	April 4, '62	
Mobley, J. A.			Died in hospital with disease June 21, '62.

Roll Company K (Pensacola Guards)—1st Florida Infantry.

(CONTINUED.)

NAMES.	MUSTERED IN	MUSTERED OUT.	REMARKS.
Morris, Warren	June 11, '61	April 4, '62	
Nall, J. A.	June 11, '61	April 4, '62	Re-enlisted in 2nd Reg. and served to close of war; woundedat Seven Pines May 31, '62.
Neely, James			
Newton, Charles A.	June 11, '61	April 4, '62	
Nicholson, J. W.			Killed at Franklin June 4, '63.
Nipper, A. F.			Corporal.; died October 20, '63.
Norris, John M.			Died, June 5, '62, in hospital.
Norris, William J.	June 11, '61	April 4, '62	
O'Neil, Peter	June 11, '61	April 4, '62	
Reese, George	June 11, '61	April 4, '62	Re-enlisted, July, in Co. A, 44th Alabama Infantry at Selma under Colonel Kent, and was elected Lieutenant.
Rodgers, J. D.			Corporal; promoted Sergeant.
Rodgers, William L.	June 11, '61	April 4, '62	
Roberts, James B.	June 11, '61	April 4, '62	
Roberts, J. D.		April 26, '65	
Rungan, William Bell	June 11, '61	April 4, '62	Promoted to 3rd Lieutenant, Co. A, Fla. and C G. R. Battalion.
Sanchus, G.			Corporal.
Seely, John W.	June 11, '61	April 4, '62	
Serra, Charles P.	June 11, '61	April 4, 62	
Smith, John A.	June 11, '61	April 4, '62	
Smith, C. P.			Corporal; promoted Sergeant..
Sparrow, Patrick S.	June 11, '61	April 4, '62	
Stevens, Burrell	June 11, '61	April 4, '62	
Stewart, Claurence H.	June 11, '61		Died in Macon, Ga., January 11, '64.
Stockwell, Samuel	June 11, '61	April 4, '62	Died August, '62, from wounds at Enterprise, Miss.
Thompson, B. W.	June 11, '61	April 4, '62	
Touart, Frank		April 26, '65	Wounded at Perryville, Ky., Oct. 8, '62; Corporal.
Touart, Francis	June 11, '61	April 4, '62	Re-enlisted and served to close of war; Corporal.
Turner, Thomas	June 11, '61	May '62	
Umphress, J. B.	June 11, '61	April 26, '65	
Walker, James	June 11, '61	April 4, '62	
Ward, Micheal	June 11, '61	April 4, '62	
Ware, James H.	June 11, '61	April 4, '62	Promoted Corporal.
Watson, William F.	June 11, '61	April 4, '62	
White, William O.	June 11, '61	April 4, '62	
Welch, Isaac		April 26, '65	
Williams, R. G.			Sergeant; died May 17, '62.
Woodburn, John A.		April 26, '65	Wounded at Jonesboro, Ga., August 31, '63; promoted Lieutenant in B and K consolidated.
Woolf, Thomas D.	June 11, '61	April 4, '62	1st Sergeant.
Worrel, R. P.		June 11, '62	
Wynn, Charles E.	June 11, '61	April 4, '62	
Ynisstra, Gregory	June 11, '61	April 4, '62	2nd Sergeant; promoted to Captain; Inspector General on Bragg's Staff.

SECOND FLORIDA INFANTRY.

The 2nd Florida Regiment, as it was first organized, was composed of ten companies as follows: Alachua Guards, Alachua county (Co. B), Capt. Lew Williams; Columbia Rifles, Columbia county (Co. C), Capt. Walter R. Moore; Leon Rifles, Leon county (Co. D), Capt. T. W. Brevard, Jr.; Hammock Guards, Marion county (Co. E), Capt. John D. Hopkins; Gulf State Guards, Jackson county (Co. F), Capt. James F. McClellan; St. Johns Greys, St. Johns county (Co. G), Capt. J. J. Daniels; St. Augustine Rifles, Putnam county (Co. H), Capt. John W. Starke; Hamilton Blues, Hamilton county (Co. I), Capt. Henry J. Stewart; Davis Guards, Nassau county (Co. K), Capt. George W. Call; Madison Rangers, Madison county (Co. L), Capt. W. P. Pillans. In the early days of July these ten companies were ordered to rendezvous near the Brick Church, just west of Jacksonville, now known as LaVilla, and on July 13 the Regiment was mustered into the Confederate service by Maj. W. T. Stockton. The Regiment was organized by the election of George T. Ward, of Leon county, Colonel; S. St. George Rogers, of Marion county,

Lieutenant-Colonel; and Louis G. Pyles, of Alachua county, Major. The following Staff appointments were then made: Dr. Thomas Palmer, Surgeon; Dr. Thomas W. Hendry, Assistant Surgeon; Capt. Edward M. L'Engle, Assistant Quartermaster; Capt. W. A. Daniel, Assistant Commissary; Lieut. R. B. Thomas, Adjutant; Edward Houston, Sergeant Major; T. W. Givens, Quartermaster Sergeant. On Monday, July 15th, the Regiment left by rail for Virginia, arriving in Richmond Sunday afternoon, July 21st. The Regiment was in Camp of Instruction, in the neighborhood of Richmond, nearly two months. On September 17, 1861, the Regiment left Richmond for Yorktown, where they were joined by the Rifle Rangers of Escambia county (Co. A), Capt. E. A. Perry. During the fall of 1861 and the winter following the Regiment was encamped near Yorktown, forming a part of Maj.-Gen. J. B. Magruder's Command. Early in October Lieutenant Thomas was ordered to report to Richmond and Lieut. Seaton Fleming was assigned to duty as Adjutant. It was at the siege of Yorktown that the Regiment received its "baptism of fire." On May 5th, at Williamsburg, the Regiment again distinguished itself by its gallant resistance to McClellan's advance. In this battle Col. George T. Ward was killed, and Companies E, D and L each lost one man, making four killed; and every company in the Regiment had one or more wounded, making thirty wounded. Among the seriously wounded was Lieut. C. S. Fleming. The 2nd Florida, being twelve months' men, were by Act of Congress required to remain in the service two years longer; this act was known as the Conscript Laws and gave them a right to reorganize by a re-election of officers, which should have taken place on May 3rd; but owing to the battle of Williamsburg reorganization did not take place until the following week or May 10th. At the reorganization Capt. E. A. Perry was elected Colonel; Maj. L. G. Pyles, Lieutenant-Colonel; and Capt. George W. Call, Major. All the companies in the Regiment changed their captains except B. and C. On May 31st the Regiment was engaged in the battle of Seven Pines, where it lost 6 officers, 4 non-commissioned and 24 privates killed. Wounded, 17 officers, 21 non-commissioned officers and 106 privates; total casualties, 178. In the battle of Seven Pines Maj. George W. Call was killed, and Lieut.-Col. L. G. Pyles was wounded and disabled. Of the eleven captains who went into the battle, four, J. H. Pooser, C. S. Flagg, A. C. Butler and T. A. Perry were killed, and six, W. D. Ballantin (Co. A), Lew Williams (Co. B), W. R. Moore (Co. C), M. G. C. Musgrove (Co. D), W. E. Caslin (Co. E) and M. J. Duncan (Co. I) were wounded. Shortly after the battle of Seven Pines Co. M. was assigned to this Regiment, making twelve companies in all. After the battle of Seven Pines followed in quick succession the battles of Cold Harbor, Gaines' Mill, Savage Station, Frazier's Farm and Malvern Hill. In the battles of Ellison's Mill and Frazier's Farm, June 26 and 27, the Regiment lost 8 killed and 52 wounded; among the killed was G. W. Parkhill, Captain of Co. M. At the battle of Frazier's Farm, June 30, the Regiment lost: Killed, 2 officers, 1 non-commissioned officer and 11 privates; wounded, 3 officers, 2 non-commissioned officers and 62 privates. Among the wounded was Col. E. A. Perry. Following the battle of Frazier's Farm came the Maryland campaign. On December 13 the battle of Fredericksburg was fought.   The Regiment lost: killed, 1 non-commissioned officer and 3 privates; wounded, 4 officers, 5 non-commissioned officers and 25 privates (casualties in Co. K not reported).   A partial report of the casualties at Chancellorsville show 3 officers and 17 privates wounded, and 3 privates killed. In the battle of Gettysburg: Killed, 6 officers, 4 non-commissioned officers and 5 privates; wounded, 6 officers, 6 non-commissioned officers and 54 privates; total casualties, 81.   There is no report accessible of the casualties during the year 1864 and 1865, and it was during these years that some of the most desperate and bloody battles were fought; and in all of them the 2nd Florida did its full measure of duty.   It was but a skeleton of a splendid regiment that surrendered at Appomatox Court House.   But 7 officers and 59 men.

Roll Field and Staff—2nd Florida Infantry.

NAMES.	MUSTERED IN.	MUSTERED OUT.	REMARKS.
Colonels—			
George T. Ward	July 13, '61		Killed at Williamsburg May 5, '62.
E. A. Perry	July 13, '61	May 9, '65	Captain Co. A; promoted Colonel May 10, '62; Brigadier-General August, '62; wounded and disabled at the Wilderness May, '64.
L. G. Pyles	July 13, '61		Wounded, Seven Pines, May 31, '62, and disabled, promoted Colonel, but never served as such on account of disability.
Walter R. Moore	July 13, '61	April 9, '65	Captain Co. C; promoted Major August, '62; Lieutenant-Colonel '63; Colonel '64.
Lieutenant-Colonels—			
S. St. George Rogers	July 13, '61	May 10, '62	Retired on reorganization, May 10, '62.
W. D. Ballantine	July 13, '61	July '65	1st Lieutenant Co. A; promoted Captain May 10, '62; Major May '63; Lieutenant-Colonel August '64; captured, Gettysburg July 3, '63.
Majors—			
George W. Call	July 13, '61		Captain Co. K; promoted Major May 10, '62; killed at Seven Pines May 31, '62.
Alexander Moseley	July 13, '61	April 9, '65	Captain; promoted Major, '64.
Surgeons—			
T. M. Palmer	July 13, '61	April 9, '65	Charge of Florida hospital June 1, '62 to close of
M. S. Thomas		April 9, '65	war.
J. C. L'Engle	July 13, '61	April 9, '65	Assistant Surgeon; promoted Surgeon, '63.
D. E. Hawes		April 9, '65	
Assistant Surgeons—			
T. G. Henry	July 13, '61	April 9, '65	Assistant Surgeon September 18, '62.
B. F. Walker		April 9, '65	
Drill Master(Captain)			
J. L. Cross	July 13, '61		Transferred to provisional army C. S.
Adjutants—			
R. B. Thomas	July 13, '61	April 9, '65	1st Lieutenant; promoted Captain; transferred to regular army '62; promoted Major; Colonel and A. A. Adjutant-General '64.
C. S. Fleming	July 13, '61		1st Lieutenant; promoted Captain Co. G Sept. 2, '62; wounded Williamsburg May 5, '62; killed, Gaines' Farm June 3, '64.
Waddy Butler	July 13, '61		Killed, Chancellorsville May 6, '63.
R. Jenckes Reed	July 13, '61		Sergeant, '61; promoted Adjutant May '63; killed at the Wilderness May 5, '63.
Quartermaster—			
E. M. L'Engle	July 13, '61	April 9, '65	Captain and A. Q. W.
Commissary—			
W. A. Daniel	July 13, '61	April 9, '65	Captain and A. C.....
Chaplains—			
J. W. Kimberlake	July 13, '61		Resigned.
Donald Frazer	July 13, '61	April 9, '65	
Sergeant-Majors—			
Edward Houstoun	July 13, '61	April 15. '65	Transferred to Florida conscript service.
Ephriam Harrison	July 13, '61	April 15, '65	
Quartermaster-Sergeants—			
Thomas W. Givens	July 13, '61	Feb. 24, '65	Promoted 2nd Lieutenant, Co. K, 8th Florida, September, 62; Captain Co. K, May, '63; wounded at Gettysburg July 2, '63.
Commissary-Sergeant—			
Hospital Steward—			
John C. Smythe	July 13, '61	Feb. 24, '65	

Roll Company A (Pensacola Rifle Rangers)—2nd Florida Infantry.

NAMES.	MUSTERED IN.	MUSTERED OUT.	REMARKS.
OFFICERS.			
Captains—			
Edward A. Perry	May 25, '61	April 9, '65	Promoted Colonel May 10, '62; Brigadier-General August, '62; wounded at Frazier's Farm June 30, '62; Wilderness May 5, '64 and disabled.
W. D. Ballantine	May 25, '61	April 9, '65	Promoted Captain May 10, '62; Major; Lieutenant-Colonel '64; wounded, Seven Pines May 31, '62 twice; Sharpsburg September 17, '62 twice; Chancellorsville May '63; also at Gettysburg July 3, '63, and captured.
1st Lieutenants—			
E. C. Humphrey	May 25, '61		2nd Lieutenant; promoted 1st Lieutenant; lost arm at Chancellorsville May 3, '63, and killed at Gaines' Farm June 27, '63 while commanding company.
William F. Lee	May 25, '61	April 9, '65	2nd Lieutenant; promoted 1st Lieutenant, and as such commanded company at Chancellorsville May 3, '63, in which he lost his right arm; then he was promoted Captain Engineers and assigned to Staff.
L. T. Landrum	May 25, '61		1st Sergeant; promoted 1st Lieutenant June, '63; Wounded at Williamsburg May 5, '62, and killed at Culpepper, Va., August, '63.
2nd Lieutenants—			
H. F. Riley	May 25, '61		Sergeant; promoted 2nd Lieutenant; re-enlisted, May 10, '62; wounded, Seven Pines; killed at Gettysburg July 3, '63.
D. F. Bradley	May 25, '61		Private; promoted Sergeant; 2nd Lieutenant; wounded, Williamsburg May 5, '62; Seven Pines may 31, '62; Frazier's Farm June 30, '62; killed Spottsylvania May 12, '64.
3rd Lieutenant—			
ENLISTED MEN.			
Aldred, J. A.	May 25, '61		
Amos, J. E.	May 25, '61		Appointed Sergeant July 13, '61; re-enlisted and transferred to Ordnance Department.
Barnes, F.	May 25, '61		Killed at Seven Pines May 31, '62.
Bobe, J. V.	Aug. 29, '61		
Bond, W.	May 25, '61		Killed at Gettysburg July 2, '63.
Bower, F. M.	Aug. 29, '61		Killed at Spottsylvania May 12, '64.
Bowers, S. A.	May 25, '61		Wounded, Fredericksburg December 13, '62; captured at Gettysburg; imprisoned at Fort Delaware.
Brewer, J. W.	May 25, '61		Promoted Corporal; May 10, '62, wounded and disabled at Seven Pines May 31, '62.
Brosnaham, George O.			Transferred to Prattville, Ala., Dragoons; promoted Assistant Surgeon of C. S. A., '64; shot at Chickamauga.
Bryan, W. C.	May 25, '61		Re-enlisted '62; wounded, Seven Pines May 31, '62; Chancellorsville May 1, '63; Gettysburg July 3, '63.
Buttz, A.	May 25, '61		Re-enlisted '62; wounded, Gettysburg July 2, '63.
Byrnes, Frank	May 25, '61		Killed, Seven Pines May 31, '62.
Byrnes, J. M.	May 25, '61	April 9, '65	
Caldwell, R. C.	Aug. 29, '61		
Christian, L.	May 25, '61		Wounded at Yorktown April '62.
Church, H.	Aug. 29, '61		Killed in Seven Days Battle June to July1, '62.
Clark, J. P.	May 25, '61		Mortally wounded at Seven Pines May 31, '62.
Clifford, G. C.	Aug. 29, '61	April 9, '65	Wounded, Seven Pines May 31, '62; Sharpsburg September 17, '62; imprisoned at Fort Delaware
Clifford, S. L.	Aug. 29, '61		Wounded at Gaines' Mill June 26, '62; Gettysburg July 3, '63.
Colson, E. W.	May 25, '61		
Conklin, J. W.	Aug. 29, '61		Deserted at Williamsburg, '62.
Cooper, C. E.	May 25, '61		Killed at Sharpsburg September 17, '62.
Cunningham, J.	May 25, '61		Wounded, Williamsburg May 5, '62; killed at Frazier's Farm June 30, '62.
Curry, R.	May 25, '61		Transferred May, '62, to Navy.
Curtis, Z. E. C.	May 25, '61		Musician; captured at Gettysburg.
Cushman, H. C.	May 25, '61	April 9, '65	Re-enlisted May, '62; wounded, Gettysburg July 3, '63.
Davis, B. B.	June 23, '61		
Deer, D. H.	May 25, '61		Mortally wounded, Gaines' Farm June 27, '62; died October, '62.
Dennison, W. H.	May 25, '61		Transferred June, '62; wounded, Seven Pines May 31, '62.
Ditmar, John	May 25, '61		Wounded, Gettysburg July 3 63.
Ditmar, Noyes	May 25, '61		Deserted at Montgomery May '61
Dixon, A. B.	May 25, '61		Died at St. Charles hospital August 29, '61.
Dow, R.	June 26, '61		Transferred June, '62, to Navy.
Ellis, C. H.	May 25, '61		Promoted Corporal.
Fenley, J. T.	May 25, '61	April 9, '65	
Flournoy, G.	Aug. 29, '61		Wounded, Seven Pines May 31, '62; Gettysburg July 2, '63; discharged August, '63, on account of wounds.
Flourney, W.	Aug. 29, '61		Killed at Sharpsburg September 17, '62.
Flowers, T.	May 25, '61		Wounded at Frazier's Farm June 3, '62; killed at Gettysburg July 3, '63.
Floyd, J. B.	May 25, '61		Died at Fort Delaware.

Roll Company A—(Pensacola Rifle Rangers) 2nd Florida Infantry.

(CONTINUED.)

NAMES.	MUSTERED IN.	MUSTERED OUT.	REMARKS.
Fowler, W	May 25, '61		Discharged for deafness.
Gee, W. A	May 25, '61		Killed at Sharpsburg September 17, '62.
Gerard, J	Aug. 29, '61		Killed, Williamsburg May 4, '63.
Givens, D. C	May 25, '61		Wounded, Frazier's Farm June 30, '62.
Glass, S	May 25, '61		
Gleason, J	May 25, '61		Killed, Gettysburg July 2, '63.
Grinnell, G. F	May 25, '61	April 9, '65	Went to Navy.
Haley, J. H	May 25, '61	April 9, '65	
Harrison, Frank M	May 25, '61	April 9, '65	Re-enlisted May '62; wounded in Seven Days' Battle, June 25 to July 1.
Harrison, J. W	May 25, '61		Transferred to Virginia Cavalry.
Harrison, W. H	May 25, '61		Wounded, Seven Pines May 31, '62.
Hendrix J S	May 25, '61		
Hernandez, A. J	Aug. 29, '61		
Hooper,			Wounded, Seven Pines May 31, '62.
Jones, J	May 25, '61		
Jordan, R. S	May 25, '61	April 9, '65	
Julian, B	May 25, '61		Killed in Seven Days battle.
Kelher, D	May 25, '61		
Kennedy, W. D	May 25, '61		Promoted Corporal; wounded, Seven Pines May 31, '62; Gettysburg July 2, '63.
Keyser, A. W	May 25, '61		Wounded, Seven Days' battle June 25 to July 1; Gettysburg July 2, '63.
Knight, B. R	May 25, '61		Discharged May, '63, for disability.
Knight, D. M	May 25, '61		Killed, Gettysburg July 2, '63.
Knight, J. C	May 25, '61		Mortally wounded at Chancellorsville May 2, '63.
Knight, J. H	May 25, '61		Wounded at Gaines' Farm June 27, '62.
Knowles, D. C	May 25, '61		Wounded at Gaines' Farm June 27, '62.
Landrum, S. M	May 25, '61	April 9, '65	
Luckie, James T	May 25, '61		Re-enlisted May, '62; wounded Gettysburg; killed at the Wilderness May 5, '64.
McKindlay, J. L	Aug. 29, '61		Killed at Sharpsburg September 17, '62.
Maura, Frank	Mch. 16, '62	April 9, '65	Sergeant.
Merrell, W. J		April 9, '65	
Merritt, J. T	May 25, '61		Killed, Williamsburg May 5, '62.
Milligan, R	May 25, '61		
Milsted, F	May 25, '61		Transferred, Confederate Navy May, '62.
Morris, J. H	May 25, '61		
Nall, J. A	May 25, '61		Wounded, Seven Pines May 31, '62.
Odam, W. H			Wounded, Seven Days' battle June 25 to July 1, '62.
Penny, A. J			Wounded, Gaines' Farm June 27, '62.
Penny, J. L			
Perry, C. H	May 25, '61		Corporal.
Philips, W. H	Aug. 29, '61		Wounded, Gettysburg July 3, '63.
Powell, J	Aug. 29, '61		
Quinn, W	May 25, '61		Deserted July, '61.
Reed, D. B. R	Aug. 29, '61	April 9, '65	Wounded, Seven Pines May 31, '63.
Riley, R	May 25, '61		Promoted Sergeant; wounded Seven Pines May 31, '62; Sharpsburg September 17, '62.
Rosson, T. N	May 25, '61		Killed at Ellison's Mill June 26, '62.
Sherman, J	Aug. 29, '61		Killed at Williamsburg May 5, '62.
Shippey, C. S	Aug. 29, '61		Killed at Seven Pines May 31, '62.
Shuttleworth, J	Aug. 29, '61		
Sills, W. B	May 25, '61		Wounded, Gaines' Farm June 27, '62; Gettysburg July 2, '63.
Squires, W. W	May 25, '61		Wounded, Frazier's Farm June 3, '62.
Taylor, D. B	July 1, '61		Transferred to Staff.
Towles, W	May 25, '61		Discharged for deafness.
Turner, L. B	May 25, '61		Wounded, Seven Pines May 31, '62.
Villar, A	Aug. 29, '61		Wounded, Gaines' Farm June 27, '62; Gettysburg July 3, '63.
Visor, George	May 25, '61		Transferred to Hospital Service.
Waters, L	May 25, '61		Re-enlisted May 10, '62; mortally wounded at Seven Pines May 31, '62.
Way, S	May 25, '61		Killed, Williamsburg May 5, '62.
Webster, W	May 25, '61		Furnished substitute.
Wilkins, M	Aug. 29, '61		

Roll Company B (Alachua Guards)—2nd Florida Infantry.

NAMES.	MUSTERED IN.	MUSTERED OUT.	REMARKS.
OFFICERS.			
Captains—			
Lew. Williams	July 13, '61		Wounded at Seven Pines May 31, '62; resigned, '63.
R. G. Jerkins	July 13, '61		4th Sergeant; promoted 1st Lieutenant May 10; Captain June '62; wounded at Seven Pines May 31, '62; killed at Gettysburg July 1, '63.
1st Lieutenant—			
Asa Clark	July 13, '61		Returned to Florida in May, '62, and deserted.

Roll Company B (Alachua Guards)—2nd Florida Infantry.

(CONTINUED.)

NAMES	MUSTERED IN.	MUSTERED OUT.	REMARKS.
2nd Lieutenants—			
Ransom Cason	July 13, '61		Resigned at reorganization;reinlisted in 7th Florida
J. J. Thompson	July 13, '61	April 9, '65	Wounded at Seven Pines May 31, '62.
J. H. Sikes	July 13, '61		Promoted from Sergeant to Lieutenant May 10; killed at Frazier's Farm June 30, '62.
ENLISTED MEN.			
Arnow, B.	July 13, '61		3rd Sergeant.
Adams, John	July 13, '61		
Baldwin, L.	July 13, '61		
Barfied, B. B.	July 13, '61		....
Beall, J. D.	July 13, '61	April 9, '65	Wounded at Williamsburg May 5, '62.
Bennett, D. H.	July 13, '61		Corporal; wounded at Seven Pines May 31, '62.
Bennett, Jacob	July 13, '61		
Bennett, R.	July 13, '61		
Blanton, Thomas	July 13, '61		Killed at Seven Pines May 30, '62.
Bleach, J. F.	July 13, '61		Wounded at Gettysburg July 3, '63.
Boytt, J. H.	July 13, '61		Promoted to Corporal; wounded at Gettysburg July 2, '63.
Bryant. H.	July 13, '61		Killed at Perryville, Ky., '62.
Bryant, J. T.	July 13, '61		Killed at Seven Pines May 31, '62.
Bryant. W. M.	July 13, '61		Wounded at Frazier's Farm June 30, '62.
Brooker, J. G.	July 13, '61		
Burnett, G. J.	July 13, '61		Corporal.
Button, James W.	July 13, '61	April 9, '65	
Caston, W. C.	July 13, '61		2nd Sergeant.
Cannon, John A.	July 13, '61		Wounded at Seven Pines May 31, '62.
Colson, Jonah	July 13, '61		Killed at Frazier's Farm June 30, '62.
Colson, J. B.	July 13, '61		Imprisoned at Fort Delaware.
Cooley, E.	July 13, '61		Imprisoned at Fort Delaware.
Cox, M. F.	July 13, '61		Promoted to Sergeant; wounded at Seven Pines May 31, '62.
Cox, R. B.	July 13, '61		Wounded at Seven Pines May 31, '62.
Crosby, Isam	July 13, '61		Promoted to Sergeant May 10; wounded Seven Pines May 31, '62.
Cummins, L. R.	July 13, '61		Wounded at Seven Pines May 31, '62.
Dinkins, C. L.	July 13, '61		
Downing, W. B.	July 13, '61		
Dunham, H. C.	July 13, '61		Killed at Chattanooga May, '63.
Ellis, A. C.	July 13, '61		Wounded at Seven Pines May 31, '62; Frazier's Farm June 30, '62.
Ellis, V. H.	July 13, '61	April 9, '65	
Evans, James	July 13, '61		Wounded at Chancellorsville May 3, '63.
Evans, Richard	July 13, '61		Musician.
Finley, T. J.	July 13, '61		Wounded at Seven Pines May 31, '62; Frazier's Farm and Gettysburg July 3, '63.
Flynn, William	July 13, '61		
Hathcox, James	July 13, '61		
Holbrook, J. P.	July 13, '61		
Holder, J. B.	July 13, '61		
Holder, T. B.	July 13, '61		
Hubbard, W. W.	July 13, '61		
Huggins, J. H. H.	July 13, '61		
Jones, B.	July 13, '61		Wounded at Gettysburg July 3, '63.
Jones, S. A.	July 13, '61		Corporal.
Kemps, J. S.	July 13, '61		Died in Fort Delaware, '63.
Lockhart, J. A.	July 13, '61		
Little, J. W.	July 13, '61		Wounded at Williamsburg May 5, '62.
Long, James T.	July 13, '61		Killed at Seven Pines May 31, '62.
McCain, J. T.	July 13, '61		Wounded at Seven Pines May 31, '62.
McDonald, E.	July 13, '61		
McKinney, James	July 13, '61		
McKinney, Joseph	July 13, '61		
McRae, W. J.	July 13, '61		
Martin, A. Calvin	July 13, '61	April 9, '65	Captured and imprisoned at Fort Delaware.
Malphurs, W. L.	July 13, '61	April 9, '65	
Miller, G. W.	July 13, '61		
Mills, Thomas	July 13, '61		Wounded at Gaines' Farm June 27, '62.
Moody, J. J.	July 13, '61		
Moore, James	July 13, '61		Wounded at Seven Pines May 31, '62.
Moore, Stephen	July 13, '61		
Odom, John	July 13, '61		
Olmstead, F. P.	July 13, '61		
Paget, E.	July 13, '61		
Parker, C. F.	July 13, '61	May '65	Wounded at Yorktown and at the Wilderness; paroled from prison.
Parker, H. C.	July 13, '61	April 9, '65	
Paschall, E. P.	July 13, '61	.62	Discharged, '62, on account of disabilities.
Pelote, C. E.	July 13, '61		
Polk, D.	July 13, '61		
Polk, J. K.	July 13, '61		
Porcell, James	July 13, '61		
Powers, D. J.	July 13, '61		Corporal.
Rawls, C. D.	July 13, '61		Wounded at Seven Pines May 31, '62.
Ray, D. C.	July 13, '61	April 9, '65	
Robinson, D. W.	July 13, '61		Wounded at Seven Pines May 31, '62.
Sanchez, S. J.	July 13, '61		Sergeant; wounded at Seven Pines May 31, '62
Sanders, J. H.	July 13, '61	April 9, '65	Wounded at Seven Pines May 31, '62.

Roll Company B (Alachua Guards)—2nd Florida Infantry.

(CONTINUED.)

NAMES.	MUSTERED IN.	MUSTERED OUT.	REMARKS.
Scott, W. P.	July 13, '61	April 9, '65	Wounded in neck Gettysburg July 3, '63; in hand
Sherley, Jasper—	July 13, '61		Wilderness May, '64.
Sparkman, G. W.	July 13, '61		
Stroble, W. E.	July 13, '61		Wounded at Gettysburg July 3, '63.
Stroble, W. W.	July 13, '61	April 9, '65	Wounded at Gaines' Farm June 27; Frazier's Farm June 30, '62.
Strock, J. E.	July 13, '61	April 9, '65	Wounded at Seven Pines May 31, '62.
Sumerlin, D. J.	July 13, '61		
Tidwell, D. H.	July 13, '61	April 9, '65	
Thomas, J. J.	July 13, '61		Wounded at Seven Plnes May 31, '62.
Took, J. W.	July 13, '61		
Ursey, A. P.	July 13, '61		
Wadkins, Crawford	July 13, '61		
White, J. M.	July 13, '61		Wounded at Gaines' Farm June 27, '62.
Weeks, J. T.	July 13, '61		Corporal.
Wescott, William	July 13, '61		
Wilkey, James	July 13, '61		Killed at Gaines' Farm June 27, '62.
Wilkey, William	July 13, '61		
Williams, J. J.	July 13, '61		Promoted Sergeant and Color Bearer.
Wilson, Nathaniel	July 13, '61		Killed at Seven Pines May 31, '62.
Younge, William H.	July 13, '61		Musician.

Roll Company C (Columbia Rifles)—2nd Florida Infantry.

NAMES.	MUSTERED IN.	MUSTERED OUT.	REMARKS.
OFFICERS.			
Captains—			
Walter R. Moore	July 13. '61	April 9. '65	Re-enlisted May 10, '02; Jan. 28, '64; wounded at Seven Pines May 31, '62; Chancellorsville'63; Gettysburg July 3, '63; promoted Major '63; Lieutenant-Colonel '63; Colonel, '64; in all principal battles of Army of Northern Virginia and fight at Cedar Keys, Fla., at which vessels loaded with railroad iron were captured.
H. E. Stokes		April 9, '65	Sergeant; promoted Captain.
1st Lieutenant—			
R. B. Thomas	July 13, '61	April 9, '65	Promoted Adjutant; 1st Lieutenant; Captain; Major P. A. C. S.
2nd Lieutenants—			
W. B. Brown	July 13, '61	April 9, '65	
W. L. Hazlett			2nd Sergeant; promoted 2nd Lieutenant.
Harrison Pratt	July 13, '61	April 9 '65	Re-enlisted May, '62; promoted 2nd Lieutenant; wounded at Gaines' Mill June 2, '62; transferred to Co. D, 4th Infantry.
3rd Lieutenants—			
P. Shealy	July 13, '62		Killed July 3, '63. In battles of Wilderness to Gettysburg; the battles of Army of Northern Virginia from May 5, '62 to July 3, '63.
J. C. Hamilton	July 13, '61		Killed at Sharpsburg September 20, '62.
Spier Allison	July 13, '61		Seriously wounded at Chancellorsville in head; disabled; lost his mind from wound.
ENLISTED MEN.			
Allen, Robert	July 13, '61	April 9, '65	Wounded at Seven Pines May 31, '62; imprisoned at Fort Delaware.
Allen, William	July 13, '61	April 9, '65	
Bateman, A. H.	July 13, '61	April 9, '65	Wounded at Gettysburg July 3, '63.
Banks, Archibald T.	July 13, '61	April 9, '65	Promoted Adjutant.
Brown, Jethro	July 13, '61	April 9, '65	
Brown, L. P.	July 13, '61	April 9, '65	
Brewer, J. W.	July 13, '61		
Bennett, Henry	July 13, '61		
Bennett, John A.	July 13, '61	April 9, '65	Wounded at Gaines' Farm June 27, '62.
Board, S. P.	July 13, '61		
Brewer, W. B.	July 13, '61		Re-enlisted May, '62; wounded Gaines' Farm June 27, '62.
Buttchaell	May		Promoted to 2nd Lieutenant Co. B, 5th Infantry.
Burns, W. P.	July 13, '61		Reported as deserter.
Cason, J. B.	July 13, '61		Corporal; killed at Seven Pines May 31, '62.
Chambliss, W. O.	July 13, '61	April 9, '65	Captured at Gettysburg; imprisoned at Fort Delaware.
Cone, D. N.	July 13, '61	April 9, '65	Wounded at Seven Pines May 31, '62.
Cutter, W. H.	July 13, 61		
Cason, H. J.	July 13, '61	'63	Wounded at Seven Pines May 31, '62; discharged on account of wounds.
Crane, M. C.	July 13, '61		Wounded at Ellison's Mill June 26, '62.

Roll Company C (Columbia Rifles)—2nd Florida Infantry.
(Continued.)

NAMES.	MUSTERED IN.	MUSTERED OUT.	REMARKS.
Daniels, W. E.	July 13, '61		
Dowling, W. W.—	July 13, '61		
Doliff, A.	July 13, '61		
Demere, John	July 13, '61		
Ellinger, A.	July 13, '61		Re-enlisted May 10, '62; and promoted Sergeant; wounded at Williamsburg.
Fernandez, A.	July 13, '61		
Gahagen, C.	July 13, '61		
Gaylard, Thomas M.	July 13, '61		
Grisham, L. M.	July 13, '61		Killed at Seven Pines.
Green, A. C.	July 13, '61		
Green, George W.	July 13, '61		
Griffin, G. A.	July 13, '61		Captured and imprisoned at Fort Delaware.
Harvey, Richard	July 13, '61	April 9, '65	
Hines, Isaac	July 13, '61	April 9, '65	Wounded in foot at Chancellorsville May 3, '63.
Hines, William	July 13, '61	April 9, '65	
Hocter Demenic	July 13, '61		Re-enlisted May, '62; wounded at Seven Pines May 31, '62.
Jackson, Thomas	July 13, '61		
Jerrold, David	July 13, '61		Killed.
Jerrold, E.	July 13, '61		
Jones, John A.	July 13, '61		Re-enlisted May, '62; mortally wounded at Gettysburg July 3, '63.
Kinsey, Luke	July 13, '61		Wounded at Seven Pines May 31, '62.
Long, Joseph	July 13, '61		Transferred 4th Florida; killed at Dallas, Ga., May 28, '64.
Low, Phillip E.	July 13, '61	April 9, '65	Sergeant; transferred Co. K, 3rd Florida.
Mack, Adam	July 13, '61		
Miller, J. T.	July 13, '61		Killed at Gaines' Farm June 27, '62; in battles of Williamsburg May 5, '62; Seven Pines May 31, '62; Ellison's Mill June 26, '62, and Gaines' Farm June 27, '62.
Mote, John A.	July 13, '61		Wounded at Ellison's Mill June 26, '62; Gaines' Farm June 27, '62; captured at Gettysburg; imprisoned at Fort Delaware.
Mote, W. F.	July 13, '61		Killed.
Mondane, Jacob	July 13, '61		
Mondane, James	July 13, '61		
More, J. C.		April 9, '65	Wounded at Ellison's Mill June 26, '62.
Nichols, Jerry	July 13, '61		
Nobles, L.	July 13, '61		
O'Brien, James	July 13, '61		
Peoples, John H.	July 13, '61		Killed at Seven Pines May 31, '62.
Peoples, W. W.	July 13, '61		Killed.
Raulerson, W. J.	July 13, '61		Transferred Co. D, 4th Regiment.
Raulerson, A.	July 13, '61		Re-enlisted May 10; wounded at Fredericksburg December 13, '62.
Rogerson, E. G.	July 13, '61		Wounded May, '63, at Fredericksburg.
Roberts, A. C.	July 13, '61		Killed at Seven Pines May 31, '62.
Robinson, James H.	July 13, '61		
Sheffield, C. H.	July 13, '61		
Shields, W. H.	July 13, '61		
Stokes, A. T.	July 13, '61		Re-enlisted May, '62; wounded at Seven Pines May 31, '62.
Strickland, M. T.	July 13, '61		
Suggs, J. T.	July 13, '61		Wounded at Gettysburg July 3, '63.
Tuely, John T.	July 13, '61		
Townsend, V. D.	July 13, '61		
Tucker, J. E.	July 13, '61		Killed at Seven Pines May 31, '62.
Tucker, E. A.	July 13, '61		
Venters, B. F.	July 13, '61		
Wilkerson			
Williams, T. W.	July 13, '61		Sergeant.
Willis, R. H.	July 13, '61		
Williams, Peter	July 13, '61	April 9, '65	
Wolfe, Frederick	July 13, '61	April 9, '65	Wounded at Seven Pines May 31, '62.
Wooten, John	July 13, '61		Deserted.

Roll Company D (Leon Rifles)—2nd Florida Infantry.

NAMES.	MUSTERED IN.	MUSTERED OUT.	REMARKS.
OFFICERS.			
Captains—			
T. W. Brevard, Jr.	July 13, '61		Retired on reorganization May, '62.
M. J. C. Musgrove	July 13, '61		Sergeant; promoted Captain May, '62; wounded at Seven Pines May 31, '62; deserted, '62.
1st Lieutenants—			
Richard B. Maxwell	July 13, '61		Resigned July, '61.
G. M. R. Cook	July 13, '61		Resigned May 15, '62.

Roll Company D (Leon Rifles)—2nd Florida Infantry.

(CONTINUED.)

NAMES.	MUSTERED IN.	MUSTERED OUT.	REMARKS.
A. J. Stewart	July 13, '61		Promoted 1st Lieutenant; wounded and disabled at Seven Pines May 31, '62; resigned May 16, '63
A. P. Barrow	July 13, '61		Promoted 3rd, 2nd and 1st Lieutenant; captured and imprisoned.
2nd Lieutenants—			
A. F. Hayward	July 13, '61		Retired at reorganization.
John Parker	July 13, '61		Wounded at Seven Pines; deserted, '62.
Joseph M. Tolbert	July 13, '61		Promoted 3rd and 2nd Lieutenants, '62; wounded at Williamsburg May 5, '62; Gettysburg July 3, '63.
3rd Lieutenant—			
G. W. Saunders	July 13, '61		Retired on reorganization.
ENLISTED MEN.			
Ambar, W	July 13, '61		
Anderson, C	July 13, '61		
Baker, Charles	July 13, '61		
Barr, J. T.	July 13, '61		
Baltzell, Franklin	July 13, '61		1st Sergeant; wounded at Sharpsburg and discharged.
Bell, W	July 13, '61		
Belvin, George	July 13, '61		
Bethell, Frank	July 13, '61	April 9, '65	
Boatwright, B. J. Q	July 13, '61		
Bond, W			
Boyde, L. L	July 13, '61		
Brevard, S. M.	July 13, '61		Sergeant.
Brown	July 13, '61	April 9, '65	
Bryant, D	July 13, '61		
Bryant, James	July 13, '61		
Burroughs, B. M.	July 13, '61		Transferred to Co. F, 1st Cavalry and promoted Captain.
Burroughs, Eben W	May '61		Wounded at Seven Pines June 30, '62 and discharged; re-enlisted, '63, in Capt. George W. Scott's Co.; was elected 2nd Lieutenant of Capt. D. W. Gwynn's Co., of Scott's Battalion.
Cameron, John			
Chester, W	July 13, '61		
Cokely, J.	July 13, '61		
Coleman, Thomas			Wounded at Seven Pines May 31, '62.
Conners, J.	July 13, '61		
Cooper, W. A	July 13, '61		
Crabtree, H.	July 13, '61		
Dauson, Henry	July 13, '61		
DeCottes, E.	July 13, '61		
Demillay, L. L.	July 13, '61		
Dortch, John	July 13, '61		Wounded at Gaines' Farm June 27, '62.
Dutton, J. L.	July 13, '61		Wounded at Seven Pines May 30, '62; Gaines Farm June 27, '62; Frazier's Farm June 30, '62; Promoted Sergeant.
Edwards, J.	July 13, '61		Wounded at Seven Pines May 31, '62.
Edwards, W	July 13, '61		
Footman, George Newell	July 13, '61		Wounded at Gettysburg July 3, '63, and captured.
Given, A	July 13, '61		
Gray, J. G	July 13, '61		Killed at Ellison's Mill June 26, '62.
Hall, R	July 13, '61		
Harrington, M	July 13, '61		Wounded at Seven Pines May 31, '62; promoted Sergeant.
Henderson, A	July 13, '61		Killed at Williamsburg May 5, '62; promoted Sergeant.
Hickman, W. E.	July 13, '61		
Horn, W. H.	July 13, '61		Wounded at Seven Pines May 31, '62.
Houck, B. M.	July 13, '61		Wounded at Seven Pines May 31, '62; promoted Corporal.
Houstoun, E.	July 13, '61		
Hunt, D. R.	July 13, '61		
Jammerson, D.	July 13, '61		
Jammerson, G.	July 13, '61		
Jarvis, W	July 13, '61		
Jett, Allison	July 13, '61		
Johnson, Charles W	July 13, '61		Promoted 1st Sergeant, and Lieutenant in command at battle of Gettysburg; killed.
Johnson, J. F.	July 13, '61		Corporal.
Johnson, O. M.	July 13, '61		Promoted 1st Sergeant.
Jones, Robert	July 13, '61		Wounded at Seven Pines.
Jones, Whitman	July 13, '61	April 9, '65	Wounded at Gettysburg July 3, '63.
Jordan, D.	July 13, '61		
Jordan, N.	July 13, '61		Wounded at Seven Pines May 31, '62.
Jordan, W	July 31, '61		
King W. R.	July 13, '61		Wounded at Williamsburg May 5, '62.
Leatherwood, S.	July 13, '61		
Ledwith, Robert	July 13, '61		Wounded at Gaines' Farm June 27, '62.
McCormick, J.	July 13, '61		Wounded at Seven Pines May 31, '62.
McKinney, J	July 13, '61		
Mangum, O. P.	July 13, '61		
Marrow, John	July 13, '61		Corporal; promoted Captain Co. H, 1st Cavalry.
Maxwell, D. E.	July 13, '61		Wounded at Seven Pines May 31, '62.
Moerring, Henry	July 13, '61		
Miller Fred	July 13, '61		
Morrison, A. J.	July 13, '61		
Moore, G.	July 13, '61		
Murphy, John	July 13, '61		Musician.
Murray, E. J.	July 13, '61		
Nichols E.	July 13, '61		Wounded at Bristow Station October 14, '63.

Roll Company D (Leon Rifles)—2nd Florida Infantry.
(CONTINUED.)

NAMES.	MUSTERED IN.	MUSTERED OUT.	REMARKS.
Page, J. L.	July 13, '61		
Rawls, R. E.	July 13, '61		
Reddick, J. M.	July 13, 61	April 9, '65	
Richardson, D.			Killed at Seven Pines.
Roberts, A. W.	July 13, '61	April 9, '65	
Russell, T. S.	July 13, '61		
Saunders, George C.	July 13, '61		Musician.
Saunders James.	July 13, '61		
Sciller, F.	July 13, '61		
Smith, A. W.	July 13, '61	April 4, '65	
Smith, S.	July 13, '61		Killed at Seven Pines May 31, '62.
Smythe, James C.	July 13, '61		Hospital Steward December 13, '62.
Stephens D.	July 13, '61		Promoted Sergeant.
Stewart, A. J.	July 13, '61		
Stewart, J. F.	July 13, '61	April 9, '65	
Stokes, Henry	Mch. '62		Killed in battle of Turkey Ridge, Va., Aug. 31, '64
Strickland, E. E.	July 13, '61		
Surey, L. S.	July 13, '61		
Thomas, William	July 13, '61	April 9. '65	....
Turner, C.	July 13, '61		
Walcott, H.	July 13, '61		
Waller, R. B.	July 13, '61	April 9, '65	
Weather, D.	July 13, '61		
Whitley, S. S.	July 13, '61		
Wightman, A.	July 13, '61		
Willis, D.	July 13, '61		
Willis, W. J.	July 13, '61		
Wilson, H.	July 13, '61		Wounded at Seven Pines May, '31, 62.
Wilson, James.	July 13, '61		Wounded at Seven Pines May 31, '62.
Wilson, John.	July 13, '61		Killed at Seven Pines May 31, '62.
Wolfe, R. J.	July 13, '61		Wounded at Seven Pines May 31, '62; also at Gettysburg July 3, '63; promoted Corporal.
Woodward, A. L., Jr.	July 13, '61		Sergeant; transferred to Co. D, Scott's Battalion Cavalry April, '62.
Wright, W.	July 13, '61		

Roll Company E (Hammock Guards)—2nd Florida Infantry.

NAMES.	MUSTERED IN.	MUSTERED OUT.	REMARKS.
OFFICERS.			
Captains—			
John D. Hopkins.	July 13, '61		Resigned at reorganization.
William E. McCaslin.	July 13, '61		2nd Lieutenant; promoted Captain; wounded, Seven Pines May 31, '62; killed at Gettysburg July 3, '63.
James H. Johnson.	July 13, '61		Promoted 1st Lieutenant, then Captain; wounded Gettysburg July 3, '63, and captured.
Patrick P. L. Todd.	July 13, '61		Sergeant; promoted 3rd Lieutenant and Captain; wounded at Gettysburg July 2, '63; killed, Orange C. H. September, '63.
1st Lieutenants—			
Allen G. Summer.	July 13, '61		Retired May 10, '62, at reorganization.
David S. Reynolds.	July 13, '61		2nd Sergeant; promoted 1st Lieutenant; killed, Seven Pines May 31, '62.
2nd Lieutenant—			
Jesse Dupree.	July 13, '61	April 9, '65	Promoted 2nd Lieutenant, wounded, Gettysburg July 3, '63; transferred to 9th Regiment; promoted Captain.
3rd Lieutenant—			
William Cox.	July 13, '61		Retired at reorganization; joined Co. H, 2nd Cav.
ENLISTED MEN.			
Alexander James A.	July 13. '61		Wounded, Williamsburg May 5, '62; killed, Seven Pines May 31, '62.
Alexander, Mordica.	July 13, '61		Wounded, Williamsburg May 5, '62; Seven Pines May 31, '62.
Allbritton, Thomas W.	July 13, '61		Wounded, Seven Pines May 31, '62; Gettysburg July 3, '63.
Allen, George P.	July 13, '61		Wounded, Frazier's Farm June 30, '62.
Allen, James A.	July 13, '61		Killed Frazier's Farm June 30, '62,
Allen, William B.	July 13, '61		
Alsobrook, Joseph.	July 13, '61		
Atkinson, J. M.			Imprisoned, Fort Delaware.
Anglin, Johnus I.	July 13, '61		
Barnes, Caleb H.	July 13, '61		Corporal.
Bellamy, James.	July 13, '61		
Biggs, Jacob.	July 13, '61		Wounded, Frazier's Farm June 30, '62.
Blitch, Alonzo E.	July 13, '61		Wounded, Frazier's Farm June 30, '62.
Bond, Sanford.	July 13, 61	April 9, '65	Transferred to Co. L, 2nd Florida.
Borchers, Nicholas B.	July 13, '61		Killed, Frazier's Farm June 30, '62,
Boyte Henry.	July 13, '61		Killed, Seven Pines May 31, '62.

Roll Company E (Hammock Guards)—2nd Florida Infantry.
(CONTINUED.)

NAMES.	MUSTERED IN.	MUSTERED OUT.	REMARKS.
Broudwater, William H	July 13, '61		Promoted 1st Sergeant May 10, '62; wounded Seven Pines.
Broome, Thomas H	July 13, '61		
Brown, Charles M	July 13, '61		Wounded, Seven Pines May 31, '62; transferred to Co. G, 9th Regiment; promoted 1st Lieutenant, '63; then Captain, '64; wounded at Olustee, while in the 9th.
Bryant, Dempsey	July 13, '61		Wounded, Gettysburg July 3, '63.
Bryant, J. H	July 13, '61		Died, Fort Delaware of disease, '63.
Burleson, Daniel D	July 13, '61	April 9, '65	
Burleson, Marion D	July 13, '61	April 9, '65	Wounded, Seven Pines May 31, '62.
Burleson, Thomas B	July 13, '61	April 9, '62	Wounded, Frazier's Farm June 30, '62.
Burns, C	July 13, '61		Killed, Chancellorsville May, '63.
Carter, George W	July 13, '61	April 9, '65	
Crankfield, Littleton P	July 13, '61		
Cross, Halcombe R	July 13, '61		Promoted Corporal; wounded, Seven Pines May 31, '62.
Dawkins, Samuel	July 13, '61		
Deger, J. H	July 13, '61		
Dickerson, James W	July 13, '61		
Driggers, Abel L	July 13, '61		
Dutton, Z. E	July 13, '61		
Dye, James H	July 13, '61		
Eichelberger, Thomas W	July 13, '61	April 9, '65	Corporal; promoted Sergeant; wounded, Williamsburg May 5, '62; Gettysburg July 3, '63.
Farmer, Benjamin D	July 13, '61		Killed, Frazier's Farm June 30, '62.
Fogg, Moses	July 13, '61		Wounded, Gaines' Farm June 26, '62; killed Chancellorsville May 4, '63.
Gardner, James G	July 13, '61		
Geiger, Henry C	July 13, '61		
Gibson, Charles F	July 13, '61		Wounded, Frazier's Farm June 30, '62.
Gorden, James G	July 13, '61		
Gradick, Diogenes W	July 13, '61		Wounded, Frazier's Farm June 30, '62.
Grinner, Nathaniel H. C	July 13, '61		
Guerry, Mark	July 13, '61		Musician.
Harrell, Alexander J. W	July 13, '61		
Hamlin, John	July 13, '61		
Hardin, Thomas H	July 13, '61		Sergeant.
Hedick, David L	July 13, '61	April 9, '65	Musician; promoted 2nd Sergeant.
Hedick, W. J	July 13, '61		
Hendricks, Lemuel H	July 13, '61		
Hogan, Andrew J	July 13, '61		Wounded, Ellison's Mills May 26, '62; Gettysburg July 3, '63.
Howard, William D	July 13, '61		Promoted Corporal.
Jones, Whitman H	July 13, '61		
King, George W	July 13, '61		
Lykes, Eugene F	July 13, '61		Wounded at Seven Pines May 31, '62.
Madden, Patrick	July 13, '61		
Massey, John P. C	July 13, '61	April 9, '65	Wounded at Gaines' Farm June 27, '62.
McKee, Sidney D	July 13, '61		
Mills, Crawford	July 13, '61		
Mills, Thomas S	July 13, '61		
Mix, S. A	July 13, '61		
Mixon, Stephen G	July 13, '61		
Moorman, William P	July 13, '61		
Neil, John	July 13, '61		
Nevitt, John M	July 13, '61		
Pogue, Daniel	July 13, '61		Wounded at Frazier's Farm June 30, '62.
Pyles, Thomas W	July 13, '61		
Rawley, C. D		April 9, '65	Corporal.
Reddick, John M	July 13, '61	April 4, '65	
Roberts, James M	July 13, '61		Captured at Gettysburg; imprisoned at Fort Delaware.
Roberts, William N	July 13, '61		
Rowe, Judson A	July 13, '61		
Slager, Julius	July 13, '61		
Starke, Reuben	July 13, '61	April 9, '65	
Starke, Thomas	July 13, '61		Corporal.
Scott, George L	July 13, '61		
Tate, B	July 13, '61		Wounded at Gettysburg July 3, '63.
Tate, Robert H	July 13, '61		Corporal; Wounded at Bristow Station October 14, '63.
Thomas, George W	July 13, '61	April 9, '65	
Thomas, Richard	July 13, '61		
Todd, Joseph A. S	July 13, '61		
Tuton, William C	July 13, '61		
Turner, John W	July 13, '61		
Turner, Joseph E	July 13, '61		
Vaughn, R. T	July 13, '61		
Venning, Robert D	July 13, '61		
Walker, Jesse C	July 13, '61		
Watkins, William B	July 13, '61		1st Sergeant.
Williams, Edward T	July 13, '61		
Williams, Eli G	July 13, '61		Corporal; died at Yorktown.
Williams, Warner	July 13, '61		
Wheeler, James F	July 13, '61		
Wenton, Henry	July 13, '61		
West, N. W	July 13, '61		

Roll Company E (Hammock Guards)—2nd Florida Infantry.
(CONTINUED.)

NAMES.	MUSTERED IN.	MUSTERED OUT.	REMARKS
Wooley, James McT	July 13, '61		
Wright, M	July 13, '61		Died in Fort Delaware prison, '63.
Yongue, Robert E	July 13, '61	April 9, '65	
Zetrouer, Solon R	July 13, '61	April 9, '65	

Roll Company F (Gulf State Guards)—2nd Florida Infantry.

NAMES.	MUSTERED IN.	MUSTERED OUT.	REMARKS.
OFFICERS.			
Captains—			
James F. McClellan	July 13, '61		Retired May 10,'62; promoted Lieutenant-Colonel,
J. Henry Pooser	July 13, '61		1st Lieutenant; promoted Captain May 10, '62; killed at Seven Pines May 31, '62.
Harrison, Tillinghast	July 13, '61		2nd Lieutenant; promoted Captain May 31, '62; wounded, Seven Pines May 31, '62; killed at Sharpsburg September 17, '62.
Ben F. Watts	July 13, '61		Promoted 2nd Lieutenant May 10, '62; 1st Lieutenant, then Captain, June, '63; wounded, Frazier's Farm June 30, '63; killed in service.
1st Lieutenants—			
George E. Pooser	July 13, '61		Promoted 1st Lieutenant July 3, .'63; wounded, Seven Pines May 31, '62; killed at Gettysburg July 3, '63.
Joe Wyatt			Promoted 3rd Lieutenant May 10, '62; 2nd Lieutenant September, '63, and 1st Lieutenant.
2nd Lieutenant—			
3rd Lieutenants—			
Charles D. Eaton	July 13, '61		Resigned May 10, '62.
James W. Brett	July 13, '61		Sergeant; promoted 1st Sergeant April, '62; then 3rd Lieutenant, June, '62; wounded at Chancellorsville May 13, '63.
ENLISTED MEN.			
Allen, Joseph F	July 13, '61		Promoted Corporal.
Ayers, John	July 13, '61		
Barnes, E. S	July 13, '61		Wounded, Seven Pines May 31, '62.
Barnes, William R	July 13, '61		Wounded, Ellison's Mill June 26, '62.
Bassett, Newten P	July 13, '61		Musician; wounded at Frazier's Farm June 30, '62.
Baty, Reuben	July 13, '61		
Bell, J. D	July 13, '61		Wounded; imprisoned at Fort Delaware.
Bell, William E	July 13, '61		Wounded at Seven Pines May 31, '62; Frazier's Farm June 30, '62.
Bell, W. R	July 13, '61		
Best, Archibald	July 13, '61		
Best, Tillman	July 13, '61		
Bird, John S	July 13, '61		1st Sergeant; promoted to Regimental Staff.
Bonner, John J	July 13, '61		
Brown, N. L	July 13, '61		
Bryan, Newten	July 13, '61		
Bryan, R. R	July 13, '61		
Bryan, William	July 13, '61		
Burger, Jeff	July 13, '61		
Burnham, Alfred	July 13, '61		
Butler, Albert C	July 13, '61		Wounded at Seven Pines May 31, '62.
Butler, Stephen	July 13, '61		
Butler, William	July 13, '61		2nd Corporal; promoted Sergeant May 10, '62; wounded at Seven Pines May 31, '62.
Champas, T. E	July 13, '61		Wounded at Fredericksburg December 13, '62.
Chance, Alexander	July 13, '61		
Cobb, Reuben	July 13, '61		Corporal; wounded, Seven Pines May 31, '62; Gaines' Farm June 27, '62; Gettysburg July 3, '63.
Collier, W. A	July 13, '61		Wounded at Seven Pines May 31, '62.
Cook, John	July 13, '61		
Coonrod, A. Mc.	July 13, '61		Wounded, Chancellorsville, '63.
Daffin, Horace	July 13, '61		Wounded, Seven Pines May 31, '62.
Daniels, William	July 13, '61		
Darcy, John T	July 13, '61		Wounded, Seven Pines May 31, '62.
Dickson, John	July 13, '61		
Dykes, A. D	July 13, '61		
Gladden, John	July 13, '61		Corporal.
Glisson, Henry J			
Harrison, William H	July 13, '61		
Hearn, Thomas C	July 13, '61		
Hinson, Hadley	July 13, '61		2nd Sergeant; promoted 1st Sergeant; imprisoned at Fort Delaware.
Howard, Abram	July 13, '61		Wounded, Frazier's Farm June 30, '62.
Howard, Richard	July 13, '61		Wounded, Seven Pines May 31, '62.
Howard, William W	July 13, '61		Wounded, Seven Pines May 31, '62: captured, Gettysburg; imprisoned. Fort Delaware.

Roll Company F (Gulf State Guards)—2nd Florida Infantry.
(CONTINUED.)

NAMES.	MUSTERED IN.	MUSTERED OUT.	REMARKS.
Irvin, Robert J.	July 13, '61		Killed, Seven Pines May 31, '62.
Jenkins, Robert N.	July 13, '61		Wounded Seven Pines May 31, '62.
Johnson, Eleazer.	July 13, '61		
Johnson, Gahazer.	July 13, '61		
Johnson, John W.	July 13, '61		
Jones, S. A.	July 13 '61		Wounded, Frazier's Farm June 30, '62.
Jordan, Richard H.	July 13, '61		Wounded, Seven Pines May 31, '62.
Kelly, John.	July 13, '61		Wounded, Chancellorsville May 13, '63.
Kemp, F. M.	July 13, '61		
Lane, William.	July 13, '61		
McAnulty, James J.	July 13, '61		Wounded, Seven Pines May 31, '62; Gaines' Farm June 26, '62.
Neil, John.	July 13, '61		Wounded, Gettysburg July 2, '63.
Oaks, John F.	July 13, '61		
Owens, J. R. B.	July 13, '61		Wounded, Seven Pines May 31, '62.
Padrick, J. G.	July 13, '61		Wounded, Frazier's Farm June 30, '62.
Parker, A. J.	July 13, '61		
Peacock, Pierson.	July 13, '61		
Peacock, W. G.	July 13, '61		Promoted Corporal; wounded Seven Pines May 31, '62.
Philips, C.	July 13, '61		Wounded, Frazier's Farm June 30, '62.
Playor, Thomas F.	July 13, '61		Wounded, Williamsburg May 5, '62; Seven Pines May 31, '62.
Pooser, Charles H.	July 13, '61		
Powell, W. J.	July 13, '61		
Pritchett, Stephen D.	July 13, '61		Killed at Gettysburg July 3, '63.
Raines, C. S.	July 13, '61		Wounded, Seven Pines May 31, '62; promoted Corporal, then Sergeant.
Register, W. B.	July 13, '61		
Reynolds, R. S.	July 13, '61		
Rhodes, W. L.	July 13, '61		Wounded, Frazier's Farm June 30, '62.
Richardson, J. H.	July 13, '61		
Roddenbery, Samson.	July 13, '61		
Russell, James.	July 13, '61		
Sauerford, W. S.	July 13, '61		
Sills, James.	July 13, '61		
Smith, J. M.	July 13, '61		
Spencer, L. W.	July 13, '61		
Taylor, William.	July 13, '61		Killed, Seven Pines May 31, '62.
Taylor, William C.	July 13, '61		Killed, Seven Pines May 31, '62.
Tuten, W. R.	July 13, '61		Seven Pines May 31, '62.
Tidwell, Edward.	July 13, '61		1st Corporal.
Tillinghast, George W.	July 13, '61		
Tillis, Demsey.	July 13, '61		Wounded, Gettysburg July 3, '63.
Thompson, W. J.	July 13, '61		Wounded, Gettysburg July 3, '63.
Underwood, P. M.	July 13, '61		
Wells, Benjamin.	July 13, '61		Wounded, Williamsburg May 5, '62.
Welsh, T.			Wounded, Fredericksburg December 13, '62.
Williams, Nathaniel.	July 13, '61		
Wood, Silas H.	July 13, '61		Wounded, Seven Pines May 31, '62.
Wright, S. H.	July 13, '61		
Wyatt, James B.	July 13, '61		

Roll Company G (St. John's Grays)—2nd Florida Infantry.

NAMES.	MUSTERED IN.	MUSTERED OUT.	REMARKS.
OFFICERS.			
Captains—			
J. Jacquelin Daniel.	July 13, '61	April 9, '65	Captain; retired at reorganization; re-enlisted '63; promoted Colonel 1st Florida Reserves.
Charles F. Flagg.	July 13, '61		1st Sergeant; promoted Captain May 10, '62; killed at Seven Pines May 31, '62.
Thomas M. Brown.	July 13, '61		Promoted 1st Lieutenant May 10, '62; Captain October, '62; wounded, Seven Pines May 31, '62; killed June 27, '62.
C. Seton Fleming.	July 13, '61		1st Lieutenant; promoted Captain August, '62; wounded, Williamsburg May 5, '62; Chancellorsville May 3, '63; killed at Cold Harbor June 4,'64
2nd Lieutenants—			
Maybanks A. Jones.	July 13, '61		Left out on reorganization May 10,
Albert J. Russell.	July 13, '61		Re-enlisted at reorganizat on, went into another department and served to close of war.
Antonio J. Mickler.	July 13, '61	April 9, '65	2nd Corporal; promoted 2nd Lieutenant May 10, '62; wounded and died in hospital at Richmond, Va.
3rd Lieutenants—			
Mathew A. Knight.	July 13, '61		Retired at reorganization.
Clayborne L. Wright.	July 13, '61		Promoted 3rd Lieutenant May 10, '62; wounded, SevenPines May 31, '62.

Roll Company G (St. John's Grays)—2nd Florida Infantry.
(CONTINUED.)

NAMES.	MUSTERED IN.	MUSTERED OUT.	REMARKS.
ENLISTED MEN.			
Ashurst, Robert J.	July 13, '61		Re-enlisted May 10, '62.
Abyr, Thomas	July 13, '61		Wounded, Seven Pines May 31, '62.
Bachlor, Charlton H.	July 13, '61		
Beardon, M. J.	July 13, '61		
Beardon, Simpson R.	July 13, '61		3rd Corporal; re-enlisted May, '62.
Beaty, John	July 13, '61		
Berant, Miles	July 13, '61		Wounded, Seven Pines May 31, '62
Booth, William J.	July 13, '61		Wounded, Seven Pines May 31, '62.
Bowden, Charles	July 13, '61		
Bowden, Uriah	July 13, '61	April 9, '65	
Brantley, John A.	July 13, '61		
Brantley, William T.	July 13, '61		
Brooman, G. R.	July 13, '61		Wounded, Gettysburg July 3, '63.
Brown, Augustus W.	July 13, '61		
Brown, George R.	July 13, '61		Wounded, Ellison's Mills June 26, '62; Frazier's Farm June 30, '62.
Brown, Moses J.	July 13, '61		Discharged '62, under age; re-enlisted Co. D, 11th Regiment.
Brown, Stephen W.	July 13, '61		Wounded, Seven Pines May 31, '62.
Broxson, Henry W.	July 13, '61		
Bryan, W. P.	July 13, '61		Wounded, Fredericksburg December 13, '62.
Callahan, William	July 13, '61		
Canova, George P.	July 13, '61		
Carr, Allen	July 13, '61	April 9, '65	
Carr, David L.	July 13, '61		Imprisoned at Fort Delaware.
Carr, John W.	July 13, '61		
Caruthers, W. R.	July 13, '61		Wounded, Fredericksburg December 13, '62.
Cason, James B.	July 13, '61		Wounded, Chancellorsville April, '63.
Caston, Stokley	July 13, '61		
Corbyn, Roland	July 13, '61		Sergeant; wounded Seven Pines May 31, '62.
Davis, Charles	July 13, '61		
Daniel, William A.	July 13, '61		
Doyle, David W.	July 13, '61		
Duval, Wilbur E.	July 13, '61		1st Corporal; imprisoned at Fort Delaware.
Edmonds, Richard	July 13, '61		Musician.
Ferguson, Thomas H.	July 13, '61		Lost arm at Chancellorsville, '63; discharged.
Ferguson, John J.	July 13, '61		
Farrell, John	July 13, '61		
Farrell, John C.	July 13, '61		
Fernandez, E. A.	July 13, '61	April 9, '65	Sergeant; wounded, Williamsburg May 5, '63.
Flynn, William H.	July 13, '61		
Fripp, Augustus D.	July 13, '61		
Flynn, James M.	July 13, '61		
Farley, Mathew	July 13, '61		
Griffith, Samuel	July 13, '61		Wounded at Seven Pines May 31, '61.
Gardner, Charles	July 13, '61		
Goston, S.	July 13, '61		Thigh broken at Chancellorsville
Higginbotham, Aaron	July 13, '61	April 9, '65	
Hogarth, Robert S.	July 13, '61	April 9, '65	
Hardin, William	July 13, '61		
Harris, A. J.	July 13, '61	April 9, '65	Musician.
Harris, Hugh	July 13, '61		Wounded at Gettysburg July 3, '63.
Harris, A. Jackson	July 13, '61		Musician.
Hurlburt, David S.	July 13, '61		Wounded at Seven Pines May 31, '62.
Johnson, James	July 13, '61		Wounded Second Manassas; promoted Captain Co. E, 2nd Regiment.
Johnson, Charles W.	July 13, '61	April 9, '65	Wounded, Seven Pines May 31, '62; Petersburg, April 2, '65.
Jordan, Manual C.	July 13, '61	April 9, '65	
Kennedy, James	July 13, '61		
L'Engle, John C.	July 13, '61		
Long, H. V.	July 13, '61		Wounded at Gettysburg July 3, '63.
Long, David	July 13, '61		Wounded at Frazier's Farm June 30, '62.
Lawrence, Alexander	July 13, '61		
Leary, Joseph W.	July 13, '61		
Lee, John	July 13, '61	April 9, '65	
Livingston, William E.	July 13, '61		Private; promoted Sergeant; wounded at Gaines' Farm June 27, '62; Gettysburg July 3, '63.
L'Engle, Edward M.	July 13, '61		Corporal; promoted Captain and Assistant Quartermaster May 10, '62; wounded at Gaines' Farm June 27, '62.
Lumpkin, J. T.	July 13, '61		Sergeant; mortally wounded at Petersburg.
Mickler, George C.	July 13, '61		Corporal May 10; killed at Seven Pines May 31, '62
Mickler, Jacob			Killed in '64.
Masters, Bartolo	July 13, '61	April 9, '65	Wounded Seven Pines May 31, '62.
McClelland, Hiram	July 13, '61	April 9, '65	Wounded Seven Pines May 31, '62; Gettysburg, July 13, '63.
McClelland, Robert	July 13, '61		Killed at Frazier's Farm June 30, '62.
McMullen, Henry	July 13, '61		
Mixon, David	July 13, '61		
McCann, Frank	July 13, '61		
Nichols, Newman	July 13, '61		
Parr, Henry	July 13, '61		
Pendarvis, George A.	July 13, '61		

Roll Company G (St. John's Grays)—2nd Florida Infantry.
(CONTINUED.)

NAMES	MUSTERED IN.	MUSTERED OUT.	REMARKS.
Raker, David, Jr.	July 13, '61	April 9, '65	
Register, James	July 13, '61		Wounded, Seven Pines May 31; Frazier's Farm June 30, '62.
Revel, John	July 13, '61		Wounded at Gettysburg July 3, '63.
Robarts, Edgar	July 13, '61		Wounded at Williamsburg May 5, '62.
Robarts, James	July 13, '61	April 9, '65	Orderly Sergeant May 10, '62: wounded Seven
Richardson, William	July 13, '61		Pines May 31. '62.
Stewart, John F	July 13, '61	April 9, '65	
Reny, D.	July 13, '61		Lost arm at Chancellorsville; discharged May 3,
Solayre, Antonio	July 13, '61	April 9, '65	'63.
Smith, William	July 13, 61		
Small, James	July 13, '61		
Syms, Robert	July 13, '61		Corporal; killed at Seven Pines May 31, '62,
Syms, John	July 13, '61		
Sapp, John J	July 13, '61		
Swan D.	July 13, '61		Promoted Sergeant; killed at Fredericksburg December 13, '62.
Turner, Benjamin H	July 13, '61		
Turney, Thomas	July 13, '61		
Turney, William T.	July 13, '61		Wounded at Frazier's Farm, June 30, '62.
Taitt, Robert	July 13, '61		
Urwich, Barnett	July 13, '61		
Wilson, Robert R.	July 13, '61		Wounded at Seven Pines May 31, '62.
Wilson, Henry C	July 13, '61		Wounded at Frazier's Farm June 30, '62.
Williams, Peter	July 13, '61		
Wright, Thomas O.	July 13, '61		

Roll Company H (St. Augustine Rifles)—2nd Florida Infantry.

NAMES.	MUSTERED IN.	MUSTERED OUT.	REMARKS.
OFFICERS.			
Captains—			
John W. Starke	July 13, '61		Retired on reorganization May 10, '62.
Alexander Moseley	July 13, '61	April 9, '65	2nd Lieutenant, re-enlisted May, '62; promoted Capt. May, '62; then Major.
A. M. Carlisle	July 13, '61		Corporal, re-enlisted May 10, '62 and promoted 1st Lieutenant, then Captain '64; wounded, Seven Pines May 31, '62.
1st Lieutenant—			
C. Seton Fleming	July 13, '61		Wounded, Williamsburg May 5, '62; captured and exchanged Aug. 5, and reported for duty, promoted Adjutant of 2nd Regiment, Captain Company G, 2nd Regiment; killed at Cold Harbor June 3, '64.
David L. Dunham	July 13, '61	April '65	2nd Sergeant, promoted, 1st Lieutenant, wounded, Seven Pines May 31, '62; Gaines' Farm June 27, '62, Frazier's Farm June 30, '62; captured at Gettysburg, imprisoned on Johnson's Island, detailed Feb. '65.
2nd Lieutenant—			
J. E. Caine	July 13, '61		Retired at reorganization.
William B. Watson	July 13, '61	April '65	1st Sergeant, promoted 2nd Lieutenant, May 10, '62
3rd Lieutenant—			
F. Baya	July 13, '61		Died on Johnson's Island Feb. 23, '64; Grave No. 159.
ENLISTED MEN.			
Alverson, J. C.	July 13, '61		
Anderson, J. P. T.	July 13, '61		
Baisden, George	July 13, '61		
Baker, F.	July 13, '61		
Baker, J. D.	July 13, '61		
Baltzell, Frank	July 13, '61		Wounded, Seven Pines May 31, '62.
Beasley, E.	July 13, '61		Wounded, Ellison's Mill June 26, '62.
Bennett, P. J.	July 13, '61		Musician.
Bishop, James E.	July 13, '61	April '65	Re-enlisted May 10, '62.
Boyde, T. C.	July 13, '61		Wounded, Seven Pines May 31, '62.
Bradley, B. H.			Imprisoned at Fort Delaware.
Bradley, R.	July 13, '61		
Brown, B. F.	July 13, '61		Re-enlisted May 10, '62; wounded, Gaines' Farm June 27, '62.
Burroughs, B. Maxwell	July 13, '61	April '65	Promoted Sergeant, re-enlisted May 10, '62; transferred to Company F, 1st Cavalry, Dismounted Tenn., and promoted Captain, wounded, Frazier's Farm June 30, '62.
Burroughs, Eben W	July 13, '61	April '65	Re-enlisted May 10, '62; wounded, **Seven Pines.** May 31, '62.
Butler, R. S.	July 13, '61		....

Roll Company H (St. Augustine Rifles)—2nd Florida Infantry.
(CONTINUED.)

NAMES.	MUSTERED IN.	MUSTERED OUT.	REMARKS.
Caine, A.	July 13, '61		Re-enlisted May 10, '62; wounded, Seven Pines May 31, '62.
Caine, C.	July 13, '61		Re-enlisted May 10, '62.
Cason, J.	July 13, '61		
Cason, W.	July 13, '61		
Chandler, J. L.	July 13, '61		Re-enlisted May 10, '62; wounded, Frazier's Farm June 30, '62; captured at Gettysburg, imprisoned at Fort Delaware.
Crabtree, Henry.	July 13, '61		Re-enlisted May 10, '62; paroled from prison at close of war.
Crabtree, James.	July 13, '61		
Davis, E.	July 13, '61		
Davis, J. J.	July 13, '61		Re-enlisted May 10, '62; wounded, Ellison's Mill June 26, '62.
Dent, W.	July 13, '61		
Drawdy, B.	July 13, '61		
Dunham, H. C.	July 13, '61		
Dupont, B. E.	July 13, '61		Re-enlisted May 10, '62; wounded, Seven Pines May 31, '65.
Dupont, T. B.	July 13, '61		
DuPont, W. Abram.	July 13, '61		Re-enlisted May 10, '62; wounded Seven Pines May 31, '62, killed in service.
Fleming, Francis P.	July 13, '61	May '65	Re-enlisted May 5, '62; transferred to western army, promoted, 1st Lieutenant and Sergeant assigned to Co. D 1st Regiment Cavalry in Tenn.
Gallagher, Joseph.	July 13, '61		Re-enlisted May '62; wounded, Seven Pines May 31, '62.
Gray, John J.	July 13, '61		Corporal, re-enlisted May 5, '62; wounded at Williamsburg May 5, '62; Gaines' Farm June 27, '62.
Grover, D L.	July 13, '61		
Harper, T. W.	July 13, '61		Re-enlisted May 5, '62; wounded, Gaines' Farm June 27, '62.
Harris, S. B.	July 13, '61		
Hatch, J. L.	July 13, '61		Corporal, wounded at Williamsburg, May 5, '62
Hawes, George E.	July 13, '61		
Hemmingway, J. A.	July 13, '61		Re-enlisted May 5, '62; killed at Frazier's Farm June 3, '62.
Hickman, H. J.	July 13, '61		Re-enlisted May 2, '62; wounded, Williamsburg May 5, '62; Frazier's Farm June 30, '62.
Hogans, J. R.	July 13, '61		
Holliman, George.	July 13, '61		Re-enlisted May 5, '64; wounded Seven Pines May 31, '62.
Hull, E.	July 13, '61		Re-enlisted May '62; wounded Gaines' Farm June 27, '62; Gettysburg July 3, '63.
Hull, J. T.	July 13, '61		Re-enlisted May, '62; wounded, Chancellorsville May '63
Humphreys, Edward C.	July 13, '61		Killed, 2nd battle of Manassas.
Ivers, John.	July, 13 '61		Re-enlisted May ,'62; killed ,Seven Pines May 31, '62.
Ivers, William.	July, 13 '61		Re-enlisted May, '62; wounded ,Seven Pines May 31, '62; transferred to Co. H 2nd Cavalry.
Jeffrey, J. A.	July 13, '61		Corporal.
Jennings, Wm. H.	July 13, '61	April 9, '65	
Joiner, J. B.	July 13, '61		
Jones, D. F.	July 13, '61		
Jones, J. H.	July 13, '61		
Jones, William.	July 13, '61		Re-enlisted May '62; wounded, Chancellorsville May, 1863.
Llambias, J. F.	July 13, '61		
Llambias, M. G.	July 13, '61		Sergeant, killed in service,
Latham, H.	July 13, '61		
Livingsten, J. H.	July 13, '61		
Maxwell, D. Elwell.	July 13, '61	April '65	Re-enlisted May, '62; transferred to 1st Dismounted Cavalry, wounded, Frazier's Farm June 3, '62; promoted Corporal May, '62; Captain '63, Company D 1st Cavalry Dismounted, Army Tenn.
Medcis, F.	July 13, '61		Re-enlisted May, '62; July 28, '64; wounded, Gettysburg July 3, '64, captured and imprisoned at Fort Delaware.
Minor, J.	July 13, '61		
Moore, A. M.	July 13, '61		
Moore, L. H.	July 13, '61		
O'Toole, J. J.	July 13, '61		
Paine, J.	July 13, '61		Musician.
Papy, Marino.	July 13, '61		Killed, Seven Pines May 31, '62.
Pellicio, Peter.	July 13, '61		Wounded, Seven Pines May 31, '62.
Perry, M. S.	July 13, '61		
Pharr, E.	July 13, '61		
Randell, W.	July 13, '61		
Redd, Raymond Jenkes.	July 13, '61		Sergeant, re-enlisted May 6, '62; Jan. 28, '64; wounded mortally at Wilderness May 5, '64; promoted 1st Lieutenant and Adjutant 2nd Florida Regiment.
Russell, J. A.	July 13, '61		
Sadler, N. B.	July 13, '61		
Sanchez, E. C.	July 13, '61		
Sanchez, M. R.	July 13, '61		Re-enlisted May, '62; wounded, Gettysburg July 4, '63.
Sapp, O.	July 13, '61		
Sapp, S.	July 13, '61		
Sharpe, J. M.	July 13, '61		
Sharpe, J. P.	July 13, '61		
Sheldon, George.	July 13, '61		

Roll Company H (St. Augustine Rifles)—2nd Florida Infantry.
(CONTINUED.)

NAMES.	MUSTERED IN.	MUSTERED OUT.	REMARKS.
Smith, George R.	July 13, '61		Re-enlisted May, '62; killed, Frazier's Farm June 30, '63.
Smith, Samuel B.	July 13, '61		
Smith, Samuel P.	July 13, '61		Wounded, Chancellorsville May 13, '63.
Spears, William	July 13, '61		
Summers, W.	July 13, '61		
Sykes, Isaac P.	July 13, '61		
Taylor, John W.	July 13, '61		
Terrell, G. W.	July 13, '61		
Tolle, P. H.	July 13, '61		
Vinzant, James J.	July 13, '61	April 9, '65	Re-enlisted May, '62; wounded, Frazier's Farm June, '62; Gettysburg July 3, '63.
Walker, A. T.	July 13, '61	April 9, '65	Promoted Sergeant.
Warren, J. C.	July 13, '61		
Wheeler	July 13, '61		Wounded, Chancellorsville May 3, '65.
Wickwire, John	July 13, '61		
Wightman, A. J.	July 13, '61		

Roll Company I (Jasper Blues)—2nd Florida Infantry.

NAMES.	MUSTERED IN.	MUSTERED OUT.	REMARKS.
OFFICERS.			
Captains—			
Henry J. Stewart	July 13, '61		Retired at reorganization May 10, '62.
Moses L. Duncan	July 13, '61		2nd Lieutenant, promoted Captain, May 10, '62; resigned October 29, '63.
1st Lieutenants—			
John Q. Stewart	July 13, '61		Retired at reorganization May 10, '62.
James M. Underwood	July 13, '61		Promoted 1st Lieutenant.
2nd Lieutenants—			
Henry De Loach	July 13, '61		2nd Lieutenant, killed at Culpepper Court House
John W. Hall	July 13, '61		Promoted 1st Lieutenant; wounded at Gettysburg July 3, '63.
ENLISTED MEN.			
Allen, McPherson B.	July 13, '61		Wounded, Frazier's Farm June 3, '62.
Bancroft, Henry	July 13, '61		
Bellotte, Henry	July 13, '61	April 9 '65	Williamsburg, May 5, '62; Frazier's Farm June 30, '62.
Bellotte, John	July 13, '61		Died in service.
Bellotte, William	July 13, '61	April 9, '65	Wounded, Seven Pines May 30, '62; Gettysburg July 3, '63.
Boyde, William I.	July 13, '61		Reported dead Feb. 28, '62.
Bryant, Brown	July 13, '61		
Bryan, Phet	July 13, '61	April 9, '65	
Bryan, Reed Asa	July 13, '61		Died in service.
Bryant, William A.	July 13, '61		
Byrd, William	July 13, '61		
Cason, Willie E.	July 13, '61	April 9, '65	Wounded, Seven Pines May 31, '62.
Cheshire, John R.	July 13, '61		Wounded mortally at Gaines' Farm June 27, '62; died in Richmond Field Hospital.
Cheshire, Nathaniel	July 13, '61		
Cheshire, Thomas	July 13, '61	Feb. 28, '62	Because insane.
Clemons, James	July 13, '61		Reported dead Feb. 28, '62.
Coalson, Ross L.	July 13, '61		Deserted.
Cockfield, Solomon	July 13, '61		Wounded, Williamsburg May 5, '62.
Cross, Benjamin F.	July 13, '61	April 9, '65	Wounded, Seven Pines May 5, '62.
Cross, Edward	July 13, '61		Reported dead Feb. 28, '62.
Calbreath, Lewis	July 13, '61		
Daniel, S. W.	July 13, '61		
Day, James H.	July 13, '61		Wounded, Frazier's Farm June 30, '62.
Day, Thomas	July 13, '61	Feb. '62	Cause: insane.
De Loach, Zachariah	July 13, '61	April 9, '65	
Demere, John F.	July 13, '61		Corporal.
Demary, Hardy S.	July 13, '61	Sept. '63	Cause: disability, wounded at Gettysburg July 3, '63; lost left arm.
Dormany, James A.	July 13, '61		
Dozier, James	July 13, '61		Reported dead Feb. 28, '62.
Elliot, James M.	July 13, '61		
Farrell, Thos.	July 13, '61	Feb. 28, '62	
Findley, James	July 13, '61		
Fletcher, Joshua E.	July 13, '61		Sergeant, died March 1, '62.
Gerry, Chas. E. W.	July 13, '61		Wounded, Frazier's Farm June 30, '62.
Grant, John	July 13, '61		
Green, Riley	July 13, '61		Reported died in prison, Feb. 28, '62.
Groonstine, Henry C.	July 13, '61		Sergeant, wounded, Gettysburg July 3, '65.
Hall, Francis M.	July 13, '61		Discharged from Fort Delaware at close of War;
Hall, James A.	July 13, '61		wounded, Frazier's Farm June 30, '62 and captured and imprisoned at Fort Delaware.
Hall, Scott N.	July 13, '61	April 9, '65	Wounded, Seven Pines May 31, '62.
Harris, Elias L.	July 13, '61		

Roll Company I (Jasper Blues)—2nd Florida Infantry.

(CONTINUED.)

NAMES.	MUSTERED IN.	MUSTERED OUT.	REMARKS.
Higden, William H	July 13, '61		Sergeant, died in service.
Holmes, Henry A	July 13, '61	April 9, '65	
Jackson, Henry D	July 13, '61	Feb. 28, '62	
Jackson, William G	July 13, '61		Reported discharged Feb. 28, '63.
Johns, A. J	May 2, '64		
Kelly, H. G. W	July 13, '61		Died in service.
Kent, Jackson	July 13, '61		Reported dead Feb. 28, '62.
Kindrick, John	July 13, '61		Wounded, Seven Pines May 31, '62.
King, Ziba	July 13, '61		Reported as a deserter Feb. 28, '62; (Record taken from roll March 1, '62; signed by Lieut.-St. Geo. Rogers and Capt. Stewart.)
Langford, George	July 13, '61		Reported discharged Feb. 28, '62.
McCormick, James	July 13, '61		Wounded, Williamsburg May 5, '62.
McInnis, Edward	July 13, '61		Died in service.
McInnis, John	July 13, '61		Wounded, Williamsburg May 5, '62.
McLeod, William H. H.	July 13, '61		Promoted Sergeant, killed at Gettysburg.
McNesee, William T. M.	July 13, '61		Wounded, Frazier's Farm June 30, '62; promoted Sergeant May 10, '62.
Matthis, Bungan	July 13, '61		Reported discharged Feb. 28, '62.
Matthis, Charlten	July 13, '61		
Matthis, Kelton	July 13, '61		Reported discharged Feb. 28, '61.
Matthis, William	July 13, '61		Wounded, Seven Pines May 31, '62.
Mitchell, Samuel A	July 13, '61	April 9, 65	
Morrow, Daniel	July 13, '61		
Nelson, Jesse	July 13, '61		Reported dead Feb. 28, '62.
Nelson, John	July 13, '61		Reported dead Feb. 28, '62.
Nobles, John A	July 13, '61	April 9, '65	
Overstreet, John C	July 13, '61	April 9, '65	Wounded, Gettysburg July 3, '63.
Overstreet, S. T.	July 13, '61	April 9, '65	Transferred to Medical Department as Assistant Surgeon April ,'63.
Overstreet, Thomas L	July 13, '61		Wounded, Seven Pines, died in service.
Overstreet, William R	July 13, '61		Discharged prior to Feb. 28, '62.
Parr, John	July 13, '61		Musician, discharged prior Feb. 28, '62.
Perry, John R	July 13, '61	April 9, '65	Wounded, Frazier's Farm June 30, '62.
Perry, Owen F	July 13, '61	April 9, '65	Imprisoned at Fort Delaware.
Purviance, John S	July 13, '61		Sergeant, discharged prior to Feb. 28, '62.
Penningten, Jesse	July 13, '61		Killed, Seven Pines May 31, '62.
Penningten, Walter P	July 13, '61		Wounded, Frazier's Farm June 3, '62.
Powell, Lewis P	July 13, '61		Re-enlisted for the War; was hung in Washington with Mrs. Suratt.
Rouse, Ira S	July 13, '61		Corporal.
Shirley, Calvin	July 13, '61	Feb. 28, '62	
Shiver, George	July 13, '61		Wounded, Gaines' Farm June 27, '62.
Shiver, Isaac —	July 13, '61	April 9, '65	
Sills, James	July 13, '61	Feb. 28, '62	
Slade, William	July 13, '61		
Starling, Thomas C	July 13, '61	April 9, '65	
Stewart, David M	July 13, '61	'63	
Stringheard, William	July 13, '61		Wounded, Gettysburg June 3, '63.
Sutton, W. R.	July 13, '61		
Taylor, James W	July 13, '61		
Thomas, Caswell	July 13, '61		Wounded, Frazier's Farm June 30, '62.
Thombley, Edward	July 13, '61		Wounded, Gettysburg July 3, '63; imprisoned at Fort Delaware.
Tootle, William W	July 13, '61		Reported dead Feb. 28, '62.
Walden, Lemuel	July 13, '61		
Walker, Berry	July 13, '61	April 9, '65	
Walker, Nathan B	July 13, '61		Corporal, Wounded, Williamsburg May 5, '62
Watson, Thomas J	July 13, '61		Killed, Gaines' Farm June 27, '62.
Watson, William C	July 13, '61		Discharged prior Feb. 28, '62.
Williams, Washington	July 13, '61		Wounded, Seven Pines May 31, '62; Frazier's Farm June 30, '62; promoted Corporal May 10, '62.
Willis, Jesse	July 13, '61		Wounded, Frazier's Farm June 30, '62.
Willis, William	July 13, '61	April 9, '65	
Worre, Pleasant	July 13, '61		Deserted to the enemy at Culerkey, Florida.
Woodle, Ansel	July 13, '61		Wounded, Frazier's Farm June 27, '62.
Woodward, M. F. F.	July 13, '61		

Incorporated in the above is a copy of a roll of Company I: Henry J. Stewart, Commander, Wynns' Mill, March 1, 1862. The facts set forth as to a death discharge, commitment to asylum and desertion are certified to by Capt. Stewart and by S. St. Geo. Rogers, Lieut. Colonel 2nd Florida and Inspecting and Mustering Officer.

Roll Company K (Davis Guards)—2nd Florida Infantry.

NAMES.	MUSTERED IN.	MUSTERED OUT.	REMARKS.
OFFICERS.			
Captains—			
George W. Call	July 13, '61		Promoted Major, May 10, '61; Killed at Seven Pines, May 31, '61.
A. C. Butler	July 13, '61		2nd Lieutenant, promoted Capt. May 10, '62; killed, Seven Pines, May 31, '62.
John B. G. Oneil	July 13, '61		Sergeant, promoted 1st Lieutenant, May 10, '62; promoted Capt. June '62 on death of Capt. Butler; wounded at Seven Pines, May 31, '62.
1st Lieutenant—			
E. C. Simkins	July 13, '61		Retired May 10, '62, at reorganization.
2nd Lieutenant—			
Oscar Stewart	July 13, '61		Promoted 2nd Lieutenant.
3rd Lieutenant—			
James F. Tucker	July 13, '61		
ENLISTED MEN.			
Adams, W. A.	July 13, '61		Wounded, Williamsburg, May 5, '62; promoted Sergeant May 10, '62.
Arnold, George	July 13 '61		Wounded, Seven Pines, May 31, '62.
Batton, Robert N.	July 13, '61		Wounded, Gettysburg, July 2, '63.
Black, Alexander	July 13, '61		Killed, Frazier's Farm June 26, '62.
Blanchard, C. W.	July 13, '61		Sergeant.
Blitch, Joseph	July 13, '61		
Bowden, James F.	July 13, '61		Corporal.
Brand, Henery	July 13, '61		
Brantley, G. C.	July 13, '61		
Brockingten, R. W.	July 13, '61		Killed at Frazier's Farm June 30, '62.
Bryan, S. P.	July 13, '61		Wounded, Seven Pines May 31, '62.
Burkeet, John	July 13, '61		
Butler, Allen	July 13, '61		Wounded at Seven Pines May 31, '62.
Butler, L. M.	July 13, '61		Sergeant.
Butler, Martin	July 13, '61		
Byce, Jonathan	July 13, '61		Wounded, Seven Pines May 31, '62.
Cameron, George	July 13, '61		
Carvane, George	July 13, '61		
Clark, Labun J.	July 13, '61		Wounded, Seven Pines May 31, '62.
Cole, Richard	July 13 '61		Wounded, Seven Pines May 31 '62.
Cooper, M. R.	July 13, '61	April 9, '65	Wounded, Frazier's Farm June 30, '62.
Cowden, Samuel	July 13, '61		
Curtis, F. O.	July 13, '61		
Darby, John W.	July 13, '61		Corporal.
De Cottes, E, F.	July 13, '61		Wounded, Seven Pines May 31, '62,.
Demot, J.	July 13, '61		
Drummond. J. B.	July 13, '61		Wounded, Gaines' Farm June 27, '62.
Duke, N. B.	July 13, '61		
Durrance, George	July 13, '61		
Edwards, J. F.	July 13, '61		Wounded, Seven Pines May 31, '62.
Edwards, T. H.	July 13, '61		
Eddy, Jock	July 13, '61		
Etkens, Loit	July 13, '61		
Floyd, Samuel	July 13, '61		
Fountain, David	July 13, '61		Musician.
Futch, Isaac	July 13, '61	April 9 '65	
Gibbs, J. C.	July 13, '61		Wounded, Gaines' Farm June 27, '62.
Gillett, Robert	July 13, '61		
Given, Thomas W.	July 13, '61	April 9, '65	Transferred, 8th., promoted 2nd Lieutenant Co. K., promoted Q. M. Sergeant.
Gray, Allen	July 13, '61		Wounded, Frazier's Farm June 30 '62.
Green, Edward	July 13, '61		
Gould, J. D.	July 13, '61	April 9, '65	1st Sergeant.
Groomstine, H. C.	July 13, '61		Wounded, Gettysburg July 3, '63.
Gwynn, James	July 13, '61		
Hall, I. J.	July 13, '61		
Harris, F. W.	July 13, '61		
Hamson, Ephnam	July 13, '61	April 9, '65	Corporal, wounded Sharpsburg Sept. 17, '62; Petersburg Sept. 8, '64.
Harville, Samuel	July 13, '61		Wounded, Bristow Station Oct. 14, '63.
Hatcher, William	July 13, '61		
Hewritt, John	July 13, '61		
Higgenbotham, Aaron	July 13, '61		
Highsmith, S. J.	July 13, '61		
Hodge, Westbury B.	July 13, '61	April 9, '65	Wounded, Gettysburg July 2, '63.
Hyams, M. E.	July 13, '61		
Jackson, Wyatt	July 13, '61		Wounded, Williamsburg May 5, '62.
Jennings, W. H.	July 13, '61	April 9, '65	
Johnson, George	July 13, '61		
Johnson, John	July 13, '61		Corporal.
Johnson, W. C.	July 13, '61	April 9, '65	Wounded, Petersburg, Va. April 3, '65.
Kilburn, Theo. E.	July 13, '61		
Koerner, P, W. O.	July 13, '61		Sergeant.
Lany, Nathaniel	July 13, '61		Killed at Seven Pines May 31, '62.
Mercer, W. J.	July 13, '61	April 9, '65	
Miller, John	July 13, '61		
Moore, E. A.	July 13, '61	April 9, '65	Wounded, Seven Pines May 31, '62.
Moore, L.	July 13, '61		Wounded, Seven Pines May 31, '62.

Roll Company K (Davis Guards)—2nd Florida Infantry.
(CONTINUED.)

NAMES.	MUSTERED IN.	MUSTERED OUT.	REMARKS.
Manson, J. M.	July 13, '61		Wounded, Seven Pines May 31, '62.
Murphy, P.	July 13, '61		
Nolan, John	July 13, '61		Wounded, Ellison's Mills June 26, '62.
Pacetti, Louis	July 13, '61		
Parrish, John W.	July 13, '61		Killed, Seven Pines May 31, '62.
Philips H. L.	July 13, '61		
Philips, W. N.	July 13, '61		Musician.
Reddick, Francis	July 13, '61		
Reddick, George	July 13, '61		Killed, Gettysburg, July 3, '63.
Reddick, Peter	July 13, '61		Wounded, Williamsburg May 5, '62.
Reed, H. C.	July 13, '61		
Rollins, Thos. N.	July 13, '61		
Rowell, W. J. J.	July 13, '61		
Roux, Edwin	July 13, '61		
Russell, R. H.	July 13, '61		
Russell, R. R.	July 13, '61		
Sabal, E. T.	July 13, '61		
Sanders, W. H.	July 13, '61		
Sanders, T. W.	July 13, '61		
Saunders, T.	July 13, '61		Wounded, Seven Pines May 31, '62.
Sheilces, Edwane	July 13, '61		
Skinner, Oliver	July 13, '61		
Salee, W. F.	July 13, '61		Wounded, Williamsburg May 5, Seven Pines May 31, '62; promoted Sergeant May 10, '61.
Speers, John	July 13, '61		Killed, Seven Pines May 31, '62.
Stewart, George	July 13, '61		
Stewart, Henery	July 13, '61		
Taylor, Ephriam	July 13, '61		Wounded, Gaines' Farm June 27, '62.
Tomlinson, N. N.	July 13, '61		
Tomlinson, William	July 13, '61		
Walker, L. F.	July 13, '61	April 9, '65	Wounded, Gettysburg July 3, '63.
Walker, P. J.	July 13, '61		
Walsh Valentine	July 13, '61		
Ward, Patrick	July 13, '61		
Wilkenson, J. W.	July 13, '61		Wounded, Gaines' Farm, June 27, '61.
Williams William	July 13, '61		
Wright, Abner	July 13, '61		
Wright, Augustus	July 13, '61		
Wright, Mitchell	July 13, '61		
Wright, William	July 13, '61		
Young, Henery	July 13, '61		

Roll Company L (Madison Rangers)—2nd Florida Infantry.

NAMES.	MUSTERED IN.	MUSTERED OUT.	REMARKS.
OFFICERS.			
Captains—			
William P. Pillans	July 13, '61		Resigned May 10, '62, at reorganization.
Thomas A. Perry	July 13, '61		1st Lieutenant; promoted Captain; killed, Seven Pines May 31, '62.
W. H. H. Rogers	July 13, '61		Corporal; promoted 1st Lieutenant May 10, '62; Captain; killed at Chancellorsville April, '63.
W. H. Croom	July 13, '61	April 9, '65	Promoted Corporal, Lieutenant, then Captain.
1st Lieutenant—			
J. R. Kimbrew	July 13, '61		Corporal; promoted 2nd Lieutenant May 10, '62; then 1st Lieutenant; wounded, Seven Pines May 31, '62 and disabled in '64.
2nd Lieutenants—			
F. J. B. Fox	July 13, '61		Sergeant; promoted 2nd Lieutenant; retired at reorganization; re-enlisted in Florida Light Artillery.
James T. Mathis	July 13, '61		Promoted 2nd Lieutenant.
3rd Lieutenants—			
T. M. Anderson	July 13, '61		Promoted 3rd Lieutenant; retired May 10, '62; died at home in '62.
L. Maynard Perry	July 13, '61	April 9, '65	1st Sergeant; promoted 3rd Lieutenant; wounded and disabled at Rappahanock Station.
ENLISTED MEN.			
Adams, J. T. C.	July 13, '61		Wounded, Ellison's Mills June 26, '62.
Allen, M. P.	July 13, '61		
Arnold, E. J.	July 13, '61		
Arnold, R. N.	July 13, '61		
Barker, Jerry	July 13, '61	April 9, '65	
Bird, J. A.	July 13, '61		Wounded at Seven Pines May 31, '62.
Bishop, J. T.	July 13, '61		Wounded at Seven Pines May 31, '62.
Boatwright, John W.	July 13, '61	April 9, '65	
Bonds, R. O.	July 13, '61		Wounded at Seven Pines May 31, '62.
Bonds, Sanford	July 13, '61	April 9, '65	
Boyette, H.	July 13, '61		

Roll Company L (Madison Rangers)—2nd Florida Infantry.

(CONTINUED.)

NAMES.	MUSTERED IN.	MUSTERED OUT.	REMARKS.
Briant, R.	July 13, '61		
Brooks, M. R. C.	July 13, '61		Sergeant; wounded, Seven Pines May 31, '62.
Bryant, W. B.	July 13, '61	April 9, '65	2nd Corporal,
Burleson, Daniel D.	July 13, '61		
Burney, C.	July 13, '61		
Carver, Elijah	July 13, '61		
Carver, J. N.	July 13, '61		
Carver, S. B.	July 13, '61		
Crawford, N.	July 13, '61		Promoted Corporal; killed at Williamsburg May 5, '62.
Cruce, T. O.	July 13, '61		
Dampeir, E.	July 13, '61		Wounded, Gettysburg July 3, '63.
Drew, J. M.	July 13, '61		Promoted Corporal; killed, Seven Pines May 31, '62.
Easters, J. S.	July 13, '61		
Edwards, Ellsbury	July 13, '61		
Edwards, Wiley.	July 13, '61		
Eggitt, J. H.	July 13, '61		
Espy, James G.	July 13, '61		Died at Danville.
Evers, David K.	July 13, '61		Musician; wounded Seven Pines May 31, '62.
Ezzell, J. H.	July 13, '61		Wounded, Williamsburg May 5, '62.
Fox, F. J. B.	July 13, '61		Sergeant.
Green, Evers E.	July 13, '61		Wounded, Seven Pines May 31, '62.
Green, R.	July 13, '61		
Hernden, G. M.	July 13, '61		Killed, Ellison's Mill June 26, '62.
Hogan, J. C.	July 13, '61		Wounded, Seven Pines May 31, '62.
Hogan, T. M.	July 13, '61		
Horten, J. J.	July 13, '61	April 9, '65	Wounded, Seven Pines May 31, '62.
Johnson, B. R.	July 13, '61		
Jordon, T. C.	July 13, '61		Discharged, '63; insanity.
Lamb, W. H.	July 13, '61	April 9, '65	Promoted Corporal.
Lanier, Benjamin	July 13, '61		Killed, Seven Pines May 31, '62.
Lanier, Clem	July 13, '61		Promoted Sergeant; discharged honorably;
Lee, John.	July 13, '61	April 9, '65	wounded Sharpsburg April 17, '62; lost left leg.
Lee, Levi	July 13, '61	April 9, '65	
Lewis, F.	July 13, '61		Wounded, Gaines' Farm June 27, '62.
Lewis, Thomas.	July 13, '61		Musician.
McAlpine, Daniel M.	July 13, '61	April 9, '65	
McLeod, Benjamin	July 13, '61		
McClamma, W. R.	July 13, '61		
Miller, L. H.	July 13, '61		
Odum, George W.	July 13, '61	April 9, '65	
Parker, Jasper	July 13, '61		
Parker, Newten	July 13, '61		Wounded, Seven Pines May 3, '62.
Parker, W. M.	July 13, '61		Wounded, Gaines' Farm June 27, '62; captured at Gettysburg; discharged from prison May, '65.
Peterson, J. B.	July 13, '61		
Pigue, John.	July 13, '61		
Quiet, J. H.	July 13, '61		Wounded, Frazier's Farm June 30, '62.
Quiet, T. P.	July 13, '61		Wounded, Seven Pines May 31, '62.
Rowell, J. R.	July 13, '61		
Rutherford, T. T.	July 13, '61	April 9, '65	
Skipper, Needhum	July 13, '61		
Smith, S. J.	July 13, '61		
Stanford, J. H.	July 13, '61		
Stephens, James	July 13, '61		
Stewart, R. L.	July 13, '61	April 9, '65	
Sutten, J. H.	July 13, '61		Sergeant; wounded, Gettysburg July 3, '63; also at the Wilderness; discharged.
Tompkins, S. D.	July 13, '61		
Tompkins, T. H.	July 13, '61		
Turner, Thomas	July 13, '61		
Wadsworth, J. M.	July 13, '61		Wounded, Seven Pines May 31, '62.
Walker, W. J. R.	July 13, '61		
Webb, A. J.	July 13, '61		
Wells, A. J.	July 13, '61		Killed, Seven Pines May 31, '62.
White, R. M.	July 13, '61	April 9, '65	Wounded, Bristow Station October 14, '63; Petersburg September 14, '64.
Wheeler, J. N.	July 13, '61		
Wilder, E. M.	July 13, '61	April 9, '65	Transferred to Gamble's Battery.
Wilder, F. W.	July 13, '61		
Wilder, J. M.	July 13, '61		Wounded, Seven Pines May 31, '62.
Wilder, J. S.	July 13, '61		Killed at Frazier's Farm June 26, '62.
Wilder, T. J.	July 13, '61		Killed at Ellison's Mill June 26, '62.
Wilder, R. H.	July 13, '61		
Watson, James	July 13, '61		
Wilson, J. T.	July 13, '61		
Wilson, Thomas	July 13, '61		
Young, Joseph A.	July 13, '61	May '62	Promoted 1st Sergeant; re-enlisted and was killed in battle of Olustee February, '64.

Roll Company M (Howell Guards)—2nd Florida Infantry.

NAMES.	MUSTERED IN.	MUSTERED OUT.	REMARKS.
OFFICERS.			
Captains—			
George W. Parkhill	Aug. 20, '61		Killed, Gaines' Farm June, '62.
Richard C. Parkhill	Ang. 20, '61		3rd Lieutenant; promoted Captain, '62; wounded at Frazier's Farm; resigned latter part of '62.
Elliott L. Hampton	Aug. 20, '61		3rd Sergeant; promoted 3rd Lieutenant December 27, '61; then Captain; killed at Gettysburg July 3, '63.
Amos Whitehead	Aug. 20, '61		Sergeant; promoted 2nd Lieutenant December '61; wounded and disabled at Sharpsburg; resigned.
John Day Perkins	Aug. 20, '61		1st Corporal; promoted Lieutenant; then Captain; wounded and disabled at Gettysburg; captured and imprisoned at Cape Henry and Point Lookout; exchanged March 9, '64.
.... Bailey			
Julian Betton	Aug. 20, '61		Promoted Sergeant December 29, '61; then Captain; wounded July 2, '63 at Gettysburg.
1st Lieutenant—			
John W. Eppes	Aug. 20, '61		1st Lieutenant; resigned May, '61; in August was commissioned as regular Surgeon in C. S. A. by James Seldon, Secretary of War; also served as Surgeon in Cavalry.
2nd Lieutenants—			
Robert H. Partridge	Aug. 20, '61		Resigned.
William A. Ball	Aug. 20, '61		Corporal; promoted Lieutenant; captured at Gettysburg.
3rd Lieutenant—			
ENLISTED MEN.			
Akard, John	Aug. 20, '61		
Alexander, Robert T	Aug. 20, '61		Deserted.
Armstrong, N. A	Aug. 20, '61	April 9, '65	Wounded at Gettysburg July 2, '63.
Avers, Henry	Aug. 20, '61		Deserted August 21, '61.
Baker, Montford J	Aug. 20, '61		
Barkley, Thadius S	Aug. 20, '61		Discharged November 23, '61, for rheumatism.
Bentley, Reid M	Aug. 20, '61	April 9, '65	
Billingsley, Henry C	Aug. 20, '61		Wounded at Gettysburg July 2, '63.
Bowen, George A	Aug. 20, '61		
Brannon, J. R. B	Aug. 20, '61		
Brown, Edd. D	Aug. 20, '61		Transferred to Co. K, then Co. A, 6th Infantry.
Brown, Gustavus	Aug. 20, '61	April 9, '65	
Bryant, Jeremiah	Aug. 20, '61		
Bryant, R	Aug. 20, '61	April 9, '65	
Campbell, Neil	Aug. 20, '61	April 9, '65	Promoted Sergeant.
Carman, Albert V	Aug. 20, '61		
Carman, Samuel A	Aug. 20, '61		
Chason, Claborn	Aug. 20, '61		Died November 7, '61.
Chason, Owen	Aug. 20, '61		
Chestnut, David	Aug. 20, '61		
Clear, William M	Aug. 20, '61		
Coker, John	Aug. 20, '61		
Connelly, Thomas	Aug. 20, '61		Deserted September 27, '61.
Corniff, Daniel	Aug. 20, '61		Wounded, Frazier's Farm June 30, '62; deserted.
Corniff, Patrick	Aug. 23, '61	April 9, '65	Wounded, Gettysburg July 3, '63; re-enlisted January 28, '64.
Demilly, John T	Aug. 20, '61		Transferred to Gamble's Battery.
Denmark, Jasper	Aug. 20, '61		
Denmark, Newton	Aug. 20, '61	April 9, '65	Promoted Corporal.
Denmark, S	Aug. 20, '61		Wounded at Gettysburg July 3, '63.
Dice, George	Aug. 20, '61		Lost an arm.
Dillon, Michael	Aug. 20, '61		Wounded at Gaines' Farm June 27, '62.
Dobson, John N	Aug. 26, '61		Wounded at Gaines' Farm June 27, '62.
Donaldson, Henry	Dec. 21, '61		
Duffy, Patrick	Aug. 23, '61		Transferred to Navy September 25, '61.
Dyke, James H	Aug. 20, '61		Died at hospital in Richmond November 25, '61.
Easters, Giles T	Aug. 20, '61		
Ellis, Charles T	Aug. 20, '61	April 9, '65	
Eppes, Nicholas W	Aug. 20, '61	April 9, '65	2nd Sergeant and Drill master; transferred to Co. C, 5th Infantry.
Falon, Patrick	Aug. 23, '61		Wounded at Frazier's Farm June 30, '62.
Footman, John Maxwell	Aug. 20, '61		Wounded at Evansport, Va., December 31, '61.
Fulford, Jordan	Dec. 21, '61	April 9, '65	Promoted Sergeant.
Fulford, P	Dec. 21, '61	April 9, '65	
Green, James	Aug. 20, '61		
Gregory, John R	Aug. 20, '61		2nd Corporal.
Hampton, B. Wade	Aug. 20, '61		Discharged December, '61; furnished substitute.
Hargrove, J	Aug. 20, '61	April 9, '65	
Hargrove, James W	Aug. 20, '61		Died in Richmond.
Herndon, Green L	Aug. 20, '61		
Herndon, James W	Aug. 20, '61		
Herndon, Jerrott	Aug. 20, '61		Wounded at Frazier's Farm June 30, '62; also at Gettysburg July 2, '63.
Herndon, Nathaniel G. L	Aug. 20, '61		
Holland, Nathaniel W	Aug. 20, '61		1st Sergeant.
Horn, R. Benjamin M	Aug. 20, '61		Wounded at Ellison's Mill June 26, '62; at Gettysburg July 3, '63.
Hoyle, William H	Aug. 20, '61		
Humphries, Charles D	Aug. 20, '61		Deserted August 21, '61.

Roll Company **M** (Howell Guards)—2nd Florida Infantry.

(CONTINUED.)

NAMES.	MUSTERED IN.	MUSTERED OUT.	REMARKS.
Ivey, James M.	Aug. 20, '61		Discharged by order of War Department December 3, '61; ill health.
Jerkins, Richard A.	Aug. 20, '61		Discharged December 3, '61.
Johnson, Abram B.	Aug. 20, '61		
Jerkins, R. A.	Aug. 20, '61		Killed at Frazier's Farm June 30, '62.
Julian, David B.	Aug. 20, '61		
Kent, Reuben.	Aug. 20, '61		
Kindon, Edward T.	Aug. 20, '61		
Kindon, T. E. W.	Aug. 20, '61		Wounded at Frazier's Farm June 30, '62.
Lawrence, Theodore.	Aug. 20, '61		Died, typhoid fever, hospital Dumphries, Va., December 21, '61.
Lee, Allen M.	Aug. 20, '61		
Lewis, Elery.	Aug. 20, '61		
Lewis, James.	Aug. 20, '61		
McCants, Joseph L.	Aug. 20, '61		Promoted to Sergeant December 29, '61; killed at Frazier's Farm June 30, '62.
Paine, A.	Aug. 20, '61		Wounded at Gaines' Farm June 27, '62.
Papy, Francisco B.	Aug. 20, '61		Discharged September 9, '61, by order of Secretary of War.
Palmer, Johnathan R.	Aug. 20, '61		Discharged October 31, '61; ill health; order Secretary of War.
Porter, Edward L.	Aug. 20, '61	April 9, '65	In hospital at surrender.
Rogers, David C.	Aug. 20, '61		Died hospital Richmond October 18, '61.
Roney, Micheal.	Aug. 20, '61		
Sealey, James J.	Aug. 20, '61	April 9, '65	
Sherrod, John.	Aug. 20, '61		Died Richmond hospital September 26, '61.
Sherrod, William J.	Aug. 20, '61		
Shewman, William W,	Aug. 20, '61		Wounded Frazier's Farm June 30, '62; Gettysburg July 1, '63.
Shine, Thomas J.	Aug. 20, '61		Transferred to Davis' Regular Cavalry as Sergeant-Major November 7, '61.
Sirles, R. W.	Aug. 20, '61		Wounded at Gettysburg July 2, '63.
Spratt, John H.	Aug. 20, '61		Died Danville, Va., December 1, '61.
Strickland, Jackson.	Aug. 20, '61		Wounded Frazier's Farm June 30, '62.
Strickland, John.	Aug. 20, '61		Died hospital Richmond September 23, '61.
Sturgis, Duhart.	Aug. 20, '61		Promoted to Corporal August 12, '61.
Sturgis, Robert D.	Aug. 20, '61		Wounded Gaines' Farm June 27; Frazier's Farm June 30, '62.
Sunns, John.	Aug. 20, '61		Deserted July 31, '62.
Sweatman, Francis M.	Aug. 20, '61		Deserted at Richmond, Va., September 27, '61.
Taylor, Green B.	Aug. 20, '61		
Taylor, John W.	Aug. 20, '61		
Triplett, Thomas W.	Aug. 20, '61		Discharged by order of General French; substitute furnished.
Turnbull, Junius.	Aug. 20, '61	April 9, '65	Promoted to 3rd Sergeant December 29, '61; promoted 1st Sergeant.
Ward, Simon P.	Aug. 20, '61		Died at hospital Richmond November 28, '61.
Williams, A.	Aug. 20, '61		Promoted Sergeant; killed at Gettysburg July 3, '63.
Williams, Chesley.	Aug. 20, '61		Died at hospital Richmond, Va., September 12, '61
Williams, George C.	Aug. 20, '61	April 9, '65	Wounded at Frazier's Farm June 30, '62.
Williams, William A.	Aug. 20, '61		Wounded at Frazier's Farm June 30, '62; captured Gettysburg.
Wilson, David C, Jr.	Aug. 20, '61		Imprisoned at Fort Delaware.
Worrell, William H.	Aug. 20, '61		

THIRD FLORIDA INFANTRY.

The 3rd Florida Regiment was organized in July, 1861, and mustered into the Confederate service August 10, 1861, on Amelia Island and was composed of the following companies: Jacksonville Light Infantry, Duval county (Co. A), Capt. Holmes Steele; St. Augustine Blues, St. Johns county (Co. B), Capt. John Lott Philips; Hernando Guards (Wild Cats), Hernando county (Co. C), Capt. Walter Terry Saxon; Wakulla Guards, Wakulla county (Co. D), Capt. Daniel L. Frierson; ˙Jefferson Beauregards, Jefferson county (Co. E), Capt. Daniel E. Bird; Cow Boys, Duval county (Co. F), Capt. Lucius A. Hardee; Madison Grey Eagles, Madison county (Co. G), Capt. Thomas Langford; Jefferson Rifles, Jefferson county (Co. H) Capt. William O. Girardeau; Dixie Stars, Columbia county (Co. I), Capt. Jesse B. Wood; Columbia and

Suwannee Guards (Co. K), Capt. William Parker. An election of officers was held July 25, 1861. William S. Dilworth was elected Colonel; Arthur J. T. Wright, Lieutenant-Colonel; Lucius A. Church, Major. They were all members of the Regiment. Colonel Dilworth had enlisted as a private in the Jefferson Beauregards. Lieutenant-Colonel Wright was in command of the Columbia and Suwannee Guards, and Major Church was Lieutenant of the Madison Grey Eagles.

The Regimental Staff was as follows: Capt. Henry R. Teasdale as Quartermaster; he was afterward promoted Major and made District Quartermaster for Florida with his station at Lake City; Capt. E. Yulee, Commissary; Hill, Surgeon; Dr. D. Carn, Assistant Surgeon; Lieut. J. O. A. Gerry, Adjutant; David Lewis, Sergeant Major; W. T. Moseley, Jr., Quartermaster Sergeant; P. E. Lowe, Commissary Sergeant.

The Blues, Captain Philips, and the Jefferson Beauregards, Captain Bird, were stationed at St. Augustine; the Jacksonville Light Infantry, Captain Steele, and the Cow Boys, Captain Hardee, were stationed at the Bluff, near the mouth of the St. Johns; the other six companies of the Regiment were stationed at Fort Clinch, on Amelia Island near Fernandina. The Regiment saw but little active service during the first year of its organization, but did a great deal of hard work throwing up sand batteries on Amelia and Tolbert Islands and the defences in the eastern part of the State.

Companies E and H, under Captain Bird, were sent during the winter to New Smyrna to protect Government stores brought in from Nassau. In March, 1862, a detachment under Capt. Mathew H. Strain, who had succeeded Girardeau, engaged a number of launches from the Federal blockading vessels, which were attempting to land and destroy the stores; nearly all the occupants of the launches were killed, wounded or captured.

Early in 1862 the Confederate Government determined to shorten its lines of defense and abandon its works at the mouth of the St. Johns River and Amelia Island, and these last were occupied by the Federals about March 12.

On the night of March 24th Lieut. Thomas E. Strange of Co. K, and Lieut. Charles H. Ross and Frank Ross of Co. I, 3rd Florida, with ten volunteers, attacked the Federal picket at the "Brick Church," which stood where LaVilla Junction now stands, killing 4 and capturing 3 of the Federals; in this skirmish Lieutenant Strange was mortally wounded. After the evacuation of Fernandina and St. Johns Bluff, the companies not engaged in the Smyrna expedition were stationed at Cedar Keys.

In May the entire Regiment for the first time was brought together in camp at Midway, Gadsden county, preparatory to taking up its march for the Western Army, then in northern Mississippi. Many of the companies had already re-enlisted for the war and under the laws enacted for the reorganization of the Confederate army the term of all was extended and it was deemed best to have a re-election of officers to serve permanently with the company.

The election resulted in the choice of the following Field Officers, Staff appointments and Captains: Colonel, W. S. Dilworth; Lieutenant-Colonel, Lucius A. Church; Major, Edward Mashburn; Quartermaster, Captain Hickman; Commissary, Capt. D. Lewis; Surgeon, Doctor Carn; Assistant Surgeon, Dr. M. C. W. Jordan; Adjutant, H. Steele; Sergeant Major, C. H. Stebbins; Commissary Sergeant, P. E. Lowe; Ordnance Sergeant, Theodore Bridier; Quartermaster Sergeant, William P. Moseley; Hospital Steward, B. Frank Moseley. Co. A, Captain, John B. Oliveres; Co. B, John Lotts Philips; Co. C, Walter Terry Saxon; Co. D, Daniel L. Freirson; Co. E, Daniel B. Bird; Co. F, Albert Drisdale; Co. G, Thomas L. Langford; Co. H, Mathew H. Strain; Co. I, Charles H. Ross; Co. K, William G. Parker.

The Regiment remained in camp about three weeks. During this time a beautiful silk banner with the motto "We Yield but in Death," was presented to the Regiment by one of the ladies of Jefferson county.

Shortly after the middle of the month of May the Regiment broke camp, marched to the Chattahoochee River and went by steamers to Columbus, then by rail to Montgomery; and after a short detention there was sent to Mobile, where the orders to proceed to Bragg's army in Mississippi were countermanded and the Regiment put on duty to guard and patrol the city, where they remained for several months.

Early in August of 1862 the Regiment was ordered to Chattanooga and went into camp at the foot of Lookout Mountain, near the Tennesse? River. After remaining there for a short time the 3rd crossed the Tennessee and was assigned to the brigade of Gen. John C. Brown of Tennessee, Gen. Patton Anderson's division. The regiments composing Brown's Brigade were the 1st and 3rd Florida and 41st Mississippi.

The Army of Tennessee encamped for a few days in the beautiful Sequatchee Valley; then it took up its line of march across the Cumberland Mountains into middle Tennessee and northward toward the Kentucky line, crossing the Cumberland River above Nashville and entered Kentucky in Monroe county. Then proceeded directly to Green River, near which a brigade of 4,000 Federal troops were captured. After a few days' delay, anticipating the approach of Buell's Army, the Army of Tennessee on September 20th moved toward Louisville, Kentucky, and for two weeks were camped at different points; part of the time a few miles from Bardstown. The movements of the Federal forces caused General Bragg to shift his position and on October 8th the two armies confronted each other at Perryville, where the 3rd lost heavily. Capt. D. B. Bird, who commanded the Regiment during most of the time after it left Chattanooga, fell mortally wounded, late on the afternoon of the 8th.

From Perryville the army fell back until it again reached Chattanooga in December, where the decimated ranks of the 1st and 3rd Regiments were consolidated, the 3rd forming the right wing of the consoldated regiment, and this it continued through all its subsequent history. The consolidated Regiment shared in all the subsequent movements of Bragg's Army back to east and forward to middle Tennessee, where, as a part of Breckinridge's Division it took part in the battle of Murfreesborough, where, out of its 531 men it lost 138 killed, wounded and miss'ng, and the other engagements of that campaign. Early in the summer of 1863 the Regiment, under Breckenridge, was ordered to Mississippi and was on the Big Black when Vicksburg was surrendered; afterward was engaged in the siege at Jackson, Miss. After the close of the Mississippi campaign the consolidated regiment returned to Northern Georgia in time to take part in the battle of Chickamauga and Missionary Ridge. The Regiment was in all the subsequent movements with the Army in Northern Georgia, which opened early in the spring of 1864 and extended from Chattanooga to Atlanta, thence onward to Middle Tennessee under Hood, and finally back through Alabama, Georgia, South Carolina and North Carolina to Durham Station, near Greensboro, N. C., April 26, 1865.

Roll, Field and Staff—3rd Florida Infantry.

NAMES.	MUSTERED IN.	MUSTERED OUT.	REMARKS.
Colonel—			
William Scott Dilworth	July 23, '61	April 26, '65	
Lieutenant-Colonels—			
Arthur J. T. Wright	July 23, '61		Retired at reorganiation May 10, 62.
Lucius A. Church	July 23, '61		Promoted from Major at reorganization; resigned '63.
E. Mashburn	July 23, '61	April 26, '65	Promoted from Major on resignation of Church.
Majors—			
E. Mashburn	July 23, '61		Promoted Lieutenant-Colonel.
John Lott Philips	July 23, '61		Promoted Major; resigned March 30, '63.
George A. Ball	July 23, '61		
Surgeons—			
Hill	July 23, '61		
D. Carn	July 23, '61		
E. G. Clay	July 23, '61		
Charles Hardee	July 23, '61	April 26, '65	
Assistant Surgeons—			
M. G. W. Jordan	July 23, '61	April 26, '65	
Adjutants—			
Lieut. J. O. A. Gerry	July 23, '61		Resigned, ill health; died of consumption.
Lieut. David Lewis	July 23, '61		Promoted to Captain and Commissary.
Lieut. Holmes Steele	July 23, '61	April 26, '65	Transferred to Medical Department.
Charles H. Stebbins	July 23, '61	April 26, '65	Promoted from Sergeant-Major.
Sergeant Major—			
David Lewis	July 23, '61		
Charles H. Stebbins	July 23, '61		Wounded at Chickamauga September 20, '63.
J. S. R. Snow	July 23, '61	April 26, '65	Wounded at Chickamauga September 20, '63.
Quartermasters—			
Capt. H. R. Teasdale	July 23, '61		Promoted Major and Quartermaster District of Florida.
Captain Hickman	July 23, '61		
Capt. Charles H. Collins	July 23, '61	April 26, '65	
Commissary—			
Capt. E. Yulee	July 23, '61		Transferred.
Capt. D. Lewis	July 23, '61	April 26, '65	Resigned November 23, '63.
Quartermaster Sergeant—			
William P. Moseley	July 23, '61	April 26, '65	
Commissary Sergeant—			
P. E. Love	July 23, '61	April 26, '65	
Ordnance Sergeant—			
Theo Bridier	July 23, '61	April 26, '65	
Hospital Steward—			
B. Frank Moseley	July 23, '61	April 26, '65	
Chaplain—			
W. J. Duval			Resigned February 1, '64.

Roll Company A (Jacksonville Lignt Infantry)—3rd Florida Infantry.

NAMES.	MUSTERED IN.	MUSTERED OUT.	REMARKS.
OFFICERS.			
Captains—			
Holmes Steele	Aug. '61		Resigned November, '61; promoted Adjutant May '62; transferred to Medical Department as Surgeon.
John B. Oliveros	July 13, '61		1st Lieutenant; promoted Captain November '61; wounded, disabled at the battle of Perryville and resigned.
Aristides Doggett		April 26, '65	2nd Lieutenant; promoted 1st Lieutenant November '61; Captain November '62.

Roll Company A (Jacksonville Light Infantry)—3rd Florida Infantry.
(CONTINUED.)

NAMES	MUSTERED IN.	MUSTERED OUT.	REMARKS.
1st Lieutenants—			
John G. Butler			3rd Lieutenant; promoted 2nd and 1st Lieutenant; lost in Kentucky.
John King	'62		Promoted 1st Lieutenant.
2nd Lieutenants—			
William Caulk			
Francis H. Sabal	Aug. '61		Corporal; promoted 3rd and 2nd Lieutenant November '62; killed between Chattanooga and Atlanta.
William Haddock		April 26, '65	Promoted 2nd Lieutenant '64.
3rd Lieutenant—			
Owens			
ENLISTED MEN.			
Allen, William H	Aug. '61		Promoted 1st Sergeant wounded at Perryville Ky., and disabled; deserted.
Andrew, Florence F		April 26, '65	
Andrew, Ignacio			
Biggs, Colin			
Booth, Richard			Musician.
Bowden, David			
Bowden, Edward			Deserted.
Bowden, William R	Aug. '61	April 26, '65	Wounded at Murfreesborough January 30; also at Kennesaw Mountains July 3, '63.
Brodnax, E. C			
Brodnax, R. R	July '61	April 26, '65	Wounded at Murfreesborough, Tenn., January 1 '63.
Bryant, William A			
Canova, A. A			
Clark, James			
Collins, C. H	Aug. '61		Sergeant.
Cubbage, Albert M	Aug. 2, '61	April 26, 65	Shot at Perryville, Ky., October 8, '62.
Curry, Robert			Mentioned for gallantry at Chickamauga.
Davis, James S	Aug. 2, '61	April 26, '65	Wounded at Missionary Ridge December 27, '63
Driver, John			
Driver, Leonard			
Dunbary, Patrick			
Duval, Virginius			
DeWaal, James M		April 26, '65	
Edwards, James			Deserted.
Falany, Benjamin			
Falany, Romain	'61		Wounded at Murfreesborough; captured; sent to Camp Chase till close of war.
Fatio, Lawrence L			
Floyd, Antonio V		April 26, '65	
Floyd, Francis		April 26, '65	Close of war.
Floyd, James H			Corporal; promoted 3rd Sergeant; deserted.
Floyd, Stephens A			Deserted.
Gilberth, David			Corporal; deserted.
Gilbert, Herrid			
Granyer, J. A		April 9, '65	
Greek, Elijah			
Hall, Robert D		April 26, '65	
Hamilton, Thomas	Aug. '61		
Hanford, G. W			
Hansy, Alexander	Aug. '61	April 26, '65	Wounded between Tunnell Hill and Dallas, Ga., '64.
Harvey, John J	Aug. '61	April 26, '65	Promoted Corporal; wounded at Marietta. Ga,, and disabled, '64.
Harvey, J. S		April 26, '65	
Hemming, Charles C	Aug. 2, '61	April 26, '65	Sergeant August, '61.
Hernandez, Antonio	Aug. 2,		
Hernandez, Frank	Aug. 2, '61		Promoted Corporal.
Hopkins, Alphonzo	Aug. 2, '61		Promoted Sergeant.
Houston, John C			
Houston, Robert E		April 26, '65	
Houston, William H		April 26, '65	Sergeant, October '61.
Huchingson, M. M. T		April 26, '65	Promoted Corporal.
Jackery, Lewis	Aug. 2, '61		
Javnigan, David	Aug. 1, '61		
Keenan, John	Aug. '61		
Keenan, Peter	Aug. '61		
Keenan, William A	Aug. 1, '61		
Kill, John	Aug. '61		
Killer, John		April 26, '61	
Lary, Joe			Promoted Sergeant.
Livingston, T. H	Aug. '61	April 26, '65	
Lopez, Andrew	Aug. '61		
Lopez, Joseph	Aug. '61		
Lord, Joseph B	Aug. '61		
Madden, John	Aug. '61		
Manusa, Mark	Aug. 1, '61		
Manusa, Philip	Aug. 2, '61		
Mather, Charles	Aug. '61		Sergeant.
Mitchell, William	Aug. '61		
Moody, Holles M	Aug. '61		1st Sergeant, August '61; deserted.
Moony, Hugh	Aug. '61		
Moony, John J	Aug. '61		
Ortagos, Predentes	Aug. '61		

Roll Company A (Jacksonville Light Infantry)—3rd Florida Infantry.
(CONTINUED.)

NAMES.	MUSTERED IN.	MUSTERED OUT.	REMARKS.
Patterson, Thomas	Aug. '61		
Perpaul, Charles	Aug. '61		Musician.
Perpaul, William O	Aug. '61		
Pinkham, Bathlib			Captured near Dallas, Ga., while on picket guard; '64; died of consumption at Fort Delaware.
Ponce, John	Aug. '61		Corporal; killed battle of Pine Mountain, '62.
Redman, James	Aug. '61	April 26, '61	Paroled from Fort Delaware close of war.
Richard, Francis M	Aug. '61		Paroled from Fort Delaware close of war.
Robion, Sidney G	Aug. '61		
Sallis, Domatio	Aug. '61		
Sheppard, W. D	Feb. '62	April 26 '65	
Shackelford, A. W			
Smith, Clarence W		April 26, '65	
Smith, Henry M		April 26, '65	
Stewart, Robert	Aug. '61		Killed on picket, near Atlanta.
Strausser, Antonio	Aug. '61		Corporal; drowned '61.
Sweet, Henry M		April 26, '61	
Walker, George A	Aug. '61		
Wasson, Charles R	Aug. '61		Deserted.
Wingate, Jerry	July 4, '61		Wounded at Perryville, Ky., October 8, '62 and captured; after remaining in hospital prison at Harrisburg until December '62, was exchanged and returned to his company.
Wingate, John G	Aug. '61		Died Chattanooga; buried Chattanooga cemetery.
Wingate, J. J	Aug. '61		
Wingate, Joseph W	Aug. '61		
Wingate, Nathan M	Aug. '61		
Wilds, Phineas	Sept. '61	April 26, '65	

Roll Company B (St. Augustine Blues)—3rd Florida Infantry.

NAMES.	MUSTERED IN.	MUSTERED OUT.	REMARKS.
OFFICERS.			
Captains—			
John Lott Philips	Aug. '61		Promoted to Major.
Charles L. Ridgeley	Aug. '61		Promoted from 2nd Lieutenant.
1st Lieutenants—			
Lawrence M. Andrews	Aug. '61		
Charles Downing Segue		April 26, '61	Promoted Lieutenant.
2nd Lieutenants—			
Irvine, Drysdale	May 17, '62		Promoted from Lieutenant Junior to 2nd Lieutenant; wounded at Perryville, Ky., October 8 '62; resigned June 6, '63.
3rd Lieutenants—			
Fatio Dunham	Aug. '61		Promoted from Sergeant to 3rd Lieutenant.
John B. Butler			Promoted 2nd Lieutenant.
ENLISTED MEN.			
Allen, James W	Aug. '61		
Anderson, Andrew	Aug. '61		
Andrew, Claudio	May '61		
Andrew, Emanuel	Aug. '61		
Andrew, Francis	Aug. '61		
Andrew, Joseph			Killed, Murfreesborough January '63.
Andrew, Laborn	Aug. '61	April 26, '65	
Andrew, Nicholas	May '61	May '63	Disability.
Arnow, Francis	Aug. '61		
Avice, Alexander	Aug. '61		
Bennett, Joseph		'62	April 26, '65	
Bennett, Stephen A	Aug. '61		Imprisoned at Fort Delaware.
Bravo, Christobal	Aug. '61		Corporal.
Bridier, Henry	Aug. '61		Killed in service.
Bridier, Louis D	Aug. '61		Wounded and died in Mobile hospital, '63.
Bridier, Theodore F	Aug. '61		Promoted Ordnance Sergeant for Regiment.
Briesh, Charles C. H	Aug. '61		
Canova, Andress	Aug. '61		
Canova, Antonio L	Aug. '61		
Canova, Stephen		April 26, '65	
Capo, Philip	Aug. '61		
Cauevas, Stephen	Aug. '61	April 26, '65	
Coles, George	Aug. '61		
Coles, William		April 26, '65	
Cook, Samuel L	May 30, '61	April 26, '65	
Crosby, James	Aug. '61		
Dunham, Harry			Sergeant; wounded September 20, '62.
Dunham, Oregon	Aug. '61		
Fante, John	Aug. '61		
Fontain, Tony	Aug. '61		Musician.
Foster, C. G		April 26, '65	
Genovar, William	Aug. '61	April 26, '65	
Genovar, Bartolo		April 26, '65	

Roll Company B (St. Augustine Blues)—3rd Florida Infantry.
(Continued.)

NAMES.	MUSTERED IN.	MUSTERED OUT.	REMARKS.
Gould, Archibald	Aug. '61		
Gould, James M	Aug. '61		
Gould, Rutledge	Aug. '61		
Handford, George W	Aug. '61		
Hernandez, Edward	Aug. '61		Sergeant.
Hernandez, Joseph V	Aug. '61		
Hinsey, Jackson		April 26, '65	Wounded in Kentucky' 62; captured and imprisoned at Camp Chase, Ohio.
Hurlburt, James			
Hussey, Genl I	Aug. '61		
Irwin, Joseph C	Aug. '61		Died Camp Chase prison, December 12, '64; Grave No. 606.
Irwin, Joseph			Died a prisoner in hospital.
Llambias, Autonio	Aug. '61		
Llambias, John	Aug. '61		
Llambias, J. M			Died in hospital at Danville, Ky.
Leonardy, Celestine	Aug. '61	April 26, '65	Wounded Knoxville, Tenn., May 17, '62.
Leonardy, John	Aug. '61		
Leonardy, Joseph	Aug. 5, '61	Dec. 13, '64	Discharged because of wounds; wounded at Perryville, Ky., October 8, '62.
Leonardy, Philip	Aug. '61	April 26, '65	Corporal.
Lopez, Alonzo	Aug. '61		Killed at Perryville, Ky., October 8, '62.
Lopez, Emanuel M	June '61	April 26, '65	Wounded in Murfreesborough January '63 and at Dallas, Ga., May 4, '64.
Masters, Disdario	Aug. '61		
Masters, James E		April 26, '65	
Master, Paul		April 26, '65	
Masters, Peter C	Aug. '61		Died in prison.
Mauncy, John	Aug. '61		
Mickler, Daniel J	Aug. '61	April 26, '65	
Mickler, D. L		April 26, '65	
Middletown, W. C		April 26, '65	
Miller, James A	Aug. '61		
Miller, James J	Aug. '61		
Miller, John	Aug. '61		
Mirander, William	Aug. '61		
Neligan, Henry H	Aug. '61		
Neligan, Michael	Aug. '61		
Osborn, Emanuel	Aug. '61		
Osteen, William E	March '62	April 26, '65	Wounded at Murfreesborough, Tenn., December 31, '62.
Pacetty, Albert	Aug. '61		
Pacetti, Bartolo		April 26, '65	
Pacetti, Elusebio			Died in Florida, '64.
Pacetty, Joseph A	Aug. '61		
Padgetti, Martin		April 26, '65	Wounded at Resaca, Ga., May 3, '64.
Papano, Isaac	Aug. '61		Musician.
Papy, Edward A	Aug. '61		
Papy, Frank			Died in hospital.
Papy, Isadora B	Aug. '61	April 26, '65	
Papy, John	Aug. '61		Died Camp Douglass prison.
Philips, John L	Aug. '61		Promoted Sergeant.
Philips, Paul G	Aug. '61		
Pinkham, Batholio			Captured near Dalton, Ga., January 23, '63; died in Fort Delaware of consumption.
Pomar, William	Aug. '61		
Ponce, Anthony	Aug. '61		
Ponce, Bartholow D	Aug. '61		Sergeant.
Ponce, James	Aug. '61		Discharged '63; re-enlisted Dickinson's Cavalry.
Ponce, James A		April 26, '65	
Ponce, Thomas	Aug. '61		
Rose, John A	Aug. '61		Sergeant.
Russell, Richard			Killed in battle.
Sanchez, James P	Aug. '61		
Solana, Joseph M	Aug. '61		
Spencer, Joseph	Aug. '61		
Stephens, B. H			September 20, '63.
Stephens, John M	March '62		Wounded and died in hospital in Kentucky '62.
Turner, Thomas M. D	Aug. '61		Transferred to Medical Department.
Usina, Micheal S	Aug. '61		
Usina, Domingo	Aug. '61	April 26, '65	
Watson, James			
Weems, Frank			Killed at Murfreesborough '63.
Whitby, John A	Aug. '61		
Wynn, George W	April '61	May '65	Wounded, Chickamauga; Jonesboro; captured, imprisoned at Camp Chase and from there paroled.
Ximanies, R. F		April 26, '65	

Roll Company C (Hernando Guards)—3rd Florida Infantry.

NAMES.	MUSTERED IN.	MUSTERED OUT.	REMARKS.
OFFICERS.			
Captain—			
Walter Terry Saxon	July '61	April 26, '65	Re-enlisted May 25, for the war.

Roll Company C (Hernando Guards)—3rd Florida Infantry.
(CONTINUED.)

NAMES.	MUSTERED IN.	MUSTERED OUT.	REMARKS.
1st Lieutenants—			
Samuel G. Frierson	July '61		Resigned at reorganization May, '62.
Joshua Stafford	July '61		Promoted from 2nd Lieutenant to 1st Lieutenant May, '62.
2nd Lieutenant—			
David H. Wall	July '61		Promoted from Sergeant May,'62; died in hospital.
3rd Lieutenants—			
William D. O'Neill	July '61		Resigned at reorganization '62.
Charles M. Lang	July '61		Promoted from Sergeant; resigned; cause, personal reasons.
Alfred N. Arline	July '61	April 26, '65	Promoted 3rd Lieutenant.
William M. Lang		April 26, '65	Promoted 3rd Lieutenant.
ENLISTED MEN.			
Allen, Lott, Sr	April 20, '61	July 15 '65	Wounded at Chickamauga, Ga., September 20, '63; at Jonesborough, Ga., August '64; at Da las, Ga., May '64; promoted Orderly Sergeant; mentioned for gallantry at Chickamauga.
Allen, William T	July '61		Died in service.
Andrews, Enoch H	July '61	April 26, '65	
Atkins, George W	July '61		Died in hospital at Columbus, Ga., December '63.
Baggett, Andrew A	July '61	April 26, '65	Corporal.
Bassett, John F	July '61	April 26, '65	Transferred, '63, to John T. Lisler's Co., Cavalry.
Bassett, Josiah B	July '61	April 26, '65	
Bates, Thomas L	July '61		Killed in battle.
Bethay, James	July '61		Died in prison.
Blackshear, Cicero S	July '61	April 26, '65	
Bowen, Right W	July '61	April 26, '65	
Bradley, Robert J	July	April 26, '65	
Breaker, Henry M	July '61		Killed by accident at Fernandina 61.
Burnham, Aaron T	July '61	April 26, '65	
Brown, Wright W	July	April 26, '65	
Byrd, Judson	July '61	April 26, '65	Wounded at Perryville, Ky., and Murfreesborough Tenn.
Calahan, Alexander B	July '61		Killed in battle.
Chance, John C	July '61		Died Camp Chase prison January 9, '65; Grave No. 723.
Clark, William R	July '61	April 26, '65	
Dan, John R	July '61		Sergeant; killed in batt.e.
Danford, George	July '61		Killed in battle.
Dyess, George	July '61	April 26, '65	
Ellis, James L	July '61		Killed in battle.
Ellis, Thomas B	July '61	April 26, '65	
Eubanks, John	July '61		Died in hospital.
Gannett, Chauncy	July '61		Died in hospital of wounds.
Hall, S. J			Died in Camp Douglass prison.
Hasbon, William I	July '61		Killed in battle.
Hay, Daniel	July '61	June '65	From Camp Douglass prison, close of war; captured at Missionary Ridge, Dec. '64; promoted Serg't.
Hay, James A	July '61	April 26, '65	
Hay, John F	July '61		Killed in battle.
Hay, Joseph M	July '61	April 26, '65	
Hay, William B	July '61	April 26, '65	Wounded at Atlanta, right cheek and neck.
Haymans, William C	July '61		Corporal; died in hospital of wounds.
Heisler, John	July '61		Killed in battle.
Hines, R. J	July '61		
Holton, T. J			
Hutzclaw, J. C	Aug. '61	April 26, '65	
Hines, Rufus I	July '61		Killed in battle.
Jackson, Evander E	July '61		Killed in battle at Resaca, Ga., '64; 1st Musician
Johnson, John R	July '61	April 26, '65	
Jumpp, Thomas	July '61	April 26, '65	
Kane, Patrick	July '61		Killed in battle.
Kersey, Thomas	July '61	April 26, '65	
Landrum, J. Turner	July '61	April 26, '65	Imprisoned at Fort Delaware.
Lang, James A	July '61	April 26, '65	
Leggett, William A	July '61	April 26, '65	
Liles, Samuel H	July '61	April 26, '65	Promoted Corporal; wounded at Peach Tree Creek.
Liles, Thomas W	July '61	April 26, '65	Wounded by accident at Fernandina, '61.
Lisk, William	Aug. '61	April 26, '65	
Long, James A	July '61		
Long, Thomas J	July '61	April 26, '65	
McKay, Diegenus	July '61		Killed in battle.
Mattan, James	July '61		2nd Musician; killed in battle.
Murden, Isham A	July '61	April 26, 65	
Nicks, Benjamin	July '61	April 26, '65	
Nicks, Francis R	July '61	April 26, '65	
Nevitt, Cornelias Q	July '61	April 26, '65	Re-enlisted in 9th Reg. Co. C.; hired a substitute but later went to Virginia in Co. C, 9th Reg.
Osborn, George	July '61		Killed in battle.
Peterson, John L	July '61	April 26, '65	Promoted 1st Sergeant; wounded and discharged.
Powell, Frank G	July '61	April 26, '65	In hospital during the entire term of service.
Rickbury, Daniel	July '61		Killed in battle.
Richbury, Nathaniel	July '61		Killed in battle.
Rooks, James	July '61		Killed in battle.
Row, William	July '61		Killed in battle.
Saxon, Benjamin	July '61		Discharged at reorganization; under age. '62.
Saxon, Franklen H. E	July '61	April 26, '65	Wounded, Perryville, Ky., '62.

Roll Company C (Hernando Guards)—3rd Florida Infantry.
(CONTINUED.)

NAMES.	MUSTERED IN.	MUSTERED OUT.	REMARKS.
Saxon, James Randolph	July '61		Killed in battle of Missionary Ridge, Nov. '63.
Simmons, Felix	July '61		Discharged at Fernandina, cause; raised a Co. of which he became Captain; (Co. F-8th Inf.).
Simmons, James R.	July '61		Transferred to Co. F, 8th Infantry.
Smith, James	July '61	April 26, '65	
Smith, William H.	July '61		Killed in battle.
Snow, Joseph R.	Aug. '61	April 26, '65	
Solis, John J.	July 61	April 26, '65	Sergeant; killed in battle.
Stafford, Eli W.	July '61		Killed in battle.
Stafford, John M.	July '61		Killed in battle.
Stafford, William H.	July '61	April 26, '65	
Strange, Daniel	July '61	April 26, '65	
Suhr, Augustus W.	July '61		Killed in battle.
Thigpin, William H.	July '61		Deserted.
Thomas, Roland	July '61	Aug. '62	Disability.
Tillett, George	July '61		Killed.
Tillett, John W.	July '61		Killed.
Zeigler, William W.	July '61		

Roll Company D (Wakulla Guards)—3rd Florida Infantry.

NAMES.	MUSTERED IN.	MUSTERED OUT.	REMARKS.
OFFICERS.			
Captains—			
Daniel L. Frierson	July '61		
John L. Ingles		April 26, '65	Sergeant; promoted Captain of consolidated Companies, D and G.
1st Lieutenants—			
Thomas F. Swearingin	July 25, '61	April 26, '65	
Richard C. McMillan	July '61		2nd Lieutenant; promoted 1st Lieutenant.
T. W. Ross			Promoted 1st Lieutenant.
2nd Lieutenant—			
3rd Lieutenants—			
William H. Walker	July '61		
Josiah R. Bostick	July '61		Promoted 3rd Lieutenant.
ENLISTED MEN			
Adkins, John	July 25, '61		
Alexander, Amos	July 25, '61		
Anderson, Charles W.	July 25, '61		
Anderson, William U.	July 25, '61		
Ashley, Berry			
Ashley, Charles			Shot through both thighs.
Bird, Henry	July 25, '61	April 26, '65	Wounded, Murfreesborough, Dec., '62.
Blackwell, W. R.	April 6, '63	April 26, '65	Wounded at Tullahoma, April 5, '63.
Boss, G. E.			Captured and paroled.
Bostick, Joseph C.	July 25, '61		Sergeant.
Boyd, John D.	July 25, '61		
Carraway, Jasper N.			Mentioned for gallantry.
Carter, Jeremiah B.			
Chanson, Joseph			
Coggins, J. H.			Died at Chattanooga.
Cogans, John	July '62		
Core, Arthur S.	July 25, '61		
Core, John J.			Wounded, Sept. 20, '63.
Core, William I.	July 25, '61		
Cuthbert, Isaac			
Cuthbert, James J.	July '61		
Cuthbert, John A.			
Cuthbert, William H.	July '61		
Counsel, William	July '61		
Dugger, James F.	July '61		Sergeant; discharged Oct. 19, '61, for disability; re-enlisted in Co. E, 2nd Cav.
Dunham, Davison			Died; Camp Chase, Jan. 31, '65; grave No. 200.
Elliot, James B.			Died at Chattanooga.
Elliot, John R.	July '61		
Faircloth, Joshua	July '61		Transferred to Co. I; 5th Regiment.
Forbes, Columbus	July '61		Corporal.
Gilchrist, William I.	July '61		
Grant, John	July '61		
Gray, J. J.			
Hair, Matthew		April 26, '65	
Harrell, William H.	July '61		
Hart, Daniel	July '61		Corporal.
Hart, Samuel D.	July '61		
Henderson, William M.	July '61		
Herning, G. W.			

Roll Company D (Wakulla Guards)—3rd Flofida Infantry.
(CONTINUED.)

NAMES.	MUSTERED IN.	MUSTERED OUT	REMARKS.
Hill, Richard W.	July 61		Sergeant; transferred to Bird's Co. K, 10th Reg. at re-organization, May, '62.
Horn, John W. H.	July '61	April 26, '65	
Hunt, Marghs D. L.	July '61		
Kellam, W. W.	June 1, '61	April 26, '65	
Langston, E. E.	June 15, '62	April 26, '65	Wounded at Bentonville, N. C.
Langston, Jesse I.	July 25, '61		
Langston, L. M. P.	July 25, '61		
Langston, William I.	July 25, '61		
Lawhorn, J. M.		April 26, '65	
Lewis, David	July 25, '61		
Lewis, John J.	July 25, '61		
Lewis, S. P.	July 25, '61		
McBride, Robert.	July '61		
McKinnon, Daniel F.	July 25, '61		
McMillan Lawrence W.	July 25, '61		
McMillan, R. C.		May 14, '65	
Mash, W. H.	July '61		
Merritt, William	Mch. '62	April 26, '65	
Milton, C. C.	Mch. '62	April 26, '65	
Moore, Francis M.	July '61	April 26, '65	
Newell, Charles	July 25, '61		Musician.
Oliver, James S.		April 26, '65	Transferred to Co. D, 2nd Reg., Cav.
Peterson, Gastarus O.	July '61		
Piggott, Robert R.	July 25, '61	June 25, '64	Disability; wounded at Resaca Ga., April 14, '64
Piggott, William N.	July '61		
Posey, Joseph W.	July 25, '61		
Revell, Elijah A.	July 25, '61		
Revell, J. A.	May 15, '61		Captured at Jonesboro, Ga., '64 and held in prison until close of war.
Revell, Samuel K.	July '61		Corporal.
Reeves, Mark A.	July 25, '61		
Roberts, Benjamin M.	July 25, '61		
Roberts, G. D.			Died, Camp Chase, Jan. 13, '65; grave No. 760.
Roberts, John H.	July 25, '61		
Roberts, John P.	July 25, '61	April 46, '65	
Roberts, Thomas.	July 25, '61		
Robertson, Robert P.	July 25, '61	April 26, '65	
Sasser, James J.	July 25, '61		
Saær, Wiilam Z.	July 25, '61	June 12, '65	Captured and imprisoned at Camp Chase, O, until close of the war.
Simmons, Hilery B. A.	July 25, '61		
Stevens, James A.	July 25, '61		
Taylor, James W.	July 25, '61		Wounded, Sept. 20, '63.
Taylor, Robert P.	July 25, '61		
Thompson, John.	July 25, '61		
Trice, Ezekiel.	July 25, '61	April 26, '65	
Uker, William.			
Ulmer, John L.			
Valize, J. F.		April 26, '65	
Vance, F. M.	Oct. '61	June 18,	Paroled From Camp Douglass, Illinois.
Vance, James W. W.	July '61		
Vance, John E.	July 25, '61		Discharged from Camp Douglass at close of war.
Walker, James W.	July 25, '61		Corporal.
Walker, Wright W.	July '61		
Whaley, Thomas E.	July 25, '61		
Whetstone, Irvine	July 25, '61		
Whetstone, Marion	July 25, '61		
Williams, Frank M.	April '61	June 18, '65	Wounded at Bentonville, N. C., March, '63.
Wood, James A.	July 25, '61		

Roll Company E—3rd Florida Infantry.

NAMES.	MUSTERED IN.	MUSTERED OUT.	REMARKS.
OFFICERS.			
Captains—			
Daniel B. Bird.			Killed at Perryville, November, '62.
Hamilton K. Walker.		April 26, '65	Corporal; promoted 1st Lieutenant, May, '62; Captain, November, '62.
1st Lieutenants—			
Marion J. Clark.			Retired at reorganization, May, '62.
John T. Bailey.			Sergeant; promoted 2nd Lieutenant, then 1st Lieutenant; mortally wounded at Murfreesborough.
2nd Lieutenants—			
William Z. Bailey.			Promoted 2nd Lieutenant; captured and paroled from Johnson's Island, June, '65.
Andrew J. Miller.			Corporal; promoted 2nd Lieutenant.

Roll Company E—3rd Florida Infantry.
(CONTINUED.)

NAMES.	MUSTERED IN.	MUSTERED OUT.	REMARKS.
3rd Lieutenants—			
Pickens B. Bird			Retired at reorganization, May, '62; then raised Company K, 10th Infantry.
Benjamin W. Edwards			Promoted May, '62.
William H. Ellis			Promoted 3rd Lieutenant.
ENLISTED MEN.			
Anderson, Asa			
Anderson, Chris			
Anderson, Moses			
Archer, A. W.			
Braden, Thomas			
Branch, William T.			
Brooks, Richard W.			
Brooks, Thomas J.			
Butler, Daniel			
Butler, Lorenzo			
Butler, Mitchell			
Cason, John B.			
Cason, William L.			
Chatman, Thomas			
Clark, M. J.			
Cosgrove, Thomas			
Craven, O. B.			Mortally wounded, died December 20, '63.
Cravey, B.			
Cuthbert, J. A.		April 26, '65	
Dixon, William H.			
Donaldson, John L.			
Donaldson, William			
Dotson, William M.			Died in '64.
Duncan, Joshua	July '61		Lost left arm at Resaca, May 28, '64 and discharged.
Duncan, William	June '61		Wounded at Franklin; captured and imprisoned until close of war.
Ellis Joseph J.			
Franklin, Leonidas W.			
Freeman, Archibald J.			
Ford, Early			
Fuguay, John			
Goettee, Robert R.			
Grey, John J.			
Grey, Minch L.			
Goza, Peter	June 27, '64	April 26, '65	
Hammell, Thomas B.			
Hancock, Augustus B.			
Hart, John			
Hart, Jacob			
Hart, Theophelus			
Hartsfield, George			
Hemmerson, William			
Hendry, Irvin R.			
Holt, Asa			
Holt, W. W.	July '61		
Horn, Joshua			
Huson, Isaiah			
Jones, A.			Wounded at Perryville, and captured; exchanged at Vicksburg.
Kellum, John W.	May '61	June '65	Wounded at Chickamaugua Georgia, Sept. 20, '63; captured at Nashville, Tennessee, December 6, '64; in prison at Camp Douglass, Illinois and paroled from there June, '65.
Kelly, John W.			
Kinsey, Joel			
Lee, W. D.	April 26, '65		
Livingston, A.	April 26, '65		
Martin, George W.		April 26, '65	
McMullen, D. J.		Feb. '64	Elected to a civil office.
Manley, B. F.		April 26, '65	
Mazingo, M. V.;B.		April 26, '65	Was captured July 22, '64 and sent to Camp Chase O. and from there paroled at close of war.
Merrill, Rufus M.			
Miller, Henry W.			
Morris, Collens D.			
Newman, George M.			
Newman, William A.			
O'Neil, Thomas			
Pellham, J. W.			Wounded, September 20, '63.
Philips, P. S.			
Porter, John T.			Sergeant.
Porter, Richard L.		April 26, '65	Corporal.
Porter, W. T.	June 21, '61	April 26, '65	Re-enlisted in same Company and paroled at close of war.
Porter, William			
Prosser, James A.			
Pruden, James H.			
Palcifer, John C.			
Ramsey, George W.			
Rhiems, William E.			
Roddenbery, A.			
Sanders, E. J.			
Sheffield, J. W.			

Roll Company E—3rd Florida Infantry.

(CONTINUED.)

NAMES.	MUSTERED IN.	MUSTERED OUT.	REMARKS.
Slauter, Henry			
Stanley, Irvin			
Stanley, Richard			
Stevens, Asher E	Jan. '64	April 26, '65	Wounded at Kennesaw Mountain, Georgia, July 20, '64.
Stephens, Hubbard			Musician.
Streety, William P			Musician.
Stokes, Bethel A			Corporal.
Stroman, John W			
Summerlin, Madison			
Tanner, William R			Killed at Murfreesborough Tennessee, Dec. 31, '62
Taylor, E. G.	Dec. 15, '61	May 9, '65	Wounded at Missionary Ridge, Tennessee.
Turner, J. C.		April 26, '65	
Ward, Isaiah			
Ward, William			
Whidden, William A			
Williams, R. L		April 26, '65	
Williamson, Judge			
Whitehurst, William			

Roll Company F (Cow Boys)—3rd Florida infantry.

NAMES.	MUSTERED IN.	MUSTERED OUT.	REMARKS.
OFFICERS.			
Captains—			
Lucius A. Hardee	Aug. '61		Resigned, May, '62; at reorganization.
Albert Drysdale			Promoted Captain, May, '62.
1st Lieutenants—			
J. E. Mickler	Aug. '61		
John C. King	Aug. '61		Promoted 1st Lieutenant.
2nd Lieutenant—			
William H. Haddock	Aug. '61		Promoted 1st Lieutenant, '63; resigned June 27, '64.
3rd Lieutenant—			
Elias Jaudon	Aug. '61		
Henry B. Goode			1st Sergeant, promoted 3rd Lieutenant.
Thomas Stratton	Aug. '61		Sergeant, promoted 3rd Lieutenant.
James C. West	May 11, '61	April 26, '65	Wounded, Perryville, October 8, '62.
Samuel H. Wienges	May '61	April 26, '65	Wounded, Decatur, Georgia, July 22, '64; promoted 3rd Lieutenant.
ENLISTED MEN.			
Allen, John G			
Allen, Lorenzo D			Musician.
Bardin, James			Discharged January 9, '63; over age.
Beggs, C. Pleasant			Corporal.
Biggs, Charles P			Died in hospital at Lake City, January 23, '63; of disease.
Bush, Clayton			
Bush, Francis F			
Bush, John C			Musician, promoted Corporal.
Cain, Dempsey			Promoted Sergeant.
Carter, Elijah			
Carter, Joseph			
Carter. Levi H		April 26, '65	Shot at Chickamauga, September 19, '63.
Clark, Stephen			
Crews, Alexander			
Crews, Harley J			
Crews, S. D	May 11, '61		Captured at Bentonville N. C, imprisoned at Point Lookout and paroled June 26 '65.
Crow, S. H			Died, Camp Chase August 15, '64; Grave No. 205.
Daniels, James M			
Davis, Timothy T			
Davis, William J			
Dewall, James M		April 26, '65	
Donald, John M			
Dowell, William			1st Sergeant.
Edwards, James W	Jan. 1, '62	April 26, '65	Shot at Murfreesborough, December 31, '63.
Falana Romain		April 26, '65	
Friar, John			Promoted Sergeant.
Gardner James		April 26, '65	
Garey, Love			
Garey, William J			
Garrett, Arthur C			
Hammond, John	Aug. '61	April 26, '65	
Hanchey, Daniel A	Aug. '61		
Hansler, Francis J	Aug. '61		
Harris, John J	Aug. '61		
Harris, William E	Aug. '61		

Roll Company F (Cow Boys)—3rd Florida Infantry.
(CONTINUED.)

NAMES.	MUSTERED IN.	MUSTERED OUT.	REMARKS.
Harris, Z. T.	Aug. '61		
Holmes, James	Aug. '61		
Hopkins, J.			Corporal.
Hopkins, H.			Corporal.
Huffingham, James	Aug. '61		
Hurlburt, Francis	Aug. '61		
Jamison, Peter M.	Aug. 1, '61	April 26, '65	Wounded, Jonesborough September, '64.
Jones, Washington L.	Aug. 1, '61		Promoted corporal, discharged January 9, '63; over age.
Jordan, Willam W.	Aug. 1, '61		Corporal, promoted 2nd Sergeant.
King, Pennelton R.	Aug. '61		
Linton, Charles A.	Aug. '61		
Livingston, Joseph	Aug. '61		
McDowell, George W.	Aug. 1, '61		Corporal.
Morgan, Richard S.	Aug. '61		
Morris, John S.	Aug. '61		Discharged January 9, '63; over age the cause.
O'Neal, W. C.	June 24, '61	April 26, '65	Shot at Perryville, October 8, '62.
O'Steen, Theodore		April 26, '65	
Padgett, Martin	May 25, '61	April 26, '65	Wounded at Resaca, Ga., May 15, '64.
Padgett, Stephen		April 26, '65	
Pigg, John W.	Aug. '61		Never left the State.
Quarterman, Robert T.	Aug. '61		
Quarterman, W. G. M.	Aug. '61		
Rainer, J. J.	Aug. '61		
Rainer, William			Corporal.
Richard, F. M.		April 26, '65	Imprisoned at Fort Delaware.
Richardson, Edmund	Aug. '61		
Richardson, John	Aug. '61		Sergeant.
Roberts, Francis M.	Aug. '61		Wounded September 20, '63.
Roberts, M.	'61	April 26, '65	ergeant, wounded at Chickamauga September 20, '63.
Roberts, Randall Z.	Aug. '61		Corporal.
Roberts, Thomas W.	Aug. '61		
Sams, Frank W.	Aug. '61		Corporal, discharged, under age; transferred ot 1st Res. Colonel Daniel.
Sparkman, William	Aug. '61		
Stansell, Nathaniel W.	Aug. '61		Sergeant.
Stratton, Samuel	Aug. '61		
Suarez, Rapheal	Aug. '61		
Sweat, Henry M.	Aug. '61	April 26, '65	Promoted Corporal, and Sergeant.
Thomas, Solomon	Aug. '61		
Thompson, Allen	Aug. '61		
Thompson, Isaiah L.	Aug. '61		
Thompson, John L.	Aug. '61		
Thompson, William F.	Aug. '61		
Townsend, Benjamin F.	Aug. '61		
Thymme, Bernard	Aug. '61		Promoted Corporal.
Unges, Samuel	Aug. '61		
Walker, William	Aug. '61		
Walmsby, T. M.	Aug. '61		
Ward, Henry	Aug. '61		
Ward, John	Aug. '61		
Warren, Thomas	Aug. '61		Lost left arm, died September 25, '63.
West, Robert	Aug. '61		Promoted Sergeant, mortally wounded September 20, '63; died September 28, '63.
Weeks, Levi R.	Aug. '61		Honorable mention, promoted Sergeant.
Wiles, Spencer B.			
Williamson, Ivy	Aug. '61		
Wingate, R. W.	'61	April 26, '65	
Withington, J. A.		April 26, '65	

Roll Company G—3rd Florida Infantry.

NAMES.	MUSTERED IN.	MUSTERED OUT.	REMARKS.
OFFICERS.			
Captains—			
Thomas Langford	Aug. 9, '61		Resigned December 5, '64.
Robert J. Bevill	July 25, '61		1st Lieutenant; promoted Captain; resigned February 11, '65.
1st Lieutenants—			
Charles Beggs			Promoted 2nd Lieutenant; 1st Lieutenant; resigned and re-enlisted Co. E, 11th Regiment and promoted Captain.
Albert R. Livingston			Sergeant; promoted 1st Lieutenant.
2nd Lieutenants—			
Edward Mashburn			2nd Lieutenant; promoted Major May 10, '62.
John M. Bryan			Sergeant; promoted 2nd Lieutenant.
Henry M. Sutton			Promoted 2nd Lieutenant.
3rd Lieutenant—			

SOLDIERS OF FLORIDA.

Roll Company G—3rd Florida Infantry.
(CONTINUED.)

NAMES.	MUSTERED IN	MUSTERED OUT.	REMARKS.
ENLISTED MEN.			
Ayers, John H			
Bell, Enoch	Sept. 2, '61		
Bell, John G			Died, Camp Chase January 19, '65.
Bennett, Samuel	July '61	April 26, '65	
Bevans, George W	Sept. 5, '61		
Bevans, W. J			
Blair, W. T	Aug. 19, '61	April 26, '65	
Brown, J. H			
Brown, Reuben			
Burnett, Cassel P			
Burnett, James H	July 17, '61		Wounded at LaGrange, Ga.
Burnett, P. P			Wounded at 1st Manassas; discharged December 24, '63.
Burnett, William			
Carraway, Frank S			
Caña, John C	Aug. 9, '61		
Cobb, John			Killed September 20, '63.
Cockran, Ancillo C			Died in service '62.
Coffee, William S	Aug. 9, '61		Wounded and died.
Collier, Oscar W	June '62		Wounded at Bentonville, N. C., March '65.
Coody, Lewis T			
Coody, Samuel			
Crosby, Wilson J			
Davis, J. R	Sept. '62	April 26, '65	
Dees, Moses W	'62		Shot, Dallas, Ga., July 22, '64; discharged.
Dyialinski, M. A			Wounded at Perryville.
Edwards, Anderson			
Ellison, Thomas J			
Gainey, B. D	Aug. 9, '61		
Golding, J. G			
Green, Charles	Aug. 9, '61		
Green, James	Aug. 9, '61	April 26, '65	Shot at Chickamauga, Ga., September '63.
Hadden, Henry			
Hamlin, Joseph			
Haddock, John S			
Haddock, Joshua			Corporal; killed at Perryville November '62.
Hammerville, A. W			
Hamilton, Joe	Aug. 9, '61		
Hardee, Theophilus			
Hart, S. B	May '61		Shot at Murfreesborough May '62.
Henderson, Jasper M			
Herring, J. E			
Higgins, James N			
Hobls, Thomas			
Horn, William N			
Howell, William W			Promoted Corporal.
Hurst, Littleton	'61	April 26, '65	Wounded at Fort Clinch, Fla., November '61.
Jenknes, Randall			
Lamb, Abram	Sept. 2, '61	April 26, '65	
Lamb, C			Died at Chattanooga from wounds; buried in cemetery at Chattanooga.
Lamb, Jarrod	Sept. 2, '61		
Lamb, William	Sept. 2, '61		Killed at Chickamauga September 20, '63; honorable mention.
Leak, John D		April 26, '65	
Lee, Farmer			
Leasly, Maddison L		April 26, '65	
Livingston, Archibald			Promoted 1st Sergeant.
McCormick, Eli	July '61		Died of pneumonia October 30, '62 at Knoxville.
McCormick, William			Corporal; killed at Chickamauga.
McCoy, Styne D			
McCullough, James M			
McCullock, John R			
McDaniel, Duncan	May '62	April 26, '65	Shot in left hip; also in left arm.
McDaniel, Francis M			
McDaniel, Samuel			
McKinney, James			Killed, September 20, '63.
McLeod, Henry W		April 26, '65	Wounded, September 20, '63.
Martin. James H			
Mathews Mathew		April 26, '65	
Mathews, Williard			
Miller, H	Aug. '61		
Miller, William J	Aug. 27, '61		
Morgan, Reuben	Sept. 2, '61		
Moseley, B. F		April 26, '65	
Moseley, Thomas			Killed, Perryville November '62.
Moseley, William P		April 26, '65	
Moon, Egbert C			
Mathis, Andrew			
Newman, M			Wounded September 20, '63.
Nichols, Bryan			
Nichols, John			
Osteen, Ezekiel B			
Osteen, Leonard			Musician.
Osteen, Thomas			
Overstreet, Stephen D			

Roll Company G—3rd Florida Infantry.

(CONTINUED.)

NAMES.	MUSTERED IN.	MUSTERED OUT.	REMARKS.
Parker, Joseph P	July 22, '61	April 26, '65	Wounded by explosion of shell in the left wrist in Georgia.
Parker, William J			
Peterson, William J			
Philips, P. S		April 26, '65	
Philips, R. A			
Philips, William H			
Porter, W. T			
Pridgen, John			
Ramsey, Joseph D	Sept. 2, '61	April 26, '65	Shot at Resaca, Ga., May 21, '64.
Ramsay, William M. J			
Rodgers, William O	Sept. '61	April 26, '65	
Rodgers, Thomas A			1st Corporal.
Rys, William W			
Sauls, Jacob			
Saunders, Samuel W			Wounded September 20, '63.
Seaver, Benjamin			
Sessions, John R			
Sessions, L. M			
Shepard, Thomas			
Shortridge, George	July '61		Killed at Perryville October 7, '62.
Smiley, John C			
Smith, Edwin L			
Smith, James W			Sergeant.
Smithwick, Robert			
Stebbins, Francis M		April 26, '65	
Sutton, John T			
Sutton, Thomas			
Sutton, W. J	Aug. '61	April 26, '65	Shot at Perryville October 8, '62.
Taylor, Jasper		April 26, '65	
Townsend, Joseph		April 26, '65	
Townsend, Samuel			
Waring, Malachi H	Mch. 28, '61	April 26, '65	Severely wounded at Dallas May 28, '64.
Warner, Fayette N			
Watts, John B			Corporal.
Webb, W. A	'63	April 26, '65	
Welch, D. A. J	April '61	April 26, '65	Wounded Chickamauga, Perryville and Atlanta.
Welch, Jackson		April 26, '65	
West, John		April 26, '65	
West, Timothy			
West, Garrett W			
Whidden, Alanson			
Whidden, Ferinand M			
Whitfield, Francis M			
Whitfield, Joseph I			
Whitfield, William W			Corporal; killed at Dallas, Ga.
White, Edward			Died, Chattanooga; buried in cemetery there.
Williams, James P			
Williams, J. M		April 26, '65	
Williams, J. W		April 26, '65	
Williams, R. L	July 4, '61	April 26, '65	Wounded at Bentonville, N. C., March 19, '65.
Winburn, Nicholas			
Witt, W, W			
Young, James M			Killed near Missionary Ridge.
Zipperer, John M			

Roll Company H (Jefferson Rifles)—3rd Florida Infantry.

NAMES.	MUSTERED IN.	MUSTERED OUT.	REMARKS.
OFFICERS.			
Captains—			
William O. Girardeau	Aug. 10 '61		Captain; resigned '62 to take charge of Jefferson Academy.
Mathew Harvey Strain	Aug. 10, '61	April 26, '65	3rd Lieutenant; promoted Captain '62.
1st Lieutenant—			
C. E. Johnson	Aug. 10, '61	April 26, '65	Re-enlisted '62 at Quincy.
2nd Lieutenants—			
Thomas L. Shehee	Aug. 10 '61		Re-enlisted '62 at Quincy; killed at Perryville, Ky., August 8, '62.
Thomas J. Moore		April 26, '65	Promoted 2nd Lieutenant.
3rd Lieutenants—			
A. Campbell McCants	Aug. 10, '61		1st Sergeant; promoted 3rd Lieutenant; failed of re-election at the reorganization May, '62, and went into the Nitre Bureau.
Aborn Harris	Aug. 10, '61	April 26, '65	Sergeant; re-enlisted '62; promoted 3rd Lieutenant,
L. Q. C. Lingo	Aug. 10, '61	April 26, '65	Promoted 3rd Lieutenant; shot at Kennesaw Mountain, June 24, '64.

Roll Company H (Jefferson Rifles)—3rd Florida Infantry.
(CONTINUED.)

NAMES.	MUSTERED IN.	MUSTERED OUT.	REMARKS.
ENLISTED MEN.			
Adams, George W	Aug. 10, '61		Promoted Sergeant at reorganization; killed at Dallas, Ga., '64.
Akridge, Asa W	Sept. 10, '61		
Aldrich, William N	Aug. 10, '61	April 26, '65	Re-enlisted at Quincy '62.
Andrews, James W	Aug. 10, '61	April 26, '65	Re-enlisted at Quincy '62.
Atkinson, Henry D	Aug. 10, '61	April 26, '65	Re-enlisted at Quincy '62.
Baker, Benjamin J	Aug. 10, '61	April 26, '65	Re-enlisted at Quincy '62.
Beal, Frank	Aug. 10, '61	April 26, '65	Re-enlisted at Quincy '62.
Braswell	Aug. 10, '61		Discharged at reorganization '62.
Bryan, Needham N	Aug. 10, '61	April 26, '65	Re-enlisted '62; wounded September 20, '63.
Bryant, William	Aug. 10, '61		Re-enlisted '62; transferred to Co. A.
Cailahan, Thomas			
Carpenter, Armour J	Aug. 10, '61		Re-enlisted '62; died in hospital '62.
Carroll, Charles Thomas	Aug. 10, '61	April 26, '65	Promoted 1st Sergeant and to Captain when in prison; in battles of Perryville, Jackson, Murfreesborough, Chickamauga, and was captured at Missionary Ridge and imprisoned at Fort Delaware.
Cassidy, Norman	Aug. 10, '61	April 26, '65	Re-enlisted at Quincy '62.
Chace, Charles F	Aug. 10, '61		Discharged for disability '62.
Charri, Charles P	Aug. 29, '61	April 26, '65	
Clarke, Thomas L			
Cole, Silas	Aug. 10, '61	April 26, '65	
Cole, William L	Aug. 10, '61		Discharged '62, under age.
Cuthbert, Isaac	Aug. 29, '61		Discharged '62, under age.
Cuthbert, John A	Aug. 29 '61		Corporal; promoted Sergeant; was in prison at Point Lookout, Md., at close of war.
Deal, Henry C	Aug. 13, '61		Discharged for disability.
Dixon, Lemuel	Aug. 10, '61		Killed at Murfreesborough.
Ellenwood, William G	Aug. 10, '61		Discharged in '62; under age.
Fennell, James J	Aug. 10, '61		Captured at Missionary Ridge, '63; and died in prison.
Gale, Alexander	Aug. 10, '61		Died in hospital.
Gale, Hiram	Aug. 10, '61	April 26, '65	Wounded in right leg and right hand at Resaca Ga. May 8, '64.
Gilchrist, William G	Aug. 10, '61		Transferred to Co. D, died in hospital at Mobile.
Gilmer, George R	Aug. 10, '61	April 26, '65	
Granger, Hiram	Aug. 10, '61	April 26, '65	
Granger, Mathew	Aug. 10, '61		Discharged 1862; disability.
Grantham, William R	Aug. 10, '61		Discharged in '63; disabled from wounds. Shot through right hip at Perryville, Ky. Oct. 8, 1862.
Green, Christopher B	Sept. 23, '61	April 26, '65	Died in hospital in '63.
Ham, Ichabod	Aug. 10, '61		Wounded. Sept. 20, '63.
Harp, Augustus C	Aug. 10, '61	April 26, '65	Discharged in '61; disabled.
Harp, John L	Aug. 10, '61		
Hassell, Solomon M	Aug. 10, '61	April 26, '65	
Hart, S. B	Aug. 10, '61	April 26, '65	
Hay, John E	Aug. 10, '61		Discharged in '62; disability.
Hay, Noah	Aug. 10, '61		Discharged in '62; disability.
Hemming, Charles C	Aug. 10, '61	April 26, '65	Transferred to Company A.
Hersch, Herman	Aug. 10, '61	April 26, '65	Captured in '64.
High, James	Aug. 10, '61		Died in hospital, '63.
Holtzchew, James	Aug. 10, '61	April 26, '65	Captured and sent to Camp Norton, Ind.
Horton, Whitmil H	Aug. 10, '61		Discharged in '62; disabled.
Houston, William S	Sept. 6, '61		Corporal.
Johnson, Benj. W	Oct. 9, '61		Discharged in '62; disabled, re-enlisted in Cavalry.
Johnson, George P	Dec. 18, '61		Died in service.
Johnson, James E	Aug. 10, '61	April 26, '65	Sergeant 1 year; returned to ranks on re-organization.
Johnson, William; R	Aug. 10, '61		Corporal, killed at Dallas, Ga.
Jordan, John W	Aug. 10, '61	April 26, '65	Corporal.
Kyle, J. W	Aug. 10, '61	April 26, '65	
Kyle, Theodore	Aug. 10, '61		Killed at Murfreesboro Jan. 2, '63.
Lastinger, Berry L	Aug. 13, '61		Discharged in '62; disability, accidental wound at New Smyrna.
Letchworth, William H	Aug. 10, '61	April 26, '65	
McAdams, James P	Aug. 10, '61		Discharged in '63; disabled, wounded in ,leg at Murfreesboro. Jan. 3, '63.
McClellan, Frank M	Aug. 10, '61	April 26, '65	
McClellan, James J	Aug. 20, '61		Died at Fernandina, '61.
McGehee, John	Aug. 10, '61		Missing at Murfreesboro.
McDermott, John	Aug. 10, '61		Captured at Dalton, Ga. May 13,'64 and died at Camp Morton, Ind. Sept. 10, '64; No. of Grave 1117, Green Lawn Cemetery.
McNeill, L		April 9, '65	
Manning, Simeon		April 26, '65	
May, Albert		April 26, '65	
Mershon, Henry	Aug. 10, '61		Discharged, '62; disabled.
Mershon, Martin L	Aug. 10, '61	April 26, '65	
Moody, Lemuel C		April 26, '65	Died Nov. 26, '99.
Moon, Egbert C	Aug. 9, '61		Killed at Dallas, Ga.
Nickols, Bryan	Aug. 10, '61		
Pacetti, Dennis J	Nov. 17, '61	April 26, '65	
Palmer, S. A	May '62		Paroled from prison, close of war.
Partridge, B. W		April 26, '65	Transferred to 15th Confederate Cavalry.
Pasco, Samuel	Aug. 10, '61	April 26, '65	Sergeant.
Peacock, Alfred J	Sept. 12, '61	April 26, '65	
Peeler, Wilbur T	Aug. 10, '61	April 26, '65	Transferred to Cavalry.
Pettus, John G	Aug. 10, '61		Killed in action.

Roll Company H (Jefferson Rifles)—3rd Florida Infantry.

(CONTINUED.)

NAMES.	MUSTERED IN.	MUSTERED OUT.	REMARKS.
Pettus, Thomas L.			Killed at Jackson, Miss., July 10, '63.
Proctor, Henry L.	Aug. 10, '61	April 26, '65	
Philips, William H.			
Raysor, Michæl O.	Aug. 10, '61		Wounded, Sept. 20, '63; died in service.
Reaves, Daniel A.	May '62		Shot through upper part of body at Chickamauga Ga. Sept. 20, '63; died October 30, '1902.
Reeves, James.	Aug. 10, '61		Died in service.
Reeves, R. G.			
Reeves, Samuel.	Aug. 10, '61		Died from disease at Ocala, '62.
Reeves, Solomon S.	Aug. 10, '61		Musician, died in service.
Richardson, William M.	Aug. 10, '61		Unaccounted for.
Roberts, John L.	Aug. 10, '61		
Roberts, John P.	Aug. 10, '61		
Rouse, John.	Aug. 10, '61	April 26, '65	
Russell, William E.	Dec. 7, '61	April 26, '65	
Sauls, Daniel.	Aug. 10, '61		Discharged Dec. 17, '61; disability.
Sauls, David.	Aug. 10, '61		Discharged in '62; disability.
Scott, Edmund G.	Aug. 10, '61	April 26, '65	Wounded in left arm at Kennesaw Mountain, July '64.
Scott, James E.	Aug. 20, '61	April 26, '65	
Scruggs, Solomon M.	May '62	April 26, '65	
Scruggs, William H.	May '62		
Sealey, Fredric W.	Aug. 10, '61	April 26, '65	Wounded and left on the field at Perryville Ky. '62; Oct. 8, shot in left hip, died Nov. 30, 1890.
Shackelford, A. W.	Aug. 10, '61		Discharged May, '62; under age.
Sheppard, William;M.	Aug. 10, '61		Discharged in 62; under age.'
Simmons, Frank R.	Aug. 10, '61		Discharged May, '62; under age.
Sledge, A. Darius.	Aug. 10, '61		Died in service, '63; Nostalgia.
Sledge, Ellsbury T.	Aug. 10, '61		Died in service, '63; Nostalgia.
Sloan, James.	Aug. 10, '61		Killed.
Sloan, Thomas M.	Aug. 31, '61	April 26, '65	
Smith, Clarence W.	Aug. 10, '61	April 26, '65	Promoted Corporal of Color Guard.
Smith, Loyd S.	Aug. 10, '61		
Smith, Wiliam J.	Aug. 10, '61	April 26, '65	
Snow, James S. M.	Aug. 10, '61	April 26, '65	Promoted Sergeant Major.
Smiley, John C.	Aug. 10, '61		
Sparks, John A.	Aug. 10, '61	April 26, '65	
Sparks, Thomas.	Aug. 10, '61	April 26, '65	
Stebbins, Charles H.	Aug. 10, '61	April 26, '65	Corporal, promoted Sergeant; Sergeant Major, Adjutant.
Taylor, Joseph O.	Aug. 10, '01		Sergeant, wounded, Chickamauga '63; elected Sheriff and discharged in '63. Died in '64.
Taylor, L. L.	Aug. 10, '61	April 26, '65	Transferred to Cavalry.
Taylor, William R.	Aug. 10, '61	April 26, '65	
Thomas, John P.	Aug. 10, '61		Died in hospital.
Tucker, Thomas Ware.	Aug. 10, '61		Died in Jackson, Miss.
Townsend, Samuel A.	Aug. 10, '61		
Ulmer, Charles P.	Aug. 10, '61		Corporal, killed at Missionary Ridge,Tenn. carrying colors of Regiment.
Walker, Alfred W.	Aug. 10, '61		Died in service.
Walker, Archibald J.	Aug. 10, '61	April 26, '65	
Walker, George.	Aug. 10, '61	April 26, '65	Honorable mention at Chickamauga and was killed at that place Sept. 20, '63.
Walker, George W.	Aug. 10, '61		Killed at Chikcamauga Tenn. '63.
Walker, Jesse W.	Aug. 10, '61	April 26, '65	
Walker, J. Wesley.	Aug. 10, '61	April 26, '65	Transferred to Co. D.
Walker, Michæl.	Aug. 10, '61		Corporal, died in service.
Walker, William B.	Aug. 10, '61	April 26, '65	
Washington, J. W.	Aug. 10, '61		
West, Henry.	Aug. 10, '61		Died in service.
West, John.	Aug. 10, '61	April 26, '65	
Weston, Joel A. T.	Aug. 10, '61		Died in hospital at Montgomery in '65.
Wethington, John W.	Aug. 10, '61	April 26, '65	Discharged in '62, under age; re-enlisted in '62 for three years. Wounded twice at Perryville, Ky., in '63.
Whitehurst, Levi J.	Aug. 10, '61		Mustered out in '62.
Williams, Charles R.	Aug. 10, '61		Died Aug. '61 at Fernandina; first death in Company after entering service.
Williams, Darius.	Aug. 10, '61	April 26, '65	
Wilford, F. M. T.	Aug. 10, '61	April 26, '65	
Wolfe, Howell.	Aug. 10, '61	April 26, '65	Wounded, Chickamauga Sept. 20, '63.

Roll Company I (Dixie Stars)—3rd Florida Infantry.

NAMES.	MUSTERED IN.	MUSTERED OUT.	REMARKS.
OFFICERS.			
Captains—			
Jesse S. Wood	Aug. '61		Resigned May 10, 1862.
Charles H. Ross	Aug. '61	April '65	2nd Lieutenant, promoted Captain and captured at Nashville.

SOLDIERS OF FLORIDA.

Roll Company I (Dixie Stars)—3rd Florida Infantry.
(Continued.)

NAMES.	MUSTERED IN.	MUSTERED OUT.	REMARKS.
1st Lieutenant—			
John L. Dozier	Aug. '61	April '65	
2nd Lieutenants—			
Green H. Hunter	Aug. '61		Transferred to Co. E, 9th Regiment.
Leroy Smith	Aug. '61		Resigned April 23, '63.
William Ross	Aug. '61		Promoted 2nd Lieutenant.
3rd Lieutenants—			
Levi Smith	Aug. '61		Promoted 3rd Lieutenant, resigned April 23, '63.
Robert S. Paschall	Aug. 10, '61	April 26, '65	Promoted Lieutenant Sept. 3, '63; wounded Sept. 20, '63.
ENLISTED MEN.			
Barber, Samuel	Aug. '61	April '65	
Beaufort, Fleming A	Aug. '61		Died in hospital at Ringgold, Ga. '63.
Bleammer, Lewis	Aug. '61		Captured in Jacksonville, '62, Mar. 5; at Brick Church.
Bowles, George	Aug. '61		
Brinkley, Allen	Aug. '61		Corporal, killed.
Brown, James	Aug. '61		
Bryan, James H	Aug. '61		
Bryan, J. Madison	Aug. '61		
Bryant, John C	Aug. '61		Mortally wounded at Perryville, Ky.
Calahan, James R	Aug. '61		Killed Murfreesboro, Jan. 2, '63.
Calahan, John C	Aug. '61		
Callahan, John W	Aug. 14, '61		Paroled from Camp Chase prison O. at close of war.
Callahan, T. J	Aug. '61		Captured at Nashville, imprisoned at Camp Chase and paroled June 13, '65.
Callahan, William S	Aug. '61		
Chastain, James T	Aug. '61		Paroled from Camp Chase June 12, '65.
Clarke, William H	Aug. '61		
Clemonds, William	Aug. '61		Musician.
Cobb, Absolem	Aug. '61		
Cook, William	Aug. '61	April '65	
Covington, Samuel	Aug. '61		
Curry, James	Aug. '61		
Edwards, James	Aug. '61		
Ellis, T. B	Aug. '61		
Fielding, James J	Aug. 10, '61		Shot at Murfreesborough Tenn. Dec. 3, '62.
Garganit, David			
Gear, William	'61		
Godfrey, John M	Aug. '61	April '65	
Grant, Osborn W	Aug. '61		
Grant, William C	Aug. '61		
Herndon, Charles S	Aug. '61		Sergeant; killed at Dallas, Ga., May 28, '64.
Herring, Daniel	Aug. '61		Died in prison.
Herring, W. W	May '62		
Hicks, Joseph	Aug. '61		
Holloway, William	Aug. '61		Wounded September 20, '63.
Horn, Elijah F	Aug. '61	April '65	
Horn, J. R			
Hunt, James A	Aug. 10, '61		Paroled from prison at Rock Island May 28, '65.
Hunt, Madison	Aug. '61		
Hunter, Thompson	Aug. '61		Died in hospital.
Hurlington, Theodecius	Aug. '61		Lost right arm at Chickamauga '63.
Hurlingson, V. W. A	Aug. '61		Wounded, Pine Moutain June 14, '64.
Huchingson, T. A	Aug. 10, '61		Lost left hand at Chickamauga September 20, '63.
Huchingson, V. W			
Inglish, Henry		April '65	
Jernigan, W. H			
Keene, Jackson			
Long T			
McCollum, Robert			Wounded at Chickamauga September 20, 63.
McCoy, Thomas			
McCullum, John D			Sergeant.
McCullum, John W			
McKensie John			
Parker, Joseph			
Peacock, John G			
Perryman, Neil A		April '61	Transferred to 26th Georgia.
Peterson, Albert			
Polk, Columbus C			
Prather, Augustus M		April '65	
Raulerson, James	Aug. '61	April '65	
Rawls, W. T	Aug. '61		
Rewis, Andrew J	Aug. '61	April '65	
Rewis, Obediah	Aug. '61		Killed.
Sellars, William L	Aug. '61	April '65	
Smith, Ezekiel C	Aug. '61		Wounded September 20, '63; killed at Perryville.
Smith, E. S		April '65	
Smith, Henry M	Aug. '61	April '65	Wounded at Perryville, Ky., October 11, '62.
Smith, John D	Aug. '61	April '65	Wounded September 20, '63.
Taylor, Joseph K	Aug. 10, '61	April '65	Transferred to Co. D, 4th Regiment; wounded at Pine Mountain, Ga., June 14, '64.
Tompkins, Donald	Aug. '61	April '65	
Tompkins, John W	Aug. '61	April '65	
Verrett, Edward	Aug. '61		
Wadsworth, Thomas C	Aug. '61		Killed at Murfreesborough January 2, '63.
Walker, Elbert	Aug. '61		

Roll Company I (Dixie Stars)—3rd Florida Infantry.
(CONTINUED.)

NAMES.	MUSTERED IN.	MUSTERED OUT.	REMARKS.
Walker, Gilbert	Aug. '61		Corporal.
Walker, Thomas	Aug. '61		
Webb, T. B.		April '65	
Williams, James W	Aug. '61		
Wiley, David M	Aug. '61		
Wiley, Gardner E	Aug. '61		
Winiges, S. H.		April '65	
Woodward, William H	Aug. '61	April '65	
Young, George W	Aug. '61	April '65	
Young, Patrick H		April '65	Shot through the liver at Meridian, Miss., '64.

Roll Company K (Columbia and Suwannee Guards)—3rd Florida Infantry.

NAMES.	MUSTERED IN.	MUSTERED OUT.	REMARKS.
OFFICERS.			
Captains—			
William G. Parker			Died.
Simon J. Stallings	Aug. '61	April '65	1st Sergeant; promoted Lieutenant; then Captain.
1st Lieutenant—			
Thomas C. Strange	Aug. '61		Killed at Brick Church near Jacksonville, Fla.
2nd Lieutenants—			
Nathan M. Daniel	'61		Resigned March 20, '63.
Melvil B. Gerry	Aug. '61	April '65	Promoted 2nd Lieutenant.
3rd Lieutenants—			
Mathew W. Postell		April '65	Sergeant; promoted 3rd Lieutenant.
Littleton Hurst			Promoted Lieutenant.
ENLISTED MEN.			
Barr, Robert	Aug. '61		
Bennett, Jesse	Aug. '61		
Bloom, George W	Aug. '61		
Block, Neil	'61		
Boyd, Calvin	'61		
Bray, Charles	'61		Honorable mention at Chickamauga.
Clements, Thomas	'61		Musician.
Cobb, Samuel S	'61		
Coleman, William	'61		
Cox, John	'61		
Craven, William B	'61		
Curl, Elisha	'61	April '65	
Curl, Jasper	'61	April '65	
Curl, William H	'61	April '65	
Dixon, Henry	'61		
Dunaway, John B	'61		
Duse, Washington	'61		
Edwards, John C	'61		
Feagle, Michael	'61		
Frazer, Samuel E	'61		
Gaining, John G	'61		
Gerry, Robert B	'61		
Godwin, Arthur	61		
Godwin, Wiley	'61		
Gray, Allen	'61		
Groover, Wesley	'61		
Guthrie, John C	'61		
Hallwanger, Elmon	'61	April '65	Corporal.
Hatch, Thomas	'61		Died at Camp Chase March 8, '65.
Haynes, James J	'61		
Holland, James	'61		
Johns, Jeremiah	'61		
Johnson, Alexander	'61		
Johnson, Thomas	'61		
Johnson, Thomas L	May 3, '61	April '65	Wounded at Perryville, Ky., October 8, '62.
Keene, Humphrey	'61		
Keene, Mills			Deserted.
Knight, John G. A		April '61	Wounded at Perryville, Ky., October 8, '62.
McCally, Pierce			
McNair, Samuel C			
Marcum, A. J	Sept. '61	April 26, '65	
Mills, John M			Corporal.
Miller, James B			Musician.
Parker, Little B			
Peacock, Washington			
Platt, William		April '65	Promoted Lieutenant in Captain Lesley's Co., 7th Florida Regiment.
Pympton, Joseph R		April '65	Promoted Sergeant; wounded at Murfreesborough, January 3, '63; disabled; shot at Resaca, Ga., May 14, '64.
Prysock, William B			

Roll Company K (Columbia and Suwannee Guards)—3rd Florida Infantry.
(CONTINUED.)

NAMES.	MUSTERED IN.		MUSTERED OUT.		REMARKS.
Rodgers, Dale D	Aug.	'61			Corporal.
Rodgers, James F	Aug.	'61			
Raulerson, Hawes	Aug.	'61			
Raulerson, Jackson	Aug.	'61			Killed at Gettysburg.
Smith, David			April	'65	
Smith, James A	Aug.	'61			
Smith, Joseph B	Aug.	'61			
Smith, Mitchell F	Aug.	'61			
Smith, William J	Aug.	'61			
Swales, James R	Aug.	'61			Corporal.
Swinny, Thomas	Aug.	'61			
Stewart, Alphonzo A	Aug.	'61			
Stewart, Ezekiel	Aug.	'61			
Traitt, William	Aug.	'61			
Tuton, Evans		'61			
Union, John F		'61			
Vass, James T		'61			
Walker, James H		'61			
Ward, James H		'61			
Witt, Adam C		'61	April	'65	
Witt, David A	July 1,	'61	April	'65	Lost hearing by explosion of shell at Missionary
Witt, Jacob	July 1,	'61	April	'65	Ridge, Tenn., November 25, '63.
Wilcox, George W		'61			
Wood, Burrzella		'61			Killed.
Wood, J. S			April	'65	
Zetterower, James W	July 1,	'61	April 26,	'65	Captured at Bentonville, N. C., March 22, '65; imprisoned at Hart's Island, N. Y., and paroled from there June 17, '65.

FOURTH FLORIDA REGIMENT.

Early in the spring of 1861 ten more companies of volunteers were organized as the 4th Florida Regiment of Infantry and mustered into service July 1, 1861, with Edward Hopkins of Jacksonville, Fla., as Colonel; M. Whitsmith, Lake City, Fla., Lieutenant-Colonel; W. L. Bowen, as Major; Lieut. Edward Badger, Adjutant; Capt. James McCay, Quartermaster; Dr. W. S. Weedon, Surgeon; J. M. Kilpatrick, Sergeant-Major; J. P. McLaughlin, Quartermaster-Sergeant; and the following companies and captains:

Capt. Charles A. Gee, Gadsden county, Co. A; Adam W. Hunter, Franklin county, Beauregard Rifles, Co. B; Capt. William H. Dial, Madison county, Co. C; William A. Shefield, Columbia county, Co. D; Thomas A. McGhee, Columbia and LaFayette counties, Co. E; James P. Hunt, New River county, (Bradford), Co, F; William Fletcher, Marion and Levy counties, Co. G; W. F. Lane, Washington and Liberty counties, Co. H; Joseph B. Barnes, Jackson county, Dixie Boys, Co. I; John T. Leslie, Hillsborough county, Co. K. Upon the completion of its organization the Regiment was assigned to duty mainly on the Gulf coast, Companies D, E and K being stationed at Tampa Bay; F at Cedar Keys; B, E and I at St. Marks; Companies H and G at Fernandina until the evacuation of that place March, 1862, when they were ordered to Camp Langford near Jacksonville. Details from Companies F and C, of the 2nd Florida under command of Capt. Walter B. Moore, on July 4, 1861, took the steamer Madison and captured three schooners loaded with railroad irons, and Major Bowen in command of Tampa captured two sloops with their crews.

In May, 1862, the Regiment was reorganized. J. P. Hunt was elected Colonel; W. F. L. Bowen, Lieutenant-Colonel; and Edward Badger Major.

Colonel Hunt died September 1, 1862, at Chattanooga, Lieutenant-Colonel Bowen becoming Colonel; Maj. Edward Badger, Lieutenant-Colonel; and Capt. John T. Leslie was promoted Major.

The 4th Regiment became a part of Bragg's Army, being assigned to General Forrest's command; and in this command were engaged at Nashville. On its return to Murfreesborough the Regiment went into camp and remained until late in December, 1862. On the morning of December 28, 1862, it was ordered to the Lebanon Pike, where it engaged the enemy. On the afternoon of December 28 the 1st, 3rd and 4th Florida were brigaded under Gen. William Preston. This brigade and Palmer's were the last of General Breckenridge's command transferred to the west side of Stone River December 31, and made the final and unsuccessful assault on the Federal center. The 1st and 3rd Florida, under Col. William Miller, gained the cedar brake so prominent in that action; and the 4th, under Colonel Bowen, advanced as far but with much heavier loss. In the engagement the 4th lost 55 killed and wounded. It captured 250 rifles from the enemy. Ordered back to the east side of the river it was again with Breckenridge January 2, 1863, where it did splendid service; being the last regiment to leave the field and made a gallant fight to save the brigade battery, sustaining heavy loss. First Lieut. S. D. Harris, commanding Co. I, was mortally wounded and left on the field. Sergt. L. N. Miller and Adj. C. C. Burke were also wounded. In this battle, Murfreesborough, the 4th, 458 strong, lost 163 killed and wounded, and 31 missing.

In May, 1863, the brigade, under Gen. M. A. Stovall, was transferred to Mississippi, under General Johnston, to relieve Vicksburg. On July 1 General Johnston reported that "a party of skirmishers of the 1st, 3rd and 4th Florida, 47 Georgians and Cobb's Battery struck the enemy's flank and captured 200 prisoners and the colors of the 28th, 45th and 53d Illinois Regiments.

On September 20 the 1st, 3rd and 4th, still with General Stovall, took part in the battle of Chickamauga and again were distrenched. At the battle of Missionary Ridge the 4th carried in 172 men, and all except 18 were either killed, wounded or captured. At Dalton, on February 23, 1864, the 4th was consolidated with the 1st Cavalry, dismounted, which had lost all its field officers, and of 200 men engaged at Missionary Ridge only 33 effective men were left. The consolidated 1st and 4th took part in all the campaigns until the final surrender in North Carolina at the close of the war. On June 9, 1862, the 4th Regiment mustered 926 men and 47 officers; on April 26 it surrendered 23 men.

Roll, Field and Staff—4th Florida Infantry.

NAMES.	MUSTERED IN.		MUSTERED OUT.		REMARKS.
Colonels—					
Edward Hopkins	July	'61			Retired at reorganization May '62.
J. P. Hunt	July	'61			Promoted Colonel May '62; died September 1, '62.
W. L. L. Bowen			April 26,	'65	Promoted Colonel; honorable mention at Chickamauga.
Lieutenant-Colonels—					
M. Whit Smith	July	'61			Resigned at reorganization.

Roll, Field and Staff—4th Florida Infantry.

(CONTINUED.)

NAMES.	MUSTERED IN.	MUSTERED OUT.	REMARKS
W. L. L. Bowen	July '61		Promoted Lieutenant-Colonel at reorganization May 10, '62.
Edgar Badger	July '61	April 26, '65	
Majors—			
W. L. L. Bowen	July '61	April 26, '65	Promoted Colonel.
John T. Leslie	July '61		Captain; promoted Major; resigned.
Jacob A. Lash	July '61		Captain; promoted Major; captured and died on Johnson Island May 21, '65; grave No. 174.
Surgeon—			
Assistant-Surgeons—			
Hamilton M. Weeden	July '61	April 26, '65	
Robert J. Bigelow			
Adjutants—			
Edward Badger	July '61	April 26, '65	Promoted Lieutenant-Colonel.
C. C. Burke	July '61	April 26, '65	1st Lieutenant; resigned November 5, '63.
Sergeant-Major—			
J. M. Kilpatrick	July '61	April 26, '65	
Quartermasters—			
James McKay	July '61	April 26, '65	
H. L. Crane			
Commissary—			
H. G. Townsend	July '61	April 26, '65	
Quartermaster-Sergeant—			
J. P. McLaughlin	July '61	April 26,'65	
Commissary-Sergeant—			
Chaplain—			
R. L. Wiggins			Resigned February 11, '65.

Roll Company A—4th Florida Infantry.

NAMES.	MUSTERED IN.	MUSTERED OUT.	REMARKS.
OFFICERS.			
Captain—			
▶ Charles A. Gee	July '61		
1st Lieutenants—			
William E. Gorman	July '61		
A. S. Owens		April 26, '65	Promoted 1st Lieutenant; honorable mention at Chickamauga.
2nd Lieutenants—			
David Gee			Retired at reorganization.
Henry H. Spear	July '61		Sergeant; promoted 2nd Lieutenant; resigned November 4, '63.
G. W. Reynolds			Promoted 2nd Lieutenant; resigned March 14, '64.
3rd Lieutenants—.			
James A. Black			
Seligman M. Davis			Corporal; promoted 3rd Lieutenant.
ENLISTED MEN.			
Alderman, David			
Alderman, Joseph J			
Andrews, Elishua	July '61		
Andrews, Owen E			
Andrews, W. H			
Black, Calvin			
Black, Wesley	July '61		
Bowman, Samuel			
Brown, Hensford D			
Bryan, Archibald B			
Cargill, Cornelius E			
Cargill, Efford E		April 26, '65	
Colleton, Charles B			
Cooper, W. P	July '61		
Decker, E. T	July '61		
Dykes, Jacob H	May 18, '62		Wounded, Stone River; Missionary Ridge; Franklin, Tenn., in '62 and '63.
Edenfield, Joseph W	June 19, '61	April 26, '65	Shot at Murfreesborough December 31, '62.
Edwards, C. B	July '61		
Evans, Reuben B			
Fletcher, George W		April 26, '65	
Flowers, Leonard W			
Filligan, James J			
Freeman, Thomas J			
Garry, John Thomas			Corporal.
Gilbourne, Henry J			
Glisson, Elbert			
Glisson, Elisha			
Gordan, William F			
Gore, James W			
Gore, William W			

Roll Company A—4th Florida Infantry.
(CONTINUED.)

NAMES.	MUSTERED IN	MUSTERED OUT.	REMARKS.
Goza, W. W.			
Hardin, Adam C.	April '61	April 26, '65	Paroled from prison at close of war.
Haas, W. A.			Honorable mention.
Hilliard, William J.			
Hinson, B. F.		April 26, '65	
Houk, George W.			
Hudson, Benjamin F.			
Jackson, T. H.		April 26, '65	
Johnson, James.			
Johnson, J, C.			
Johnson, John H.	July '61	April 26, '65	Wounded at Resaca, Ga., '63.
Johnson, Martin.			
Johnson, Stephen.			
Johnson, W. F.		...April 26, ' 65	
Keadle, William H.			Musician.
Long, Wesley.			
Luckie, Alonzo T.			Sergeant.
McCardel, James.			
McCardel, William.			
McIntosh, James D.		April 26, '65	
McIntosh, S.			
McKenzie, John W.			
McLaughlin, John P.			1st Sergeant.
McMullen, John.			Musician.
McPhatter, Archibald.	July '61		
McPhatter, John A.			
Martin, Nathaniel.			
Mathews, George M.			Died Camp Chase February 15, '65; grave No.
Mathews, John C.			1298.
Matthews, Thomas F.			
Matthews, William.			
Morgan, Richard M.		April 26, '65	Promoted from Corporal to 1st Sergeant.
Myers, Herman.			
Owens, Silas S.			
Peacock, Mitchell.			
Peters, Andrew J.			
Perkins, James P.			
Pittman, Edward E.			
Posten, J. W.	July '61		
Reagan, George.	July '61		
Regan, Robert.	May '61	April 26, '65	Wounded at Murfreesborough, Tenn., Jánuary 2
Rowan, William.			'63.
Richards, Jacob D.			
Rossiter, James.	July '61		
Rossiter, William.			
Shaw, R. G.	July '61		
Smith, Francis M.			
Spear, T. B.	July '61		
Standley, John.			
Stoudamayer, Ansel T.			
Strickland, Alssmon M.			
Strickland, David.			
Temple, Mark H.			
Thomas, P. F. M.	April 18, '62		
Thompson, Tobias.	April 18, '62		
Truman, S. P.		April 26, '65	
Turner, J. D.		April 26, '65	
Turner, Alonzo D.		April 26, '65	Promoted Corporal.
Turner, Nathan.			
Wadkins, George W.			Corporal.
Warren, William.			
Weeks, John F.			
Whethersby, John T.			
Whaley, James S.			
Whaley, Milton.	July '61		
Whitson, James E.	July '61		
Whittle, James B.			
Williams, John.			
Wilson, James.			

Roll Company B (Beauregard Rifles)—4th Florida Infantry.

NAMES.	MUSTERED IN.	MUSTERED OUT.	REMARKS.
OFFICERS.			
Captains—			
Adam W. Hunter.			
Robert Knickmeyer.			Sergeant; promoted Captain.

Roll Company B (Beaureguard Rifles)—4th Florida Infantry.
(CONTINUED.)

NAMES.	MUSTERED IN.	MUSTERED OUT.	REMARKS.
1st Lieutenant—			
Reuben L. Harrison			
2nd Lieutenants—			
John Richards	April 30, '61	Aug. '64	Discharged for disability; promoted Lieutenant.
William H. Flower			
Reuben. H. Hall			
3rd Lieutenant—			
Sanders Myers		April 26, '65	Wounded at Missionary Ridge, Tenn., November 25, '63; promoted 3rd Lieutenant.
ENLISTED MEN.			
Albritton, Green			
Anderson, John B			
Anderson, Robert	July '61		
Barnett, William			
Beattel, James			
Bethel, Alexander G			
Bird, Isreal			Prisoner of war.
Bowles, Thomas J			Died in service.
Bray, Hamilton W			
Brown, William C			
Bufkins, Sylvester			
Burke, Charles			Corporal.
Calhoun, Francis J			
Clifton, James			
Coupe, Edward			Corporal.
Cousins, Thomas			Corporal.
Daniels, Shilman			
Daniels, J. S		April 26, '65	....
Davis, James			
Donahue, William		April 26, '65	
Emmerson, Charles			
Flemming, Martin			
Fillchett, John K			
Flower, Jonah B			Musician.
Friel, John			
Gibson, William			
Hall, James H			
Hall, John M			
Harden, James			Died Camp Chase April 4, '65; grave No. 1817.
Harrison, Benjamin K			1st Sergeant.
Herndon, James			Prisoner of war.
Holm, Peter			
Horten, Thomas			
Iles, Francis			
Johnson, Andrew			
Kelber, Luther			
Kennedy, John			
Key, William			Musician.
Kruter, Daniel S			
Lee. Paul			
Lenighans, John			
Leverman, William B			
Lightfoot, Henry B			Corporal.
Lord, Lewis			
McCardle, Abel G			
McCardle, Mirabeau B			
McCardle, Russin			
McCauley, James O			
McClennon, James E			
McDonald, John			
McPhadder, Wiley			Prisoner of war.
Maddox, Joseph Y			
Mahoney, Cain			
May, Albert			
May, William			
Millengin, Edward			
Moon, Thomas			Sergeant.
Muller, Thomas R			
Mullin, John J			
Murkein, Fred			
Norham, Robert			
Oliver, Henry F			
Paulson, Jacob			
Pendleton, Stephen P			
Pennington, S. P	April 25, '61	April 26, '65	Shot in right arm at Murfreesborough, Tenn. December 31, '63.
Piles, Henry			
Powell, Elijah		April 26, '65	Wounded right leg and eye at Missionary Ridge December 27, '63, and captured.
Register, Anthony J			
Rohlink, Henry			
Sallig, Robert S			Corporal; disabled.
Sanders, Myers			Sergeant.
Shalby, August			
Shariot, Benjamin R			
Sheppard, George W			
Sherdan, James			

Roll Company B (Beauregard Rifles)—4th Florida Infantry.
(Continued.)

NAMES.	MUSTERED IN.	MUSTERED OUT.	REMARKS.
Sullivan, Jerry			
Thomas, Henry			
Thomas, James			
Wentworth, Charles W			
Wentworth, George W		April 26, '65	Scalped by a piece of shell at Murfreesborough Tenn., January 2, '63; captured and sent to prison at Nashville, Tenn.
Wentworth, William			Prisoner of war.
Williams, George			
Wingate, Thomas L			Honorable mention; promoted Sergeant.
Worthington, James			
Worthington, Joseph			

Roll Company C—4th Florida Infantry.

NAMES.	MUSTERED IN.	MUSTERED OUT.	REMARKS.
OFFICERS.			
Captains—			
William H. Dial		May 9, '65	Promoted Major of 1st Florida Reserves.
J. A. Lash			1st Lieutenant; promoted Captain, then Major; died on Johnson's Island, May 21, '65; grave No. 179.
James B. Parramore			Promoted 1st Lieutenant; then Captain, Transferred to General Finnegan's Staff as Inspector General, '64.
John L. Ingles		May 26, '65	Promoted Captain; '64.
1st Lieutenant—			
Aaron S. Pope			Honorable mention at Chickamauga; promoted 1st Lieutenant.
2nd Lieutenants—			
John M. Beggs			
Nathaniel T. Elliot			
George C. Dickle			Honorable mention at Chickamauga.
William H. Edwards			Promoted Jr. 2nd Lieutenant.
John H. Stephens			Corporal; promoted 2nd Lieutenant for meritorious conduct.
ENLISTED MEN.			
Adams, George M		May 9, '65	
Bentrol, Casper			Died at Chattanooga, buried in cemetery there.
Bond, Alford		May 9, '65	Wounded at Chickamauga, Ga., and at Dallas, Ga.
Bond, Nelson			
Boyett, William H			
Braden, J. H		May 9, '65	
Brim, J. B		May 9, '65	
Brins, John			
Brinson, Charles H		May 9, '65	
Brinson, John			
Borch, Gilson H			
Brock, William G			
Brown, John		May 9, '65	
Bunker, Seth H			Sergeant.
Bykard, Edmund C			Sergeant.
Caruth, William L		May 9, '65	Shot through side at Murfreesborough, Tenn., January 2, '63.
Clanten, James B			
Clemons, Jasper W			
Coats, Edward B		May 9, '65	Shot in arm at Dallas, Ga., May 28, '63.
Coats, P. G		May 12 '65	Wounded at Missionary Ridge, Tenn., December 27, '63.
Coats, William W		April 26, '65	
Clayton, Samuel B	Sept. 5, '61	April 26, '65	
Cochrun, William P			
Collins, John		April 26, '65	
Coats, Philip G			
Cope, Edmond		April 26, '65	
Daniel, J. S		April 26, '65	
Davis, George W			Sergeant.
Dean, Charles E			
Dean, James			
Devane, Benjamin F			
Devane, Samuel R			
Dougerts, James A			
Driggers, Elishu			
Driggers, John I			
Driggers, William			
Ernest, Lippman			
Farnell, John			
Farnell, William B			
Flynn, Daniel B			

Roll Company C—4th Florida Infantry.
(CONTINUED,)

NAMES.	MUSTERED IN	MUSTERED OUT.	REMARKS.
Frier, A.			Imprisoned at Fort Delaware.
Frier, Newlin A.			Died Camp Chase, O., April 7, '65; grave No. 1827.
Futwell, H. T.		April 26, '65	
Garnly, William R.			Corporal.
Gomto, James D.			
Gornto, Thomas J.			
Harmmerly, James W.		April 26, '65	Honorable mention.
Humpton, A. P.		April 26, '65	
Harken, John T.			
Haskey, William R.			
Hinson, B. F.		April 26, '65	
Hinton, Thomas J.			
Hinton, William.			
Howard, Francis M.			
Huammaly, James W.			
Ives, W. M.			Promoted Sergeant-Major of consolidated Regiment, '65.
Jones, Brown V.			
Kesey, James M.			
Kilbride, Dennis.			Musician.
Kilpatrick, John M.			
Kirkpatrick, James W.			Sergeant.
Kirkpatrick, John O.			
Lacquey, Jefferson.		April 26, '65	
Latner, Lawrence.			Died, Camp Douglass, buried in Oakwood Cemetery, Chicago.
Livingston, A.		April 26, '65	
Lynch, Elijah.			
Lynch, Hesekiah.			
Ginty, James M.		April 26, '65	
McLeary, Fred S.		April 26, '65	Shot through right elbow at Murfreesborough, Jan. 2, '63.
McLeod, Henry R.		April 26, '65	Discharged at Tullohoma, Tenn., '63 for Rheumatism.
Mattair, R. B.		April 26, '65	
Moat, J. W.			Died, Camp Douglass Prison, buried Cemetery, Chicago.
Mooney, John.		April 26, '65	
Newman, William H.			
Odum, Nathan.			
Page, Jackson J.	Sept. 5, '61	April 26, '65	Wounded at Chickamauga, Ga., Sept. 20, 1863.
Parramore, W. L.		April 26, '65	
Patterson, Andrew E.			
Patterson, Archibald.			Died Camp Chase, Nov. 16, '64; grave No. 624.
Patterson, Henry.			
Patterson, John F.			
Peet, Henry B.	Aug. 12, '61	April 26, '65	
Pemberton, Moses C.		April 26, '65	Musician.
Powder, Benjamin F.		April 26, '65	
Powell, Oliver H.			
Pierson, William H.		April 26, '65	Wounded in thigh at Snake Gape, Ga.
Raybon, Charles.			
Revels, Owen J.		April 26, '65	
Rutherford, Samuel.			
Rykard, Edmund C.			Promoted Orderly Sergeant, wounded at Murreesborough, Tenn. Jan. '63; died at Vicksburg, Miss. May '63. Buried at Oak Hill Cemetary at Evansville, Ind.
Salis, Asa N.			
Sessions, Samuel R.			
Severitt, William J.			
Shaffer, Michæl G.			
Skipper, James W.			
Smith, James.			
Smith, William.		April 26, '65	
Sowell, Joshua J.			
Sowell Laton.			
Stephens, John H.		April 26, '65	Corporal.
Stephens, John K.			Corporal.
Townsend, H. G.		April 26, '65	
Walker, Hiram A.			
Warneck, James D.			
Webb, Axam.			
Webb, Fenton B.		April 26, '65	Was captured and exchanged during war.
Webb, James.			
Webb, William.		April 26, '65	
Weeks, S. W.		April 26, '65	
Whittle, William J.			
Williams, William.			Corporal.
Wimberly, James R.		April 26, '65	

Roll Company D—4th Florida Infantry.

NAMES.	MUSTERED IN.	MUSTERED OUT.	REMARKS.
OFFICERS.			
Captains—			
William A. Sheffield	Sept. 7, '61		Retired at reorganization May 10, '62.

Roll Company D—4th Florida Infantry.
(CONTINUED.)

NAMES.	MUSTERED IN.	MUSTERED OUT.	REMARKS.
John D. Miot	Sept. 7, '61		Succeeded Sheffield at reorganization May, '62; honorable mention at Chickamauga.
1st Lieutenant—			
Andrew B. Hagan	Sept. 7, '61	April 26, '65	Wounded, Jonesboro Ga. Aug. 31, '64; 1st Lieutenant at reorganization May, '62. Promoted Captain April 9, '65.
2nd Lieutenants—			
Lawrence W. Whitehurst		April 26, '65	Retired at reorganization May, '62.
George W. Brown	Sept. '61		1st Sergeant promoted to 2nd Lieutenant at reorganization.
3rd Lieutenants—			
Epaminondus, Brown		April 9, '65	Retired at reorganization May, '62; re-enlisted fall of '62, 1st Battalion, 10th Florida.
John P. Goodbread		June '65	Promoted 3rd Lieutenant at re-organization May 62; captured, imprisoned at Johnson's Island, O. and from there paroled June ,'65.
Elias D. Waldron			Promoted from private to 3rd Lieutenant, '64.
ENLISTED MEN.			
Alberton, John T	Sept. 7, 61		Discharged at Camp Douglass, Ill, May,'65, prison.
Anderson, John		April 26, '65	
Andrews, E. D		April 26, '65	
Arnold, Burton			
Arnold, John B	Sept. 7, '61	Oct. '63	Discharged for disability, lost right hand at Chickamauga Ga., Sept. 20, '63; honorable mention.
Arnold, Newton T		April 26, '65	
Bailey, Jesse		April 26, '65	
Barfield, Needham	Jan. '61		
Beasley, Raymond J	Feb. 1, '62	April 26, '65	Wounded at Missionary Ridge, Tenn., Dec. 27, '63.
Bigelow, Robert	Jan. '61	April 26, '65	
Brannon, Henry	Jan. '61		
Brannon, Joseph S	Jan. 1, '61	April 26, '65	Wounded in R. R. wreck July 22, '62.
Combs, John R	Oct. 13, '61	July '65	Wounded at Tampa in April, '62.
Cook, John M			
Fletcher, Jesse R			
Foy, John F			
Foy, Thomas S			
Goodbread, J. S	Sept. '61	April 26, '65	
Hatcher Jackson J			
Harris, T. C. B	Sept. 7, '61	April 26, '65	Wounded at Dallas, Ga. Feb. 25, '64.
Harris, T. C. B	Oct. 14, '61	July, '65	
Harris, Thomas H		April 26, '65	
Hays, Robert			
Hunter, James			
Hunter, Silas			
Irvy, Henry M			
Ives, Wash. M			Q. M. Sergeant, promoted Sergeant-Major 1st and 4th consolidated Jan. 3, '64.
Johns, John		April 26, '65	
Jones, Harrison			
Jones, J. K. P			Wounded, Murfreesborough; died of consumption, '64.
Jones, James J		April 26, '65	
Keen, Harrod		April 26, '65	
Keene, Jackson			
Keene, Jesse		April 26, '65	
Keen, P. O		April 26, '65	
Kennady, William J			
King,-Rufus L		April 26, '65	
Knowles, Angus M	Sept. 7, '61	April 26, '65	Wounded at Chickamauga, Ga. Sept. 20, '63.
Lauramore, J. C	Feb, '62	May 4, '65	Wounded in R. R. wreck July 23, '62.
Long, John F			Killed at Dallas, Ga. Jan., '64.
Madison, W. H			
Mercer, John M			
Mercer, Screven		April 26, '65	Musician.
Moore, T. H			
Parnell, Caleb			
Parnell, Jacob		April 26, '65	
Parnell, John W	Sept . 1, '61	April 26, '65	Shot at Chickamauga, Tenn. Sept. 20, '63.
Parnell, Joshua M	Sept. 1, '61	Dec. '62	Discharged for disability.
Payne, Cyrus D			Killed at Murfreesborough, Jan. 2, '63.
Payne, William			
Pratt, George W			
Pratt, Henry W		April 26, '65	
Raulerson, Samuel			
Raulerson, W. J		April 26, '65	
Revels, O. J		April 26, '65	Transferred from Co, A 1st Cav. to Co. D 4th Inf.
Reynolds, Charles W			
Roberts, H. L. R	Sept. 14, '61		Discharged from prison June 1st ,'65.
Rutherford, J. J			
Sanders, Jeremiah			
Sandlin, Henry N			Sergeant.
Sandlin, Wiley B			Killed at Murfreesborough, Tenn.
Shedd, James T			
Shuford, G. W		April 26, '65	
Silcox, D. L	Sept. 1, '61	April 26, '65	Captured at Chickamauga, Ga. Sept. 20, '63 and imprisoned at Camp Douglass, Ill.
Smart, William P			
Thomas, John B			

Roll Company D—4th Florida Infantry.
(Continued.)

NAMES.	MUSTERED IN.	MUSTERED OUT.	REMARKS.
Thomas, Louis R		April 26, '65	
Thompson, Henry M			Deserted, '64.
Walker, David S			Killed in action.
Waldren, E. D		April 26, '65	
Waldren, Keilty S			Discharged at Murfreesborough Dec. 28, '63.
Walker, L. F	Aug. 12, '61	April 26, '65	
Walker, W. W		April 26, '61	
White, James L		April 26, '65	
Williams, William	Sept. 7, '61	April 26, '65	Promoted 1st Sergeant.
Willis, George		April 26, '65	

Roll Company E—4th Florida Infantry.

NAMES.	MUSTERED IN.	MUSTERED OUT.	REMARKS.
OFFICERS.			
Captains—			
Thomas J. McGehee			Retired at re-organization.
William H. Edwards		April 26, '65	3rd Lieutenant, promoted Captain at re-organization May 10, '62.
1st Lieutenants—			
William Forsyth Bynum	Jan. '61	April 26, '65	Retired at re-organization.
Nathaniel T. Elliot		April 26, '65	2nd Lieutenant, promoted 1st Lieutenant; retired at re-organization, and transferred to 15th Con. Cavalry, '63.
William M. T. Johnson			Sergeant, promoted 1st and 3rd Lieutenant; killed in service and honorable mention at Chickamauga.
2nd Lieutenant—			
Benjamin F. Lyons	Sept. 15, '61	April 26, '65	Promoted 2nd Lieutenant, captured Feb., near Blakely, Ala. imprisoned at Camp Douglass.
3rd Lieutenants—			
William M. Lyons			Corporal, promoted 3rd Lieutenant; killed in service.
George W. Lyons			Sergeant, promoted 3rd Lieutenant; resigned, '63.
ENLISTED MEN.			
Adams, George W			Captured at Missionary Ridge, Nov. 22, '63; imprisoned at Rock Island, while there lost eyes from disease.
Allison, George W		April 26, '65	
Andrews, James		April 26, '65	
Arnold, Charles			
Barnett, John N	Sept. 1, '61	April 26, '65	Musician, promoted Corporal.
Barrington, Elicius T	June '61		Wounded at Kennesaw Mt.
Beazley, William			
Bell, Enoch	June '61		
Bell, Lucius C	June '61		Killed.
Bennett, Joseph H	June '61		
Bennett, Reuben W	June '61		
Black, Jack			Corporal.
Blanton, Elbert C	June '61		
Blanton, W. J		April 26, 65	
Blanton, James J	June '61		
Boatwright, Jacob C	June '61		
Boatwright, J. W	Aug. 26, '61	April 26, '65	Transferred, '62 to Co. A, 8th Regiment; captured at Gettysburg, imprisoned at Fort Delaware.
Bond, A		April 26, '65	
Brannan, Robert H	June '61		
Brun, John		April 26, '65	
Brown, William M	June '61		
Carlton, Robert R	Aug. '61		Discharged May 20, '62 for disability.
Carraway, William S			Promoted 1st Sergeant, killed.
Clark, John T			Died of measles at Chattanooga, Oct., '63.
Cooper, William P	June 22, '61	April 26, '65	
Cowart, J. Nathaniel			
Cox, D. N			
Dean, Charles E	June 22, '61		
Dean, James	June 22, '61		
Delaughter, J. P			Promoted 2nd Lieutenant.
Devane, Benjamin F	June 22, '61		
Devane, Samuel R	June 22, '61		
Dougerts, James A	Jan. '61		
Driggers, John J	Jan. '61		
Foster, Ransom S		April 2, '65	Corporal.
Foster, Milton G			
Foster, Watkin N		April 2, '65	
Fugua, Don			
Grace, G. M		April 2, '65	
Hall, Joseph			
Hall, Nathaniel L	Sept. 1, '61	April 2, '65	Shot at Murfreesborough, Tenn. Jan. 2, '63.
Hall, William			
Haney, W. H	Mar. '61	April 2, '65	

Roll Company E—4th Florida Infantry.
(CONTINUED.)

NAMES.	MUSTERED IN.	MUSTERED OUT.	REMARKS.
Henelry, William E.			
Hendry, William J.			
Herring, Joseph.			
Hill, Green.			Killed.
Hinton, William E.			
Hodges, Robert T.			
Howard, Seaborn.			
Hunter, George W.			
Jones, Matthew A.			Right arm amputated, injuries received while chasing deserters.
Lamb, John B.		April 2, '65	
Larrimore, William.			Died in Camp Douglass Prison, buried at Oakwoods cemetery, Chicago.
Latner, L. K.			Died, Camp Douglass Prison.
Lawhorn, Drewery.			
Lewis, H. B.	Oct. '63		
McAlpin, Malcivin.			Corporal.
McCall, Robert F.		April 26, '65	
McCall, William.		April 26, '65	
McCarmna, John.			
McClemma, John M.			Died at St. Andrews Bay during the war.
McCullus, William.			
Mickler, John H.		April 26, '65	
Mills, H. Kelly.		April 26, '65	Honorable mention.
Mims, Valentine.			Wounded, Dallas, Ga. May 28, '64; deserted.
Mims, William J.			
Montgomery, J. G.		April 26, '65	
Morgan, John M.			
Morgan, Joseph W.			
Morrison, Alexander.			
Page, Marion.			
Parker, William B.			
Poppell, William B.	Jan. 15, '63	April 26, '65	
Rabun, John.			
Reams, Josiah.		April 26, '65	
Roberts, Berry.	'61		
Roberts, Francis W.	'61		
Rodgers, Benjamin.		April 26, '65	
Rowell, W. J.		April 26, '65	
Sapp, Bartley W.			Died at Chattanooga.
Sapp, John.	Sept. 10, '61	April 26, 65	
Sapp, Newton.		April 26, '65	Reported a deserter.
Shepherd, Robert N.	'61		
Sherod, Lony J.	'61		Sergeant.
Simmons, John W.	'61		
Smith, John A.		April 26, '65	
Sparks, William B.		April 26, '65	
Sparks, William D.	Nov. '62	April 26, '65	
Stanton, Alexander A.	'62		
Stewart, Daniel J.	Sept. 10, '62	April 26, '65	Shot at Murfreesborough, Tenn. Jan. 2, '63.
Stewart, Edward.		April 26, '65	
Stewart, James W.	'62		
Tillis, Willoughby.	'62		
Tyner, James W.	'62		
Vann, William L.		April 26, 65	
Underwood, J. N.		April 26, '65	
Wagner, Andrew J.	'62		
Walker, David M.		April 26, '65	
Walker, Isaac.	'62		
Walker, J. A.		April 26, '65	
Ward, Abram.	'62		Sergeant.
Watson, Tilman.			
Watson, William C.	July '62		Discharged for disability, '63.
Whidden, G. W.	'63	April 26, '65	
Wilson, Alexander.	'61		
Wilson, Enoch.	'61		
Woods, Henry G.		April 26, '65	
Yawn, Green P. J.	Sept. '63		Discharged Aug. 3, '64; for disability.

Roll Company F—4th Florida Infantry.

NAMES.	MUSTERED IN.	MUSTERED OUT.	REMARKS.
OFFICERS.			
Captains—			
James P. Hunt.	July '61		Promoted Colonel May, '62; died at Chattanooga September 1, '62.
F. W. Williams.	July '61		Promoted Captain.

SOLDIERS OF FLORIDA.

Roll Company F—4th Florida Infantry.
(CONTINUED.)

NAMES.	MUSTERED IN.	MUSTERED OUT.	REMARKS.
George R. Langford	July '61	April 26, '65	1st Lieutenant; promoted Captain; shot in breast and legs.
1st Lieutenant—			
W. W. Mathews		April 26, '65	Promoted 1st Lieutenant.
2nd Lieutenants—			
William T. Weeks		April 26, '65	
Richard K. C. Weeks	July '61		Promoted 2nd Lieutenant; died on Johnson's Island January 17, '64; grave No. 137.
Jeremiah Moody	May 1, '61	April 26, '65	Promoted 2nd Lieutenant; resigned November 4, '63.
M. L. Brown	July '61		Promoted 2nd Lieutenant.
3rd Lieutenant—			
John W. Osteen	July '61	April 26, '65	Promoted 3rd Lieutenant.
ENLISTED MEN.			
Abbott, W. W	July '61		
Biglowe, D. R		April 26, '65	Promoted Sergeant.
Bird, John			Died in service.
Bird, William			Deserted.
Bird, William M	May '61	April 26, '65	Wounded at Murfreesborough and captured; paroled from Rock Island.
Bond, Isreal	July '61		
Bond, William	July '61		
Boyd, James O	July '61		
Branning, William O	July '61		Honorable mention at Chickamauga.
Brinson, D. A	July '61		Corporal.
Brown, William L	July '61		Sergeant.
Bryan, Joseph S	July '61		
Carlton, Joseph R. M	July '61		
Cason, George W	July '61		Musician; promoted Corporal.
Cason, William F	July '61		
Clyatt, G. W		April 26, '65	
Crews, P. M	July '61		
Denmark, James	July '61		
Dobson, Seaborn			Paroled from prison at close of war.
Donahue, William J	Aug. 31, '61	April 26, '65	Wounded at Jackson, Miss., July 21, '63.
Douglass, C			Died at Chattanooga; buried in cemetery there.
Ellis, Joseph H	July '61		
Gatlin, Benjamin	June '61		
Gay, Gilbert	May 10, '62		Paroled from prison at close of war.
Gay, Lewis F	May '62		Corporal; imprisoned at Fort Delaware; paroled at close of war.
Gay, W. H			Paroled from prison at close of war.
Hall, J. O. E	July '61		Sergeant.
Handcock, H. M	July '61		
Hayle, John	July '61		
Hazel, John T	July '61	April 26, '65	Wounded at Murfreesborough, Tenn., September 31, '62.
Hendricks, James B	July '61		
Hormann, Samuel	July '61		Deserted.
Hodges, S. J		April 26, '65	
Holland, J. G	July '61		
Hull, William C	July '61		
Hunt, Davis	July '61		Died at Camp Chase February 15, '65; grave No. 126.
Hunter, Thomas D	July '61		Died in service.
Jackson, William T	July '61		
Johns, George T	July '61		
Johns, Jeremiah J	July '61		
Jones, A. W	July '61		Corporal.
Jones, William N			Shot through lung and captured at Murfreesborough, Tenn., December 31, '62; died January 23, '63.
Julin, Alexander	July '61		Died Camp Douglas prison.
Knight, W. L			
Knowles, Wiley	Feb. 16, '63		Wounded at Kennesaw Mountain, Ga., May 28, '64; deserted.
Lacquey, Jefferson		April 26, '65	Wounded at Atlanta, July 22, '64; died December 12, '89.
Langford, S. L	May 17, '61	May 17, '65	Paroled from Fort Delaware.
Langford, Silas T	April 15, '61	April 26, '65	
Lastinger, D. B	July '61		
Linsey, John D	July '61		Deserted.
Mansell, Samuel T	July '61		Musician.
Mattair, Robert B	July '61	April 26, '65	Prisoner of war.
Matthews, J. H	May '61	April 26, '65	Wounded at Stone River, Tenn., December 31, '62.
Mickler, J. H		April 26, '65	
Murphy, J. H			
Murphy, W. J			
Newsome, D. P		April 26, '65	Promoted 1st Sergeant.
Newsome, Sol		April 26, '65	
Newman, Willis	May '61	April 26, '65	
Odorn, A. C		April 26, '65	Prisoner of war.
Osteen, William N	July '61		
Padgett, Samuel	July '61		
Parrish, Benjamin A	July '61	April 26, '65	Wounded three times at Murfreesborough, Tenn. December 31, '62.
Parrish, George W			Deserted.
Partin, R. C		April 26, '65	

Roll Company F—4th Florida Infantry.
(CONTINUED.)

NAMES.	MUSTERED IN.	MUSTERED OUT.	REMARKS.
Pingston, David W	July '61		
Pingston, James B	July '61		
Poer, John S	July '61		
Poer, William L	July '61		Deserted.
Prevatt, Morgan	July '61		
Price, George W	July '61		
Pierce, John David	May 14, '61	April 26, '65	
Punott, John	July '61		
Punott, Thomas J	July '61		
Renfro, James D. C			Died Camp Douglas prison.
Renfro, M. W			Died in service.
Roberts, B. J	July '61		Prisoner of war.
Roberts, M	July '61		
Roberts, Stephen	July '61		Promoted Corporal and Sergeant; prisoner of war.
Ruff, J. D. C	May 26, '62	April 26, '65	
Scott, James C	July '62	April 26, '65	Corporal; wounded at Missionary Ridge, Tenn., November 25, '63.
Shans, Thomas J. W	July '62		
Sheffield, D. B	July '62		Promoted Sergeant.
Simmons, Benjamin J	July '62		
Simmons, James T	July '62		
Simmons, Thomas	July '62		
Simpson, Thomas			Died in service.
Smith, Joseph D	July '62		
Smith, William L	July '62		
Stanaland, D. L			
Stewart, Joseph	April '62		Died May 1, '64.
Shinger, Docter F	July '62		
Stringer, E. Z	July '62		
Stringer, Ira	July '62		
Stringer, James	July '62		Died in service.
Sturgis, Ira	April '62	April 26, '65	Wounded at Missionary Ridge, Tenn., December. 27, '63.
Sturgis, J			Died in service.
Sturgis, William	May 4, '62	April 26, '65	
Thomas, C. R	May '62		Prisoner of war.
Thomson, Street	May '62		
Weekham, G, R	May '62		
Weeks, Ezekiel	May 20, '62	May 27, '65	Captured at Resaca, Ga., May 27, '64; imprisoned at Rock Island, Ill., and paroled from there March 27, '65.
Weeks, F. M	July '62		1st Sergeant.
Weeks, O. D	July '62		
Weeks, Silas	July 10, '62	April 26, '65	Wounded at Murfreesborough, Tenn., January 3, '63.
Weeks, William H. H	July '61		
Wells, Israel J	May '62	April 26, '65	Wounded at Chickamauga, Ga., September 20, '63; promoted 1st Sergeant.
Wickham, David L	Nov. '62	April 26, '65	
Wilson, Henry			
Wingate, R. B			
Wynne, Isaac			
Young, Charles A	July '62		

Roll Company G—4th Florida Infantry.

NAMES.	MUSTERED IN.	MUSTERED OUT.	REMARKS.
OFFICERS.			
Captains—			
William L. Fletcher	'61	April 26, '65	Retired on reorganization May 10, '62.
Samuel O. Howse	June '61	April 26, '65	1st Lieutenant; promoted Captain; resigned March 25, '62.
Thomas J. Rawls	June '61	April 26, '65	1st Lieutenant; promoted Captain.
1st Lieutenants—			
James O. Brown		April 26, '65	2nd Lieutenant; promoted 1st; resigned March 31, '63.
Henry N. Clark	June '61		Sergeant; promoted 1st Lieutenant.
2nd Lieutenants—			
Berry Mills	June '61	April 26, '65	Promoted 2nd Lieutenant; resigned April 2, '63.
B. F. Overman			
Cullin Curle	June '61		Resigned March 12, '64.
William H. McCardell	June '61	May 10, '65	Transferred to Co. H, 2nd Florida Cavalry.
3rd Lieutenants—			
J. W. Dyches		April 26, '65	Promoted Corporal of Color Guard; 3rd Lieutenant.
John R. Scott	Aug. '61	April 26, '65	Promoted 3rd Lieutenant.
William H. Bingham	June '61	April 26, '65	Promoted 1st Sergeant; 3rd Lieutenant.
ENLISTED MEN.			
Addison, John S	June '61		Died in service.
Andos, Amos K			
Badger, E. N			Promoted Lieutenant-Colonel.

Roll Company G—4th Florida Infantry.
(CONTINUED.)

NAMES	MUSTERED IN.	MUSTERED OUT.	REMARKS.
Badger, John	June '61		
Barnes, Harrison H	June '61		
Bingham, S. P		April 26, '65	Died in service.
Boyles, Henry J	June '61		Died in service.
Bruce, George W	June '61		Deserted.
Bridges, S. M			Died in service.
Carter, George R	June '61		Transferred to Co. K, 7th Regiment.
Carter, John B	Sept. '61	April 26, '65	Wounded Chickamauga, Ga., September 20, '63.
Carter, Joseph	June '61	April 26, '65	
Carlton, Alderman G. W	June '61		Died in service.
Carlton, Thomas W	June '61		Died in service.
Chandler, Thomas J	June '61	April 26, '65	1st Sergeant; prisoner of war.
Clark, H. N	June '61	April 26, '65	
Clark, John H	June '61		
Colding, Samuel	June '61		Died in service.
Colding, Thomas E	June '61		Died in service.
Colson, Abraham	May '61		Discharged from Rock Island prison at close of war.
Cook, James H	June '61		Died in service.
Conyers, Francis M	July '61		Wounded, Atlanta, '64; paroled from prison '65.
Conyers, I. N			Honorable mention at Chickamauga.
Counts, William	June '61		Died in service.
Daniels, J. S			Member of band.
DeBruhle, Stephen C	June '61	April 26, '65	Sergeant.
Driggers, Charles W	Mch. 20, '62		Honorable discharge.
Driggers, Mathew N	Mch. 20, '62		Deserted at West Point, Ga.
Dye, Francis	June '61	April 26, '65	
Dye, Joseph E	June '61		Paroled from prison.
Dunn, John F	June '61		Transferred to Co. K, 7th Regiment.
Dunn, William A	June '61		Transferred to Co. K, 7th Regiment.
Evans, Charles G	June '61	April 26, '65	Corporal.
Fields, G. W		April 26, '65	
Fretwell, Hiram T	June '61	April 26, '65	
Fretwell, John E	June '61	April 26, '65	
Gamble, S. J		April 26, '65	Corporal.
Gainey, Richard R	June '61		Died in service.
Graham, Lorentus M	June '61	April 26, '65	
Grantham, Elijah	June '61		Honorably discharged.
Griggs, Philip T	June '61	April 26, '65	
Gunter, Aaron	June '61		Died in service.
Hagin, Peter		April 26, '65	
Heart, Stephen W	June '61	April 26, '65	
Herl, William	June '61		Died in service.
Hickman, Henry W	June '61		Musician; reported that he went to the enemy.
Holley, W. B		April 26, '65	Wounded, Murfreesborough, December 28, '62.
Hogg, Joseph T	June '61		
James, Warren	June '61		
James, Washington L	June '61		
Jones, J. F		April 26, '65	
Jones, Lamar	June '61		Died in service.
Jones, Warren	June '61		Died in service.
Jones, Watkins	June '61		Died in service.
Knight, Samuel N	June '61		Corporal; died in service.
Knoblock, Jasper J	June '61		Died in service.
Leggitt, John	June '61		
Lee, J. E	June '61		Died in service.
Leonard, S. S			Paroled from prison.
Logan, Thomas L	June '61		Died in service.
Long, Nathan	June '61		Died in service.
Lovell, W. A			Died, Chattanooga; buried in cemetery there.
Lyles, Louis	June '61		
McCredie, David		April 26, '65	Severely wounded Murfreesborough, December 31, '62.
McCredie, James		April 26, '65	Captured December 15, '64; imprisoned and paroled from Camp Chase, O., May 14, '65.
McDougal, Neil P	June '61		
Marlow, Albert D	June '61		Died in service.
Mathews, J. C		April 26, '65	
Mock, William B	July 5, '61	April 26, '65	Wounded, Murfreesborough, December 28, '62;
Mills, Benjamin	June '61	April 26, '65	imprisoned and paroled from Camp Chase April 13, '65.
Mills, James F	June '61		Died in service.
Millican, Pinckney W	June '61		Died in service.
Morelle, Joseph W	June '61	April 26, '65	
Mundon, Isham	June '61	April 26, '65	
Oberry, Reuben B	June '61		
Padgett, Clark	June '61		Died in service.
Pendarvis, J. S			Deserted.
Pendarvis, Silas	June '61		Deserted
Pendarvis, William	June '61		Deserted.
Peters, S. J		April 26, '65	
Pounds, Robert J	June '61		Died in service.
Quatlebaum, William D	June '61		Died in service.
Rainer, Hardy		April 26, '65	Wounded, Murfreesborough, December 31, '62.
Rawls, Q	June '61		

Roll Company G—4th Florida Infantry.
(CONTINUED.)

NAMES.	MUSTERED IN.	MUSTERED OUT.	REMARKS.
Rawls, Sam	June '61		Honorably discharged.
Redding, Lee R	June '61		Died in service.
Riggs, J. A.		April 26, '65	
Riggs, J. W.	Aug. 15, '61		Captured; imprisoned and paroled from Camp Chase May 14, '65.
Roberts, Daniel L	June '61		Died in service.
Roberts, R.	June '61	April 26, '65	
Russell, Ichabod C	June '61		Died in service.
St. Legar, Butler	June '61		Died in service.
Scott, James E	June '61		Imprisoned and paroled at Fort Delaware at close of war.
Shaw, Daniel	June '61		Honorably discharged.
Sherouse, Jackson	June '61		Died in service.
Simpson, James W	June '61		Died in service.
Sims, William C	June '61	April 26, '65	
Smith, Alfred H	June '61		Died in service.
Smith, B. F.		April 26, '65	
Smith, Calvin H	June '61		Honorably discharged.
Smith, David W	June '61		Died in service.
Smith, Frank	June '61		Died in service.
Smith, William W	June '61		Died in service.
Stenter, James W	June '61		
Streeter, J. Wynman			Deserted.
Strickland, William	June '61		Died in service.
Stivender, Arthur	June '61		Died in service.
Watkins, Charles F	June '61		Sergeant.
Watkins, Thomas W	June '61		
Wells, John T			Died, Camp Douglass prison; buried Oakwood cemetery.
White, Charles H	June '61	April 26, '65	Promoted Sergeant.
Wiggins, G. A.			Paroled from prison.
Williams, Shade	June '61		Died in service.
Williams, Thomas	June '61	April 26, '65	
Wrenn, John J	June '61		Died in service.

Roll Company H (Washington County Invincibles)—4th Florida Infantry.

NAMES.	MUSTERED IN.	MUSTERED OUT.	REMARKS.
OFFICERS.			
Captains—			
William F. Lane	Sept. 13, '61		Died at Lake City, Fla.
Bernard Laspeyre	Sept. 13, '61		Promoted Captain; died of disease.
George W. Cook	Sept. 13, '61	April 26, '65	Lost arm at Murfreesborough, Tenn.; wounded at Franklin, Tenn.; promoted 2nd Lieutenant and elected Captain.
1st Lieutenants—			
Joseph Summerlin			Promoted 2nd and 1st Lieutenant; wounded at Murfreesborough, Tenn., January 2, '63 and died January 16, '63.
Thomas J. Russ	Sept. 13, '61	April 26, '65	Promoted 1st Lieutenant.
2nd Lieutenants—			
Daniel D. McLean	Sept. 13, '61		Died in service.
Joseph B. Canell	Sept. 13, '61		Corporal; promoted 2nd Lieutenant; resigned March 31, '63.
3rd Lieutenants—			
LaFayette Irvin	Sept. 13, '61		Retired at reorganization.
Wilson L. Raley	Sept. 13, '61	April 26, '65	Sergeant; promoted 3rd Lieuetnant.
ENLISTED MEN.			
Abbott, Robert S	Sept. 13, '61		
Anderson, Henry		'61	April 26, '65	Shot at Chickamauga, Ga., September 20, '63.
Anderson, Lewis	Sept. 13, '61		
Beasley, Clayton	Sept. 13, '61		
Bond, J. E. F.			
Bower, Mark A	Sept. 13, '61	April 26, '65	
Brock, W. A.	Sept. 13, '61		
Burke, Jeremiah	Sept. 13, '61		
Carmichal, J. W.	Sept. 13, '61		
Carter, Felix K	Sept. 13, '61	April 26, '65	
Carter, James	Sept. 13, '61		
Carter, John	Sept. 13, '61		
Carter, R. F.	Sept. 13, '61		
Chance, S.	Sept. 13, '61		
Chestnut, James M. D	Sept. 13, '61		
Curlee, J.	Sept. 13, '61		
Curlee, William	Sept. 13, '61		
Danly, James J	Sept. 13, '61		
Davis, Elbert	Sept. 13, '61		
Dertch, Henry J	Sept. 13, '61		Died in hospital February 12, '62.
Dukes, Albert M	Sept. 13, '61		

Roll Company H (Washington County Invincibles)—4th Florida Infantry.
(CONTINUED.)

NAMES.	MUSTERED IN.	MUSTERED OUT.	REMARKS.
Easters, Sherod	Sept. 13, '61		
Evans, David	Sept. 13, '61		
Evans, Lambert	Sept. 13, '61		
Ferguson, J.	Sept. 13, '61		
Fulford, Randal	Sept. 13, '61		
Griffin, Abner G.	Sept. 13, '61		
Hagans, Hiram W. J.	Sept. 13, '61		
Hagans, James L.	Sept. 13, '61		
Hogan, Isham H.	'61	April 26, '65	Promoted 1st Corporal; wounded at Jackson, Miss., July 10, '63.
Hall, Henry J.	Sept. 13, '61		Musician.
Harris, James	Sept. 13, '61		
Harvey, Allen	Sept. 13, '61		
Hays, E.	Sept. 13, '61		
Hewitt, Ephriam L.	Sept. 13, '61		
Hewitt, Robert W.	Sept. 13, '61		
Hewitt, William E. C.	Sept. 13, '61		
Howard, Stephen	Sept. 13, '61		Promoted Corporal.
Howell, William W.	Sept. 13, '61	April 26, '65	
Hudson, Hale B.	Sept. 13, '61	April 26, '65	
Hudson, James T.	Sept. 13, '61		
Irvin, James S.	Sept. 13, '61		
Johns, William H. H.	Sept. 13, '61	April 26, '65	
Johnson, S. C.			Died, Camp Chase February 12, '65; grave No. 1629.
Kent, Theophelus	Sept. 13, '61	April 26, '65	
Laryford, Edward	Sept. 13, '61		
Lanier, James S.	Sept. 13, '61		
Lanier, Lewis H.	Sept. 13, '61		Corporal; killed at Nashville, Tenn.
Lewis, Thomas B.	Sept. 13, '61		
McCormick, John D.	Sept. 13, '61		
McKiethon, Washington J.	Sept. 13, '61		
Maddox, G. W.	Sept. 13, '61		
Martin, Duncan M.	Sept. 13, '61		
Mathews, David	Sept. 13, '61		
Mayhn, D. W.	Sept. 13, '61		
Melvin, Daniel V.	Sept. 13, '61	April 26, '65	
Melvin, Grivin	Sept, 13, '61		
Merritt, David A.	Sept. 13, '61		
Miller, James	Sept. 13, '61		Discharged from Rock Island prison at close of the war.
Miller, John M.	Sept. 13, '61		Sergeant.
Miller, Levi N.	Sept. 13, '61		Killed at Murfreesborough, Tenn.
Miller, Lewis H.	Sept. 13, '61		Promoted 1st Sergeant; killed at Murfreesborough.
Milton, Isreal R.	Sept. 13, '61		
Mills, Hiram	Sept. 13, '61		
Moody, William G.	Sept. 13, '61		
Morris, M.	Sept. 13, '61		
Norris, D.	Sept. 13, '61		
Ousburn, Calvin F.	Sept. 13, '61		Lost left leg at Murfreesborough December 30 '62, and discharged.
Owens, William D.	Sept. 13, '61	April 26, '65	
Palmer, David William	Sept. 13, '61		Died at pneumonia at Fernandina, Fla., November 28, '61.
Parker, John	Sept. 13, '61		
Parker, Peter F.	Sept. 13, '61		Killed at Jonesboro.
Parker, R.	Sept. 13, '61		
Parker, William N.	Sept. 13, '61		
Pierce, Stephen G.	Sept. 13, '61		
Pippin, Johnson	Sept. 13, '61		Honorable mention at Chickamauga.
Pippin, Solomon	Sept. 13, '61		
Potter, W. R. F.	Sept. 13, '61		
Posey, Alfred	Sept. 13, '61		
Provost, Richard V.	Sept. 13, '61		
Railey, James E.	Sept. 13, '61		
Roberts, John H.	Sept. 13, '61		
Russ, James L.	Sept. 13, '61	April 26, '65	Leg broken.
Russ, John J.	Sept. 13, '61		
Russ, John R.	Sept. 13, '61	April 26, '65	Promoted Sergeant.
Singleton, William E.	Sept. 13, '61		
Skipper, Joel	Sept. 13, '61		
Skipper, Reddick W.	Sept. 13, '61		
Stewart, Alexander	Sept. 13, '61		
Tanner, J. T.	Sept. 13, '61		
Taylor, Andrew J.	Sept. 13, '61	April 26, '65	Shot at Dallas, Ga., May 18, '64.
Taylor, David	Sept. 13, '61		Killed at Franklin, Tenn., November 30, '64.
Taylor, F.	Sept. 13, '61		
Taylor, James	Sept. 13, '61		
Taylor, Johnathan	Sept. 13, '61		
Taylor, Robert H. J.	Sept. 13, '61		
Taylor, Washington	Sept. 13, '61		Corporal.
White, J. G.	Sept 13, '61		Corporal.
White, John M.	Sept. 13, '61		
Whittle, S. N.	Sept. 13, '61		
Willis, Hiram	Sept. 13, '61		
Wood, Joseph W.	Sept. 13, '61		

Roll Company I (Dixie Boys) — 4th Florida Infantry.

NAMES.	MUSTERED IN.		MUSTERED OUT.			REMARKS.
OFFICERS.						
Captains—						
Joseph B. Barnes	July	'61				Resigned.
Marmaduke M. Dickson			May	1,	'65	Promoted Captain.
1st Lieutenants—						
Seaborn D. Harris						1st Sergeant; promoted 1st Lieutenant; killed January 2, '63.
Charles C. Burke			May	1,	'65	Promoted 1st Lieutenant.
2nd Lieutenant—						
W. H. Dickson			May	1,	'65	Sergeant; promoted 2nd Lieutenant.
3rd Lieutenants—						
Thadeus G. H. Dekle						Died, '62.
S. L. Owens						Promoted 3rd Lieutenant.
William J. Banks			May	1,	'65	Sergeant; promoted 3rd Lieutenant; honorable mention.
ENLISTED MEN.						
Alexander, Daniel	July	'61				
Anderson, Jefferson F						
Arnold, Chilsey			May	1,	'65	
Avery, John						
Baldeora, Ambrose						
Baldeora, Richard						
Barkly, Albert T			May	1,	'65	Wounded in hand and head; promoted Corporal.
Barkley, Britten L						Musician.
Barnes, Henry T			May	1,	'65	Wounded, Chickamauga, September 20, '63.
Bassford, J. W			May	1,	'65	
Bassford, L. Samuel			May	1,	'65	
Baxter, James D. W						
Balyes, Irwin						
Bell, John R						Died, Camp Chase, January 20, '65; grave No. 818.
Blackman, Charles M						
Bowers, Thomas O						
Branford, Lorenzo R						
Brogden, George W						
Brogden, John T						
Brown, Thomas						
Bryan, Green L			May	1,	'65	Color bearer; promoted Corporal, honorable mention.
Burnham, William B						
Cannon, James J						
Clark, Henry						
Coonrod, T. T	July	'61				
Conner, Reuben M						
Dickson, James W						Sergeant.
Dickson, W. F			May	1,	'65	Promoted Sergeant.
Digby, Talbot W						
Dikes, William H						
Dudley, William D						
Eleby, Edward A						
Ethridge, Josiah	July	'61	May	1,	'65	
Evans, Jesse T	July	'61	May	1,	'65	
Everitt, Samuel D	July	'61	May	1,	'65	Corporal; promoted Sergeant.
Faghan, W. H	July	'61	May	1,	'65	
Fillman, Daniel	July	'61	May	1,	'65	
Gardiner, Joseph W	July	'61	May	1,	'65	
Gaylan, W. H	July	'61	May	1,	'65	
Grant, Zacariah	July	'61	May	1,	'65	
Grantham, Daniel	July	'61	May	1,	'65	
Grice, H	July	'61	May	1,	'65	
Grumbles, Jesse F	July	'61	May	1,	'65	
Hall, J. C	July	'61	May	1,	'65	
Hamilton, Archibald	July	'61	May	1,	'65	
Harrison, Robert W	July	'61	May	1,	'65	
Hart, David	July	'61	May	1,	'65	
Hart, William M	July	'61	May	1,	'65	Corporal; promoted Sergeant.
Jennings, Jasper S	July	'61	May	1,	'65	
Johnson, Benjamin F	July	'61	May	1,	'65	
Johnson, Daniel F	July	'61	May	1,	'65	
Johnson, James C	July	'61	May	1,	'65	Wounded in elbow at Murfreesborough, June, '62
Johnson, James W	July	'61	May	1,	'65	
Jones, John B	July	'61	May	1,	'65	
Keen, Thomas	July	'61	May	1,	'65	
Keen, W. R	July	'61	May	1,	'65	
Lacy, James M	July	'61	May	1,	'65	
Lacy, William W	July	'61	May	1,	'65	
Lott, William C	July	'61	May	1,	'65	Died at Chattanooga.
Meercer, James T	July	'61	May	1,	'65	Corporal; promoted Sergeant.
Minchen, Edward D	July	'61	May	1,	'65	
Michen, Joseph L	July	'61	May	1,	'65	
Morrison, A. James	July	'61	May	1,	'65	
Moseley, Levy M	July	'61	May	1,	'65	Corporal.
Padgett, J. W	July	'61	May	1,	'65	
Pare, Curry	July	'61	May	1,	'65	
Pare, Ebinezer C	July	'61	May	1,	'65	
Petterson, William L	July	'61	May	1,	'65	
Peacock, George M	July	'61	May	1,	'65	

Roll Company I (Dixie Boys)—4th Florida Infantry.
(CONTINUED.)

NAMES.	MUSTERED IN.	MUSTERED OUT.	REMARKS.
Paxton, Richard E.	July '61	May 1, '65	
Peacock, William J.	July '61	May 1, '65	
Parker, Daniel.	July '61	May 1, '65	
Parker, Nathaniel.	July '61	May 1, '65	
Pinder, Drew W.	July '61	May 1, '65	
Rawls, James.	July '61	April 15, '65	
Rawls, Junius.	July '61	April 15, '65	Promoted 1st Sergeant.
Roberts, Rutledge.	July '61	May 1, '65	
Rodgers, David.	July '61	May 1, '65	
Shanklin, Augustus N.	July '61	May 1, '65	
Sills, James A.	April 1, '61	May 1, '65	Wounded at Murfreesborough, Tenn., December 31, '62.
Simms, Charles W.	July '61	May 1, '65	
Simpson, John.	Ju.y '61	May 1, '65	
Simpson, Joseph.	July '61	May 1, '65	
Smith, Anderson.	July '61	May 1, '65	
Smith, Leonidus.	July '61	May 1, '65	Sergeant.
Thomas, Benjamin.	July '61	May 1, '65	Musician.
Trayler, John M.	July '61	April 15, '65	
Trayler, William M.	July '61	May, 1, '65	
Turner, John.	July '61	May 1, '65	
Watts, Thomas.	July '61	April 15, '65	
Watford, M.	July '61	May 1, '65	
Webb, Nathaniel E.	July '61	May 1, '65	Corporal; promoted Sergeant.
Weeks, F. J.	July '61	'64	Discharged for disability.
Wester, Samuel.	July '61	April 15, '65	
Wilson, C. A.	July '61	April 15, '65	
Wilson, George M.	July '61	May 1, '65	
Wood, Almerina J.	July '61	May 1, '65	
Yerty, Henry J.	July '61	May 1, '65	
Young, W. L.	July '61	May 1, '65	
Yon, Terril H.	July '61	May 1, '65	

Roll Company K—4th Florida Infantry.

NAMES.	MUSTERED IN.	MUSTERED OUT.	REMARKS.
OFFICERS.			
Captains—			
John T. Leslie.	July '61		Promoted Major; resigned.
Henry L. Mitchell.	July '61	April 26, '65	1st Lieutenant, promoted Captain; resigned Nov. 30, '64.
Charles W. Hendry.	July '61		Sergeant, promoted 3rd Lieutenant; then Captain
1st Lieutenants—			
John E. Spencer.	July '61		3rd Lieutenant, promoted 1st Lieutenant.
Francis M. Mitchell.	July '61		Sergeant, promoted 2nd Lieutenant, then 1st Lieutenant; killed in action.
2nd Lieutenant—			
William E. Sweat.	July '61		
3rd Lieutenant—			
Calfrey L. Wilder.	July '61		Promoted 3rd Lieutenant.
ENLISTED MEN.			
Andrew, Floire F.	July '61		
Bethel, Joseph.	July '61		
Bowen, William M.	July '61		Sergeant.
Brandon, James H.	July '61		Promoted Corporal, Sergeant; honorable mention.
Carney, Robert J.	July '61		
Collins, James N.	July '61		
Collins, Jesse.	July '61		Corporal.
Collins, John.			
Cook, Charles.	July '61		
Cowart, Henry.	July '61		
Cothran, Thomas.	July '61		
Crane, H. C.		April 26, '65	
Crews, Berry M.	July '61		
Davis, Stafford.	July '61		
Davis, W. R.			
Dease, William.	July '61		
Driggers, Dennis.	July '61		
Eady, Joseph.	July '61		
Fillmon, Darlington.		April 26, '65	
Finley, John.	July '61		
Finley, Thomas J.	July '61		
Fisher, Amos J.	July '61		
Futch, Henry.	July '61		
Gant, G. W.		April 26, '65	
Godwin, William.	July '61		
Griffin, Francis M.	July '61	April 26, '65	Wounded at Franklin, Nov. 30, '64.
Griffin, George W.	July '61		Wounded at Atlanta, Ga. July 22, '64.

Roll Company K—4th Florida Infantry.
(CONTINUED.)

NAMES.	MUSTERED IN.		MUSTERED OUT.	REMARKS.
Grillon, Adet			April 26, '65	
Gullion, Olliot	July	'61		
Hamilton, James	July	'61		
Handcock, George W. D.	July	'61		
Haskins, James P. B.	July	'61		Sergeant.
Harris, Joseph	July	'61		Corporal.
Haskell, J. T.			April 26, '65	
Heard, George S.	July	'61		Musician.
Hendry, Charles W	July	'61		Sergeant.
Henry, John M.	July	'61		
Johnson, James 1st.	July	'61		
Johnson, James H. 2nd.	July	'61		
Johnson, Thomas M.	July	'61	April 26, '65	
Jowers, Patterson	July	'61		
Keen, Perry O.	July	'61		
Lacter, Robert P.	July	'61		
Lumacks, William W.	July	'61		
Lynch, Charles	July	'61		
Lynn, J. A.			April 26, '65	
McLeod, Henry R.	July	'61		Discharged at Tullohoma, Tenn., for disability.
McLeod, Hiram A.	July	'61		
Marsh, Middleton	July	'61		
Mellon, John.				
Miley, Samuel A.	July	'61	April 26, '65	Wounded at Murfreesborough, Tenn., Jan. 3, '63.
Mobley, John B.	July	'61		
Moody, John D.	July	'61		
Moody, Nathaniel M.	July	'61	April 26, '65	
Moody, Simon B.	July	'61		Corporal.
Philips, Joseph F.	July	'61		
Platt, Francis M.	July	'61		
Pollard, Thomas A.	July	'61	April 26, '65	
Prine, James E.			April 26, '65	
Rice, Benjamin L.				Musician.
Rice, George R.	July	'61		
Robinson, George	July	'61		
Robels, Michæl F.	July	'61		
Rockner, Julius				Promoted 1st Sergeant.
Sheppard, William E.	July	'61		
Sloan, Jasper	July	'61		
Smith, Henry	July	'61		
Sparkman, William W.	July	'61		
Spencer, T. K.	July	'61	April 26, '65	Musician, discharged, '62, under age; captured and imprisoned at Fort LaFayette, N. Y. Exchanged and re-enlisted in Jno. T. Lesley's Co.
Strode, John	July	'61		
Thomas, James	July	'61		
Thomas, Robert W	July	'61		
Trull Samuel D	July	'61		
Tully, Joseph	July	'61		
Turner, Benjamin M.	July	'61		
Varn, W. B.			April 26, '65	
Watson, Alexander G.	July	'61		
Weeks, John A.	July	'61	April 26, '65	Wounded in foot at Murfreesborough, Tenn. Dec. 31, '62.
Weeks, Samuel W.	July	'61		
Whidden, Wiloughby	July	'61		
White, Elbert	July	'61		
Wiggins, James	July	'61		
Wilder, John W.	July	'61		
Wilder, W.				Died, Camp Chase, Oct. 15, '64; grave No. 314.
Williams, Matthew H	July	'61		
Young, Joseph H.	July	'61		

FIFTH FLORIDA REGIMENT.

The 5th Florida Regiment was organized in 1862, and mustered into service with J. C, Hately as Colonel; Thompson B. Lamar as Lieutenant-Colonel; B. F. Davis as Major; Capt. W. H. Baker as Quartermaster; and Capt. R. W. Reed as Commissary. The companies were commanded by Captains A. Z. Bailey (Co. A) Garrant Vanzant (Co. B), W. D. Bloxham (Co. C), A. J. Lee (Co. D), John W. Hollyman (Co. E), John Frink (Co. F), W. J. Bailey (Co. G), W. T. Gregory (Co. H), Sam A. Spencer (Co. I), and Richmund N. Gardner (Co. K). Immediately upon its organization the Regiment was ordered to Virginia, where it joined the 2nd Florida, being assigned to Pryor's Brigade; with which it took part in the Second Battle of Manassas and in the Maryland campaign and won distinction at Sharpsburg. After the return from Maryland the 5th was brigaded with the other Florida regiments and became a part of Perry's immortal brigade, surrendering at Appomatox Court House with but 6 officers and 47 men, the only representatives left for duty at that time of a magnificent regiment.

Roll Field and Staff—5th Florida Infantry.

NAMES.	MUSTERED IN.		MUSTERED OUT.		REMARKS.
Colonel—					
J. C. Hateley	Mch.	'62			Wounded and disabled at Sharpsburg September 20, '62; resigned July 6, '63.
Thompson B. Lamar	Mch.	'62			Promoted Colonel, vice Hateley disabled; killed at Petersburg '64.
Lieutenant-Colonel—					
Thompson B. Lamar	Mch.	'62			
Major—					
B. F. Davis	Mch.	'62	April 9,	'65	Wounded at Chancellorsville, Va.
Surgeons—					
R. E. Sapp	Mch.	'62			
J. D. Godfrey	Mch.	'62	April 9,	'65	Transferred to 6th N. C. Infantry.
Assistant Surgeon—					
Adjutants—					
1st Lieut. William Scott	Mch.	'62			
1st Lieut. Thomas W. Shine	Mch.	'62	April 9,	'65	Acting Adjutant; surrendered at Appomatox.
Sergeant-Majors—					
Quartermaster—					
Capt. W. H. Baker					
Commissary—					
Captain R. R. Reed					
Chaplain—					
Quartermaster-Sergeant—					

Roll Company A—5th Florida Infantry.

NAMES.	MUSTERED IN.		MUSTERED OUT.		REMARKS.
OFFICERS.					
Captains—					
Abram Z. Bailey	Mch.	'62			Resigned '62.
William K. Partridge	Nov.	'61	April 9,	'65	Promoted Captain; shot at Petersburg October, '64, and disabled.
1st Lieutenant—					
Samuel J. Turnbull			April 9,	'65	
2nd Lieutenant—					
James Collins			April 9,	'65	
3rd Lieutenant—					
George L. Odum			April 9,	'65	Sergeant; promoted 3rd Lieutenant; wounded, Gettysburg July 2, '63.
ENLISTED MEN.					
Allen, Joseph M					
Almon, Mathew					
Annear, George S					
Barker, Isaac	May 18, '63		May 15,	'65	Transferred to Captain Barwick's Company, 1st Reserves, August '64.
Barker, Jeremiah			May 15,	'65	Wounded at Petersburg June, '64.
Baxley, James					
Bellamy, Marsden D					
Bellamy, Richard					
Bennett, G. W					
Blakeley, Mathew P					
Blount, Allen					
Bonhart, Joseph					
Brown, David					
Bryant, Joseph					
Budd, W. A					Captured and imprisoned at Fort Delaware.
Burnett, William					
Byshot, Joseph	April 15, '62				Wounded, Sharpsburg September 17, '62; imprisoned at Fort Delaware; paroled June 9, '65.
Clark, Erastus W					Sergeant.
Clayton, Daniel M					Corporal; wounded, Gettysburg. July 3, '63.
Clayton, Dilman					

Roll Company A—5th Florida Infantry.

(CONTINUED.)

NAMES.	MUSTERED IN.	MUSTERED OUT.	REMARKS.
Clayton, John J	'62		Became blind while in prison at Point Lookout October ,'64; paroled from there.
Cooper, John F	July 15, '61	April 9, '65	Lost left arm at Gettysburg, July 3, '63.
Crosby, L. W			
Cummings, Joshua		April 9, '65	
Davis, Elisha	July 20, '63		Lost leg at Culpepper Court House, August 13,'63 and discharged.
David, James			
Depratter, Marianna			
Ellenwood, Albert A			
Elliett, William			
Ellis, James M			
Ellis, N. B		April 9, '65	
Gainey, Burrell D		April 9, '65	
Gause, George W		April 9, '65	
Gibbens, Hiram			
Hale, Henry G			
Hammock, W. A		April 9, '65	
Hamilton, A. T		April 9, '65	
Hamilton, James A		April 9, '65	
Harris, Sylvester H			
Harris, William W		April 9, '65	Wounded at North Anna River, May 26, '64.
Hinsey, Henry E		April 9, '65	Wounded at Sharpsburg, September 17, '62.
Hinsey, John R		April 9, '65	
Holly, James		April 9, '65	
Holton, George W			
Holton, Josiah	Jan. '62	April 9, '65	
Holtzclaw, J. C	Jan. 5, '61	April 9, '65	Wounded at Sharpsburg, Md., September 17, '62.
Hughey, N. D		April 9, '65	
Hurst, William L			
Jarvis, Andrew J			Imprisoned at Fort Delaware.
Kinsey, Martin		April 9, '65	Injured in charge at Cold Harbor, June, '64.
Kirkland, Albert			
Lanier, Francis M			Died in prison at Elmira, N. Y., December 5, '64.
Lavall, Patrick			
Lee, Benjamin H			Wounded at Gettysburg, July 3, '63.
Lewis, Benjamin W			Wounded at Gettysburg, July 3, '63.
Lewis, Jesse		April 9, '65	Wounded at Chancellorsville, May 4,'63.
Lewis, Llewellyn			
Lord, Albert			
Lord, John A			
Lord, Zachariah			
Louisiana, Joseph		April 9, '65	
McClellan, Richard H			Wounded at Gettysburg, July 3, '63.
McClellan, William			
McGruder, C. B		April 9, '65	
Madox, Lemuel			
Malone, Drewry	Mch. '63	April 9, '65	
Mays, John R			Wounded at Bristow Station, October 14, '63.
Moore, Lewis			
Morison, A. G		April 9, '65	
Neally, James T		April 9, '65	
Norris, William S		May '65	
Odom, Elkanuh			
Potts, Robert			Wounded at Gettysburg, July 3, '63.
Pratton, M. D			Wounded at Gettysburg, July 3, '63.
Roberts, William L			
Rogers, J. A		June '62	Disability.
Rowell, David R			
Rowell, John C			Died in hospital Lake City, Fla., July 18, '62.
Samson, William			
Scott, David W			Killed at Gettysburg, July 3, '63.
Slaughter, J. D	Jan. '62	April 9, '65	Wounded at the Wilderness, Va., May 6 '64.
Slaughter, Samuel B			
Sloan, Malachi		April 9, '65	
Smith, David J			
Smith, I. W			Imprisoned at Fort Delaware.
Smith, James			
Smith, John Patrick			1st Sergeant.
Smith, Lorenzo D			
Smith, Patrick H		May 25, '65	Sergeant.
Snead, Lawson			
Sparks, John			
Sparks, Martin			
Sparks, Thomas			
Stanley, Hillary			Sergeant; killed at Petersburg '64.
Staughten, James			
Staughten, Thomas			
Stevins, Birch R			
Stewart, John G			
Stewart, R. J	Feb. '61	April 10, '65	
Stewart, William F	Dec. 11, '61	April 9, '65	
Summers, H. M		April 9, '65	
Summers, P. B. W		April 9, '65	

Roll Company A—5th Florida Infantry.
(CONTINUED.)

NAMES.	MUSTERED IN.	MUSTERED OUT.	REMARKS.
Turnbull, Theodore			1st Sergeant.
Wade, Lewis H			
Webb, Isaiah T			Corporal; killed at Sharpsburg, September 17, '63.
Wheeler, C. P		April 9, '65	
Whitmore, Martin			
Willie, J. J		April 9, '65	
Windham, Elias C			Corporal.
Windham, John H			

Roll Company B—5th Florida Infantry.
(CONTINUED.)

NAMES	MUSTERED IN.	MUSTERED OUT.	REMARKS.
OFFICERS.			
Captains—			
Garrett Vanzant		April 9, '65	Resigned May 26, '63.
John H. Tolbert			Promoted Captain from 2nd Lieutenant; killed.
1st Lieutenant—			
William T. Bacon	'61	April 26, '65	
2nd Lieutenants—			
John G. Raulerson	'61		Junior 2nd Lieutenant; killed at Chancellorsville May 3. '63.
T. W. Hart		April 9, '65	Promoted Lieutenant Co. B, 5th Florida.
ENLISTED MEN.			
Allison, Humphrey D	'61		
Anderson, John J	'61		
Anderson, Zacariah	'61		
Arnow, Peter	'61		
Barnes, James A	'61	April 9, '65	promoted 1st Sergeant; wounded Sharpsburg September 13, '62.
Barnes, Robert R	'61		Killed, Gettysburg July 3, '63.
Barr, William T	'61	April 9, '65	
Beaufort, Washington	'61	April 9, '65	
Bivin, Miles M	'61		Killed, Briston Station October '63.
Blume, LaFayette	'61	April 9, '65	
Blume, Watson W	'61		
Brown, Hugh	April 8, '62	April 9, '65	Wounded at the Wilderness, Va., May 6, '64; also at Petersburg, Va., September 17, '64; promoted Sergeant.
Browning, Alexander M	'62	April 9, '65	Prisoner at Elmyra, '64.
Bryant, Joseph	April '62	April 9, '65	
Bryant, Sylvester J		April 9, '65	
Bryant, W. N		April 9, '65	
Carver, Henry	'61	April 9, '65	Wounded, Chancellorsville, May 4, '63.
Chambers, William H	'61		
Coon, John C			
Coon, M			Wounded at Gettysburg, July 3, '63.
Cribb, Thomas D	'61		
Dekle, Thomas G	'61		
Douglass, Alexander J	'61	April 9, '65	
Douglass, F. M	'61	April 9, '65	Wounded, Chancellorsville, May 4, '64.
Douglass, H. J		April 9, '65	
Douglass, Martin L	Mch. 8, '62	April 9, '65	In prison in New York State '00 (Hart's Island).
Drawdy, B. F		April 9, '65	
Duke, David L	'61		Killed, Gettysburg, July 3, '63.
Edwards, Andrew J			
Edwards, Hiram			
English, Henry	May '62		Discharged in '62; cause, substitute; re-enlisted in Mummerlyn's Battalion and served until close of the war.
English, James		Apri 9, '65	
Faircloth, John M		April 9, '65	
Feagle, Andrew		April 9, '65	Discharged from Fort Delaware at the close of the war.
Feagle, Mark H		April 9, '65	
Field, John			Wounded, Gettysburg, July 3, '63.
Futch, John A			
Gaines, Widlis			
Geer, D. D		April 9, '65	
Geer, David L	Nov. 14, '62	April 9, '65	Wounded at Chancellorsville '63; also Petersburg November '64.
Geer, Frederic S		April 9, '65	Wounded, Gettysburg July 3, '63 and captured; paroled from prison at Elmira, N. Y.
Geer, T. J. C	Feb. 15, '62	April 9, '65	Wounded at Wilderness, Va., May 6, '64.
Gerrel, Bennett			
Gilliard, James D			
Gilliard, Lawrence			
Godwin, James			Wounded mortally at Sharpsburg September 17, '62; died December 1, '62.
Goens, Jesse		April 9, '65	
Goens, Stephen O			

Roll Company B—5th Florida Infantry.

(CONTINUED.)

NAMES.	MUSTERED IN.	MUSTERED OUT.	REMARKS.
Griffin, F. M.		April 9, '65	
Griffin, James A.	Mch. '61	April 9, '65	Captured at Gettysburg and paroled from prison at Fort Delaware at close of the war.
Grisham, Columbus C.		April 9, '65	
Groover, Rowan J.	Mch. 8, '62	April 9, '65	Wounded at Gettysburg; afterwards captured at Wilderness May 6, '64 and paroled at close of the war.
Gwin, Augustus.			
Gwin, William.			
Hardee, J. H.	June 5, '61	April 9, '65	
Henry, Francis C.		April 9, '65	
Holtywonger, James C.			
Hobzendolf, William H.		April 9, '65	
Hunt, Thomas V.			
Hurst, John.	'61		
Hurst, Macon S.	'61		
Keen, Allen.	'61		
Keen, George D.	'61		
Keen, George W.	'61	April 9, '65	
Keen, John.	'61		Deserted December '63.
Keen, J. J.		April 9, '65	
Keen, Moses H.			Wounded at the Wilderness, Va., May 6, '64; captured and died in prison at Elmira, N. Y., November 15, '64.
Keen, Wiley		April 9, '65	
Kinard, Wiley A.			Discharged, '63, disability; wounded at Gettysburg July 3, '63.
Langford, F. M.			Died in hospital at Lynchburg, Va., April 13, '63.
Lea, F. S.		April 9, '65	
Lee, J. L.		April 9, '65	
Lee, P. S.		April 9, '65	
Long, William H.	'63		Discharged, '63, disability; wounded at Culpepper August 1, '63.
Manning, George W.	'63	April 9, '65	
Melton, Robert.	April '62	May 16, '65	
Mennett, William H.			
Merritt, J. M.			Wounded at Gettysburg July 3, '63, and left on field.
Milligan, John.			Died July 6, '62.
Moore, James W.		Apri 9, '65	Promoted Sergeant.
Moore, Jacob T.		April 9, '65	
Moore, Philip G.		April 9, '65	Wounded, Gettysburg July 3, '63.
Morgan, Pliney			Killed in Seven Days Battle '62.
Niblack, James L.	Mch. 7, '62		Died in Jacksonville, Fla, smallpox, July 25, '62.
Niblack, James S.			Discharged, '63, disability; wounded, Gettysburg July 3, '63.
Niblack, Joel.	' 61		
O'Cain, William H.		April 9, '65	
Owens, W. J.		April 9, '65	
Perry, James W.			Killed in Virginia.
Polhill, William H.	Mch. 3, '62	April 9, '65	Wounded at Sharpsburg, Md., September 17, '62.
Powell, Joseph.	Mch. '62		Killed at Sharpsburg, Md., September 17, '62.
Raulerson, Elias.			Killed in Virginia.
Raulerson, Jackson.			
Rausson, Henry W.	'61		Discharged, '62; wounded, Sharpsburg September 13, '62, and disabled.
Reid, Marion K.	'61		Captured and imprisoned at Fort Delaware
Reid, William F.			
Register, Mitchel.	'61		Wounded, Gettysburg July 3, '63.
Richard, James R.	'61	April 9, '65	
Roberts, R. B.		April 9, '65	Re-enlisted in 1st Reserves Reg. J. J. Daniel.
Rodgers, R. F.			
Ross, A. H.	April 21, '62	April 9, '65	
Rowling, John.	'61		
Selers, William L.	'61	April 9, '65	
Smith, Coleman,	'61		
Smith, James M.	Mch. '62	April 9, '65	Captured near close of war and paroled.
Snellgrove, G. M.		April 9, '65	
Spicer, John R.		April 9, '65	
Tatum, Robert W.		April 9, '65	Wounded, Chancellorsville May 3, '63.
Taylor, Robert.	April 1, '62	April 9, '65	Wounded at Sharpsburg, Md.
Therman, Joseph W.			
Truluck, Jason.	'61	April 9, '65	
Tyre, Lewis.	'61		
Umstead, George W.	'61	April 9, '65	Wounded and captured at Petersburg, '63, and imprisoned at Point Lookout.
Vinard, W. A.		April 9, '65	
Waldron, J. C.		April 9, '65	
Ward, William P.	'61	April 9, '65	
Waters, Isaac	'61	April 9, '65	
Williams, John.	Mch. '61	April 9, '65	Wounded at Gettysburg, Pa., captured and remained in prison until close of the war.
Witt, A. J.			Imprisoned at Fort Delaware.
Wrey, William.	'61		

Roll Company C—5th Florida Infantry.

NAMES.	MUSTERED IN.	MUSTERED OUT.	REMARKS.
OFFICERS.			
Captains—			
William D. Bloxham	April '62		Transferred to Quartermaster Department, Madison, Fla.
Council A. Bryan	April '62		1st Lieutenant; promoted Captain December '62; elected to Legislature and resigned November 19, '64; afterward joined Co. C, Scott's Battalion talion, and served to close of the war.
1st Lieutenant—			
I. McQuenn Auld	April '62	April 9, '65	2nd Sergeant; promoted 1st Lieutenant after battle of Sharpsburg September, 17, '62; commanded company at surrender.
2nd Lieutenants—			
Mathew Lively			Discharged, '62, for disability.
Alexander L. Bull	April '62		1st Sergeant; promoted 3rd Lieutenant; then 2nd Lieutenant.
3rd Lieutenants—			
James D. Galbraith			Discharged, '62, for consumption.
Leroy Allen	Feb. 27, '62	April 9, '65	Promoted 3rd Lieutenant; wounded at Cold Harbor June 5, '64.
ENLISTED MEN.			
Allen, Joseph	Feb. 27, '62	April 9, '65	Promoted Sergeant.
Alligood, Charles S	Mch. 28, '62	April 9, '65	Shot at Gettysburg July 3, '63.
Alligood, James			Wounded, Chancellorsville May 4, '63.
Atkinson, Stephen			
Atkinson, Wiley L			Wounded, Gettysburg July 3, '63.
Barefoot, Thomas B			
Barlow, John S			
Bariman, Elias			Killed, Gettysburg July 3, 63.
Barnes, Elias			
Brown, William J	'61	'62	Expiration of term; re-enlisted August, '62, in W. D. Bloxham's Co.; shot at the Wilderness, Va.
Bruce, Robert L			
Bryan, Joseph L	Feb. 22, '62	April 9, '65	Promoted Sergeant; wounded at Petersburg, Va.
Carroll, William			
Comparett, John B			Killed, Charlottsville; buried in cemetery of the University of Virginia.
Conner, Martin C			
Daughtery, James			
Daughtery, William			
Davis, Washington J			
Dudley, Rufus M			Wounded, Gettysburg July 3, '63.
Eppes, Nicholas W			Transferred from Co. M, 2nd Regiment; appointed Sergeant-Major; promoted 2nd Lieutenant, for gallantry at the battle of Gettysburg and transferred to 1st Cavalry.
Fairbanks, Henry			
Farady, James W			Killed, Chancellorsville May 4, '63.
French, James W			Wounded, Gettysburg July 3, '63.
Gause, George W		April 9, '65	
Gorman, Robert B		April 9, '65	
Gramlin, J. W			Discharged from Fort Delaware prison.
Grandy, Mike K			
Gray, Edward			
Hall, L. H			Imprisoned, Fort Delaware.
Hargrove, Samuel T			
Hart, John R			Sergeant.
Hartsfield, Moses			Wounded, Bristow Station Oct. 14, '63.
Harvey, Mike L			
Henby, James T	Mar. '61		Shot at Sharpsburg, Maryland, disabled and discharged, '63.
Hicks, S. J			Died, Fort Delaware prison, '63.
Hinson, John H			
Holland, Thomas			Killed, Chancellorsville, May 5, '63.
Holt, Asa H		April 9, '65	
Holt, Christopher C			
Horne, H. M		April 9, '65	
Howell, John W			Wounded, Gettysburg, July 3, '63.
Isler, D. C			Wounded, Gettysburg July 3, '63.
Isler, Fredrick W			
Isler, John F		April 9, '65	
Isler, Thomas J		April 9, '65	
Isler, W. M		April 9, '65	
Isler, W. M	April '62	April 9, '65	
Jenkins, Samuel M		April 9, '65	Wounded and captured, paroled from prison.
Johnson, James W			
Jones, Charles S			
Jones, William L			Killed at Gettysburg July 3, '63.
Kyle, Christopher C	Mar. '62		Discharged June, '63 from Fort Delaware prison.
Kyle, C. C. Jr			Imprisoned at Fort Delaware.
Lee, John A			
Levy, Alfred			
Levy, David			Corporal.
Levy, Henry			
Levy, Richard			
Livingston, J. F		April 9, '65	
Maxwell, Francis Oliver	'62		Died, Richmond Va., Nov. 14, '62.
Mobley, Robert S	May '62		Wounded, Chancellorsville May 4, '63; paroled.
Norris, Henry H		April 9, '65	Wounded, Gettysburg July 3, '63.
Oliver, Arvin			Killed, Gettysburg July 3, '63.

Roll Company C—5th Florida Infantry.

(CONTINUED.)

NAMES.	MUSTERED IN.	MUSTERED OUT.	REMARKS.
Oliver, James		April 9, '65	1st Sergeant.
Owens, Calvin S.			Corporal.
Page, Benjamin F.		April 9, '65	Promoted Corporal, wounded Gettysburg July 3, '63.
Page, James J.			
Page, John W.			
Page, Sherod P.			
Pittman, William			
Pitts, Joseph.			
Purvis, John N.			Died at Staunton, Va. Sept. 18, '62; of pneumonia.
Redd, Toliver C.			
Redd, Washington W.			
Renfro, James P.			
Rickerson, James M.			
Roberts, Richard			
Roberts, Robert E.			
Roberts, William			
Robinson, Larkin		April 9, '65	Shot at Petersburg Oct. 9, '64.
Russell, Daniel W.			Imprisoned at Fort Delaware.
Russell, Jesse Daniel	Mar. 22, '62	April 9, '65	Wounded, Gettysburg July, '63; captured and imprisoned at Fort Delaware.
Scott, Allen		April 9, '65	Wounded, Petersburg Va.
Scott, John R.		April 9, '65	
Smith, R. B.	Mar. 11, '62	April 9, '65	Shot, Chancellorsville May 3, '63.
Smith, W. D.			Wounded, Gettysburg July 3, '63.
Stanford, H.			Wounded, Gettysburg July 3, '63.
Sutton, John A.	Mar. 15, '62	April 9, '65	Wounded, Gettysburg July 3, '63.
Sutton, S. M.		April 9, '65	Wounded, Gettysburg July 3, '63.
Thomas, W. H.		April 9, '65	
Tomberlin, James E.		April 9, '65	
Tomberlin, Samuel		April 9, '65	
Troup, George.			
Verris, Farnwell W.			
Walters, William H.			
Watkins, Robert M.			
White, A. J.		April 9, '65	Wounded, Gettysburg July 3, '63.
White, S. H.			Killed, Gettysburg July 3, '63.
Whitley, Thomas		April 9, '65	Corporal.
Wilson, James B.			
Wiggins, Dan	April 1, '62	April 9, '65	Wounded severely, Gettysburg July 3. '63.

Roll Company D—5th Florida Infantry.

NAMES.	MUSTERED IN.	MUSTERED OUT.	REMARKS.
OFFICERS.			
Captains—			
A. J. Lea			
O. F. Peake		April 26, '65	2nd Lieutenant, promoted to Captain Co. D.
1st Lieutenants—			
J. S. Cockran			
Hill Bryan Coffee		April 9, '65	Promoted 1st Lieutenant.
2nd Lieutenants—			
J. A. Shaw			Wounded at Gettysburg July 3, '63.
A. DeLaughter		April 9, '65	Promoted 2nd Lieutenant.
3rd Lieutenants—			
George I. Devane		April 9, '65	
G. W. Odum			Sergeant, promoted 3rd Lieutenant; became blind.
ENLISTED MEN.			
Ashley, Edward			
Baker, William F.			
Bell, Abram	June '63		
Bellamy, Calvin B.	'61		Died in hospital at Richmond, Va. April, '63.
Bennett, David W.			
Bennett, George W.		April 9, '65	
Bennett, James A.			
Blanton, E. C.	April '62	April 9, '65	
Blanton, J. B.		April 9, '65	Wounded at Chancellorsville May 3, '63.
Bonds, Sanford			
Brannon, S. J.			
Brown, Arthur			
Brown, Reuben			Imprisoned at Fort Delaware.
Brown, Thomas J.			
Brown, William S.			
Browning, J.			Wounded at Chancellorsville May 4, '63.
Burgess, R. W.			
Burnett, G. M.			
Burney, James			Killed at Gettysburg July 3, '65.
Campbell, J. R.		April 9, '65	

Roll Company D—5th Florida Infantry.
(CONTINUED.)

NAMES.	MUSTERED— IN.	MUSTERED OUT.	REMARKS.
Carlton, Thomas A.	'62	April 9, '65	
Carter, Alex.	Mar. '62	April 9, '65	Wounded at Culpepper Court House, Va.
Carter, Archibald M.			Corporal.
Catlage, William		April 9, '65	
Clark, Eli.			
Collins, Archibald M.			Sergeant.
Coper, Silas L.			
Dees, Marion.			
DeLaughter, J. P.			
Denmark, Jasper.			
Devane, G. F.			Wounded at Gettysburg July 3, '63.
Dewey, Richards.			
Drane, Benjamin T.			
Drew, Benjamin R.			
Drew, Thomas F.		April 9, '65	
Drew, Willis.			
Driggers, Bartimirs.			
Duer, William.			
Dulton, Andrew L.		April 9, '65	Promoted Corporal, wounded at Gettysburg July 3 '63.
Edwards, Edward.			Imprisoned at Fort Delaware.
Edward, Samuel.			
Ellis, N. B.			
Ellis, Nathaniel B.	April 7, '62		Wounded at Sharpsburg, Md. Sept. 17, '62.
Elliot, George E.	April 7, '62	April 9, '65	Wounded at Antietam, Md. Sept. 17, '62.
Ellison, J. D.			
English, Mathew J.	'62		Killed in battle at Sharpsburg, Md. Sept. 17, '62.
English, Redding.	'62		Killed in battle at Sharpsburg, Md. Sept. 17, '62.
English, William.			Sergeant.
Ezell, E. F.			
Farmer, Richard.			
Faulkner, Z. T.		April 9, '65	
Flowers, Benjamin.	'62	April 9, '65	Shot at Sharpsburg, Md. Sept. 17, '62.
Flowers, Henry.			
Flowers, Joseph.		April 9, '65	Wounded at Chancellorsville, Va. May 3, '63 and died next day.
Grambling, C. W.			
Gramling, Joel F.	Mar. 15, '62	April 9, '65	Shot at Wilderness, Va. May 6, '64.
Gramling, William J.	Dec. '62		Died of disease at Land's Mill, Va. Nov. 1, '62.
Goza, Peter.			
Hall, A. K.			Wounded at Bristow Station Oct. 14, '63.
Hawkins, D. D.		April 9, '65	
Hawkins, M.			
Hawkins, W. D.		April 9, '65	
Henderson, John.			
Hendrix, John G.			
Hinely, Edward S.			
Hinely, J. H.			Wounded at Gettysburg July 3, '63.
Howren, William D.			Shot at battle of Wilderness.
Humphries, Robt. B.			Sergeant.
Jarvis, A. J.	Jan. '61	April 9, '65	Captured at Gettysburg, Pa., and imprisoned at Fort Delaware until close of war.
Jarvis, James N.			
Kelly, John I.			
Lanier, F. S.			
Lanier, M. V. B.		April 9, '65	
Leak, A. B.			Sergeant; killed at Chancellorsville May 3, '65.
Leak, Elzie.			Promoted 1st Sergeant.
Lee, John.			
Lee, Josiah.			
Lee, S. I.			
Lewis, C. J.			Corporal.
Lewis, John.		April 9, '65	
Lewis, J. G.			
Lindsay, Henry W.			
Lindsay, Neway.			
Livingston, J. F.			
McDaniel, F. M.			Killed at Chancellorsville May 4, '63.
Matthew, David L.		April 9, '65	
Montgomery, B. H.			
Montgomery, James H.		April 9, '65	Transferred to Captain Bird's Company E.
Montgomery, M. T.			
Morgan, J. H.			Wounded at Gettysburg July 3, '63.
Morgan, Olin M.			
Newton, William H.			
Odom, Nathan.		April 9, '65	Shot in leg and back at Sharpsburg Sept. 17, '62.
O'Quinn, J. R.			
O'Quinn, V. J.			
Page, Marion W.	Mar. 26, '62		Promoted Sergeant; wounded at Sharpsburg, Md. lost right leg Sept. 17, '62; discharged Mar. 13, '63.
Painter, John J.	Mar. 10, '62	April 9, '65	Paroled from Hart's Island; N. Y. prison.
Parker, M. W.			
Parker, William T.		April 9, '65	
Patterson, David B.			
Patterson, Thomas.			

Roll Company D—5th Florida Infantry.

(CONTINUED.)

NAMES.	MUSTERED IN.	MUSTERED OUT.	REMARKS.
Peacock, Isham			
Pert, Elias		April 9, '65	
Pickles, Robert			
Porter, Allen			
Porter, B. J			
Porter, J. A		April 9, '65	
Power, F. E			
Poynter, John			
Reams, Joshua			
Redden, Thomas J			
Roberts, John P		April 9, '65	
Robertson, J. R			Wounded at Gettysburg July 3, '63.
Robinson, John B			Corporal.
Rowe, James P			
Rowell, Henry A			
Rykard, Robert			
Sealey, James W		April 9, '65	
Shaw, Thomas J		April 9, '65	Wounded at Bristow Station Oct. 14, '63.
Sherod, Seburn			Sergeant.
Shortridge, J. W			
Silas, David			
Simmons, J. W			
Skipper, Robert R		April 9, '65	
Skipper, Thomas		April 9, '65	
Sloan, Malachai	April '62	April 9, '65	Shot at Wilderness, Va. May 5, '64.
Sloan, Samuel J			
Sloan, William R	Mar. 1, '62	April 10, '65	
Strickland, A. B			
Strickland, T. J			
Tatem, John F			
Thomas, William H		April 9, '65	
Walker, D. L. M			Wounded at Chancellorsville, May 4, '63.
Webb, Samuel S		April 9, '65	Died in Va. in summer of '63.
Weeks, Sam B			
Wentworth, J. H			Sergeant; wounded, Gettysburg July 3, '63.
Wicker, Daniel			
Wishard, A. J			
Wynburn, John			

Roll Company E—5th Florida Infantry.

NAMES.	MUSTERED IN.	MUSTERED OUT.	REMARKS.
OFFICERS.			
Captain—			
John W. Holleyman			
1st Lieutenants—			
mBenjamin F. Davis			Promoted 1st Lieutenant.
T. J. Vann		April 9, '65	
2nd Lieutenant—			
William A. Livingston			
3rd Lieutenant—			
John A. Jenkins			Killed at Gettysburg July 3, '63.
ENLISTED MEN.			
Allison, Robert F			
Ambero, John			
Arnold, Perris D			
Arnolds, William			
Barnett, James S	April '62		
Bailey, Joseph			
Bailey, W. H		April 9, '65	
Bowers, P			Wounded at Gettysburg July 3, '63.
Boyt, William			
Brantley, Anthony			
Brown, Thomas		April 9, '65	
Brown, William G		'62	Disability; lost right arm at Sharpsburg September 17, '62.
Brown, William W			
Bryant, William			
Burnett, Thomas			
Butler, Thomas E			Promoted Corporal.
Calhoun, C. W			Died at Chancellorsville, buried at the cemetery of the University of Virginia.
Calhoun, L. H			Killed at Gettysburg July 3, '63.
Calhoun, Thomas		April 9, '65	
Campbell, Benjamin F			
Campbell, J. R		April 9, '65	
Carrod, John O		April 9, '65	
Cash, R. C			Killed at Gettysburg July 3, '63.

Roll Company E—5th Florida Infantry.

(CONTINUED.)

NAMES.	MUSTERED IN.	MUSTERED OUT.	REMARKS.
Cash, Richard E.	Feb. '62	April 9, '65	Imprisoned at Fort Delaware.
Cason, W.			Wounded at Gettysburg July 3, '63.
Cliate, George W.			
Cliate, Robert A.			
Coffee. James			
Collins, G. L.			
Coody, James		April 9, '65	Corporal; wounded at 2nd battle of Fredricksburg, Va., captured at Petersburg and imprisoned at Fort Delaware until close of war.
Cox, D. N.	Mch. '62	April 9, '65	
Cubbage, George Frank	'61	April 9, '65	
Davenport, J. A.		April 9, '65	
Dees, Moses W.		April 9, '65	
Drew, J. E.		April 9, '65	
Dukes, W. L.		April 9, '65	
Duncan, Andrew J.			Promoted Musician.
Ellison, Henry	'62	April 9, '65	
Flynn, James E.		April 9, '65	Corporal.
Flynn, Sam B.		April 9, '65	Sergeant.
Goodson, Wilson	Feb. '62		Discharged '62; Rheumatism.
Goolesby, Alvin.			
Grambling, Marques M.			
Hancook, Jackson			Musician.
Hassie, Bryant P.			
Henderson, Ed. J.		April 9, '65	
Henderson, John.		April 9, '65	Sergeant.
Henderson, Samuel C.	Feb. '62	April 9, '65	Captured at the Wilderness, Va. May 6, '64; sent to Point Lookout, Md. and remained until Nov.
Hicks, Levi		April 9, '65	Wounded at Gettysburg July 3, '63.
Hudson, E.			
Hudson, John A.			
Hudson, Richard.			Killed at Gettysburg July 3, '63.
Hughey, John.			
Hughey, N. D.		April 9, '65	
Izler, I. P.			
Johnson, John C.		April 9, '65	
Johnson, John W	Feb. '62	April 9, '65	Wounded at Gettysburg July 3, '63.
Jones, Isaiah			Wounded at Gettysburg July 3, '63.
Kelly, George C.			
Lanier, Byrd			
Lanier, F. M.			Captured at Spottsylvania Court House May 5; died in prison at Elmira, N. Y. Dec. 9, '64.
Lanier, Lamb.			
Lanier, Luke P.			
Lanier, Martin Vanburen	May 13, '62		Wounded severely at Wilderness, Va., May 25, '63; promoted Sergeant.
Lee, John T.			
Leggett, John F.	Mar. '62	April 9, '65	Wounded near spinal column at Gettysburg, Pa., Juy 2, '63; and captured; paroled from Fort Delaware.
Leinten, Hugh.			Killed at Gettysburg July 3, '63.
Leinten, James T.			
Livingston, J. F.		April 9, '65	
Loyd, Joseph P.			
McClellan, J. H.	Feb. 28, '62	April 9, '65	
McDaniel, Duncan.			
McGhin, H.		April 9, '65	
McNair, James W.			Corporal.
Moseley, Boaz W.			Wounded at Gettysburg July 3, '63.
Norris, H. H.			
Parsons, Josiah.			
Philips, Benjamin W.			
Philips, Joseph T.			
Philips, Robert A.		April 9, '65	
Ponder, Benjamin F.	Aug. '62	April 9, '65	Transferred from Co. E, 4th Regiment, to 5th Regiment; shot at St. Marks, also at Sharpsburg, Md. Sept. 17, '62.
Ponder, Ephriam D.			Sergeant.
Ponder, W. J.		April 9, '65	
Ramsey, J. C.		April 9, '65	
Rayborn, James F.			
Renew, G. A.	Feb. '62	April 9, '65	Shot at the Wilderness May 6, '64; also at Brandy Station, Va. Aug. 1, '63.
Renew, William			
Revels, Alfred	Mar. '62	April 9, '65	
Revels, Riley	'62	April 9, '65	Killed at Gettysburg, Pa. July 3, '64.
Richardson, William			
Rogers, W. C. Preston			
Sauls, James R.	Feb. 15, '62		Discharged by parole from prison Point Lookout, Md. July 1, '65.
Scott, Warren			
Senice, B.			Killed at Gettysburg July 3, '63.
Sessions, Mezenar R.			
Smith, Stephen M.			
Solls, James			
Solls, Jeremiah F.			
Stewart, Robert J.	April '62	April 9, '65	Wounded under left arm.
Strickland William J.			
Thigpen, Jesse	'64	April 9, '65	

Roll Company E—5th Florida Infantry.
(CONTINUED.)

NAMES.	MUSTERED IN.	MUSTERED OUT.	REMARKS.
Thompson, Alexander			
Vann, John W		April 9, '65	
Warren, Josiah			Sergeant.
Webb, George P			
Webb, William			
Wiglesworth, Joseph			
Williams, Benjamin			
Williams, I. V		April 9, '65	
Williams, James W			
Williams, Owen			
Withington, D. E			Wounded at Gettysburg July 3, '63.
Whitlock, Charles A			
Worrell, Benjamin			

Roll Company F—5th Florida Infantry.

NAMES.	MUSTERED IN.	MUSTERED OUT.	REMARKS.
OFFICERS.			
Captains—			
John Frink			Killed, Gettysburg July 3, '63
R. W. Adams		'61	Promoted Captain.
1st Lieutenant—			
Evan S. Wiley		'61	
2nd Lieutenants—			
Edwin F. Wrede		'61	April 9, '65	
Francis M. Selph		'61	
E. F. Woods		April 9, '65	Promoted 2nd Lieutenant Co. F, 5th Florida.
William A. Shands		April 9, '65	Promoted 2nd Lieutenant Co. F, 5th Florida.
ENLISTED MEN.			
Adams, James L		'61	Died of disease at Fredericksburg, Va. Dec. 14,'62.
Adams, Willoughby		'61	
Allen, Brittan			Corporal.
Allison, Robert F		April 9, '65	
Allman, William F		April 9, '65	Wounded in left hand, captured and imprisoned at Fort Delaware.
Ashe, George C	Mar. '62	April 9, '65	Wounded, Gettysburg July 3, '63; captured at Wilderness, Va. May 6, '64, imprisoned at Elmira, N. Y. and paroled there July 1, '65.
Averett, Henry	June '61		
Averett, J. E	April '62		Wounded at North Anna River, Va. '64.
Baker, John H		'61	1st Sergeant.
Barker, Jerry		April 9, '65	
Bell, James		'61	
Bellflower, Robert R		'61	
Bembry, Henry L	Feb. '62	April 9, '65	
Bembry, Thomas N	Feb. 14, '62	April 9, '65	Wounded at Fredericksburg, Va., '62.
Bishop, Joseph		April 9, '65	
Black, William		'61	Corporal.
Bonds, Sanford			
Boon, Stephen H	April '65	April 9, '65	
Brown, F. M		'61	April 9, '65	Promoted 1st Sergeant.
Burton, William		'61	
Cameron, John		'61	
Cheshire, David		April 9, '65	Imprisoned at Fort Delaware.
Cheshire, William R		'61	April 9, '65	
Clark, J. M		April 9, '65	
Coulson, Joseph		'61	
Cribbs, D. J		April 9, '65	
Danford, Thomas			
Dees, Elijah	Mar. '61		Discharged for disability, '62.
Dees, James			
Demerie, Paul		'61	
Dempsey, Elvin W		'61	Wounded, Gettysburg July 3, '63.
Dorman, George H		April 9, '65	
Ellis, N. B	Mar. '62		Discharged, '63; shot at Sharpsburg, Md. Sept. 17, '62.
Faircloth, Benjamin P		'61	
Faircloth, Caleb	Mar. '61	April 9, '65	Wounded in Virginia and died Oct. 29, '63.
Farweel, Augustus P		'61	Musician.
Farweel, James		'61	
Fennell, James			Captured at Spottsylvania May 5, '64; died at Elmira, N. Y., imprisoned Oct., '64.
Ferguson, Thomas			Shot at Petersburg, Va. Oct., '64; promoted Sergeant.
Fields, Kin		April 9, '65	
Flowers, Benjamin	Mar. 10, '61		
Green, D. D		April 9, '65	
Haddock, William		'61	
Hall, Elijah			
Harris, W. W		April 9, '65	

Roll Company F—5th Florida Infantry.
(CONTINUED.)

NAMES.	MUSTERED IN.	MUSTERED OUT.	REMARKS.
Herndon, H			Wounded, Chancellorsville May 3, '63.
Herndon, James	May 10, '62		Wounded, Chancellorsville May 3, '63; captured,
Hill, J. A	'61	April 9, '65	imprisoned at Fort Delaware.
Hillhouse, Barton N	'61		Wounded, Gettysburg July 3, '63.
Hodges, M. W		April 9, '65	
Horn, Henry M	'61		
Hunter, Miles M. C	'61		
Hunter, William M	'61		
Jackson, B. F		April 9, '65	
Jackson, Henry S			
Jackson, James O	'61	April 9, '65	Corporal, wounded at Culpepper Court House, Va.
Johns, W. R	'61		Aug. 1, '63.
Jones, William J	'61		Sergeant.
Kelly, James E	'61		
Kent, James L	'62	April 9, '65	Wounded at Wilderness, Va. May 6, '64; also at
			North Anna River, Va. May 25, '64.
Kendrick, George C		April 9, '65	Paroled from hospital.
Lewis, Daniel M	'61		Sergeant.
Lindsey, Henry F	March 14, '62	April 9 '65	
Lindsey, Wm. A			
Locke, George W	'61		
McCall, Benjamin F	'61	April 9, '65	Sergeant; imprisoned at Fort Delaware.
McCullons, Henry	'61		
McCullons, Mathew	'61		
Newson, James	'61	April 9, '65	
Oliver, Alfred		April 9, '65	
Padgett, Zacariah	'61		
Paynne, Joseph	'61		
Purviance, John S		April 9, '65	
Rawles, A	'61		Wounded, Gettysburg July 3, '63.
Register, C. A		April 9, '65	Captured and imprisoned at Elmira, N. Y. until
			close of war.
Revels, Henry	May '62		Discharged Dec. '64; disease.
Robinson, William		April 9, '65	
Roebuck, James H	'61		Musician.
Royal, Alex	May '62		Wounded at Gettysburg, Pa. July 3, '63; imprison-
Rudd, William A	'61		ed at Fort Delaware.
Sanders, Joel	'61	April 9, '65	
Çadders, Wm. M			Wounded at Sharpsburg, Va.
Shands, William A	'61		Sergeant.
Shaw, W. J	'61		
Sharpe, Charles W	'61		
Shiver, James A	'61		Corporal.
Simpson, Aaron	'61		
Simpson, Elijah M	'61		
Simpson, Henry		April 9, '65	Wounded at Gettysburg, Pa.
Simpson, James			
Sistrunk, Henry E	'61		
Sistrunk, William E	'61	April 9, '65	
Sloan, Isaac	'61		
Smith, Owen C	'61		
Smith, William Wilder	'61	April 9, '65	
Smith, William Willoughby	'61		
Swilly, Reason A	'61		
Taylor, Alexander	'61		Killed at Chancellorsville May 3, '63.
Taylor, Jerry B	'61	April 9, '65	
Taylor, Lanban J	'61		
Taylor, Lewis	'61		
Taylor, Nathaniel	'61		
Thompson, William J	'61		
Tyre, Nathaniel	'61		
Umstead, John W			Furloughed and died while at home in '64.
Webb, John	'61		
Wide, Edwin F		April 9, '65	
Williams, Alfred		April 9, '65	
Williams, David	'61		
Yates, J	'61		Wounded, Chancellorsville May 3, '63.
Zipperer, Solomon E	'61		
Ziperer, Stephen G	'61		

Roll Company G—5th Florida Infantry.

NAMES.	MUSTERED IN.	MUSTERED OUT.	REMARKS.
OFFICERS.			
Captains—			
William J. Bailey	'62		Wounded at Gettysburg July 3,'63; died in prison.
George D. Raysor	'62	April 9, '65	1st Lieutenant, promoted Captain '63.
1st Lieutenant—			
George R. Walker			Mortally wounded at Gettysburg July 3, '63.

Roll Company G—5th Florida Infantry.
(CONTINUED.)

NAMES.	MUSTERED IN.	MUSTERED OUT.	REMARKS.
2nd Lieutenant—			
Alexander Gill			Died in Petersburg, Va.
3rd Lieutenant—			
John Wood			Deserted to the enemy.
ENLISTED MEN.			
Abbott, William W	Oct. 1, '61	April 9, '65	
Albritton, Jasper B			
Arnold, Dawson W	'62		
Arnold, Edmond I	'62		
Arnold, Francis M	'62		
Arnold, Robert H	'62	April 9, '65	
Ayers, Ira			Killed at Sharpsburg Md. Sept. 17, '62.
Ayers, John H	'62		
Baker, Montford I			
Bannerman, C. W	Mar. 3, '62		Wounded at Wilderness Va.; promoted 1st Sergeant and Sergeant-Major.
Baugh, John	Oct. '61		Killed at Gettysburg July 2, '63.
Baysor, Edgar H			Sergeant.
Beasley, C. I			
Bellinger, William			
Billingsley, H. C		April 9, '65	
Bishop, Eli			Killed at Sharpsburg, Md. Sept. 17, '62.
Bishop, Elijah			Killed at Sharpsburg, Md. Sept. 17, '62.
Bishop, E. M			
Bishop, George D			
Bishop, Hilary	Mar. 4, '6_	April 9, '65	Wounded at Sharpsburg, Md., at Cold Harbor and at Petersburg, Va.
Blackburn, Joseph E			Imprisoned at Fort Delaware.
Bolen, W. E			Corporal; wounded at Chancellorsville May 4, '63.
Boseman, S. A			
Brooker, John H	'62		
Brooks, John		April 9, '65	Wounded at Wilderness, Va., promoted Corpora.
Brown, William H		April 9, '65	
Bryant, James		April 9, '65	Wounded, Gettysburg July 3, '63; and left on field.
Carroll, John M			
Carroll, William J		April 9, '65	
Clarke, John M			Discharged, '64; disability.
Childers, L. J	Dec. '61	April 9, '65	Wounded severely at Wilderness, Va. May 6, '64.
Clarke, John M		'64	Discharged for disability.
Cole, G. W	Oct. 1, '61		Wounded, Gettysburg July 3, '63.
Cole, W. J			Wounded at the Wilderness, Va. May 6 '64; and died from wound at Charlottsville May 24, '64, and buried in the Cemetery of the University of Virginia.
Cribb, Austen S			
Crosby, Marider			
Crosby, Thomas W		April 9, '65	
Denmark, Jasper			Appointed Corporal; '62.
Denmark, N		April 9, '65	
Dice, George			Lost right arm at Gettysburg, Pa. July 2, '63.
Duncan, James	Mar. '62	April 9, '65	Killed at Wilderness.
Earnest, James M			Sergeant; discharged '64, disability.
Faget, John M			Musician.
Freman, John			Appointed Corporal, '61; died in service.
Freman, Thomas J		April 9, '65	
Granger, Irvin A	Mar. 8, '62	April 9, '65	Shot at Sharpsburg, Md. Sept. 17, '62.
Grantham, D. P			
Gray, J. J		April 9, '65	
Grubbs, Samuel G	'62	April 9, '65	
Hamrick, D. J	Nov. '61		Paroled, May '65.
Hamrick, J. M		April 9, '65	
Hamrick, W. A		April 9, '65	Wounded at Gettysburg July 3, '63.
Hawin, James T			
Hightower, Jesse			
Hightower, Richard B	May '62	April 9, '65	Discharged from Fortress Monroe.
Hill, William			
Huggins, George	Mar 10, '65		
Huggins, Thomas	Mar. 10, '63		Discharged at Tallahassee, Fla., disability caused by measles.
Johns, James M	Sept. '61		Killed in battle of Sharpsburg, Md. Sept. 17, '62.
Johnson, Duncan	May '61	April 9, '65	
Johnson, James P			
Johnson, Joseph W			
Johnson, Samuel N.			Wounded, Gettysburg July 3, '63.
Johnson, S. W			
Jones, Saborn	April '61	April 9, '65	
Kailey, James			
King, A			
King, John J		April 9, '65	Wounded at Sharpsburg, Md. Sept. 17, '62.
Kinsey, William A	Dec. '61	April 9, '65	
Lacy, Archibald			Discharged Oct. 15, '62; disability.
Lang, Lemuel			Wounded at Gettysburg July 3, '63.
Lanier, Clem		April 9, '65	
Lanier, M. P. B		April 9, '65	
LeRoy, A		April 9, '65	
Lightsey, Archibald		April 9, '65	

Roll Company G—5th Florida Infantry.
(CONTINUED.)

NAMES.	MUSTERED IN.	MUSTERED OUT.	REMARKS.
Lindsay, W. A.		April 9, '65	
Livingston, John S.			Corporal.
Long, L.	Oct. '61		Wounded, Gettysburg July 3, '63.
McLean, John.			
McMullen, John.			
Milton James.	Oct. '61		Wounded, Gettysburg July 3, '63.
Morris, H. W.		April 9, '65	Imprisoned at Fort Delaware.
Pollard, John.			
Poppell, George.			
Poppell, H. D.			
Poppell, John W.		April 9, '65	Transferred, Battalion Cavalry; died from disease in Camp Jackson, Fla. Dec. 25, '62.
Poppell, Pharoah.			
Raynolds, George W.			Corporal.
Reese, Drew W.			
Reichert, J. D.		April 9, '65	
Reichert, J. T.		April 9, '65	Promoted Sergeant.
Richards, William B.			Corporal, promoted Sergeant; deserted.
Richardson, W. M.		April 9, '65	
Roach, Charles W.			Imprisoned at Fort Delaware.
Roach, George W.			
Roach, James B.		April 9, '65	
Rhodes, W. N.			
Robertson, James J.			
Rosser, George D.			
Sattonstall, William G.			
Sealy, D. P.			
Spears, James.		April 9, '65	
Stralin, Alford.			
Strickland, J. P.		April 9, '65	Wounded, Gettysburg July 3, '63.
Strickland, Nathan W.		April 9, '65	Promoted Corporal, '64.
Taylor, W. B.			
Truman, T. J.		April 9, '65	
Walker, D. M.		April 9, '65	
Walker, Isham J.	Mar. '63	April 9, '65	
Walker, James A.			Promoted 1st Sergeant; discharged '63; for accidental injury to spine.
Walker, John T.		April 9, '65	Wounded at Sharpsburg Sept. 17, '62.
Walker, Sittle B.			Wounded, Gettysburg July 3, '63.
Ward, K.	Oct. '61		Wounded at Petersburg, Va. '62.
Watts, A. J.	Feb. '62	April 9, '65	
Wheeler, James H.			
Wheeler, John C.		April 9, '65	
Whitfield, Benjamin.		June '63	Captured at Reams Station, Va., paroled from prison.
Whitehurst, Absalom.			
Willie, J. J.			
Woods, F. M.		April 9, '65	Shot at Gettysburg July 3, '63.
Woods, Thomas J.			
Woods, William M.		April 9, '65	Imprisoned at Fort Delaware.
Wooten, James T.			

Roll Company H (Liberty Guards)—5th Florida Infantry.

NAMES.	MUSTERED IN.	MUSTERED OUT.	REMARKS.
OFFICERS.			
Captains—			
William T. Gregory	Mar. 10, '62		Wounded at Sharpsburg, Md. Sept. 17, '62; was furloughed from hospital and reached home '62; where he died Dec. 18, '62.
James G. Shuler	Mar. 10, '62	April 9, '65	Promoted from 3rd Lieutenant to Captain; wounded at Gettysburg July 3, '63; captured and died on Johnson's Island Dec. 11, '63. Grave 121
1st Lieutenant—			
Benjamin F. Wood	Mar. 10, '62	April 9, '65	Wounded at Gettysburg July 3, '63.
2nd Lieutenants—			
William H. Speight	Mar. 10, '62		Resigned Sept. '62.
Benjamin T. Rich	Mar. 10, '62	April 9, '65	Promoted Lieutenant.
John W. Hosford	April 19, '62	April 9, '65	Clerk, promoted 2nd Lieutenant.
3rd Lieutenant—			
ENLISTED MEN.			
Anglin, Thomas.	April 19, '62		
Atkins, Francis M.	April 19, '62	April 9, '65	
Atkins, Samuel N.	April 19, '62		
Ayers, David.	April 19, '62		
Ayers, J. S.	April 19, '62	April 9, '65	Wounded at Gettysburg July 3, '63.
Ayers, John.	April 19, '62		
Ayers, Solomon.	April 19, '62		

Roll Company H (Liberty Guards)—5th Florida Infantry.
(CONTINUED.)

NAMES	MUSTERED IN.	MUSTERED OUT.	REMARKS.
Ayers, Thompson	April 19, '62		
Barr, James A	April 19, '62	April 9, '65	Wounded at Sharpsburg, Md. Sept. 17, '62.
Barr, Thomas G	May 5, '62	April 9, '65	
Bateman, B. M			
Bateman, Calvin	April 10, '62		
Bateman, Wiley W	Mar. 10, '62		
Beck, William H	April 19, '62	April 9, '65	Shot at Gettysburg July 3, '63.
Bentley, R. M		April 9, '65	
Bird, Andrew	April 11, '62		
Bowlin, J			
Bowlin, W			
Branch, Henry			
Branch, James N	April 19, '62		Wounded at Charlottsville, buried in the cemetery of the University of Virginia.
Brown, A	Oct. 20, '62		Discharged and re-enlisted in '62; Co. D, 10th Reg.
Brown, John			
Bryant, Edward J	April 19, '62		
Bryant, George W	April 19, '62	April 9, '65	Wounded at Petersburg July 30, '64.
Bryant, John R	April 19, '62	April 9, '65	Wounded at Gettysburg July 3, '63.
Buckhalter, William	Mar. 10, '62		
Burnes, B			
Burnes, Samuel	Mar. 10, '62	April 9, '65	
Cannon, James			Imprisoned at Fort Delaware.
Carraway, James D	April 19 '62		Sergeant.
Caurdle, John	April 19, '62		
Chance, S			
Chestnut, John	April 19, '62		
Clark, William B	Mch. 10, '62	April 9, '65	
Conner, D			
Conner, James		April 9, '65	
Crosby, Isham			
Davis, Henry	April 19, '62		
Davis, John			
Dillard, John L	April 19, '62		Corporal; killed in action.
Driggors, Willam W		April 9, '65	
Dudley, Aaron		April 9, '65	
Dudley, Alexander C	Mch. 10, '62		
Dudley, Jesse	April 19, '62	April 9, '65	
Durham, William C	Mch 10, '62	April 9, '65	
Edenfield John	April 19, '62		
Edwards, John W	April 14, '62		
English, Samuel	April 14, '62		
Ethridge, James	April 14, '62		
Evans, William L	Mch. 10, '62		Corporal; promoted Sergeant.
Ferguson, Alexander M	April 19, '62		
Fort, James E	'62		
Franklin, Cicero D	April 14, '62		
Glasque, Benjamin F	April 19, '62		
Glenn, Thomas S	Mch. 10, '62		Discharged for disability.
Golden, Osco	'62		
Goodson, G. W	Jan. '65	April 9, '65	Wounded between hips and lower ribs on right side.
Graham, John R. B	April 19, '62		Sergeant; died Nov. 11, '62, at hospital.
Green, John W	April 19, '62		
Green, Thomas N	'62		
Gwinn, E. H			Imprisoned at Fort Delaware.
Hagan, George W. B	Mar. 13, '62		
Hagan, Henry D	Mar. 13, '62		
Hawkins, Jackson J	April 19, '62	April 9, '65	
Hawkins, Thomas J	April 19, '62	April 9, '65	Commissary, promoted 1st Sergeant.
Hentz, William			
Herndon, W. S			
Hill, William			
Holmes, John	Mar. 10, '62	April 9, '65	Wounded at Cold Harbor June 3, '64.
Holt, John	Mar. 10, '62		Captured at Gettysburg '63; died at Fort Delaware Feb. 25, '64.
Hasford, Robert F	Mar. 13, '62	April 9, '65	Promoted Corporal and Sergeant; wounded at the Wilderness May 6, '64.
Hosford, Thomas J	'62		
Hofsord, William H			Musician.
Howard, A. J			
Hudson, James R	April 9, '62		Sergeant; killed at Sharpsburg.
Inman, B			
Jackson, T. H			
Johns, Francis M	April 10, '62		
Johnson, John W	Mar. 13, '62		
Jones, William	Mar. 10, '62		
Jordan, T. C			
Kelly, James L. R	April 19, '62		
Kirkland, Caleb			
Lamb, James	April 19, '62		
Larkins, G	'62		
Larkins, Dearborn			
Lee, Ichabod	April 19, '62		Wounded at Chancellorsville, May 4, '63.
Lewis, John W	April 19, '62		
Lewis, Timothy			
Licelt, Lemuel G	'62		

Roll Company H (Liberty Guards)—5th Florida Infantry.
(CONTINUED.)

NAMES.	MUSTERED IN.	MUSTERED OUT.	REMARKS.
Little, Asa	April 19, '62		
Littlefield, John	April 19, '62		
McDonald, George L	April 19, '62		
McKnight, A. C.			
McPhaul, Neil L	April 1, '62	April 9, '65	
McQuaigge, Daniel	'62		Wounded at Chancellorsville, May 4, '63.
Martin, Aaron	April 19, '62		
Mathews, John J	April 19, '62		Imprisoned and paroled from Fort Delaware June 10, '65.
Meacham, Joseph	April 19, '62		Promoted Sergeant; killed at Chancellorsville, May 4, '63.
Mercer, J. C.			
Moore, Edward	April 19, '62		
Morgan, William	Mar. 10, '62		
Morgan, William W	April 19, '62		
Morris, W. C.			Sergeant.
Morris, T. J.			
Murray, George	Mar. 10, '62		Wounded at Chancellorsville, May 4, 63.
Nixon, James N	April 19, '62		
Niel, W. H. H.			
Oats, H.			
Owens, H. P.		April 9, '65	
Owens, M.			
Parker, John	'62	April 9, '65	
Peacock, John W	April 19, '62	April 9, '65	
Peters, H. J.			
Pickett, F.			
Pope, Thomas M	Mar. 10, '62		
Reaves, Joseph	April 19, '62		
Rhodes, John			1st Sergeant; killed in action.
Rich, John F	Mar. 10, '62	April 9, '65	
Ritter, Madison L	April 19, '62		
Robertson, John W	April 19, '62		Imprisoned at Fort Delaware.
Rogers, Joseph	April 19, '62		
Sansom, Bennett T	April 19, '62	April 9, '65	
Shuler, William E	April 19, '62		
Smith, James F	April 19, '62		
Smith, James W	'62		
Smith, R. R.			
Spears, John M	April 19, '62		
Spears, William J	April 19, '62		
Stemly, Daniel			
Stone, Shade S	April 19, '62		Wounded at Sharpsburg Sept. 17, '62; Cold Harbor June, '64; and captured, paroled from prison July 4, '65.
Strickland, Fayette	Mar. 10, '62		
Taff, Joseph D	'62		
Teat, A. F.	April 19, '62		
Thomas, L. Jackson			Killed at Gettysburg July 3, '63.
Thomas, William A. J	Mar. 10, '62		
Vinzant, G. W		April 9, '65	
Williams, W. W			1st Corporal; transferred to Gregory's Co.; lost left leg at Sharpsburg and discharged.
Yon, Newton	April 19, '62		

Roll Company I—5th Florida Infantry.

NAMES.	MUSTERED IN.	MUSTERED OUT.	REMARKS.
OFFICERS			
Captains—			
Samuel A. Spencer			Resigned.
James A. Kinlock			1st Lieutenant promoted Captain; killed at the Wilderness.
John Hill		April 26, '65	1st Sergeant, promoted 1st Lieutenant, then Captain.
1st Lieutenant—			
John O. Morris			2nd Lieutenant, promoted 1st Lieutenant.
2nd Lieutenant—			
M. B. Swearengen	Mar. '62	April 26, '65	Promoted 2nd Lieutenant; wounded at Gettysburg July 2, '63 and again at Sharpsburg, Md. Sept. 17, '62.
3rd Lieutenants—			
Willam H. Walker			Transferred from 3rd Regiment, Co. D., went out on reorganization.
George M. Ferguson			Corporal, promoted 3rd Lieutenant; killed in action.
Anderson Peeler			Promoted 3rd Lieutenant.
ENLISTED MEN.			
Allen, J. M		April 26, '65	
Allen, Leroy		April 26, '65	

Roll Company I—5th Flor'da Infantry.

(CONTINUED.)

NAMES.	MUSTERED IN.	MUSTERED OUT.	REMARKS.
Alligood, C. S.		April 26, '65	
Anderson, William H.			
Ashley, John B. L.			
Ashmore, Robert W.	May '62	April 26, '65	Wounded, July 3, '63.
Barrs, James M.	July '63	April 26, '65	Wounded at Gettysburg July 2 '63.
Bartleote, John			
Benton, William N.		April 26, '65	
Blitchington, William			
Brasswell, Henry H.		Apri 26, '65	
Brombly, Bennet			
Brown, William			
Bryan, J. L.			
Butler, Daniel			
Butler, Green B.			
Bird, Alexander			
Calaghan, Charles			
Calaghan, Thomas			
Campbell, W.			Wounded at Bristow Station Oct. 14, '63.
Carter, Jesse			
Coleman, John			Killed at Petersburg Va. July 4 '64.
Condelary, Peter			Killed in front of Petersburg, Va. '64.
Condelary, William	'62		Killed at Gettysburg July 3, '63.
Cox, James C.			
Crowson, Moses			
Curry, Joseph			
Davis, A. P.			
Davis, Levi			
Davidson, James			
Deas, John S.			
Dudley, Milton			
Ellis, William R. L.			
Eubanks, John			
Evers, Henry A.			
Faircloth, Joshua		April 26, '65	Transferred from 3rd Reg. to Co. D.
Faircloth, Richard			Promoted 1st Sergeant.
Farr, William L.			
Fountaine, Green			
Fuquay, Cornelius			
Fuquay, George M.			
Gilchrist, James M.			
Grant, Philip G.			
Grant, Washington			Died at Charlottsville and buried in the cemetery of the University of Virginia.
Homer, I. A.			Killed at Bristow Station Oct. 14, '63.
Jenkins, Joseph			
Johnson, Hugh			
Langston, Jesse			Sergeant; transferred from Co. D. 3rd Regiment.
Langston, William I.			Transferred from Co. D. 3rd Regiment.
Lewis, Jesse			
Lohner, John P.			
McCarthy, John T.			Sergeant.
McKinnon, John I.			
McSwain, Charles			
Marion, Joseph			
Munson, A. G.		April 6, '65	
Murray, John			Discharged June 1, '62 for disability; re-enlisted in Engineer Corps and wounded at Olustee Feb. '64.
Norton, William			
Pedworth, David			Corporal.
Raulerson, James T.			Wounded, Bristow Station Oct. 14, '63.
Raulerson, William			Sergeant.
Remington, A. H.			Captured, imprisoned at Fortress Monroe; paroled May 6, '65.
Revell, S. C.			
Revell, Bisney E.	Mar. 1, '62	April 28, '65	Wounded at the Wilderness May, '64 and died May 9, '65.
Richardson, Sol. B.			Wounded and lost right leg at Sharpsburg Sept. 17, '62 and discharged.
Roath, Clifford D.		April 26, '65	Wounded at Gettysburg July 2, '63.
Robertson, Benjamin F.			
Ronalds, Hiram			
Sealey, Jesse			
Stanford, Eli		April 26, '65	
Stanford, J. H.		April 26, '65	
Stevens, William H.			
Stewart, Wiley			
Sweat, James G.			Corporal; died at Charlottsville and buried in the cemetery of the University of Virginia.
Thomas, Daniel J.			
Thomas, John C.			Died in hospital at Richmond, Va. of disease, June '64.
Toole, J. J.	Feb. '62		
Tucker, Charles P.			
Van Brunt, Francis S.		April 26, '65	Transferred to Co. F. 20th Ga. Cavalry; shot at Hall's Shop, Va. June 1, '64.
West, George H.			
Wrede, E. F.		April 26, '65	
Wood, William F.			

Roll Company K (Dixie Yeomen)—5th Florida Infantry.

NAMES.	MUSTERED IN.	MUSTERED OUT.	REMARKS.
OFFICERS.			
Captains—			
Richmond N. Gardner			Lost left arm at Gettysburg July 2, '63.
James B. Conner			Corporal, promoted 3rd Lieutenant then Captain.
1st Lieutenant—			
Joel C. Blake			Killed at Gettysburg July 3, '63.
2nd Lieutenant—			
Junius L. Taylor			
3rd Lieutenant—			
W. R. Blake			Promoted 2nd Lieutenant; resigned Mar. 17, '63.
ENLISTED MEN.			
Atkins, Robert R.		April 9, '65	Severly wounded at the Wilderness May 6, '64.
Aldridge, Richard M.		April 9, '65	
Aldridge, Thomas		April 9, '65	
Austin, Benjamin		April 9, '65	
Austin, John C.		April 9, '65	Corporal.
Averitt, Jesse Jr.			Sergeant; killed at the Wilderness.
Averitt, Walter H.	Mar. 30, '62		Lost left arm at Gettysburg July 2, '63 and discharged.
Baggett, M. W.		April 9, '65	Wounded at Gettysburg July 2, '63.
Berry, A. F.		April 9, '65	Wounded at Gettysburg July 3, '63.
Blake, Isham M.	April '62	April 9, '65	Transferred from 5th Regiment to Company B., 1st Cavalry, Captain of said Company shot at Sharpsburg, Md. Sept. 17, '62; also wounded at Dalton Ga. while Captain of Company B.
Boles, William D.			Died in service.
Bond, Walter L.		April 9, '65	
Branch, Henry E.		April 9, '65	
Bradford, John			Discharged.
Brown, George T.	Feb. 20, '62		Wounded at the Wilderness, Va. May 6, '64 and discharged for injuries, June, '64.
Brown, Jeff			Furnished substitute.
Brown, John H.			Furnished substitute.
Bryan, William H.		April 9, '65	
Burney, John T.			
Burney, Willis P.		April 9, '65	Wounded at Chancellorsville May 4, and Gettysburg July 2, '63.
Caldwell, Robert			Deserted.
Carr, Charles H. ½			Sergeant, died in service.
Carter, M.			
Cay, Thomas		April 9, '65	
Clark, E. W.		April 9, '65	Promoted Sergeant.
Clark, John Wesley	Feb. 20, '62		Paroled from Fort Delaware.
Clark, William P.			Deserted at Petersburg.
Cromartie, John A.			Imprisoned at Fort Delaware.
Davis, William W.		April 9, '65	Sergeant.
DeVaughn, Felix K.		April 9, '65	Imprisoned at Fort Delaware.
Felkel, Daniel C.		April 9, '65	Wounded at Gettysburg July 2, '63.
Felkel, John Y.			Discharged.
Felkel, Wade O.			Died in service.
Felkel, Wesley R.			Killed at Sharpsburg Sept. 17, '63.
Ferrill, Gabriel			Killed.
Fleming, George A.		April 9, '65	
Fletcher, J. P.			Deserted at Petersburg.
Folsom, Israel		April 9, '65	
Folsom, W. T.	May '63	April 9, '65	
Gaskins, William			Wounded at Sharpsburg Sept. 17, '63 and died.
Grace, Ben.			Killed.
Grace, Jordan F.			Died in service.
Grace, Glenn		April 9, '65	Sergeant
Gramling, Irwin		April 9, '65	
Gramling, John L.			Wounded and captured at Gettysburg July 2, '63, paroled from Fort Delaware at close of war.
Gramling, J. W.		April 9, '65	Wounded at Gettysburg July 4, '63.
Gramling, Wilber W.		April 9, '65	
Gray, Jackson J.			
Gray, William H.	Mar. 11, '62		Discharged June 15, '62; for disability, re-enlisted on Gun Boat Spray and paroled at close of war.
Hammet, Radford		April 9, '65	
Harrod, Jacob			Killed at Cold Harbor.
Hines, J. W.		April 9, '65	
Hinson, J.			Killed.
Isler, Thomas J.		April 9, '65	Wounded at Gettysburg July 3, '63.
Isler, Nathaniel			Died in service.
Jeffcoat, George W.	Oct. '61	April 9, '65	Shot at Reams Station June 23, '64.
Jenkins, James H.		April 9, '65	Imprisoned at Fort Delaware.
John, Daniel S.			Died in Richmond.
Joiner, Joseph R.		April 9, '65	Musician.
Lastinger, E.		April 9, '65	
Leger, Hamilton		April 9, '65	
Lewis, Willis			Died.
Lipscomb, Edward P.			Wounded at Atleas Station and died.
Lynch, James F.		April 9, '65	
Mazingo, John			Discharged.
Merritt, J. W.			Wounded at BristowStation Oct. 15, '63.

Roll Company K (Dixie Yeomen)—5th Florida Infantry.
(CONTINUED.)

NAMES.	MUSTERED IN.	MUSTERED OUT.	REMARKS.
Montford, Thomas			Killed at Gettysburg July 3, '63.
Nash, John W		April 9, '65	Transferred to Western Army and made Captain of Co. I; wounded at Gettysburg July 2, '63.
Perkins, John H			Discharged for disability, fall of '64.
Perkins, William			Furnished a substitute.
Puller, Mallard L			Musician; discharged.
Peagan, A			Killed.
Shine, Thomas W		April 9, '65	1st Sergeant; wounded at Gettysburg July 4, '63.
Shores, Franklin I		April 9, '65	Imprisoned at Fort Delaware.
Snipes, William M. D		April 9, '65	Wounded at the Wilderness.
Strickland, William L		April 9, '65	
Stringer, Daniel F		April 9, '65	
Sweatman, F. M		April 9, '65	Corporal.
Thompson, A			
Walker, Benjamin F			Corporal; imprisoned at Fort Delaware.
Wheeler, A. H			Wounded at Gettysburg July 2, '63 and died.
Wilford, John H	Feb. 20, '62	April 9, '65	
Willis, Patrick			Died.
Willis, Robert M			Died.
Zeigler, Vann			

SIXTH FLORIDA INFANTRY.

Early in the spring of 1862 the 6th Florida Regiment was organized at Chattahoochee by the election of Jesse J. Finley as Colonel; Angus McLean, Lieutenant-Colonel; Daniel Kenan, Major. This Regiment was organized by the State and immediately turned over to the Confederate service and ordered to report to Gen. E. Kirby Smith at Knoxville, who was then Commander of the Department of East Tennessee. There the 6th and 7th Florida Regiments and the 1st Florida Cavalry, Dismounted, were placed under the command of William G. M. Davis as senior Colonel.

In the early spring of 1862 General Smith, with his command, was ordered to join General Bragg in his march into Kentucky in pursuit of General Buel, who was then under retreat. The 6th Florida Regiment went through the Kentucky campaign when General Bragg retreated from the State before General Buel, who had been heavily reinforced and who had again assumed he offensive. Coming out of Kentucky, Colonel Finley was ordered to occupy and defend Cumberland Gap against a possible approach by the enemy. The 6th Florida Regiment was afterward relieved by General Gracie's Brigade, and the 6th was ordered back to Knoxville where it remained in winter quarters during the winter of 1862-63.

The Regiment remained in Knoxville until the following summer, when General Smith's command was ordered to report to General Bragg at Chattanooga In the meanwhile, however, Colonel Davis was commissioned a Brigadier General and the 54th Virginia was added to the Brigade, and Colonel Trigg was assigned to the command of the Brigade as senior Colonel.

The 6th Florida Regiment was in the bloody battle of Chickamauga, in the reserve corps of the first day's fight and ordered to make a charge on a Federal battery of artillery. This charge was made by the Regiment alone through an old field—the battery of the enemy being on the crest of a ridge about the center of the field. In making the charge it was enfiladed by the battery of the enemy to its left, which was near enough to use cannister and grape-shot. The Regiment carried the position and the battery in front retreated. It was now about sun-down, when the Regiment received preemptory orders to retire from the field,which it did bivouacking just outside of the field. In making the charge the Regiment bore itself with distingushed firmness and gallantry.

In the next day's battle the 6th Florida Regiment and the 54th Virginia were supporting a battalion of Confederate artillery, which was not then engaged, when they were ordered to the right to reinforce Gen. Patton Anderson and General Kelly, whose pickets only were then engaged, their ammunition being nearly exhausted.

When the two Regiments came up General Anderson gave them their proper alignment for moving squarely upon the enemy, which they did; and about sun-down they cleared the heights of Chickamauga and about five hundred (500) of the enemy, who were armed with Colt's revolving rifles, surrendered—Colonel Trigg, the Brigade commander, and the 7th Florida Regiment under Colonel Bullock having first come up. This was about the last fighting on the second day's battle of Chickamauga. The army under the command of General Bragg achieved a complete victory over the enemy, but remained a day on the battle field after the battle.

In the meantime Federal General Thomas rallied the fleeing forces of the enemy and occupied the strong fortifications at and around Chattanooga; and General Bragg, occupying Missionary Ridge, laid siege to the beleaguered city.

During the winter the Confederate Army was reorganized and all the Florida Regiments, then in the Army of Tennessee, were brigaded together, comprising the 6th Florida Regiment, under the command of Colonel McLean; the 7th Florida Regiment, under the command of Colonel Bullock; the 1st and 3d Regiments (consolidated), under the command of Colonel Dilworth; the 4th Florida Regiment, under the command of Col. W. L. Bowen; the 1st Cavalry, Dismounted, under the command of Col. George Troup Maxwell; and Colonel Finley was commissioned Brigadier-General and assigned to the command thereof.

At the battle of Missionary Ridge, in which the Brigade participated, the 6th Florida Regiment and the 1st and 3d Regiments were in the main Confederate line of battle on the crest of the Ridge; while the 7th Regiment and the 4th Regiment and the 1st Florida Cavalry, Dismounted, were on the picket line in the valley under orders on the advance of the Federal forces to fall back to the intrenchments at the foot of the Ridge; this they executed and they were driven out of the intrenchments by the overwhelming numbers of the enemy and a large portion were captured in ascending the steep acclivities of the Ridge.

The 6th Florida Regiment and the 1st and 3rd Regiments were posted in the dip of the Ridge near General Bragg's headquarters, and occupied their position on the fire line until peremptorily ordered to retire—they being about the last of the Confederate troops to leave the Ridge. The Confederate Army then fell back to Dalton; there it went into winter quarters, and Gen. Joseph E. Johnston, succeeding General Bragg, assumed command of the Army.

The Brigade was in the battle of Rocky Face in front of Dalton in Febuary, when, after two days fight, General Sherman fell back to Chattanooga to wait reinforcements. Having received reinforcements, he advanced again in May with superior numbers and, after a two days' battle and an attempt to flank General Johnston's army, the latter commenced the famous retreat under General Johnston to Atlanta.

The army then fell back to Resaca and deployed into line of battle in a strong position and, after a two days' battle (in which General Finley was wounded). again took up the line of retreat. And, not to be tedious—the Brigade was in all the battles from Dalton to Atlanta, bearing itself with its customary intrepidity and bravery.

It was then that General Johnston was removed from the command of the Army and was succeeded by General Hood. The Brigade participated in the battles of Atlanta and Jonesboro, in which last battle General Finley was again wounded.

The Brigade was with Hood in his unfortunate and disastrous campaign into Tennessee; and after the retreat of the Confederate Army from Nashville, it was transferred, with General Hood's command, to North Carolina and was in the battle of Bentonville just before the surrender of General Lee at Appomatox.

Col. Daniel Kenan, in the battle of Bentonville, was wounded in the leg so severely that amputation was necessary; and Col. Angus McLean was killed in the battle of Dallas on the retreat from Dalton to Atlanta.

It may be truly said that the Florida troops, in both the Tennesseee Army and in Virginia, conducted themselves with patriotism and gallantry.

Roll, Field and Staff—6th Florida Infantry.

NAMES.	MUSTERED IN.	MUSTERED OUT.	REMARKS.
Colonels—			
Jesse Johnson Finley	April 15, '62	April 26, '65	Promoted Brigadier-General.
Angus McLean	April 15, '62		Killed at Dallas, Georgia.
Daniel L. Kenan	April 15, '62		Wounded and disabled at Bentonville.
Lieutenant Colonels—			
Angus McLean	April 15, '62		Promoted Colonel Dec., '63.
R. H. M. Davidson	April 15, '62		Severely wounded and disabled at Dallas, Ga. May 28, '64; promoted to Lieutenant Colonel, '64.
Daniel L. Kenan	April 15, '62		Promoted Colonel.
Majors—			
R. H. M. Davidson	April 15, '62		Promoted Lieutenant Colonel; vice McLean killed.
Daniel L. Kenan	April 15, '62		Promoted Lieutenant Colonel; vice Davidson disabled.
Surgeon—			
J. T. Holder	April 15, '62	April 26, '65	
Assistant Surgeons—			
——Perry	April 15, '62		
Adjutants—			
John R. Ely	April 15, '62		
Frank Philips	April 15, '64	April 26, '65	
Sergeant Major—			
Commissary—			
John P. Jordan	April 15, '62		
Chaplains—			
——Tomkies	April 15, '62		
——Giles	April 15, '62		
Silas Cooper	April 15, '62		Resigned, April 24, '63.
Quartermasters—			
Alexander Smith	April 15, '62		
Jeff Coleman	April 15, '62		Killed at Resaca, Georgia.
William Gunn			
Quartermaster Sergeants—			

Roll, Field and Staff—6th Florida Infantry.
(CONTINUED.)

NAMES.	MUSTERED IN.	MUSTERED OUT.	REMARKS.
Ordnance Sergeant—			
Hospital Steward—			
1st Lieutenant and Ensign—			
Benjamin S. G. Smith			Promoted Ensign at Chickamauga, captured at Nashville Dec. 16; imprisoned on Johnson's Island.

Roll Company A—6th Florida Infantry.

NAMES.	MUSTERED IN.	MUSTERED OUT.	REMARKS.
OFFICERS.			
Captains—			
Robert H. M. Davidson	Mar. 12, '62	April 26, '65	Promoted Major; Lieutenant-Colonel.
C. E. L. Allison	Mar. 12, '62	April 26, '65	Promoted Captain; shot at Chickamauga, Ga.
———McNicolson	Mar. 12, '62	April 26, '65	Promoted Captain.
1st Lieutenant—			
Anderson M. Harris	Mar. 12, '62	April 26, '65	2nd Lieutenant; promoted 1st Lieutenant.
2nd Lieutenant—			
Hugh Black	Mar. 12, '62	April 26, '65	3rd Lieutenant, promoted 2nd Lieutenant; shot at Chickamauga.
William C. Gunn	Mar. 17, '62		Corporal, promoted Sergeant; 3rd and 2nd Lieutenant; wounded.
3rd Lieutenant—			
Edward B. White	Mar. 17, '62	April 26, '65	1st Sergeant;; promoted 3rd Lieutenant, wounded.
ENLISTED MEN.			
Barker, J. S.			Died in Kentucky, buried in Lexington Cemetery.
Black, Neil G.	Mar. 17, '62	April 26, '65	
Boykin. James C.	Mar. 17, '62	April 26, '65	
Bracewell, Joseph	May 9, '62	April 26, '65	Shot at Atlanta, Ga. July 22, '64.
Brown, E. D.			
Bryant, J.			Corporal; died in service.
Butler, Jesse R.	Mar. 12, '62		Died in Kentucky, buried in Lexington Cemetery.
Butler, John	May '62	April 26, '65	
Campbell, John C.	Mar. 15, '62		Promoted 1st Sergeant; mortally wounded.
Cannon, David			Honorable mention at Chickamauga.
Cannon, Jacob C.	April 18, '62	April 26, '65	Wounded at Kennesaw Mt. Ga. June, '64.
Cannon, Thomas H	Mar. 12, '62		
Carroll, William	Mar. 12, '62		
Cowan, John J.	Mar. 12, '62	April 26, '65	Shot at Chickamauga, Ga. Sept. 20, '63.
Crawford, George W	Mar. 18, '62	April 26, '65	
Crawford, James	Mar. 12, '62		
Crosby, Henry A.	Mar. 12, '62		Corporal.
Crosby, Isham J.	Mar. 25, '62		Promoted Corporal; died in service.
Davis, William	Mar. 12, '62		
Dugger, Simeon	Mar. 12, '62		Captured at Kennesaw Mt. July 1, '64; carried to Camp Morton Ind. and there lost right eye from disease; paroled from prison.
Edenfield, Elias J.	Mar. 17, '62		
Eubanks, Darlie	Mar. 17, '62		
Fair, William	Mar. 12, '62		
Ferrell, W. J.	Mar. 12, '62		Corporal; captured at Nashville, Dec. 15, '64 imprisoned and paroled at Camp Douglass June '65.
Fillingin, John I.	Mar. 12, '62		
Fletcher, Joseph C	Mar. 4, '62		
Flowers, Henry	Mar. 12, '62		
Freeman, Richard	Mar. 12, '62		
Gatlin, Thomas	Mar. 12, '62		
Gatlin, William	Mch. 12, '62	April 9, '65	Transferred to Smith's Cavalry.
Glover, George K	May 15, '62	April 26, '65	
Goldmire, Robert L	April 12, '62		
Gora, W. W.		April 26, '65	
Grubb, Thomas L	April 12, '62		Promoted 1st Sergeant; wounded.
Hair, John	Mch. 12, '62		
Harden, James T.	Mch. 12, '62		
Harrington, William			Killed at Missionary Ridge December 27, '63.
Harris, Samuel H	Mch. 24, '62		
Holloway, Benjamin F		April 26, '65	
Horne, Henry F.	Mch. 24, '62	April 26, '65	Sergeant.
Howard, John F.	Mch. 13, '62	April 26, '65	
Howe, John H.		April 26, '65	
Johnson, William M.	Mch. 12, '62		
Jones, R. Emmett	Mch. 12, '62	April 26, '65	Corporal.
Jordan, John P.		April 26, '65	Promoted Sergeant; April 18, '62, then Regimental Q. M.
Karkein, William J.			
Keadle, John H.	Mch. 12, '62		
Kenan, Daniel L.	Mch. 12, '62		1st Sergeant; promoted Major, Lieutenant-Colonel, and Colonel; lost leg at Bentonville.
Kenardy, J. T. H.	Mch. 20, '62		

Roll Company A—6th Florida Infantry.

(Continued.)

NAMES.	MUSTERED IN	MUSTERED OUT.	REMARKS.
Kennedy, Thomas	Mch. 20, '62	April 26, '65	Wounded at Dallas, Ga., May 28, '64.
King, Henry	Mch. 20, '62		
Kirkland, S. H.	Mch. 20, '62		Promoted 1st Sergeant; wounded mortally.
Kirkland, William J.	Mch. 20, '62		
Laird, Henry	Mch. 20, '62	April 26, '65	
Laird, James	Mch 20, '62	April 26, '65	Transferred from 1st Ala.
Lambert, Benjamin	Mch. 20, '62		Died at Cumberland Gap.
Lambert, Thomas	Mch. 20, '62	April 26, '65	Corporal.
Langston, Jacob R	Mch. 13, '62	April 26, '65	
Langston, James			
Langston, Jonathan B	June 1, '61		Discharged May, '63, for disability.
Long, Charles E	Mch. 22, '62		
McAlily, Samuel	Mch. 19, '62		
McAlpin, Arlington	Mch. 19, '62	April 26, '65	
McClellan, A	Mch. 19, '62	April 26, '65	
McCullers, Hardy	Mch. 12, '62		
McLeod, Alexander	Mch. 12, '62	April 26, '65	Imprisoned at Fort Delaware.
McNair, F. L.	Mch. 12, '62	April 26, '65	
McPhaul, Hamilton	Mch. 12, '62	April 26, '65	Wounded at Bentonville, N. C., March 19, '64.
McPherson, Alexander M	Mch. 20, '62	April 16, '65	Musician.
McPherson, Archibald	Mch. 20, '62		Died of pneumonia at Knoxville May 10, '63.
McPherson, James	Mar. 20, '62	April 16, '65	
Martin, Jeremiah J	Mar. 20, '62	April 26, '65	
Martin, M. L	Mar. 20, '62	April 26, '65	
Nicholson, Angus	Mar. 20, '62	April 26, '65	
Owen, L. S	Mar. 20, '62	April 26, '65	
Parramore, Adam J	Mar. 12, '62		
Parker, Stephen A	Mar. 12, '62		
Penny, John J	Mar. 12, '62		
Peters, A. J.	Mar. 21, '62		
Peters, Francis M	Mar. 21, '62		
Peters, Hardy	Mar. 21, '62		Died at Camp Chase Feb. 11, '65; Grave No. 1152.
Pittman, John C	Mar. 21, '62		Corporal.
Poindexter, John W	Mar. 15, '62		
Pringle, Byardam G	Mar. 14, '62	April 26, '65	
Renew, Timothy	Mar. 14, '62		
Revell, Stephen	Mar. 6, '62		
Richards, W. N.	Mar. 6, '62	April 26, '65	
Robinson, William E	Mar. 12, '62		Promoted Sergeant; came near killing General
Robinson, William U	Mar. 10, '62	April 26, '65	Forrest while on picket near Murfreesborough
Rudd, Jerry	Mar. 12, '62		Tennessee.
Rudd, Samuel	Mar. 12, '62	April 26, '65	
Sanders, John C	Mar. 12, '62	April 26, '65	Promoted 2nd Sergeant.
Sapp, Asa	Mar. 4, '62		
Shephard, B. F.	Mar. 12, '62	April 26, '65	
Shepard, Fountain H	Mar. 12, '62	April 26, '65	Wounded at Missionary Ridge Dec. 27, '63 and
Smith, William J	Mar. 13, '62		discharged.
Smith William T	Mar. 12, '62		
Suber, Lemuel P	Mar. 5, '62	April 16, '65	
Thomas, P. T. M. T	Mar. 21, '62		
Thomas, W. A	Mar. 21, '62	April 26, '65	Wounded in the hip, in Georgia.
Thompson, Tobias	Mar. 12, '62		
Tolar, John R	Mar. 12, '62		Discharged, '63; for cause unknown.
Vendrick John	Mar. 28, '62		
Vendrick, Nathan	Mar. 28, '62		
Wade, William H	Mar. 12, '62		
Walden, Lemuel J	Mar. 12, '62	April 26, '65	Promoted Sergeant; wounded at Chickamauga Sept. 20, '63.

Roll Company B—6th Florida Infantry.

NAMES.	MUSTERED IN.	MUSTERED OUT.	REMARKS.
OFFICERS.			
Captains—			
Samuel B. Love	Mar. 12, '62		Resigned, '63, in Tennessee.
Malcolm Nicholson	April 5, '61	April 26, '65	Sergeant, promoted Captain.
1st Lieutenants—			
William H. Scott	April 18, '65		Resigned.
Raburn H. Reeves		April 26, '65	2nd Lieutenant, promoted 1st Lieutenant.
2nd Lieutenant—			
Theophilus S. Luckie		April 26, '65	Sergeant promoted 2nd Lieutenant.
3rd Lieutenant—			
Donald W. Nicholson	April 5, '61		Resigned.
ENLISTED MEN.			
Albert, Joseph			Died in prison at Columbus, O. March 1, '65; Grave No. 82.
Barefoot, Thomas			Died in prison, buried in Oakwood Cemetery,
Bustick, William			Chicago.

Roll Company B—6th Florida Infantry.

(CONTINUED.)

NAMES.	MUSTERED IN.	MUSTERED OUT.	REMARKS.
Boykin, Lott C.			
Bradley, Solomon			
Brown, John			Wounded at Olustee.
Caldwell, Bryan			
Campbell, Alexander F.			
Campbell, William J.			
Chandler, Joseph C.	April '64	April 26, '65	Promoted Sergeant.
Chester, George H.			Musician.
Chester, Marion A.			
Copeland, James			
Crabbs, Richard			
Crosby, Richard			
Elliot, Joseph D. P. S.			
Elliot, Nixon		April 26, '62	Corporal; honorable mention at Chickamauga.
Ferrell, Daniel			
Ferrell, W. J.			
Fleishman, Simon			
Gibburn, Daniel			
Gibburn, Henry J.			
Gorries, Charles			
Goza, Thomas	Mar. 12, '62		Discharged Aug. 1, '62 for disability.
Green, Thomas			
Hall, Iradell A.	Mar. 12, '62	April 26, '65	
Harrison, James			Musician.
Harrison, William S.			
Henly, Thomas N.			Sergeant.
Hill, Thomas			Died in Camp Chase Nov. 12, '64; Grave No. 453.
Holly, Lewis			
Holloway, Franklin G.			
Howell, John			
Howell, Henry			
Ingram, Daniel R.			
Johnston, George W.			
Johnson, Irvin W.			
Johnson, John W.			
Johnson, William F.			
Johnson, W. G.	Mar. 1, '62	April 26, '65	
Jones, C. H.			... .
Jones, William B.			
Joyner, Lawrence R.		April 26, '65	
Lawrence, William			
Lawrence, William C.			
Lott, Zackariah M.		April 26, '65	
McCall, Sherod			Sergeant; hired a substitute.
McElly, Albert B.			
McDougal, James			
McKenzie, Archibald B.			
McKenzie, Daniel J.			
McPhaul, Archibald			
Mann, Jesse C.		April 26, '65	Promoted Corporal.
Mann, Milton M.		April 26, '65	Promoted Corporal.
Martin, Jeremiah			
Mathis, Marcus			
Miller, Andrew J. Jr.			
Mitchell, William		April 26, '65	
Moore, Nickelby B.			
Moore, Deabourn			
Morton, John E.			
Nelson, James B.	May '62	April 26, '65	Wou at Resaca, Ga. May 14, 64.
Nicholson, Angus	'62	April 26, '65	
Owens, Henry M.			
Parrott, W. B.			
Perkins, William H.			
Rich, Jacob			
Rich, John B.			
Robertson, W.		April 26, '65	
Rogers, James M.			Corporal, promoted Sergeant.
Schwarzenback, Franklin			
Show, Nathaniel G.			
Smith, Alexander L.			
Smith, Andrew J.		April 26, '65	Sergeant.
Smith, T. S.		April 26, '65	Promoted 1st Sergeant.
Strickland, Abel			Discharged June 8, '63 for disability.
Strickland, Green B.		April 26, '65	
Strickland, John			
Timmons, Samuel B.			Corporal.
Tomberlin, William H.			
Truluck, David M.			
Warnock, George W.			
Warnock, William J.			Sergeant; died in service.
Wood, John			
Whidden, Alfred			Died at Camp Chase June 4, '65.
Whidden, Bennett			

Roll Company B—6th Florida Infantry.
(CONTINUED.)

NAMES.	MUSTERED IN.	MUSTERED OUT.	REMARKS.
White, Thomas J.			
Weakely, John W.	May '62	April 26, '65	Shot at Stone Mt. Ga. July 22, '64.
Weakely, Paul		April 26, '65	
Weakely, Silas		April 26, '65	
Wray, William F.			
Wry, John			

Roll Company C—6th Florida Infantry.

NAMES.	MUSTERED IN.	MUSTERED OUT.	REMARKS.
OFFICERS.			
Captain—			
James C. Evans			
1st Lieutenants—			
W. B. Malone			
William B. Forman		April 26, '65	Wounded at Chickamauga, Ga. Sept. 20, '63; promoted 1st Lieutenant from 2nd Lieutenant.
2nd Lieutenant—			
John M. Thomas			Shot through the liver at Dallas, Ga., May 28, '64.
ENLISTED MEN.			
Albert, J. J.			
Austen, B. W.			
Boykin, George H.			Died in Kentucky, buried in Lexington Cemetery.
Boykin, John W.	Mar. '62	April 26, '65	Shot at Missionary Ridge, Tenn. and captured, sent to Rock Island, Ills., and exchanged Mar. 20 '65.
Boykin, John A.			
Brichaman, M.			
Brown, Benjamin F.			
Brown, L.			
Brown, C. B.			
Brouning, John S.			
Burkett, John A.			Died at Camp Chase Prison, May 19, '65; Grave No. 1984.
Campbell, William			Corporal; wounded at Bristow Station, Oct. 14, '63.
Cannon, John			
Cloud, J.			
Cowan, John E.			Died in Kentucky, buried in Lexington Cemetery.
Calton, Burrel			
Dalton, Bailey			
Darby, J. A.			
Darby, T. H.			
Davis, William			Sergeant.
Dean, Thomas W.			
Dudley, J. S.			
Dunn, H. D.		April 26, '65	
Dunn, J. E.			
Dyer, G. W.	May 5, '62		Wounded severely at Chickamauga, Ga. Sept. 19, '63
Dyke, John T.			
Fair, F. W.			
Ferrell, W. D.			
Gee, Walker			
Gillis, M. M.			Sergeant.
Harris, J. H.			Musician.
Jeter, Joseph F.			
Johnson, Daniel			
Jones, Charles H.		April 26, '65	
Jones, Thomas P.			
Kemp, B. A.		April 26, '65	Wounded at Dallas, Georgia., May 28, '64.
Kennedy, A. F.			
Kennedy, S. G.			
Kile, Christopher			
Lang, W. R.			
Lester, H. W.			
Love, W. W.			
McBride, A. S.			Corporal.
McDonald, John A.			Honorable mention.
McDonald, D.			
McDonald, F. J.			
McDougal, J.			
McIver, John			
McRæ, D. G.			Killed May 28, '64, at Dallas, Ga.
Malone, A. F.			Sergeant.
Mathews, William H.	May '62		Died in Tenn., Sept., '63.
Mathews, John			
Mercer, Asa J.			
Mercer, John J.			
Mills, David			
Mills, John S.			
Mitchell, William			

Roll Company C—6th Florida Infantry.
(Continued.)

NAMES.	MUSTERED IN.	MUSTERED OUT.	REMARKS.
Mole, John A		April 26, '65	
Muse, A. H			Musician.
Nicholson, Angus		April 26, '65	
Oneal, J. B			Corporal.
Owens, W. J			
Pittman, John C			
Rawls, A. J			Sergeant.
Reeves, J. S			
Richards, W. N	May 15, '61	April 26, '65	
Roach, Robert			Died at Camp Chase Prison, Feb. 13, '61; Grave No. 1222.
Rowan, S. T			Died in Kentucky, buried in Lexington Cemetery.
Sadler, John			
Sadler, John W			
Santapher, Jacob			
Smart, John H			
Smith, B. S. G		April 26, '65	
Smith, F. M			Sergeant.
Spear, H. L			
Sylvester, William M			Corporal; Camp Chase Prison, Mar. 11, '61; Grave No. 1622.
Thomas, E. J			
Thomas, H. D			
Thomas, William H		April 26, '65	
Temple, J. J			
Tharple, E. J			
Whaley, John			
Whaley, Thomas			
Wynn, Filed			
Yates J. J			

Roll Company D—6th Florida Infantry.

NAMES.	MUSTERED IN.	MUSTERED OUT.	REMARKS.
OFFICERS.			
Captains—			
Jesse J. Finley	Mar. 17, '62		Promoted Colonel, Brigadier General.
John L. Hayes	Mar. 18, '62		1st Lieutenant, promoted Captain; killed, Dallas Ga. '64.
J. B. Anderson	Mar. 18, '62	April 26, '65	2nd Lieutenant, promoted Captain.
1st Lieutenant—			
James Hays	Mar. 17, '62		2nd Lieutenant, promoted 1st Lieutenant.
2nd Lieutenant—			
John W. Butt			Resigned, April 30, '63.
3rd Lieutenant—			
Robert L. Dickson	Mar. 17, '62		
ENLISTED MEN.			
Armstead, Thomas J	Mar. 18, '62		
Baxter, F. G	Mar. 17, '62		
Baxter, John J	Mar. '62	April 26, '65	
Barnes, Jesse B	Mar. 17, '62	April 26, '65	
Beauchamp, J. A			Died at Camp Chase Prison, Mar. 31, '61; Grave No. 1645.
Bowden, Samuel	Mar. 17, '62	April 26, '65	Corporal.
Brantley, John D	Mar. 17, '62		
Brett, John W	Mar. 18, '62		Sergeant.
Brower, William	Mar. 17, '62		
Cain, Augustus C	Mar. 18, '62		
Cain, John S	Mar. 18, '62		
Caldwell, George	Mar. 17, '62		
Carter, Wyatt S	Mar. 17, '62		
Carraway, John M	Mar. 17, '62		
Cawthorn, Stephen J	Mar. 18, '62		
Chisholm, Robert	Mar. 17, '62		Commissary Sergeant.
Collier, James	Mar. 17, '62		Corporal.
Compton, Charles F	Mar. 17, '62		Corporal.
Conner, Edward J	Mar. 18, '62		
Conner, Willis A	Mar. 18, '62		
Conrad, D. S			Died at Camp Douglass Prison, buried Oakwood Cemetery.
Culbreth, David			
Daniel Elijah J	Mar. 17, '62		
Daniel, Jonas	Mar. 17, '62		
Deason, Abram	Mar. 17, '62		
Devone, Leonard H	Mar. 18, '62		
Dickson, John J	Mar. 17, '62		Wounded, Aug. 20, '64; was at home on furlough when Lee surrendered.
Drummond, James	Mar. 17, '62		
Dykes, John J	Mar. 17, '62		

Roll Company D—6th Florida Infantry.
(Continued.)

NAMES.	MUSTERED IN.	MUSTERED OUT.	REMARKS
Ellis, E. W.			Died at Camp Chase, O., Nov. 10, '64; Grave No. 445.
Ely, John R.			
Garrett, Henry K.	May '62	April 26, '65	Wounded at Chickamauga, Ga., Sept. 19, '63
Glover, G. K.		April 26, '65	
Grant, J. C.		April 26, '65	
Hand, Zacariah.	Mar. 18, '62		
Harper, Wilson.	Mar. 18, '62	April 26, '65	Imprisoned at Fort Delaware.
Hare, Green B.	Mar. 17, '62		Corporal.
Hawthorn, Benjamin.	Mar. 17, '62		
Hawthorn, Robert.	Mar. 17, '62		
Hawthorn, William M.	Mar. 17, '62		
Hibbard, Wilson.	Mar. 18, '62		
Hickman, George W.	April 3, '62		
Higswith, Daniel J.	Mar. 18, '62		
Holden, J. T.	Mar. 18, '62	April 26, '65	
Holloway, William J.	Mar. 18, '62		
Holton, William H.	Mar. 18, '62		
Irwin, Allen.	Mar. 18, '62		
Jackson, M. V. B.	Mar. 17, '62		
Jewell, Daniel W.	Mar. 17, '62		Died at Camp Douglass Prison.
Johnson, John D.	Mar. 18, '62		
Johnson, John W.	Mar. 18, '62	April 26, '65	
Johnsey, Charles B.	Mar. 17, '62		
Jonas, Andrew.	June '62	April 26, '65	Wounded at Resaca, Ga., May 14, '64.
Jones, Jonas.	Mar. 17, '62		
Jonas, William P.	Mar. 17, '62		
Kilgore, Arthur W.	Mar. 17, '62		
King, John P.	Mar. 17, '62		Killed at Atlanta, Aug. 7, '64.
Kittleband, John.	Mar. 17, '62		
Koonce, Thomas B.	Mar. 18, '62		
Lashley, Peter.	Mar. 18, '62		
Lawrence, Peter P.	Mar. 17, '62		
Lockhart, J. R.	Mar. 17, '62	April 26, '65	
McClendon, Andrew J.	Mar. 18, '62		
McDaniel, Samuel M.	Mar. 17, '62		
McLellan, Alex.	Mar. 17, '62	April 26, '65	
Meadows, John W.	Mar. 18, '62		
Minchen, Nathaniel C.	Mar. 17, '62		
Mitchell, Thomas J.	Mar. 17, '62	April 26, '65	Sergeant.
Nickles, Joseph I.	Mar. 17, '62		
Oliver, Joshua.	Mar. 17, '62		
Perry, John J.	Mar. 18, '62		
Pynes, Lewis W.	Mar. 17, '62		
Ridley, Joseph D.	Mar. 18, '62	April 26, '65	
Richardson, James N.		April 26, '65	
Riley, William T.	Mar. 17, '62		
Rogers, Francis M.	Mar. 17, '62		
Rogers, Peter L.	Mar. 17, '62		
Rogers, Thomas L.	Mar. 17, '62		
Scott, Samuel F.	Mar. 17, '62		
Sexton, Alfred.	Mar. 17, '62	April 26, '65	
Shepherd, B. F.	Mar. 17, '62		
Simmons, Mercer.	Mar. 17, '62		
Stanton, Samuel F.	Mar. 17, '62		Sergeant.
Smith, Francis P.	Mar. 17, '62		
Snell, Robert F.	Mar. 17, '62		
Speights, Green.	Mar. 17, '62		
Stapleton, David.	Mar. 17, '62		
Starling, Solomon.	Mar. 17, '62	April 26, '65	Wounded at Chickamauga, Georgia.
Steed, John R.	Mar. 17, '62		
Stone, John B.	Mar. 17, '62		
Strickland, Simeon J.	Mar. 17, '62		
Toole, Calvin.			
Toole, Hezekiah I. I.			
Waters, Frederick.	Mar. 18, '62		
Wills, John W.	Mar. 18, '62		
Wooten, Amos J.	Mar. 17, '62		
Yon, Wesley C.	Mar. 18, '62		

Roll Company E—6th Florida Infantry.

NAMES.	MUSTERED IN.	MUSTERED OUT.	REMARKS.
OFFICERS.			
Captain—			
Henry O. Bassett.			Killed in Marianna raid.
1st Lieutenant—			
William M. A. Harrell.			Resigned April 8, '63.

Roll Company E—6th Florida Infantry.
(CONTINUED.)

NAMES.	MUSTERED IN	MUSTERED OUT.	REMARKS.
2nd Lieutenants—			
Frank Philips Jr			Promoted Captain and Adjutant, 6th Regiment.
William W. Brown Jr		May '65	2nd Lieutenant.
Hentz C. Lewis			1st Sergeant promoted 2nd Lieutenant.
3rd Lieutenant—			
W. W. Brown	Mar. '62		Promoted 3rd Lieutenant, Company E.
ENLISTED MEN.			
Bassett, G. W		April 26, '65	
Bennett, D. T			
Benton, Joseph H			
Bradley, Jesse		April 26, '65	
Bracewell, Joseph		April 26, '65	
Bray, W. W	Mar. '62	April 26, '65	
Bullock, Nathan			
Bunch, Daniel			
Bush, P. C			Died in Camp Chase, June 5, '65 grave No. 706.
Carson, James			
Cooley, Seaborn			
Comerford, James E	Feb. 1, '62		Captured July 22 '64 at Atlanta, held a prisoner until April 1, 65; paroled for exchange a few days before the close of the war.
Courtney, John			Died, Camp Chase, July 14, '65; grave No. 763.
Courtney, William			
Cutts, Joseph J			
Cutts, William F			
Davis John T			
Deason, Abraham	Mar. 15, '62	April 26, '65	
Dykes, James R			
Everett, Robert P			
Faw, James			
Gavin, Stephen B	Mar. 28, '62	April 26, '65	Shot at Tunnell Hill, Ga., Feb. 18, '64.
Gibson, Martin			
Gibson, William			
Giles, J. J	Mar. '62		Discharged Nov. '64; cause, disability.
Griffin, Jefferson	Mar. '62	April 26, '65	Shot at Atlanta, Ga., July 22, '64.
Hall, Daniel		April 26, '65	
Ham, Patrick	Magr. 10, '6	April 26, '65	
Ham, William D	Dec. '62		Died in hospital at Knoxville, Tenn., Jan., '63.
Hartsfield, James W			
Harden, Felix G			
Harrell, J. H		April 26, '65	
Harrell, William	Mar. 28, '62	April 26, '65	
Hermett, E. D		April 26, '65	
Hill, Denley		April 26, '65	
Hinson, Andrew			
Holden, J. T		April 26, '65	
Jackson, Thomas			Died in Kentucky, buried in Lexington Cemetery.
Jackson, W. A		April 26, '65	
Jenkins, Emanuel		April 26, '65	
Johnson, Gazaway	April '62	April 26, '65	
King, John J			
Lacy, John			
Lacy, Love			
Lasiter, James M			Died, Camp Douglass.
Lastinger, Clayton			
Latner, L. R			Died, Camp Douglass Prison.
Lewis, Arthur			
Lockhart, J. R		April 26, '65	
McCrean, Elbert			
McCrean, John			Died in hospital of disease, Sept. 25, '62.
McDaniel, Doss		April 26, '65	
McDonald, Daniel			
McDonald, William P		April 26, '65	Shot at Chickamauga, Ga., Sept. 19, '63.
Mais, David J			
Mays, James T			
Miller, Enoch			
O'Conner, William	May 18, '62	April 26, '65	
Pate, Washington			
Peacock, Abraham	May '62		Died of disease at Richmond, Va., Aug. 24, '64.
Pitman, Amon			
Pitman, T. Harman		April 26, '65	
Pitman, Thomas			
Register, John D			
Register, Thomas		April 26, '65	
Richardson, J. N		April 26, '65	
Rivers, Joel			
Rivers, Louis			
Royals, William			Honorable mention.
Sapp, Anthony	Nov. '62	April 26, '65	Wounded at New Hope Church, Ga., Mar. 28, '63.
Sapp, Renford		April 26, '65	
Sexton, J. W		April 26, '65	Wounded at Chickamauga, Tenn., Sept. 19 '63;
Shepherd, William H			died Dec. 2. '62.
Shie, Alexander			
Simms, Henry G	April '62	April 26, '65	

(CONTINUED.)

NAMES.	MUSTERED IN.	MUSTERED OUT.	REMARKS.
Simpson, P. A.	May 7, '62	April 26, '65	Shot at Chickamauga, Sept. 19, '63.
Simpson, W. D.	May 7, '62	April 26, '65	
Smith, John W.			Sergeant.
Stewart, John		Apri 26, '65	
Taylor, Jasper		April 26, '65	
Tindall, Moses	Mar. 15, '62	April 26, '65	Shot at Missionary Ridge, Tenn., Nov. 10, '63.
White, Joseph		April 26, '65	Wounded severely in left shoulder and left hip.
Whittle, Ellison A.			
Wilson, James Franklin	May 12, '61	April 26, '65	Wounded at Chickamauga, Ga., Sept. 19, '63; captured at Atlanta, Ga., Aug. 5, '64; carried to Camp Chase, O., where he died Jan. 21, '65 of small-pox, grave No. 833.
Williams, George F.	May '61	April 26, '65	Wounded slightly during service.
Williams, S. J.			Died in Kentucky, buried in Lexington Cemetery.
York, John			

Roll Company F (Magnolia State Guards)—6th Florida Infantry.

NAMES.	MUSTERED IN.	MUSTERED OUT.	REMARKS.
OFFICERS			
Captains—			
Lawrence M. Attaway	Oct. 16, '61		Died at Columbus, Ga., hospital July 9, '62.
Joseph M. White		April 26, '65	1st Lieutenant, promoted Captain; wounded at Chickamauga and disabled.
1st Lieutenant—			
William D Simmons	Oct. 16, '61		Promoted 1st Lieutenant, wounded and disabled.
2nd Lieutenant—			
George W. Lesley			Killed at Chickamauga, Sept. 20, '63.
3rd Lieutenants—			
Junius L. Snellgrove			Sergeant, promoted 3rd Lieutenant; killed at Knoxville.
Hentz Lewis			Promoted 3rd Lieutenant, captured in May.
James Maloy	Oct. 16, '61		Promoted 3rd Lieutenant,
ENLISTED MEN.			
Battle, Henry	Oct. 16, '61		
Beasley, John	Oct. 16, '61		
Battey, James W.	Oct. 16, '61		Corporal.
Blair, William F.			
Boswell, Richard L.			
Britte, John			
Buchanan, Thomas			
Bullock, G. K.			Died, Camp Chase, Nov. 13, '64; grave No. 446.
Busby, John			
Butler, Job			Musician.
Butler, John			
Carpenter, James		April 26, '65	
Carpenter, William		April 26, '65	
Chaunel, John			
Chance, S.	Oct. 16, '61		Corporal.
Clark, William G.			
Cloud, Martin			
Cook, Hardy		April 26, '65	Wounded at Chickamauga, Sept. 19, '63.
Crawford, Archibald			
Davis, Jordan W.			
Davis, Wesley J.			
Devane, Robertson C.			
Derrick, H. M.			
Dickerson, DeKalb	Oct. 16, '61		
Dykes, Moses	June 15, '62		Wounded at Dallas, Ga., May 28, '64, and discharged for disability June, '64.
Emanuel, Asa			
Emanuel, John			
Folsome, Francis M.			Died, Camp Chase, O. 10,'64; grave No. 590.
Gable, J. D.		April 26 '65	
Gable, J. H.		April 26, '65	
Gabriel, Andrew J.			
Gabriel, James			
Garbett, Erasmus			Sergeant.
Garbett, Samuel			
Gay, John			
Gay, Lewis D.			
Gay, Thomas B.			Corporal
Gibson, John	Oct. 16, '61		
Glisson, Dennis			
Glisson, Marion			
Glisson, William			
Goodman, Green G.			
Goodman, M.	Oct. 16, '61		
Griffin, Len	Mar. 1, '62	April 26, '65	

Roll Company F (Magnolia State Guards)—6th Florida Infantry.
(CONTINUED.)

NAMES.	MUSTERED IN.	MUSTERED OUT.	REMARKS.
Grinsley, Felix A		April 26, '65	1st Sergeant.
Ham, Patrick		April 26, '65	
Hamilton, Levi			Died, Camp Chase, O., Feb. 16,'65; grave No. 1287.
Hamilton, Z. H.			
Hill, Dempsey		April 26, '65	
Holden, J. T. (M. D.)		April 26, '65	Promoted Surgeon, C. S. A.
Hollis, Thomas	Oct. 16, '61		
Hollister, William H.	Aug. '61	April 26, '65	Transferred to Abell's Battery, '65; shot through lung at Chickamauga, Ga., Sept. 19, '63; promoted Corporal.
Howard, Newton	Oct. 16, '61		
Ingram, Benjamin			
Jackson, William			Musician.
Johnson, Zackledge		April 26, '65	
Jones, A. B	Oct. 16, '61		
Kemp, J. C	Mar. '62	April 26, '65	Wounded at Dallas, Ga., May 28, '64.
Keel, Green			
Keller, John			
Lamb, Edward I.			
Lasiter, L. W			
McDonald, Daniel P		April 26, '65	
Maddox, Elijah			Died in Kentucky, buried in Lexington Cemetery.
Maddox, John			
Martin, John-D			Corporal.
Mathews, John			
Mercer, Asa			
Mercer, J. C			Died in Kentucky, buried in Lexington Cemetery.
Mercer, J. H			
Mercer, Josiah L			
Myrick, Litt	Oct. 16, '61		1st Sergeant.
Nall, James			Died in Kentucky, buried in Lexington Cemetery.
Pelt, Obedeah			
Pelt, Robert			Corporal.
Pelt, William W			
Player, Aaron F			
Player, Daniel H	Feb '61	April 26, '65	Wounded at Missionary Ridge, again at Bentonville, N. C.
Player, W. J		April 26, 65	
Potter, William R. F			Killed at Chickamauga, Sept. 13, '63.
Revels, George W			
Sansom, J. T. L	Mar. 15. '62		Captured at Nashville, Tenn., '64; sent to prison at Camp Douglass, Ill., from there paroled June, '65.
Scott, McGilberry			
Shores, Joseph D			
Simms, Henry G		April 26, '65	
Simms, Isaac		April 26, '65	
Sims, Samuel	Mar. '61	April 26, '65	Wounded at Dallas, Ga.
Sims, William H			Sergeant.
Simmons, J. T	May 3, '62	April 26, '65	Shot at Chickamauga, Ga., Sept. 20, '63.
Simmons, Mills			
Slade, George W			
Stanley, N. J	Oct. 16, '61		
Stephens, James			Discharged for disability.
Stephens, James B			
Stephens, William D		April 26, '65	
Straus, S	Oct. 16, '61		Sergeant.
Strickand, N. L			
Vanderford, Thomas			
Varner, Elijah			Died in Kentucky, buried in Lexington Cemetery.
Wadford, William			
Williams, Daniel			
Wood, Right			
Young, A. N			

Roll Company G—6th Florida Infantry.

NAMES.	MUSTERED IN.	MUSTERED OUT.	REMARKS.
OFFICERS.			
Captain—			
Henry B. Grace	Mar. 11, '62	April 26, '65	
1st Lieutenant—			
John E. Wilson	Mar. 11, '62		
2nd Lieutenant—			
Charles L. Herring	Mar. 11, '62		
3rd Lieutenant—			
Daniel McGill	Mar. 11, '62		
ENLISTED MEN.			
Alford, James W	Mar. 11, '62		
Ayers, Daniel	Mar. 11, '62		
Barefoot, Noah	Mar. 11, '62		

Roll Company G—6th Florida Infantry.

(CONTINUED.)

NAMES.	MUSTERED IN.	MUSTERED OUT.	REMARKS.
Baty, Reuben	Mar. 11, '62		
Baty, William	Mar. 11, '62		
Beaman, Noah W	Mar. 11, '62		
Bell, Andrew L	Mar. 11, '62		
Bell, John D	Mar. 11, '62		
Bell, Zacariah	Mar. 11, '62		
Berry, Harney	Mar. 11, '62		
Birch, John E	Mar. 11, '62		
Brett, Robert B. G	Mar. 11, '62		Corporal.
Brett, Wiliam H	Mar. 11, '62	April 26, '65	
Brown, George W	Mar. 11, '62		
Brown, H. Harris	Mar. 11, '62		
Buck, John E	Mar. 11, '62		
Budd Jefferson	Mar. 11, '62		
Burkett, John	Mar. 11, '62	April 26, '65	Wounded at Chickamauga, Ga., Sept. 19, '63.
Cook, Barnabas B	Mar. 11, '62	April 26, '65	
Coonrod, Charles L	Mar. 11, '62		
Coonrod, Joseph M	May '62	April 26, '65	
Coonrod, William H	Mar. 11, '62		Killed at Missonary Ridge, Tenn., Dec. 27, '63.
Connelly, Franklin B	Mar. 11, '62		
Connelly, George W	Mar. 11, '62		
Connelly James H	Mar. 11, '62		
Connelly, Jesse	Mar. 11, '62		
Connelly, Joseph W	Mar. 11, '62		
Dater, Charles	Mar. 11, '62		Sergeant.
Davis, Daniel	Mar. 11, '62		
Davis, Francis M	Mar. 11, '62		
Davis, John M	Mar. 11, '62		
Davis, Stafford	Mar. 11, '62		
Davis, T. Allen	Mar. 11, '62		Sergeant.
Dickerson, Benjamin R	Mar. 11, '62		
Dickerson, DeKalb	Mar. 11, '62		
Dickerson, Joseph F	Mar. 11, '62		
Dukes, William H	Mar. 11, '62		
Duncan, Charles	Mar. 11, '62		Died, Camp Chase, Oct. 16, '64; grave No. 304
Faircloth, Wilson	Mar. 11, '62		Sergeant.
Gilbert, Joseph	Mar. 11, '62		Corporal.
Gilbert, Thomas J	Mar. 11, '62		
Goodwin, James	Mar. 11, '62		
Glover, George K	Mar. 11, '62	April 26, '65	
Grant, Calvin P	Oct. 17, '62		Discharged April 12, '63, cause, disability.
Grant, Edwin	Oct. 17, '62	April 26, '65	
Grant, Jefferson C	Mar. 11, '62	April 26, '65	Wounded at Chickamauga, Ga., '62; promoted Sergeant.
Green, Thomas Jr	Mar. 11, '62		
Grimsley, F. A	Mar. 11, '62	April 26, '65	
Hall, Daniel	Mar. 11, '62		
Hall, Elam L	Mar. 11, '62		Corporal.
Hall, Hamilton	Mar. 11, '62		
Hathaway, Benjamin F	Mar. 11, '62	April 26, '65	Wounded and captured at Atlanta, '64; held in prison until close of war.
Hathaway, Gustavus M	Mar. 11, '62		Died at Camp Chase, O., Nov. 9, '64; grave No. 417
Hathaway, Simon B	Mar. 11, '62	April 26, '65	
Harden, Daniel M	Mar. 11, '62		
Haney, Nathaniel H. B	Mar. 11, '62		
Hicks, James W	Mar. 11, '62	April 26, '65	Wounded at Chickamauga, Ga., Sept. 19, '63.
Hilliard, George	Mar. 11, '62		
Holman, Francis M	Mar. 11, '62		
Hodspeth, Conegal	Mar. 11, '62		Musician.
Hyatt, Edward M	Mar. 11, '62	April 26, '65	Shot at Chickamauga, Ga., Sept. 19, '63; also at Atlanta, Ga., July 22, '64; promoted Corporal.
Johnson, John W	Mar. 11, '62		
Kickers, James L	Mar. 11, '62		
Knight, Cooper	Mar. 11, '62		
Knight, Thomas S	Mar. 11, '62		
Knight, William	Mar. 11 '62		
Lacy, A	Mar. 11 '62		
Laslie, John C	Mar. 11 '62		
Lockhart, J. R	Mar. 11 '62	April 26, '65	
Lolly, Joel	Mar. 11 '62		
McDaniel William	Mar. 11, '62		Musician.
McGill, Cornelius A	Mar. 11 '62		Sergeant.
McNeil, John E	Mar. 11 '62		
Miles, William M	Mar. 11 '62	April 26, '65	Shot at Atlanta, Ga., July 22, '64; also at Chickamauga, Ga., Sept. 19, '63; promoted Sergeant.
Miller, John	Mar. 11, '62		
Morris, James E. D	Mar. 11, '62		
Newton, Daniel H	Mch. 11, '62		
Newton, Reuben B	Mar. 11, '62		
Niell, I. W	Mar. 11, '62	April 26, '65	
Owens, John W	Mar. 11, '62		
Parker, James	Mar. 11, '62		
Parker, John A	Mar. 11, '62		
Pen, Joseph I	Mar. 11, '62		
Pennington, S. P	Mar. 11, '62	April 26, '65	
Philips, George W	Mar. 11, '62	April 26, '65	

Roll Company G—6th Florida Infantry.
(CONTINUED.)

NAMES.	MUSTERED IN.	MUSTERED OUT.	REMARKS.
Powell, Bryant H.	Mar. 11, '62		
Rich, George W.	Mar. 11, '62		
Richards, Daniel T.	Mar. 11, '62		
Rudd, Henry.	Mar. 11, '62		
Rudd, John.	Mar. 11, '62		
Rudd, Jefferson.	Mar. 11, '62		
Slater, Alexander.	Mar. 11, '62	April 26 '65	
Slater, Charles.	Mar. 11, '62		
Slater, Lundon.	Mar. 11, '62		
Slater, S.	Mar. 11, '62		
Slapper, Daniel A.	Mar. 11, '62		
Seals, Edwia.	Mar. 11, '62	April 26, '65	
Still, William.	Mar. 11, '62		
Strickland, Thomas.	Mar. 11, '62		
Taylor, Asa.	Mar. 11, '62		
Taylor, William H.	Mar. 11, '62	April 26, '65	
Taylor, Jasper S.	Mar. 11, '62	April 26, '65	
Tedder, Eli.	Mar. 11, '62		
Toole, Calvin.	Mar. 11, '62	April 26, '65	Shot at Atlanta, Ga., July 22, '64.
Toole, Isaac M.	Mar. 11, '62		Corporal; wounded at Chickamauga, Ga., Sept. 19, '63; promoted Sergeant
Vanderford, Thomas.	Mar. 11, '62		Discharged Aug.,'64; disability, wounded near Dallas, July1, '64. Honorable mention at Chickamauga.
Vickers, James T.	Mar. 11, '62		
Weatherby, Seaborne.	Mar. 11, '62		Surrendered at Wilmington, Sergeant.
Webb, Jasper N.	Mar. 11, '62		
Webb, Marion J. L.	Mar. 11, '62		
Webb, Williford.	Mar. 11, '62		
Whitaker, James T.	Mar. 11, '62	April 26, '65	
Whitaker, John D.	Mar. 11, '62		
Whitefield, Benjamin H.	Mar. 11, '62		
Whitefield, Francis M.	Mar. 11, '62		
Whitefield, George W.	Mar. 11, '62	April 26, '65	
Whitefield, John A.	Mar. 11, '62	April 26, '65	

Roll Company H—6th Florida Infantry.

NAMES.	MUSTERED IN.	MUSTERED OUT.	REMARKS.
OFFICERS.			
Captains—			
Angus D. McLean	April 2, '62		Promoted Lieutenant-Colonel and Colonel, killed at Dallas, Ga.
Stephen Cawthon	April 2, '62		Promoted from 1st Lieutenant to Captain.
1st Lieutenant—			
2nd Lieutenants—			
James J. P. McClellan	April 2, '62		Died of brain fever at Knoxville, Tenn., Aug. 20 '62.
Alexander G. McLeod			3rd Lieutenant, promoted to 2nd Lieutenant.
3rd Lieutenant—			
P. D. McSwain	April 2, '62	April 26, '65	Promoted 3rd Lieutenant.
ENLISTED MEN.			
Bedsole, Mathew	April 2, '62		
Bell, Robert.	April 2, '62		
Bird, James A.	April 2, '62		Discharged, disability and injuries from a fall Aug. 9, '62.
Bray, William.	April 2, '62		
Birk, Mark.	April 2, '62		
Birk, William.	April 2, '62		
Bugby, William F.	April 2, '62		
Burgess, J. H.		April 26, '65	
Burks, Joseph F.			
Campbell, Daniel.		April 26, '65	
Campbell, John A.	April 2, '62		
Campbell, W. L.	April 2, '62	April 26, '65	
Campbell, William M.	April 2, '62		Corporal.
Cannon, Henry M.	April 2 '62		
Cannon, Henry R.	April 2, '62		
Carter, Emanuel.	April 2, '62		
Chestnut, Calvin.	April 2, '62	Jan. 15, '64	Disability.
Clary, William P.	April 2, '62		
Cook, George W.	April 2, '62	April 26, '65	Wounded, Nov. 30, at Franklin, Tenn., promoted to Lieutenant, in Laspier's Company.
Crain, Harvey.	May 10, '62		
Crain, Wash.			
Crawford, W. Patrick.	April 2, '62	April 26, '65	
Daniel, Thomas P.	April 2, '62		
Davis, Isaac.	April 2, '62		
Divine, Robert D.	April 2, '62		
Edge, Jesse.	April 2, '62	June 12, '65	From Camp Chase, O., prison.
Edge, Obediah.	April 2, '62		Corporal; discharged at Knoxville, Tenn. disability.

Roll Company H—6th Florida Infantry.

(Continued.)

NAMES.	MUSTERED IN.	MUSTERED OUT.	REMARKS.
Foley, Zion	April 2, '62		Died in Kentucky, buried in Lexington Cemetery.
Fountain, Daniel	April 2, '62		
Gainer, James	April 2, '62		
Garrett, James	April 2, '62		
Garner, Joseph	April 2, '62	April 26, '65	
Garner, T. G.	'64	April 26 '65	
Gillis, Angus D.	April 2, '62		
Gillis, William C.	April 2, '62		
Gillis, Norman W	April 2, '62		
Gordon, Angus	April 2, '62		
Gregory W. T.	April 2 '62		Wounded at Sharpsburg, Md., Sept. 17, '62 and died Dec. 17, '62.
Hall, Lawrence	April 2, '62		
Hall, Rayford	April 2, '62		
Hart, William H.	April 2, '62		
Herring, Hardy J.	April 2, '62		
Hustle, Isaac C.	April 2, '62		Sergeant.
Jones, W. B.	April 2, '62	April 26, '65	
Jordan, Lorenzo D.	April 2, '62		
Kimmons, James M.	April 2, '62		
Kimmons, William J.	April 2, '62	April 26, '65	
Kinnington, John.	April 2, '62		
Kinnington, John H.	April 2, '62		
Kirkland, Reese	April 2, '62		
Levins, Richard	April 2, '62		
Linn, John W.	April 2, '62		Musician.
Londay, Francis A.	April 2, '62		
Londay, Stephen	April 2, '62		
Lott William	April 2, '62		
McCaskell, Finley	April 2, '62		
McCaskill, Spear	April 2, '62		
McCurley, William	April 2, '62		
McDonald, Daniel P.	April 2, '62	April 26, '65	Shot at Chickamauga, Ga,. Sept. 19, '63.
McDonald, Daniel L.	April 2, '62		
McDonald, D. T.	April 2, '62	April 26, '65	
McDonald, P. P.	July 16, '62	April 26, '65	Wounded at Dallas, Ga., May 28, '64.
McLeod, D. G.		April 26, '65	
McLeod, John D.	April 2, '62		Sergeant.
McLeod, John G.	April 2, '62		Sergeant.
McPherson, Malcolm	April 2, '65		
Meeks, William			
Minger, John.	April 2, '62		
Morrison, Archibald G	April 2, '62		1st Sergeant.
Morrison, Daniel	April 2 '62	April 26, '65	
Morrison, John P.	May '62	April 26, '65	
Nichols, Wiley	April 26, '62		
Padgett, Dozier	April 2, '62		
Padgett, George W	April 2, '62		
Padgett, Isham	April 2, '62	April 26, '65	Shot near Chattanooga, Tenn., July,'64.
Perry, Samuel	April 2, '62		
Powell, Daniel B.	April 2, '62		
Preachers, George	April 2, '62		
Ray, Colin G.	April 2, '62		
Ray, Colin G. Jr	April 2, '62		
Ray, Dunsan C.	April 2, '62	April 26, '65	
Reeves, B. F.	April 2, '62	April 26, '65	
Rice, James H.	April 2, '62		Sergeant.
Roling, John L.	April 2, '62		
Rutherford, John	April 2, '62		
Simmons, John J.	April 2, '62		
Simmons, Thomas	April 2, '62		
Smith, Green R.	April 2, '62		
Stafford, John	April 2, '62	April 26, '65	
Turner, William A.	April 2, '62		
Vaughn, W. M.	April 2, '62		Died, Camp Chase, Nov. 20, '65; grave No. 1717.
Walch, John			
Ward, Andrew J.	April 2, '62		
Ward, George T.	April 2, '62		
Weeks, Jacob	April 2, '62		
West, Robert H.	April 2, '62		
White, Kinnon E.	April 2, '62	April 26, '65	Captured, '64; confined at Camp Douglass prison and paroled from there at the close of war.
William, John E.	April 2, '62		
Williamson, Rice	April 2, '62		Musician.
Williamson, Seth	April 2, '62		
Woodham, Uriah	April 2, '62	April 26, '65	
Yeashy. W. J.	April 2, '62		
Yon, C. T.	April 2, '62	April 26 '65	
Znin, John W	April 2, '62		

Roll Company I—6th Florida Infantry.

NAMES.	MUSTERED IN.	MUSTERED OUT.	REMARKS.
OFFICERS.			
Captains—			
Harrison K. Hagan	Mch. 14, '62		
Samuel Yerger Finley	Mch. 14, '62	April 26, '65	1st Lieutenant, promoted Captain.
1st Lieutenant—			
Thomas H. Pittman	Mch. 14, '62	April 26, '65	Sergeant, promoted 1st Lieutenant.
2nd Lieutenant—			
Robert D. Snelling	Mch. 14, '62		
3rd Lieutenant—			
Archibald Gillis	Mch. 14, '62		
ENLISTED MEN.			
Babb, James	Mch. 14, '62		
Barton, J. W	Mch. 14, '62		Died, Camp Chase, Mch. 1, '65; grave No. 1493.
Blakeman, A	Mch. 14, '62		Captured and died at Camp Douglass prison.
Braxton, George W	Mch. 14, '62		
Braxton, John W	Mch. 14, '62		
Broxton, Thomas	Mch. 14, '62		
Brown, John W	Mch. 14, '62	April 26, '65	
Bryan, J. S	May '62	April 26, '65	Shot at Dalton, Ga., '64.
Burgess, Joel	Mch. 14, '62		
Callahan, Haynes	Mch. 14, '62		
Calhoun, Henry	Mch. 14, '62		
Carroll, Marshall W	Mch. 14, '62		
Cassity, David	Mch. 14, '62		
Cassity, William	Mch. 14, '62		
Chapman, Moses	Mch. 14, '62	April 26, '65	
Chapman, Noah	Mch. 14, '62		
Chapman, Simon	Mch. 14, '62		Discharged '63; for disability.
Clennon, William G. B			Corporal.
Davis, John	Mch. 14, '62		
Davis, Owen	Mch. 14, '62		
Dixon, Jasper	Mch. 14, '62		
Dyson, Evan	Mch. 14, '62		
Dyson, Jefferson	Mch. 14, '62		
Ethridge, Joseph W	Mch. 14, '62		
Ethridge, Peter	Mch. 14, '62		
Everett, Henry	Mch. 14, '62		Died in hospital at Knoxville of typhoid fever July, '62.
Everett, William T	Mch. 14, '62		
Gillis, Malcolm	Mch. 14, '62		Sergeant.
Gillis, Malcolm Jr	Mch. 14, '62		
Graves, Samuel	Mch. 14, '62		Sergeant.
Hall, Seaborn A. J	Mch. 14, '62		Corporal; honorable mention at Chickamauga.
Hall, John T	Mch. 14, '62		
Hamilton, Solomon			
Harris, C. H	May '62		Captured at New Hope Church, Mch. 18, '64 and paroled from Rock Island, close of the war.
Harris, Henry P	Mch. 14, '62	April 26, '65	
Hiedelberg, Drury W			Died at Camp Chase, Feb. 23, '63; grave No. 1401.
Hewett, Andrew L		April 26, '65	
Hewitt, Ethelred D		April 26, '65	
Hewett, H. M	Mch. 14, '62	April 26, '65	
Hewett, Jeptha	Mch. 14, '62	April 26, '65	Wounded at Missionary Ridge, Nov. 10, '63.
Hewett, Moses	Mch. 14, '62	April 26, '65	
Hewett, Thomas	Mch. 14, '62		Killed in battle at Knoxville, Sept. 2, '62.
Hobbs, Isaac	Mch. 14, '62		
Hurd, Aaron B	Mch. 14, '62		
Hurley, Joshua H			
Jordan, Richard D	Mch. 14, '62		1st Sergeant, died of typhoid fever at Knoxville Jan. 25, '63.
Keith, Aaron	Mch. 14, '62		
Keith, Warren	Mch. 14, '62		
Lammon, John M	Mch. 14, '62		
McClang, George	Mch. 14, '62		
Martin, John R	Mch. 14, '62		Honorable mention.
Mattox, William M	Mch. 14, '62		
Mays, Richard	Mch. 14, '62		Died of pneumonia at Chattahoochee, April 3, '63.
Merritt, James E. J	Mch. 14, '62		Corporal.
Morrison, Daniel	Mch. 14, '62	April 26, '65	
Norris, Benjamin	Mch. 14, '62		Musician.
Norris, Felix	Mch. 14, '62		
Norris, James	Mch. 14, '62		
Norris, William	Mch. 14, '62		
Padgett, Henry	Feb. 15, '62		Discharged for disability, Oct., '64.
Padgett, W. Dawson	Mch. 14, '62		Wounded at Murfreesborough and at Powder Springs, Ga., and paroled from prison July 21, '65.
Parish, Judge	Mch. 14, '62		
Pearce, Peter W	Mch. 14, '62		Died in Kentucky, buried in Lexington Cemetery.
Pickerson, William H	Mch. 14, '62		
Pittman, William C	Mch. 14, '62		
Royal, William	Mch. 14, '62		
Sellers, Benjamin E	May 10, '62	April 26, '65	
Sellers, C. E	May 10, '62		Imprisoned at Fort Delaware.
Sowell, Green M	Mch. 14, '62		Corporal.
Sowell, Willis J	May 10, '62		
Stanley, A. W	April '62	April 26, '65	
Stanley, David C	Mch. 14, '62	April 26, '65	Wounded severely at Missionary Ridge, Nov. 25, '63
Sutton, Benjamin	Mch. 14, '62		
Sutton, J. S	April '62		Discharged for disability, Feb. '65.

Roll Company I—6th Florida Infantry.

(Continued,)

NAMES.	MUSTERED IN	MUSTERED OUT.	REMARKS.
Taylor, John Z.	April 14, '62		
Wall, James G.	Mch. 14, '62	April 26, '65	Lost left arm at Cold Harbor, June 3, '64.
Ward, E. J.	Mch. 14, '62	April 26, '65	Died, Camp Chase; buried in Oakwood Cemetery,
Ward, John R.	Mch. 14, '62	April 26, '65	Chicago.
Ward, J. J.			
Williams, Osteen	Mch. 14, '62		
Wilson, Henry H.	Mch. 14, '63	April 26, '65	

Roll Company K—6th Florida Infantry.

NAMES.	MUSTERED IN.	MUSTERED OUT.	REMARKS.
OFFICERS.			
Captain—			
Angus McMillan	Mch. 17, '62		Captured and imprisoned on Johnson's Island, Ill. until the close of the war, and discharged from there.
1st Lieutenant—			
Robert Russ	Mch. '62		
2nd Lieutenant—			
W. B. Jones	Mch. '62		
3rd Lieutenant—			
Thomas H. Gainer	Mch. '62		
ENLISTED MEN.			
Alsabrook, Isaiah L.	Mch. '62		
Ard, James W.	Mch. '62		
Armstrong, James	Mch. '62		
Atkinson, John	Mch. '62		Buried at Cave Hill Cemetery, Louisville, Ky.
Barton, Louis	Mch. '62		
Brown, Benjamin B.		'62	
Coleman, J. J. E.	Mch. '62		Sergeant.
Coleman, Larry	Mch. '62		Corporal.
Cravey, James W.	Mch. '62		
Dennis, Solomon O.	Mch. '62		Musician.
Davis, Thomas L.	Mch. '62		
Dorsey, James S.	Mch. '62		
Dorsey, John R.	Mch. '62		
Evans, Julius			April 26, '65
Everett, William	Mch. '62		
Fau, James	Mch. '62		
Faulk, L. M.	Mch. '62		
Furgerson, James	Mch. '62		
Furgerson, W. L.	Mch. '62	April 26, '65	
Finch, William	Mch. '62	Mch. 4, '65	Wounded at Missionary Ridge, Dec., '63 and captured.
Folsom, Thomas	Mch. '61	April 26, '65	
Gainer, Thomas H.	Mch. 2, '62	April 26 '65	Wounded at Jonesboro, Ga., '64.
Gainer, W. R.			April 26, '65
Hand, John T.	Mch. '62		
Hays, Etharl	Mch. '62		Died in Kentucky, buried in Lexington Cemetery.
Hewitt, Dennes M.	Mch. '62		
Hicks, Adam	Mch. 22, '62	Oct. '63	Lost leg at Chickamauga, Ga., Sept. 17, '63.
Hicks, Armstead	Mch. '62		
Hix, William	Sept. '62	April 26, '65	Shot at Missionary Ridge, Tenn., Nov. 2, '63.
Holsom, Thomas	Mch. '62		
Howard, Henry	Mch. '62		
Isræl, Timothy	Mch. '62	Oct. '63	Lost left arm at Chickamauga, Sept. 18, '63.
Jeffries, William T.	Mch. '62	'63	Discharged for disability, re-enlisted as Captain of Scouts; was captured and taken to prison at Elmira, N. Y., where he remained until the close of the war.
Jones, William B.	Mch. '62		
Larfield, George W.	Mch. '62		
Levens, Alexander	Mch. '62		
Levens, William J.	Mch. '62		Sergeant.
McCormick, William	Mch. '62		
McEachern, William	Mch. '62		
McKenzie, W. C.	Mch. '62		
McMillan, Archibald	Mch. '62	April 26, '65	
Mallory W. H.	Mch. '62		
Martin, John R.	Mch. 8, '64	April 26, '65	Shot in right shoulder, Nov. 30, '64, Franklin, Tenn., honorable mention at Chickamauga.
Mashburn, R. B.	Mch. '62	May 28, '65	Discharged from Rock Island prison.
Mathis, John A.	Mch. '62		Sergeant.
Miller, Levi M.	Mch. '62		Sergeant.
Miller, W. J.	Mch. '62		
Newsom, Jacob	Mch. '62		
Pate, Bennett	Mch. '62		
Pate, David	Mch. '62		
Perry, George W.	Mch. '62		Corporal.
Pitts, John B.	Mch. '62		
Pitts, Louis	Mch. '62		

Roll Company K—6th Florida Infantry.
(Continued.)

NAMES.	MUSTERED IN.		MUSTERED OUT.	REMARKS.
Porter, Joseph M	Mch.	'62		
Posey, Elbert	Mch.	'62		
Prunphow, Louian	Mch.	'62		
Rainey, Alison	Mch.	'62		
Rainey, W. W	Mch.	'62		
Rhodes, James	Mch.	'62		Musician.
Richardson, J. N			April 26, '65	
Riley, George W	Mch.	'62		
Riley, P. B	Mch.	'62		
Roberts, Absalom	Mch.	'62		
Roberts, Thomas J	Mch.	'62		
Russ, R. S			April 26, '65	
Sealey, John	Mch.	'62		
Simmons, Jesse	Mch.	'62		Corporal.
Simmons, John T	Mch.	'62	April 26, '65	
Slay, John	Mch.	'62		
Teller, Craton	Mch.	'62		
Teller, Seaborn	Mch.	'62		Corporal.
Timothy, J	Mch.	'62		
Thomson, C			April 26, '65	
Wachob, Joseph F			April 26, '65	
Wachob, W. A				Discharged, Jan. '62; expiration of term and disability.
Wadsworth, M. C	Mch.	62		
Walker, James W	Mch.	'62		
Watts, Thomas Y	Mch.	'62	April 26, '65	
Wilks, James				
Wood, Dallas	Mch.	'62		
Wood, Jabez B	Mch.	'62		1st Sergeant.
Young, Edmond	Mch.	'62		

SEVENTH FLORIDA INFANTRY.

The 7th Regiment was mustered into service at Gainesville, Florida, in April, 1862, with ex-Gov. Madison S. Perry as Colonel; Robert Bullock as Lieutenant-Colonel, and Tillman Ingram as Major. The companies were commanded by Captains Roland Thomas (Roland Thomas resigned immediately and was succeeded by Henry T. York), Co. A; James Gettes, Co. B; Philip B. H. Dudley, Co. C; Simeon Vanlandingham, Co. D; Nathan S. Blount, Co. E; William W. Sloan, Co. F; S. D. McConnell, Co. G; Wade H. Eichelberger, Co. H; A. S. Moseley, Co. I; R. B. Smith, Co. K. The companies forming this Regiment had been on duty at various points in Florida for several months prior to their consolidation as the 7th Regiment, notably at Tampa and New Smyrna, where they did excellent service. Soon after being mustered in they were ordered to Tennessee to join Bragg's Army, with which it took part in all the campaigns of the Army of Tennessee and surrendered but a handful of men with Johnston at the close of the war.

Roll, Field and Staff—7th Florida Infantry.

NAMES.	MUSTERED IN.		MUSTERED OUT	REMARKS.
Colonels—				
M. S. Perry	April	'62		Resigned June 2, '63.
Robert Bullock	April	'62	April 26, '65	Promoted Colonel June, '63.
Lieutenant Colonels—				
Robert Bullock	April	'62		
Tillman Ingram	April	'62	April 26, '65	
Majors—				
Tillman Ingram	April	'62		Promoted Lieutenant-Colonel vice Bullock promoted Colonel.

Roll, Field and Staff—7th Florida Infantry.

(CONTINUED.)

AMES	MUSTERED IN.	MUSTERED OUT.	REMARKS.
Nathan S. Blount	April '62	April 26, '65	Promoted Major vice Ingram promoted Lieutenant-Colonel.
Surgeons—			
Thomas W. McCaa	April '62	April 26, '65	
Thomas P. Gary			
Assistant Surgeon—			
J. L. Lewis	April '62	April 26, '65	
Adjutants—			
1st Lieut. D. P. Holland	April '62		
1st Lieut. Poschall	April '62	April 26, '65	
Sergeant Major—			
Quartermaster—			
George Arnow	April '62	April 26, '65	
Commissary—			
John McPhaul	April '62	April 26, '65	
Chaplain—			
W. J. McCormick			Resigned April 22, '63.
Quartermaster Sergeant—			
Hospital Steward—			

Roll Company A—7th Florida Infantry.

NAMES.	MUSTERED IN.	MUSTERED OUT.	REMARKS.
OFFICERS.			
Captains—			
Roland Thomas	Mch. 8, '62		Resigned when the Regiment was ordered to Tennessee.
Henry F. York	Mch. 8, '62		1st Lieutenant; promoted Captain; wounded at Missionary Ridge and captured; paroled from prison on Johnson's Island at close of war.
1st Lieutenant—			
Lemuel B. Rhodes	Mch. 8, '62	April 26, '65	2nd Lieutenant; promoted 1st Lieutenant.
2nd Lieutenant—			
Rance Carson	Mch. 8, '62	April 26, '65	Promoted 2nd Lieutenant.
3rd Lieutenants—			
W. J. D. Prevatt	Mch. 8, '62		Promoted 3rd Lieutenant; died August 9, '62.
James Harrell	Mch. 8, '62	April 26, '65	Promoted 3rd Lieutenant.
Thomas W. Sweat	Mch. 8, '62	April 26, '65	Promoted 2nd and 1st Sergeants; then 3rd Lieut.
ENLISTED MEN.			
Addison, William			Honorable mention at Chickamauga.
Alvers, James	Mch. 8, '62		
Ammons, James	Mch. 8, '62		
Anderson, Leonard	Mch. 8, '62		
Anderson, William			
Barry, Nicholas J.	Mch. 15, '62	April 26, '65	Wounded at Atlanta July 22, '64.
Bohanan, Nathaniel	Mch. 8, '62		
Branning, Benjamin	Mch. 8, '62	April 26, '65	
Bradham, Henry	Mch. 8, '62		Died in hospital at Knoxville December 1, '62.
Brooks, George W	Mch. 8, '62		Sergeant.
Brooks, John A	Mch. 8, '62		Corporal.
Brown, Benjamin J	Mch. '62		1st Sergeant.
Brown, Jerry F	Mch. 8, '62		
Brown, John, Jr	Mch. 8, '62		
Buckhart, George			Died, Camp Chase March 13, '65; grave No. 1884.
Burnett, S. H	Mch. 8, '62	April 26, '65	
Carlton, Stephen S	Mch. 8, '62	April 26, '65	Shot at Resaca, Ga., May 1, '64.
Cone, Alfred D	Mch. 8, '62		
Cone, Lewis	Mch. 8, '62		
Craft, Charles	Mch. 8, '62	April 26, '65	
Craft, John	Mch. 8, '62		Corporal; promoted Sergeant; lost left leg at Dallas. Ga., April 5, '64, for which he was discharged May, '64.
Crawford, D. C.			
Crews, Pliny O	Mch. 8, '62	April 26, '65	Wounded at Resaca, Ga., May, '63.
Driggers, Simeon	Mch. 8, '62		Died, Camp Chase prison February 9, '65; grave No. 1140.
Dyre, Abraham	Mch. 8, '62		
Dukes, George W	Mch. 8, '62		
Fowler, Aaron	Mch. 8, '62		Died in Kentucky; buried in Lexington Cemetery.
Fowler, James	Mch. 8, '62		
Fralie, John	Mch. 8, '62		
Futch, D. J.			
Granthan, John W	Mch. 8, '62		Wounded at Franklin, Tenn., November 30, '64.
Groves, John	Mch. 8, '62		Discharged '64, disability; wounded, Jonesboro, Ga., August 31, '64.
Hadsock, Richard M	Mch. 8, '62		
Hamilton, Roderic P	Mch. 8, '62		
Hammonds, James L	Mch. 8, '62		Discharged, July, '62; disability.

Roll Company A—7th Florida Infantry.
(CONTINUED.)

NAMES.	MUSTERED IN.	MUSTERED OUT	REMARKS.
Hancock, William	Mch. 8, '62		
Harrod, Winburn A.	Mch. 8, '62		
Hinson, George W.	Mch. 8, '62		While at home on furlough he volunteered in Captain Hutchinson's Co. and went into the fight at Natural Bridge and there was shot in right thigh.
Holbrook, J. I.			
Johns, Colonel A.	Mch. 8, '62		
Johns, James R.	Mch. 8, '62	April 26, '65	Wounded at Chickamauga, Ga., September 2, '63.
Johns, Jesse	Mch. 8, '62		
Johns, Richard B.	Mch. 8, '62		
Kelly, Joseph.	Mch. 8, '62		
Kerce, Richard B.	Mch. 8, '62		
Kerce, William C.	Mch. 8, '62		Wounded at Chickamauga, Ga., September 19, '63.
Kinsey, Lucius	April '62	April 26, '65	
Kite, James M.	April '62		
Knowles, James T.	Mch. 8, '62		
Lamb, John, Jr.	Mch. 8, '62		
Lea, Jackson	Mch. 8, '62		Discharged December '62; disability.
Lenord, Anderson	Mch. 8, '62		4th Corporal.
McKenny, Mathew L.	Mch. 8, '62	April 26, '65	
McLeod, John B.			
Mann, Arrabel J.	Mch. 8, '62		
Mann, Benjamin D.	Mch. 8, '62		Captured at Missionary Ridge, Tenn., November 27, paroled from Rock Island prison June 22, '65.
Mann, William J.	Mch. 8, '62		Died at Knoxville, Tenn., '63; disabled.
Markey, Adam L.	Mch. 8, '62		
Markey, John H.	Mch. 8, '62		Wounded at Murfreesborough, Tenn., December 8, '64.
Mizell, Andrew W.	Mch. 8, '62	April 26, '65	Wounded at Missionary Ridge, Tenn., November 25, '65.
Moore, J. H.			
Morgan, Oren L.	Mch. 8, '62		
Morgan, Sloman D.	Mch. 8, '62		
Neal, Roan	Mch. 8, '62	April 26, '65	
Norman, Daniel G. W.	Mch. 8, '62	April 26, '65	
Norman, Francis N.	Mch. 8, '62	April 26, '65	Wounded at Buzzard Roost Gap, Ga.
Norman, John C.	Mch. 8, '62	April 26, '65	Shot at Buzzard Roost, Ga., February 25, '64.
Norman, I. N.	Mch. 8, '62	April 26, '65	Wounded near Marietta, Ga., July 2, '64; again at Murfreesborough, Tenn., December '64.
Osteen, Elias E.	Mch. 8, '62		
Palmer, Richard	Mch. 8, '62		
Parrish, James	Mch. 8, '62	April 26, '65	Shot at Atlanta, Ga., July 22, '64.
Parrish, Oden	Mch. 8, '62		
Partin, H. S.	Mch. 8, '62	April 26, '65	
Pinholster, J. W.	Mch. 8, '62	April 26, '65	
Pope, W. W.	Mch. 8, '62	April 26, '65	Captured and imprisoned at Rock Island, Ill.; paroled from there June 22, '65.
Redding, William A.		April 26, '65	Wounded near Dallas, Ga., February, '64.
Roberts, John	Mch. 8, '62		
Roberts, John J.	Mch. 8, '62		
Roberts, Simeon	Mch. 8, '62		
Sauls, Abram J.	Mch. 8, '62		
See, Jackson	Mch. 8, '62		
Shirley, William	Mch. 8, '62		
Simson, John	Mch. 8, '62		
Smith, Edward W.	Mch. 8, '62	April 26, '65	Was prisoner at Rock Island, Ill.; paroled from there June 21, '65.
Stricklin, William	Mch. 8, '62		
Surrency, H. C.	Mch. 8, '62	April 26, '65	Wounded at Resaca, Ga., May 14, '64, and at Nashville, Tenn., December 16, '64.
Sweat, John	April 2, '62	April 26, '65	
Sweat, Nathan	Mch. 8, '62		
Tatum, John	Mch. 8, '62		Corporal.
Thomas, Edward W.	Mch. 8, '62		Corporal.
Tillman, John	Mch. 8, '62		
Trail, David W.	Mch. 8, '62		
Tucker, George R. A.	Mch. 8, '62		Promoted Sergeant.
Varn, Jacob E.	Mch. 19, '62		Lost a hand at Chickamauga, Ga., September 19 '63, and discharged.
Waters, Isaac		April 26, '65	
Williams, Hezekiah C.	Mch. 8, '62	April 8, '62	Died at Frankfort, Ky., October, '62.
Whitehead, John J.	Mch. 8, '62		Died at Knoxville, '63.
Wilkson, John	Mch. 8, '62		
Williams, Abiham	Mch. 8, '62		
Williams, H. C.	Mch. 8, '62		
Williams, James B.	Mch. 8, '62		
Willis, Thomas C.	Mch. 8, '62		
Willis, William B.	Mch. 8, '62		Died in a Georgia hospital, '65.
Wynn, Ashley L.	Mch. 8, '62	April 26, '65	

Roll Company B (South Florida Infantry)—7th Florida Infantry.

NAMES.	MUSTERED IN.	MUSTERED OUT.	REMARKS.
OFFICERS.			
Captains—			
James Gettis	April 10, '62		Resigned, April 17, '63.

Roll Company B (South Florida Infantry)—7th Florida Infantry.
(Continued)

NAMES.	MUSTERED IN.	MUSTERED OUT.	REMARKS.
Thomas Mitchell	April 10, '62		Promoted from private to 3rd Lieutenant, to 2nd Lieutenant, to 1st Lieutenant, to Captain; died in service.
W. E. Sweet	April 10, '62		Promoted from private to 3rd Lieutenant, to 2nd Lieutenant, to 1st Lieutenant, to Captain.
Willis M. Johnson	April 10, '62		Promoted Captain Co. B 7th Florida.
1st Lieutenants—			
William B. Henderson	April 10, '62	April 26, '65	Resigned, '63.
John A. Henderson	April 26, '65	April 10, '62	Promoted 1st Lieutenant, on resignation of W. B. Henderson and resigned.
2nd Lieutenant—			
Robert F. Nurrey	April 10, '62		3rd Lieutenant, promoted to 2nd Lieutenant, on resignation of J. A. Henderson.
3rd Lieuteunants—			
William O. Pass	April 10, '62	June 22, '65	Promoted to 3rd Lieutenant, then 2nd Lieutenant.
J. D. Riggs	April 10, '62		Promoted 3rd Lieutenant, vice Mitchell promoted 2nd Lieutenant.
ENLISTED MEN.			
Addison, David J	April 10, '62		
Allen, Hiram	Mch. '62	April 26, '65	
Atkins, Eli	Mch. '62		
Atkins, Hiram	Mch. '62		
Barnes, David W	Mch. '62		Died, Camp Chase, Jan. 31, '63; grave No. 999.
Beal, George M	Mch. '62		
Boyett, George W	'62		Shot at Kennesaw Mt. June, '64; captured, imprisoned at Camp Chase, O. Discharged by parole from prison, March, '65; disability.
Brannon, F. L	Mch. '62	April 26, '65	Wounded at Missionary Ridge, Tenn., Nov. 25, '64.
Brockway, Simeon L	Mch. '62		Corporal.
Brown, William H	Mch. '62		1st Sergeant.
Buchanan, William E	May 17, '62		Paroled from Camp Chase, close of war.
Campbell, Alfred S	Mch. 10, '62	April 26, '65	Shot at Missionary Ridge, Ga., Nov. 25, '63; promoted 2nd Sergeant and 1st Sergeant.
Campbell, William N	April '62		
Carming, Robert	April '62	April 26, '65	Sergeant.
Carney, William	April '62		
Coleman, John	April '62		
Cowart, Alexander J	April '62		
Cowart, Benjamin F	April '62	April 26, '65	
Douglass, Robert	April '62		
Ellis, T. B		April 26, '65	
Gago, Alexander	April '62		
Givins, Jasper T	April '62		Musician.
Givins, Joseph J	April 10, '62		
Graham, Alexander	April '62		
Graham, Daniel G	April '62	April 26, '65	
Graham, George W	April '62		
Grice, John A	April '62		
Gunter, John B	Mch. 15, '62	April 26, '65	
Henderson, Andrew A	Mch. 15, '62		Musician.
Hendry, I. M		April 26, '65	Captured at Murfreesborough, Tenn., Dec. 7, '64 and confined at Camp Chase, O., and paroled in '65.
Hendry, John H			Honorable mention.
Jameson, Daniel	April '62		
Johnston, Levi D	April '62		
Keen, Joseph	April '62		
Kersey, George	April '62		
Krause, John H			
Lanier, John H	April '62		
McKay, John A		April 26, '65	Sergeant.
McLeod, Daniel	April '62		
McLeod, John B	April '62	April 26, '65	Wounded at Chickamauga, Ga., Sept. 19, '63.
McLeod, J. Ferdinand	April '62	April 26, '65	Wounded at Murfreesborough, Tenn., Dec. '64.
McLeod, William	April '62	April 26, '63	
Masters,	April '62		Corporal.
Masters, Lawrence H	April '62	April 26, '65	Corporal.
Mizell, Enoch E	April '62		
Monte-de-Oca, Charles	April '62		
Pagas, Joseph	April '62		
Pappy, Charles	April '62		
Platt, George	April '62		
Pollock, Thomas	April '62		
Pool, Thomas	April '62		
Powell, Ambrose	April '62		
Prine, Henry D	April '62		
Prine, James E	April '62		
Rawls, William A. L	April '62	April 26, '65	
Ressey, George	April '62		
Riley, James F	April '62		
Rogers, Julius D	April '62	May 3, '65	
Ross, Lonnzo D	April '62		
Rum, Joseph	April 10, '62		
Rushing, Theodore H	April '62		
Rye, Erasmus	April '62		

Roll Company B (South Florida Infantry)—7th Florida Infantry.
(CONTINUED.)

NAMES.	MUSTERED IN.	MUSTERED OUT.	REMARKS.
Ryner, Gasper	April '62		
Sauls A. J.		April 26, '65	
Simmons, George	April '62		
Sistrunk, Moses	April '62		
Sloan, Elbert	April '62	April 26, '65	
Sloan, Orvil	April '62		
Smith, George W	April '62		
Stafford, Columbus			Died of pneumonia, Feb. 27, '63.
Stephens, Berrien	April '62		
Stephens, James A		April 26, '65	
Stephens, John W	April '62		
Stone, John P	April '62		
Tanner, Nathan	April '62	May 10, '65	
Tanner, Vincent	April '62		
Thomas, James H	April "62	April 26, '65	
Thomas, Lewis A	April '62		Sergeant.
Townsend, Adolphus	April '62		
Townsend, Elijah Jr	April '62		Corporal.
Townsend, Lonnzo D	April '62	April 26, '65	Corporal.
Tuner, Arthur C	April '62		
Vipper, Gildeon	April '62		
White, Abraham B	April '62		
Whidden, Bennett	April '62		
Whidden, Elias	April '62		Shot at Franklin, Tenn., Nov. 10, '64; also Benton-
Whidden, James	April '62		ville.
Whidden, William	April '62		
White, Abram B	April 10, '62		
White, John F	April '62		
White, James Houston	Mch. '62		Captured at Missionary Ridge, Dec. 27, '63; carried
White, William B	April '62		to Camp Chase where he died in '65.
Whitehurst, Lonnzo D	Mch. '62		
Whitton, Jesse	Mch. '62		
Whitten, Wiloby	Mch. '62		
Wiggins, John R	Mch. '62		
Wiggins, M. L.		Sept. 12, '65	
Wiggins, William J	Mch. '62		
Williams, James	April '62		
Williams, James G	April '62		

Roll Company C—7th Florida Infantry.

NAMES.	MUSTERED IN.	MUSTERED OUT.	REMARKS.
OFFICERS.			
Captains—			
Philip B. H. Dudley	Mch. 20, '62		
William E. June	Mch. 20, '62		3rd Lieutenant; promoted Captain.
1st Lieutenants—			
Sam B. McLin	Mch. 20, '62		
Joseph J. Jones	Mch. 20, '62	April 26, '65	Private; promoted 1st Lieutenant.
William F. Sheffield	Mch. 20, '62		Promoted 1st Lieutenant; shot at Jonesboro, Ga., August 30, '64, and died in hospital at Macon, Ga., October 2, '64.
James Doig	Mch. 20, '62	April 26, '65	1st Sergeant; promoted 1st Lieutenant.
2nd Lieutenant—			
Solomon Warren	Mch. 20, '62	April 26, '65	
3rd Lieutenant—			
ENLISTED MEN.			
Adams, Jesse T	Mch. 20, '62	April 26, '65	Wounded at Nashville December 15, '64.
Alexander, William E	Mch. 20, '62	April 26, '65	
Beckham, Marion J	Mch. 20, '62	April 26, '65	
Beckham, Robert J	Mch. 20, '62		Captuerd, imprisoned and discharged from Rock Island prison June '65.
Bennett, Joseph A. R	Mch. 20, '62		Sergeant.
Bennett, L. Hiram	Mch. 20, '62	April 26, '65	
Bennett, Noah	Mch. 20, '62		
Bennett, William	Mch. 20, '62		
Bevil, R. H	Mch. 20, '62		
Blair, Isaac F	Mch. 20, '62		
Bradshaw, John A	Mch. 20, '62		
Brinkley, Nathan G	Mch. 20, '62		
Brown, James J	Mch. 20, '62	April 26, '65	
Bryant, Asberry	Mch. 20, '62		
Bucker, J	Mch. 20, '62		
Burmucker, James L	Mch. 20, '62		Sergeant.
Burnett, John W	Mch. 20, '62		

Roll Company C—7th Florida Infantry.
(CONTINUED.)

NAMES.	MUSTERED IN.	MUSTERED OUT.	REMARKS.
Carter, Henry	Mch. 20, '62		
Cathcart, James	Mch. 20, '62		
Cheasser, Joe	Mch. 20, '62		
Cheasser, Mathew	Mch. 20, '62		Corporal.
Chitty, M. J	Mch. 20, '62	April 26, '65	
Clark, Elishua H	Mch. 20, '62		
Coulter, Alexander			Discharged Nov. '62 and re-enlisted in 2nd Cav-
Davis, Robert	Mch. 20, '62		under Captain Chambers and served to close war.
Dawson, George	Mch. 20, '62		Captain of company; 4th and 5th Consolidated.
Dickinson, Mathew P	Mch. 20, '62		
Denton, H. C	Mch. 20, '62	April 26, '65	
Downing, Thomas W	Mch. 20, '62	April 26, '65	
Dudley, James V. R	Mch. 20, '62		Killed at Missionary Ridge Nov. 25, '63.
Duffey, James	Mch. 20, '62		
Enfinger, William E	Mch. 20, '62		
Gaissom, J. R. W	Mch. 20, '62	April 26, 65	
Garrett, Drury B	Mch. 20, '62		
Geiger, Enoch G	Mch. 20, '62		
Geiger, Joshua D	Mch. 20, '62		
Gornto, James M	Mch. 20, '62		
Gunnell, Edwin S	Mch. 20, '62		
Guthrey, John J	Mch. 20, '62		
Hague, Archilaus	Mch. 20, '62		
Hague, Henry B	Mch. 20, '62	April 26, '65	
Hague, John R	Mch. 20, '62	April 26, '65	Wounded at Chattanooga, Dallas, Ga., May 27,
Hall, Daniel E	Mch. 20, '62		'64; Bentonville, N. C.
Heidt, Joshua	Mch. 20, '62	April 26, '65	
Hill, William John	Mch. 20, '62		
Hill, William	Mch. 20, '62		
Holder, J. J. B	Mch. 8, '62		Captured near Harrodsburg, Ky., Oct. 2, '64; im-
Jackson, Andrew	Mch. 20, '62	April 26, '65	prisoned and paroled at close of war.
Jackson, Andrew G	Mch. 20, '62		
Jordan, Edward P	Mch. 20, '62		Corporal.
Jones, Charles Mc	Mch. 20, '62		Died in Kentucky, buried in Lexington Cemetery.
Jones, Joseph A	Mch. 20, '62		
Keene, Moses	Mch. 20, '62	April 26, '65	Wounded at Mill Creek Gap, Ga., Feb. 22, '64.
Kennedy, Thomas S	Mch. 20, '62	April 26, '65	Sergeant.
Knight, Thomas B	Mch. 20, '62	April 26, '65	Wounded at Bentonville, N. C. Mar. 9, '65.
Koonie, Francisco	Mch. 20, '62		
Kriminger, W. M	Mch. 20, '62		
Law, Robert Y. H	Mch. 20, '62		
Link, Jacob	Mch. 20, '62		Wounded at Jonesborough, Ga., Aug. 31, '64.
Lisle, Andrew J	Mch. 20, '62		
McCreight, James A	Mch. 20, '62	April 26, '65	
McKenstry, J. F. S. Sr	Mch. 20, '62	April 26, '65	
McKinney, George W	Mch. 20, '62		
McKinney, James H	Mch. 20, '62	April 26, '65	
McRory, James A	Mch. 20, '62	April 26, '65	
Malphurs, Jathan	Mch. 20, '62		
Malphurs, William T	Mch. 20, '62	April 26, '65	
Mann, Edward B	Mch. 20, '62	April 26, '65	
Miller, John M	Mch. 20, '62		Corporal.
Mooney, Pinkney J	Mch. 20, '62	April 26, '65	
Moore, Jeremiah H	Mch. 20, '62	April 26, '65	
Odum, Edward	Mch. 20, '62		
Ormand, Robert T	Mch. 20		
Parchman, James M	Mch. 20, '62		Transferred Co. C, 2nd Cavalry, Captain Chambers.
Pheiffer, John W	Mch. 20, '62		
Pheiffer, Samuel U	Mch. 20, '62		
Phillips, J. T	Jan. 13, '62	April 26, '65	Wounded at Dallas, Ga., May 28, '63.
Polk, Henry	Mch. 20, '62	April 26, '65	Wounded at Tunnell Hill, Ga., February '64.
Polk, John	Mch. 20, '62		
Polk, Samuel	Mch. 20, '62		Captured at Kingston, Ga., December 17, '64 and imprisoned at Camp Chase, O., till close of war.
Prescott, Samuel T	Mch. 20, '62	April 26, '65	Wounded at Atlanta, Ga., July 22, '64.
Prescott, James H	Mch. 20, '62	April 26, '65	
Renfroe, Nathan G	Mch. 20, '62	April 26, '65	
Riggs, George S	Mch. 20, '62		
Richardson, Henry	Mch. 20, '62		
Robbins, John J	Mch. 20, '62	April 26, '65	
Robinson, J. H	Mch. 20, '62	April 26, '65	
Robinson, S. McB	Jan. '62	April 26, '65	
Robertson, William H	Mch. 20, '62	April 26, '65	
Roseman, George W	Mch. 20, '62		
Sapp, Elias	Mch. 20, '62	April 26, '65	
Sapp, Henry H	Mch. 20, '62	April 26, '65	Wounded at Atlanta, Ga., July 20, '64.
Sapp, Russell	Mch. 20, '62	April 26, '65	Discharged February '64 for disability, but re-
Sapp, Shadrick	Mch. 20, '62		enlisted.
Seagle, F. V	Mch. 20, '62	April 26, '65	
Shuford, G. W	Mch. 20, '62	April 26, '65	
Shuttleworth, Thomas	Mch. 20, '62		
Slaughter, Samuel	Mch. 20, '62		
Stakes, Compton W	Mch. 20, '62		

Roll Company C—7th Florida Infantry.
(CONTINUED.)

NAMES.	MUSTERED IN.	MUSTERED OUT.	REMARKS.
Stuart, Jones Murray	Mch. 20, '62	April 26, '65	Transferred 1st Battalion, Hopkins' 10th Florida Regiment.
Stephens, William E.	Mch. 20, '62		
Sturman, James E.	Mch. 20, '62		Sergeant.
Swindle, Henry	Mch. 20, '62		
Swindle, Owen	Mch. 20, '62		Captured, imprisoned and paroled from Camp Chase at close of the war.
Thomas, Charles	Mch. 20, '62		
Thigpen, John C	Mch. 20, '62		
Tompkins, John H	Mch. 20, '62		
Thompson, Isaac L	Mch. 20, '62		
Thompson, W. Nayler	Mch. 20, '62	April 26, '65	
Tilles, Tapley	Mch. 20, '62	April 26, '65	
Turner, Elias	Mch. 20, '62	April 26, '65	
Turner, William	Mch. 20, '62		
Vanlandingham, James M	Mch. 20, '62	April 26, '65	
Vanlandingham, W. M.	Mch. 20, '62	April 26, '65	Wounded twice at Kennesaw Mountain July, '64; Nashville, '65.
Valantine, Jesse M	Mch. 20, '62		
Vaughn, Willis H	Mch. 20, '62		
Watlington, George M	Mch. 40, '62		Corporal.
Watson, Joshua G	Mch. 20, '62		
Watson, Samuel N	Mch. 20, '62		Discharged from Camp Douglass at close of war.
Watson, W. J	Mch. 20, '62		
Williams, James W	Mch. 20, '62		Sergeant.
Williams, John W	Mch. 20, '62	April 26, '65	
Wynn, Richard E	Feb. '62		Died of disease at Knoxville, Tenn., November 19, '62.
Zetrover, Albert T	Mch. 20, '62		
Zetrover, James C	Mch. 20, '62		

Roll Company D (Alachua Rebels)—7th Florida Infantry.

NAMES.	MUSTERED IN.	MUSTERED OUT.	REMARKS.
OFFICERS.			
Captains—			
Tillman Ingram	April 2, '62		Elected Major, promoted Lieutenant-Colonel.
S. C. Vanlandingham	April 2, '62		Promoted Captain, died in prison hospital, Aug. 8, '64.
Daniel C. Hart	April 2, '62	April 26, '65	Promoted 3rd Lieutenant, April, '62, promoted Captain, Aug., '64.
1st Lieutenants—			
Archibald A. Maulden	April 2, '62		Promoted 1st Lieutenant, killed Aug. 31, '64.
John Clowney	April 2, '62		Resigned, Mar., '62.
James A. Grigsby	April 2, '62	April 26, '65	Promoted 1st Lieutenant, Sept., '64.
2nd Lieutenant—			
Andrew E. Burnside	April 2, '62		Elected 2nd Lieutenant; resigned Jan., '64.
3rd Lieutenant—			
ENLISTED MEN.			
Armstoff, John	April 2, '62		
Arnow, George J	April 2, '62		Promoted Reg. Q. M., rank of Captain.
Avera, Alexander	April 2, '62		
Avera, Joseph H	April 2, '62		Shot at Resaca, Ga., April 13, '64.
Avery, James A	April 2, '62		
Bailey, Casermo O	April 2, '62		
Bailey, Charles	April 2, '62		
Baker, F. T	April 2, '62	April 26, '65	
Baxter, William M	April 2, '62	April 26, '65	Shot at Marietta, Ga., May 10, 6⁴
Bennett, Harry L	April 2, '62		
Bennett, Noah	April 2, '62		
Bennett, Jake	April 2, '62		
Bennett, W. M	April 2, '62		
Blitch, Marion	April 2, '62		
Blitch, Thomas L	April 2, '62		
Clarke, James A	April 2, '62		
Clark, John	April 2, '62		
Compton, Thomas			
Daugherty, Peter	April 2, '62		
Davis, John G	April 2, '62		
Denton, Harris C	April 2, '62		
Denton, James I	April 2, '62		
Driggers, Noah H	April 2, '62		
Eunis, Mathew	April 2, '62		
Fletcher, William G	April 2, '62		
Floyd, Marion G	April 2, '62		
Freeman, George	April 2, '62		
Galbreath, John A	April 2, '62		
Gore, John	April 2, '62		
Grissom, Walter J	April 2, '62		
Guthrie, Abram	April 2, '62		

Roll Company D (Alachua Rebels)—7th Florida Infantry.
(CONTINUED.)

NAMES.	MUSTERED IN.	MUSTERED OUT.	REMARKS.
Hithcox, Joseph B.	April 2, '62		
Highsmith, John M.	April 2, '62		
Hinnant, William Q.	April 2, '62		Musician.
Hinson, Robert H.	April 2, '62	April 26, '65	
Hodge, Elishua			
Hodge, James T.	April 2, '62		Killed in battle.
Horn Bennett.	April 2, '62		
Horn, Henry.	April 2, '62		Killed in battle.
Horn, William A.	April 2, '62		
Howell, Kinchen H.	April 2, '62		
Hudson, James B.	April 2, '62		
Huggins, George S.			
Ingram, Frank G.	April 2, '62		
Jackson, Benjamin F.	April 2, '62		
Jenkins, Nicholas.	April 2, '62		
Jonas, Andrew.	April 2, '62		
Jones, Henry.	April 2, '62		
Lewis, James.	April 2, '62		
McCain, Julius C.	April 2, '62	April 26, '65	
McCain, Littleberry.	April 2, '62		
McKinney, Charles J.	April 2, '62	April 26, '65	Wounded at Missionary Ridge, Peach Tree Creek, Ga. and Saultsburg, N. C.
Malphurs, Isham.	April 2, '62		
Malphurs, Jason.	April 2, '62		
Malphurs,	April 2, '62		
Malphurs,	April 2, '62		
Marshall, Robert.			
May, M. M.	April 2, '62	April 26, '65	
Mills, J. C. H.	April 2, '62	April 26, '65	
Mills, William R.	April 2, '62	April 26, '65	
Moore, Lewis H.	April 2, '62		
Nobles, Ananias.	April 2, '62		
Nobles, Joshua.	April 2, '62		Died of pneumonia at Knoxville, Tenn., Nov. 2, '62
Nobles, Leonard.	April 2, '62	April 26,	
Ogelsby, John J.	April 2, '62		
Orbits, Louis.	April 2, '62		
Pardee, Frank A.	April 2, '62	April 26, '65	
Pardee, H. E.	Apr 1 2, '62		Sergeant.
Parker, B. F.	April 2, '62	April 26, '65	
Pearce, Bryant.	April 2, '62		
Pearce, Edwin.	April 2, '62		
Pettes, William H.	April 2, '62		
Philips, Henry A.			
Philips, J. T.	April 2, '62	April 26, '65	
Pinkston, Willis K.	April 2, '62		
Raulerson, Moses L.	April 2, '62		Corporal.
Revil, John R.	April 2, '62		
Richardson, Henry S.	April 2, '62		
Richardson, John G.	April 2, '62		Sergeant; killed in battle.
Richardson, William T.	April 2, '62	April 26, '65	Wounded at Resaca, Gc., May 13, '64; also at Nashville, Tenn., Dec. 17, '64, promoted Serg't.
Rooks, Frank.	April 2, '62		
Rooks, James F.	April 2, '62		
Sapp, Josiah.	April 2, '62		
Sapp, William.	April 2, '62		
Shaw, Henry.			
Shuford, George W.	April 2, '62	April 26, '65	Sergeant.
Shearrouse, Lewis.	April 2, '62		
Seagle, F. V.	April 2, '62	April 26, '65	
Simonds, Harvey.	April 2, '62		Musician.
Slade,	April 2, '62		
Smith, Martin.	April 2, '62		
Sparkman, Edward.	April 2, '62	April 26, '65	
Sparkman, Frank M.	April 2, '62		
Sparkman, Lewis.	April 2, '62		
Sparkman, Lewellyn.	April 2, '62		
Sparkman, William M.	April 2, '62		
Strickland, William.			
Sweat, John.	April 2, '62	April 26, '65	
Thorton, Moses.			
Tillis, Joseph D.	April 2, '62		
Tillis, Thomas B.			
Tillman, Daniel M.	April 2, '62		Imprisoned at Camp Douglass, Ill. and paroled from there June 27. '65.
Thomas, Charles.	April 2, '62	April 26, '65	Died, Camp Chase. Mar. 24, '65; grave No. 1743; honorable mention.
Turner, Benjamin C.	April 2, '62		
Turner, Elias.	April 2, '62		
Turner, James S.	April 2, '62		
Turner, Jonathan G.	April 2, '62		1st Sergeant.
Turner, T. O.	April 2, '62		Died from wound received in battle.
Turner Thomas T.	April 2, '62		Wounded, captured, and died in prison.
Varnadoe, I. L.	April 2, '62	April 26, '65	
Whidden, Bennett.	April 2, '62		Wounded at Chickamauga and Murfreesborough captured and paroled from Camp Chase, O.
Whidden, John.	April 2, '62		Captured at Nashville, Dec. 16, '64; paroled a close of war.
Wiggins, Benjamin.	April 2, '62		
Wiggins, Burrel.			

Roll Company D (Alachua Rebels)—7th Florida Infantry.
(CONTINUED.)

NAMES.	MUSTERED IN.	MUSTERED OUT.	REMARKS.
Wiggins, George	April 2, '62		
Wiggins, Perry	April 2, '62		
Willie, Mark	April 2, '62		
Wilkie, William	April 2, '62		
Wilkinson, Charlton			
Yearty, Jacob	April 2, '62		Killed in battle.
Yearty, William E	Apr l 2, '62	April 26, '65	Wounded at Franklin, Tenn.; Bentonville, N. C.

Roll Company E (South Florida Bull Dogs)—7th Florida Infantry.

NAMES.	MUSTERED IN.	MUSTERED OUT.	REMARKS.
OFFICERS.			
Captains—			
Nathan S. Blount	April 10, '62		Promoted Major.
John W. Whidden	April 10, '62	April 26, '65	1st Lieutenant; promoted Captain.
1st Lieutenant—			
Simon Turman	April 10, '62		Promoted 1st Lieutenant '63.
2nd Lieutenants—			
Zachariah Seward	April 10, '62		Resigned June 20, '63.
Solomon D. Johnson	April 10, '62		Corporal, promoted 2nd Lieutenant.
3rd Lieutenants—			
William H. Mansfield	April 10, '62		Resigned June 21, '63.
W. H. Johnson		April 26, '65	Sergeant; promoted 1st Sergeant; 3rd Lieutenant.
ENLISTED MEN.			
Altman, Lewis	April 10, '62	April 26, '65	
Altman, William	April 10, '62		
Barton, Washington J	April 10, '62		
Blount, Owen R	April 10, '62		
Brown, Daniel M	April 10, '62		
Brown, Rigdon	April 10, '62		Died in Kentucky; buried in Lexington Cemetery.
Brown, William	April 10, '62	April 26, '65	
Campbell, A. S		April 26, '65	
Carlton, Reuben	April 10, '62		
Carlton, Wright	April 10, '62	April 20, '65	
Cuthcart, William R	April 10, '62		
Cook, Wilson	April 10, '62		
Coplin, Jacob J	April 10, '62		
Cornelius, Levi W	April 10, '62		Sergeant.
Crum, D. J	Mch. 7, '62		Died of pneumonia in hospital at Columbus, Ga., June 20, '62.
Davis, James	April 10, '62		
Driggers, Henry W	April 10, '62		
Durrance, Uriah R	April 10, '62		
Ferguson, James D	April 10, '62		
Fletcher, James L	April 10, '62		
Friar, William H. H	April 10, '62		
Gaskins, James	April 10, '62		
Gay, Williard H	April 10, '62		1st Sergeant.
Geiger, Joshua D	Mch. 10, '63		Died at Greenville, Tenn., April 13, '63.
Hancock, James T	April 10, '62		
Hancock, Jeremiah	April 10, '62		
Hancock, Morton J	April 10, '62		
Hendry, Albert J	April 10, '62		
Hendry, Edward T	April 10, '62		
Hendry, James M	April 10, '62		
Hill, Henry R	April 10, '62		Lost eye from smallpox while in prison at Camp Chase, O., paroled from there at close of war.
Hilliard, William A	April 10, '62		
Hooker, William J	April 10, '62		
Hull, Stephen	April 10, '62		Corporal.
Jackson, John S	April 10, '62		
Johnson, William R	April 10, '62		Sergeant.
Jordan, Daniel C. B	April 10, '62		
Keen, Andrew J	April 10, '62		
Keen, James M	April 10, '62		
Killpatrick, George W	April 10, '62		
McAuley, Robert W	April 10, '62	April 26, '65	Corporal.
McAuley, William M	April 10, '62		Promoted Sergeant.
McClelland, Mayfield	April 10, '62		Corporal.
McClelland, Silas L	April 10, '62		
McClelland, William	April 10, '62		
Marsh, William P	April 10, '62		
O'Neil, John C	April 10, '62		
Parker, Lewis H	April 10, '62		
Patrick, Archibald	April 10, '62	April 26, '65	Wounded at Jonesborough, Ga., August 31, '64.
Pearce, Thomas C	April 10, '62		Sergeant.
Phillips, J. T		April 26, '65	
Platt, David H	April 10, '62		
Platt, William C	April 10, '62		

Roll Company E (South Florida Bull Dogs)—7th Florida Infantry.
(CONTINUED.)

NAMES.	MUSTERED IN.	MUSTERED OUT.	REMARKS.
Pitts, James B.	April 10, '62		
Pitts, William C.	April 10, '62		
Pollard, John J.	April 10, '62		
Rogers, William P.	April 10, '62		
Romer, Alexander	April 10, '62		
Seward, Felix J.	April 10, '62		Sergeant.
Seward, James R.	April 10, '62		
Seward, Richard A.	April 10, '62		
Shepherd, William H.	April 10, '62		
Shepherd, William W.	April 10 '62		
Smith, James E.	April 10, '62		
Sullivant, Reley B.	April 10, '62		
Thompson, E. W.	April 10, '62	April 26, '65	
Underhill, John	April 10, '62		
Varn, Josiah	April 10, '62		
Varn, William B.	April 10, '62		
Waldron, Daniel	April 10, '62	April 26, '65	
Weeks, Carry P.	April 10, '62	Apri 26, '65	Wounded at Resaca, Ga., '64.
Welch,	April 10, '62		
Whidden, Maxwell	April 10, '62		
Williams, James W.	April 10, '62		
Wi liams, John A.	April 10, '62	April 26, '65	
Williams, Nathan	April 10, '62	April 26, '65	Wounded at Jonesborough July 2, '64.
Woodward, John C.	April 10, '62		

Roll Company F—7th Florida Infantry.

NAMES.	MUSTERED IN.	MUSTERED OUT.	REMARKS.
OFFICERS.			
Captains—			
William W. Slone			Resigned May 18, '63.
J. R. Mizell		April 9, '65	Promoted from 1st Lieutenant to Captain and captured at Missionary Ridge.
1st Lieutenants—			
Michael J. Doyle		April 26, '65	Promoted from 1st Sergeant to 1st Lieutenant.
C. C. Hart		April 26, '65	Promoted 1st Lieutenant, Co. F, 7th Florida Regiment.
2nd Lieutenant—			
3rd Lieutenant—			
George W. Collins			
ENLISTED MEN.			
Alsabrook, Thomas T.			Corporal.
Alsabrook, James A.			
Aneritt, Luke		April 26, '65	
Barrington, John S.			
Barton, James W			
Bass, Crawford			
Baker, Joseph F.			
Baker, John D.			
Bennett, William S.			
Bennett, James L.		April 26, '65	Wounded at Jonesborough, Ga., '64.
Black, G. E.		April 26, '65	
Bumink, Miles			
Branch, William B.			
Crenshaw, James M.			Corporal; died Camp Chase prison November 4, '65; grave No. 1544.
Champlin, Levy G.			
Collins, David			
Collins, James A.			
Cook, William			
Crum, David			
Curry, James			
Cuvrey, Russell			
Daniels, Wiley R.			
Daniels, William A.	April '62	May 14, '65	Wounded at Chickamauga, Ga.; captured and imprisoned at Rock Island, Ill., until close of war.
Drawdy, Benjamin			
Emanuel, Amos	June '61	Apr l '65	
Fussell, Bryant			
Fussell, Benjamin A.			
Fussell, James			
Fussell, James C.			
Fussell, Obed			
Fussell, William S.	Mch. '62		Died in hospital, Knoxville, Tenn., November, '62.
Glenn, John R.	Sept. 18, '62	April '65	Shot at Stone Mountain, Ga., August, '64.
Grant, Christopher C.		April '65	Promoted Corporal.
Harris, Stephen		April '65	
Harris, Thomas			
Hawkins, Joseph R.		April 26, '65	Discharged from Camp Chase, at close of war.
H ays, George F.		April 26, '65	

Roll Company F—7th Florida Infantry.
(CONTINUED.)

NAMES.	MUSTERED IN.	MUSTERED OUT.	REMARKS.
Hodges, James S			
Hodges, William			
Houston, J. R		April 26, '65	
Ivey, D. C		April 26, '65	
Jenkins, John T			
Joiner, Mathew J			
Joiner, Randall			
Jones, David C	'61	April 26, '65	
Jones, John R			
Jones, William R			
Kershaw, Cade			Corporal; captured, imprisoned at Rock Island and died in prison.
Lee, A. Y		April 26, '65	
Lee, Eli A		April 26, '65	
Lisk, William			Honorable mention.
McLaughlin, Littleton			
Masters, Edwin D			
Masters, Luke			
Matchett, John W		April 26, '65	
Meeks, William S		April 26, '65	
Merritt, Josiah			Died in Kentucky, buried in Lexington Cemetery.
Merritt, Luke	Mch. '61	April 26, '65	
Merritt, William			
Minshen, Archibald			
Mitchell, James	April '62	April 26, '65	Wounded at Atlanta, July, '64.
Mobley, George R			
Moorman, W. P		April 26, '65	
Mott, Luke		April 26, '65	
Murphy, William W			
Nesbit, William R			
Padgett, Hopkins			
Padgett, John		April 26, '65	
Pierce, John N			
Prevatt, Charles M		April 26, '65	Shot at Peach Tree Creek, Ga., July 19, '64; and died June 19, '73.
Prevatt, John M			Sergeant.
Purdum, William J		April 26, '65	
Rauterson, Wade H			
Rauterson, William J			
Reddit, John T		April 26, '65	
Roberts, Robert W		April 26, '65	
Robinson, Chesterfield G			
Robinson, William J			
Simmons, Andrew J			
Simmons, Robert W		April 26, '65	
Simmons, William I			
Smith, Henry A		April 26, '65	
Smith, Lewis			
Smith, Warren A		April 26, '65	Corporal; promoted 1st Sergeant, wounded Aug., '64; and in hospital at Macon, when surrendered.
Snow, Lewylen E			
Solomon, William			
Spier, Edward W			Sergeant.
Spivey, George W		April 26, '65	Corporal.
Studing, William J			
Sylvester, Ramon H			
Sylvester, Rollin			
Townsend, Edward			
Townsend, John			
Tucker, James M			
Waters, John W		April 26, '65	
Weeks, Charles F			
Wheeler, James F			1st Sergeant; wounded and disabled.
Williams, Abraham F			
Williams, Alexander K			
Williams, Blaney			
Williams, Irvin J		April 26, '65	Died in hospital at Knoxville, Tenn., of brain fever May 30, '63.
Williams, R. F		April 26, '65	
Williams, William S			
Wills, Hartley			
Willson, J. W			
Wofford, John			
Yates, James F			

Roll Company G—7th Florida Infantry.

NAMES.	MUSTERED IN.	MUSTERED OUT.	REMARKS.
OFFICERS.			
Captains—			
Robert Bullock	April 11, '62		Promoted Colonel.

Roll Company G—7th Florida Infantry.
(CONTINUED.)

NAMES.	MUSTERED IN.	MUSTERED OUT.	REMARKS.
Samuel D. McConnell	April 11, '62	April 26, '65	Promoted Captain; wounded at Chickamauga, Franklin, Tenn., also at Resaca, Ga., May 14, '64.
1st Lieutenant—			
Benjamin F. Priest			Wounded at Resaca, Ga.
2nd Lieutenants—			
Dozier Broome			Promoted Ordnance Officer for Regiment.
Edward Roux			Promoted 2nd Lieutenant; wounded at Resaca, Ga.
3rd Lieutenants—			
Simon Helvingston	April 11, '62		
Charles Pasley			Promoted 3rd Lieutenant; Appointed adjutant; killed at Nashville, Tenn.
ENLISTED MEN.			
Atkinson, Edward			Captured at Missionary Ridge.
Barco, Thomas			
Barnes, John A	April 11, '62		Corporal.
Baucknight, Caleb	April 11, '62		Sergeant.
Bauknight, Ottis A	April 11, '62		
Blackman, John	April 11, '62		Wounded at Bentonville, N. C., March 19, '65.
Broome, John D	April 11, '62		Sergeant.
Browne, Zephinah	April 11, '62		Captured at Frankford, Ky., and died in prison.
Blitch, James S	April 11, '62		
Bruton, Napoleon B	April 11, '62		
Bruton, Samuel B	April 11, '62		
Canefield,	April 11, '62		
Carter, George	April 11, '62		Died at Knoxville, Tenn.
Carter, Ira	April 11, '62		
Carter, John	April 11, '62		Captured at Missionary Ridge.
Carter, J. M. T	April 11, '62	April 26, '65	Shot at Franklin, Tenn., '64.
Carter, Michael	April 11, '62		Captured at Jonesboro.
Caulfield, James S	April 11, '62		Imprisoned at Fort Delaware.
Chandler, William A	April 11, '62		
Clarke, John I	April 11, '62		
Colding, Henry H	April 11, '62		Wounded near Decatur, Ga., July 22, '64.
Cothran, Jackson	April 11, '62		
Creroson, Walter R	April 11, '62		
Crutchfield, Ansom B	April 11, '62		
Crutchfield, Pomp	April 11, '62		Wounded at Franklin, Tenn.
Deas, Benjamin	April 11, '62		
Deas, Joshua	April 11, '62		Died in Kentucky, buried in Lexington Cemetery.
Dickinson, Elijah	April 11, '62		
Dunn, John F	April 11, '62		
Dupree, Louis F	April 11, '62		
Dunning, William Sumter	April 11, '62		Corporal; captured at Frankford, Ky.
Eunis, Ervin	April 11, '62		Killed at Peach Tree Creek, July 20, '64.
Eunis, Henry	April 11, '62		
Floyd, Erwin	April 11, '62		
Fort, Josiah J	April 11, '62		
Geiger, Alexander	April 11, '62		Killed at Resaca, Ga.
Geiger, George	April 11, '62		Died at Knoxville, Tenn.
Geiger, Harmon	April 11, '62		
Goss, Jesse H	April 11, '62		
Gordon, N. A. J	May	'62	Paroled from prison, close of war.
Ham, William S	April 11, '62		Color bearer; wounded at Chickamauga.
Harris, Henry William	April 11, '62		Died in prison.
Hearn, William	April 11, '62		
Heath, Henry	April 11, '62		
Hogan, William	April 11, '62		
Holly, Frank S	April 11, '62		Wounded at Jonesboro, Ga., August 31, '64.
Holly, Joe	April 11, '62		Died, Knoxville, Tenn.
Holly, Robert	April 11, '62		Captured at Perryville, Ky.
Holly, William Granvil	April 11, '62		Died at Knoxville, Tenn.
Holsenback,	April 11, '62		
Johnson, Henry	April 11, '62		Killed at Atlanta, August 7, '64.
Johnson, Madison S	April 11, '62		Killed at Jonesboro, August 30, '64.
Jones, John F	April 11, '62		Wounded twice at Missionary Ridge, captured,
Kettle, Laurence	April 11, '62		imprisoned at Rock Island and paroled from there, close of war; June, '65.
Kileres, Pinkney	April 11, '62		Killed at Resaca, May 14, '64.
King, Tom	April 11, '62		
King, Solomon S	April 11, '62		
Laveigne, William J	April 11, '62		Captured at Missionary Ridge and died at Camp Chase, February 24, '65; grave No. 1420.
Lewis, James S	April 11, '62		
Lewis, Philip I	April 11, '62		
McLain, Thomas		April 26, '65	
McLain, William	April 11, '62		
Marlow, John R	April 11, '62		
Marlow, Lexington	April 11, '62		
Marsh, George W	April 11, '62		
Mattair, Henry P	April 11, '62	April 26, '65	Wounded at Missionary Ridge.
Mattair, John T	April 11, '62	April 26, '65	Wounded at Missionary Ridge, November 25, '63.
Meyer, Frederick	April 11, '62		
O'Farrell, Hugh H	April 11, '62		
Patterson, Martin D	April 11, '62		
Payne, John M	April 11, '62		

Roll Company G—7th Florida Infantry.

(CONTINUED.)

NAMES.	MUSTERED IN.	MUSTERED OUT.	REMARKS.
Perkins, Henry W	April 11, '62		
Pounds, William T	April 11, '62		Sergeant.
Priester, John A	April 11, '62		
Pyles, William B	May '62	April 26, '65	
Rivers, Sylvester	April 11, '62		
Robinson, Richard R	April 11, '62		
Shaw, John D	April 11, '62		
Shelino, Simon	April 11, '62		
Sims, William	April 11, '62		
Sistrunk, Henry	April 11, '62		
Smith, John H	April 11, '62		
Smith, Rull	April 11, '62		
Smith, Wirt	April 11, '62		Killed at Murfreesborough, December 7, '64.
Smith, West	April 11, '62	April 26, '65	
Sparkman, Lewis M	July '61		Captured at Tullahoma, Tenn., imprisoned and
Standley, William D	Aug. '62	April 26, '65	paroled from Camp Douglass, Ill. at close of
Tate, W. H	April 11, '62	April 26, '65	war.
Thomas, George W	April 11, '62		
Todd, J. Calvin C	April 11, '62		Bugler.
Tyner, Barnetto T	April 11, '62		
Tyner, David Y	April 11, '62		
Voyt, Daniel	April 11, '62		
Wammock, John M	April 11, '62		
Waters, John W	Mch. '62	April 26, '65	Shot at Chickamauga, Ga., September 20, '63.
Watkins, Tom	April 11, '62		Wounded at Chickamauga, Ga.
Watkins, William	April 11, '62		Died in hospital.
Watkins, William Charles	April 11, '62		Lost arm at Dallas, Ga., May 7, '64.
Weathers, Seaborn	April 11, '62		Captured at Nashville, Tenn.
Wells, Simon H	April 11, '62		
White, Andrew J	Mch. 13, '62	April 26, '65	Wounded at Chickamauga, September 18, '63; also
White, Calvin	April 11, '62		at Egypt, Miss., captured February 29, '65.
Wiggins, George T	April 11, '62		Corporal.
Withers, John S	April 11, '62		
Young, Alcanah	April 11, '62		Killed at Missionary Ridge.
Young, James	April 11, '62		Died at Frankford, Ky.

Roll Company H (Marion Hornets)—7th Florida Infantry.

NAMES.	MUSTERED IN.	MUSTERED OUT.	REMARKS.
OFFICERS.			
Captains—			
Wade Eichelberger	April 12, '62		Died at Knoxville, Tenn.
J. H. Counts	April 12, '62		3rd Lieutenant; promoted Captain.
Henry H. Hudgens	April 12, '62		Resigned.
Henry Houseal	April 12, '62		1st Lieutenant; promoted Captain; died at Chattanooga.
1st Lieutenant—			
M. Richard G. Stephens	April 12, '62		2nd Lieutenant; promoted 1st Lieutenant; resigned June 17, '63.
2nd Lieutenant—			
Pickens Creswell	April 12, '62		Promoted 2nd Lieutenant; severely wounded at Atlanta July 22, '64.
3rd Lieutenant—			
A. G. Rutherford	April 12, '62		Promoted 1st Sergeant; then 3rd Lieutenant
ENLISTED MEN.			
Agnew, James	April 12, '62		Promoted 1st Sergeant; captured at Nashville.
Armstrong, Daniel M	April 12, '62		Seriously wounded at Jonesborough September, '64.
Armstrong, George O	Mch. '62		Died of pneumonia at Chattanooga, Tenn., July, '62.
Aultman, David	Mch. '62		Discharged at Wautuga, Tenn., for disability.
Barber, Jack	April 12, '62		Deserted at Lindon, Ky., July 26, '63.
Barnett, James			Killed at Savanah while attacking Gun Boat "Water Witch."
Bauknight, Curry	April 12, '62		Wounded at Jonesborough, Ga., September, '64.
Bauknight, Hilliard	April 12, '62		
Bauknight, W. R	April 12, '62		
Beard, James	April 12, '62		Died at Chattanooga, Tenn.
Boyd, John T	April 12, '62		Promoted Hospital Steward.
Brooks, Spencer	April 12, '62		Killed.
Brown, John H	April 12, '62		Died in Knoxville April, '63, of pneumonia.
Buckston William	April 12, '62		Captured and died in prison.
Burlerson, H. H			
Calhoun, Samuel	April 12, '62		Promoted Sergeant; killed at Missionary Ridge '63.
Carmon, William B	April 12, '62		
Carroll, Benjamin	April 12, '62		
Carroll, John			Captured at Frankfort; died in prison.
Chilty, Martin J	April 12, '62	April 26, '65	Promoted Sergeant; wounded at Franklin, Tenn.
Conyers, Isaac N			
Cress, Andrew	April 12, '62		Died at Knoxville, Tenn.

Roll Company H (Marion Hornets)—7th Florida Infantry.
(CONTINUED.)

NAMES.	MUSTERED IN.	MUSTERED OUT.	REMARKS.
Curry, James N.	Mch. 13, '62	April 26, 65	
Curry, Richard	April 12, '62		Transferred to Engineer Corps.
Dunn, Harley	April 12, '62		
Dunn, John	April 12, '62		Captured at Nashville, Tenn.
Dunn, William A.	April 12, '62		Captured in Kentucky and died in prison November 11, '62; buried in the Danville Cemetery.
Duncan, George W.	April 12, '62		Killed at Atlanta, '64.
Duncan, John R.	April 12, '62		Killed on Missionary Ridge, '63.
Eichelberger, J. W. F.	April 20, '62	April 26, '65	
Evans, John W.	April 12, '62		
Fogg, Daniel J.	Mch. '62		Shot at Kennesaw Mountain, Ga., June 17, '64.
Fort, Isaiah J.	Mch. '62	April 26, '65	Wounded at Lookout Mountain, Tenn., November, '63.
Fort, Robert	May 2, '62	April 26, '65	Wounded at Chickamauga, Ga., September 23, '63.
Freeman, Albert A.			Corporal.
Freeman, Doc.			Died in prison.
Frink, Albert A.	Apri, 12' 62'		
Fussell, William	April 12, '62		Killed on Missionary Ridge, '63.
Fyson, Stewart			Died at Louden, Tenn.
Garner, James			Killed in front of Atlanta.
Geiger, Eli W.			
Geiger, Wade A.	April 12, '62		Promoted Corporal; captured at Murfreesborough December 7, '64.
Gray, John	April 12, '62		Captured at Nashville, Tenn.
Hammond, Berry W.	April 12, '62		Captured at Atlanta July 22, '64.
Hodges, Elias	April 12, '62		Deserted.
Holder, William			Killed in front of Atlanta.
Holland, John M. S.	April 12, '62		Promoted Corporal; captured at Atlanta July 22 '64.
Jackson, John	April 12, '62	April 26, '65	
Jeffords, W. C.	April 12, '62	April 26, '65	Promoted Corporal.
Joiner, James M.			Died at Louden, Tenn.
Jordan, Newton	April 12, '62		Transferred to Engineer Corps.
Kennedy, James	April 21, '62		Wounded and disabled at Atlanta July 22, '64.
Killgore, John	April 12, '62		Sergeant; died at Knoxville, Tenn.
Kirkland, LaFayette	April 12, '62		Died at Knoxville, Tenn.
Knoblock, H. N.	April 12, '62	April 26, '65	
Knoblock, Owen	April 12, '62		Died at Knoxville, Tenn.
Lowe, John T.			
Lucius, Samuel Lewis	April 12, '62		Died at Chattanooga.
Lucius, William	April 12, '62	April 26 '65	
Luker, Charles			
Lutta, Jones F. M.			
McAllen, William			Captured at Missionary Ridge November 25, '63.
McAteer, William B.	April 12, '62		Captured on Missionary Ridge November 25, '63; paroled from prison at close of the war.
McCardel, Joshua	April 12, '62	April 26, '65	Transferred to Commissary Department.
McErven, W. A.			
McFall, John			
May, Mack	April 12, '62		Captured at Atlanta July 22, '64; paroled from prison at close of the war.
Mills, Elbert	April 12, '62		Captured at Atlanta August 7, '64; imprisoned at Camp Chase and died October 29, '64; grave No. 378.
Mills, John B.	April 12, '62	April 26, '65	Transferred to Engineer Corps.
Mixon, Charles J.			Promoted Sergeant; wounded and died.
Mixon, James J.	April 12, '62	April 26, '65	Seriously wounded at Jonesborough, Ga.
Mixon, Jones	April 12, '62		Mortally wounded at Atlanta July 22, '64.
Monroe, James	April 12, '62		Killed on Missionary Ridge November 25, '63.
Moody, Roger	April 12, '62		Captured at Frankfort, Ky., October, '62; died in prison.
Moorman, William	April 12, '62		Discharged at Cumberland Gap for disability.
Nelson, Samuel T.	April 12, '62		Sergeant; captured in Kentucky; died in prison.
Newman, Charmick			
Perry, M. C.			Killed in front of Atlanta.
Perry, Payne			Killed at Peach Tree Creek July 20, '64.
Perry, Thomas J.	April 12, '62		Promoted Corporal; wounded at Atlanta July 22, '64.
Perry, William H.	April 12, '62		
Potts, James	April 12, '62		Captured at Frankfort October 1, '62; died in prison.
Reid, John D.	April 12, '62		Captured at Murfreesborough December 7, '64.
Rhodes, Jeremiah			
Rhodes, Terry			Died in Tennessee.
Ridout, John W.	April 12, '62		1st Sergeant; died at Knoxville, Tenn.
Roach, Azro			Killed at Atlanta.
Roach, Joseph A.	April 12, '62		Died at Camp Chase October 25, '65; grave No. 358.
Ross, Abraham	April 12, '62	Apr 1 26, '65	Ambulance driver.
Rutherford, A. G.	Apr 1 12, '62	Apr 1 26, '65	
Shaw, George R. W.	Aug. '63	April 26, '65	
Shaw, Nehamiah			
Smith, Samuel	April 12, '62	April 26, '65	Wounded at Resaca, Ga., October, '64.
Sturdevant, Charles S.	April 12, '62		Died from accident.
Swindle, Willis			
Tanner, Henry C.			

Roll Company H (Marion Hornets)—7th Florida Infantry.
(CONTINUED.)

NAMES.	MUSTERED IN.	MUSTERED OUT.	REMARKS.
Tanner, K.			Died at Knoxville, Tenn.
Tison, Stewart	April 12, '62		Wounded at Chickamauga Septemper 20, '63, and died at Louden, Tenn., from his injuries.
Thomas, R. Y. H.	April 12, '62		1st Sergeant; discharged at Chattanooga for disability.
Turner, G. D.			Corporal.
Turner, John	April 12, '62		Promoted 1st Sergeant; killed at Missionary Ridge November 25, '63.
Waites, William F.			
Waldon, John F.	April 12, '62	April 26, '65	
Walker, Joseph E.			
Weathery, J. S.		April 26, '65	
Whitmire, George S.	April 12, '62		Promoted Corporal; died on his way home.
Williams, Ben			Died at Chattanooga.
Williams, Jacob E.			
Williams, Joe B.			
Williams, Lawson			
Williams, William P.	April 12, '62		
Worley, Jacob			

Roll Company I—7th Florida Infantry.

NAMES.	MUSTERED IN.	MUSTERED OUT.	REMARKS.
OFFICERS.			
Captains—			
A. S. Moseley	April '62		
N. Norton	April '62		Promoted Captain; succeeded Moseley.
1st Lieutenant—			
G. W. R. McRæ	April '62	April 26, '65	Resigned April 22, '63.
2nd Lieutenants—			
C. C. Seyle	April '62		
R. W. Jenkens	April '62		Shot at Murfreesborough, December 4, '64; died December 13, '64; promoted Lieutenant, Company I, 7th Regiment.
3rd Lieutenant—			
B. L. Wall		April 26, '65	Promoted 3rd Lieutenant, Company I, 7th Regiment.
ENLISTED MEN.			
Alvers, W. C.	April '62	April 26, '65	
Anerd, A.		April 26, '65	
Ashley, C. C.	April '62	April 26, '65	Lost arm at Jonesboro, Ga., August 3, '63 and discharged September, '64; 1st Sergeant.
Ashley, H. A.	April '62		
Basford, James C. L.	April '62	April 26, '65	
Bates, B.	April '62		
Beck, J. J.	April '62	April 26, '65	Lost right eye from small-pox in Tenn.
Beck, Wilson	April '62		
Bonhanon, M.	April '62		
Cason, Noah	April '62		Died in hospital at Chattanooga of measels.
Cassels, J. H.	April '62		
Cassell, T. A.	Mch. 2, '62	April 26, '65	Wounded at Murfreesborough, December, '64; also at Dallas, Ga., May 25, '64.
Cassels, W. B.	Mch. '62		Died, Camp Chase prison, February 2, '65; grave No. 1010.
Caudory, L. H.	Mch. '62		
Clinton, C. M.	Mch. '62		
Cook, H. D.	Mch. 2, '62	April 26, '65	Wounded at Dallas, Ga., May 26, '64.
Copher, E. M.	Mch. '62		
Coward, W. J.	Mch. '62		
Cribb, M. C.	Mch. '62		
Dacosta. Raymond	Mch. '62		
Davis, J. N.	Mch. '62		
Drummond, C. C.	Mch. '62		
Durance, W. H.	Mch. '62		
Eubanks, R. S.	April '62		Corporal.
Fowler, W.	April '62		
Gaskins, S. V.	April '62	April 26, '65	
Geiger, L. P.	April '62		
Green, Archibald	April '62		
Hall, W. H.	April '62		
Hancock, J.	April '62		
Hatchet, S. A.	April '62		
Hawthorn, J. L.	April '62		
Higginbothim, E.	April '62		
Higgenbothim, J.	April '62		Corporal.
Hilliard, Samuel	April '62		
Hilliard, Silas	April '62		
Johnson, J. A.	April '62		
Johnson, W. W.	April '62		
Lane, F. M.	April '62		Sergeant.

Roll Company I—7th Florida Infantry.
(CONTINUED.)

NAMES.	MUSTERED IN	MUSTERED OUT.	REMARKS.
Lane, S. A.	April '62		
Lee, Lewis	April '62		
Love, S. M.	Mch. 8, '62	Oct. 30, '62	Disability.
McCramy, Nathan		'63	Disability.
Manning, John	April '62		
Manning, Moses	April '62		
Markey, J. H.		April 26, '65	
Molten, Benjamin	April '62		Captured at Missionary Ridge, Tenn., November 25, '63; sent to Camp Morton, Ind., paroled there close of war.
Mizzell, N. B.	April '62		
Moseley, O. S.	April '62		
Napier, W. R.	April '62		Sergeant.
Nobles, E.	April '62		
North, Caleb		April 26, '65	
North, John		April 26, '65	
Parlin, Henry S.	May 18, '62	June 3, '65	
Perry, B. F.	May 18, '65		
Perry, J. F. C.	May 18, '62		
Petterson, F. M.	May 18, '62		
Peterson, M.	May 18, '62		
Priest, G. W.	May '62		Corporal.
Riles, Lewis	May '62		
Rentfrœ, Green	'61	April 3, '65	
Roundtree, H.	May '62		
Roundtree, Isaac	May 23, '62		Discharged at Knoxville, August 7, '62; spinal trouble.
Sanders, J. G.	May '62	April 3, '65	
Sanders, W. H.	May '62		Corporal; wounded at Chicamauga, Ga., captured and sent to Camp Douglass, Ill., paroled, close of war.
Sheppard, J. H.	May '62		
Smith, E. W. S.		April 26, '65	
Sparkman, J. W.	April '62		
Sparkman, L. A.	April '62		
Spear, W.	April '62		Sergeant.
Spiers, H.	April '62		
Stallings, S. S.		April 26, '65	
Suggs, E.	April '62	April 26, '65	
Suggs, W.	April '62	April 26, '65	
Sweat, Edmund			Died of pneumonia at Frankfort, Ky., September 6, '63.
Thomas, Charles		April 26, '65	
Thomas, Thomas W.	Mch. '62	April 26, '65	Prisoner of war for 18 months at Rock Island, Ill.
Thompson, T. W.	April '62		
Thornal, A. A.	April '62	'63	
Timmons, L. E.	April '62		Sergeant.
Timmons, S. A.	April '62		
Turner, J. W.	April '62		
Vause, C. F.	April '62		Died, Knoxville, Tenn., November 6, '63; of pneumonia.
Vause, D. H.	April '62		
Vause, Samuel	April '62		
Vinyard, A. G.	April '62		
Weathersbee, Preston	April '62	April 26, '65	
White, G. W.	April '62		
Wilkison, Elijah	April '62	April 26, '65	Wounded at Chickamauga, Ga., September 20, '63.
Wilkison, Elisha	April '62		
Wilks, J. S.	April '62		
Williams, H. R.	April '62		
Williams, Issiah	April '62	April 26, '65	

Roll Company K—7th Florida Infantry.

NAMES.	MUSTERED IN.	MUSTERED OUT.	REMARKS.
OFFICERS.			
Captain—			
Robert B. Smith	April '62		
1st Lieutenant—			
Walter C. Malency	April '62	April 26, '65	
2nd Lieutenants—			
John A. Bethel	April '62	April 26, '65	Captured, August, '64.
Samuel B. Ashley	April '62		
ENLISTED MEN.			
Abburg, Benjamin	April '62		
Allison, John	April '62		Sergeant.
Amon, Manuel	April '62		
Anderson, Charles	April '62		
Anderson, George	April '62		
Barneet, James	April '62	April 26, '65	Wounded in side by shot which caused death September 23, '86; transferred to Navy.
Barthlum, James	April '62	April 26, '65	Transferred to Navy, Confederate Ram; "Savannah."
Bell, Louis Jr.	Mch. '62	April 26, '65	
Berry, Charles H.	April '62		Sergeant.

Roll Company K—7th Florida Infantry.
(CONTINUED.)

NAMES.	MUSTERED IN.		MUSTERED OUT.	REMARKS.
Bishop, Asa	April	'62		
Bryson, Robert	April	'62		
Butler, Thomas	April	'62		
Burnes, Thomas	April	'62		
Chabert, Jules	Jan. 1,	'62	April 26, '65	Transferred C. S. Navy, (Ram Savannah); shot through body in a fight with U. S. War Ship "Water Witch;" June 3, '64.
Chapman, Charles	April	'62		
Cole, Joseph E.	April	'62		Sergeant.
Collins, J. E.	April	'62		
Comb, Charles	April	'62		
Cowart, R. A.			April 26, '65	
Curry, Joseph	April	'62		
Curry, Samuel	April	62		
Curry, William	April	'62		
DeLaunay, J. A.			April 26, '65	
DeLaunay, St.John	April	'62		
Dorsey, Edward	April	'62		
Duprey, John	April	'62		
Edwards, George W.	April	'62		
Fallis, Rofina	April	'62		Corporal.
Fagan, Joseph	April	'62		
Franklin, William	April	'62		
Guerro, Miguel	April	'62		
Gibley, William T.	April	'62		
Hawkins, Daniel L.	April	'62		
Herrymand, William	April	'62		
Jackson, John B.	April	'62	April 26, '65	
Josselyn, William	April	'62		
Lee, Edmund	April	'62		
Lovett, James	April	'62		
Lowe, Alfred	April	'62	April 26, '65	Transferred to Ram Savannah; C. S. N.
Lowe, John T.	April	'62	April 26, '65	Transferred to Confederate Navy.
Lowe, William E.			April 26, '65	
McLaughlin, William	April	'62		
McLean, John L.	April	'62		
Mason, John	April	'62		
Merrilac, Augustus	April	'62		Corporal.
Miller, Charles	April	'62		
Monte-De-Oca, Manuel	April	'62		
Morrison, John	April	'62		
Moss, Josephus	April	'62		Honorable mention at Chickamauga.
Oliveri, Marcus	April	'62		
O'Neil, William	April	'62		
Pent, John		'62	April 26, '65	Shot at Missionary Ridge, Tenn., December 25, '63.
Pratt, Benjamin	April	'62		
Richards, George	April	'62		Died Camp Chase prison, April 17, '65; grave No. 1884.
Roddenberry, J.				Died Camp Chase, March 8, '65; grave No. 1592.
Russell, John	April	'62		
Russell, Thomas	April	'62		
Sands, John B.	April	'62		
Sawyer, William	April	'82		Corporal.
Swain, Benjamin	April	'62		
Thompson, N. S.				Died Camp Chase, September 17, '64; grave No. 253.
Wadsworth, Melchi	April	'62		Sergeant.
Watson, Robert	April	'62		
Weathersford, Jeremiah	April	'62		
Williamson, J. P.	April	'62		
Woodruff, Joseph	April	'62		
Wood, Anderson	June	'62	April 26, '65	Captured, '62; and exchanged, '63.
Woods, James	June	'62		

EIGHTH FLORIDA INFANTRY.

The 8th Regiment of Infantry was mustered into the Con'ederate service in May, 1862, with R. F. Floyd as Colonel; John M. Pons as Lieutenant-Colonel, and W. I. Turner as Major. With the following companies commanded by Captains, Burrel A. Bobo, Co. A; R. A. Waller, Co. B David Lang, Co. C; William Baya, Co. D: Thomas E. Clarke. Co. E; Felix Simmons, Co. F; J. C. Stewart, Co. G; Jam·s Tucker. Co. H; John M. Pons Co. I; Frederick Worth, Co. K. Shortly after the organizat on of the Reg ment it was ordered to Virginia where it joined the 2nd and with that Regiment and the 5th, fought in the Second Battle of Manassas, August 30, 1862, where, as General Prior reported: "The 5th and 8th Florida Regiments, though never under fire before, exhibited the cool and collected courage of veterans." Crossing the Potomac near Leesburg, early in September, the Brigade, which consisted of the 2nd, 5th and 8th Florida, 12th Virginia and 14th Alabama, marched through Frederick City, over South Mountain into Pleasant Valley, and participated in the investment and capture of the Federal forces at Harper's Ferry, thence they hurried to the field of Sharpsburg, September 17, where they shared the service of R. H. Anderson's division in that battle. In this engagement Colonel Hateley and Lieutenant-Colonel Lamar, of the 5th, were wounded; the former so severely that he retired from service. On the return of the army to Virginia, the 8th Regiment was brigaded with the other Florida regiments under command of E. A. Perry, who had been promoted to Brigadier-General. The Brigade remained in R. H. Anderson's division, in Longstreet's corps, until after Chancellorsville, when it became a part of Ambrose P. Hill's corps. At Fredericksburg December 11, 1862, the 8th Regiment, under command of Captain David Lang, went to the support of the two Mississippi Regiments under Barksdale, at the river where the Federals were endeavoring to lay their bridges. In General McClellan's report he says: "It (the 8th) acted gallantly and did good service." Toward noon Captain Lang was severely wounded, and Capt. Thomas R. Love, of Co. B, took command, and the position although very much exposed was maintained until they were ordered back at 4 p. m. A detachment of three companies under Captain Baya were also engaged, and he and Lieut. H. C. Simmons and 20 men were captured. The companies under Captain Lang lost 7 killed and 24 wounded During the early part of the Chancellorsville campaign Perry was on duty near Fredericksburg; May 2, 1863, the Brigade, after an exhausting march and skirmishing, rejoined the Division in time to march to the Furnace at daylight on May 3. They took part in the gallant fighting of May 3 and 4, and General Anderson in his report paid a special tribute to "Brigadier-General Perry and his heroic little band of Floridians who showed a courage as intrepid as that of any others in their assault upon the enemy in his entrenchment on the third and in their subsequent advance on Chancellorsville." In General Perry's report he says: "The conduct of both officers and men of my command through the tiresome marches and continued watching, as well as while engaging the enemy, was such as to meet high praise. The firm and steadfast courage exhibited, especially by the 5th and 2nd Florida Regiments in charge at Chancellorsville, attracted my particular attention." The General especially noted the services of Capt. W. E. McCassland, H. F. Riley, Lieut. D. B. Taylor, Lieut. William Scott, Maj. T. C. Elder and Maj. D. W. Hinkle, Staff officers and voluntee a des. The 8th lost 11 killed and 35 wounded. Among the latter were Capt. B. F. Whitner, Lieuts. J. M. Nelson and T. S. Armestead. The 2nd lost 3 killed, includ ng Adj. Woody F. Butler, and 29 wounded; and the 5th lost 6 killed and 22 wounded, among the latter Maj. B. F. Davis.

At the battle of Gettysburg the Brigade was commanded by David Lang, of the 8th, the heroic fighter of Fredericksburg, who had been promoted to Colonel (promoted September 18, 1862), General Perry being disabled by typhoid fever.

General Lang in his report of the battle of Gettysburg said: "Since the battle I have had no staff at all except David Wilson. The Adjutant of the 8th has been acting for me. There are now but 22 line officers and 233 enlisted men for duty in the Brigade. Our loss has been 455, aggregate killed, wounded and missing. I th'nk that a large number of missing are men who have been captured unhurt, as there were a large number of men who were exhausted by the rapidity with which the first charge was made, who were unable to keep up on the retreat."

In the battle of Fredericksburg the 8th lost their colors; the Color-bearer and the entire color guard of the 8th were killed or wounded and their colors left on the field. Owing to the fact that several colors of other Br gades fell back with the Florida Brigade, the 8th did not miss their colors until after it was too late to secure them. During the night a Federal Lieutenant of artillery, whose command had been moved up to the position, was examining the ground n front of them, discovered two pieces of artillery belonging to a Federal battery. In moving these pieces, which owing to the proximity of the Confederate line had to be done by hand, Sergeant Horen of the 72nd New York Vo'unteers, picked up the flag of the 8th from where it lay on the ground by the dead Color-bearer.

Colonel Lang in this report mentions the fact that the 2nd Regiment also lost its colors and the greater part of its men. The flag of the 2nd was a silk one presented by the ladies; it was the Confederate battle flag with this exception—the intersection of the cross in the center of the flag was surrounded by a golden sun-burst.

In the Gettysburg fight the 5th Florida lost 17 killed and 76 wounded; among the killed were Capt. John Frink, and Lieuts. J. A. Jenkins and J. C. Blake; among the wounded, Capts. William Bailey and R. N. Gardner, Lieuts. G. L. Odum, J. C. Shaw and George Walker. The 2nd lost 11 killed and 70 wounded. The 8th 5 killed and 65 wounded. Among the wounded were Capts. T. R. Love, J. Mizell and T. B. Livingston; Lieuts. Hecter Bruce, W. W. Wilson, E. J. Dismukes, John Malone, F. M. Bryan and T. W. Givens.

At the battle of Bristow Station, October 14, 1863, the Brigade was conspiciously engaged, loosing a considerable number killed and wounded; among the latter Lieutenant-Colonel William Baya, commanding Regiment, and Sergeant Major Arnow of the 8th Regiment.

In the campaign of the Wilderness May, 1864, the Florida Brigade lost 250 men. Among the wounded, was General Perry, who was compelled on that account to retire from service. In the campaign of 1864, which followed that of the Wilderness, the old Brigade continued to add to its laurels. After General Perry retired Colonel Lang again became the Brigade commander and remained such until the remnant of Perry's Brigade was consolidated with Finnegan's Brigade about June 1, 1864; from that time until the surrender the Florida Brigade was known as Finnegan's Brigade. The story of the service of the 2nd, 5th and 8th, Perry's Brigade, is so closely interwoven that the story of one is practically the story of them all; they differ in details only. For this reason the story of the 8th has been made fuller that it might take in its gallant compatriots, who wrote the name of Florida high up on a scroll of fame and in characters that can only fade when time shall cease to be. At Appomattox the 2nd Florida surrendered 9 officers and 59 men; the 5th Florida 6 officers and 47 men; the 8th 4 officers and 28 men. This record needs nothing added to tell the world the gallantry of the men who marched under Florida's standard.

Roll, Field and Staff—8th Florida Infantry.

NAMES.	MUSTERED IN.	MUSTERED OUT.	REMARKS.
Colonels—			
Richard F. Floyd	May '62		Resigned on account of ill health.
David Lang	May '62	April 9, '65	Captain Co. C; promoted Colonel September 17 '62.
Lieutenant-Colonels—			
John M. Pons	May '62		Resigned.
William Baya	May '62	April 9, '65	Wounded, Bristow Station October, '63.
Majors—			
William J. Turner	May '62		Resigned, '62.
Thomas E. Clark	May '62	April 9, '65	
Surgeon—			
R. P. Daniel	May '62	April 9, '65	
Assistant Surgeons—			
Theodore West	May '62	April 9, '65	
Du P. Hooper			Died while on duty at Fredericksburg December 12, '63.
Adjutant—			
1st Lieut. B. F. Simmons	May '62	April 9, '65	
Sergeant-Major—			
E. P. Dismukes			
Quartermaster—			
Capt. J. T. Bernard	May '62	April 9, '65	
Commissary—			
Capt. H. T. Baya	May 62	April 9, '65	
Quartermaster-Sergeant—			
Samuel C. Woodbury	May '62	April 9, '65	
Commissary-Sergeant—			
——— Kaul			
Chaplain—			
B. I. Johnson			
Hospital Steward—			
Ordnance Sergeant—			
R. H. Randolph			

Roll Company A—8th Florida Infantry.

NAMES.	MUSTERED IN.	MUSTERED OUT.	REMARKS.
OFFICERS.			
Captain—			
Burwell A. Bobo			Cashiered for cowardice on November 11, '62.
1st Lieutenant—			
James M. Robinson			Deserted, August 16, '62.
2nd Lieutenants—			
Charles S. Livingston			Resigned, October 15, '62.
I. M. Nelson	May 8, '62		Wounded at Gettysburg, July 3, '63; resigned.
N. M. Redding	May 8, '62		Promoted 2nd Lieutenant; November 22, '62; killed at N. Anna Road, May, '64.
3rd Lieutenant—			
ENLISTED MEN.			
Albritton, Jasper			Died at Charlottsville; buried in the Cemetery of the University of Virginia.
Albritton, Joseph			Deserted, November 1, '62.
Allmans, Aug. C			
Allmans, John E.			
Allmans, J. A.			
Allmans, M. G.			Promoted Corporal.
Allmans, William H.			Promoted Sergeant; imprisoned at Fort Delaware
Barington, S.			Wounded at Gettysburg, July 3, '63.
Bishop, Berry	May 8, '62		Deserted at Thomasville, '62.
Bishop, Eli.			
Black, N. G.			

Roll Company A—8th Florida Infantry.
(CONTINUED.)

NAMES.	MUSTERED IN.	MUSTERED OUT.	REMARKS.
Boatwright, Benjamin	May 8, '62		
Boatwright, John W	May 8, '62		
Brown, J. A. M.			
Bryant, Francis M	May 8, '62		Wounded at Gettysburg, July 3, '63.
Campbell, William			
Cason, David	May 8, '62		Deserted at Camp Leon, July 16, '62.
Cattell, William I	May 8, '62		Deserted June 1, '62.
Clements, J. G.		April 9, '65	
Clyatt, William H.			
Coker, James	May 8, '62		Deserted May 25, '62 from Station 5.
Coaker, L. A.	May 8, '62		Deserted May 25, '62 from Station 5.
Coaker, William P			Deserted May 25, '62 from Station 5.
Corrine, David	May 8, '62		Wounded at Chancellorsville, May 4, '63.
Corrine, W. W	May 8, '62		Unaccounted for, October, '62.
Crawley, George W	May 8, '62	April 9, '65	Paroled from Elmira prison, N. Y.
Douglass, Joseph	May 8, '62		
Levi, Drawdy	May 8, '62		
Driggers, Dennis	May 8, '62		Deserted at Camp Leon, June 30, '62.
Driggers, James E.	May 8, '62		
Dugger, William			Wounded at Chancellorsville, May 4, '63; unaccounted for, October 30, '62.
Edwards, W. W	May 8, '62		
English, R.			
Espey, Joseph H	May 8, '62		Wounded at 2nd Manassas, August 30, '62 and disabled; re-enlisted August 20, '63; Company F 5th Battalion, Captain A. J. Dozier.
Flitch, Jacob	May 8, '62		Unaccounted for, October 30, '62.
Fletcher, John	May 8, '62		
Feidling, J. N	May 8, '62		Sergeant; wounded at Fredericksburg, December 13, '62.
Futch, A. J	May 8, '62		
Futch, John E.	May 8, '62		Deserted at Camp Leon, June 30, '62.
Galloway, J. T	May 8, '62		
Goodman, Robert	May 8, '62		Unaccounted for.
Goff, W. E.	May 10, '62		1st Sergeant; transferred to Company K, 5th Regiment, January 1, '63.
Grant, John H	May 10, '62	April 9, '65	
Hall, Elishua			
Hodges, L. A	May 8, '62		
Hoolsclough, D. C.	May 8, '62		
Horrell, David R.	May 8, '62		
Hurts, Thomas F	May 8, '62		
Jones, John			Wounded by accident, discharged October 15, at Culpepper.
Jordan, T. L			
Jywes, J. P			Died October 10, at Winchester.
Keene, N	Nov. 8, '62		Deserted at Camp Leon, June 30, '62.
King, Elisha			
Lamb, Thadeus			
Lamb V. W	Nov. 8, '62		
Lassiter, C	Nov. 8, '62	April 9, '65	
Lewis, James P.	Nov. 8, '62		
Lisle, A. J.	Nov. 8, '62		Died September 7, at Gordonville.
Long, John H	Nov. 8, '62		Corporal; deserted October 1, '62.
Long, Leonard	Nov. 8, '62		Shot at the Wilderness, May 4, '64.
Lyon, J. P	Nov. 8, '62		
McDowell, John	Nov. 8, '62		Promoted Corporal; deserted November 1, '62.
McInnis, James	Nov. 8, '62		Promoted Sergeant; deserted November 11, '62.
McClamma, William R.			
Mathis, D. S.	Nov. 8, '62	April 9, '65	
Mickler, P. T.	Nov. 8, '62	April 9, '65	
Miller, G. C.	Nov. 8, '62		Discharged August 23, from Richmond.
Miller, Jacob	May 8, '62		
Mills, James	May 8, '62		
Newman, G. C.		April 9, '65	Promoted 1st Sergeant; lost right leg by accident R. R. after war.
Newman, Pat.	May 8, '62		
Newman, W. H	May 15, '62	April 9, '65	Promoted Corporal; shot at Gettysburg July 3, '63.
Outlaw, B.	May 8, '62	April 9, '65	
Owen, W. J		April 9, '65	
Parnell, J.			Killed at Chancellorsville, May 4, '63.
Pickell, J.	May 8, '62		Deserted at Tallahassee, July 16, '62.
Pouder, B. F.		April 9, '65	
Redding, B. J	May 8, '62		
Ross, G. B.	May 8, '62		Died in hospital at Richmond, '63.
Ross, J. W	May 8, '62		Sergeant.
Sapp, John			
Sapp, William J	May 8, '62		
Smith, A. M	May 8, '62		
Smith, Moses			
Strawn, J. L	May 8, '62		
Strickland, Abner	May 8, '62		Unaccounted for.
Strickland, William	May 8, '62		Corporal.
Sullivan, S.	May 8, '62		Musician, discharged Oct. 15 at Culpepper.
Sullivan, William	May 8, '62		Paroled from Fort Delaware.
Summers, H. M	May 8, '62	April 9, '65	
Sumers, P. P			
Taylor, James			
Thompson, John	May 8, '62		2nd Sergeant.

Roll Company A—8th Florida Infantry.
(CONTINUED.)

NAMES.	MUSTERED IN.	MUSTERED OUT.	REMARKS.
Tina, S.	May 8, '62		Wounded at Bristow Station, Va., October 14, '63.
Triblet Eli.	May 8, '62		Deserted at Thomasville, July, '62.
Tucker, James.			
Watkins, G. W.	May 8, '62		
Walker, G. W.			
Webb, William.	May 8, '62		
Williams, Alfred.	May 8, '62	April 9, '65	Captured and imprisoned at Fort Delaware when paroled.
Williams, R. B.	May 8, '62		Discharged November 10,
Winn, Joseph.	May 8, '62		

Roll Company B (Young Guards)—8th Florida Infantry.

NAMES.	MUSTERED IN.	MUSTERED OUT.	REMARKS.
OFFICERS.			
Captains—			
R. A. Waller.	May 10, '62		Killed at Sharpsburg, September 17, '62.
Thomas R. Love.	May 10, '62		1st Lieutenant; promoted Captain, September, '62; killed at Gettysburg, July 3, '63.
mHector Bruce.	May 10, '62	April 9, '65	Promoted 1st Lieutenant; then Captain 63,wounded at Fredricksburg, December 13, '62, Gettysburg July 3, '63 and captured, imprisoned at Fort Delaware; escaped and returned to his command.
1st Lieutenants—			
John W. Booth.	May 10, '62		2nd Lieutenant, promoted 1st Lieutenant; resigned, '62.
W. M. Barrineau.	May 10, '62		Promoted 2nd Lieutenant, 1st Lieutenant; wounded at Gettysburg, '63, killed at the Wilderness, May 6, '64.
2nd Lieutenants—			
E. P. Dismukes.	May 10, '62		1st Sergeant, promoted Lieutenant; wounded at Gettysburg, July 3, '63.
John W. Malone.	May 10, '62		Sergeant, promoted 2nd Lieutenant; wounded at Gettysburg, July 3, '63.
3rd Lieutenants—			
Thomas W. Brown.	May 10, '62		
Benjamin E. Russell.	May 10, '62	April 9, '65	Promoted 3rd Lieutenant.
ENLISTED MEN.			
Andrews, F. William.	May 10, '62		Wounded at Gettysburg July 3, '63.
Arline, A. W.	May 10, '62		
Barfield, Levi.	May 10, '62		
Barineau, J. E.	May 10, '62		
Barineau, J. S.	May 10, '62		1st Sergeant; killed at Cold Harbor, June 3, '64.
Barrinton, S.	May 10, '62		Wounded at Gettysburg, July 3, '63.
Barton, John.	May 10, '62		Died in Charlottsville, and buried in the Cemetery of the University of Virginia.
Blan, C.	May 10, '62		Imprisoned at Fort Delaware.
Bleach, J. T.	May 10, '62		Wounded at Gettysburg July 2, '63.
Blount, C. W.	May 10, '62		Imprisoned at Fort Delaware.
Blount, Neil.	May 10, '62		
Boutwell, J. D.	May 10, '62		
Boyd, William.	May 10, '62		Reported dead October 1, '62.
Bradshaw, J. J.	May 10, '62		
Bradshaw, J. M.	May 10, '62		
Bradshaw, S. J.	May 10, '62		Died and buried in the Cemetery of the University of Virginia.
Bracewell, J. P.	May 10, '62		Wounded at Fredericksburg December 13, '62.
Bradwell, A. M.	May 10, '62		Imprisoned at Fort Delaware.
Brock, Abram.	May 10, '62		
Brock, J. R.	May 10, '62		
Brock, Martin.	May 10, '62	April 9, '65	Wounded and disabled at Petersburg, Va., Sept-'64; re-enlisted in militia to guard prisoners.
Campbell, J. W.	May 10, '62	April 9, '65	
Campbell, M. M.	May 10, '62		Killed at the Wilderness, April 6, '63.
Campbell, William.	May 10, '62		Promoted Corporal; wounded at Gettysburg July 3, '63; at Bristow Station October 14, '63.
Castillo, David.	May 10, '62		Wounded at Chancellorsville May 4, '63.
Castillo, John.	May 10, '62		
Chason, Jonathan.	May 10, '62		Wounded at Gettysburg July 4, '63.
Chester, D. H. C.	May 10, '62		
Collins, Ben C.	May 10, '62		Severely wounded at Chancellorsville, May 4, '63.
Connell, J. W.	May 10, '62		
Connell Manley.	May 10, '62		
F.	May 10, '62		
C.	May 10, '62		Wounded at Gettysburg July 3, '63.

Roll Company B (Young Guards)—8th Florida Infantry.
(CONTINUED.)

NAMES.	MUSTERED IN.	MUSTERED OUT.	REMARKS.
Cox, J. T.	May 10, '62		Wounded at Gettysburg July 3, '63; imprisoned at Fort Delaware.
Cox, J. H.	May 10, '62		Wounded at Fredricksburg December 13, '62.
Cox, Simon	May 10, '62		
Cox, William G.	May 10, '62		
Davis, T. P.	May 10, '62		Wounded at Chancellorsville May 4, '63; at Bristow Station October 14, '63.
Dixon, William	May 10, '62		
Dollar, Francis W.	May 10, '62		
Dollar, James	May 10, '62		
Dollar, William	May 10, '62		
Donaldson, J. B.	May 10, '62		
Dudley, H. C.	May 10, '62		
Dudley, Ivan	May 10, '62		
Eaton, John E.	May 10, '62		
Eaton, W. H.			Killed at Culpepper, '63.
Freeman, Ivan	May 10, '62		
Freeman, Jacob W.	May 10, '62		
Gandy, Blacksher	May 10, '62		Deserted at Sharpsburg.
Gandy, Theophilus	May 10, '62		
Ganons, Lemuel	May 10, '62		
Ganons, Michæl	May 10, '62		Wounded at Chancellorsville May 3, '63.
Gibson, B. H.	May 10, '62		Wounded at Gettysburg July 3, '63.
Goddin, Thomas	May 10, '62		
Gray, J. M.	May 10, '62		Killed at Fredericksburg December 13, '62.
Gray, Thomas	May 10, '62		
Green, J. R.	May 10, '62		
Green, W. F.	May 10, '62		
Griffin, D. R.	May 10, '62		
Griffin, Jesse R.	May 10, '62		
Hall, P. W.	May 10, '62		
Hannah, Calvin	May 10, '62		
Hannah, H.	May 10, '62		Killed at 2nd Manassas August 30, '62.
Harper, H. W.	May 10, '62		Wounded at Fredericksburg December 13, '62.
Harrell, Darius	May 10, '62		
Harrell, Elias	May 10, '62		
Harrell, Jabez	May 10, '62		
Harrell, J. J.	May 10, '62		
Harrell, John G.	May 10, '62		
Harrell, Lyttleton	May 10, '62		
Harrell, M. P.	May 10, '62		
Hatcher, L. G.	May 10, '62		
Hicks, Putnam	May 10, '62		
Ingram H. H.	May 10, '62		Wounded at Sharpsburg and left on field.
Ingram, J. M.	May 10, '62		Wounded at Sharpsburg.
Ingram, W. J.	May 10, '62		
Jarvis, J. S.	May 10, '62		Killed at Sharpsburg.
Johnson, James R.	May 10, '62		
Johnson, W. W.	May 10, '62		Wounded at Gettysburg July 3, '63.
Kemp, John K.	May 10, '62		Killed at Chancellorsville May 4, '63.
Lambert, Benjamin	May 10, '62		
Lambert, D. S.	May 10, '62		
Lambert, G. S.			Wounded at Fredericksburg December 13, '62.
Lambert, Moses	May 10, '62		Lost right arm at Gettysburg July 2, '63.
Lambert, N. L.	May 10, '62		Wounded at Gettysburg July 3, '63.
Love, A. B.	May 10, '62		Captured at Gettysburg July 3, '63; imprisoned at Fort Delaware until close of war.
Love, A. D.	May 10, '62		Promoted Corporal; killed at Chancellorsville May 4, '63
Love, J. J. R.	May 10, '62		Promoted Sergeant; captured at Gettysburg and paroled from Fort Delaware at close of the war.
Love, H. H.	May 10, '62	April 9, '65	Wounded at Gettysburg, July 3, '63, at Petersburg, Sept. 18, '64.
Lutten, John E.	May 10, '62		Corporal.
McCall, T. Chalmers	May 10, '62		Promoted Corporal; wounded at Fredericksburg December 13, '62.
McConnell, T. F.	May 10, '62		Killed at Sharpsburg.
McDaniel, A.			
McDougald, John	May 10, '62		
McElvy, H. S.	May 10, '62		Discharged at Camp Leon May ,'62.
McGowin, James A.	May 10, '62		Died in hospital at Liberty, Va., February 2, '62.
McJunkins, James	May 10, '62		
McLaughlin, James	May 10, '62		Died at Fredericksburg.¶
McPherson, Colin	May 10, '62		
Marshall, J. N.	May 10, '62		
Marshall, T. M.	May 10, '62		Killed at Fredericksburg December 13, '62.
Messer, H. D.	May 10, '62		
Messer, W. F.	May 10, '62		Wounded at 2nd Manassas August 29, '62.
Morgan, T. A.	June '62		Wounded at Gettysburg July 3, '63; imprisoned at Fort Delaware and paroled from there at close of the war.
Morris, T. J.	May 10, '62		
Morris, W. C.	May 10, '62		Corporal.
Muire, David	May 10, '62		
Nixon, J. J.	May 10, '62		
Pickett, Charles	May 10, '62		
Porter, W. P.	May 10, '62	April 9, '65	

Roll Company B (Young Guards)—8th Florida Infantry.

(CONTINUED.)

NAMES.	MUSTERED IN.	MUSTERED OUT.	REMARKS.
Prevatt, T. K.	May 10, 62		Wounded at Fredericksburg December 13, '62.
Randolph, R.	May 10, '62		
Redd, C. S.	May 10, '62		Wounded at Chancellorsville May 4, '63.
Reaves, John M.	May 10, '62		Wounded and captured at Gettysburg ,imprisoned at Fort Delaware and died April 3, '64.
Rich, D. T.	May 10, '62		
Roberts, George	May 10, '62		Captured at Gettysburg July 3, '63; imprisoned and paroled at Fort Delaware at close of war.
Roberts, Jackson	May 10, '62		
Roberts, W. C.	May 10, '62		
Russell, J.	May 10, '62		Wounded at Gettysburg July 3, '63.
Shaw, D. A.	May 10, '62		Died at Leesburg hospital December 2, '62.
Shaw, N. D.	May 10, '62		Killed at Chancellorsville May 4, '63.
Shirley, H. W.	May 10, '62		
Simpson, J. J.	May 10, '62		Killed at Sharpsburg September 17, '62.
Simpson, J. P.	May 10, '62		
Smith, Abner W.	May 10, '62	April 9, '65	Sergeant; transferred May 7, '63 to Smith's Co., 5th Cavalry Battalion.
Spingler, John	May 10, '62		Wounded at Sharpsburg September 17, '62.
Spooner, William	May 10, '62		
Stone, H. S.	May 10, '62		Wounded at Gettysburg July 3, '63.
Strange, B. F.	May 10, '62		
Strickland, Jones	May 10, '62		Died, Lynchburg hospital December 21, '62.
Swicord, S. W.	May 10, '62		
Sylvester, J. H.	May 10, '62		
Taylor, Green B.	May 10, '62		
Taylor, John M.	May 10, '62		Died of dropsy in hospital at Richmond, Va., November 27, '62.
Thomas, W. S.	May 10, '62		Discharged, '62.
Vinson, Josiah	May 10, '62		
Watters, J. P.	May 10, '62		
Wescott, L. R.	May 10, '62		Killed at Sharpsburg.
Wilson, D. C.	May 10, '62		
Wilson, W. W.	May 10, '62	April 9, '65	
Wimberly, E.	May 10, '62		Wounded at the 2nd Manassas.
Woodbury, S. C.	May 10, '62		
Woodward, Edward W.	May 10, '62	April 9, '65	
Wright, B. R.	May 10, '62		Mortally wounded at Sharpsburg September 17, '62.

Roll Company C—8th Florida Infantry.

NAMES.	MUSTERED IN.	MUSTERED OUT.	REMARKS.
OFFICERS.			
Captains—			
David Lang	May 10, '62		Wounded at Fredericksburg December 13, '62; promoted Colonel; and was in command of the Brigade '62, '64 and commander at surrender.
Benjamin F. Whitner	May 15, '62		3rd Lieutenant; promoted Captain, wounded at Chancellorsville May 4, '63.
1st Lieutenants—			
H. R. Hull	May 10, '62		Died at Martinburg September 27, '62.
Craven Lassiter	May 10, '62	April 9, '65	
2nd Lieutenant—			
William J. Oats	May 10, '62	April 9, '65	
3rd Lieutenant—			
Benjamin F. Whitner	May 10, '62	April 9, '65	Wounded at Chancellorsville May 3-4, '63.
ENLISTED MEN			
Adams, James W.	May 10, '62	April 9, '65	
Adams, John Q.	May 10, '62		
Allison, Robert F.			
Amerson, J. T.	May 10, '62	April 9, '65	
Amerson, Redding	May 10 '62		
Amerson, Samuel T.	May 10, '62		Wounded at Chancellorsville May 4, '63; then near Petersburg December 25, '64.
Bass, A. J.	May 14, '62		
Bevan, W. R.		April 9, '65	
Blackman, A.	May 10, '62		
Blackman, Cullen	May 10, '62		Died in camp February 9, '63.
Blackman, Joab	Mch. 10, '62	April 9, '65	Corporal.
Blue, D. McQueen	May 10, '62		Wounded at Gettysburg July 3, '63.
Callahan, William	May 14, '62		
Carraway, Arthur	May 10, '62		Died at Richmond October 20, '62.
Carraway, John H.	May 10, '62		Wounded at Chancellorsville May 4, '63.
Carter, John B.	May 10, '62		
Clements, Henry W.	May 14, '62		
Curle, Elijah	May 10, '62		Wounded at Fredericksburg December 13, '62.
Curry, James	May 14, '62		
Daniels, James E.			

Roll Company C—8th Florida Infantry.

(CONTINUED.)

NAMES.	MUSTERED IN.	MUSTERED OUT.	REMARKS.
Dalrymple, J. D.	May 10, '62	April 9, '65	
Daugherty, Hardy	May 10, '62		Fredericksburg December 13, '62.
Daughtry, Joseph	May 10, '62		
Deese, George W.	May 10, '62	April 9, '65	
Deese, Zacariah	May 10, '62		
Fletcher, Charles	May 10, '62		
Gibbs, James	May 10, '62		
Glisson, John	May 10, '62		
Grant, John H.	May 10, '62	April 9, '65	Wounded at Chancellorsville May 4, '63.
Grantham, B. E.	Mch. 10, '62		Corporal; died in Florida prior to March 1, '63.
Green, Arnold W.	May 10, '62		
Green, Charles H.	May 10, '62		Sergeant; died at Richmond October 30, '62.
Griffin, C. Bryant	May 10, '62		Killed at Sharpsburg September 17, '62.
Hall, John	May 10, '62		
Hamilton, John C.	May 13, '62		
Hatch, Isaac	May 13, '62		Deserted.
Hatch, Joseph	May 13, '62		Deserted.
Hatch, Paul	May 13, '62		Promoted Corporal; wounded at Gettysburg July 3, '63, imprisoned at Fort Delaware.
Hatch, Azra	May 10, '62		
Herrington, Jasper	May 14, '62		
Holdee, Leeread			
Holland, Benjamin	May 10, '62		Died at Front Royal November 21, '63.
Howell, C. W. P.	May 10, '62	April 9, '65	Sergeant.
Haggins, William J.	May 10, '62		Wounded at Chancellorsville May 4, '63.
Hurst, Thomas Y.	May 10, '62	April 9, '65	Shot at the Wilderness, May 6, '63.
Irvins, B. F.		April 9, '65	
Johnson, A. L.	May 15, '62		Promoted 5th Sergeant.
Johnson, John H.			Transferred from Powers' Company to 8th Regiment.
Jones, Abner	May 15, '62		
Jones, Jonas			
Jones, S. C.	May 5, '62		Died at Richmond September 6, '62.
Jones, W. H.	May 15, '62		Died at Richmond August 17, '65.
Jordan, E. W.	May 15, '62		
Jordan, J. F.	May 15, '62		
Kellam, W. W.		April 9, '65	
Lane, L. A.	Mch. 10, '62		Corporal; wounded at Sharpsburg.
Lawson, Lewis	May 10, '62		
McKenzie, Hugh	May 15, '62		
McKenzie, William	May 10, '62		
McNeil, James	May 15, '62		
Mattair, Downing J.	May 10, '62		
Moore, Augustine	May 10, '62		
Nichols, John	May 10, '62		
Oats, Young P.	May 10, '62		Sergeant.
Owens, B. F.	May 11, '62	April 9, '65	Wounded at Orange Court House September 1, '64.
Owen, J. W.	May 10, '62		2nd Sergeant.
Parker, W. T.			Captured and imprisoned at Fort Delaware.
Parnell, James	May 14, '62		
Polk, E. Frank	May 11, '62		Wounded at Chancellorsville May 4, '63.
Ponchier, Joseph	May 15, '62		Wounded at Chancellorsville May 4, '63; captured at Fredericksburg, Md.
Riley, Jasper	May 10, '62		
Roebuck, John R.		April 9, '65	
Sanders, J.			Wounded at Fredericksburg December 13, '62.
Sanders, Thomas R.	May 13, '62		Wounded at Fredericksburg Died December 12,'62.
Sapp, Russell		April 9, '65	
Slaughter, William	May 15, '62		Killed at Gettysburg July 3, '63.
Smith, M. Wesley	May 13, '62		
Stewart, H. G.	May 13, '62	April 9, '65	Corporal.
Sular, H.			Wounded at Gettysburg July 3, '63.
Thompson, Amos	May 10, '62		
Thompson, John H.	May 15, '62	April 9, '65	Promoted Surgeon.
Thompson, William	May 15, '62		
Tillis, James	May 10, '62		
Tillis, Willoughby	May 14, '62		Deserted.
Truett, William	May 10, '62		
Tuten, R. J.	May 15, '62		
Urquhart, I. Capers	May 10, '62		
Walker, Thomas	May 15, '62		
Waters, Emanuel	May 15, '62	April 9, '65	Wounded at Richmond, '64.
Waters, William		April 9, '65	
Ward, Abraham	May 15, '62		Imprisoned at Fort Delaware.
Wood, A. L.		April 9, '65	
Wood, H. M.	May 10, '62		1st Sergeant; wounded at Sharpsburg September 17, '62.
Wood, William H.			1st Sergeant.
			This Company mustered in May 15, '62.

Roll Company D—8th Florida Infantry.

NAMES.	MUSTERED IN.	MUSTERED OUT.	REMARKS.
OFFICERS.			
Captains—			
William Baya	Nov. 18, '61	April 9, '65	Promoted Captain; Major '62, Lieutenant-Colonel June, '63.
J. Anthony Pacetty			1st Lieutenant; promoted Captain, February 17, '63.
1st Lieutenant—			
2nd Lieutenant—			
I. P. Irwin	July '62		
3rd Lieutenant—			
Peter L. Bennett	Aug. '61		Dropped from Army rolls by order of Secretary of War; February 24, '63.
ENLISTED MEN.			
Andrew, Antonio			
Baker, Franklin			Captured and imprisoned at Fort Delaware.
Baker, M. L.	July '62		Wounded at Gettysburg.
Batton, Green	Aug. '61		
Batton, Samuel	Aug. '61		
Baya, H. F.		April 9, '65	
Baya, Joseph F.	Aug. '61	April 9, '65	
Bennett, Casinero	Aug. '61		Killed at Appomatox Court House May, '65.
Blackwilder, Wiley	Aug. '61		
Capella, Mariano			
Capella, Severus	Aug. 18, '61		1st Sergeant.
Capo, Lewis	Aug. '61		
Capo, William	Aug. '61		
Craft, James T	Aug. '61		Promoted Sergeant; wounded at Fredericksburg December 13, '62.
Curl, John	Aug. '61		Captured at Gettysburg ,imprisoned at Fort Delaware.
Dial, Aldrich	Aug. '61		Wounded at Chancellorsville May 4, '63.
Dial, Alexander	Aug. 18, '61		Wounded at Chancellorsville May 3, '63; Gettysburg July 3, '63.
Dial George	Aug. '61		
Dugger, Emanuel	Aug. '61		Killed at Chancellorsville May 4, '63.
Erwin, John A.	Aug. '61		Sergeant; wounded at Gettysburg July 3, '63.
Foster, Godfrey	July '62		Corporal.
Foster, William	July '62		
Gomez, Nichols	July '62		
Gomez, Philip L.	July '61		1st Sergeant; promoted, '62, killed at Chancellorsville May 4, '63.
Gonzales, Augustine	July '61	April 9, '65	Wounded at Gettysburg July 3, '63; captured and imprisoned at Fort Delaware.
Griffis, Berry	July '62		
Griffis, Charles	July '62		
Griffis, Charles B.	July '62		Captured and imprisoned at Fort Delaware, paroled at close of war.
Griffis, John	July '62		
Hamens, Antonio	July '62		
Hanson John M.	July '62		Sergeant; died in prison after battle of Antietam.
Harper, Calvin	July '62		Wounded at Gettysburg July, '63.
Harper, Francis	July '62		Wounded at Gettysburg, '63.
Harper, Jacob	July '62		
Hull, James F.	July '62		
Irving, John A	July '62		Wounded at Gettysburg July 3, '63; died in service.
Lacy, I.	July '62		Sergeant.
Livingston, David	July '62		Promoted Corporal November, '62; wounded at Fredericksburg December 13, '62.
Lopez, Alfonzo	July '62		Killed in service.
Lopez, Andrew M.	Dec. '61		Promoted 2nd Sergeant; shot at Culpepper Court House August 1, '63.
Lopez, A. M.	July '62	April 9, '65	
Lopez, Antonio	July '62		Killed in service.
Lopez, Ignatius			Sergeant.
Lopez, John P.	July '62	April 9, '65	
Lucas, Bartolio	July '62		
McEvin, John	July '62		
McMullen, John		April 9, '65	Courier; wounded at Appomatox.
Masters, B.	July '62		
Masters, Francis	July '62		
Newman, Henry	July '62	April 9, '65	
Othello, C.	July '62		Wounded at Gettysburg July 3, '63.
Pacetty, Bartolo A.	July '62	April 9, '65	
Pacetty, Dennio	July '62		
Pacetty, Edward	July '62		
Pacetty, Felix	July '62	April 9, '65	Corporal.
Padgett, E.	July '62		Wounded at Gettysburg July 3, '63.
Peacock, M.	July '62		
Pelliceo, James	July '62		
Ponce, James B.	July '62		Sergeant.
Powers, James	July '62		
Prior, J.			Wounded at Gettysburg July 3, '63.
Quigley, Owen	July '62		
Quigley, Thomas	July '62		
Quincy, Henry	July '62		
Rante, Felix	July '62		Promoted Corporal; '62, wounded at Chancellorsville; killed at Petersburg, Va., '64.
Rogers, M.	July '62		
Seque, Bartolo	July '62		Corporal.

Roll Company D—8th Florida Infantry.
(CONTINUED.)

NAMES.	MUSTERED IN.	MUSTERED OUT.	REMARKS.
Seque, John	July '62		
Smith, Hardy	July '62		Promoted Corporal.
Smith, Richard C	July '62		
Sparkman, Stephen S	July '62		
Spear, Edward	July '62		
Southwick, S. Decatur	July '62		
Tracy, Pete	July '62		
Triay, Hernatio			Died in prison.
Triay, Victorius	July '62		
Ximanes, Antonio	July '62	April 9, '65	

Roll Company E—8th Florida Infantry.

NAMES.	MUSTERED IN.	MUSTERED OUT.	REMARKS.
OFFICERS.			
Captains—			
Thomas E. Clark	May 13, '62	April 9, '65	Wounded at Fredericksburg December 15,'62; promoted to Major, May, '62.
Francis M. Farley	May 13, '62		Promoted from 1st Lieutenant to Captain, May, '62; resigned, November 2, '63.
Whisley H. DuBose	May 13, '62	April 9, '65	Promoted 1st Lieutenant, then Captain, in '63; from 2nd Lieutenant.
1st Lieutenant—			
Thomas S. Armistead	May 13, '62	June 17, '65	Promoted from 1st Sergeant to 3rd Lieutenant, May, '62; 2nd Lieutenant, '63 and 1st Lieutenant in '64; wounded at Chancellorsville May 4, '63 '64 and captured, imprisoned at Fort Delaware.
2nd Lieutenants—			
Anthony Armistead	May 13, '62		Promoted 2nd Lieutenant from 3rd Lieutenant; killed at Sharpsburg September 17, '62.
James M. Cumbaa	May 13, '62	April 9, '65	Promoted 2nd Lieutenant from Corporal; 2nd Sergeant, 1st Sergeant, and 3rd Lieutenant.
3rd Lieutenant—			
W. W. Wilson	May 13, '62		Promoted 3rd Lieutenant; wounded at Gettysburg July 3, '63.
ENLISTED MEN.			
Allen, Jas. M			
Allen, J. T			..
Arnold, William			
Ayers, Jesse W			
Bailey, Jesse W			Captured and imprisoned at Fort Delaware.
Bailey, Samuel D			Killed at Chancellorsville May 4, '63.
Barcley, Oscar J			
Barcley, William C			
Barnes, George W			Wounded at Bristow Station October 15, '63.
Barnes, Thomas J			
D Gainney			Killed at Sharpsburg.
Bell, Greenberry			
Bevis, James P			
Bevis, Martin L			Captured and imprisoned at Fort Delaware.
Boyett, Josiah D			
Britton, Francis G			Killed at Sharpsburg September 17, '62.
Brock, Wesley A			
Brogden, Jesse		April 9, '65	From prison at close of war.
Brown, Edward G	May 13, '62	April 9, '65	Wounded at Sharpsburg September 17, '62.
Bush, B			
Cannon, Samuel D	May 13, '62		
Cason, Henry C	May 13, '62		
Cawthron, Hosia B	May 13, '62	April 9, '65	
Cox, Henry			
Cox, Jesse	May 13, '62		Left at Tallahassee by order of General Finnegan.
Crawford, Lewis W	May 13, '62		Killed at Fredericksburg December 13, '62.
Crawford, W. F	May 13, '62		
Croom, John J	May 13, '62		Wounded at Gettysburg July 3, '63; imprisoned at Fort Delaware.
Croom, William F	May 13, '62		Taken prisoner in Maryland.
Cumbaa, Perceval	May 13, '62	April 9, '65	Promoted 1st Lieutenant; captured at Gettysburg and imprisoned at Fort Delaware until close of war.
Daniels, William J	May 13, '62		Killed at Sharpsburg September 17, '62.
Davis, J. L. B	May 13, '62		
Drummond, Eugenius E	May 13, '62		1st Sergeant, October 1, '62; killed at Chancellorsville May 4, '63.
Dykes, Henry G	May 13, '62		Lost right arm at Hatcher's Run February 5, '65.
Falkner, John	May 13, '62		
Fields, John C			Corporal; transferred to Navy at Wilmington February 27, '62.
Green William	May 13, '62		

Roll Company E—8th Florida Infantry.
(CONTINUED.)

NAMES.	MUSTERED IN.	MUSTERED OUT.	REMARKS.
Hair, William	May 13, '62		Wounded at Chancellorsville May 4, '63.
Harrell, G. William	May 13, '62	April 9, '65	
Harrell, Isaac B.	May 13, '62		
Henderson, John B.	May 13, '62		Absent without leave October 31, '62.
Hewitt, Benjamin N.	May 13, '62		
Hewitt, John M.	May 13, '62		Deserted.
Hewitt, James N.	May 13, '62		Deserted.
Hill, John W.	May 13, '62		Died in hospital at Richmond, '63.
Howard, Allen	May 13, '62		
Jenkins, Moses	May 13, '62		Died at Mount Jackson hospital November 2, '62.
Jenkins, Wilbur F.			
Johnson, Joshua S.	May 13, '62		Promoted Corporal; killed near Petersburg.
Kidd, Robert	May 13, '62		Corporal, promoted Sergeant; deserted, applied for, and took the oath of allegiance while imprisoned at Fort Delaware; captured at Gettysburg July 3, '63.
Killgore, Andrew J.	May 13, '62		Corporal; killed at Gettysburg July 3, '63.
King, Angus	May 13, '62		
King, Daniel	May 13, '62		Died in hospital at Richmond.
Knowles, Henry S.	May 13, '62		Wounded at Sharpsburg September 17, '62.
Knowles, William K.	May 13, '62		
Lassiter, Luke W.	May 13, '62		
Lewis, Mathews W.	May 13, '62		Killed at Fredericksburg December 15, '62.
Lloyde, Andrew J.	May 13, '62		Died in camp December 11, '62.
Long, Aaron	May 13, '62		Discharged at Montgomery White Sulphur Springs for disability.
Lovelace, W. S.			Wounded at Fredericksburg December 13, '62.
McNeily, George W.	May 13, '62		Wounded at Sharpsburg.
McNeily, Isaac W.	May 13, '62		
McNeily, Sidney	May 13, '62		....
McNeily, Sidney	May 13, '62		
Maloy, John E.			
Manetoly, James M.			
Maultsby, Joseph M.	May 13, '62	April 9, '65	Wounded at Amelia Court House, captured 2 or 3 days before surrender.
Morris, Sidney	May 13, '62		Absent without leave October 31, '62.
Neely, J. T.		April 9, '65	
Nichols, Richard R.	May 13, '62		
Padgett, Alfred	May 13, '62		
Padgett, Ellis	May 13, '62		
Pickney, Thomas W.	May 13, '62		
Pitts, Riley			
Pitts, William G.	May 13, '62		
Pittman, John D.			2nd Sergeant; killed at the 2nd battle of Manassas August 3, '62.
Pledger, C. B.	May 13, '62		Corporal, August, '62; wounded at Gettysburg July 3, '63; captured and sent to hospital at Baltimore, paroled August 22, '63 and returned to Petersburg where he was furloughed and discharged.
Porter, Ellsworth E.	May 13, '62		Died in hospital at Richmond January 25, '63.
Porter, William R.	May 13, '62		Wounded at Battle of Wilderness May 6, '64
Redd, William J.			Corporal; reduced to ranks.
Roebuck, William T.	May 13, '62		Wounded at Gettysburg July 3, '63.
Savage, F. E.			
Sharritt, James H.	May 13, '62	April 9, '65	
Sharritt, Josiah L.	May 13, '62	April 9, '65	Corporal; promoted 2nd and 1st Sergeant.
Slagner, D. W.			
Smith, George W.		April 9, '65	Absent without leave February 28, '63.
Smith, James H.			
Snellings, James W.			Corporal.
Stayner, Daniel W.	May 13, '62		Deserted.
Stephens, Halcombe	May 13, '62		
Stephens, Philip	May 13, '62		
Stewart, Charles G.	May 13, '62		
Still, Thomas L.			Wounded at Richmond July 2, '63 and discharged.
Stone, Henry S.	May 13, '62		
Suails, Pleasant			Wounded at Fredericksburg December 11, '62.
Suails, William T.			Killed at Chancellorsville May 4, '63.
Taylor, Charles	May 13, '62		Wounded at Manassas August 30, '62.
Thorpe, Samuel	May 13, '62	April 9, '65	Wounded at Gettysburg July 3, '63.
Tucker, E. D.			
Turner, Isaac J.	May 13, '62		
Vickery, F. H.			
Vickery, William C.	May 13, '62	April 9, '65	Wounded at Sharpsburg September 17, '62; at Bristow Station October 15, '63.
Wachob, Arthur Mc.	May 13, '62		Died at Tallahassee.
Wachob, Francis M.	May 13, '62		Died in hospital near Fredericksburg.
Wachob, Joseph F.	May 13, '62	April 9, '65	Wounded at Culpepper Court House August 1, '63.
Waldon, Joseph	May 16, '62	April 9, '65	Captured and imprisoned at Fort Delaware.
Waldon, Samuel P.	May 16, '62	April	Captured at Gettysburg July 2, '63; soon paroled.
Ward, John			Deserted near camp at Fredericksburg February '62.
West, Joel		April 9, '65	Wounded at Gettysburg July 3, '63.

Roll Company E—8th Florida Infantry.
(CONTINUED.)

NAMES.	MUSTERED IN.	MUSTERED OUT.	REMARKS.
West, Theodore			Sergeant.
Whittle, Seaborn W			Left sick at Richmond August 9, '63; not since heard from.
Wilkerson, James			
Wilson, George W. S	May 13, '62		
Williams, Irwin	May 13, '62		Wounded at Chancellorsville May 4, '63.

Roll Company F—8th Florida Infantry.

NAMES.	MUSTERED IN.	MUSTERED OUT.	REMARKS.
OFFICERS.			
Captains—			
Felix Simmons	May 17, '62		Resigned, on account of age.
H. C. Simmons	May 17, '62		Promoted from 2nd Lieutenant to Captain; February 17, '63.
1st Lieutenant—			
Marshall, B. Holland	May 17, '62		
2nd Lieutenant—			
3rd Lieutenant—			
Warren, W. Andrews	May 17, '62		Promoted 3rd Lieutenant; resigned June 10, '63.
ENLISTED MEN.			
Acosta, A. J	May 17, '62		Promoted Sergeant.
Aldrick, Whipple	May 17, '62		
Anderson, M	May 17, '62		
Andrews, William O			Left in Tallahassee.
Arrow, Henry H	May 17, '62		
Barnhill, W. C	May 17, '62		Died in hospital October 20, '62.
Birdlong, Alfred	May 17, '62		Died in Augusta, Ga.
Bryant, F. M	May 17, '62		Promoted Sergeant.
Campos, Joseph E	May 17, '62		Wounded at Fredericksburg December 13, '62; Bristow Station October 15, '63.
Chambers, Charles J	May 17, '62		
Chambers, John R			
Conner, George	May 17, '62		
Chambers, William J	May 17, '65		Wounded at Chancellorsville May 4, '63.
Conner, George	May 17, '62	Nov. 15, '62	
Crews, W			Wounded at Gettysburg July 3, '63; captured and imprisoned at Fort Delaware.
Cross, Seaborn	May 17, '62		
Daley, John	May 17, '62		
Darrah, Charles	May 17, '62		Deserted July 22, '62.
Decotts, Edward A	May 17, '62		Killed at Sharpsburg September 17, '62.
Dorman, John	May 17, '62		
Dowling, John D	May 17, '62		Paroled from prison, close of war.
Duncan, George	May 17, '62		
Ellis, T. B			
Ellison, John A			
Freeman, J. W	May 17, '62		Died at Charlottsville and buried in the Cemetery of the University of Virginia.
Frier, Samuel H			
Griffin, J. R	May 17, '62	April 9, '65	
Handley, Alexander	May 17, '62		Deserted December 11, '62.
Haselden, Samuel J	May 17, '62		
Haselman, Theodore	May 17, '62		Captured in Maryland.
Hardee, Thomas E	May 17, '82		Transferred to Cavalry, killed near Pensacola, Fla., Partridge's Cavalry; 15th Confederate.
Hawkins, Thomas D	May 17, '62		Hospital Steward.
Hinton, John			
Hopkins, Charles	May 17, '62		
Hunter, Jeremiah M	May 17, '62		
Hunter, John L	May 17, '62		
Hunter, L. L			Killed at Bristow Station October 14, '63.
Jeffords, A. H	May 17, '62		
Kaul, Benjamin H	May 17, '62		
Kernan, John	May 17, '62		
Kernan, Thomas J	May 17, '62		
Knight, William	May 17, '62		Left in Tallahassee.
Latham, George A	May 17, '62	April 9, '65	
Lewis, G. S	May 17, '62		
Lewis, John W			
Long, James	May 17, '62		Corporal; wounded at Chancellorsville May 3, '63.
Lucas, Henry	May 17, '62		Deserted.
Lyons, James			Corporal.
McKiver, James	May 17, '62		
McLeod, Columbus	May 17, '62		
McTeer, Barnard			1st Sergeant; killed at Chancellorsville May 4, '63.
Marion, John	May 17, '62		
Mason, Folen	May 17, '62		
Mathews, Solomon	May 17, '82		
Mora, Joseph	May 17, '62		Deserted July 16, '62.
Newman, William			Transferred to Company F from Company H.
O'Mally, John	May 17, '62		

Roll Company F—8th Florida Infantry.
(CONTINUED.)

NAMES.	MUSTERED IN.	MUSTERED OUT.	REMARKS.
Ormand, Arthur W	May 17, '62		
Pelion, Pablo	May 17, '62		Deserted July 16, '62.
Pirtle, R. S	May 17, '62		
Polk, James H	May 17, '62		Died November 30, '62.
Prevat, James W	May 17, '62		Corporal.
Quinn, Willam W	May 17, '62		
Roberts, D. B	May 17, '62		Sergeant.
Rose, Michæl	May 17, '62	Aug. 29, '62	Corporal.
Rowe, John			Killed at Gettysburg July 3, '62,
Samis, Francis	May 17, '62		
Samis, Thomas			
Sheffield, Samuel	Oct. 5, '61		
Simmons, George M. T	May 17, '62		
Smith, Mitchel	May 17, '62		
Snowball, J. A. L	May 17, '62		
Strickland, Cornelius	May 17, '62		
Syms, Charles	May 17, '62		
Taylor, David L	May 17, '62		
Temple, William C	May 17, '62		Absent without leave.
Thigpen, James C	May 17, '62		
Thigpen, William			Died June 22, '62.
Tidwell, Benjamin F	May 17, '62		
Tompkins, Donald	May 17, '62		
Tompkins, John W	May 17, '62		Captured from Maryland.
Turner, Riley	May 17, '62		Died in hospital at Winchester October 21, '62.
Walsh, John	May 17, '62		
Ward, William	May 17, '62		
Welsh, T			Wounded at Fredericksburg December 13, '62.
Wilds, George B	May 17, '62		
Wilds, John W			Wounded, died January 15, '63 at Charlottsville and buried in the Cemetery of the University of Va.
Wilkerson, James M	May 17, '62		
Wilkinson, John W	May 17,³ '62		Left in Thomasville, Ga.
Williams, Elias	May 17, '62		Wounded at Gettysburg July 3, '63 and captured and imprisoned at Fort Delaware.
Wingate, Cornelius	May 17, '62		Discharged for wounds received at Chancellorsville May 3, '63.
Wingate, John A	May 17, '62		Sergeant; wounded at Gettysburg July 3, '63; died in hospital August 1, '63.
Wingate, O. L	May 17, '62		1st Sergeant; died November 9, '62.
Youn, Samson	May 17, '62		

Roll Company G—8th Florida Infantry.

NAMES.	MUSTERED IN.	MUSTERED OUT.	REMARKS.
OFFICERS.			
Captains—			
J. C. Stewart			
Joshua Mizell			Promoted from 1st Lieutenant to Captain; wounded at Gettysburg, captured and imprisoned on Johnson's Island, Ohio; and died in prison April 17, '64; grave No. 168.
1st Lieutenant—			
2nd Lieutenants—			
James K. Stewart			
E. J. Hull			Resigned April 10, '63.
W. W. Wilson			Promoted 2nd Lieutenant.
3rd Lieutenant—			
Richard Stewart			
ENLISTED MEN.			
A , James A			Deserted July 25, '62.
Alderman, David			
Ballard, Wiley C			Deserted December 11, '62.
Barnhart, William R			
Barton, James W			
Bennett, Simmons			
Bradford, Hampton			
Brantly, W. M			
Brian, William P			Wounded at Fredericksburg December 13, '62.
Buchan, Joseph D			
Cardle, Alvin M			Sergeant.
Cannon, James			Deserted July 15, '62.
Carthus, J. H			
Carthus, Nathan R			
Carlisle, Jœl N			
Carlisle, L. L. J	May 11, '62		Deserted May 11, '62.
Caruthers, W. R			Wounded at Fredericksburg December 13, '62.
Clarke, Joseph J			

Roll Company G—8th Florida Infantry.
(CONTINUED.)

NAMES	MUSTERED IN.	MUSTERED OUT.	REMARKS.
Collins, George W			
Cox, W. G			Wounded at Gettysburg July 3, '63.
Dann, Howard L			
Delk, William P			Died at Tallahassee July 15, '62.
Drawdy, William J			Died December 16, '62.
Driggers, Edward		July 13, '62	Disability.
Driggers, William F			Died at Richmond hospital.
Ellis, L. J			Killed at the battle of Manassas August, '62.
Galloway, Thomas M			Killed at Gettysburg July 3, '62.
Greegs, John G			
Hall, Isaiah			Deserted.
Hall, William B			imprisoned at Fort Delaware.
Hardee, James C			Wounded at Chancellorsville May 4, '63.
Harris, John			Deserted June 4, '62.
Hartley, Daniel			
Hawthorn, K			Died at Lake City July 20, '62.
Hobbs, W. P			
Hodges, John R			
Hodges, Samuel			
Holland, N. W			Transferred to Company ''G'' from Company ''F'' October 29, '62.
Hooker, James W			Wounded mortally at Fredericksburg December 13, '62; died December 20, '62.
Hooker, S. J. L			
Hooker, W. P			Captured and imprisoned at Fort Delaware; paroled from there at close of war.
Hooker, William J			
Hubbard, John D			
Hull, William B			Wounded at Chancellorsville May 4, '63.
Jackson, Ben F			Sergeant; wounded at Chancellorsville May 3, '63; lost some teeth by explosion of shell.
Jerkins, Richard F			Sergeant.
Joiner, Thomas J		Oct. 18, '62	Discharged for disability.
Kilgore, William C. G			Captured April 6, '65; imprisoned at Point Lookout, until June, '65.
Kirkland, R. L			
Lancaster, Oliver P			Corporal.
Lippman, S. D			
Long, Reuben			Wounded at Sharpsburg, Md., Sept. 17, '62
Luffman, Shad			Deserted July 15, '62.
Luffman, Disney			Deserted July 15, '62.
McKinnie, James W			By parole, close of war.
Mercer, William			
Miller, Benjamin W			Died December 16, '62.
Miller, Thomas			Died January 30, '63.
Mizell, David W		Jan. 14, '63	Corporal.
Mizell, Morgan M			Paroled, close of war.
Nelson, Joseph			
Newberry, Hiram J	June 1, '61		Deserted July 15, '62.
Nichols, Richard G			
Oberry, Wesley C			
Pillan, Richard			
Prescott, Robert			Deserted Ju.y 15, '65.
Richards, James R			
Robinson, Charles A			Wounded at Sharpsburg, Md., September 17, '62.
Robinson, Henry			Promoted Sergeant; October 1, '62.
Rogers, Middleton D			Transferred to Watson's Cavalry in Fla., paroled.
Savage, James W		Aug. 12, '62	Disability.
Savage, Richard B			
Savage, Robert B			Deserted.
Savage, Thomas E			
Simon, G. F			Wounded at Gettysburg July 3, '63.
Simmons, George W			
Simmons, Philip M			Sergeant; deserted July 15, '62.
Simmons, W. R			
Smith, K. D			Discharged from hospital for disability.
Sowell, Thomas J			Died in Maryland.
Stephens, William			Deserted July 15, '62.
Stewart, Asa A			Deserted.
Stewart, David B			
Stewart, John J			Paroled, close of war.
Stewart, John W			Died in Tallahassee July 30, '62.
Stewart, Philinan B			
Stewart, T. A			Paroled, close of war.
Story, Reed			Deserted July 15, '62.
Swan, David H			Promoted Sergeant; killed at Fredricksburg December 13, '62.
Tanner, Mathew			
Trapwell, William W			
Tucker, E. D			
Tuner, David			
Turner, Robert			1st Sergeant; imprisoned at Fort Delaware
Unchurch, C			
Wheeler, Charles M			
Wiggins, E. W			Wounded at Gettysburg July 3, '63
Wilson, Henry			
Williams, Thomas M			
Wright, Selestin C			Missing at battle of Fredericksburg.

Roll Company H—8th Florida Infantry.

NAMES.	MUSTERED IN.	MUSTERED OUT.	REMARKS.
OFFICERS.			
Captains—			
James Tucker	April 12, '62		Resigned September 3, '62.
Zacheus Shepard	April 12, '62		1st Lieutenant, promoted Captain, September 29, '62; resigned January 24, '63; wounded at Fredericksburg December 13, '62.
T. B. Livingston	April 12, '62		Promoted Captain from 2nd and 3rd Lieutenant; wounded at Gettysburg, captured and paroled at close of war.
1st Lieutenants—			
William Scott		April 9, '65	Promoted 1st Lieutenant.
Donald T. Livingston	April 12, '62		Promoted 1st Lieutenant; September 27, '62. from 2nd Lieutenant.
2nd Lieutenant—			
J. M. Bryant			
3rd Lieutenant—			
William P. Pigman			1st Lieutenant; promoted 3rd Lieutenant, September 30, ''62.
ENLISTED MEN.			
Adams, J. B.			
Adkins, James L	June '62		
Allen, Robert		April 9, '65	Promoted 1st Sergeant; October 1, '62.
Alderman, David G	April 12, '62		Promoted Corporal.
Arnow, Henry H	Oct. 5, '61		Transferred from Company ''F'', October 1, '62; promoted Sergeant October 15, '62.
Barber, George W			
Barrons, James J	April 12, '62		Wounded at Petersburg, Va., August 21, '64.
Barrons, Robert	April 12, '62		
Barrington, Milton	April 12, '62		Promoted Sergeant.
Barrington, Walter J			Sergeant; wounded at Fredericksburg December 13, '62.
Bassett, Andrew J. D	April 12, '62		
Bell, Abram	May '62		Discharged for disability.
Bell, Patrick, R.			
Bevan, William R	April 12, '62	April 9, '65	
Blanton, D. T.			
Boyet, Edward J	April 12, '62		
Boyd, M.			
Bowen, Henry D	May '62		
Brown, James A. M	June 24, '62	April 9, '65	
Brown T.			Wounded at Fredericksburg December 13, '62.
Bryan, D. S.			
Bryan, P. N.		April 9, '65	
Burroughs, Cornelius T	April 12, '62		Corporal; promoted Sergeant.
Byrd, A. J.	April 12, '62		Corporal.
Byrd, Evander	June 1, '62		Shot at Sharpsburg, Md., September 18, '62.
Clark, W. B.			
Clayton, Milledge G	April 12, '62	April 9, '65	Corporal.
Corbin, William	May 17, '62		Deserted.
Curl, Jesse			
Davenport, James A	April 12, '62		
Deese, James	April 12, '62		Transferred from Company ''I.''
Deese, John M			
Deas, Samuel M	April 12, '62		Corporal; lost left arm at Chancellorsville, Va. May 3, '63.
Deas, T. M.			Wounded at Fredericksburg December 13, '62.
Dice, H.			Wounded at Gettysburg July 3, '63.
Eddison, T.			Wounded at Fredericksburg December 13, '62.
Ellison, James	May 7, '62		Transferred from Company ''I;'' wounded at Fredericksburg ,Va., December 13, '62.
Ellison, John L	May 5, '62		Transferred from Company ''I;'' discharged July 15, '62.
Fort, Elias N	Apr l 12, '62		Sergeant.
Fletcher, C. N.		Apr l 9, '65	
Fletcher, W.		April 9, '65	
Glover, Alfred J	April 12, '62		Discharged January 12, '63.
Gill, Joseph			
Green, John	April 12, '62		
Hagen, Urban			
Hall, Elisha		Apr l 9, '65	
Hall, N. S.		Apr l 9, '65	
Hammond, Elias	May 28, '62		Transferred from Company ''I.''
Hammond, Seymore	May 15, '62		
High, Henry	Apr l 12, '62		Wounded at Fredericksburg December 13, '62.
Holland, William W	June 7, '62		
Horn, William J	May 20, '62		
Hurst, T. T.		April 9, '65	
Hyers, Philip L	June 20, '62	April 9, '65	
Hysler, William	Mch. '62		Transferred from Company ''I.''
Irvin, John H	April 12, '62		
Irving, Washington L	April 12, '62		
Ivey, Jasper N	April 12, '62		
Ivey, Robert A	April 12, '62		Discharged February 26, '63.
Jarrell or Gerrold, Samuel	June 1, '62		Deserted.
Jenkins, Thomas G	April 12, '62		Sergeant.
Jordan, Thomas L.			Musician.
Johnson, Benjamin J	April 12, '62		

Roll Company H—8th Florida Infantry.
(Continued.)

NAMES.	MUSTERED IN.	MUSTERED OUT.	REMARKS.
Jowers, Calvin I.	April 12, '62		Wounded at Chancellorsville May 4, '63.
Kelly, W lliam M.	July 1, '63	April 9, '65	
Keen, David.			Killed at Weldon R. R., Va., August 22, '64.
Lomerick, James.			
Lomerick, George.			
Langford, James J.			
Langford, John B.	May '62		
Lee, Charles.	April 12, '62		
Lee, George H.	April 12, '62		Died at Richmond, Va., August 15, '62.
Lee, Levi.	April 12, '62		Discharged October 7, '62 for disability.
Lee, William.	Apr l 12, '62		
McLeod, John J.			Promoted Corporal.
May, Daniel.			
Mills, William.	April 12, '62		Killed at Chancellorsville May 4, '63.
Milton, James.			
Mimms, James.			
Moat, Isaac N.			
Moseley, Alexander.	April 12, '62		
Nail, Joseph R.	April 12, '62		Sergeant.
Newborn, William.	May 12, '62		Transferred from Company "I."
Newman, William.	May 10, '62		Transferred from Company "F," Sept. 30, '63.
Nicholson. James.	April 12, '62		
Nicholson, Robert W.	April 12, '62		
Nicholson, Sylvester.	April 12, '62		
Overstreet, William R.			Died in prison at Fort Delaware, '63.
Parramore, Isaac B.	April 12, '62		Corporal.
Pigman, Charles.	April 12, '62		Musician; discharged December 19, '62.
Rawlins, Daniel.	April 12, '62		
Rimes, David A.		April 9, '65	
Roberts, Jackson.	April 12, '62		
Roberts, John J.	June '62		Discharged for disability.
Robinson, William.	April 12, '62		
Sanders, Ashford G.	May '62		
Sanders, George.			
Saunders, W. M.		April 9, '65	
Sawyers, Demsey.			Discharged for disability.
Simmons, T. F.		April 9, '65	
Smith, James D.			
Smith, John F.			
Smith, Robert B.	April 12, '62		
Snyder, John B.	April 12, '62		
Spires, Richard.	April 12, '62		
Stanaland, T. B.	Aug. 15, '63	May 10, '65	Wounded at Hanover Junction, Va., May 15 '63.
Stanford, Eli.	April 12, '62	April 9, '65	
Suggs, Elijah.	May '62		
Townsend, James E.	May '62	April 9, '65	Wounded at Fredericksburg December 13, '62.
Wester, Samuel S.	April 12, '62		
West, James M.	April 12, '62		
White, Stephen K.	April 12, '62		Killed at Sharpsburg September 19, '6 .
Young, Adam.	June '62		Wounded at Chancellorsville May 4, '63.
Young, Dan G.	June '62		Sergeant.

Roll Company I—8th Florida Infantry.

NAMES.	MUSTERED IN.	MUSTERED OUT.	REMARKS.
OFFICERS.			
Captains—			
John M. Pons.	May 14, '62		
Benjamin F. Roberts.	May 14, '62		1st Lieutenant; promoted Captain.
1st Lieutenant—			
John Thomas.	May 14, '62		2nd Lieutenant; promoted 1st Lieutenant.
2nd Lieutenants—			
Elias G. Jaudon.	May 14, '62		
Julian J. Acosta.	May 14, '62	April 9, '65	Promoted 2nd Lieutenant; wounded at Fredericksburg December 13, '62.
3rd Lieutenant—			
ENLISTED MEN.			
Acosta, Arcadio.	May 14, '62		Discharged July 6, '62, for disability.
Acosta, Joseph E.	May 14, '62		
Adams, George W.	May 14, '62		Deserted July 26, '62.
Adkerson, Woodman.	May 14, '62		
Andrew, Jerome C.	May 14, '62		Musician.
Andrew, Thomas.	May 14, '62		Sergeant.
Barbee, Joseph A.	May 14, '62		Deserted at Augusta, Ga., July 23, '62.
Barber, Isaac.	May 14, '62		Imprisoned at Fort Delaware.
Barton, John.	May 14, '62		
Bearden, John.	May 14, '62		Left sick near Harper's Ferry.

Roll Company I—8th Florida Infantry.

(CONTINUED.)

NAMES.	MUSTERED IN.	MUSTERED OUT.	REMARKS.
Bennett, Elias R.	May 14, '62		Killed at Sharpsburg September 17, '62.
Bennett, John G.	May 14, '62		Deserted July 23, '62.
Bennett, Wiley	May 14, '62		Shot at the Wilderness; on furlough when war closed.
Bennett, William	May 14, '62		
Bird, Melican	May 14, '62		Deserted July 14, at Camp Leon.
Bird, William	May 14, '62		
Black, William	May 14, '62		
Braddock, William G.	May 14, '62		Sergeant.
Broadnax, T.	May 14, '62		
Brodnax, William H.	May 14, '62		Killed at Fredericksburg Decembtr 11, '62.
Bryan, H.	May 14, '62		Wounded at Gettysburg July 3, '63.
Buckles, John	May 14, '62		Wounded at Chancellorsville May 3, '63; also at Richmond and died of wounds received December, '64.
Burnsed, Gideon	May 14, '62		
Burnsed, John E.			Died in hospital Nov. 5, '62.
Campbell, Henry F.	May 14, '62	April 9, '65	
Campbell, Wesley	May 14, '62		Wounded at Bristow Station October 14, '63.
Canova, Bartolo	May 14, '62		
Carter, Darling	May 14, '62		
Carter, E. C.	May 14, '62		
Carter, George W. H.	May 14, '62		Deserted at Camp Leon July 20, '62.
Carter, Jesse H.	May 14, '62		
Cary, W. H.	May 14, '62		
Cox, Hatch	May 14, '62		
Craroty, Levy	May 14, '62		Died in Fort Delaware prison, '63.
Crews, C.	May 14, '62		Killed at Gettysburg July 3, '63.
Crews, Samuel	May 14, '62		Deserted July 13, '62.
Crews, William P.	May 14, '62		Died November, '62.
Curry, Moses	May 14, '62		Discharged October 1, '62 for disability.
Curry, William	May 14, '62		
Danford, Isaac	May 14, '62		Wounded at Sharpsburg, Pa., September 17, '62.
Davis, George	May 14, '62		Killed at Sharpsburg September 17, '62.
Davis, John G.	May 14, '62		
Deese, James	May 14, '62		
Deese, John H.	May 14, '62		Discharged October 1, '62 for disability.
Deloche, Edmund	May 14, '62		
Dibble, Charles H.	May 14, '62		
Dixon, J. J.	May 14, '62		
Doile, F. William	May 14, '62		Sergeant.
Doggett, S. F.	May 14, '62		1st Sergeant.
Doggett, Forbes I.	May 14, '62		Corporal.
Doyle, David W.	May 14, '62		
Drawty, Levy	May 14, '62		
Ellison, James	May 14, '62		
Ellison, John L.	May 14, '62		
Fitzgerald, James	May 14, '62		Musician; killed at Fredericksburg December 17, '62.
Fitzpatrick, Patrick	May 14, '62		
Fitzpatrick, William	May 14, '62		
Flinn, George B.	May 14, '62		Wounded at Sharpsburg September 17, '62.
French, Edwin	May 14, '62		
Gardner, Alfred	May 14, '62		
Gardner, George	May 14, '62		
Garrold, J.	May 14, '62	April 9, '65	Wounded at Fredericksburg December 13, '62.
Goreka, Henry	May 14, '62		
Gillen, William	May 14, '62		
Green, Salathiel	May 14, '62		Deserted at Camp Leon July 17, '62.
Griffiths, Juniper	May 14, '62		Deserted at Camp Leon July 14, '62.
Hammonds, Elias	May 14, '62		
Hammonds, Seymour	May 14, '62		
Hammond, William R.	May 14, '62		
Harrison, Jonah G.	May 14, '62		Discharged October 28, '62 for disability.
Harrison, Josiah E.	May 14, '62		
Harris, John N.	May 14, '62		Corporal; wounded at Sharpsburg September 17, '62.
Harris, Richard	May 14, '62		
Heisler, William	May 14, '62		
Hendrick, William H.	May 14, '62		
Herndon, John R.	May 14, '62	April 9, '65	
Hernandez, Joseph	May 14, '62		Deserted at Camp Hunt May 19, '62.
Hicks, Bryant	May 14, '62		Wounded at Gettysburg July 2, '63.
Hicks, Robert C.	May 14, '62		Wounded at Chancellorsville May 4, '63.
Hinn, G. B.	May 14, '62		Wounded at Fredericksburg December 13, '62.
Hogans, Reuben	May 14, '62		
Hoggins, John	May 14, '62		
Hoggans, Robert	May 14, '62		
Holmes, Alexander	May 14, '62		
Johnson, F'ancis A.	May 14, '62		Promoted Chaplain; died at Richmond, Va., March 29, '63.
Kennedy, Francis M.	May 14, '62		Wounded at Chancellorsville May 4, '63.
King, Charles	May 14, '62		Deserted March 16, '62 at St. John's Bluff.
Kirby, William A.	May 14, '62		
Lacourse, Joseph	May 14, '62		
Laurimore, Richard M.	May 14, '62		Died at hospital September 1, '62.
Laurimore, Robert O.	May 14, '62		
Lawerence, F. M.	May 14, '62		

Roll Company I—8th Florida Infantry.
(CONTINUED.)

NAMES.	MUSTERED IN.	MUSTERED OUT.	REMARKS.
Lawerence, J.	May 14, '62		Captured at Gettysburg, imprisoned at Fort Delaware.
Lay, James	May 14, '62		
Lowe, Archibald	May 14, '62		Deserted July 19, '62.
McCormick, Aaron T.	May 14, '62		
McCormick, W. B.	May 14, '62		
Marcus, B.	May 14, '62		
Murray, Archibald	May 14, '62		Killed at Sharpsburg September 17, '62.
Murray, John	May 14, '62		Wounded at Sharpsburg September 17, '62.
Newborn, William	May 14, '62		
Newmans, John	May 13, '62		Deserted at Camp Leon July 14, '62.
Newmans, William A.	May 14, '62		
Oliver, William	May 14, '62		
O'Neil, Henry	May 14, '62		
Osteen, Richard	May 14, '62		Corporal.
Osteen, Riley	May 14, '62		Wounded at Gettysburg July 3 '63.
Othello, Charles	May 14, '62		
Padgett, Daniel	May 14, '62		Deserted July 14, '62.
Padgett, William	May 14, '62		Discharged at Tallahassee August 10, '62 for disability.
Parker, Daniel I.	May 14, '62		
Parish, Hiram	May 14, '62		Wounded at Gettysburg July 3, '63.
Peterson, Archibald	May 14, '62	April 9, 65	
Peterson, John	May 14, '62		
Petty, George A.	May 14, '62		
Philips, Robert	May 14, '62		
Pifer, Joseph H.	May 14, '62		Deserted March 16, at St. John's Bluff and went to the Yankees.
Plummer, James Alexander	May 14, '62		Killed near Richmond, Va., May 29, '64.
Prescott, John H.	May 14, '62		Wounded at Chancellorsville and disabled.
Raulerson, William	May 14, '62		Wounded at Bristow Station October 14, '6°
Rhoden, Henry H.	May 14, '62		Deserted July 14, '62.
Rhoden, Isham J.	May 14, '62		Imprisoned at Fort Delaware.
Rhoden, James T.	May 14, '62		Deserted July 14, '62.
Rhoden, John A. J.	May 14, '62		Deserted July 14, '62.
Rhoden, John H.	May 14, '62		
Rhoden, Levi J.	May 14, '62		Wounded at Sharpsburg September 17, '62
Roberts, Andrew J.	May 14, '62	April 9, '65	Wounded at Antietam, Md., September 17, '62.
Roberts, Conner	May 14, '62		Wounded at Sharpsburg September 13, '62, also at Fredricksburg, Va., December 13, '62.
Roberts, Cornelius	May 14, '62	April 9, 65	
Roberts Isaiah	May 14 '62	April 9, '65	Wounded at Sharpsburg September 17, '62.
Roberts, Joseph Garrett	May 14, '62		Discharged October 4, '62, for disability.
Roberts, Josiah	May 14, '62	April 9, '65	Wounded at Sharpsburg, Md., September 17, '62.
Roberts, Ulysses M.	May 14, '62		Sergeant.
Robertson, Stephen I.	May 14, '62		Deserted at Camp Leon July 14, '62.
Robinson, William	May 14, '62	Apr 1 9, '65	Shot at Bristow Station, Va., August 20, '63.
Russell, John	May 14, '62		Wounded at Chancellorsville May 3, '63
Russell, William	May 14, '62		
Sanger, Henry C.	May 14, '62		Musician.
Scott, Edward	May 14, '62		
Silcox, Isaac	May 14, '62		Wounded at Chancellorsville May 3, '63; captured and imprisoned at Fort Delaware.
S lcox, Wade	May 14, '62	Apr 1 9, '65	Wounded at Chancellorsville, Va., May 3, '63; promoted Corporal.
Sparkman, Alfred	May 14, '62		Captured and imprisoned at Fort Delaware.
Sparkman, Luke	May 14, '62		
Sparkman, William C.	May 14, '62		
Spearing, John N.	May 14, '62		1st Sergeant.
Spence, Charles	May 14, '62		
Stanley, Henderson	May 14, '62	Apr 9, '65	Wounded at Sharpsburg September 17,
Starling, Thomas	May 14, '62		Deserted July 26, '62, at Blackshear
Strickland, Abraham	May 14, '62		Discharged July 5, '02, for disability.
Strickland, Jonathan	May 14, '62		Promoted Sergeant; wounded at Sharpsburg September 17, '62.
Summerall, John W.	May 14, '62		Deserted July 23, '62.
Sweat, Alfred J.	May 14, '62		Wounded at Sharpsburg September 17. '62.
Sweat, Freeman	May 14, '62		Deserted July 23, '62.
Sweat, James	May 14, '62		Captured and died in prison at Hilton Head, S. C.
Sweat, James A.	May 14, '62		
Tanden	May 14, '62		Promoted Sergeant; wounded at Fredricksburg December 13, '62.
Thompson, William J.	May 14, '62		Deserted at Camp Leon July 14, '62
Tumplin, John H.	May 14, '62		
Tumplin, Samuel W.	May 14, '62		Wounded at Sharpsburg September 17, '6
Tyler, J. B.	May 14, '62		Captured at Gettysburg and imprisoned at Fort Delaware.
Vaughn, William	May 14, '62		
West, Mangum B.	May 14, '62		Killed at Sharpsburg September 17, '62.
West, Moses C.	May 14, '62		Died at Chimborazo hospital August 15, '62.
West, William H.	May 14, '62		
Whitaker, Jacob M.	May 14, '62		Sergeant.
Whitman, Martin	May 14, '62		Sergeant.
Wilkinson, Elishu	May 14, '62		Wounded at Sharpsburg September 17 '62.
Wilkinson, Gadsen	May 14, '62		Deserted June 15, '62: at Camp Hunt.
Wilkinson, Joseph	May 14, '62		Promoted Sergeant.
Wilkinson, Joseph Jr.	May 14, '62		
Wilkinson, William	May 14, '62		Deserted July 14, '62 at Camp Leon.

Roll Company I—8th Florida Infantry.
(CONTINUED.)

NAMES	MUSTERED IN.	MUSTERED OUT.	REMARKS.
Williamson, John E	May 14, '62		
Wilson, James B	May 14, '62		Captured at Gettysburg, died at Fort Delaware, '64
Winegourd, Eleazer	May 14, '62		Discharged October 4, '62 for disability.
Winegourd, James	May 14, '62		
Wood, James	May 14, '62		
Woodman, Atkinson	May 14, '62		
Worley, George W	May 14, '62		
Youngblood, S. S	May 14, '62	April 9, '65	Captured and imprisoned at Fort Delaware.

Roll Company K—8th Florida Infantry.

NAMES.	MUSTERED IN.	MUSTERED OUT.	REMARKS.
OFFICERS.			
Captains—			
William J. Turner			Promoted Major.
Frederick Worth		Apr l 9, '65	Promoted Captain; wounded at Hanover Junction through the lungs May 24, '64.
1st Lieutenant—			
Francis H. Warren	June '61		Promoted 1st Lieutenant; shot at Sharpsburg September 17, '62 and disabled.
2nd Lieutenants—			
Jones Thompson			Promoted 2nd Lieutenant; resigned on account of consumption; died.
Thomas W. Givens		April 9, '65	Promoted 2nd Lieutenant; September, '62; captured at Gettysburg July 3, '63, sent to Rock Island; exchanged February 24, '65.
3rd Lieutenant—			
F. M. Bryant		April 9, '65	Promoted 3rd Lieutenant; wounded at Gettysburg July 3, '63.
ENLISTED MEN.			
Allen, W	Oct. 21, '61		Transferred, promoted Sergeant.
Altman, Jesse	Oct. 21, '61		Imprisoned at Fort Delaware.
Andrews, J. P	Oct. 21, '61		
Arnold, F. D			Died at Charlottesville and buried in the Cemetery
Blocker, William	Oct. 28, '61		of the University of Virginia.
Carpenter, W			
Caruthers, E			
Cox, E	Oct. 26, '61		
Crews, Joshua	May 15, '62		
Driggers, E	Oct. 26, '61		
Gandy, G. W	May 15, '62		
Garrison, G. A	Oct. 27, '61		
Gill, F. M	May 15, '62		
Hall, R. B			
Harn, A			
Harn, H. B	Oct. 27, '61		
Harm, James	Oct. 21, '61		2nd Sergeant.
Hatfield, T. H	Oct. 27, '61		
Hilliard, E. J	Nov. 10, '61		Promoted Corporal.
Hilliard, H			Wounded at Gettysburg July 3, '63.
Lawerence, F	Oct. 27, '61		Wounded at Sharpsburg September 17, '62.
Lenair, C. H	May 15, '61		Absent without leave.
Lenair, D. S			
Lewis, H. H	May 15, '62		Corporal; wounded at Fredericksburg December 11 '62.
Lewis, W. H	May '62		Wounded at Fredericksburg December 11, '62; died at Richmond May 20, '63.
Manley, J	Nov. 5, '61		Wounded at Fredericksburg May 11, '62.
Manley, Jas. M		April 9, '65	
Martin, Luther A	May 15, '62		
Mathews, H. H	Oct. 27, '61		
Miley, D. M	Oct. 27, '61		Killed at Petersburg.
Mizell, T. E	Nov '61		Promoted 1st Sergeant.
Parker, W. P	Nov. 27, '61		
Peirce, J	Nov. 2, '61		Wounded at Fredericksburg December 13, '62.
Prine, H	Mch. 10, '62		Wounded at Gettysburg July 3, '63.
Prine, J	Oct. 27, '61		
Rawles, W. C	Oct. 27, '61		
Read, D. D	Oct. 27, '61		
Roberts, S	Oct. '61		
Simmons, A	Oct. 27, '61		
Smith, B. M	Oct. 27, '61		Wounded at Sharpsburg September 17, '62.
Smith, G. W			
Smith, J	Oct. 27, '62		
Stallins, W. W	Oct. 27, '61		Sergeant.
Symes, S. R. J	May 15 '62		1st Sergeant; missing after 1st battle of Manassas.
Trice, W			Corporal.
Tyner, S. T	Oct. 27, '61	April 9, 65	Captured and imprisoned at Fort Delaware.

Roll Company K—8th Florida Infantry.
(CONTINUED.)

NAMES.	MUSTERED IN.	MUSTERED OUT.	REMARKS.
Tyner, W.	Oct. 21, '61		Corporal; wounded at Sharpsburg September 17,
Walker, A.	Oct. 27, '61		'62.
Walker, G. W.	Oct. 27, '61		
Walker, O.	Oct. 27, '61		Wounded at Bristow Station October 14, '63.
Wamsbey, L. W.	May 15, '62		Wounded at Chancellorsville May 4, '63.
Weeks, J.			
Weeks, L.	May 1, 62		Promoted Corporal.
Whidden, Bennett.	Nov. 15, '61		Died at Richmond, Va., '62.
Willingham, William	May 15, '62		Wounded at Gettysburg July 3, '63.
Youngblood, S. S.	Oct. 27, '62	April 9, '65	

NINTH FLORIDA INFANTRY.

Early in May, 1864, Gen. Patton Anderson, commanding the District of Florida, received from the War Department an orde to send a good brigade to Richmond with all possible expedition. Gen. Joseph Finnegan was ordered to immediately proceed to Virginia with his brigade, consisting of 1st Battalion, Lieut.-Col. Charles Hopkins; 2nd Battalion, Lieut.-Col. Theodore Brevard; 4th Battalion, Lieutenant-Colonel McClellan; and 6th Battalion, Lieut.-Col. John M. Martin. The order was obeyed immediately and the Brigade arrived at Richmond May 25, 1864, and joined Anderson's Division, of which Holmes was then commander, and Hill's Corps at Hanover Junction May 28, 1864. On June 8,.the troops were organized into two regiments as follows: The 1st Florida Battalion, six companies, and the companies of Captains Mays, Stewart, Clark and Powers of the 2nd Battalion, formed the 10th Regiment, Colonel Hopkins commanding. The 4th Florida Battalion, seven companies, the companies of Captains Ochus and Robinson, of the 2nd Battalion, and Captain Cullens' unattached company formed the 11th Regiment, Col. Theodore Brevard commanding. The 6th Florida Battalion, seven companies, and the three independent companies, Capts. J. C. Eichelberger, John McNeil, and B. L. Reynolds, formed the 9th Regiment, Colonel Martin commanding. The seven companies that formed the 6th Battalion before organizing as such, had served as independent volunteer companies in different parts of the State; they were commanded by Captains John C. Chambers, John W. Pearson, Samuel Hope, James Tucker, A. A. Stewart, J. C. DuPree, S. M. G. Gary. At the battle of Olustee these companies were formed into a battalion commanded by Maj. Pickens Bird. In concentrating the troops between Waldo and Jacksonville, after the battle of Olustee, Lieutenant-Colonel Martin was placed in command of the Battalion, and upon the arrival of the Battalion in Virginia the Regiment was formed and the companies named, became A, B, C, D, E, F and G, under their respective captains. To these companies were added the company of B. L. Reynolds, which became Co. H; John McNeil, Co. I; Jacob Eichelberger, Co. K; John M. Martin was promoted to Colonel, John W. Pearson to Lieutenant-Colonel, and Pickens B. Bird became Major. Major Bird was killed at Cold Harbor June 3, 1864, as was Captain Reynolds of Co. H and Lieut. Ben B. Lane of Co. I. Regimental Adjutant Owens, Captain

Tucker, of Co. D, and Lieut. R. D. Harrison, commanding Co. B, were seriously wounded. After the battle of Cold Harbor Finnegan's Brigade, which now consisted of the 2nd, 5th, 8th, 9th, 10th and 11th Regiments, took up the line of march for Petersburg. On June 23 they moved from the breastworks, under a heavy fire of shells and canister, and marched down the Weldon Road, six miles below, and drove back the enemy, who were tearing up the road. On June 30 the battle of Ream's Station was fought. A Florida Brigade marched, reached the battle field at day-break and attacked the enemy, driving him back in a running fight four miles, capturing seven pieces of artillery, many horses, a few prisoners, and 1300 negroes. On the morning of the 21st August the Florida brigade advanced within one hundred yards of the Federal breast-works on the Weldon Railroad, where the enemy were strongly entrenched. Repeated charges were made to dislodge them, but failed. The loss in killed and wounded was very severe. Lieut.-Col. John W. Pearson, of the 9th Regiment, was so severely wounded that he died in Augusta, Ga., while on his way home.

The death of Colonel Pearson left the 9th Regiment with no Field Officers, except the Colonel. An attempt was made to have outsiders appointed to these positions, but Colonel Martin objected on the ground that captains in his regiment had earned promotion and were entitled to the offices; bu for some reason the War Department failed to make these deserved promotions and the 9th Regiment served to the close of the war without either Lieutenant-Colonel or Major. On December 7, 1864, the Florida Brigade, of which the 9th was a part, made a forced march of 50 miles and struck the enemy at the Bellfield on the 9th; but the enemy numbering 20,000, who had been on a raid declined to accept the gage of battle, and retreated, and the Brigade returned to camp foot-sore, having marched over frozen roads, and through sleet and snow more than one hundred miles. Early in February, 1865, the 9th was engaged at Hatcher's Run, opposing the Federal attempt to extend their line of battle. In this engagement S. W. Crowson was seriously wounded. The Brigade was now ordered to winter quarters; but before reaching them received orders to return to reinforce General Gordon south of Hatcher's Run. In this engagement the Brigade numbered but 3,500 effective men. After a charge the enemy fled in confusion and night ended the battle. On the morning of April 2 General Lee's lines were broken and the retreat began. The 9th Regiment retreated by way of High Bridge and marched to Farmville; being crowded it halted and fortified for an attack, which was repulsed with heavy loss to the enemy. This was the last battle in which the 9th was engaged. The Regiment surrendered at Appomatox, 15 officers and 109 men.

Roll, Field and Staff—9th Florida Infantry.

NAMES.	MUSTERED IN.	MUSTERED OUT.	REMARKS.
Colonel—			
John M. Martin	Sept. 4, '63	April 9, '65	
Lieutenant-Colonel—			
John M. Martin	Sept. 4, '63		Promoted Colonel.
Majors—			
Pickens Bird	Sept. 4, '63		Killed at Cold Harbor June 3, '64.

Roll, Field and Staff—9th Florida Infantry.
(CONTINUED.)

NAMES.	MUSTERED IN.	MUSTERED OUT.	REMARKS.
Surgeons—			
Assistant Surgeons—			
Simmons	Sept. 4, '63		Transferred to hospital.
T. D. Hawkins	Sept. 4, '63		Transferred of buspital.
Pickerton	Sept. 4, '63	April 9, '65	
Adjutants—			
James Owens	Sept. 4, '63		
M. A. Rogers	Sept. 4, '63		Killed at Cold Harbor June 3, '64.
1st Lieut. Ben. F. Parker	Sept. 4, '63	April 9, '65	
Sergeant Major—			
Charles Pearson	Sept 4, '63	April 9, '65	
Quartermaster—			
James H. Johnson	Sept. 4, '63	April 9, '65	
Commissary—			
Quartermaster Sergeant—			
Commissary Sergeants—			
Chaplain—			
James Little	Sept. 4, '63	April 9, '65	
First Lieutenants—			
R. G. McEwen-Ensign			Discharged for ill health.
Rufus King-Ensign			
			This regiment had no Lieutenant-Colonel or Major after the promotion of Colonel Martin and the death of Major Bird owing to the fact that General Finnegan wished to promote outsiders to the position. Colonel Martin protesting against such appointment on the ground that he had fine officers who had won promotion by their gallantry.

Roll Company A—9th Florida Infantry.

NAMES.	MUSTERED IN.	MUSTERED OUT.	REMARKS.
OFFICERS.			
Captains—			
John C. Chambers	Mch. 15, '62		Resigned, '63.
Dr. Enos E Davis	Mch. 15, '62		Died in hospital at Richmond June, '64 from disease contracted from exposure at the battle of Cold Harbor, June 3, '64.
Samuel H. Worthington	Mch. 15, '62		Promoted from Corporal to 3rd Lieutenant; then Captain, resigned March 1, '65,
1st Lieutenant—			
Benjamin Lane	Mch. 15, '62		Promoted 1st Lieutenant from 2nd Lieutenant; killed at Cold Harbor, June 3, '64.
2nd Lieutenant—			
Haile,	Mch. 15, '62		Promoted 2nd Lieutenant from 3rd Lieutenant; died in Virginia, '64.
3rd Lieutenant—			
Willis R. Meadlin	Mch. 15, '62		
ENLISTED MEN.			
Baldwin, Joseph	Mch, 15, '62		
Beck, Mathew A	Mch, 15, '62	April 9, '65	Captured and imprisoned at Fort Warren, Mass.; paroled at close of war,
Bryant, Lewis H	Mch, 15, '62		
Chesser, John W	Mch, 15, '62	May '65	Discharged from Broodsville, Fla.
Chesser, Thomas W	Mch, 15, '62		
Chesser, William H	Mch, 15, '62		
Clark, Alexander W	Mch, 15, '62		
Clark, Elias B	Mch, 15, '62		
Cylatt, Marion F	Mch, 20, '62		Corporal.
Clyatt, Montgomery N	Mch, 26 '62		
Collier, James	Mch, 15, '62	April 9, ,65	Promoted Sergeant.
Comancher, Joseph	Mch, 15, '62		
Compton, Thomas R	Mch, 17, '62		
Conden, Samuel	Mch, 17, '62		Musician.
Corrigan, Edward J	Mch, 20, '62		
Corrigan, Owen	Mch, 20, '62		
Dean, W, H, H.	Mch, 20, '62		
Dixon, James M	Mch, 20, '62		Corporal.
Dixon, John	Mch, 20, '62		Sergeant.
Duncan, Wiley W	Mch, 20, '62		
Garrard, Jacob			Killed at Petersburg June 10, ,64.
Gordette, Eugene.	Mch, 24, '62		
Haddock, William H	Mch. 15, '62		
Harilson, Garrett V.			
Higginbotham, Aaron	Nov. '62		Lost right arm at Bay Port, Fla., February, '63.
Higginbotham, Caleb	Mch. 15, '62		

Roll Company A—9th Florida Infantry.

(CONTINUED.)

NAMES.	MUSTERED IN.	MUSTERED OUT.	REMARKS.
Higginbotham, Joseph		April 9, '65	
Hill, Henry L	Mch. 15, '62		
Hill, John J	Mch. 15, '62		
Hill, William A	Mch. 15, '62		
Hopkins, George W	Hch. 15, '62		
Hogan, Edmund D	Mch. 15, '62		
Hogan, Llewelyn J	Mch. 15, '62		
Hogan, Stephen W			
Hudson, James B	Mch. 15, 62		
Hudson, Samuel I	Mch. 19, '62		
Jackson, John F	Mch. 15, '62		1st Sergeant.
Johnston, Abraham	Mch. 15, '62		
Johnston, Henry	Mch. 15, '62		
Kelley, Henry	Mch. 25, '64	April 9, '65	
Kirkand, Oscar H. Perry	Mch. 15, '62		1st Sergeant.
Lewis, L. B	Mch. 15, '62		Musician.
Lynn, George W	Mch. 15, '62		
McCaskill, Peter H	Mch. 15, '62		
McLeod, Alexander	Mch. 20, '62	April 9, '65	
Malphurs, John R	Aug. 15, '63	April 9, '65	Shot at Olustee, Fla., February 20, '64; imprisoned at Point Lookout, Md., during the war.
May, David F	Mch. 15, '62		
May, Reuben	Mch. 15, '62		
Meadlin, Elias H		April 9, '65	Corporal.
Miller, John	Mch. 17, '62		
Munden, Isaac		April 9, '65	
Munden, William	Mch. 15, '62		
Oglesby, Joseph F			
Oglesby, Lewis A			
Parish, Robert O	Mch. 15, '62		
Peterson, Timothy	Mch. 30, '62		
Reaves, James A	Mch. 15, '62		Corporal.
Richardson, William S	Mch. 15, '62		
Roberts, Allen	Mch. 15, '62	April 9, '65	Shot near Petersburg, '64, while on picket duty.
Scarborough, Allen S	Mch. 15, '62		
Shirley, Thomas	Mch. 15, '62		
Slaughter, Charles L	Mch. 15, '62		
Smith, Hampton	Mch. 15, '62		
Smith, Milton	Mch. 15, '62		
Smith, Thomas P	Mch. 15, '62		
Smith, William H	Mch. 15, '62		
Tindale, John W		April 9, '65	
Tindale, Matheio	Mch. 15, '62		
Tindale, Willis F	Mch. 15, '62		
Took, John G	Mch. 15, '62		
Weeks, Cabal	Mch. 17, '62		
Weeks, John G	Mch. 19, '62		
White, James	Mch. 19, '62		
White, John B	Mch. 20, '62	April 9, '65	
White, William C	Mch. 15, '62		
Wilson, Jerome	Mch. 15, '62		
Wilson, William		April 9, '65	
Wilson, William, Jr	Mch. 15, '62		
Worthington, Granville H		April 9, '65	
Worthington, Samuel H			

Roll Company B—9th Florida Infantry.

NAMES.	MUSTERED IN.	MUSTERED OUT.	REMARKS.
OFFICERS.			
Captains—			
J. W. Pearson			Promoted Lt.Col.; wounded at Reames' Station Aug. 21, '64 and died at Augusta, Ga., on his way home.
R. D. Harrison		April 9, '65	Promoted Captain; wounded at Cold Harbor June 3, '64.
1st Lieutenant—			
Francis McMeekin		April 9, '65	Promoted 1st Lieutenant; wounded at Cold Harbor June, '64.
2nd Lieutenant—			
3rd Lieutenants—			
David Hall			Died in service in Virginia, '64.
M. A. Rogero			Promoted 3rd Lieutenant; Adjutant-General after Owens was killed at the battle of Green Station.
ENLISTED MEN.			
Bankright, W. K			
Blue, Archibald C	June 21, '62		
Blount, R			
Boyles, L. C			
Brinson, J. S			
Browning, Noah	April '63		Shot at Olustee, Fla., February 22, '64.

Roll Company B—9th Florida Infantry.
(Continued.)

NAMES.	MUSTERED IN.	MUSTERED OUT.	REMARKS.
Bullock, P.			
Caldwell, Robert A.			Died in hospital June 11, '63, of typhoid fever at
Caldwell, Robert C.			Tampa.
Cason, A. J.			
Cathron, W. D.			
Clemons, Henry.	May '62	April 9, '65	
Congers, D.			
Daniels, W. H.			
Ellis, Aaron.			
Ellis, G. N.			
Ellis, James.			
Ellis, John.			
Ferguson, R. H.			
Frier, F. L.			
Futch, S.			
Galbrath, D. C.		April 9, '65	Sergeant.
George, L.			
Gillis, John.			Sergeant; surrendered but died before reaching
Gillis, Neil.			home.
Grantham, John.			
Grantham, John W.			
Haggins, John.			
Hall, B.			
Hall, J. J.			Sergeant.
Hall, John W.			Shot at Olustee, Fla., February 24, '64.
Hampton.			
Harrison, John.			
Hawthorn, W. L.			
Henderson, Levi.			
Hill, M. N.			
Hill W.			
Hinson, Allen W.			Corporal; shot at Petersburg, Va., August 21, '64.
Hobkerk, James.			Corporal.
Hull, Isaac I.			
Hunter, J. R.			Musician.
Hunter, R. G.			Corporal.
Ivey, R. L.			
John, C. S.			
Johnson, J. A.			
Key, W.			
Lockler, Irwin.			
Luffman, W. H.			
Manning, J. E.			
Manning, J. M.			
Marsh, G. W.			
Martin, H. E.			1st Sergeant.
Martin, J. S.		April 9, '65	
Mason, William H.		April 9, '65	
Matchett, Enoch.			
Matchett, L.			
Matchett, S. T.		April 9, '65	
May, Joseph N.		April 9, '65	Wounded at Turkey Ridge, Va., '64.
McBride, A. M.		April 9, 65	
McCradie, John L.			
McDermett, Hiram.		April 9, '65	
McErvin, Joseph C.		April 9, '65	
McEwen, Robert G.	May 1, '62	April 9, '65	Wounded at Cold Harbor, Va., June 3, '64.
McNeil, Joseph.			
McRae, Angus.			
McRae, J.		April 9, '65	
Mitchell, D. T.		April 9, '65	
Murphy, E.			
Murphy, John.			
Parker, L. H.		April 9, '65	
Pearson, C. G.			
Pearson, P. G.			Musician.
Pike, S. H.			
Sapp, O.			
Sanders, Fred.			1st Sergeant.
Scott, G. L.			
Scott, J. B.			
Seque, Charles Downing.			
Shaler, S. T.			
Sherouse, W. M.		April 9, '65	
Sherouse, James.			
Shurouse, Marion.			
Shorter, William F.		April 9, '65	
Shores, Joseph.			
Sikes, A. D.			
Sikes, Isaah.			
Sikes, Joseph.			
Simmonds, T. F.			
Smith, Adam.			
Smith, John.			

Roll Company B—9th Florida Infantry,
(CONTINUED.)

NAMES.	MUSTERED IN.	MUSTERED OUT.	REMARKS.
Stevens, Christopher C.		April 9, '65	
Stevens, S.			
Strickland, A.			
Sylvester, W.			
Tompkins, Alfred D.	May '62	April 9, '65	
Tompkins, John W.	Mch. '62	April 9, '65	Shot on Weldon Railroad, Va., August 21, '64.
Turner, George W.		April 9, '65	Wounded at Petersburg, Va., August 22, '64.
Waldron, David E.	May '62	April 9, '65	
Waldron, M.			
Walker, Elias.		April 9, '65	
Waterbury, Horace W.		April 9, '65	
Wells, A. A.			
Wells, George W.		April 9, '65	
Wells, S. J.			
Wells, T. N.			
Wimberly, J. T.			
Wimberly, J. I.		April 9, '65	
Whidden, John H.		April 9, '65	
Williams, Thomas W.		April 9, '65	

Roll Company C—9th Florida Infantry.

NAMES.	MUSTERED IN.	MUSTERED OUT.	REMARKS.
OFFICERS.			
Captain—			
Samuel E. Hope	June 21, 62	April 9 '65	Wounded at Petersburg August 25, '64; resigned November 1, '64.
1st Lieutenant—			
Horace H. Hale.		April 9, '65	
2nd Lieutenants—			
Thomas I. Hill.			Promoted 2nd Lieutenant from 3rd Lieutenant; killed at Olustee February 28, '64.
E. Allen Hill.		April 9, '65	Promoted 2nd Lieutenant; wounded at Petersburg August 25, '64,
3rd Lieutenant—			
James L. Colding.		April 9. '65	
ENLISTED MEN.			
Alford, J. L.	Oct. '62		
Allen, E. A.			
Allen, Early A.		April 9, '65	
Allen, David A.		April 9, '65	
Allen, Eason W.			
Allen, John J.			Killed on picket line in Virginia, '64.
Allen, Jesse Wesley.		April 9, '65	
Allen, Z. E.	June 21, '62		Killed at Cold Harbor June 3. '64.
Alexander, Stephen S.		April 9, '65	
Alsobrook, Thomas M.		April 9, '65	
Anderson, Charles.			Killed at Cold Harbor June 3, '64.
Baker, Robert.			
Baker, William J.	June 21, '62	April 9, '65	Transferred to Captain Lesley's Company.
Bassett, John G.		April 9, '65	
Bassett, Josiah F.		April 13, '65	
Bates, George W.		April 13, '65	
Bates, Robert J.		April 13, '65	
Bates. Thomas M.		April 13, '65	
Boyett, John G.			
Boyett, William E.		April 13, '65	
Britton, Samuel.	June 21, '62		Died in Virginia.
Brown, E.			
Carter, Thomas.			Killed at Olustee February 20, '64.
Colding, James L.		April 13, '65	
Curry, Benjamin.		April 13, '65	
Curry, Joseph K.			Killed at Olustee February 20, '64.
Crum, Richard R.		April 13. '65	Transferred from 3rd Regiment, Co. C.
Dann, Stephen.			
Day, Thomas W.		April 13, '65	
Deas, George.	June 21, '62	April 13, '65	
Deas, Moses.			
Duke, G. F.		'63	Disability.
Dykes, George W.		April 13, '65	
D. W. H.			
Edwards, Henry D.		April 13, '65	
Edwards Marvin.		April 13, '65	
Edwards, Obidiah E.	June 21, '62	April 13, '65	
Enocks, Andrew S.		April 13, '65	Corporal.
Eubanks, William D.	June 21, '62		
Fillman, Martin D.	June 21, '62	April 13, '65	
Frierson, James J. E.		April 13, '65	
Garland M. W.		April 13, '65	

Roll Company C—9th Florida Infantry.
(CONTINUED.)

NAMES.	MUSTERED IN.	MUSTERED OUT.	REMARKS.
Godwin, Berrien			Wounded at Olustee February 22, '64; died in Va., in service.
Godwin, Samuel			Died in Virginia.
Godwin, William		April 13, '65	
Hancock, Durham		April 13, '65	
Hancock, James M. J		April 13, '65	
Hart, Isaiah			Musician; died in service.
Hart, John		April 13, '65	
Hay, Isaac		April 13, '65	
Hays, William	June 21, 62	April 13, '65	
Hil, Chelsey D		April 13, '65	
Hill, Elisha A		April 13, '65	
Hill, Malcolm N		April 13, '65	
Hill, Robert M		April 13, '65	
Hope, Michæl			Died in hospital at Lake City, Fla.
House, Hill W	June 21, '62	April 13, '65	Wounded at Olustee February 20, '64.
Jackson, J. F			
Johns, John P		April 13, '65	
Johnson, Simpson		April 13, '65	
Leggett, David		April 13, '65	
McGeachy, Edward C		April 13, '65	Sergeant.
McGeachy, Malcolm		April 13, '65	
McKewin, Greg	June 21, '62		Killed at Cold Harbor June 3, '64.
McKeown, C. Leroy			Discharged for disability, lost arm.
McKinney, Richard C		April 13, '65	
McMinn, William L		April 13, '65	Transferred from Com any "C," 3rd.
Mason, Calvin H		April 13, '65	
Mason, William		April 13, '65	Wounded at Petersburg August 10, '63.
Messer, George C		April 13, '65	
Messer, Henry		April 13, '65	
Mickler, Jacob B		April 13, '65	
Mizell, Osias		April 13, '65	Captured at Jacksonville, Fla., sent on parole.
Moore, Daniel F		April 13, '65	
Morrison, J. B	June 21, '62	April 13, '65	
Morrison, John P		April 13, '65	Promoted 3rd Sergeant.
Nevitt, Cornelius Q		April 13, '65	Transferred from Company "C," 3rd Regiment.
ONeil, William D		April 13, '65	
Osborn, David		April 13, '65	
Nicks, William R		April 13, '65	
Olford, Jason		April 13, '65	
Parker, Robert H	June 21, '62	April 13, '65	
Peterson, Henry		April 13, '65	
Phelps, Fletcher		April 13, '65	
Pinkston, Daniel W		April 13, '65	
Revils, Jeremiah F			Musician.
Rogers, Joel W		April 13, '65	
Shipman, James		April 13, '65	
Smith, A. H		April 13, '65	
Smith, Edward		April 13, '65	
Smith, Green		April 13, '65	
Smith, William F	Jpne 21, '62	April 13, '65	
Smith, William Seaborn	June 21, '62	April 13, '65	
Stafford, Will am H	Nov. 1, '62	April 13, '65	Wounded at Cross Roads, Va., August 10, '64; also twice in thigh at Cold Harbor May 20, '63.
Stappleton, Francis		April 13, '65	
Strickland, William		April 13, '65	
Tucker, Jesse B			Killed.
Tucker, Jesse H		April 13, '65	
Tucker, Pleasant T		April 13, '65	
Turnbull, Charles W		April 13, '65	Corporal.
Vickers, W. R		April 13, '65	
Wall, William W		April 13, '65	
Washington, George P		April 13, '65	
Wells, George W		April 13, '65	
Wells, John		April 13, '65	
Whitehurst, Berrien D		April 13, '65	
Willis, Richard T		April 13, '65	
Willis, George W			
Wilson, James B		April 13, '65	
Wilson, Norman		April 13, '65	
W lliamson, William W		April 13, '65	
Winegourd, C. W		April 13, '65	
Winn, Thomas		April 13, '65	

Roll Company D—9th Florida Infantry.

NAMES	MUSTERED IN.	MUSTERED OUT.	REMARKS.
OFFICERS.			
Captains—			
John Bryan	'62		Resigned.

Roll Company D—9th Florida Infantry.
(CONTINUED.)

NAMES.	MUSTERED IN.	MUSTERED OUT.	REMARKS.
James Tucker	'62		Promoted Captain May 10, '62; wounded at Cold Harbor June 3, '64.
1st Lieutenants—			
Joseph D. Bryan			Resigned at reorganization May 10, '62.
William Scott		April 9, '65	Promoted 1st Lieutenant.
2nd Lieutenants—			
T. J. Padget			Resigned at reorganization May 10, '62.
Joseph Perry			Promoted 2nd Lieutenant; killed at Olustee February 24, '64.
Young,			
Jesse Turner			
William P. Burns		April 9, '65	2nd Lieutenant; commanding Company at surrender.
3rd Lieutenant—			
James R. Finnigan			Promoted 3rd Lieutenant.
ENLISTED MEN.			
Bethea, Foster C.			
Blanton, D. T.		April 9, '65	Promoted 1st Sergeant.
Boyett, E. J.			
Brown, D. C.			
Bryan, D. S.			Sergeant.
Bryan Hardee			
Bryan, N. G.			
Bryan, P. N.			Sergeant.
Bryan, T. J.			
Chaney, E.			
Cowart, David			
Cowart, William A.			Promoted Corporal.
Crews, Benjamin			
Crews, Henry			Corporal.
Crews, J. B.			Musician.
Crews, Joseph			
Crews, M. L.			
Crews, S. L.			
Deas, Joseph	April '63		Paroled at close of war.
Ellis, E. H.	Aug. 15, '63		Was at home, sick, at the surrender.
Fletcher, C. N.			
Fletcher, Newton			
Fulford, William B.			
Ginn, C. W.			
Gluner, J. E.			
Griffis, Joel			
Hall, N. S.			
Hancock H.			
Hancock, S.			
Harris, John			
Hints, David			
Hunter, E.			
Hunter, George			
Hunter, Hamilton			
Hunter, Silas			
Hurnage, John C.			Corporal.
Johnston, J. E.			
Johnston, John			
Johnson, William			Killed at Cold Harbor, Va., June, '64.
Johnston, W. A. P.			....
Johnston, W. R.			
Johnston, W. S.			
Keen, David			Corporal.
Keen, Thomas			Corporal; killed at Olustee February 24, '64.
Kibez, Ira			
Knowis, R. Alexander			Sergeant.
Lancaster, Joseph D.			
Lee, Henry			
Lewis, E.			
Lewis, Williard			
McCall, C. F.			
McCall, J.			
McCaskill, A. W.			
McClellan, George E.	May '61	April '65	
McDaniel, Thomas T.	June '64	April '65	
McEwen, W. A.		April '65	
McLane, William T.			
Meeks, H. C.		April '65	
Mitchell, Thomas J.	Oct. '63	April '65	Wounded at Olustee February 20, '64.
Mixon, J. G.			
Mixon, William		April '65	
Newborn, Benjamin			
Newlan, J.			
Newlan, J. R.		April '65	Musician.
Odum, A.			
Owens, Joseph P.		April '65	
Ogelsby, Francis			
Padgett, E.			
Padgett, John			

Roll Company D—9th Florida Infantry.
(CONTINUED.)

NAMES.	MUSTERED IN.	MUSTERED OUT.	REMARKS.
Parker, W. T.			
Peacock, M.			
Rhymes, David			Sergeant; wounded and died at Olustee.
Roberts, W. N.			
Sandlin, Jesse R.			1st Sergeant; killed at Cold Harbor June, '64.
Sandlin, W. D.			Sergeant.
Shirley, Warren			
Sill, Newton			
Stapleton, Alexander			
Stapleton, Jackson			
Starling, Thomas			
Summers, J. W.			
Tomberlin, William			
Tyler, Stephen J.			
Williams, Willis			
Willis, William		April 9, '65	Sergeant.

Roll Company E—9th Florida Infantry.

NAMES.	MUSTERED IN.	MUSTERED OUT	REMARKS.
OFFICERS.			
Captains—			
A. A. Stewart	'62		Resigned June 7, '64.
G. H. Hunter			Promoted 1st Lieutenant; then Captain; wounded at Cold Harbor and resigned.
J. L. Dozier		April 9, '65	Promoted 1st Lieutenant; then Captain.
1st Lieutenants—			
J. W. Pearce			Promoted 1st Lieutenant from 2nd Lieutenant, killed at Farmville April 7, '65.
J. W. Barnett		April 9, '65	Promoted 1st Lieutenant.
2nd Lieutenants—			
3rd Lieutenants—			
Robert B. Roberts		April 9, '65	Re-enlisted, Company "E," 9th Regiment; promoted 1st Sergeant, then 3rd Lieutenant.
ENLISTED MEN.			
Alford, W. A.			
Altman, T.			
Arnow, W. J.			
Barber, J.			
Beasley, J. F.		April 9, '65	Transferred to Company "H," B. L. Reynolds' Company.
Brannan, Benjamin W.			
Boyd, William	April 11, '63	April 20, '63	Discharged for disability.
Bryant, D.			
Burnside, E.			
Cobb, W. C.			Transferred to Captain Reynolds' Company.
Combs, W.			
Couter, P. J.			
Condley, W. B.			
Crawford, J. L.			
Curl, J.			
Dacosta, John		April 20, '63	
DeBouse, E. D.		April 20, '63	
Deese, L. B.			
Dinkins, B. R.		April 20, '63	
Douglass, James			Killed at Petersburg, Va., August, '64.
Easton, H. P.		April 20, '63	
Forsom, John M.		April 20, '63	
Forsom, Thomas		April 20, '63	
Fuqua, L. D.		April 20, '63	
Fuqua, R.		April 20, '63	
Godwin, H. O.			
Godbolt, J. S.		April 9, '65	
Greek, William		April 9, '65	
Green, W. J.		April 9, '65	
Griffin, J. S.		April 9, '65	Sergeant.
Griffin, Thomas C.	Feb. '63	April 9, '65	
Hancock, J. W.		April 9, '65	
Hancock, S.		April 9, '65	
Harris, Henry		April 9, '65	Wounded at Petersburg, Va., September, '64.
Harvey, W. B.		April 9, '65	
Harvey, Washington H.	April 15, '63	April 9, '65	
Hawthorn, W. A.		April 9, '65	Wounded in foot.
Herndon, J. B.		April 9, '65	
Holmes, William		April 9, '65	
Hull, N.		April 9, '65	
Hurst, F.		April 9, '65	
Hurst, T. T.		April 9, '65	

Roll Company E—9th Florida Infantry.
(CONTINUED.)

NAMES.	MUSTERED IN.	MUSTERED OUT.	REMARKS.
Jones, W. L.			Killed in Virginia.
Keen, W. R.		April 9, '65	
Knight, M. A.		April 9, '65	1st Sergeant.
Koon, Frederick H.		April 9, '65	
Langford, J. B.		April 9, '65	
Langford, L. W.		April 9, '65	
Liddon, Abraham		April 9, '65	Wounded in right hand.
McClellan, William H.		April 9, '65	
McEwing, W. A.		April 9, '65	
Manning, George W.			Discharged March, '65 for disability.
Mattair, Downing		April 9, '65	Courier.
Mott, J. M.			Corporal; deserted, '64.
Norman, W.		April 9, '65	
Ogden, George K.		April 9, '65	Discharged from Captain Roberts' Company, on
Owens, W. J.		April 9, '65	account of being frost bitten; re-enlisted in
Parnell, James T.	'62	April 9, '65	Stewart's Company.
Parnell, K.			Transferred to 4th Regiment.
Parnell, T.			Transferred from 4th Regiment.
Parnell, William King	Mch. 4, '63	April 9, '65	
Prevatt, A. J.		April 9, '65	Sergeant.
Prevatt, J.		April 9, '65	
Prevatt, M.		April 9, '65	
Poer, D. M.		April 9, '65	
Renfrow, A. S.		April 9, '65	
Roberts, K.		April 9, '65	
Roberts, J. K.		April 9, '65	
Roberts, Nathan		April 9, '65	Transferred from 3rd Battalion.
Roberts, Reuben S.	Feb. '63	April	Transferred to Reynold's Company and died of disease in hospital at Petersburg, Va., August, '64.
Roberts, Stephen W.		April 9, '65	Musician.
Roberts, W. P.			Sergeant; killed at Reams Station.
Roen, John A.		April 9, '65	Killed at Cold Harbor, Va., June 3, '64.
Russell, J. W.		April 9, '65	
Scott, David		April 9, '65	
Scott, J. R.		April 9, '65	
Shaw, H. D.			Corporal; deserted, '64.
Sheppard, Z. F.		April 9, '65	
Smith, J. L.		April 9, '65	
Smith, J. W.		April 9, '65	
Smith, T. J.		April 9, '65	
Smith, W. H.		April 9, '65	
Sparkman, S.		April 9, '65	
Sweat, Allen	Feb. '63	April 9, '65	Wounded at Weldon R. R. August 17, '63.
Taylor, H. D. L.		April 9, '65	
Taylor, James A.	Feb. '63	April 9, '65	Corporal; wounded at Cold Harbor and at Petersburg.
Taylor, James S.		April 9, '65	Corporal.
Taylor, William M.	Feb. 15, '63	April 9, '65	Wounded at Cold Harbor, Va., June 3, '64.
Tyler, S. J.			Corporal; deserted.
Tyre, Jesse	Feb. 1, '63	April 9, '65	Transferred to Captain Samuel May's Company,
Tyre, William H.		April 9, '65	"B" Battalion; wounded at Cold Harbor, Va.
Tompkins, Giles	May 1 '63	April 9, '65	June 3, '64.
Walters, J. W.		April 9, '65	
Waters, Isaac		April 9, '65	
Weeks, O. M. D.		April 9, '65	
Welch, Bryant R.	'63		Wounded at Cold Harbor, Va., June, '64 and died July 30, '64.
Wilson, George S.		April 9, '65	
Wiley, J. J.		April 9, '65	
Williams, A. T.	Feb. '62	April 9, '65	Discharged May '62 for sickness and being under
Williams, W. P.		April 9, '65	age; re-enlisted in A. A. Stewart's Company
Young, E. J.		April 9, '65	"E," shot at Weldon R. R., Va., August 2, '64.
Youman, M. M.		April 9, '65	

Roll Company F—9th Florida Infantry.

NAMES.	MUSTERED IN.	MUSTERED OUT.	REMARKS.
OFFICERS.			
Captains—			
A. P. Mooty	'62		Wounded and disabled at Olustee February 20, '64.
J. C. DuPree	'62	April 9, '65	Promoted Captain March, '64; from 1st Lieutenant.
1st Lieutenant—			
2nd Lieutenants—			
S. M. Love			Resigned October 30, '63.
J. D. Hopkins		April 9, '65	

Roll Company F—9th Florida Infantry.
(Continued.)

NAMES.	MUSTERED IN.	MUSTERED OUT.	REMARKS.
3rd Lieutenant—			
Dr. Johnson	Feb. '62		Resigned.
ENLISTED MEN.			
Adkins, E. A.	Feb. '62	April 9, '65	Wounded at Seven Days' battle, Va.
Alderman, Hiram	Aug. '62	April 9, '65	
Baker, Thomas	April '63	April 9, '65	
Barton, William		April 9, '65	
Bates, John	'63		
Caldwell, John M.			
Carlton, William T.	'62	April 9, '65	
Causey, Leighton E.			
Cawthorn, George T.	April 18, '61		
Crosby, W. C.	'63		Shot at Petersburg, Va., August. '64
Driggers, James A.	Mch. '63		
Driggers, Ed. T.			
Driggers, John F.	'61	April 9, '65	Slightly wounded twice.
Drummond, E. L.			
Fleming, John F.	'62	April 9, '65	Shot at Appomattox Court House April 7, '65.
Fulford, W. R.			
Galbreath, Charles H.			
Gaskins, J. J. H.		Feb. 16, '62	
Gaskins, T. J. H.			
Gill, Joseph	Mch. '62		Wounded at Petersburg, Va., July 15, '64.
Goodson, A.			
Green, W. J.	Mch. 4, '63	Aug. 18, '64	Discharged for disability.
Harper, M.	Sept. '64		Killed in battle, '64.
Holmes, Daniel	Jan. '62		Discharged for disability, '64.
Johnson, W. W.			
Madden, Patrick		April 9, '65	
Mann, James A.	'62		Died of measles at Lake City, Fla., April 15, '64.
Marsh, J. J.	Mch. '63	April 9, '65	Shot at Olustee, Fla., February 22, '64.
Peterson, G. W.	'61	April 9, '65	
Price, Laban	Feb. '62	April 9, '65	
Redding, W. H.		April 9, '65	
Register, Ivy		April 9, '65	
Rivers, Thomas	July '62	April 9, '65	
Sharouse, Israel	'62	April 9, '65	
Shaver, D. M.		April 9, '65	
Sill, Joseph		April 9, '65	
Smith, J. F. Sr.		April 9, '65	
Smith, J. F. Jr.		April 9, '65	
Saunders, Z. M.		April 9, '65	
Terrell, James			Killed at Olustee February 20, '64.
Thompson, W. L.		April 9, '65	
Vogt, D. A.		April 9, '65	
Waits, Calvin	'62	April 9, '65	Accidentally shot at Camp Finnegan, Fla., November 7, '63; promoted 2nd Corporal.
Webb, J. B.	July 27, '63	April 9, '65	

Roll Company G—9th Florida Infantry.

NAMES.	MUSTERED IN.	MUSTERED OUT.	REMARKS.
OFFICERS.			
Captains—			
S. M. G. Gary	'62		Transferred to Staff of General Martin Gary with rank of 1st Lieutenant.
Charles M. Brown	'62		Promoted 1st Lieutenant from 2nd Lieutenant; then Captain, wounded at Seven Pines May 31 '62; Olustee, February 20, '64 and at Reams Station June 3, '64.
1st Lieutenants—			
Thomas			Promoted 1st Lieutenant.
Joseph E. Barco			Captured near Baldwin February 7, '64; sent to Johnson's Island, N. Y. where he died in '64.
2nd Lieutenant—			
3rd Lieutenant—			
E. D. Williams	'62		Wounded at Seven Pines May 31, '62, Olustee February 20, '64; discharged.
ENLISTED MEN.			
Armstrong, M. L.	June '63		
Armstrong, M. S.			
Beasley, J. F.			
Brooks, Joseph			Sergeant; died in service.
Brooks, Spencer			Sergeant; mortally wounded.
Brown, E. F.	Mch. 16, '64	April 9, '65	
Brown, S. R.	April '64	April 9, '65	
Buxton, L. H.	April 20, '63		Transferred to Company "K" 1st Reserves.
Carter, J. W.			

Roll Company G—9th Florida Infantry.

(CONTINUED.)

NAMES.	MUSTERED IN.	MUSTERED OUT.	REMARKS.
Dean, Thadeus R.	Mch. '62		
Dugger, Robinson B.			Killed at Olustee February 20, '64.
Fant, Valentine	Sept. '62	April 9, '65	
Frink, Albert H.			
Goin, S. M.	Mch. '64		
Goolsby, Peter.			
Hall, John W.			
Hudgens, H. H.			
Kilgore, S. H.			
Long, M. C.	April 18, '62	April 9, '65	
McGrath, W. J.			2nd Sergeant; deserted.
McKinney, G. W.	'62		Killed at Cold Harbor, Va.
Marston, John W.	Mch. 4, '64	April 9, '65	Wounded at Reams Station June 3, '64.
Martin, John U.	Feb. 19, '63	April 9, '65	
Milligard, C.		April 9, '65	
Morgan, T. D.		April 9, '65	
Moorman, W. P.		April 9, '65	
Noble, Jesse.	Oct. '63	April 9, '65	Lost left leg in service.
Perkins, Henry.	Mch. '63	April 9, '65	
Plummer, Joseph.	June 3, '63	April 9, '65	
Potts, Allen.	Mch. 15, '63		Discharged from prison June 27, '65.
Roberson, Charles A	Mch. '62	April 9, '65	Lost arm at Antietam, Md., September 17, '62.
Russell, William.	'61	April 9, '65	Shot at Cold Harbor, Va., June 19, '64.
Savage,			Sergeant.
Shaw, Henry R.		April 9, '65	
Smith, Solomon.		April 9, '65	
Spearing,			Sergeant.
Tanner, T. R.	'62		Wounded at Cold Harbor, Va., June 3, '64, and died June 30, '64.
Tison, George W.			Killed at Cold Harbor June 3, '64.
Thompson, William L.		April 9, '65	
Turnipseed, E. A.			1st Sergeant; killed in battle.
Wallace, Thomas J.			Wounded at Olustee February 20, .64, and died from effects of wounds March 20, '64.

Roll Company H—9th Florida Infantry.

NAMES.	MUSTERED IN.	MUSTERED OUT.	REMARKS.
OFFICERS.			
Captains—			
B. L. Reynolds	'62		Killed at Cold Harbor June 3, '64.
Mathew A. Knight	Feb. '63		Promoted 1st Lieutenant; then Captain, transferred to Company "H" October, '63.
1st Lieutenant—			
2nd Lieutenants—			
W. W. McCall			Resigned January 5, '65.
A. J. Prevatt		April 9, '65	In command of Company at surrender.
3rd Lieutenant—			
ENLISTED MEN.			
Alford, Miles		62	Shot at Petersburg, '63; White House, Va., August 5, '65.
Altman, John	April '64	April 9, '65	Wounded at Cold Harbor June 3, '64.
Bryan, Hardee.			
Caldwell, John M.			Killed January 4, '64.
Cobb, William C.	Sept. 1, '63	April 9, '65	
Coon, Hartwell.			
Croner, William L.	'63		Wounded at Cold Harbor June 6, '64.
Dees, L. B.			
Dukes, Silas E.	Mch. 15, '62		Captured at Howard's Grove, Va., and held until July 2, '65.
Koon, Hattwell.	Aug. '63		
Liddon, Abraham	Sept. '63	April 9, '65	Wounded at Gaines' Farm June 10, '64.
Polk, F. R.		April 20, '63	
Predatt, E. M.		April 9, '65	
Raulerson, B. E.		April 9, '65	
Smith, David.		April 9, '65	
Weeks, O. M. D.	June '61	April 9, '65	
White, William H.	Oct. '63	April 9, '65	Wounded at Olustee, '64.

Roll Company I—9th Florida Infantry.

NAMES.	MUSTERED IN.	MUSTERED OUT.	REMARKS.
OFFICERS.			
Captains—			
John McNeil	'62		Wounded at Olustee February 20, '64 and disabled.
E. E. Hill			1st Lieutenant, promoted Captain; killed at Reams Station June 30, '64.
William L. Frierson			Promoted Lieutenant; then Captain.
1st Lieutenant—			
William J. Baker	'62		Resigned.
2nd Lieutenants—			
James McNeil	'62		In command of the Company.
Ford Finnegan	'62	April 9, '65	Promoted 2nd Lieutenant; '64, from 3rd Lieutenant.
3rd Lieutenant—			
G. E. Kellam		April 9, '65	
ENLISTED MEN.			
Barry, E. E.			
Gaskins, Lewis			
Giddens, Andrew J.	Sept. '62		
Giddens, Ezekiel J.	July '62		
Jackson, Thomas B.			
Kellam, W. W.			
Lang, William M.	July 25, '63	April 9, '65	
McKinnon, Christopher W.	Dec. 20, '62	April 9, '65	Lost his right arm.
Merritt, William		April 9, '65	
Mobley, Byrd	Mch. '62	April 9, '65	Lost arm at Cold Harbor June 5, '64.
Morris, James E.	Mch. 15, '62	April 9, '65	
Overstreet, G. W.		April 9, '65	
Safford, W. D.		April 9, '65	
Smith, Allen		April 9, '65	
Smith, A. H.	Jan. '63	April 9, '65	Wounded at Culpepper Court House May 6, '64.
Stafford, Samuel Y.	Sept 1, '63	April 9, '65	Shot at Reams Station August 21, '64.
Vaughn, Jonathan	'62	April 9, '65	Teamster.
Wells, George W.	'62	April 9, '65	
Wilder, A. J.			Killed at Fredericksburg.
Williams, John W.	'61		Paroled June 1,'65 from hospital in Va.
Wilson, Thomas J.	Mch. '63	April 9, '65	

Roll Company K—9th Florida Infantry.

NAMES.	MUSTERED IN.	MUSTERED OUT.	REMARKS.
OFFICERS.			
Captain—			
Jacob C. Eichelberger	Sept. 4, '63		Captured near Baldwin, Fla., February, '64; sent to Johnson's Island, N. Y., where he remained until the close of war.
1st Lieutenant—			
James Porter Smith	Sept. 4, '63	April 26, '65	
2nd Lieutenant—			
Henry W. Long	Sept. 4, '63	April 26, '65	Wounded at Olustee February 20, '64.
3rd Lieutenants—			
Joseph Caldwell	Sept. 4, '63		Resigned, '63 or '64.
G. H. Grimes		April 26, '65	Corporal; promoted 3rd Lieutenant for gallant conduct at Olustee.
N. G. V. Grinner	Sept. 4, '63		1st Corporal; promoted 3rd Lieutenant for gallant conduct at Olustee.
ENLISTED MEN			
Bateman, A. H.			
Blount, S. J. C.	April '62	April 26, '65	
Brown, E.			
Brown, John M.	May 10, '61	April 26, '65	
Carrol, Ben B.			
Crews,	Sept. 4, '63		Corporal.
Crowson, J. W. S.	Sept. 4, '63		Sergeant.
Eichelberger, A. L.			
Forbes, H. B.	Sept. 7, '63		
Frink, M. P.			
Geiger, Elias	Sept. 4, '63		2nd Corporal.
Goin, Aaron			Sergeant.
Hillhouse, W. H.			Captured April 1, '65, carried to Point Lookout; paroled from there July ,'65.
Howard, Wiley	Sept. 3, '63		Lost right arm at Cold Harbor.
Hudgens, Henry H.	Sept. 4, '63	April 26, '65	2nd Sergeant.
King, James N.			Wounded at Olustee February 20, '64.
Luffman, W. H.	'63	April 26, '65	
McDermott, Hiram		April 26, '65	
McDonald, Edward	Nov. '63	April 26, '65	Wounded at Olustee February 22, '64; Cold Harbor June, '64.
McDonald, J. R.		April 26, '65	

Roll Company K—9th Florida Infantry.
(CONTINUED.)

NAMES.	MUSTERED IN.	MUSTERED OUT.	REMARKS.
Osteen, Orlando	Sept. 4, '63		1st Sergeant.
Owen, W. J.		April 26, '65	
Parish, John E.		April 26, '65	
Prevatt, L. M.	Oct. '63	April 9, '65	
Proctor, John	'62	April 26, '65	Shot at Olustee February 20, '64.
Pyles, Thomas W	Sept. '62	April 26, '65	
Roberts, James		April 26, '65	
Sapp,	Sept. 4, '62		Sergeant.
Smith, Solomon		April 26, '65	
Smith, Welba	Sept. 4, '62		Corporal; promoted Sergeant.
Wallace, Thomas J.		April 26, '65	Wounded at Olustee February 20, '64; died March
Warren, Josiah	Oct. 7, '62	April 26, '65	20, '64.
Waters, John	'62	April 26, '65	
Waters, Thomas C.	Oct. '62	April 26. '65	Wounded at Weldon R. R.
Witt,			Sergeant.

TENTH FLORIDA INFANTRY.

The 10th Regiment was composed of the 1st Battalion, Captains J. C. Richard, Co. A; C. J. Jenkins, Co. B; William P. Frink, Co. C; Thomas E. Buckman, Co. D; William H. Kendrick, Co. E; Wash W. Scott, Co. F; and four companies from the 2nd Battalion, commanded by Captains Sam W. May, Co. G; John Q. Stewart, Co. H John Westcott, Co. I, and Marion J. Clark, Co. K. The Regiment was commanded by Lieut.-Col. Charles Hopkins, promoted Colonel; Capt. Wash W. Scott promoted to L eutenant-Colonel, and John Westcott promoted Major. Up to April 2. 1865, when General Lee's lines were broken, the stories of the 9th, 10th and 11th Regiments are almost identical in their general features The 10th Florida surrendered at Appomatox 18 officers and 154 men.

Roll, Field and Staff—10th Florida Infantry.

NAMES.	MUSTERED IN.	MUSTERED OUT	REMARKS.
Colonel—			
Charles F. Hopkins	'62	April 9, '65	This Regiment was discharged from service at close of war.
Lieutenant-Colonel—			
W. W. Scott	'62	April 9, '65	
Majors—			
John Wescott	'62	April 9, '65	
Richard Lewis	'62	April 9, '65	
Surgeon—			
W. J. D. Danzler	'62	April 9, '65	
Assistant Surgeon—			
M. J. D. Danzler			
Adjutant—			
John C. Buffington	'62	April 9, '65	
Sergeant-Major—			
James C. McCabe	'62	April 9, '65	
Quartermaster—			
B. F. Solee	'62	April 9, '65	
Commissary—			
Quartermaster-Sergeant—			
George N. Cline		April 9, '65	
Commissary-Sergeants—			
Chaplain—			
Hospital Steward—			

Roll Company A—10th Florida Infantry.

NAMES.	MUSTERED IN.	MUSTERED OUT.	REMARKS.
OFFICERS.			
Captain—			
J. C. Richard			Discharged at Appomattox April 9, '65.
1st Lieutenant—			
M. G. Murphy			
2nd Lieutenants—			
R. B. Subrent			Resigned.
H. N. Richard			Wounded at St. John's Bluff, Fla., November, '62; discharged at Appomattox April 9, '65.
3rd Lieutenants—			
R. E. Jones			Deserted at Camp Finnegan.
R. F. Lewis			Discharged at Appomattox April 9, '65.
A. M. Pasco			
ENLISTED MEN.			
Adam, J. W.		April 9, '65	
Adams, Hilman W.	Sept. '61	April 9, '65	Wounded in Va., toward close of war.
Adams, William D.	Sept. '61		
Adams, John Q.			
Addison, John W.	April '64	April 9, '65	Wounded at Petersburg, Va., July 30, '64.
Alexander, William			
Anderson, William	May 12, '62		Wounded at High Bridge, Va., April 1, '65.
Andrews, J. A.			Wounded at St. John's Bluff, '63.
Beasley, B. S.	Sept. 14, '61	April 9, '65	Corporal.
Beasley, M. R.		April 9, '65	
Benton, T. F.			
Bennett, B.			
Bennett, R. H.			
Bennyfield, M.			
Boothe, E.			
Brooker, William H.	Feb. 15, '63	June 6, '65	Captured at Petersburg, Va., September 10, '64; carried to Point Lookout, Md., and remained there until paroled.
Brown, Jerome		April 9, '65	
Bryan, A.			
Bryant, T. C.			
Campbell, F. F.			
Campbell, Henry F.		April 9, '65	
Carrera, Gasper			Killed at Petersburg, Va.
Carter, Isaac			
Cason, A. J.	April '63	April 9, '65	Wounded in Virginia.
Cate, T. H.			
Cate, H. C.			
Chestnut, James	Sept. '61	April 9, '65	Wounded at Olustee, Fla., February 20, '64.
Crews, Joseph			
Culpepper, B. S.			
Davenport, J. T.			
Deas, Calvin A.	Nov. '62		Shot at Olustee, Fla., February 20, '64.
Dees, Franklin P.	Nov. '61		Shot at Olustee, Fla., February 20, '64.
Deas, H.			
Dees, Miles C.			
Delaberly, Joseph T.			Wounded severely at Cold Harbor, Va., June 3, '64.
Denison, D. C.		'63	Disability.
Dennison, T. M.		April 9, '65	Wounded at Petersburg, Va., July, '64.
Diog, M. C.			
Dukes, Silas E.			
Durden, T. J.	Sept. 3, '62		Wounded at Olustee February 20, '64.
Eddy, William F.			
Edge, A. J.			
Edwards, William			
Elks, Thomas S.			
Emmerick, Joseph			Killed in battle.
Farnell, Daniel			
Forsythe, F. M.		April 9, '65	
Forsythe, J. V.			
Forsythe, M. I.			
Forsythe, William T.		April 9, '65	
Gatlin, George		April 9, '65	
Gatlin, John			
Gommelion, A. F.			
Gommelion, J. B.			
Hagan, David			
Hall, Elisha			
Hall, John	Sept. 25, '61		Shot at Cold Harbor, Va., June 4, '64; promoted Sergeant.
Hardee, Joseph			
Harris, John			
Hilliard, James			
Hodge, R. C.			
Hollingworth, Gilbert	Sept. 28, '61	April 9, '65	
Hollingworth, William			
Hosford, R. F.			
James, James T.	'62		
Johns, Jackson J.		April 9, '65	Wounded at Cold Harbor, Va., February 14, '63.
Johns, William			
Johns, Levi	Sept. '61	April 9, '65	
Johnson, W. H.		April 9, '65	
Jones, Charles			
Jones, James T.	Sept. 1, '61	April 9, '65	

Roll Company A—10th Florida Infantry.

(Continued.)

NAMES.	MUSTERED IN.	MUSTERED OUT.	REMARKS.
Jones, T. J.		April 9, '65	
Kelley, J. G.		April 9, '65	
Kelley, Wesley W.			
Kennedy, Augustus.		April 9, '65	
Kennedy, James H.			Sergeant.
Kennedy, B. K.			
Kyle, David.			Sergeant.
Landing, Thomas P.	'61		Lost left eye.
Lewis, Richard F.		April 9, '65	
Long, J. V.		April 9, '65	
McGlin, H.		April 9, '65	
Malphurs, Edward.			
Malphurs, James E.	Mch. '62	July 1, '65	From hospital in Va.
Masturs, C. P.		April 9, '65	
Minton, J. T.			
Moore, James A.			
Moore, J. W.		April 9, '65	
Morgan, Thomas L.	May '62	April 9, '65	
Muller, C. P.			
Murphy, T. M.		April 9, '65	
Nobles, Benjamin.		April 9, '65	
Nobles, John.			
Nobles, J. T.			
Nobles, Isam.	Sept. 18, '62	April 9, '65	
Padgett, William.			
Parker, Mathew.	'62	April 9, '65	Shot in Virginia.
Pomar, Peter.	'62	April 9, '65	
Pool, Samuel.			
Poour, A.			
Prescott, J. D.	June '62	April 9, '65	
Prevatt, J. K.		April 9, '65	
Price, H. G.			
Revels, William E.			
Richburg, Isaac.		April 9, '65	Wounded at Crater near Petersburg July, '64.
Richard, H. M.			Sergeant.
Riggs, J. M.			Died in hospital at Savannah, Ga., '64.
Roberts, James E.	July '64		
Robinson, L. M.			
Robinson, J. R.			Promoted 1st Sergeant.
Sever, J. N.	Sept. '62	April 9, '65	
Simms, Edward.			
Simms, Joseph.		April 9, '65	
Simms, W. A.			
Smith, A. P. Dr.	'62	April 9, '65	Appointed Assistant Surgeon of 2nd Regiment Cavalry; Colonel Smith, and served as such until war ended.
Smith, S. E.			
Smith, William H.			Sergeant.
Smythe, W. J.		April 9, '65	
Stoble, W. W.		April 9, '65	
Strickland, R.			
Strickland, A. J.			
Strickland, E. M.			
Subrent, F. L.			
Sullivan, Francis.		April 9, '65	
Sullivan, Henry M.	June '61	April 9, '65	Re-enlisted in Captain Maxwell's Company.
Sutton, J. W.		April 9, '65	
Taylor, John.			
Tailor, William M.		April 9, '65	
Tidwell, John C.	'63	April 9, '65	
Trueluck, J. F.			
Varnes, William A.	'61	April 9, '65	Wounded at St. John's Bluff, '64.
Warren, W. J.			
Waters, Isaac.		April 9, '65	
West, Jason.			
West, John M.			Promoted Sergeant; deserted.
West, W. S.	Mch. 1, '62	April 9, '65	
White, George.			
White, R. F.			
White, Thaddeus.	'61		Discharged for disability September 9, '64.
Williams, John R.	'62	April 09, '65	Captured and imprisoned at Newport News, Va
Williams, Jeptha V.	Feb. '63	April 9, '65	Shot at Petersburg, Va., '63.
Wilson, Jasper N.		April 9, '65	
Wilson, Joseph.			Corporal.
Windon, Joseph H.		April 9, '65	
Youngblood, Isoiah.	Sept. '61	April 9, '65	Died at Tallahassee April, '62; of pneumonia.

Roll Company B—10th Florida Infantry.

NAMES.	MUSTERED IN.	MUSTERED OUT.	REMARKS.
OFFICERS.			
Captain—			
Charles J. Jenkins			Killed at Cold Harbor.
1st Lieutenants—			
Henry Stephens			Retired at reorganization.
John Hatcher	Mch. '62	April 9, '65	Promoted 1st Lieutenant from 1st Sergeant.
2nd Lieutenants—			
Samuel K. Collins			
V. R. Collins		April 9, '65	Surrendered, 2nd Lieutenant.
3rd Lieutenants—			
James Blalock			Retired at reorganization.
John B. Stallings			
ENLISTED MEN.			
Arnold, Daniel			
Arnold, Frank			
Arnold, Perry			
Arnold, Redding			
Arnold, Samuel			
Ayers, Frank			1st Corporal.
Barnard,			
Bass, Moses			
Blair, William			
Blalock, Jefferson			
Blalock, Thomas			
Blount, Samuel			
Boyd, Macon			
Bradshaw, John			2nd Sergeant.
Cason, Harley			
Cason, Henry			
Cheshire, Richard			Wounded at Petersburg.
Cornwell, George			
Cribbs, Darrell J	May 2, '62	May '65	
Cribbs, Jordan	May 2, '62	May '65	
Cribbs, Owen B	May 2, '62	May '65	
Cribbs, Thomas	May 2, '62	May '65	
Culpepper, Benjamin			
Curlbreth, Obediah			
Curlbreth, Thomas C			
Daniels, Elias			
Dease, Mathew			
Downing, Elk			
Downing, William			
Farnell, Daniel	Sept. 1, '61		
Green, Daniel D			5th Sergeant.
Green, James			
Hardee, Cornelius			
Hardee, Isaac			
Hardee, Joseph H			
Harrison, Thomas B	Sept. '61		Wounded at Olustee, Fla.
Hogans, Edward			
Hogans, Samuel			
Hogans, Tiny			Wounded at Petersburg, Va., June 19, '64.
Hogarty, John			
Horn, Eli C			
Horn, Mallory			
Horn, Simeon			
Hudgens			
Hunter, Luke			
Jackson, Andrew			3rd Sergeant.
Jackson, Henry			
Jackson, Dock			
Jackson, James			
Jackson, Rufus			....
Jackson, Thomas			
Jackson, William			
Kendrick, James			
Knight, Jonathan			
Knight John			
Lamb, William			
Lee, Palmer			
McCall, Jesse			
McCall, Joel			
McCall, Thomas	Mch. 21, '62		Shot at Petersburg December, '64; captured and paroled from prison at Newport News June 21, '65.
McCormick, Mathew			Wounded at Olustee February 20, '64.
McCormick,			
McNeal,			
Matthis, Dock			
Mobley, Hardee			
Ogelsby, Frank			
Ogelsby, James			
Ogelsby, John			
Ogelsby, Marion			
Padgett, George			

Roll Company B—10th Florida Infantry.
(CONTINUED.)

NAMES.	MUSTERED IN.	MUSTERED OUT.	REMARKS.
Powell, George W	Aug. '61		2nd Sergeant; transferred to Signal Corps;
Prayther, J. Y		April 9, '65	wounded four times, twice seriously.
Prather, Pope			
Prather, William			
Register, Abe			
Register, Chester A			
Register, David			
Register, Francis		Apri, 9, '65	
Register, Samuel			
Register, William	Mch. '62	April 9, '65	Shot at Weldon R. R. August 25, '64.
Roebuck, Willis			
Rollins, Robert			
Scott, George A. K			Wounded at Olustee February 20, '64.
Seavens, Fielding			
Shaw, Crawford			
Shaw, Densey			
Shaw Elbert			
Shaw, Greenberry			
Sharp, Thomas M		April 9, '65	
Shiver, Bonaparte			
Shiver, Green			4th Sergeant.
Smith, Gabriel			
Smith, Wilder			
Starling, Jasper			
Stevens, Floy		April 9, '65	
Thompson, Edward			
Wilson,			
Wilson			
Woods, Pleasant			
Woods, William			
Woods			
Woodward, Mathew			
Zipperer, T. J		April 9, '65	

Roll Company C—10th Florida Infantry.

NAMES.	MUSTERED IN.	MUSTERED OUT.	REMARKS.
OFFICERS.			
Captains—			
William P. Frink			
Edwin West			Promoted Captain from 1st Lieutenant.
1st Lieutenant—			
George Robinson			Promoted 1st Lieutenant from 1st Sergeant.
2nd Lieutenants—			
Alexander A. Stewart			Resigned.
S. G. Burk			Promoted 2nd Lieutenant; died, '64.
3rd Lieutenants—			
J. L. Morgan			Promoted 3rd Lieutenant; died while at home on
H. A. Blount			furlough.
ENLISTED MEN.			
Allen, J. J			
Allen, R. H			
Allison, J. W	June '61	April 9, '65	
Allison, R. F		April 9, '65	
Anderson, William		April 9, '65	
Averitt, J. M		April 9, '65	
Barr, J. A			
Blackman, Joab			
Blair, W. W			
Bohanon, John			
Bohannon, W		April 9, '65	Corporal.
Brown, F. J			
Brown, Jesse			
Brown, Mathew			
Bryant, T. J		April 9, '65	
Bryan, J. W		April 9, '65	
Bullock, Josiah			
Burke, W. W			Promoted 2nd Sergeant.
Burge, W. G			
Burnham, William			
Cannon, E, M			
Cannon, T. C			
Cannon, S. H			
Carraway, Joseph			
Carruth, J. L			1st Sergeant.
Chamberlain, John			
Cheshire, W		April 9, '65	

Roll Company C—10th Florida Infantry.
(CONTINUED.)

NAMES.	MUSTERED IN.	MUSTERED OUT.	REMARKS.
Chixkers, William			
Coker, J. M		April 9, '65	1st Corporal.
Coleman, William			
Crews, John			
Cribbs, D. L			
Davenport, James R		April 9, '65	Corporal; promoted Sergeant.
Davenport, Seth. G		April 9, '65	Promoted Sergeant; wounded at Cold Harbor June 3, '64.
Davenport, William			Sergeant.
Davis, C. A		April 9, '65	
Day, Joseph		April 9, '65	
Day, William	Oct. '61	July '64-'65	Re-enlisted in Quincey Stewart's Company.
Dees, F. Perry		April 9, '65	
Dempsey, Andrew		April 9, '65	Wounded at Olustee February 20, '64.
Davery, J. R			
Dorman, D. H			
Dorman, George H		April 9, '65	
Driver, William			
Duncan, W. W		April 9, '65	
Ferguson, William			
Fields, W. H			
Fishbon, E. C			
Fishbon, W. F			
Frink, G. W			Sergeant.
Gibbs, William M			
Gill, Edward		April 9, '65	
Gill, John			Wounded severely near Petersburg, Va., March, '65.
Gordy, George			
Green, D. D			
Green, Samuel		April 9, '65	Wounded at Olustee February 20, '64.
Green, W. Thomas		April 9, '65	
Ham, Aaron			
Handry. A. J			
High, William			
Hodges, R. C			Promoted 1st Sergeant.
Hodges, William			
Hodges, T. W		April 9, '65	
Inabreth, James N	Sept. 6, '61	April 9, '65	Wounded in shoulder April 7, '61 at Sailor's Creek, Va.
Ishum, W. L			
Johnson, B			
Johnson, G. H			
Johnson, W. L			
Jones, James			
Jowers, John H			
Keith, J. E			
Lee, H. W			
Lewis, J. M			
Lindsay, J. M			
McGauley, D			
Monk, H			
Moore, Joseph			
Morgan, Joseph			
Oliver, Alfred			Corporal.
Parrish, G. V			Sergeant.
Parrish, William			
Parrott, W. O			
Payne, Robert			
Stewart, Alexander A			Promoted 2nd Lieutenant, Company "A," 10th.
Stewart, A. W			
Stroman, William			Corporal.
Wadsworth, J. W			
Williams, John			
Williams, William			
Willis, James			
Wishard, W. H			
Woodward, J. H			Corporal.
Yates, William			

Roll Company D—10th Florida Infantry.

NAMES.	MUSTERED IN.	MUSTERED OUT.	REMARKS.
OFFICERS.			
Captains—			
Thomas E. Buckman			Promoted to general staff.
Thomas M. Mickler			Promoted Captain; from 2nd Lieutenant.
1st Lieutenants—			
John C. Buffington			Promoted Adjutant from 1st Lieutenant.

Roll Company D—10th Florida Infantry.

(CONTINUED.)

NAMES.	MUSTERED IN.	MUSTERED OUT.	REMARKS.
E. Martin		April 9, '65	Promoted 1st Lieutenant; from 3rd and Second.
2nd Lieutenant—			
W. B. Ratcliff		April 9, '65	
3rd Lieutenant—			
John M Taylor		April 9, '65	
ENLISTED MEN.			
Adams, J. W	Feb. '62	April 9, '65	
Adams, Joseph W		April 9, '65	
Barber, John			
Blalock, T. F.			
Booth, John			
Booth, Benjamin			Corporal.
Bronson, G. W.			
Brown, A		April 9, '65	Imprisoned at Fort Delaware.
Brown, John			
Case, John			
Clark, T. W	Sept. 27, '61		Wounded at Chattahooche River July, '63.
Clark, Wesly			
Clemens, James C		April 9, '65	2nd Corporal; wounded at Farmville, Va.
Clements, J. C		April 9, '65	
Clements, J. G			
Conner, A. S.			
Cooper, Isam			Corporal.
Cooper, Robert			
Crews, A			
Crews, D. W			
Crews, H. C.			
Crews, Samuel			
Darling, John J		April 9, '65	
Deas, F. P.			
Davis, W. M.			
Diog, M. C.			
Douglass, Elisha			Musician.
Evers, Jesse			
Eveloth, E.		April 9, '65	
Ferrand, Stephen W			Wounded at Fernandina June, '62 and discharged; re-enlisted in Ordnance Department.
Fowler, Moses			
Gilson, George			
Gilson, John	Oct. 11, '61	April 9, '65	Wounded at Olustee February 20, '64.
Geifford, William			
Geiger, John A			
Grey, Charles H.			
Griffiths, C. B.			
Haisten, William J	Mch. 4, '61		Discharged for disability.
Hannerhan, E.			
Hanhaw, B. D.			
Hardee, Joseph			
Hernandez, A			Sergeant.
Humphries, Charles D			
Humphreys, William			
Hunter, Hiram		April 9, '65	Wounded in head and foot in Va., '63.
Hutchins, William			
Ingerville, James			
Johnson, William L.			
Johnson, James			
Keene, Joseph B.			
Kennedy, James			Sergeant.
Knowles, A. J.			
Knowles, George			
Knowles, T. A	Oct. 14, '61	April 15, '65	Captured, '64, and imprisoned at Hilton Head S. C., until close of war.
Lewis, M. D	Mch. '63	April 9, '65	Wounded at Turkey Ridge, Va., 15, '64.
McCabe, James M.			1st Sergeant.
McGowan, D. L	Dec. '61	April 9, '65	Wounded by R. R. cars May 1, '64.
McGowan, J. N		April 9, '65	
McLaws, John K		April 9, '65	
Mickler, Daniel			
Mickler, John H			Corporal.
Mickler, Peter T		April 9, '65	
Mickler, Robert			
Mickler. Samuel C			
Morris, W. C		April 9, '65	2nd Sergeant.
Munson, W		April 9, '65	
Oliver, William			
Owens, W. J		April 9, '65	
Parker, Simon			
Parker, William			
Parmenter, D. M.			
Price. Davis			
Ratcliff, Carter			Promoted Sergeant.
Ratcliff, W. B.			
Roe, John T		April 9, '65	3rd Corporal.
Scarborough, W. A	Mch. 4, '62	April 9, '65	Wounded at Cold Harbor May 5, '62.
Sessions, Joseph			

Roll Company D—10th Florida Infantry.
(CONTINUED.)

NAMES.	MUSTERED IN.	MUSTERED OUT	REMARKS.
Sharpton, A. M.		April 9, '65	
Shepherd, William A.		April 9, '65	Shot at Cold Harbor June 3, '64 and died in hospital at Richmond, Va.
Smith, David		April 9, '65	
Smith, Isaac			
Smith, Joseph			
Sowell, John V.		April 9, '65	Wounded by R. R. accident at Tallahassee, Fla. March 10, '62.
Stukey, James			
Summerall, T. J.			Imprisoned at Fort Delaware.
Summerall, Henry			
Sweat, Alfred			
Sykes, Joseph			
Thompson, E. F.		April 9, '65	1st Corporal.
Thompson, James			Musician.
Tracy, W. Irvin			
Turner, Owin			
Tucker, Willoughby			
Tyre, John			
Varnes, W. A.		April 9, '65	
Whittle, J. N.		April 9, '65	
Wilkerson, A.			Corporal.
Wilkerson, Bryant		April 9, '65	
Wilkerson, E.		April 9, '65	
Wilkerson, John		April 9, '65	Wounded at Olustee February 20, '64.
Willis, Joseph			
Williams, George J.			
Wince, George C.			
Worth, Wilson			

Roll Company E—10th Florida Infantry.

NAMES.	MUSTERED IN.	MUSTERED OUT.	REMARKS.
OFFICERS.			
Captains—			
W. H. Kendrick			
B. O. Grenard			Promoted from 2nd Lieutenant to Captain; wounded at Cold Harbor.
1st Lieutenants—			
W. W. Kellam			
John B. Starlin	'61	April '65	Promoted 1st Lieutenant; lost left arm at Hatcher's Run, Va., October 28, '64.
John G. G. Hamilton			Promoted 1st Lieutenant; lost right leg at Petersburg, Va., '64.
2nd Lieutenant—			
John Evans			
3rd Lieutenants—			
D. C. Cook		April 9, '65	Sergeant; promoted 3rd Lieutenant.
E. A. Hill			Promoted 3rd Lieutenant.
ENLISTED MEN.			
Allison, Robert F.			
Baker, C.			
Barber, W. W.			
Bass, J.			
Bell, W. P.		April 9, '65	
Black, N. R. G.		April 9, '65	
Blue, A.	'61		
Buck, R.			Sergeant.
Calvert, J. D.		April 9, '65	1st Sergeant.
Caruthers, Andrew Y.	Sept. '61	April 9, '65	
Caruthers, Wiley W.			
Clifton, G. W.			
Colbert, W. P.			Corporal.
Crum, T. L.			
Daniels, Elias	Sept. 15, '61	April 9, '65	
Dann, E. S.			
Dean J.			
Dorman, Geo. H.			
Driggers, James A.			
Ellis, Richard	'62		Wounded at Petersburg. Va., August 21, '64.
Fussell, B.			
Garner, Jackson			
Garner, James		April 9, '65	Corporal.
Garner, John		April 9, '65	Corporal.
Gibbens, J. J.		April 9, '65	Corporal.
Gillis, M.			
Golden, John			
Gordy, George			
Gough, J. H.			
Grant, L. G.			
Hall, D. K.			1st Sergeant; discharged, over age.

Roll Company E—10th Florida Infantry.

(CONTINUED.)

NAMES.	MUSTERED IN.	MUSTERED OUT.	REMARKS.
Hamilton, Auswell T	Sept. 26, '62	April 9, '65	
Harris, W. S.		April 9, '65	1st Corporal.
Hiatt, G.			
Hodges, J. S.			
Hutchinson, Joseph		'62	Wounded at Petersburg October 27, '64; promoted Sergeant.
Hutchinson, L. B.	June '62	April 9, '65	Wounded twice at Ream's Station, Va., August 21, '64.
Ivey, James			
Ivey, W. H.			
Johns, B.		April 9, '65	
Johns, C.		April 9, '65	Corporal.
Johns, Levi Martin			
Johnson, David B.	Mch. '62	April 9, '65	Shot at Cold Harbor June 3, '64; promoted 1st Sergeant.
Johns, T.			
Jones, W.			
Jowers, John H.	Sept. 1, '61		Was blown up by a shell which passed under feet at Richmond, Va., '64.
Kellum, Amassa		April 9, '65	
Kellum, R.		April 9, '65	2nd Sergeant.
Lamb, Hiram W.	Dec. '61		Wounded at Olustee by spent ball.
Lancaster, B. F.			
Law, S. B.			
Lee, E.			
Lee, Jesse			
Lee, J. H.			
Lindsay, M.			
Loner, J.			Sergeant.
Lyons, P.			
McDavid, A.		April 9, '65	
McEndin, W.			
McLaughlin, J. H.		April 9, '65	Corporal.
Mansell, James		April 9, '65	
Meredith, A. J.			
Mitchell, J.			
Miller, Timothy		April 9, '65	Died of disease in the hospital at Lake City, '64.
Mims, H. S.			
Monroe, James		April 9, '65	
Monroe, P.			
Monroe, S.			
Newberry, H.			
Oxner, S. J.		April 9, '65	Sergeant.
Patrick, W. W.		April 9, '65	
Prescoat, T.			
Prevatt, J. S.			Corporal.
Ratcliff, J. F.	Sept. '61	April 9, '65	
Rawlins, Robert		April 9, '65	
Richard, H. N.		April 9, '65	
Roberts, R. R.		April 9, '65	
Roe, J.			
Royster, S. W.			
Savage, John			
Savage, R.			
Savage, Robert			
Shiver, D.			
Silvester, E.			
Simmons, W.			
Smith, A. H.		April 9, '65	
Smith, C.			
Solomons, W.			
Speer, Arthur A.		April 9, '65	Wounded severely at Olustee, Fla., February 20, '64.
Sumner, James		April 9, '65	
Thomas, B. F.			
Thomas, B. R.			
Tiner, S.			
Turner, J.			
Underhill, H.			
White, W. M.			
Wilkerson, H.			
Williams, J.			
Wilson S.			

Roll Company F—10th Florida Infantry.

NAMES.	MUSTERED IN.	MUSTERED OUT.	REMARKS.
OFFICERS.			
Captains— Wash W. Scott			Promoted Colonel of the 10th Florida on the formation of that Regiment under Southern Confederacy.

Roll Company F—10th Florida Infantry.
(CONTINUED.)

NAMES.	MUSTERED IN.	MUSTERED OUT.	REMARKS.
John H. Ellis			Promoted Captain from 2nd Lieutenant; died during the war.
1st Lieutenants—			
William B. Wimberly			
Thomas O. Stewart		April 9, '65	Promoted 1st Lieutenant.
2nd Lieutenant—			
O. Williams			Promoted 2nd Lieutenant.
3rd Lieutenants—			
A. Elerson			Promoted Lieutenant.
H. W. Pooser			Promoted 3rd Lieutenant from 1st Sergeant.
ENLISTED MEN.			
Adams, James M.			
Adams, J. W.			
Adderhold, John			
Allen, J. T.			
Allison, Robert F.			
Ayers Asa			
Ayers, Ben	Sept. 15, '62	'64	Discharged for disability.
Ayers, John		April 9, '65	Wounded by accident on way to Olustee February 15, '64.
Ayers, W. M.			Died at Alum Bluff, Fla., Dec. 16, '62.
Barnes, James			
Beanen, John			
Bennett, James			
Bennett, John			
Benton, Richard			
Berry, Edward G.			
Bigham, Samuel			
Blalock, T. F.			
Brinkley W. B.			
Burnett, F.			
Burton, George		April 9, '65	
Bush, M. D.			
Bush, Marscue		April 9, '65	
Bush William R.			
Cason, A.			
Cason, Benjamin			
Campbell, R.			Wounded at Petersburg, Va., August 21, '64.
Cato, Homer C.	Aug. 24, '64		
Cato, T. C.		April 9, '65	
Cato, T. H.			
Chessir, Daniel			
Cline, George N.		April 9, '65	Quartermaster-Sergeant.
Cole, Edward			
Colson, John			
Colson, Thomas W.			
Colson, W. H.			
Corbin, John			
Conner, Alfred			
Cruise, C. B.			
Darden, J.			
Davis, E. M.			
Davis, A. H.			Killed at Olustee.
Davis, Robert M.		April 9, '65	
Davis, R. F.			Wounded near Petersburg February 5, '63.
Davis, W. M.			Wounded at Gaines' Farm, Va,. July, '64.
Deason, John			
Dees, C. A.			
Downing, Henry T.	July '62		
Downing, James			
Downing, Joseph			
Ellis, Thomas S.		April 9, '65	1st Corporal.
Farmer, James M.			
Fitts, Henry			
Fleming, Dominick			
Fletcher, J. B.		April 9, '65	
Fletcher, Peter			
Fletcher, William			
Gamble, John			
Goodrun, Simon			
Goodrich, A. S.		April 9, '65	
Gorie, Jerome			2nd Sergeant.
Hagin, John			
Hagin, Morrison			
Hale, Thomas			
Hart, J.			
Hart, Thomas			
Heath, Frank			
Holland, C. M.		April 9, '62	
Hogue, I.			
Huggins, Henry		April 9, '65	
Huggins, John			
Huggins, Martin		April 9, '65	
Huggins, W.			
Jackson, J. F.			

Roll Company F—10th Florida Infantry.

(CONTINUED.)

NAMES.	MUSTERED IN.	MUSTERED OUT.	REMARKS.
Jones, James T.			
Long, Jesse		April 9, '65	
Lowman, George W		April 9, '65	Promoted Sergeant; wounded in '64.
McAaliby, John D.		April 9, '65	
McDonell, Perceval			
McGee, James			
McLin, Jerome N			Sergeant.
McLin, N. B.			1st Sergeant.
Malphus, James			
Mickel, Allen		April 9, '65	Wounded at Olustee February 20, '64.
Mickel, Solomon		April 9, '65	
Mickler, T. M.		April 9, '65	
Moody, F. D. A		April 9, '65	
Moody, James A		April 9, '65	Wounded at Petersburg June, '64.
Moore, A. J		April 9, '65	
Money, Alfred			Musician
Money, I. A.			
Mott, Benjamin			
Mott, W. W.			
Oliver, Alfred	Sept. '61	April 9, '65	Wounded at Olustee February 20, '64.
Oneal, Douglass			
Overstreet, J. C.		April 9, '65	2nd Corporal.
Pendarvis, Daniel B			
Penderois, E. L.			Corporal; killed in service.
Penderois, I. B.			Corporal.
Perry, John			
Pitts, James			
Pooser, A. E.		April 9, '65	Corporal; promoted 1st Sergeant; wounded at Weldon.
Pooser, A.			
Power, Edward R.			
Renfroe, Green			
Ritter, William H.		April 9, '65	
Ruvers, William			
Russell, A. W.			
Sanchez, F. R.			
Sanchez, H. H.			
Sanchez, John G.			
Scarborough, Mathew W			Sergeant.
Sessions, A. M. R.	Feb. 13, '61	April 9, '65	
Sessions, S. T.		April 9, '65	
Shepherd, J. C.		April 9, '65	
Shirley, Andrew J		April 9, '65	Shot at Weldon R. R. Va., August 21, '64.
Shirley, I.			
Shirley, John			
Spires, R.			
Smith, Henry			
Smith, H. T.		April 9, '65	
Smith, W. W.		April 9, '65	
Stanly, John R			
Steverson, Samuel			Corporal.
Stuart, James M		April 9, '65	Died February 20, '64.
Stroble, D. A.		April 9, '65	1st Sergeant.
Summerlin, A. J			
Summerlin, D. I			
Sweat, Thomas W			
Swiney, Thomas			
Tidwell, Charles K			
Tindale, Hill S.		April 9, '65	
Tindale, Henry			
Tindale, Samuel			Corporal.
Tucker, R. S.		April 9, '65	
Tucker, Samuel C			
Vaughn, John			
Vaughn, Willis			
Wadsworth, V. E.		April 9, '65	Wounded at Gaines' Farm May, '63; Va., also at Weldon R. R. August 21, '64.
Walker, G.			
Walker, V.			
Whitehurst, F. L			
Wiggins, Burrel		April 9, '65	
Wilkerson, James			
Woodland, James			
Woodland, Joseph			
Wynn, Ashbey			Died of consumption November, '64.

Roll Company G—10th Florida Infantry.

NAMES.	MUSTERED IN.	MUSTERED OUT.	REMARKS.
OFFICERS.			
Captain—			
Samuel W. Mays			

Roll Company G—10th Florida Infantry.
(CONTINUED)!

NAMES.	MUSTERED IN.	MUSTERED OUT.	REMARKS.
1st Lieutenants—			
Nathan Norton			
Lucien S. Duval			Promoted from 2nd Lieutenant to 1st Lieutenant
2nd Lieutenant—			
John S. Purviance		April 9, '65	Promoted 2nd Lieutenant.
3rd Lieutenant—			
William W. Tumberlin		April 9, '65	
ENLISTED MEN.			
Alderman, George F			
Alligood, George		May '65	
Anderson, A. M			
Anderson, L. B			
Bardin, J. M			Imprisoned at Fort Delaware.
Baya, Tays			
Becks, Berrien W		April 9, '65	Corporal.
Beresford, W. W		April 9, '65	
Blount, William B			
Bolling, R. T		April 9, '65	Sergeant.
Bundy, Arthur R		April 9, '65	Corporal; promoted Sergeant.
Canow, George P			
Cavedo, Lewis D			
Caves, James P			
Dalton, Williamson W			
Darley, J. F		April 9, '65	
Davis, Alexander L		April 9, '65	
Davis, George M			
Dean, H. H		April 9, '65	
Dunham, David A		April 9, '65	Sergeant.
Eubanks, James			
Eubanks, John			
Eubanks, William N			
Fletcher, General			Lost leg at Petersburg, Va., 26, '64; died August 6, '64.
Fountain, John		April 9, '65	
Gatlin, John			
Geiger, Aaron		April 9, '65	
Geiger, Abraham B			
Geiger, Eli W			
Gillen, Robert			
Gould, Archibald			
Green, John			
Green, Samuel			Wounded at Cold Harbor, Va., sent to hospital June 3, '64, and died July 3, '64.
Grinsby, Owen M			
Harris, William H			
Hardee, Joseph		April 9, '65	
Hawthorn, William S		April 9, '65	Sergeant.
Hazell, John			
Heogans, Daniel			
Higgenbothem, Lewis W			
Hunter, William			
Hynson, P. N			
Johnson, Christopher			
Johnston, James S			
Johnston, John M			
Johnston, Stephen			
Johnston, William W		April 9, '65	
Kirkland, S. D		April 9, '65	
Lewis, Jacob			
Long, George W			
Lucas, George			Corporal.
Lucas, W. H		April 9, '65	
McConn, Alexander			
McConn, Hector			
McElvy, Daniel R		April 9, '65	
McElvy, David E			
McCalhem, Joseph I		April 9, '65	
Mincher, William			
Morgan, John J. F			
Mott, Richard			
Myers, Jesse L			
Nettles, John			
Norton, Columbus			
Norton, Nathan Jr			
Norton, Willis			
O'Hern, Michael			
Owens, Martin			
Owens, William J. W			
Osteen, Shiboleth D			
Osteen, William			
Perkins, James D			
Priest, Granville W			
Proctor, Thomas J			
Register, Aaron		April 9, '65	
Revels, William R			
Roberts, Lewis			

Roll Company G—10th Florida Infantry.
(CONTINUED.)

NAMES.	MUSTERED IN.	MUSTERED OUT.	REMARKS.
Roberts, William			Corporal.
Roe, James E		April 9, '65	
Roe, Peter	Aug. '62	April 9, '65	
Russell, Charles B			
Sapp, James			
Sauls, James			
Smith, Henry			
Sparkman, William			
Stafford, R. F			
Stafford, Joseph E			
Sweat, John			
Tedder, Andrew J			
Temples, G. W			
Thomas, James A	July '62		Died in hospital at Lake City of measles May 10
Thompson, D. W		April 9, '65	'63.
Tyer, Jesse		April 9, '65	
Usina, John			Sergeant.
Walker, Andrew J			
Walker, James B			
Walker, Samuel H			
Wheeler, R. J			
Wilds, Nathaniel			
Wilds, Spicer B			
Wilson, James			
Wilson, Jesse		April 9, '65	
Wright, Abner		April 9, '65	Corporal.

Roll Company H—10th Florida Infantry.

NAMES.	MUSTERED IN.	MUSTERED OUT.	REMARKS.
OFFICERS.			
Captain—			
John Q. Stewart			
1st Lieutenants—			
F. M. Selph			Resigned.
W. B. Brown			Promoted 1st Lieutenant from 2nd Lieutenant.
2nd Lieutenants—			
E. Brown			Promoted 2nd Lieutenant.
A. E. Willard		April 9, '65	Surrendered 2nd Lieutenant.
3rd Lieutenant—			
D. M. Stewart			Resigned January 5, '61.
ENLISTED MEN.			
Allen, Norman			
Blalock, J. S			Promoted Sergeant.
Bird, Arthur			
Brannon, James			Imprisoned at Fort Delaware.
Brinkley, W. B			
Brown, D. C			Sergeant.
Brown, E			
Brown, J. A			
Brown, J. L			
Brown, J. V			
Browning, A. J		Oct. '63	Disability.
Bryan, T. J			
Bush, W. L			Sergeant.
Burnett, Richard		April 9, '65	
Chambers, J. W		April 9, '65	
Clark, Lewis			
Clark, T. S			
Cook, J. J			
Crews, Elias			
Curry, J. M			
Curry, J. C			
Daniels, J. B			
Davis, H. L			
Davis, J. L			
Day, William			
Dicks, T. D			
Driggers, B. A			
Driggers, Edward F		April 9, '65	
Dougherty, William			
Duke, G. F			
Faircloth, B			
Feagles, Drayton			
Ferrin, G. L			
Ferrand, John			
Ferrin, S. W			

SOLDIERS OF FLORIDA.

Roll Company H—10th Florida Infantry.

(CONTINUED.)

NAMES.	MUSTERED IN.	MUSTERED OUT.	REMARKS.
Foster, James, Sr			
Foster, J. M		April 9, '65	Wounded at Jacksonville, Fla., February 24, '63.
Futch, E. M	Mch. 8, '63		Discharged June 29, '65 from Point Lookout prison in Maryland.
Gaylard, J. W			
Gailliard, J. Lawrence		April 9, '65	
Green, J. O			
Graham, Thomas			
Grisson, J. L			
Hall, E		April 9, '65	Captured near Petersburg September 10, '64; imprisoned at Point Lookout.
Hane, Urban H		April 9, '65	Sergeant; wounded at St. Johns Bluff, Fla., again at Petersburg.
Harris, Henry H			Wounded at Petersburg, Va., August, '64 and disabled.
Herrington, W. M			
Herndon, Charles			
Herndon, Daniel			
Hooker, Stephen J. L			
Howard, J. C			
Hull, William B			
Humphries, R. A			
Hunter, R. H			
Hutchinson, M. M		April 9, '65	
Johns, Mathew	Aug. 1, '62		Wounded at Petersburg, Va., Aug. 2, '64.
Johnson, Stephen			
Jones, G. J			Sergeant.
Keen, J. B			
Keen, J. J			
Knight, John			
Knight, J. R. C	Aug. '62		Wounded at Petersburg August 4, '64.
King, J. B			
Lane, B. A			
Landford			Corporal.
Lee, James			
Lewis, J. S			Promoted Corporal.
Lowe, J. T			Corporal.
McColors, O		April 9, '65	
McGraudey, William			
Mann, H. H			
Marlow. J. S			Imprisoned at Fort Delaware.
Mickler, W. J			
Mixon, W. W			
Morgan, B. L		April 9, '65	Corporal.
Morgan, W. L		April 9, '65	
Moseley, H. H		April 9, '65	
Newborn, Alfred			
Nobles A			
Padgett, Henry		April 9 '65	
Patterson, John			
Reeves, David		April 9, '65	
Roberts, N. H			1st Sergeant; died in service; killed in Virginia '64.
Robinson, C			
Ruff, H. B		April 9, '65	
Ruff, S. A		April 9, '65	
Sapp, John			
Saunders, A. G			
Shirley, C			
Slater, J			
Smith, M. B			
Starling, W. R			
Stewart, A. A		April 9, '65	Captured, '64.
Stokes, Henry			Killed at Turkey Ridge, Va., May, '64.
Sweeney, Thomas		April 9, '65	
Tice, W. H			
Truelock, H. H			
Tompkins, Donald			
Tompkins, Giles			
Tison, Adam		April 9, '65	
Tyson, William H		April 9, '65	
Tucker, E. A			
Tucker, W. J			
Tyner, Edward			
Underwood, W. H		April 9, '65	Sergeant.
Wadsworth W. B			
Warren William		April 9, '65	
Waters, Isaac			
Williams, A			
Williams, E			
Williams, James			
Williams, W. P			
Wilkerson, Charlton			
Yelvington, Aaron		April 9, '65	
Young, J. E			

Roll Company I—10th Florida Infantry.

NAMES.	MUSTERED IN.	MUSTERED OUT.	REMARKS.
OFFICERS.			
Captains—			
John Westcott			
Samuel Agnew			Promoted Captain; wounded at Petersburg, Va.
Albert E. Willard			Promoted Captain.
1st Lieutenants—			
George C. Bowers			
W. O. Hampton			Private; promoted 1st Lieutenant '64; resigned March 18, '65.
2nd Lieutenants—			
Oscar F. Bradford			
Robert D. Mickler			
Burton Williams			Surrendered 2nd Lieutenant.
3rd Lieutenant—			
ENLISTED MEN.			
Arnow, James B			
Ashton, Samuel			
Bacon, George			
Bacon, Sylvester			
Blair, Samuel T			
Black, Alexander			
Black, James			
Bourne, Richard			
Bowers, George C		April 9, '65	
Braddock, Oscar F	Nov. '62	Mch. '64	Resignation commission.
Braddock, Spicer C			
Braziel, John			
Brown, Asbury		April 9, '65	
Brumhaus, William			
Canova, B. C			
Carroway, Joshua			
Carman, John A			
Carter, John			Was killed at Weldon Railroad, Va., August 22, '63.
Carrera, Gasper	April '62		Killed at Petersburg, Va., '64.
Cason, D		April 9, '65	
Clark, George W			
Clark, Thomas			
Cobb, Thomas			
Cluntos, Sabeo			
Crawford, D. C			Promoted Sergeant of Litter Bearers; wounded at Petersburg, Va.
Darley, J. F			
Dickerson, W. M			
Emery, Caleb			
Farron, Joseph			
Firns, Stephen			Sergeant.
Floyd, Andrew			Killed in service.
Floyd, A. V			
Floyd, Joseph B			
Floyd, Joseph F			Sergeant.
Flynn, Charles			
Fussell, Jacob			
Gailson, Ephraim			
Gamble, David F			
Gardner, Charles F		April 9, '65	
Gardner, John A			
Gardner, William			
Gaston, F		April 9, '65	
Geiger, John			
Grace, Major			Corporal.
Grace, Tilman			
Grace, Thomas			
Graham, Thomas J		April 9, '65	Sergeant.
Genter, Daniel			
Haddock, Zackariah			
Hammond, W. R			
Hanford, Charles C			Corporal.
Hartley, Benjamin			Sergeant.
Hartley, Francis			
Hartley, Joseph			
Hartley, George A	Mch. '63		Captured March 20, '63 and died in hospital at Fort Delaware, Md., August 28, '63.
Hartley, Joseph A			
Hendricks, William			
Henderson, J. M			
Hentley, Gabriel			
Hentley, George W			
Hernandez, Francis T		April 9, '65	
Hernandez, Joseph			
Hertley, James W			
Hogan, Joseph R			
Hogan, L. D			
Hudnall, Francis			
Hudnall, James			
Hudnall, Samuel			
Hugin, Anthony			

Roll Company I—10th Florida Infantry.

(CONTINUED,)

NAMES.	MUSTERED IN	MUSTERED OUT.	REMARKS.
Hysler, G. W.			
Jones, Hillard, Jr.			
Jones, Redding B.			
Johnson, John H.			
Lamee, William.			
Landing, T. P.	June 15, '63		Lost left eye at Weldon Railroad May 15, '64.
Linton, Charles.			Sergeant.
Linten, William Y.			
McGran, Robert M.			
McNeil, Joshua.			
Mallett, William B.			Corporal.
Masters, Cassimero.		April 9, '65	
Masters, D.		April 9, '65	
Masters, William.			
Mills, James T.			
Mixon, Thomas.			Corporal.
Obagus, Peter.			
O'Quinn, Daniel F.		April 9, '65	Shot at Horseshoe, Va., August 21, '64.
Ormand, Alex W.		April 9, '65	
Ormand, A. O.		April 9, '65	
Overstreet, G. W.		April 9, '65	
Parramore, R. W.			
Philips, A. B. Dr.		April 9, '65	
Pinkard, J. R.		April 9, '65	
Plummer, Edward D.		April 9, '65	Sergeant.
Plummer, Simeon.		April 9, '65	
Pomar, K.		April 9, '65	
Ponce, Tolemdy.		April 9, '65	
Ponce, William G.			
Price, John L.			
Quigley, Jesse M.			
Railey, George.			
Roberts, A.		April 9, '65	
Pogeo, John.			
Ruffin, John C.			
Rutherford, J. J.		April 9, '65	
Simms, Joseph.			Wounded at Ream's Station August 22, '64.
Simms, Varden.			
Speer, J.		April 9, '65	
Squires, Samuel.		April 9, '65	
Starling, Benjamin.			
Stanling, Abraham.			
Stephens, Constant.			
Stone, Charles.			
Stone, David.			
Summerstien, E. P.			Shot at Weldon Railroad, Va., August 20, '64.
Thomas, Colon.	June 15, '63	April 9, '65	Killed at Jacksonville, Fla., March 18, '63.
Turner, Fielding T.			Shot at Jacksonville, Fla., March 17, '63; died in
Turner, Thomas F.			hospital at Lake City, Fla., March 20, '63.
Tyler, Richard R. R.			
Wakeman, A. B.			
Walker, Clark.			
Whatton, Francis J.			1st Sergeant.
Wheetman, Bernard.			
Wheetman, Philip.			
Williamson, John.		April 9, '65	
Williams, W.		April 9, '65	Corporal.

Roll Company K—10th Florida Infantry.

NAMES.	MUSTERED IN.	MUSTERED OUT.	REMARKS.
OFFICERS.			
Captains—			
Pickens B. Bird.			Promoted Major; mortally wounded at Cold Harbor June 3, '64, died at Harmory Grove Hospital June 5, '64.
Marion J. Clark.		April 9, '65	Promoted Captain from 1st Lieutenant.
1st Lieutenant—			
Rich W. Hill.		April 9 '65	
2nd Lieutenant—			
W. R. Yates.		April 9 '65	Promoted 2nd Lieutenant from Sergeant.
3rd Lieutenant—			
ENLISTED MEN.			
Alderman, George F.		April 9, '65	
Aldrick, Thomas.		April 9, '65	

Roll Company K—10th Florida Infantry.
(Continued.)

NAMES.	MUSTERED IN.	MUSTERED OUT	REMARKS.
Aldrich, W. U.		April 9, '65	Belonged to the Confederate Navy but was attached to Company "K," 10th Regiment at surrender.
Albritton, James M.			
Aldridge, Thomas			
Anderson, James M.			
Andrews, Valentine E.		April 9, '65	
Baurick, Ridding.			
Benton, S. J.			Corporal.
Berry, H. H.		April 9, '65	Sergeant.
Blanchard, C.			
Blanton, E. C.			
Butler, J.		April 9, '65	
Carver, H. R.		April 9, '65	
Chase, Charles F.			
Chase, Thomas J.			Sergeant.
Clark, Jno. M.		April 9, '65	
Cuthbert, Isaac J.			
Cuthbert, J. G.		April 9, '65	Sergeant.
Darley, James.			
Davis, Elisha.			
Dawkens, Washington.			
DeMott, Abram.			
Devane, J. J.		April 9, '65	
Danford, George W.			
Dickson, L. R.		April 9, '65	
Easters, John.			
Edwards, Benjamin W.			
Edwards, Oscar.			
Edwards, Thomas H.			
Evans, James R.			
Farrell, Alex. M.			
Folson, J. N.			
Folsome, Pennerouth.		April 9, '65	
Folsom, W. J.			
Gamble, David.			
Gamble, Daniel F.			
Girardeau, W. M.			
Ham, Hardy H.			Died, '64.
Hammell, Thomas.			
Hancock, Sidney.			
Harrell, W. H.			
Harp, J. L.		April 9, '65	
Henderson, Hiram.		April 9, '65	Wounded at Cold Harbor June 3, '64.
Henderson, William.		April 9, '65	
Hening, George W.			
Herring, Henry C.		April 9, '65	Promoted Corporal.
Hill, James G.		April 9, '65	1st Sergeant.
Hill, Theophilus.			
Hagan, John H.			
Holder, James.			
Howell, Caswell.			
Howard, Solomon W.			
Hudson, J. J.			
Joiner, H. G.		April 9, '65	
Joyner, John.			
Jones, Nathaniel L.			
Kemp, Jeremiah.			
Kersy, William.			
King, Willis P.			
Long, S. K.		April 9, '65	
Lord, Culling.			
Lord, Sol. W.			
Lord, William R.			
McCall, George T.			
McCants, A. C.			
McDuffie, Daniel.			
McKinnon, John.			Sergeant.
McLeod, David.		April 9, '65	
McMullen, David G.		April 9, '65	
McMullen, Thomas J.		April 9, '65	
Maulden, J.		April 9, '65	
Miller, Martin V.			
Mixon, John T.			
Morris, Harmon W.		April 9, '65	
Moore, H. W.		April 9, '65	
Montgomery, James.			
Neely, Samuel W.			Transferred to Company "A" Confederate Cavalry.
Norwood, Daniel J.			
O'Neal, Jou B.			
O'Quinn, D. F.			
Porter, W. F.		April 9, '65	
Prather, S. W.		April 9, '65	
Powell, J. F.		April 9, '65	
Powell, S. G.		April 9, '65	
Procter, Henry.			

Roll Company K—10th Florida Infantry.
(CONTINUED.)

NAMES.	MUSTERED IN.	MUSTERED OUT.	REMARKS.
Rheames, William E.			
Rodgers, Joseph B.		April 9, '65	
Rodgers, J. M.		April 9, '65	
Rowell, Darling.			Wounded mortally April 20, '64.
Rozier, Charles.			
Sapp, Moses W.		April 9, '65	
Scott, James E.		April 9, '65	
Scott, Samuel W.			
Scruggs, James.			
Simpkins, T. B.		April 9, '65	
Simmons, F. R.		April 9, '65	
Simmons, James.			
Sloan, T. M.		April 9, '65	
Smith, Albert D.			
Smith, J. W.		April 9, '65	
Smith, O. P.		April 9, '65	Wounded in Va., '62.
Smith, T. W.		April 9, '65	Sergeant.
Spell, W. H.		April 9, '65	
Taylor, H. J.			
Vickery, Green G.			
Ward, James.		April 9, '65	
Wheeler, C. P.		April 9, '65	Wounded at Hatcher's Run December, '64.
Williams, James.			Corporal.
Wooten, Reeding.			

ELEVENTH FLORIDA INFANTRY.

The 11th Florida Regiment was composed of the 4th Florida Battalion, seven companies, the companies of Captains Ochus and Robinson, of the 2nd Battalion, and Cullen's unattached company. There is some confusion in the records that makes the assignment of two of the companies in this Regiment uncertain. W. J. Robinson was Captain of Co. A; Adams A. Ochus, of Co. D; Charles Beggs, of Co. E; John Tanner, of Co. F; G. W. Bassett, of Co. G; W. E. Anderson, of Co. H; Joe J. Chaires, of Co. I; D. D. McLean, of Co. K. Like the 10th the story of the 11th follows closely that of the 9th until the fateful April 6, when this Regiment with the 5th and 8th, under the command of Colonel Brevard, was sent by Colonel Lang, then in command of the Brigade, Finnegan having been transferred to Florida, by order of General Lee to protect the wagon train These Regiments were captured by General Custer's Cavalry. This accounts for the Regiment surrendering but 4 officers and 19 men on the morning of April 9 at Appomatox.

Roll, Field and Staff—11th Florida Infantry.

NAMES.	MUSTERED IN.	MUSTERED OUT.	REMARKS.
Colonels—			
T. W. Brevard.			Promoted Brigadier-General.
Lieutenant-Colonels—			
Majors—			
Surgeons—			
Assistant Surgeons—			
D. S. Boyle.			
C. S. Sample.			
Adjutants—			
Sergeant-Majors—			

Roll, Field and Staff—11th Florida Infantry.
(CONTINUED.)

NAMES.	MUSTERED IN.	MUSTERED OUT.	REMARKS.
Quartermasters—			
Commissary—			
Quartermaster-Sergeant—			
A. M. Nathans		April 9, '65	
Commissary-Sergeant—			
Z. Brown		April 9, '65	
Chaplains—			
Hospital-Steward—			

Roll Company A—11th Florida Infantry.

NAMES.	MUSTERED IN.	MUSTERED OUT.	REMARKS.
OFFICERS.			
Captain—			
W. J. Robinson			Resigned January 14, '64.
1st Lieutenant—			
John M. Erwin			
2nd Lieutenant—			
John Padgett			Resigned February 11, '64.
3rd Lieutenants—			
E. J. Mancill			Resigned January 12. '64,
James W. Gainer			
ENLISTED MEN.			
Baxter, Israel			Corporal.
Beckwith, Joshua			
Beckwith, William			
Bennett, Silas			
Bennett, Taylor			
Boggs, John G. W. G.			
Brown, B. B.			
Brown, Henry			
Bure, James A			Sergeant.
Carter, J. F.			
Carter, J. W.			
Cherry, M. K.			
Christmas, J. M.			
Cloud, D. I.			
Cloud, John		April 9, '65	
Coonrod, John	June 1, '62	April 9, '65	
Crawford, William R.			
Daniel, James			
Daniel, Lumpkin M.			
Davis, H. B.			
Davis, William E.			
Deckle, Littleton			
Dickson, Columbus			Corporal.
Dickson, J. A.			
Dickson, Lewis			
Dykes, Joseph C.		April 9, '65	Paroled from Point Lookout Prison.
Edenfield, W. M.			
Endfinger, John			
Endfinger, Vick			
Everett, Henry C.			
Everett, William	April '63	Jan. 11, '65	
Fink, J. E.			
Futch, John E.			
Folsom, J. Y.			
Gainer, J.			
Godwin, John			
Gomillian, Andrew J.			Died of disease at Marianna, Fla., January 5, '64.
Griffin, A. J.			
Griffin, Silas			
Grubbs, William		April 9, '65	
Hagin, James H.			
Hancock, James			
Hatton, S. J.			
Heming, A. C.			
Hinson, Burt A.			
Irwin, Henry			
Jacobs, Allerson			Wounded at Petersburg, Va., June 13, '64; d ed in hospital August 20, '64.
Jackson, M. A.			
Jackson, M. V.			

Roll Company A—11th Florida Infantry.
(CONTINUED.)

NAMES.	MUSTERED IN.	MUSTERED OUT.	REMARKS.
Johnson, J. P.			
Johnson, Stephen E.			
Johnson, Thomas			
Jones, D. G.		April 9, '65	
Jones, James M.			
Jones J. Pittman			Killed in battle at the ''Crater,'' Va., '64.
Kemp, D. A.			Corporal.
Knowles, A. S.			
Knowles, Charles			
Launivze, Russell			
Launioxe, Thomas H.			
Launioze, Zacariah			
Lee, Amasiah			Died; (date not given).
Ledger, Moses S.			
Lifford, William E.			
Lockhart, J. M.	Aug. '61		Promoted Corporal; wounded at Petersburg August 22, '64.
Malambre, J. A.			Sergeant.
McClelland, Daniel			
McClelland, John P. M.			
McDaniel, A. J.			
McDaniel, Columbus			
McDaniel, James			
McDaniel, Lumpkin C.			
McDonald, Lumpkin		April 9, '65	
McMath, H		April 9, '65	
McMillan, B. F.			
Mercer, Silas N.			
Mercer, W. T.			
Newsome, Dred		April 9, '65	
Newsome, E. D.		April 9, '65	
Nickols, J. J.			
Nixon, Daniel G.			
Nixon, James			
Owens, William E.	...		
Padgett, William			Sergeant.
Padgett, John W.			
Page, Callen			
Pitman, Irvin			
Porter, John H.			
Ramsey, John A.			
Register, Burrell		April 9, '65	
Rigsby, J. A.		April 9, '65	
Rigsby, T. W.		April 9, '65	
Rob nson, J. C.			
Scott, James F.		Aug. 15, '63	Disability.
Sketœ, Warren			
Sketœ, Willoughby			
Slater, Sanden			
Silcox, D.		April 9, '65	
Sowell, Jesse	Feb. 3, '63	Feb. 28, '65	Disability.
Sowell, Worley		April 9, '65	
Snead, A.			Corporal.
Stephens, James			
Strange, William			
Taylor, John W.	Dec. '62	April 9, '65	
Tyus, P. P			Sergeant.
Tyus, P. G.	Aug. '61	April 9, '65	From prison at Elmira, N. Y.
Wade, Daniel			
Wade, Samuel			
Wadford, Michael		April 9, '65	Shot at Richmond, Va., Petersburg, '64.
Walding, Seaborn			
Yearby, William J	Jan. '63	April 9, '65	Transferred to Captain Farmer's Company.
York, Thomas			

Roll Company C—11th Florida Infantry.

NAMES.	MUSTERED IN.	MUSTERED OUT.	REMARKS.
OFFICERS.			
Captain—			
E. P. Melvin		April 9, '65	Promoted Captain.
o Lieutenant—			
2nd Lieutenant—			
3rd Lieutenant—			
ENLISTED MEN.			
Burgess, J. H.		April 9 '65	

Roll Company C—11th Florida Infantry.

(CONTINUED.)

NAMES.	MUSTERED IN.	MUSTERED OUT.	REMARKS.
Canant, M. D.		April 9, '65	
Lee, J. G.		April 9, '65	
Rabon, R.		April 9, '65	

Roll Company D—11th Florida Infantry.

NAMES.	MUSTERED IN.	MUSTERED OUT.	REMARKS.
OFFICERS.			
Captains—			
Adams A. Ochus			Resigned, '64.
John Price Jr			Promoted 1st Lieutenant, then Captain' '64; Captured April 6, '65, imprisoned on Johnson's Isandl; paroled June 19, '65.
1st Lieutenant—			
Moses J. Brown			Re-enlisted in Company G, 2nd Infantry; promoted 1st Lieutenant, '64.
2nd Lieutenants—			
James L. Winter			Elected 2nd Lieutenant; died in Va., '64.
James M. Price			Promoted Sergeant, then Lieutenant; '64.
3rd Lieutenant—			
J. D. O'Hearn			Resigned, '64.
ENLISTED MEN.			
Adams, George Wash			Honorably discharged.
Adams, John Q			Honorably discharged.
Andrew, Jerome C			Honorably discharged.
Andrew, Thomas A		April 9, '65	
Anderson, George W	'63		
Aubert, Edward			Honorably discharged.
Baber, J.			
Barron, John			Deserted.
Barron, William			Deserted.
Beck, E.			Deserted.
Bell, W. P.			
Borrsky, John			Deserted.
Bory, Maxey			Deserted.
Box, John S.			Deserted.
Bradley, Ben			Captured, and paroled from prison.
Bradley, John			
Broer, John.			Honorably discharged.
Brown, G. C.			Corporal.
Brown, J. C.			Captured and paroled from prison June 19, '65.
Burney, William C			Deserted.
Burbank, D. L.			
Carmicheal, J. G.			Deserted.
Canova, R.			Honorably discharged.
Canova, Taylor			
Champlin, John W			Captured April 6, '65 and paroled from prison June 19, '65.
Copeland, Charles			Deserted.
Christopher, John			
Crenshaw, H. C.			
Crenshaw, Musco C			Killed at Petersburg.
Crimeshold,			
Danford Isaac			Deserted.
Danford, Thomas			Deserted.
Davis, John			Captured April 6, '65; paroled from prison June '65.
Ellack, William			
Flynn, James			Honorably discharged.
Flynn, J. E.			Deserted.
Gardner, Isaac			Died in '63.
Griffis, James H			Deserted.
Hammond, Elias			Deserted.
Hawkins, S. M.			
Herndon, Urbin C			Sergeant; wounded and was home on furlough at close of war.
Higgenbotham, Lewis			
Hogan, John E.			
Holgerson, R. H.		April 9, '65	
Houston, Lewis	May '63		Sergeant; wounded at Petersburg and the Wilderness; imprisoned and paroled at close of war.
Houston, Lewis C.			
Hurlbert, Henry			
Hursey, Samuel			Honorably discharged.
Jackman, Joseph F			Honorably discharged.
Jackson, James			Deserted.
Jackson, William			Deserted.
Johns, Isaac			Deserted.
Jones, Hilarie			Lost arm at Weldon R. R August 21, '64.
Jones, James A			Honorably discharged.

Roll Company D—11th Florida Infantry.
(CONTINUED.)

NAMES.	MUSTERED IN	MUSTERED OUT.	REMARKS.
Knowles, A. J.			Deserted.
Lamb, T. B.		April 9, '65	Sergeant.
Land, F.			Sergeant; honorably discharged.
Lowe, Wesley.			Deserted.
Lowe, Columbus.			Deserted.
Lucus, James C.			Corporal; honorably discharged.
McCall, S. W.			Corporal.
McCormick, A. T.	Feb. '63		Discharged October, '64, for disability.
McCormick, F.			
McCormick, W. B.		April 9, '65	
McGee, Benjamin.			Discharged for disability.
McKinley, John D.			Discharged; furnished substitute.
Mays, George H.		April 9, '65	Wounded, White House Station, Va., August 21 '64.
Mead, George.			
Mixon, W.			Deserted.
Moldwin, D. E.			
Moody, H. M.			1st Sergeant; deserted.
Murray, Orrick B.	April 1, '63		Wounded August 21, '64, captured April 6, '65; imprisoned at Newport News, paroled June 19, '65.
Neason, J. P. E.			Captured April 6, '65; paroled June 19, '65.
Nolan, John.			
Nowling, N.			
Ormand, J. N.	July '64	April 9, '65	
Ormand, M. H.		April 9, '65	
Padgett, John.		April 9, '65	
Passmore, A. G.			Captured at Petersburg.
Patterson, James H.			Captured at Petersburg.
Pickett, H. C.			
Pickett, John W.			Deserted.
Pickett, William L.			Promoted 1st Sergeant.
Pickett, W. S.			Sergeant; deserted.
Pope, John.	Mch. 1, '63	April 9, '65	Wounded in battle by falling timbers, near Petersburg.
Plummer, Robert.			Corporal; deserted.
Prescott, W.			Deserted.
Reed, Charles.			Honorably discharged.
Register, Aaron.			Honorably discharged.
Roberts, Bethel.	Feb. '63	April 9, '65	Hand crushed, caught between gunwale of boat and piling at Green Cove Springs, Fla., August, '63.
Roberts, C.			
Roberts, Emmeric.			
Roberts, Frank M.			Honorably discharged.
Roberts, Thomas.			Deserted.
Ross, John.			
Sieball, Jacob.			Corporal.
Silcox, James.			Honorably discharged.
Sparkman, Alfred.			Deserted.
Sparkman, John.			Deserted.
Spiers, William.			Deserted.
Stuckey, John.			Killed.
Taylor, James.			
Tedder, Benjamin.			Honorably discharged.
Tedder, George W.			Captured April 6, '65; paroled June 19, '65.
Tedder, John.			
Urwich, Burnett.	July 13, '61		
Williams, Alfred.			Deserted.
Wingate, Robert.			
Wingate, Wilson.			
Witcher, C.			
Woodlin, A. B.			Deserted.

Roll Company E—11th Florida Infantry.

NAMES.	MUSTERED IN.	MUSTERED OUT.	REMARKS.
OFFICERS.			
Captain—			
Charles Beggs.			Promoted Captain; resigned March 1, '65.
1st Lieutenant—			
A. J. Coffee.			
2nd Lieutenant—			
Oneal McLeod.		April 9, '65	
3rd Lieutenant—			
ENLISTED MEN.			
Adams, Riley.	Mch. '63		Died of measles at hospital in Virginia June 3, '64.
Blair, W. B.			

Roll Company E—11th Florida Infantry.
(Continued.)

NAMES.	MUSTERED IN.	MUSTERED OUT.	REMARKS.
Blair, W. T.		April 9, '65	Corporal.
Blalock, T. J.			
Bradley, Jesse J.	'63		
Campbell, Alex N.	Feb. '63	April 9, '65	
Clark, G. W.			
Caulk, J. J.	Feb. '63		Was home on furlough at close of war.
Davis, J. R.			
Devane, James.			
Dukes, W. L.	Mch. '63		
Dukes, William T.	Mch. '63		
Everitte, John L.	Mch. 8, '63	April 9, '65	
Gaudy, H. R.	Sept. '63	April 9, '65	
Herring, I. E.			
Hinely, Lewis L.			
Jarvis, Reuben.			
Lee, Farmer.			
McCall, Thomas J.		April 9, '65	
McDaniel, B. F.		April 9, '65	
McDavid, Benjamin F.		April 9, '65	
McGrew, John C.		April 9, '65	
Mason, H. G.		April 9, '65	
Morrow, James A.			Died at home September 9, '64, whle on furlough.
Pert, William A.	Feb. 28, '63		Paroled from prison July, '65.
Powell, J. R.	June '62	April 9, '65	Wounded at Petersburg, Va., Feb. 20, '65.
Rutherford, J. J.			
Shuen, Malachi.		April 9, '65	
Snipes, Urich.	Aug. 15, '62		Wounded at Weldon Railroad, Va., August 21, '63; again at High Bridge, Va., April 6, '64.
Stanton, Thomas.		April 9, '65	
Sutton, David S.		April 9, '65	Discharged-for disability, '64.
Tedder, Daniel W.		April 9, '65	
Thomas, John S.		April 9, '65	
Thomas, L. A. M.	'63	April 9, '65	Promoted Sergeant.
Townsend, E.		April 9, '65	
Townsend, Joseph.			
Townsend, L.	Feb. 28, '63	April 9, '65	Shot at Petersburg, Va., July 9, '64.
Walker, James.		April 9, '65	
Washington, R. T.	Feb. '65	April 9, '65	
White, R. M.		April 9, '65	
Young, Thomas.			Killed at Weldon Railroad, Va., August, '64.

Roll Company F—11th Florida Infantry.

NAMES.	MUSTERED IN.	MUSTERED OUT.	REMARKS.
OFFICERS.			
Captain—			
John Tanner			
1st Lieutenant—			
Y. J. Malone			
2nd Lieutenant—			
Whitmill Curry			
3rd Lieutenant—			
Lafayette McClellan			
ENLISTED MEN.			
Anderson, D.			Promoted Sergeant; deserted.
Atwell, Z.			Captured.
Avery, F.			Wounded at the Weldon Railroad.
Averry, M.		April 26, '65	
Baker, D.			Died at Richmond, Va.
Baker, W. A.		April 9, '65	2nd Corporal.
Berch, D.			Deserted.
Berch, Moses.			Deserted.
Best, John E.	May '63	'64	Disability.
Best, W. A.			
Brown.			
Burton, C.			1st Corporal; deserted.
Burton,		April 9, '65	
Cain, W. E.			
Cain.			
Cain.		April 9, '65	
Cook.			
Cooley, A.		April 9, '65	
Collier, W. A.			2nd Sergeant.
Cooper, William H.			
Cradock, H.			3rd Sergeant.
Cruchfield, John.	May '63	'63	Disability.
Crumple.			

Roll Company F—11th Florida Infantry.
(CONTINUED.)

NAMES.	MUSTERED IN.	MUSTERED OUT.	REMARKS.
Daniels, J. A			4th Corporal.
Davis		April 9, '65	
Dennis			Captured at the downfall.
Duncan, J		April 9, '65	
Ellis, Joseph		April 9, '65	
Elmore, J		April 9, '65	
Falana, G. K			
Finch, John E			
Fowler, D			Deserted.
Fowler, J			Deserted.
Fowler, W			Deserted.
Glison, H			
Godwin, A			
Glover, L. T			1st Sergeant; captured at Petersburg, '65.
Hall, D			Deserted.
Hall, John		April 9, '65	
Hall, West		April 9, '65	
Hinson, Francis			
Hinson, G. A			4th Sergeant; promoted.
Hinson, James H		April 9, '65	
Houston, J. W		April 9, '65	
Jackson, W. A			5th Sergeant.
Jacobs, William Alason			Wounded at Petersburg and died July 13, '64.
Jones, W. C			
Jordan, J			
Kimbol			
Kyser, P			
Lassiter, Brevard			
McKnight,			
Mills, J			
Mills, R		April 9, '65	
Miller		April 9, '65	Wounded at Petersburg.
Mooney, E		April 9, '65	
Nash, W. F	May '62	April 9, '65	Captured at Petersburg August 10, '64; imprisoned at Point Lookout, Md.; exchanged at close of war.
Newsome, E. D		April 9, '65	From Newport News prison.
Nichols, J			
Nichols, Z			
Parish, E			
Parish, Eli			
Parish, H			
Parish, James K			
Paul, John W		April 9, '65	Shot at Petersburg, Va., September 15, '64.
Paul, Wilborn		April 9, '65	
Paulk, D			
Paulk, Micajah		April 9, '65	
Peters, W			Deserted.
Pilcher, Dwin			
Pilcher			
Prevatt, D			
Pitcher, S			
Price, John		April 9, '65	Captured at Farmville April 6, '65; imprisoned on Johnson's Island; paroled June 19, '65.
Register, Burkel		April 9, '65	3rd Corporal,
Register, E			
Register, T			
Register, W. J		April 9, 65	
Ridley, J. W			
Shiver			
Semlin, L			Deserted.
Slater, S			
Smith, B			
Taylor			
Walding, Seaborn		April 9, '65	
Watford, J			Died at Savannah, Ga., hospital.
Watford, Nelson	April '63	April 9, '65	
Williams, W			
White, J		April 9, '65	Captured at Petersburg.
Yearby, W			
Yawn, H. G. D	May '63	April 9, '65	Captured April 6, '65 and imprisoned at Newport News until paroled June 16, '65.

Roll Company G—11th Florida Infantry.

NAMES.	MUSTERED IN.	MUSTERED OUT.	REMARKS.
OFFICERS.			
Captain—			
G. W. Bassett			

Roll Company G—11th Florida Infantry.

(CONTINUED.)

NAMES.	MUSTERED IN.	MUSTERED OUT.	REMARKS.
1st Lieutenant—			
C. F. Hollyman		April 9, '65	
2nd Lieutenant—			
Ira S. Rouse		April 9, '65	Promoted Lieutenant.
3rd Lieutenant—			
E. M. Smith		April 9, '65	Promoted Lieutenant.
ENLISTED MEN.			
Beauchamp, Simeon	'62	April 9, '65	Captured by Sheridan's Cavalry April 6, '65; imprisoned at Point Lookout for two months.
Bell, Abraham			
Brown, S. M.			
Christman, J. M.			
Clark, George W		April 9, '65	Shot at Appomatox Court House April 6, '65.
Dilman, Jefferson			
Dixon, James J.	Dec. '62		Severely wounded at Petersburg August 20, '64, and was home on furlough when war closed.
Drew, James E.			Promoted Corporal; discharged for disability.
Downing, George	May '62		
Downing, G. W.	April '63		Discharged December, '64, for disability.
Edwards, W. B.	April '63		Died September 1, '64, of disease.
Goff, John.			
Goff, W.			
Hays, Jefferson			Killed in railroad accident in South Carolina.
Herndon, Levy H	April '62	April 9, '65	Wounded in Virginia, '63.
Hodges, M. W.			
Jackson, M. V.	Feb. '63		
Kendrick, E. C.	'63		
McCalmma, John.			Died February 8, '64.
McDaniel, Hamilton	April '63	April 9, '65	Promoted Sergeant; wounded at Petersburg July 22, '64.
Newman, P. M.		April 9, '65	Promoted 2nd Sergeant.
Peacock, Abraham	Feb. '63		Died in hospital at Richmond, Va., August 24, '64.
Pert, Elias	June '63		Wounded in Virginia, '63, and discharged.
Philips, Sion W	June 15, 63	April 9, '65	
Roberts, David	Mch. 25, '63	April 9, '65	Wounded at Petersburg June 2, '64.
Slater, J.		April 9, '65	
Slater, J. M.		April 9, '65	
Snipes, Uriah		April 9, '65	
Squier, Samuel		April 9, '65	
Cann, Washington Edward			Died at Point Lookout October 25, '64.
Warr, W. H.		April 9, '65	
Waters, George W	April '62		Died of pneumonia at Richmond, '65.
Waters, William		April 9, '65	
Webb, Samuel S.			Died at Richmond September, '64, of disease.
Webb, W. A.		April 9, '65	
Smith, W. J.		April 9, '65	
Dukes, W. L.			
Moseley, M.		April 9, '65	

Roll Company H—11th Florida Infantry.

NAMES.	MUSTERED IN.	MUSTERED OUT.	REMARKS.
OFFICERS.			
Captains—			
W. E. Anderson	Feb. '63		Resigned November 27, '63.
George W. Bassett	Feb. '63		Promoted Captain.
1st Lieutenant—			
E. G. Earnest	Feb. '63	April 9, '65	2nd Lieutenant; promoted 1st Lieutenant.
2nd Lieutenant—			
3rd Lieutenants—			
Cullen Curl	Feb. '63		Resigned.
D. B. Lislie	Feb. '63		Promoted 3rd Lieutenant.
ENLISTED MEN.			
Beauchamp, S. A.	Feb. '63	April 9, '65	
Flower, J. B.		April 9, '65	
Musgrove, Jasper	Mch. 11, '63		Discharged September 26, '64, for disability.
Sharpton, Alex M.	Mch. '63	April 9, '65	

Roll Company I—11th Florida Infantry.

NAMES.	MUSTERED IN.	MUSTERED OUT.	REMARKS.
Captains—			
Joseph J. Chaires			
———— Shine			
T. J. Key	May 1, '61		Transferred to 11th Regiment.
ENLISTED MEN.			
Allen, Joseph M			
Alexander, A. M	Mch. 10, '63		Wounded at Weldon Railroad June 10, '64.
Critchfield, E. D	May '63		Wounded at Petersburg, Va.; paroled from prison.
Ferrell, William			
McMath, H			Promoted 1st Sergeant.
Mears, G. W		April 9, '65	
Mears, Henry S			
Morrison, A. G		April 9, '65	
Roberts, A. S	April 3, '63	May 17, '65	Wounded at Petersburg June 1, '64.
Skipper, C. D		April 9, '65	
Smith, George W	May 10, '62	April 9, '65	Wounded at Cold Harbor August 17, '64.

Roll Company K—11th Florida Infantry.

NAMES.	MUSTERED IN.	MUSTERED OUT.	REMARKS.
OFFICERS.			
Captain—			
D. D. McLean			
ENLISTED MEN.			
Alsobrook, A. T	Mch. 10, '63		Wounded in right foot Jaunary 15, '64.
Bowen, M. A			
Fi———, James			
Gainer, George F			
Johnson, David			
Melvin, E. P		April 9, '65	
Payne, James		April 9, '65	Imprisoned at Point Lookout; released on parole October, '64.
Taylor, G. T	Mch. '64	April 9, '65	Shot at Reames' Station June 29, '64.
Taylor, John W	Mch. 28, '63	April 9, '65	
Taylor, N. P		April 9, '65	

Roll Company——th Florida Infantry.

NAMES.	MUSTERED IN.	MUSTERED OUT.	REMARKS.
OFFICERS.			
Captain—			
James A. Pickett			
1st Lieutenant—			
John W. Brady			
2nd Lieutenants—			
James L. Winter			
Joseph McR. Baker			
3rd Lieutenant—			
ENLISTED MEN.			
Bacon, Sylvester			
Bardin, John			Corporal.
Bareington, Americus			
Brown, E. B			Corporal.
Byrnes, John			
Burney, Meshack			
Cannon, David			
Cameron, James A			
Canova, Bartolo			
Carling, John			
Cellenn, James			
Crawford, David			
Curtis, Richard			
Danford, Thomas			
Elliott, W. H			
Emmory, Caleb			
Falana, Fernando			
Falana, Isaac			
Flynn, Charles			
Gardner, John			

Roll Company——th Florida Infantry.
(CONTINUED.)

NAMES.	MUSTERED IN.	MUSTERED OUT.	REMARKS.
Gardner, Albert			
Gardner, Isaac			
Giger, John			
Gordon, William			
Hagin, John			
Hagin, Joseph			
Hanford, Charles			Bugler.
Hall, William T			Corporal.
Hartley, George W			
Hernandez, Joseph			
Hudnell, Frank			Corporal.
Hudnell, James			Sergeant.
Laicye, John			
Landon, Henry			
Landon, William			
Leary, Daniel E			
Lord, Philip P			
McDowell, James			
McGrath, Robert			
Miranda, Thomas			
Ortagus, Peter			
Patterson, Thomas			
Peterson, Archibald			
Peterson, Michael			Blacksmith....
Pickett, William H			
Ramsuers, James			Farrier.
Richardson, James			
Roberts, John			
Rouse, William A			
Sanders, Ashford			
Sanders, Daniel			
Sparkman, Alfred			
Sparkman, Lake			
Silbury, James			
Silcox, Isaac			
Silcox, Wade			
Turknette, Lawrence			1st Sergeant.
Turner, Adin W			Sergeant.
Turner, Benjamin			Sergeant.
Turner, Edward			
Tyler, Richard R			
Tyler, William L			
Walton, Robert			
Weedman, Barnard			
Weedman, Philip			
West, Morgan			
West, William H			
West, William N			
Wilder, John			
Williamson, John J			

Roll Capt. William J. Turner's Company, Hillsborough County.

NAMES.	MUSTERED IN.	MUSTERED OUT.	REMARKS.
OFFICERS.			
Captain—			
William J. Turner			
1st Lieutenant—			
Milton W. Johnson			
2nd Lieutenant—			
John E. Ferrell			
3rd Lieutenant—			
John Mooney			
ENLISTED MEN.			
Allen, William			
Andrew, John P			Sergeant.
Attman, Jesse			
Blocker, William M			
Branch, John			
Brannon, Milledge			Sergeant.
Brown, William H			Corporal.
Bryant, Francis M			
Buffoon, Rich V			
Chandler, Shadrick M			
Daniels, James W			
Dishong, George G			

Roll Capt. William J. Turner's Company, Hillsborough County.
(CONTINUED.)

AMES	MUSTERED IN.	MUSTERED OUT.	REMARKS.
Driggers, Elisha W			
Driggers, Jacob A			
Duffield, Thomas			Blacksmith.
Garrison, Green A			
Garner, Andrew W			
Gill, Francis M			
Givens, John J			Bugler.
Green, Samuel L			
Hair, Anson M			
Hall, Isaiah			
Ham, Alonzo			
Ham, Henry B			
Ham, James, Sr			
Ham, James N			
Harris, Joseph			
Hagen, Reuben			
Hollingworth, Timothy			
Jamerson, Daniel			
Johnson, Benjamin A			Sergeant.
Johnston, Columbus M			
Lawrence, Francis			
Lowe, Allen			
Lowe, John			
Lowe, Nathan			
Lowe, William			
McClelland, William			
McLenathan, William, Sr			
McLenathan, William, Jr			
McLeod, Ferdinand			
McMunn, William L			Corporal.
Main, David			
Mathews, Henry H			
Mathews, William			
Miley, David M			
Montes-de-Oca, Charles			
Nettles, Isaac A. M			
Parker, Pinckney P			
Platt, George I			
Pope, John C			
Powell, Charles M			
Prime, John			
Pawls, William C			
Riley, James F			
Robberts, Samuel A			
Silvester, Henry			
Simmonds, Abram			
Smith, Baxter M			
Smith, George W			
Smith, James			
Smith, John			
Smith, Wilber W			Sergeant.
Stallins, William W			
Stephens, John W			
Tiner, Stewart			
Tiner, Wilson			
Tison, George			
Tison, John M			
Thomas, James H			
Thomas, Lewis R			
Thompson, James C			Corporal.
Underhill, John			
Walker, Allen			
Walker, George W			
Walker, Oliver A			
Warren, Francis H			
Whidden, John W			Corporal.
Whidden			
Whidden, William			
White, Abram B			
White, William B			
Williams, James			
Worth, Frederick			Musician.
Youngblood, Daniel A			
Youngblood, Leoman S			

FIRST FLORIDA CAVALRY.

The 1st Florida Cavalry was composed of ten companies from various parts of the State. Co. A, Capt. Arthur Roberts, Columbia county; Co. B,

Capt. John G. Haddock, Nassau county; Co. C, Capt. John A. Summerlin, Clay county; Co. E, Capt. Charles F. Cone, Suwannee county; Co. F, Capt. William M. Footman, Leon county; Co. G, Capt. Nicholas S. Cobb, Levy county; Co. H, Capt. Noble A. Hull, Duval county; Co. I, Capt. W. D. Clarke, Alachua county; and Co. K, Capt. David Hughes.

The Regiment was assembled at Camp Mary David, six miles south of Tallahassee, where it went into camp of instruction and was mustered into service in July, 1861. The Regiment was organized by the election of William G. M. Davis, Colonel; George Troupe Maxwell, Lieutenant-Colonel; and William T. Stockton, Major. Colonel Davis was promoted to Brigadier-General November 4, 1862, and Lieut.-Col. George T. Maxwell became Colonel, and William T. Stockton Lieutenant-Colonel, and Captain Footman acting Major. The Regiment did service in Florida until the spring of 1862, when it was ordered to Chattanooga. Before leaving Florida seven companies, B, C, D, G, H, I and K, voluntarily dismounted and served through the war as infantry, being known as the 1st Florida Cavalry, dismounted. Cos. A, E and F remained mounted until 1864, when they dismounted and rejoined the Regiment. While mounted these companies did excellent service, under Captain Footman, as scouts. The mounted battalion was engaged in the battle of Richmond, Ky., August 30, 1862, and the seven dismounted companies took part in the battle of Perryville October 8, 1862. The story of the 1st Florida dismounted is so interwoven with that of the 1st, 3d, 4th, 6th and 7th, that to tell the story of one is to tell that of each of the splendid organizations from Florida that shed luster on the State in the war of the sixties. At Missionary Ridge the 1st Cavalry lost heavily in killed and wounded and captured; among these last were all the Field Officers of the Regiment. Out of the 200 men the Regiment went into the battle with, there was 33 officers left. The gallant band was so reduced that it was consolidated with the 4th Infantry at Dalton, Ga., February 23, 1864, and the little remnant surrendered with Johnston's at Army Greensborough April 26, 1865.

Roll, Field and Staff—1st Florida Cavalry.

NAMES.	MUSTERED IN.	MUSTERED OUT.	REMARKS.
Colonels—			
William George M. Davis	July '61	April 26, '65	Promoted Brigadier-General.
George Troup Maxwell	July '61	April 26, '65	Lieutenant-Colonel, promoted Colonel '62; captured at Missionary Ridge, imprisoned on Johnson's Island.
Lieutenant-Colonels—			
George Troup Maxwell	July '61	April 6, '65	Promoted Colonel.
William T. Stockton	July '61	April 26, '65	Promoted Lieutenant-Colonel; vice Maxwell promoted, wounded at Chickamauga, captured at Missionary Ridge and imprisoned on Johnson's Island until August, '65.
Majors—			
William T. Stockton	July '61		Promoted Lieutenant-Colonel.
Surgeon—			
Holmes			
Assistant-Surgeon—			
Adjutant—			
Whitner			
Sergeant-Major —			
Edmond W. Gillen			
Quartermaster—			
Maxwell			

Roll, Field and Staff—1st Florida Cavalry.
(CONTINUED.)

NAMES.	MUSTERED IN.	MUSTERED OUT.	REMARKS.
Commissary—			
Quartermaster-Sergeants—			
Commissary-Sergeants—			
Chaplain—			
R. L. Wiggins			
Hospital Steward—			

Roll Company A—1st Florida Cavalry.

NAMES.	MUSTERED IN.	MUSTERED OUT.	REMARKS.
OFFICERS.			
Captains—			
Arthur Roberts	May 12, '61		Resigned '62, March, '63; on account of age.
Martin I. Coxe	May 12, '61	May 26, '65	Wounded May 26, '64 at Dallas, Georgia; enlisted as a private; promoted 2nd Lieutenant, May, '62, 1st Lieutenant March '63 to Captain at Missionary Ridge November 24, '63. Captured at Somerset, Ky., March 30, 63, imprisoned at Camp Chase and Fort Delaware; exchanged April 10 at City Point, Va.
1st Lieutenants—			
Reuben H. Charles	May 12, '62		Resigned on reorganization.
M. I. Coxe			Promoted Captain.
2nd Lieutenants—			
James E. Young	May 12, '61		Retired on reorganization.
P. C. Osteen			
3rd Lieutenants—			
William L. Jones			Transferred to 5th Infantry and killed at Gettysburg July 3, '63.
Paul C. Osteen	May 12, '61		Promoted Lieutenant and resigned.
W. H. L. Townsend		April 26, '65	Wounded at Atlanta, Ga., August 3, '64, promoted Lieutenant.
ENLISTED MEN.			
Allen, George D.			Bugler; discharged, under age.
Barnes, Aman	May 12, '61	April 26, '65	
Bell, Kinchen	May 12, '61		Corporal; discharged '61, a minor.
Bebefield, Eli H.	May 12, '61	April 26, '65	
Blitch, George W.	May 12, '61		Died, '62.
Boyd, William B.		'61	Company physician; resigned at reorganization May 10, '62.
Browen, Berry A.		'61	April 26, '65
Brooks, James O.	Oct. 12, '61	April 26, '65	
Brooks, John A.	Oct. 12, '61		Killed at Missionary Ridge November 25, '63.
Bryant, Edward	May 12, '61		Died at Ferguson's Gap, W. Va., '62.
Bryant, James L.	May 12, '61	April 26, '65	
Bryant, Rizan V.	Dec. '61	April 26, '65	Shot at Missionary Ridge, Tenn., November 63.
Bryan, Ezekiel J.	Oct. 12, '61		Died in Kentucky, '62.
Bryant, William	May 12, '61	April 26, '65	Farrier; discharged, over age.
Carlton, Dawson	May 12, '61	April 6, '65	
Carlton, D. E. L.	May 12, '61		Died.
Carter, J. E.	Oct. 12, '61	May '62	Under age; re-enlisted August, '63 in E. A. Fernandez.
Carver, William	May 12, '61	April 26, '65	Sergeant.
Carraway, Adair	May 12, '61		Died in Knoxville, Tenn., '62.
Charles, Reupert	May 12, '61	April 26, '65	Somerset, Ky.; wounded.
Charles, Aman L.	May 12, '61		Captured at Missionary Ridge, '63; imprisoned at Rock Island, Ill.
Coon, Wiley L.	May 12, '61		Wounded.
Coxe, William A.	Sept. '61	April 26, '65	Wounded at Dallas, Ga., March 28, '64.
Cresswell, James M.	Oct. 12, '61	April 26, '65	
Dexter, Jacob S.			Transferred to Company "B," 5th Regiment, killed at the Wilderness.
Douberly, Jacob J.	May 12, '61	June 1, '65	From Camp Chase prison, captured December 7, '64.
Duboise, J. Isaiah	May 12, '61	April 26, '65	
Ellis, Joseph P.	Oct. 12, '61	April 26, '65	
Everett, David L.			
Feagle, William J.		April 26, '65	Captured at Missionary Ridge November 25, '63.
Goodman, Green B.	Oct. 12, '61	April 26, '65	Wounded at Dutton Hill, Ky., March 30, '63; promoted Corporal.
Griffin, John		April 26, '65	Wounded at Bentonville, N. C., March 19, '65.
Grisham, Columbus		April 26, '65	
Harris, Stanhope	Oct. 1, '61		Discharged at Chattanooga, April '62; over age.
Harvey, William B.			Discharged for disability, May, '62.

Roll Company A—1st Florida Cavalry.

(CONTINUED.)

NAMES.	MUSTERED IN.	MUSTERED OUT.	REMARKS.
Hawkins, T. H.		April 26, '65	
Herring, John W	'61		Killed at Chickamauga; honorable mention.
Herrod, John L			Died in service.
Herrod, Samuel			Killed at Kennesaw Mt. June 29, '64.
Hogans, J. S.		April 26, '65	Died in service.
Horn, James R.	Oct. '61		Captured at Murfreesborough, Tenn., put in prison at Camp Chase, O; paroled from there.
Hunt, William F.	Oct. 12, '61	Oct. 12, '62	Disability.
Ingraham, Francis M	Oct. 12, '61	April 26, '65	
Jenkins, Daniel F.	Oct. 12, '61	April 26, '65	From Rock Island prison.
Jenkins, J. F.	May 12, '61	April 26, '65	
Johnson, Nelson	'62	April 26, '65	Shot at Atlanta, Ga., August 3, '64.
Jones, Pickney	'61		
Kinard, Shelton G.		April 26, '65	Captured at Nashville December 16, '64; sent to Camp Chase, Ohio.
Kinard, Irving G.	Oct. 12, '61	April 26, '65	Shot at New Castle, Ky., September 20, '62 and disabled.
Lee, Freeman	Oct. 12, '61		Died in prison.
Leggett, R. J.	Oct. 12, '61	April 26, '65	Captured at Frankfort, Ky., '62; imprisoned at Rock Island, Ills., until February, '65.
McCoy, Church	Sept. 12, '61		Killed at Resaca, Ga., May 15, '64.
McKay, Joseph	Oct. 12, '61		Captured at Bentonville, N. C., '65; returned to his command.
Marcun, William A	May 12, '61	April 26, '65	Sergeant; transferred to 2nd Florida Cavalry.
Markham, Reuben L	May 12, '61	April 26, '65	
Meaks, Benjamin F	Oct. 12, '61		Wounded at Somerset, Ky., '62 and captured; paroled from Rock Island prison June, '65.
Morgan, W. F.	May 12, 61	April 26, '65	Wounded at Kennesaw Mountain June 3, '64.
Moseley, William L	May 12, '61		Discharged; over age.
Neal, Clinton	May 12, '61		
Neal, Obediah	May 12, '61		Died in service, '62.
Nickols, Mark	May 12, '61	April 26, '65	Wounded at Atlanta August 4, '64; also at Ringgold, Ga, December, '63.
Niblack, John F.	May 12, '61	April 26, '65	1st Sergeant.
Oats, Stephen W	May 12, '61		Died, '63, at Louden, Tenn.
Ogden, George R	May 12, '61	April 26, '65	Transferred to Florida Reserves because he was a minor.
Osteen, Bennett D.	May 12, '61		Captured near Murfreesborough, '64; died in Camp Chase prison April 9, '65; grave No. 1845.
Parrish, Henry	Oct. 12, '61	April 26, '65	under age.
Parrish, Robert H.	Oct. 12, '61	April 26, '65	Shot at Missionary Ridge, at Kennesaw Mountain, Ga., and at Bentonville, N. C.
Pearce, Levi T	May 12, '61		1s Sergeant; killed at Franklin, Tenn., September 30, '64.
Ponchier, John A	May 12, '61		Died of pneumonia at Strawberry Plains, Tenn., March 29, '63.
Powell, James	May 12, '61		Discharged; '62, over age.
Powell, William L	May 12, '61		Captured.
Powell, Temrle	Aug. 12, '61	July '64	Disability, wounded June 2, '64.
Roberts, H. L. R	May 12, '61	April 26, '65	Promoted Sergeant; captured at Murfreesborough December 4, '62.
Revels, O. J.	May 12, '61	April 26, '65	Transferred to Parramore's Company, 4th Regiment.
Reynolds, B. L.	Oct. 12, '61	April 26, '65	Sergeant.
Rivers, Lewis W	May 12, '61		Corporal; captured and sent to Camp Chase prison where he was paroled at close of war.
Roberts, George W	May 12, '61		Killed in battle of Missionary Ridge November 25, '63
Roberts, Henry C	May 12, '61	April 26, 65	Discharged, '62; under age.
Roberts, John D	May 12, '61	April 26, '65	Wounded at Dallas, Ga., May 26, '64.
Roberts, Robert B.	'62		Discharged, disability, re-enlisted February 20, '63. A. A. Stewart's Company, "E," 9th Infantry; promoted Orderly Sergeant.
Roberts, Thomas L.	May 12, '61		Sergeant; wounded at Missionary Ridge November 25, '63; captured, sent to Rock Island prison where he died November 20, '64.
Robson, Wiley	May 12, '61	April 26, '65	Captured.
Robertson, Joseph H	'61	April 26, '65	Transferred to Company "C," 7th Infantry.
Scott, Andrew	'61		Killed at Bentonville, N. C. March 19, '65.
Scott, Wilson	'61	April 26, '65	Wounded at New Castle, Ky., September 22, '62.
Singleton, John S.	May 12, '61		Killed near Atlanta, Ga., August 3, '64; before this he was promoted Orderly Sergeant.
Tedder, John H.	'61		Captured at Franklin, Tenn., November 30, '64,
Tillis, Temp	May 12, '61	April 26, '65	
Thoams, D. D	May 12, '61	April 26, '65	
Thomrkins, Henry C	Oct. 12, '61	April 26, '65	
Tompkins, J. T.	Oct. 12, '61	April 26, '65	Captured near Marietta, Ga., July 3, '64; sent to Camp Douglass, Ill. prison, remained there until June 14, '65.
Vinzant, John	May 12, '61	April 26, '65	1st Sergeant; lost right leg at Murfreesborough December 4, '64; captured and imprisoned until June, '65.
White, James W	May 12, '61	April 26, '65	Transferred to Navy.

Roll Company A—1st Florida Cavalry.

(CONTINUED.)

NAMES.	MUSTERED IN.	MUSTERED OUT.	REMARKS.
Williams, William F	Oct. 12, '61	April 26, '65	Wounded.
Witt, James S			Wounded at Missionary Ridge November 25, '63.
Witt, Jasper H	Mch. 4, '62		Discharged, October, '62, disability; re-enlisted October, '63, 9th Regiment, Company K; April 9, '65; lost arm at Missionary Ridge November 25, '63.

Roll Company B—1st Florida Cavalry.

NAMES.	MUSTERED IN.	MUSTERED OUT.	REMARKS.
OFFICERS.			
Captains—			
John G. Haddock	June '61		
1st Lieutenant—			
Joseph H. Haddock	June '61		
2nd Lieutenants—			
Crozier C. Jones	June '61		
W. W. Shedd		April 26, '65	
3rd Lieutenant—			
Daniel R. Howell	June '61		
ENLISTED MEN.			
Barnard, Bradley G	June '61		Farrier.
Beatty, James	June '61		Sergeant.
Blue, James	June '61		
Braddock, Henry E	June '61	May '65	
Braddock, Huteo, L		'64	Disability; shot at Pine Mountain February, '64
Braddock, James A	June '61	May '65	Wounded at Dallas, Ga.
Braddock, John S	June '61		
Braddock, Joseph	June '61	April 26, '65	
Braddock, William S	June '61		
Brooks, John	Dec. 18, '61	April 26, '65	Wounded at Missionary Ridge, Tenn.
Burnseed, P			
Carmichæl, James D	June '61		
Cawthorn, Samuel		April 26, '65	
Charney, Gill	June '61	—	
Cooks, John G	June '61		
Colson, Abram H	June '61		
Cox, William M	June '61		
David, S. R	June '61	April 26, '65	
Davis, Earl	June '61	April 6, '65	
David, G. R	June '61	April 26, '65	Wounded at Franklin, Tenn., November 30, '64 and captured, paroled from Camp Chase prison.
Davis, Jackson J	June '61		
Davis, John W	June '61	April 26, '65	
Drawdy, L		April 26, '65	
Fearless, John	June '61		Corporal.
Ford, George W	June '61		Corporal.
Gaines, J. S			
Gillin, Edward W	June '61	April 26, '65	Sergeant.
Green, David	June '61		
Griffiths, James H	June '61		
Haddock, J. N		April 26, '65	
Hammond, Francis M	June '61		
Hagin, David G	June '61		
Hagin, Jackson	June '61		
Hagin, Joseph	June '61		Blacksmith.
Higgenbothem, James H	June '61		
Higgenbothem, Madison	June '61		Corporal; promoted Sergeant, mentioned for gallantry at Chicakmauga.
Higgenbothem, Bourbon S. S	June '61		
Hogan, George W	June '61		
Holgerson, R. H		April 26, '65	
Howard, Mathew A. B	June '61		
Howell, William H. H	June '61		
Hughs, Reuben	June '61	April 26, '65	
Hunt, Jefferson F	June '61	April '61	
Hunt, John M	June '61		
Hunt, Samuel W	June '61	April 26, '65	Shot at Bentonville.
Jones, Augustus	June '61		Sergeant.
Jones, Drery	June '61		
Jones, John H	June '61	April 26, '65	
Johnson, Nathaniel T	June '61		
Jones, Stephen	June '61		Died at Camp Chase prison November 23, '64; grave No. 509.
Jones, William	June '61		
Jones, Wiley	June '61		
Kelly, George	June '61		
Land, Richard	June '61		
Lloyd, James B	June '61		Bugler.

Roll Company B—1st Florida Cavalry.

(CONTINUED.)

NAMES.	MUSTERED IN.	MUSTERED OUT.	REMARKS.
Lloyde, John F	June '61		Sergeant.
Lloyde, Henry William	June '61		
McKendre, James	Nov. '61	April 26, '65	Bugler; died of typhoid fever April 9, '62.
McKendree, Mark L	June '61		
Musselwhite, James R		April 26, '65	
Nettles, John	June '61		
Norton, Lewis Jr	June '61		
Osteen, Archibald S	June '61		
Osteen, Ezekell	June '61		
Philips, Riley W	Oct. '61	April 26, '65	Lost an arm at Chickamauga September 19, '63.
Pickett, James E	Oct. '61	April 26, '65	
Pickett, John W	Oct. '61		Sergeant.
Pope, Jacob	Oct. '62		
Price, James M	Oct. '62	April 26, '65	Sergeant.
Richardson, John	Oct. '62		
Rollins, John	Oct. '62		
Rollins, Peter		April 26, '65	
Rollins, William	Oct. '62	April 26, '65	
Rowe, Azell	June '61		
Rowe, William	June '61		
Russell, Samuel	June '61		Corporal.
Smith, David D	June '61		
Smith, John	June '61		
Stevens, Constant	June '61		
Stratton, David	June '61		
Tanner, Benjamin	June '61		
Tanner, Cornelius	June '61		
Tanner, Joshua	June '61		
Thomas, Eli	June '61	April 26, '65	
Thomas, William	Oct. 15, '61	April 26, '65	Wounded at Missionary Ridge, Tenn., November 25, '63.
Thomas, D. D.	Oct. 15, '61	April 26, '65	Wounded at Chickamauga September 19, '63.
Thomas, Daniel	June '61		
Thomas, Dixon	June '61		
Thompson, John C	June '61		
Tison, Isaac	June '61	April 26, '65	Captured at Missionary Ridge November 23, '63 imprisoned at Rock Island until July, '65.
Turnett, William	June '61		
Wainwright, Edward J	June '61	April 26, '65	Wounded at Chickamauga September 19, '63; promoted Sergeant.
West, William	June '61		
Wilson, D. B.		April 26, '65	
Williams, Stephen	May 29, '61	April 26, '65	Captured at Nashville, Tenn., December 15, '64; paroled from Federal prison at close of war.
Williamson, W. H.		April 26, '65	
Williamson, Stephen W	May 29, '61		
Wingate, James A	May 29, '61		
Wingate, James B	May 29, 61		
Wingate, John	May 29, '61		
Wingate, William H	May 29, '61		
Wright, John M	May 29, '61		

Roll Company C—1st Florida Cavalry.

NAMES.	MUSTERED IN.	MUSTERED OUT.	REMARKS.
OFFICERS.			
Captain—			
John A. Summerlin	July 1, '61		
1st Lieutenants—			
W. Mc Queen Saunders	July 1, '61	April 26, '65	
Daniel B. Knight	July 1, '61	April 26, '65	Promoted from 2nd Lieutenant to 1st Lieutenant was captured three times, once at Missionary Ridge, but he escaped each time.
2nd Lieutenants—			
Jacob Johns	July 1, '61		
C. M. Lang			Resigned April 22, '62.
ENLISTED MEN.			
Arich, Thomas H	May '61		
Beach, Joseph	Oct. 28, '61	May 12, '62	Disability.
Booth John	May '61		
Britt, Amos	May '61		
Blackweldon, David	May '61		
Bloodworth, Martin E	May '61		
Broer, George W	April 1, '61	'62	Injury, re-enlisted August, '63; in 2nd Cavalry, Captain Stephen's Company "B," shot at Shiloh
Brooker, W. H.		April 26, '65	
Branning, George W	May '61	April 26, '65	Tenn., April 6, '62.
Brown, Hezekiah	May '61		
Carter, Elisha W			Farrier.

Roll Company C—1st Florida Cavalry.
(CONTINUED.)

NAMES.	MUSTERED IN.	MUSTERED OUT.	REMARKS.
Chalken, Excellison C.			
Benjamin, Chambers L.	July '61		Blacksmith.
Conway, John M.			
Dias, John.	July '61		
Dickerson, Henry.	July '61		
Dickerson, William.	July '61		
Dillaberry, Francis.	Oct. '61		Bugler.
Faland, George.	July '62	April 26, '65	
Fonts, George W.	July '61	April 26, '65	
Ginard, Claiborn.	July '61		
Gunter, Daniel.	July '61		
Hardenbrook, James H.	July '61		Corporal.
Haws, George W.	July '61		
Holder, James B.	Oct. 1, '61	April 26, '65	
Houston, James.	July '61		Corporal.
Johns, Isaac.	July 1, '61		
Johns, Jeremiah.	July '61		
Johns, Luke.	July '61		Captured and imprisoned at Camp Chase, O.; died there February 1, '65; grave No. 1168.
Johnson, William.	Oct. '61		Shot at Chickamauga, Ga. September 20, '63.
Kellum, David.	July 1, '61		
Kellum, Thomas.	July '61		
Kite, John.	July 1, '61		
Kite, Robert.	July 1, '61		
Knight, James R.	July 1, '61		Sergeant.
Knight, Willliam H.	July 1, '61		
Knowles, Henry.	July 1, '61		
Knowles, Manuel.	July 1, '61	April 26, '65	
Livingston, Calvin.	July 1, '61		Corporal.
Long, George W.	July 1, '61		
Long, Joseph.	July '61		
McCluskie, Patrick.	July 1, '61		
McRae, Norman H.	July 1, '61		
Mathews, W. E.		April 26, '65	
Mobley, James C.	July 1, '61		
Moor, William B.	July '61		Corporal.
Morrison, Dan.		April 26, '65	
Owens, Zacariah.	July 1, '61		
Quin, James T.	July 1, '61		
Regester, William.		April 26, '65	
Rollins, Peter.	July 1, '61		
Roberts, David.	July 1, '61		
Silcox, Henry O.	July 1, '61		Sergeant.
Simpson, John.	July 1, '61		
Silvester, John P.	July 1, '61		
Swift, Simeon D.	July 1, '61		
Taland, Joshua E.	July '61		Sergeant.
Thomas, Carroleus.	July 1, '61		
Wilson, John.	July 1, '61		
Wilson, Josiah.	July 1, '61		
Wilson, William.	July 1, '61		Sergeant.
Wood, Warren.	July 1, '61		
Wright, John.	July 1, '61		

Roll Company D—1st Florida Cavalry.

NAMES.	MUSTERED IN.	MUSTERED OUT.	REMARKS.
OFFICERS.			
Captains—			
John Harvey.	May '61		
George Troup Maxwell.		April 26, '65	Promoted Captain Co. D; then Colonel 1st Florida Cavalry.
D. Elwell Maxwell.	May '61		Promoted Captain August, '63.
1st Lieutenants—			
Joseph T. Pons.	May '61		
Francis P. Fleming.	July 13, '61		Transferred from Co. H. 2nd Infantry; promoted 1st Lieutenant.
2nd Lieutenant—			
A. B. Canood.	May '61		
3rd Lieutenants—			
James Burnsed.	May '61		
Phin Burnsed.		April 26, '65	Promoted 3rd Lieutenant.
W. H. Wingate.		April 26, '65	Promoted 3rd Lieutenant Co. D, 1st Florida Cavalry; afterward consolidated with 4th Florida Regular Infantry.
ENLISTED MEN.			
Alford, William.	May '61		
Beasley, Berry.	May '61		

Roll Company D—1st Florida Cavalry.
(CONTINUED.)

NAMES.	MUSTERED IN.		MUSTERED OUT.		REMARKS.
Beasly, Hiram	May	'61			
Beal, Nathaniel	May	'61			
Beasly, William	May	'61			
Benton, Thomas	May	'61			
Berry, Henry D	May	'61			Farrier.
Blackwelder, Moses	May	'61			Sergeant.
Byrd, W. M. T.					
Bohannan, Duncan	May	'61			
Bohannan, John D	May	'61			
Burnseed, James	May	'61	April 26, '65		
Burnsed, James W	May	'61			
Burnsed, John E	May	'61			Sergeant.
Canova, B					Sergeant.
Carlton, Lewis	May	'61			
Combs, James	May	'61			
Combs, William	May	'61			
Crews, Samuel	Aug. 18,	'61			Shot at Missionary Ridge, Tenn., November 18, '63; again at Nashville, Tenn., December 15, '64.
Davis, Earl	Aug. 18,	'61	May 8,	'65	
Davis, John C					Died in hospital of disease July 6, '63.
Davis, Richard B	May	'61			
Dobson, Benjamin C					
Dowling, Berien	May	'61			
Dowling, William H	May	'61			
Driggers, A					
Driggers, William M	May	'61			Corporal.
Dugger, Aaron	May	'61			
Dugger, R. B	May	'61			
Dukes, William D	May	'61	April 26, '65		
Falany, John	May	'61			Musician.
Falany, Joseph	May	'61			
Fraser, James	May	'61			
Green, Aaron R	May	61			
Green, William					Discharged at expiration of term; reenlisted in Co. E, 9th Regular Infantry, Capt. Asa Stewart.
Garrett, William	April	62	April	'65	
Guthrie, Aaron	May	'61	April 26, '65		
Gwalthrey, Aaron	April	'61	April 26, '65		
Hagg, Francis	May	'61			Corporal.
Harvey, James A	May	'61			
Harvey, John W	May	'61			
Hodges, James M	Sept.	'61			Shot at Peach Tree Creek, Ga., July 22, '64.
Hunter, Elishu	Sept.	'61			
Hunter, Henry	Sept.	'61			
Hunter, James D	Sept.	'61			Corporal.
John, Reuben H	Sept.	'61	April 26, '65		
Johns, William B	Sept.	'61			
Johnson, Josiah	Sept.	'61			
Johnson, Stephen	Oct.	'61	April 26, '65		From prison.
Kemp, Joshua F	April	'62			Wounded at Camp Walton, Fla., April 27, '62 and discharged.
Lee, Jeremiah	May	'61			
Lee, Simeon	May	'61			
Lee, William	May	'61			Blacksmith.
Long, David	May	'61			Paroled from prison at Rock Island, Ill.
Mathis, John	April	'62	April 26, '65		
Motes, Henry	May	'61			
Motes, William	May	'61			
Norman, D. G. W			April 26, '65		
Osteen, Noah	May	'61			
Partin, James B	May	'61	April 26, '65		
Phillips, Henry	May	'61			
Philips, Riley	Oct. 16,	'61			Lost left arm at Chickamauga and discharged.
Philips, William R					Mentioned for gallantry at Chickamauga.
Rautherson, Jacob	May	'61			
Rawles, Micheal	May	'61			Musician.
Roberts, Johnathan	May	'61			
Sallas, Gomocende	May	'61			Corporal.
Sebastian, Sebasthin	May	'61			
Shaw, James T	May	'61			Died of pneumonia at Lynchburg, Va., April, '63.
Smith, Jackson W					
Sweat, W. F	May	'61	April 26, '65		
Thoams, D. D			April 26, '65		From Camp Douglass prison, Ill.
Thomas, John J	Mch.	'64	June	'65	Wounded at Griswoldville, Ga., December, '64.
Townsend, William A	Oct.	'64	April 26, '65		
Trage, Francis	May	'61			
Triay, Francis A	Nov. 17,	'61	April 26, '65		Shot at Atlanta, Ga., July 22, '64.
Valley, John	May	'61			
Vame, Andrew L	May	'61			
Varne, Isaac	May	'61			
Walker, Jerrimiah	May	'61	April 26, '65		Was at home on sick furlough at surrender.
Wells, Fred	Oct. 18,	'61	April 26, '65		Discharged from hospital.
Wells, Henry	Oct. 18,	'61	April 26, '65		Paroled from Camp Chase, O., prison.
Wells, William J	May	'61			
Yarborough, Thomas	May	'61			

Roll Company E—1st Florida Cavalry.

NAMES.	MUSTERED IN.	MUSTERED OUT.	REMARKS.
OFFICERS.			
Captain—			
Charles F. Cone			
1st Lieutenant—			
Wilay Lee			
2nd Lieutenants—			
William B. N. Crews	July '61		
Emanuel Smith		April 26, '65	
N. L. Bryan			Promoted 2nd Lieutenant Co. E, 1st Regiment Cavalry.
ENLISTED MEN.			
Bell, David	July '61		Sergeant.
Bennett, John	July '61		
Bethea, Fortes	July '61		
Bell, Thomas N			
Brooks, Jacob W	July '61		Corporal.
Bruner, James W	July '61		Farrier.
Bryan, Benjamin	July '61		
Bryan, Joseph	July '61		Bugler.
Carbin, Anterrio	July '61		
Cheshire, Charles W	July '61		
Cheshire, James	July '61		
Craig, Columbus D	July '61		Sergeant.
Crews, Henry	July '61		
Crews, Joseph	July '61		
Cribbs, Solomon B		'62	Disability.
Crews, John L			Lost a leg at Atlanta August 10, '64; died '88.
Crews. I. N			
Darrell, Sampson	Nov. '61		Captured at Missionary Ridge, Tenn.; imprisoned at Rock Island until close of the war.
Daugherty, John			
Davis, Lawson G	July '61		
Donald, John O	July '61		
Dowling, John M	Nov. '61	April 26, '65	
Durrence, John	Nov. '61		
Goodbread, J. S			
Guin, Robert E	July '61		
Gulp, John D	July '61		
Hair, George	July '61		
Hayes, George	July '61		Bugler.
Hayes, Robert	July '61		Sergeant.
Hines, Isaac			
Hogan, Joseph S	Nov. '61		
Hogans, Lewis	Nov. '61		
Humphreys, John T	July '61		
Hunter, David	July '61		Blacksmith.
Hunter, George	July '61		
Hunter, Robert	July '61		
Jackson, Benjamin C	July '61		Sergeant.
Jackson, James M	July '61		
Jenkins, D. F			
Johns, Levy M	April '61		
Johnson, Louis A	July '61		
Johnson, Moses	July '61		
Johnson, William R	July '61		
Kelly, George	July '61		Died Camp Chase February 25, '65; grave No. 1443.
Kite, John C	July '61		
Lee, Edward M	'61	April 26, '65	
Lee, H. M			
Leggett, Robert J			
Lewis, George W			Mentioned for gallantry.
Lovell, Sampson			
McInnis, Hilliard	Oct. 1, '61	April 26, '65	
McKenney, James	July '61		
Martin, Jesse			Died at Chattanooga.
Mathis, Daniel			By parole from prison at Rock Island May, '65, and died on way home.
Mitchell, Charles			Corporal; died April, '62.
Mobley, Samuel E			Died of "Bone Scurvy" at Camp Chase, Morton Ind., January 29, '65; captured at Missionary Ridge.
Newman, William M		April 26, '65	Captured at Missionary Ridge; imprisoned Rock Island and from there paroled June '65.
Padgett, Isam	July '61		
Pickett, J. D		April 26, '65	
Polk, Joseph F	July '61		
Register, Francis	Nov. '61	April 26, '65	
Roberson, James L	July '61		
Roberson, Wiley		April '65	
Roberts, David	July '61		
Roberts, John H	Nov. 14, '62	April 26, '65	
Sapp, Raiford			
Sills. William	April '61	April 26, '65	Shot in head and right hand.
Smith, Hezekiah	Nov. '61	April 26, '65	Captured Missionary Ridge November 20, '63; imprisoned at Rock Island; exchanged at Richmond, Va., March, '65.
Smith, Jacob			Died Camp Chase February 24, '65; grave No. 1432.

Roll Company E—1st Florida Cavalry.
(CONTINUED.)

NAMES.	MUSTERED IN.	MUSTERED OUT.	REMARKS.
Smith, James T.	July '62		
Stokely, W. G.			Died Camp Chase February 8, '65; grave No. 417.
Tarrell, Samson	July '61		
Taylor, Lewis L.	Mch. '62	April 26, '65	
Thompson, Edward	July '61		
Turner, Lem.		April 26, '65	
Tyner, Edward.	July '61		
Watson, Thomas.	July '61		Corporal.
Weeks, Stephen		April 26, '65	Promoted 2nd Lieutenant, Co. G, 1st Florida;
Willis, William W.	July '61	April 26, '65	then Captain.
Yelverton, Gideon.			
Yelverton, Jesse.		April 26, '65	Captured in Kentucky; sent home on parole.

Roll Company F—1st Florida Cavalry.

NAMES.	MUSTERED IN.	MUSTERED OUT.	REMARKS.
OFFICERS.			
Captains—			
William M. Footman			Promoted Major.
B. M. Burroughs			Transferred from Company H, 2nd Infantry and promoted Captain.
1st Lieutenant—			
Richard B. Maxwell			
2nd Lieutenants—			
Joseph H. Sappington			
Joseph J. C. Chaires			
3rd Lieutenants—			
Thomas N. Footman		April 26, '65	From prison on Johnson's Island, O; promoted 3rd Lieutenant.
J. Bradley McLeod	Nov. '61	April 26, '65	Promoted 3rd Lieutenant.
ENLISTED MEN.			
Adams, Elijah			
Ashley, Thomas			
Ball, Hart T.			
Bell, Stephen			Promoted Corporal.
Benton, James F.			Corporal.
Bugg, William S.			Promoted Corporal.
Burns, Ball.			
Burns, Michael.			
Collins, William.			
Cox, Thomas V.			
Davis, Allen B.			
Davis, Elishu.			
Davis, Thomas F.			
Durrance, John A.			
Ellison, Joseph D.			
Ellison, Joshua H.			
Faulkner, James N.	Nov. 25, '61		Discharged after one year's service, disabled by chronic inflammation of the bowels; re-enlisted in Taylor County and became Captain of 5th Florida Battalion; formerly Carraway Smith's Company.
Footman, John M.			Promoted Captain of some other Company in this Regiment.
Giles, James M.	Jan. '61		Captured at Peach Tree Creek, Ga., July 22, '64; imprisoned at Camp Chase, O., until March, '65; paroled.
Godwin, Stephen.	Nov. 24, '61		Died of pneumonia January 1, '63.
Gwaltney, William F.			
Hines, John W.	Nov. 24, '61	April 26, '65	Wounded at Nashville, Tenn., December, '64.
Hurst, William M.			
Hurst, John M.			
Hurst, Thomas H.	Nov. '61	April '62	Cause; disability, re-enlisted in '64 in William J. Bailey's, then in Fernandez's Company; ''Home Guards.''
Jackson, William.			
Jackson, Newton.			
Jackson, George W.			
Johnson, Milton.			
Kersey, William.			
Kinsey, J. Irvin.	'62	April 26, '65	
Lamb, Samuel H.			Sergeant.
Lester, B. E.			Promoted Lieutenant; Company ''C,'' 5th Battalion; Scott.
Lynn, John F.			
Lynn, William N.			
McDowell, Franklin.			
McDowell, William.			
McLeod, John B.			Sergeant.

Roll Company F—1st Florida Cavalry.
(CONTINUED.)

NAMES.	MUSTERED IN.	MUSTERED OUT.	REMARKS.
Mattair, Henry			
Mathis, John G			
Meeks, Amos H			
Miller, Frank			
Nis, Elijah			Musician.
Paley, E. W		April 26, '65	
Parker, Daniel			
Parker, John	Jan. '61		Sergeant; died of measles May 3, '63.
Powell, Isaac A			
Raker, John M			
River, David			
Rodgers, W. O		April 26, '65	Transferred to Company "G," 3rd Infantry; Thos. Langford.
Sallis, David			
Scott, Daniel W			Sergeant.
Sherrod, John			Corporal.
Silas, John		April 26, 65	
Singleton, Richard			
Slanton, Richard W			
Smith, Asa B			Bugler.
Spencer, William J			
Stephens, James C			
Stokeley, John B			
Stokeley, John E			
Sylvus, James			
Treeman, Simon			
Tully, George W		April 26, '65	Mentioned for gallantry.
Tully, W. C			
Walker, Henry W			
Whigham, David			
Woods, Henry G			
Youngblood, Abram W			

Roll Company G—1st Florida Cavalry.

NAMES.	MUSTERED IN.	MUSTERED OUT.	REMARKS.
OFFICERS.			
Captains—			
Nicholson S. Cobb	July 13, '61		
D. E. Maxwell	July 13, '61		Transferred from Company H, 2nd Regiment Cavalry and promoted Captain; Company G, 1st Cavalry, '64.
1st Lieutenant—			
Henry Bradford	July 13, '61		
2nd Lieutenant—			
John G. Rawls	July 13, '61		
3rd Lieutenants—			
Burrell Stokes	July 13, '61		
Thomas Pedrick			Promoted Lieutenant.
J. F. Hart			Promoted Lieutenant.
ENLISTED MEN.			
Apple, Louis	July 13, '61		
Beck, Robert D	July 13, '61		
Benefield, Eli	July 13, '61	April 26, '65	
Brock, James A	July 13, '61		
Daniels, Louis	July 13, '61		
Davis, Daniel J	July 13, '61		
Everett, Arthur E	July 13, '61		
Faircloth, Daniel	July 13, '61		
Faircloth, Sanford	July 13, '61		
Gainer, John	July 13, '61		
Gaines, John	July 13, '61		
Harris, Joseph B			
Hairs, John R	July 13, '61		Corporal.
Harvall, Joseph B	July 13, '61		Sergeant.
Highsmith, Isaac	July 13, '61		
Hogans, Monroe	July 13, '61		Farrier.
Holden, Daniel P	July 13, '61		Corporal.
Hudson, Garrett	July 13, '61		
Hurst, J. M			
Johns, James W	July 13, '61		Shot at Chickamauga September 20, '63.
Kelly, Archibald E	July 13, '61		
Lang, Edward	July 13, '61		
Lang, Levi	July 13, '61		
Lofton, Jesse	July 13, '61		
Lynn, Andrew J	July 13, '61		
McGehee, Samson	July 13, '61		
McLeaud, Alexander	July 13, '61		

Roll Company G—1st Florida Cavalry.
(CONTINUED.)

NAMES.	MUSTERED IN.	MUSTERED OUT.	REMARKS.
McLeaud, Neil	July 13, '61		
Martin, Harrison	July 13, '61		
Meddus, Green	July 1, '61		
Nobles, Saunders	July 1, '61		Corporal.
Parish, James	July 1, '61		
Patrick, Thomas	July 1, '61		
Philpot, Anderson	July 1, '61		
Philpot, James J.	July 1, '61		
Price, Barnett	July 1, '61		Bugler.
Renfrow, Nathaniel J.	July 1, '61		Corporal.
Roddenbery, William	July 1, '61		
Shepherd, Miles	July 1, '61		
Shipp, William	July 1, '61		Blacksmith.
Sparksman, Henry	July 1, '61		
Starling,	July 1, '61		
Starling, Thomas	July 1, '61		
Strawn, David	July 1, '61		
Thomington, Thomas	July 1, '61		
Tiner, E. J.			Mentioned for gallantry at Chickamauga.
Walker, Eanah	July 1, '61		
Walker, Isham	July 1, '61		Bugler.
Walker, Landrie A.	July 1, '61		
Waters, Richard	July 1, '61		
Weeks, James T.	July 1, '61		Sergeant.
White, Haser	July 1, '61		
Wilkinson, James H.			Sergeant.
Wilkinson, Lewis	July 1, '61		
Wilkinson, William R.	July 1, '61		
Wilkinson, Willis	July 1, '61		
Williamson, Cornelius	July 1, '61		
Williamson, John	July 1, '61		
Williamson, Stephen	July 1, '61		
Williamson, William	July 1, '61		
Wood, Absalom B.	July 1, '61		
Wood, Igdolio N.	July 1, '61		

Roll Company H—1st Florida Cavalry.

NAMES.	MUSTERED IN.	MUSTERED OUT.	REMARKS.
OFFICERS.			
Captains—			
Noble A. Hull	July '61		Resigned.
D. E. Maxwell			Promoted to Captain; Company "H," 1st Cavalry.
1st Lieutenants—			
Joseph R. Haddock	July '61		
Ira L. McCollum	Oct. 16, '61	June 19, '65	Wounded and captured at Murfreesborough, Tenn., December 4, '64; imprisoned at Fort Delaware until paroled; promoted 1st Lieutenant.
James P. Morgan		April 26, '65	Promoted 1st Lieutenant.
2nd Lieutenant—			
Daniel C. Sanders	July 1, '61		
3rd Lieutenant—			
William Edwards	July '61		
ENLISTED MEN.			
Baker, George W.	July 1, '61		Sergeant.
Bass, Benjamin			Captured at Missionary Ridge, Tenn., Nov. 25, '63, and died in prison at Rock Island, March 4, '64.
Bell, Thomas N.			Captured at Missionary Ridge, Tenn., November 25, '63; imprisoned at Rock Island.
Boasman, Joseph H.	July '61		
Bowen, William	July '61		
Brock, James A.	Dec. '60		Discharged for disability, re-enlisted in Captain Lutterloh's Company; promoted 1st Lieutenant Company "I," 1st Cavalry and again 1st Lieutenant in Lutterloh's Company.
Brock, Merideth	July '61		Sergeant.
Brooks, George W.			
Bronson, S. P.	Dec. '61		Died, November 4, '64.
Conner, William O.			
Corbin, James W.	Dec. 1, '61		Wounded at Chickamauga, Ga., September 19, '63.
Cowart, John F.			Captured and sent to prison at Rock Island where he died February 28, '64.
Carl, Jesse Sr.	July '61		Farrier.
Carl, Jesse Jr.	July 1, '61		
Davenport, William B.	July 1, '61		Corporal.
Dawson, James H.	July 1, '61		
Dees, Nathaniel M.	July 1, '61		

Roll Company H—1st Florida Cavalry.
(CONTINUED.)

NAMES	MUSTERED IN.	MUSTERED OUT.	REMARKS.
Demere, Vinclau	July 1, '61		Corporal.
Dempsey, Sylvester	July 1, '61		
Dupree, George W	July '61		Corporal.
Ellis, Joseph A	July 1, '61		
Feilding, John T	July '61		
Forsom, Patrick H	July '61		
Forsom, William G	July '61		
Fuqua, James	July 1, '61		
Goff, William C			Died in hospital during the war.
Goodbread, Thomas	July '61		
Greene, B. H		April 26, '65	
Hair, Rowland			Killed at Dallas, Ga., May 28, '64.
Hatch, Silas			Captured at Missionary Ridge, taken to Rock Island prison, Ill., remained there until close of war.
Hawkins, T. H	Nov. '61	June 19, '65	Discharged from Rock Island prison.
Herring, Henry H	July '61		Sergeant.
Holland, D			
Jenkins, D. F.		April 26, '65	
Johnson, Alexander L	July '61		
Johnson, James	July '61		
Kelly, Robert W	July '61		
Lee, Jesse			Died at Chattanooga, Tenn., May 1, '62.
Leech, Baxton M	July '61		
Lochlin, Gideon	July '61		
Lochlin, John	July '61		
Lochlin, William	July '61		
Low, Thomas M	July '61		
McClellan, Charles	July '61		
Martin, G. W	Jan. '62	April 26, '65	Captured at Missionary Ridge, paroled from prison May 20, '65.
Mathews, Zackeriah B	July 1, '62		
Owens, Benjamin F	July 1, '62		
Parker, Owen W	July 1, '62		Blacksmith.
Parker, Walter M	July 1, '62		
Peacock, J. A		'64	Discharged for disability; shot at Missionary Ridge December 27, '63.
Pedder, Thomas	July 1, '62		
Rawls, J. W	Oct. 1, '62	April 26, '65	Captured at Olustee, imprisoned at City Point and Washington City until close of war.
Reese, Thomas A	July 1, '62		Musician.
Roberts, J. D		April 26, '65	Promoted Corporal.
Sheffield, D. B		April 26, '65	
Simmons, G. W			Sergeant; mentioned for gallantry.
Simmons, Moses N	July '61		
Smith, H. M		April 26, '65	
Smith, John L	July '62		
Smith, Lovett	July '62		
Smith, Robert R	July '62		
Smith, S. A		April 26, '65	
Smith, Simon S	July '62		
Swinnney, Thomas	July '62		
Tedder, Thomas R	Nov. 28, '62	April 26, '65	
Tavell, Sampson		April 26, '65	Captured at Missionary Ridge, Tenn., November 24, '63; imprisoned at Rock Island, Ill.
Walker, Benjamin	July '62		
Walker, George P	July '62		
Walker, James M	June '62		Discharged, disability, '64.
Walker, William T	July '61		
Wiley, Isaac J	July '62		Corporal.
Wright, George	July '62		
Yates, Needham	July 1, '61		

Roll Company I—1st Florida Cavalry.

NAMES.	MUSTERED IN.	MUSTERED OUT.	REMARKS.
OFFICERS.			
Captain—			
W. D. Clark	July '61		
1st Lieutenant—			
Samuel J. Kennard			
2nd Lieutenant—			
James Weeks			
3rd Lieutenants—			
Stephen Weeks			Promoted Captain Co. G; resigned March 20, '63.
R. B. Weeks		April 26, '65	
ENLISTED MEN.			
Allen, James			Sergeant.
Anderson, William			

Roll Company I—1st Florida Cavalry.
(CONTINUED.)

NAMES	MUSTERED IN.	MUSTERED OUT.	REMARKS.
Appel, Louis	Dec. '61	April 26, '65	Wounded at Murfreesborough December 4, '64;
Avery, C. S.			captured and sent to Camp Chase, O; paroled
Barry, Joseph H			from there '65.
Barry, W. F			Shot and captured; died in prison at Chattanooga
Barker, James A			November, '63; promoted Sergeant.
Beale, William M			
Beck, R. D	Jan. '62	April 26, '65	Wounded at Chickamauga, Ga., September 20, '63
Bennefield, Eli Hardy	Jan. '61		Wounded at Atlanta July 22, '64; also bayonet in
Barry, Frank			arm.
Bigham, W. C			
Boune, James H			Discharged, '63; disability incurred in line of duty.
Cale, George			
Cale, John			
Cason, Bartholomow			
Chaistwell, James M			
Cheser, Leroy			
Cheser, William W			
Coker, Egbert Beville	June '61		Shot at New Hope Church, Ga., June 10, '64.
Davis, Daniel J	Dec. '61		Discharged at Knoxville December, '62, for injury
			to knee.
Denkins, William H			Blacksmith.
Dorman, John G			
Dunaway, John			
Ennis, James M			
Ennis, Mathew			
Faircloth, Daniel D	Feb. '62	April 26, '65	
Frier, A. A			Captured at Missionary Ridge, Tenn.
Fussell, Arnold			
Gaskins, William H			
Giddens, Andrew			
Gibson, Elisha	Mch. '62	April 26, '65	
Grimes, John	Jan. '62	April 26, '65	By parole from Rock Island prison at close of the
Guest, Mathew	Mch. '61	May 9, '65	war; mentioned for gallantry.
Hagin, Peter T. J	Oct. '61	'64	Discharged on account of wounds; wounded four
			different times in battle, at Resaca, Missionary
Hall, William			Ridge, Chickamauga and near Rome, Ga., the
Hamilton, Calvin			last a fracture of the skull.
Hamilton, Irwin			Corporal.
Hamilton, Sherod M			
Heagy, Henry			
Hester, William W			
Hogan, Henry		April 26, '65	
Hogan, Peter J. M			
Howell, E. T. (L.)			
Jackson, John A			
Johns, James W	Dec. 20, '61		Shot at Chickamauga, Ga., September 20, '63.
Jones, John	Oct. '61		Shot in Kentucky August '62.
Kelly, Jacob			Corporal.
Kelly, John O			
Kennard, James J			1st Sergeant.
Lee, Jesse			
Loftin, Jesse	'61		Wounded at Resaca, Ga., May 15, '64.
Lynn, A. J			
Lynn, William			
McGlor, David		April 26, '65	
McRae, James W		April 26, '65	
Mattcair, James		April 26, '65	
Merritt, Lucus		April 26, '65	
Miller, William		April 26, '65	
Mobley, Micajah		April 26, '65	Corporal.
Mobley, Ransom D		April 26, '65	
Moore, Jackson		April 26, '65	
Moore, James			
Moore, Riley		April 26, '65	
Morgan, Thomas		April 26, '65	
Nelson, I. T			Died in service.
Nobles, Alfred			
North, John			
Odom, John			
Parker, Richard			
Pennel, G. B	Mch. '62	May '65	
Prevatt, Reuben			
Pringle, Thomas D		April 26, '65	
Register, George			Sergeant.
Richards, Job T			
Roberson, Hardy			
Roberts, James L			
Shipp, William	Dec. 5, '61	April 26, '65	Wounded at Savannah.
Sanchez, Frank H	'61	April 26, '65	Wounded at Missionary Ridge, Tenn., December
			'63.
Stanton, George W	Jan. '62	April 26, '65	Wounded at Chickamauga, Ga., September 19, '63.
Stewart, Henry G			
Strobbles, Jacob G			Sergeant.

Roll Company I—1st Florida Cavalry.
(CONTINUED.)

NAMES.	MUSTERED IN.	MUSTERED OUT.	REMARKS.
Thomas, James E.	'62		Died in service '62.
Tomlinson, Naan		April 26, '65	
Tranthem, W. P.		April 26, '65	
Tyer, John			
Tyner, Edward J.			
Walker, Isham		April 26, '65	
Ward, Richard			
Weeks, George W.			
Weimer, Daniel			
Weiner, Tounsend			
White, H.			Died at Camp Chase February, '65; grave No. 1304
Wilkerson, J. H.		April 26, '65	
Williams, Stephen	Dec. '61	April 26, '65	
Williamson, Stephen	Dec. '61	April 26, '65	
Willis, R. T.		April 26, '65	

Roll Company K—1st Florida Cavalry.

NAMES.	MUSTERED IN.	MUSTERED OUT.	REMARKS.
OFFICERS.			
Captains—			
David Hughes	July 1, '61		Resigned '62; disability.
G. Finley	June '61		Promoted Captain '62.
1st Lieutenants—			
Emmet E. Barry	July 1, '61		
Andrew G. LaTaste			1st Sergeant; promoted 1st Lieutenant; resigned April 24, '64.
2nd Lieutenant—			
William Hughes	July 1, '61		Resigned April 24, '64.
3rd Lieutenant—			
William Platt	July 1, '61		
ENLISTED MEN.			
Adams, William F.			Blacksmith.
Barber, Elbert E.	July 1, '61		Musician.
Barber, William W.	Dec. '62	April 26, '65	
Bradley, R. J.	Jan. 1, '62	April 26, '65	Sergeant.
Combee, Hampton	July 1, '61		
Crews, Micajah			
Crews, W. A.	July 1, '61		
Crews, William B.			
Colbert, Benjamin F.	July 1, '61		
Colbert, Felming	July 1, '61		
Colding, J. L.		April 26, '65	
Cooper, James M.	July 1, '61		
Crichton, John W.		April 26, '65	
Darby, John W.		April 26, '65	
Darby, Thomas J.	July 1, '61		
Drew, William C.	July 1, '61		
Futch, J. W.		April 26, '65	Corpor
Futch, William	Jan. 20, '62	April 26, '65	Bugler.
Gideon, Morris	July 1, '61		
Goddard, Harvey J.	Jan. 18, '61		Mentioned for gallantry; wounded September 19, '63; was not in army service after that date; discharged at reorganization at Chickamauga;
Gold, Andrew	July 1, '61		something about right arm; mentioned for Corporal.
Godwin, Iverson	Mch. '61	April 25, '65	
Harris, Samuel B. S.	Mch. 1, '61		Corporal.
Harville, David L.			
Hendry, William M.	Mch. 1, '61		
Holton, Thomas J.	Jan. 1, '62	April 26, '65	
Hull, Stephen	July 1, '61		Corporal.
McKinney, Samuel	July 1, '61		
McLellan, William	July 1, '61		
McNeil, James	Jan. 1, '62	April 26, '65	
Malvin, William		April 26, '65	Sergeant.
Miley, James T.	Jan. '62	April 26, '65	Shot through body at Missionary Ridge December 27, '63.
Monroe, John	July 1, '61		
Peele, Jerry	July 1, '61		
Peele, Lemuel	July 1, '61		
Peters, Allison W.	July 1, '61		
Peters, George	July 1, '61		
Phan, James	July 1, '61		
Pollock, John	July 1, '61		
Purvis, William	Jan. '61	May '63	Disability.
Smith, Simon	July 1, '61		
Tanner, John W.	Jan. 20, '62	April 26, '65	Promoted Sergeant.
Tyer, Hillary	July 1, '61		Corporal.
Wade, Andrew E.	Jan. '62	April 26, '65	
Hopkins M.	July 1, '61		

Roll, Field and Staff—2nd Florida Cavalry.

NAMES.	MUSTERED IN.	MUSTERED OUT.	REMARKS.
Colonel—			
Carraway Smith			
Lieutenant-Colonel—			
Abner H. McCormick			
Major—			
Robert Harrison			
Surgeon—			
J. W. Epps			Transferred to Georgetown hospital.
Assistant-Surgeons—			
A. P. Smith			
J. A. Williams			With Co. H, Detached.
A. P. Lippford			
P. H. Hudson			Detached from Campbell's Artillery.
J. M. McCall			
Adjutant—			
William M. Ledwith			
Sergeant-Major—			
W. A. Forward			
Quartermaster—			
——Dozier			
Commissary—			
Chaplain—			
J. C. Ley			
Quartermaster-Sergeant—			
W. W. Willis			
Commissary-Sergeant—			
Hospital Steward—			

Roll Company A (Milton Dragoons)—2nd Florida Cavalry.

NAMES.	MUSTERED IN.	MUSTERED OUT.	REMARKS.
OFFICERS.			
Captain—			
Clinton Thigpen	Mch. 10, '62		
1st Lieutenant—			
Frederick N. Fuller	Mch. 10, '62		
2nd Lieutenants—			
William A. Jeter	Mch. 10, '62	May 20, '65	Promoted Captain Co. E, 5th Florida Battalion Cavalry.
Hiram N. Pace	Mch. 10, '62		
3rd Lieutenant—			
ENLISTED MEN.			
Adams, J. M.	Mch. 10, '62	May 20, '65	Thrown from horse and wounded in October, '64.
Adams, William			
Alender, Augustus R.	Mch. 10, '62		Sergeant.
Armstrong, George M.			
Austin, William			
Baker, Robert G.	Mch. 10, '62		Sergeant.
Bateman, Malachi	April 10, '62	May 20, '65	
Bauldrew, Frederic	April 1, '62		
Bolin, John	April 1, '62		
Bolin, William	April 1, '62		
Broughton, J.			
Brown, C. W.			
Buie, D. C.			
Buie, John N.			
Cash, James D.	Mch. 10, '62		
Castlebery, Elias			
Castlebery, Milton			
Colley, Beasley			
Conner, David	Mch. 10. '62		
Contie, Nicholas			
Darby, Retey G.			
Davis, Andrew J.	June 15, '63	May 20, '65	
Davis, John M.	Mch. 10, '62		
Davis, Riley	April 1, '62		
Dennis, John W.	Mch. 1, '63	May 20, '65	
Driggers, B. A.	July 1, '61	May 20, '65	Transferred September 4, '61, to Capt. James Faulkner's Company.
Ferguson, Archibald C.	April 1, '62		
Field, Augustus M.	Mch. 10, '62		
Foster, Sheppard	Mch. 10, '62		
Fowler, Asa F.	Mch. 10, '62		
Franklin, Francis M.	April 1, '62		
Gannon, John			
Glenn, J. H.	Mch. 1, '61	May 20, '65	

Roll Company A (Milton Dragoons)—2nd Florida Cavalry.
(CONTINUED.)

NAMES.	MUSTERED IN.	MUSTERED OUT.	REMARKS.
Hagan, F. B.			
Harrison, Reuben L.			
Hatcher, James	Oct. '61		
Hentz, William	April 10, '62		
Hinson, G. W.			Wounded at Natural Bridge March 4, '65.
Hobart, Charles E.			
Hobart, John H.	Mch. 10, '62		1st Corporal.
Hockstrasser, Charles E.	Mch. 10, '62		
Howell, M. T.			
Howard, Volney	April 10, '62		
Hudson, Hubbard	Mch. 10, '62		
Humphrey, J. C.			
Humphries, William			
Hyatt, E. N.			
Ingram, Sam	Mch. 10, '62		
Jackson, T. H.			
Jenia, John			
Jones, James T.	Mch. 10, '62		
Jones, Joshua C.	April 10, '62		
Jordan, James C.	Mch. 10, '62	May 20, '65	Transferred to Jeter's Company E, 5th Battalion.
Jourdan, James F.			
Jordan, John E.	'61		Wounded at Gainesville, Fla., '64.
Kelly, Pleasant	Mch. 10, '62		
Kendrick, Zebulen R.	April 1, '62		
Keen, George			
King, James	April 1, '62		
King, M. D.			
Lambeth, Allen M.	April 10, '62		
Lambeth, John J.	April 10, '62		
Larkins, Seaborn	April 10, '62	May 20, '65	
Lawrence, Joseph	Mch. 10, '62		Corporal; transferred, '63 to Company E, 5th Battalion Cavalry under Captain Jeter; paroled from prison at close of war.
Lipford, John H.			
Looper, Edward	April 10, '62		
Looper, John	April 1, '62		
Longer, William			
Lucas, Benjamin			
McIntosh, William			
McCardy, A. F.		May 20, '65	
McLendon, John A.	Mch. 10, '62		
McMillan, Archibald	April 10, '62	May 20, '65	
McMillan, Henry	April 10, '62		
McMillan, John	Mch. '62	May 20, '65	Wounded at Natural Bridge.
McNelty, James			
Maddox, William S.	Mch. 10, '62		Corporal.
Messer, Peter	'62	May 20, '65	
Mills, M.	Dec. 20, '62	May 20, '65	
Mitchell, Colby C.			
Murat, John			
Murphy, Alexander N.	April 10, '62		
Myers, Mathew R.	Mch. 10, '62		1st Sergeant.
Niel, W. H.		May 20, '65	
Patton, George A.		May 20, '65	
Pearson, John W.	Mch. 10, '62		
Pickett, Hiram W.	April 1, '62		
Piles, William	Mch. 10, '62		
Pinner, James		May 20, '65	
Pope, George W.	April 10, '62		
Powell, John			
Powell, William			
Raney, Edward J.	Mch. 10, '62		Corporal.
Rhaumes, James B.	April 1, '62		
Rhaimes, Nathan	April 10, '62		
Richards, Daniel U.	April 1, '62		
Richards, John	April 1, '62		
Rigby, James	April 1, '62		
Rogers, Cornelius	Mch. 10, '62	May 20, '65	
Rogers, Henry	April 1, '62	May 20, '65	
Rogers, John	April 10, '62		
Russell, Henry	April 10, '62		
Sasio, Alexander A.			
Scott, Jacob	Mch. 10, '62		
Shaw, William D.	April 1, '62		
Shuler, William E.		May 20, '65	
Silas, Thomas B.	Mch. 10, '62		
Smith, James M.	April 10, '62		
Smith, James P.	April 10, '62		
Smith, Malcolm N.	April 10, '62		
Smith, Peter			
Smith, Richard D.	Mch. 10, '62		
Smith, Robert R.	Mch. 10, '62		
Stanfill, James		May 20, '65	
Strange, Thomas W.	Mch. 10, '62	May 20, '65	
Summers, Jacob A.	April 1, '62	May 20, '65	

Roll Company A—2nd Florida Cavalry.
(CONTINUED.)

NAMES.	MUSTERED IN.	MUSTERED OUT.	REMARKS.
Tate, Madison	April 10, '62		
Thigpen, John T	Mch. 10, '62		Sergeant; severely wounded at Natural Bridge.
Tisser, Albert			
Toole, Calvin		May 20, '65	
Turner, R. L			
Urquhart, Norman B	Mch. 10, '62	May 20, '65	
Vinzant, Frank		May 20, '65	
Vinzant, John		May 20, '65	
Watson, Benjamin F	April 1, '62	May 20, '65	Transferred, '63 to A. C. Smith's Company, 5th Battalion.
Whitehurst, C. J	April 1, '63		Discharged for disability, October 1, '64.
Whiteside, G. H			
Willis, Joseph			
Witherspoon, J. S	Mch. 10, '62	May 20, '65	
Witherspoon, James T	Mch. 10, '62		
Witherspoon, R. A			
Wood, William L	Mch. 10, '62		
Worthington, William	Mch. 10, '62		
Yent, Sam	Mch 10, '62		

Roll Company B—2nd Florida Cavalry.

NAMES.	MUSTERED IN.	MUSTERED OUT.	REMARKS.
OFFICERS.			
Captains—			
Winston Stephens	April 62		Killed at Cedar Creek near Jacksonville March 1, '64.
Ben Hopkins	Nov. '61		
H. A. Gray	April '62	May 20, '65	Promoted from 1st Lieutenant to Captain.
1st Lieutenant—			
R. H. McLeod Jr			Promoted from 2nd Lieutenant to 1st Lieutenant
2nd Lieutenant—			
S. B. W. Stephen	'82		Promoted 2nd Lieutenant.
3rd Lieutenants—			
William W. Shedd		April 25, '65	Promoted 1st Lieutenant; captured and paroled at Jacksonville April 25, '65.
M. Smith	April '62	May 20, '65	Promoted 3rd Lieutenant.
ENLISTED MEN.			
Alvarez, D. G	April '62	May '65	
Alvarez, J. R	April '62	May '65	
Barnes, James F			
Barratte, A	April '62	May '65	
Baya, Joseph	April '62	May '65	Captured at Olustee and imprisoned at Fort Delaware.
Bagley, T. C	April '62	May 22, '65	Shot at Olustee March, '64.
Beasley, E	April '62	May '65	
Becks, J. L	April '62	May '65	
Bennett, R. L	April '62		
Boer, John	April '62	May 20, '65	
Bomshier, Mathaias			
Braddock, John			
Braddock, Joseph			
Braddock, William			
Bradley, B. H	'63		Paroled from prison.
Bradshaw, James B			
Branning, D. L	April '62	May 20, '65	
Branning, T. J	April '62	May 20, '65	Promoted Sergeant.
Bryant, D. H	April '62	May 20, '65	
Brower, G	April '62	May 20, '65	
Brown, Simon S			
Cannon, James		May 20, '65	
Cannon, Reddick	April '62	May 20, '65	
Cappo, Mitchell	April '62		
Carpenter, Samuel	April '62		Corporal.
Carter, John R	April '62		
Carter, William	April '62		
Connell, James R		May 20, '65	
Cook, E	April '62	May 20, '65	
Cook, George	April '62	May 20, '65	
Corbett, John	April '62		
Dardis, James	April '62	May 20, '65	
Dellaberry, F	April '62	May 20, '65	
Dellaberry, W	April '62	May 20, '65	
Denmark, William H	April '62		
Donaldson, George W	April '62		
Donaldson, John F	April '62	May 20, '65	
Dukes, J. J	April '62	May 20, '65	

Roll Company B—2nd Florida Cavalry.
(CONTINUED.)

NAMES.	MUSTERED IN.		MUSTERED OUT.		REMARKS.
Durrance, William	April	'62			
Dykes, Duncan	April	'62	May 20, '65		Corporal.
Dykes, E. D.					
Dykes, Jackson T.	April	'62			
Eubanks, W. N.	April	'62	May 20, '65		
Fleming, F. A.	April	'62	May 20, '65		
Flood, Patrick	April	'62			
Forward, Henry H.	April	'62			
Futch, James W.	April	'62			
Gaines, J.	April	'62	May 20, '65		
Gibson, Denis W.	April	'62			Sergeant.
Glisson, D. W.	April	'62	May 20, '65		
Glisson, W. Riley	April	'62	May '65		
Goodson, Madison					
Granger, H.	April	'62	May 20, '65		
Granger, John A.	June	'61	May 20, '65		
Granger, Meredith	April	'62	May 20, '65		
Granger, Meredith D.	April	'62			
Greely, J. C.	April	'62			
Griffith, H.	April	'62	May 20, '65		
Griffith, S.	April	'62	May 20, '65		
Griffin, Jeremiah	April	'62			
Groom, J.	April	'62	May 20, '65		
Grooms, Riley	April	'62			
Hewett, Joe M.	April	'62			
Hires, Joe M.	April	'62			
Hopkins, Henry T.	April	'62	May 20, '65		Captured at Olustee and imprisoned at Fort Delaware.
Hopkins, Joseph	April	'62			
Houston, D. P.	April	'62	May 20, '65		
Houston, J. R.	April	'62	May 20, '65		
Hunter, Archibald	April	'61	May 20, '65		
Jennings, Edward S.	April	'61	May 20, '65		
Johns, H. A.	April	'61			
Jones, William T.	April	'62	May 20, '65		
Killingsworth, C. L.	April	'62			Corporal.
King, J. A.	April	'62	May 20, '65		
Lancy, J. R.	April	'62	May 20, '65		
Lane, James	April	'62			
Lee, Daniel B.	April	'62			
Lee, George W.	Jan. 2,	'63	May 20, '65		
Lee, Thomas J.	April	'62			
L'Engle, Edward	April	'62	May 20, '65		
Livingston, Morgan	April	'62			
Livingston, Warren	April	'62			
Livingston, William	April	'62			
Lucas, William H.	April	'62	May 20, '65		
McLeod, D. C.	April	'62	May 20, '65		
McRae, George W.	April	'62			
Malette, F. F.	April	'62	May 20, '65		
Metts, Jefferson A.	April	'62	May 20, '65		
Metts, Lafayette	April	'62	May 20, '65		
Metts, Reddon	April	'62	May 20, '65		Sergeant.
Mizell, John	April	'62			Farrier.
Moats, Henry	April	'62			
Moats, John	April	'62	May 20, '65		
Monroe, P.	April		May 20, '65		
Moody, Berrian	April	'62			
Moody, Jacob	April	'62			
Olesby, D. O.	April	'62	May 20, '65		
Olesby, C.	April	'62	May 20, '65		
Osteen, John A.	April	'62			
Perry, Abram	April	'62			
Priest, Gabriel W.	April	'62			Promoted Bugler.
Priest, James C.	April	'62			
Priest, John	April	'62	May 20, '65		
Priest, William	April	'62	May 20, '65		
Pinner, James	April	'62	May 20, '65		
Purdam, James H.	April	'62			Captured August 4, '63; paroled from prison at close of war.
Reelingsworth, C. L.	April	'62	May 20, '65		Sergeant.
Revels, W. E.	April	'62	May 20, '65		
Roberts, Evans	April	'62	May 20, '65		
Rollerson, Mathew	April	'62			
Sanders, M.	April	'62	May 20, '65		
Shally, J. H.	April	'61	May 20, '65		Promoted Corporal.
Shally, Thomas	April	'62			
Shook, B. F.	April	'62			Blacksmith.
Sibley, L. G.	April	'62	May 20, '65		
Smith, F. B.	April	'62	May 20, '65		Promoted Corporal.
Snowdon, Edward	April	'62			
Soland, Mathew	April	'62			
Solowinsky, Frederick	April	'62			
Sparkman, C. W.	April	'62	May 20, '65		

Roll Company B—2nd Florida Cavalry.

(CONTINUED.)

NAMES.	MUSTERED IN.		MUSTERED OUT.			REMARKS.
Standley, Isham	April	'62				
Stephens, Charles	April	'62				
Stephens, Naaman	April	'62				
Stephens, Swepston	April	'62				Corporal.
Tompkins, James A			May	20,	'65	
Tompkins, W. P			May	20,	'65	Promoted 1st Sergeant.
Trouell, M. J	April	'62	May	20,	'65	Promoted Corporal.
Tyner, Jesse C	Oct.	'61	May	20,	'65	Bugler.
Tyner, Willis R	April	'62	May	20,	'65	
Wall, B. S	April	'62	May	20,	'65	
Wall, S. Jackson	April	'62	May	20,	'65	
Wall, Lawrence D	April	'62	May	20,	'65	Promoted Corporal.
Waterbury, H. W	April	'62	May	20,	'65	
Watson, B. F			May	20,	'65	
Weathersbee, George	Oct.	'61	May	20,	'65	
Weathersbee, Joshua	April	'62				
Weineer, J. D. A	April	'62	May	20,	'65	
Wilkerson, H	April	'62	May	20,	'65	
Wilkerson, John	April	'62	May	20,	'65	Promoted Sergeant.
Wilkerson, William	April	'62				
Wingate, A. A	April	'62	May	20,	'65	
Wingate, Isaac	April	'62	May	20,	'65	
Wingate, W. H	April	'62	May	20,	'65	
Yelvington, Richard	April	'62	May	20,	'65	

Roll Company C—2nd Florida Cavalry.

NAMES.	MUSTERED IN.		MUSTERED OUT.			REMARKS.
OFFICERS.						
Captain—						
William E. Chambers		'62	May	20,	'65	
1st Lieutenants—						
H. A. McCormick		'62				
Samuel C. Reddick			May	20,	'65	Promoted from 2nd Lieutenant to 1st Lieutenant.
2nd Lieutenant—						
Thomas P. Boulware	Aug. 12,	'64	May	20,	'65	
3rd Lieutenant—						
ENLISTED MEN.						
Adams, K. P		'62	May	20,	'65	
Atkinson, Ira D. M		'62	May	20,	'65	
Atkinson, M		'62	May	20,	'65	
Beckett, Edward M	June 1,	'62	May	20,	'65	
Bevill, Robert H		'62	May	20,	'65	
Bevill, Stephen C		'62	May	20,	'65	
Black, David		'62	May	20,	'65	
Blake, Thomas H	April	'62	May	20,	'65	Bugler.
Blitch, S. H		'62	May	20,	'65	
Blitch, William H		'62	May	20,	'65	
Boatwright, John J		'62	May	20,	'65	
Boulware, Benjamin P	Oct. 1,	'61	May	20,	'65	
Boulware, Robert P		'62	May	20,	'65	
Bowers, T. J		'62	May	20,	'65	
Bradshaw, J. B		'62	May	20,	'65	
Brad'ord, James J		'62	May	20,	'65	
Bradford, Thomas		'62	May	20,	'65	
Brevard, Edward C		'62	May	20,	'65	
Brooks, John H		'62	May	20,	'65	
Brown, B. W		'62	May	20,	'65	
Buckman, William	Oct.	'64	May	20,	'65	
Carter, Jesse		'64	May	20,	'65	
Cassady, A. J		'64	May	20,	'65	
Cassady, Benjamin F		'64	May	20,	'65	
Casady, Wilson W	July	'61	May	20,	'65	
Cauthen, Andrew J		'62	May	20,	'65	
Chapman, Gillis P	May 3	'62	Dec.	27,	'62	Discharged for disability; died of measles at Fernandina, Fla., November 4, '63.
Chamberlain, George S		'62	Dec.	27,	'62	
Chestnut, James		'62	Dec.	27,	'62	
Chesser, J. W		'62	May	20,	'65	
Clark, Absalom C		'62	May	20,	'65	
Cook, Anzeo W		'62	May	20,	'65	
Collins, Henry M		'62	May	20,	'65	
Colson, Barnard		'62	May	20,	'65	
Connell, James R		'62	May	20,	'65	
Connell, William R		'62	May	20,	'65	
Coolter, Alexander		'63	April		'65	
Cromer, William L		'62	May	20,	'65	
Crews, Samuel P		'62	May	20,	'65	

Roll Company C—2nd Florida Cavalry.
(CONTINUED.)

NAMES.	MUSTERED IN.	MUSTERED OUT.	REMARKS.
Demere, Raymond		'62 May 20, '65	
Dickison, Charles B		'62 May 20, '65	
Dixon, Josiah B	April	'61 May 20, '65	
Dogan, John	Sept.	'62 May 20, '65	
Dupries, J. S		'62 May 20, '65	
Edwards, Adeniram J		'62 May 20, '65	
Edwards, John S		'62 May 20, '65	
Ellerbe, Richard P		'62 May 20, '65	
Emmerson, Andrew J		'62 May 20, '65	
Feaster, Jacob M		'62 May 20, '65	Corporal.
Feaster, John P		'62 May 20, '65	Farrier.
Gambrell, William W		'62 May 20, '65	
Gansy, Henry M		'62 May 20, '65	
Girt, Robert T		'62 May 20, '65	
Graddick, Nicholus	Sept.	'61 May 20, '65	
Hadsock, William	Sept. 15,	'62 May 20, '65	Shot at Petersburg, Va., September 15, '64.
Haile, Edward		'62 May 20, '65	
Haile, John		'62 May 20, '65	
Harris, John M		'62 May 20, '65	
Harrison, Henry C	April	'62 May 20, '65	
Harrison, J. K		'62 May 20, '65	
Harville, Jesse S		'62 May 20, '65	
Hawthorn, Elijah T		'62 May 20, '65	
Haynes, Bunberry		'62 May 20, '65	
Ives, William		'62 May 20,	
Jackson, L. W	June	'62 June '65	Wounded while pursuing deserters January 5, '65.
Johnson, Robert E		'62 May 20, '65	Bugler
Johnson, Thomas A		'62 May 20, '65	
Johnson, William E	Aug.	'61 May 20, '65	
Jones, James M		'62 May 20, '65	
Kilgore, James F		'62 May 20, '65	Sergeant.
King, John W. F		'62 May 20, '65	Sergeant; promoted 1st Sergeant.
Kincaird, James		'62 May 20, '65	
Kinster, Hugh		'62 May 20, '65	
Knoblock, William		'62 May 20, '65	
Lee, George M		'62 May 20, '65	
Leonard, Alexander H		'62 May 20, '65	
Lewis, Wilbur G		62 May 20, '65	
Lewis, Thomas B		'62 May 20, '65	
Lewis, Thomas W		'62 May 20, '65	
Lewis, William B		'62 May 20, '65	1st Sergeant.
Lewis, William E		'62 May 20, '65	Corporal.
Letford, William		'62 May 20, '65	1st Sergeant.
Lovell, Burazillar		'62 May 20, '65	
McAteer, A. J	Sept. 9,	'62 May 20, '65	
McAteer, Jessee S		'62 May 20, '65	
McClure, Robert L		'62 May 20, '65	
McLeod, Alexander	Mch.	'62 May 20, '65	Captured and confined at Fort Delaware until close of war.
McLeod, Daniel O		'62 May 20, '65	
Marsh, Moses		'62 May 20, '65	
Mathews, John L	July	'64 May 20, '65	Shot at Marshall Swamp March 12, '65.
Mathews, John T		'62 May 20, '65	
Mattox, George O		'62 May 20, '65	
Miller, John J		'62 May 20, '65	
Mixon, John B		'62 May 20, '65	
Mixon, Miles G		'62 May 20, '65	
Moody, Daniel B		'62 May 20, '65	
Monroe, Augustus		'62 May 20, '65	
Newson, Andrew J		'62 May 20, '00	
Nix, James P		'62 May 20, '65	
Parker, James P		'62 May 20, '65	
Payne, M. L		May 20, '65	
Perry, John S	Sept. 20,	'61 May 20, '65	Wounded at Olustee by fall of horse, February 22. 64.
Pheiffer, John W		'61 May 20, '65	
Price. Alex. P	April	'61 May 20, '65	Transferred to Morgan's Cavalry; paroled from prison.
Price, H. C		'61 May 20, '65	
Priest, G		'61 May 20, '65	
Purdom, J. H		'61 May 20, '65	
Rouse, Benjamin P		May 20, '65	Wounded February 14, '64 at Olustee, Fla.
Row, S. F		'61 May 20, '65	
Ruff, George C. W		'61 May 20, '65	
Ruff, Joseph H		'61 May 20, '65	
Sistrunk, G. M		'61 May 20, '65	
Sistrunk, Henry I		'61 April 26, '65	
Sistrunk, James S		'61 May 20, '65	
Sistrunk, Thomas W. J		'61 April 20, '65	
Shuford, William T		'61 May 20, '65	
Sligh, Jacob M		'61 May 20, '65	
Shettlesworth, William P		'61 May 20, '65	
Simpson, Henry G		'61 May 20, '65	
Speer, John B		'61 May 20, '65	
Sperry, Norman S		'62 May 20, '65	
Stokes, John H		'62 May 20, '65	

Roll Company C---2nd Florida Cavalry.
(CONTINUED.)

NAMES.	MUSTERED IN.	MUSTERED OUT.	REMARKS.
Tanner, S. V.	'62	May 20, '65	
Varnadoe, Leondard	April 30, '62		Transferred from 7th Regiment, Vandlandingham's Company; discharged for disability, '64.
Waldo, J. W.	'62	May 20, '65	
Warren, James E.	'62	May 20, '65	
Weeks, John G.	'62	May 20, '65	
Weeks, Sherrod S.	'62	May 20, '65	Re-enlisted from Company H, 1st Infantry.
Whitaker, John	'62	May 20, '65	
Whitaker, Thomas	'62	May 20, '65	
Wincoff, William F.	'62	May 20, '65	Corporal.
Worthington, John R.	'62	May 20, '65	Sergeant.
Worthington, Milton J.	'62	May 20, '65	
Yongue, Alexander H.	'62	May 20, '65	Corporal.
Zetroman, A. T.	'62	May 20, '65	

Roll Company D (Captain Scott's Company)—2nd Florida Cavalry.

NAMES.	MUSTERED IN.	MUSTERED OUT.	REMARKS.
OFFICERS.			
Captains—			
P. B. Brokaw	Mch. 5, '62		Resigned.
G. W. Scott	Mch. 5, '62		
D. B. Maxwell	Mch. 5, '62		Promoted Captain.
1st Lieutenant—			
D. W. Gwynn	Mch. 5, '62		
2nd Lieutenant—			
E. A. Hart	Mch. 5, '62		
3rd Lieutenant—			
D. W. Scott			
ENLISTED MEN.			
Alderman, A.	Mch. 5, '62		
Andrews, J. A.	Mch. 5, '62		4th Sergeant.
Boswell, A. W.	April 19, '62		
Barber, John W.	Mch. 5, '62	April '65	Absent sick, August 14.
Barber, W.	Oct. 24, '62		Transferred October 24 from Captain Milton's Co. F (M. T. A.), Volunteer Battery and clothing money paid.
Barber, W. M.			
Barco, P. T.			Discharged September 1, having furnished P. H. McCook as substitute.
Barno, Peter	Mch. 5, '62		
Billingsley, J. S.	Mch. 17, '62		
Bond, Elbert	Mch. 5, '62	April '65	
Bradley, G. W.	Mch. 5, '62		Absent sick October 13.
Bradford, W. M.	Mch. 5, '62		
Branch, J. H.	Oct. 14,		Absent sick October 14; bounty due.
Braswell, M. M.			
Chaires, Samuel	April 14, '62		
Chaires, T. P.	Sept. 1,		
Coleman, W. K.	April 12,		Accidentally lost four fingers August 24, '63.
Council, John C.	Mch. 5,		
Croom, A. C.	Mch. 5, '6		3rd Corporal; absent sick October 18; promoted July 8, from 4th Corporal.
Cromartie, J. Q.			Discharged October 26 by civil authorities.
Crowder, A. H.	Mch. 5,		
Crowder, R. H.	April 19,		
Dugger, I. L.	Mch. 5,		
Dugger, J. L.	Sept. 20, '63	May 6, '65	Captured October 1, '64; paroled from prison at close of the war.
Dugger, Thomas	Mch. 5,		
Dugger, N. M.	Mch. 5,		
Denham, William	Oct. 1,		Absent sick October 7; bounty due.
Ferril, A. M.	April 19,		
Ferril, J. S.	Mch. 5,		5th Sergeant.
Finklea, A. J.	Mch. 5,		
Fletcher, J. M.	Mch. 5,		Sent to general hospital May 8.
Fletcher, M. N.	Mch. 5,		
Fletcher, R. R.	Mch. 5,		Thrown from horse and injured in back.
Floyd, George C.			
Floyd, W. H.	June '63		Transferred September 1 to Captain Gamble's Co. in exchange for T. P. Charies.
Galpin, J. M.			2nd Sergeant.
Grambling, J. W.			
Gray, J. H.	Mch. 5,		
Gregory, H. C.	Mch. 5,		
Green, T. J.	Mch. 10, '62		Paroled.
Grice, J. A.	Mch. 5,		Absent sick August 19.
Harris, A. F.	April 9,		
Hand, C. D.	Mch. 5,		

Roll Company D (Captain Scott's Company)—2nd Florida Cavalry.
(CONTINUED.)

NAMES.	MUSTERED IN.	MUSTERED OUT.	REMARKS.
Hand, W.	Mch. 5,		
Harris, W.	April 19,		
Hart, B. F.	June 4,		
Houstoun, E. M.	Mch. 5,		
Humphries, J. D.			
Jenkins, B. W.	Mch. 5,		
Jenkins, J. H.	May 22,		
Johnson, C. C.			Discharged by order civil authorities, being a minor.
Joyner, B. H.	Mch. 5,		Paroled.
Kindon, G. A.	Mch. 5,		Detailed in Ordnance Department by Special Order No. 836 August 2.
Kirksey, L. H.	Mch. 5,		
Laing, W. E.	Mch. 5,		
Laing, R. C.			
Lasch, C.	Mch. 5,		
Lester, John S.			Discharged August 1, having furnished S. A. McCook as substitute.
Lester, W. G.	Mch. 5,		3rd Sergeant; absent sick October 27.
Lester, R. E.	Mch. 5,		4th Corporal; promoted July 8 from the ranks.
McCook, S. A.	Aug. 1,		Received August 1 as substitute for John S. Lester.
McCook, P. H.	Sept. 1,		Received September 1 as substitute for P. T. Barco.
McCullum, E. S.	Mch. 5,		
McEachin, J. M.	Mch. 5,		Absent sick October 1.
McIntosh, B. M.			
Munro, Robert	Mch. 5,		
Myers, C. A.	Mch. 5,		
Mashburn, J.	Mch. 5,		
Mathison, J. L.	Mch. 29,		
Mathews, S.	April 9,		
Maxwell, John W.			Paroled.
Miller, C. K.	Mch. 5,		1st Sergeant.
Moore, C.	Mch. 5,		
Munroe, Robert			
Munroe, Thomas F.			
Myers, C. A.			
Oliver, J. L.	April 19,		Absent sick September 16.
Owens, T. W.	Mch. 5,		1st Corporal; absent sick October 13.
Parkhill, Samuel.	Mch. 5,		Corporal.
Parramore, R. W.			
Posey, Noah	Mch. 5,		Died, '65 while in prison at Ship Island, Miss.
Raker, M. D.			Paroled.
Raker, T. J.	Mch. 5,		
Randolph, W. D.	April 19,		Absent sick October 12.
Randolph, T. H.			Corporal; transferred July 8 to Waller's Co, 8th Florida in exchange for James Sylvester.
Randolph, H.	Mch. 5,		
Rawles, S.	April 19,		
Ridder, E. B.			
Robinson, F.	Mch. 5,		Absent sick October 15.
Robinson, D. F.	Mch. 5,		
Robinson, Charles.	Mch. 5,		
Rhodes, E.	Mch. 5,		
Strowman, J. L.	April 19,		
Strickland, A. J.	Mch. 5,		
Strickland, G. B.	Mch. 5,		
Shelfer, G. W.	Mch. 5,		
Shelfer, W. H.	Mch. 5,		Sent to general hospital October 15.
Shelfer, Joseph	July 15,		Bounty due.
Stephens, J. A.	Mch. 5,		
Saunders, M.	Mch. 5,		
Saunders, F. L.	Mch. 5,		
Saunders, Robert	May 5,		
Shehee, S. B.	Mch. 5,		2nd Corporal.
Shaw, James K.			
Smith, A.			Wounded in jaw.
Spiller, A. F.	Mch. 5,		Sent to general hospital October 30; detailed in general hospital May 24; returned October 1.
Spears, W. S.	April 12,		
Scott, A. M.	April 12,		
Story, Isaac			
Sylvester, James	July 8,		Transferred July 8 from Captain Waller's Co, 8th Florida Volunteers.
Tatum, T. P.	April 19,		Claims exemption as practical druggist.
Tully, W. C.			
Vickers, E.	Mch. 5,		
Vickers, J.	Mch. 5,		
Walsh, Bryant	Mch. 5,	April 7, '65	
Walsh, Patrick			Captured October 8, '64; released June, '65.
Watson, J. H.	Mch. 5,		
Watson, J. J.	April 19,		
Wamack, W.	Mch. 5,		
Woodward, W. W.	April 19,		Acting Hospital Steward of Co. from May 8.
Woodward, A. L.	Mch. 5.		
Whetstone, N.	April 16,		
Whetstone, J. C.	April 19,		
Wilson, A. J.	April 19,		
Wilson, W. R.			

Roll Company E (Beauregard Rangers)—2nd Florida Cavalry.

NAMES.	MUSTERED IN.	MUSTERED OUT.	REMARKS.
OFFICERS.			
Captain—			
Haley T. Blocker	May 8, '62		
1st Lieutenant—			
J. W. Oliver	May 8, '62		
2nd Lieutenant—			
S. E. Conyers	May 8, '62		
3rd Lieutenant—			
R. C. Booth	May 8, '62		
ENLISTED MEN.			
Allen, Lucius	May 8, '62		
Archer, Hugh	May 8, '62		1st Sergeant.
Ashman, Lanford			
Bell, W. I.	May 8, '62	May 10, '65	
Bell, J.	May 8, '62		
Blalock, W. H.	May 8, '62		
Blocker, John R.	May 8, '62		
Bratcher, Andrew	May 8, '62		
Bruton, W. A.	May 8, '62		Sergeant.
Browning, J.	May 8, '62		
Colson, James	May 8, '62		
Connell, Thomas	May 8, '62		
Cook, W. G.	May 8, '62		
Daniels, Robert	May 8, '62		Sergeant.
Dassy, J.	May 8, '62		
Dassy, J. R.	May 8, '62		
Davis, H. C.	May 8, '62		
Drake, James R.	May 8, '62		
Dugger, J. F.	May 8, '62		
Dukes, C. E.	May 8, '62		
Dunham, J. F.	May 8, '62		
DuPont, A. S.	May 8, '62		
DuPont, C. W.	May 8, '62		Corporal.
DuPont, J. H.	May 8, '62		2nd Sergeant.
DuVal, Philip	May 8, '62		
English, John W.	May 8, '62		
English, R.	May 8, '62		
Edwards, O. B.	May 8, '62	May 10, '65	
Felkel, W. W.			Wounded at Natural Bridge.
Futchwanger, A.	May 8, '62		
Gallagher, Edward Y.	May 8, '62		
Gee, Richard C.	May 8, '62		Musician.
Gibbons, C. M.	May 8, '62		
Goodson, George W.	May 8, '62		Corporal.
Goodson, Joseph	May 8, '62		
Goodson, L.	May 8, '62		
Goodson, Madison	Oct. '61	May 10, '65	Reenlisted in Blocker s Co.; transferred to W . H. Milton's Co.
Goodson, R.	May 8, '62		
Goza, J. M.	April 8, '62		
Gwynn, Thomas	May 8, '62		
Handley, G. W.	May 8, '62		
Handley, J.	May 8, '62		
Havis, James R.	May 8, '62		
Hawthorne, John C.	May 8, '62		
Hawthorne, W. B.	May 8, '62		
Hernanes, J. W.	May 8, '62		
Higdon, J. J.	May 8, '62		Corporal.
Hodges, J. J.	May 8, '62		
Holloman, J. W.	May 8, '62		
Hunter, M. B.	May 8, '62		Corporal.
Hutchins, D. B.	May 8, '62		
Jones, A. L.	May 8, '62		
Kemp, W. B.	May 8, '62		
Kersey, David E.	May 15, '61		Captured, '64; imprisoned till close of the war at Ship Island, Miss.
King, J. H.	May 8, '62		
King, W. C.	May 8, '62		
Lang, A. C.	May 8, '62		
Lassiter, J. B.	May 8, '62		
Lassiter, J. J.	May 8, '62		
Lassiter, W. A. B.	May 8, '62		
Lipford, A. T.	May 8, '62		
McElvy, A. B.	May 8, '62	May 10, '65	
McElroy, S. W.	May 8, '62		
McKinnon, J. B.	May 8, '62		
Martin, Jabez	May 8, '62		
Maxwell, D. W.	May 8, '62		
Merritt, J. W.	May 8, '62	May 10, '65	
Mills, John M.	May 8, '62	May 10, '65	
Moore, A.	May 8, '62		
Munroe, B. H.	May 8, '62		
Muse, C. H.	May 8, '62		
Nasworth, George W.	May 8, '62	May 10, '65	
Nasworth, H. W.	May 8, '62	May 10, '65	
Owens, J. M.	May 8, '62		

Roll Company E (Beauregard Rangers)—2nd Florida Cavalry.
(CONTINUED.)

NAMES.	MUSTERED IN.	MUSTERED OUT.	REMARKS.
Packard, D. C.	May 8, '62		
Pickett, F.	May 8, '62		
Pickett, J.	May 8, '62		
Pickett, James R.	May 8, '62	May 10, '65	
Powell, H. G.	May 8, '62		Bugler.
Rainey, W. C. H.	May 8, '62		
Rich, Thomas D.	May 14, '62	May 10, '65	
Robertson, J. B.	May 8, '62		
Robertson, William.	May 8, '62		
Robertson, William L.	May 8, '62		
Roland, Stephen C.	May 8, '62		Died of disease at Camp Finnegan March 1, '64.
Sanborn, Ira W.	May 8, '62		
Saunders, Wright W.	Aug. '61	May 10, '65	
Scott, William L.	May 8, '62		
Sealey, John E.	May 8, '62	May 10, '65	
Sealey, J. J.	May 8, '62		
Simmons, H. B.	May 8, '62		
Singleton, W. H.	May 8, '62		
Smith, F. T.	May 8, '62	May 10, '65	
Smith, T. Y., Jr.	May 8, '62	May 10, '65	
Smith, W. W.	Mch. 2, '62	May 10, '65	
Spears, D. S.	May 15, '62	May 10, '65	
Spears, Z.	May 8, '62		
Stanaland, George N.	Aug. 1, '61	May 10, '65	
Taylor, John L.	May 8, '62		Sergeant.
Towers, C. D.	May 8, '62		
West, Thomas H.	May 8, '62		
Whittle, A. H.	May 8, '62		
Williams, J. W.	May 8, '62		

Roll Company F—2nd Florida Cavalry.
(CONTINUED.)

NAMES.	MUSTERED IN.	MUSTERED OUT.	REMARKS.
OFFICERS.			
Captain—			
Samuel F. Row.			
1st Lieutenant—			
George M. Whetstone.			
2nd Lieutenants—			
John B. Dell.			
George B. Ellis, Jr.			
3rd Lieutenant—			
ENLISTED MEN.			
Anders, J. R.		April '65	
Andrews, C. J.		April '65	
Andrews, R. J.		April '65	
Banknight, J. A.		April '65	
Barrow, L. C.		April '65	
Beach, David C.	May 17, '62	April '65	
Beach, John L.	May 17, '62	April '65	
Beach, L. J.		April '65	
Beach, T. W.	June 17, '62	April '65	
Bell, Francis A.	May 15, '63	May 17, '65	
Belch, C. Davis.			
Bevill, W. James.	May 17, '62	May 15, '65	
Biviam, I. J.		April '65	
Blitch, N. A.		April '65	
Blitch, W. H. H.		April '65	
Boston, K. W.		April '65	
Brewer, M. E.		April '65	Corporal.
Brown, W. Bartimas.		April '65	
Bryan, David S.	May 15, '62	April '65	
Bryan, T. J.	Sept. 6, '61	April '65	
Buck, David C.		April '65	
Burnett, James F.		April '65	
Cassidy, L. A. F.		April '65	Sergeant.
Cauthon, Andrew J.		April '65	
Coker, John B.		April '65	
Collins, Charles H. W.		April '65	
Collins, Mortimer H.		April '65	
Colson, John G.		April '65	
Colson, O. W.		April 9, '65	
Cone, H. M.		April '65	
Cosby, O. John		April '65	Corporal.
Dampier, Stephen.	Feb. '61		

Roll Company F—2nd Florida Cavalry.
(CONTINUED.)

NAMES.	MUSTERED IN.	MUSTERED OUT.	REMARKS.
Davis, Robert		April '65	
Drum, Doctor R	May 15, '62	April '65	
Ellis, George B		April '65	
Ellerbe, Richard B		April '65	
Fennell, James, Jr	May 12, '62	April '65	
Fennell, John		April '65	
Fleming, John T		April '65	
Fussell, W. W		April '65	Sergeant.
Gamble, James		April '65	
Gary, Thomas		April '65	
Geiger, Luther D	'62	April '65	
Graddick, Edward W		April '65	
Graddick, H. P	Mch. 1, '62	April '65	Sergeant.
Graham, M. E		April '65	
Griffin, John J		April '65	
Hennis, Davis G		April '65	
Hickson, Ezekiel P	May 17, '62	April '65	
Hickman, E. P	'64	April '65	
Krimmerger, Jacob L		April '65	
Lee, William H		April '65	
Limbaugh, Rufus K		April '65	
Lindsey, Patrick H		April '65	
Lites, John		April '65	
Markey, Thomas J		April '65	
McNair, Francis M		April '65	
McAteer, S. J		April '65	
McIntosh, William R		April '65	
Mathews, J. C		April '65	
Mickell, Solomon		April '65	
Osteen, William		April '65	
Overstreet, Albert H		April '65	
Perry, J. P		April '65	
Pongree, A. H		April '65	
Pooser, Francis D		April '65	
Pooser, James M		April '65	
Prichard, Robert S	April 15, '61	April '65	
Ramsey, George W		April '65	
Reynolds, Benjamin L		April '65	
Roberts, Anderson	May 2, '62	April '65	
Row, A. B		April '65	
Row, Michael H	May 2, '62	May '65	
Sellers, J. E		April '65	
Simmons B. J		April '65	
Smith, James M		April '65	
Smith, John		April '65	
Smith, Thomas W		April '65	
Stafford, Ezekiel C	May 17, '62	April '65	
Standley, James W		April '65	
Stokes, Bindley		April '65	
Stokes, John R		April '65	
Stokes, William M		April '65	
Thomas, Edward W	Nov. 10, '62	April '65	
Tillman, Jesse		April '65	
Tillman. J. L	May 17, '62	May '65	
Tillman, M. M		April '65	
Tillman, W. D	Feb. '63	April '65	
Tison, William O		April '65	
Tucker, Benjamin E		April '65	
Tucker, S. C		April '65	
Tuten, Patrick H		April '65	
Vaught, William B		April '65	
Vinzant, William B		April '65	
Ward, Erma P		April '65	
Weeks, Francis M		April '65	
Weeks, Johnathan H		April '65	Corporal.
Willis, William W	May 17, '62	April '65	1st Sergeant.
Wrede, Martin L		April '65	Corporal.

Roll Company G (Capt. William H. Cone's Company)—2nd Florida Cavalry.

NAMES.	MUSTERED IN.	MUSTERED OUT.	REMARKS.
OFFICERS.			
Captain—			
W. H. Cone	Aug. 12, '63		
1st Lieutenant—			
W. A. Sheffield	Aug. 12, '63		
2nd Lieutenants			
Solomon Warren	Aug. 12, '63		

Roll Company G (Capt. William H. Cone's Company)—2nd Florida Cavalry.
(CONTINUED.)

NAMES.	MUSTERED IN.	MUSTERED OUT.	REMARKS.
W. T. Weeks	Aug. 12, '63		
ENLISTED MEN.			
Barrenton, H	Aug. 12, '63		
Bethea, F. C.	Aag. 12, '63		
Beilling, John W	Aug. 12, '63		Artificer; absent sick.
Bevill, S. P.	Feb. 1, '65		Absent sick.
Bevill, John R.	Jan. 31, '64		Corporal; absent sick.
Brooks, John W	Aug. 12, '63		
Bryant, L.	Aug. 12, '63		Absent with leave.
Bryant, J. L.	Aug. 29, '63		
Bryant, T. I.	Dec. 9, '64		
Cone, C. F	Dec. 2, '63		...Farrier.
Canova, A. B	April 12, '63		Corporal.
Cone, J. B.	Sept. 2, '63		Absent with leave.
Cheshire, A.	Aug. 12, '63		
Cheshire, J. P	Feb. 16, '63		
Colson, M. D.	Oct. 12, '63		Absent with leave.
Colson, S. B.	Oct. 14, '63		Absent sick.
Fetner, J. Z.	Aug. 29, '63		
Fannell, J. P.	Aug. 15, '63		Absent sick.
Feagle, H.	Aug. 29, '63		Absent with leave.
Floyd, D.	Aug. 12, '63		Bugler.
Goodbread, J. S.	Jan. 13, '64		
Goodbread, J. T.	Dec. 9, '64		
Gaylard, N. R.	Aug. 12, '63		Absent on special duty.
Geiger, J. W.	May 16, '62		
Hunt, Thomas H.	Aug. 12, '63		Absent sick.
Hunt, A.	Aug. 29, '63		
Hunt, W. N	May 20, '64		
Higginbotham, E. C.	Sept. 1, '64		
Hancock, G. W	Aug. 12, '63		
Howard, H.	Aug. 12, '63		Absent without leave.
Jackson, W. B.	Aug. 29, '63		Prisoner of war.
Jackson, Isham	Aug. 17, '63		Absent sick.
Jordan, David	Aug. 12, '63		Corporal.
Keith, C. H.	Aug. 29, '63		
Love, P. E.	Aug. 10, '61		
Lee, E. S.	Jan. 25, '64		Absent with leave.
Lee, H. M.	Jan. 25, '64		....
Limeberger, L. W	Dec. 6, '64		
Lamb, J. J.	Aug. 12, '63		Absent without leave.
Langford, Taff.	April 1, '65		Absent without leave.
May, Thomas I.	Aug. 12, '63		Absent without leave.
McCaskill, Thomas	Aug. 12, '63		
Mickler, William	Aug. 12, '63		Absent on special duty.
Milton, H. R.	Aug. 12, '63		
Milton, William H			Imprisoned at Newport News; paroled July, '65.
Morgan, L. M.	May 16, '62		
McKay, Jit.	Nov. 15, '63		Absent on special duty.
McInnis, Samuel	Aug. 12, '63		Sergeant.
O'Neill, C. C.	Feb. 1, '65		Absent without leave.
Parrish, R.	Aug. 12, '63		
Pennington, W. P	Feb. 12, '64		
Pratt, W. H.	Aug. 12, '63		
Parker, R. C.	Sept. 3, '63		
Pickett, J. L.	Sept. 1, '62		
Redding, T. C.	Feb. 20, '65		Absent sick.
Renfroe, J. E.	Aug. 12, '63		
Ramsey, Eli	Aug. 12, '63		
Ramsey, C. A.	Nov. 25, '63		Bugler.
Rogero, E.	Aug. 12, '63		
Rousseau, J. L.	Jan. 28, '64		
Smith, E. M.	April 12, '63		Sergeant.
Smith, J. G.	Aug. 12, '63		Absent sick.
Smith, N.	Aug. 12, '63		Absent on special duty.
Smith, A. S.	Aug. 12, '63		Corporal.
Smith, F. M.	Jan. 11, '63		
Sutton, W. B.	Aug. 12, '63		Prisoner of war.
Stancil, J. P.	Aug. 12, '63		Absent sick.
Stephens, J. K.	Aug. 12, '63		Absent without leave.
Swift, Thomas	Aug. 12, '63		
Sanford, M. J.	Aug. 12, '63		
Seigler, M.	Aug. 12, '63		Absent without leave.
Thompson, J. E.	Aug. 12, '63		Absent sick.
Turner, L.	July 29, '64		
Turner, O. L.	Dec. 1, '64		
Thomas, E.	April 1, '65		Absent without leave.
Wimberly, W. B.	Aug. 12, '63		Absent sick.
Waldron, K. S.	Aug. 15, '63		
Warren, J. J.	May 11, '62		Absent with leave.
Whilden, M. J.	Nov. 13, '64		

Roll Company G (Capt. William H. Cone's Company)—2nd Florida Cavalry.
(Continued.)

NAMES.	MUSTERED IN.	MUSTERED OUT.	REMARKS.
Wingate, J. B.	Dec. 9, '64		Absent without leave.
DESERTED.			
Alford, W. R.	Aug. 12, '63		
Daniels, N.	Aug. 12, '63		
Raulerson, Frank	Aug. 12, '63		

Roll Company H—2nd Florida Cavalry.

NAMES.	MUSTERED IN.	MUSTERED OUT.	REMARKS.
OFFICERS.			
Captain—			
J. J. Dickison	Aug. '62		
1st Lieutenant—			
W. A. McArdle	Aug. '62		
2nd Lieutenant—			
D. F. S. Brantley	Aug. '62		Resigned June 11, '63.
3rd Lieutenant—			
W. J. McEaddy			
ENLISTED MEN.			
Anderson, David	'63	May 20, '65	Wounded at Gainesville, Fla., July, '64.
Arnold, Daniel J	May 16, '63		
Barnard, A. E.			Sergeant.
Barnard, C. J.			
Barnard, C. O.	Aug. '62		Sergeant.
Barrow, Elijah	July '63	May 20, '65	
Baugham, E.			
Bauknight, J. P.			
Baya, Joseph			Imprisoned at Fort Delaware, '64 and paroled from there.
Bell, J. B.			
Bennett, Daniel			Promoted 1st Sergeant.
Berry, Sampson			
Blackwilder, D.			
Blackwilder, F.			
Blount, J. L.			
Boroughs, R. B.			Surgeon.
Boyles, George W	Jan. '65		
Braddock, H. E.			
Brantley, W. A.			
Brantley, William M.			
Brock, R. D.			
Brown, John			
Brown, S. R.			
Cain, W. D.			
Carlton, J. A.			
Caruthers, A. L.			
Caruthers, William W	Aug. '62	May 20, '65	
Cassels, William H.	Aug. 1, '64	May 20, '65	
Casson, J.			
Clifton, Daniel Jr.			
Clifton, F. M.			
Clifton, Henry J.			
Clifton, J. C.			
Cooper, Eli	Oct. '62		
Cox, William			Sergeant.
Crews, Joseph C.	Oct. 22, '64		Wounded at No. 4, near Cedar Keys, Fla.
Crow, E. H.			
Curry, Lawton			
Dell, J. M.			
Denton, G. S.			
Dicker, L. M.			
Dickison, Charles B.	Aug. '62		Sergeant; killed at Palatka August 2, '64.
Dozier, H. C.			Sergeant.
Douglass, William			
Fort, Joseph	'64	May 20, '65	
Fussell, J. W.			
Geiger, John F.			
Gibson, C. T.			
Grantham, E.			
Hall, B. A.			
Hall, J.			
Hall, Lloyde			
Hall, William M.	Aug. 15, '62		Wounded by accident at Palatka February 1, '63 near Green Cove Springs; again at Gainesville August 17, '64.
Harden, J.			
Harris, John			
Harris, William R.			
Harrison, James			

Roll Company H—2nd Florida Cavalry.
(CONTINUED.)

NAMES.	MUSTERED IN.	MUSTERED OUT.	REMARKS.
Harrison, William H	'63		
Hewett, J. L		May 20, '65	
Hinson, A. J			
Hiers, David O			
Hiers, J. M			
Hodges, E. D			
Johns, Andrew J		May 20, '65	
Johns, Ervin	Aug. '62	May 20, '65	
Johns, Jacob			
Johns, J. M			
Johns, Lewis			
Johns, Perry			
Johnson, John			
Jones, Robert			
Josephs, M. G			
Kite, John	Sept. 17, '62	May 20, '65	
Lanier, James			
Lanier, John			
Lanier, J. S			
Lanier, John W			
Lanier, Robert			
Low, L. Samuel	May 20, '62	May 20, '65	
Marsh, R		May 20, '65	
Medici, F. A			
Meyer, B F			Corporal.
Miller R. W			
Monroe, D. S			
Morgan, J. P			
Odum, L. W			
Osteen, W		May 20, '65	Promoted Lieutenant and Acting Commissary of
Peters, A. H	'63	May 20, '65	1st Regiment, Cavalry.
Piggott, T. G			Corporal.
Powell, L			
Prevatt, James			
Pruden, H. J			
Richardson, B			
Rivers, John P		May 20, '65	
Roberts, W. N			Corporal.
Robertson, John M	Sept. '63	May 20, '65	
Rogers, Albert		May 20, '65	
Rogers, John		May 20, '65	
Royal, Ivey	Sept. '63	May 20, '65	
Rozier, C. H			
Sabote, Paul E		May 20, '65	
Sanders, McQuenn			
Shaw, D			
Sheldon, R. S			
Simpson, J. H			Corporal.
Sligh, Samuel P		May 20, '65	
Smith, E. W		May 20, '65	
Smith, R. H		May 20, '65	
Spivey, G. W		May 20, '65	
Stewman, W. D	'63	May 20, '65	
Strickland, J. B	Sept. '63	May 20, '65	
Taylor, Alexander		May 20, '65	
Thomas, A. M		May 20, '65	
Thomas, Charles	Sept. '62	May 20, '65	
Thomas, James M	Oct. 00	May 20, '65	
Thomas, John		May 20, '65	
Thomas, Joseph R	Nov. 15, '64	May 20, '65	
Tyner, Benjamin	Aug. '62	May 20, '65	Captured at Tampa, Fla., March 22, '64; confined at Key West, then carried to Ship Island where he remained until the close of the war.
Ward, J. J	Aug. '62		Sergeant.
Watson, M. D	Aug. '62	May 20, '65	
Weathersbee, George		May 20, '65	
Weeks, R. B		May 20, '65	
Wood, J. A. J. W	Aug. 15, '62		
Wood, Warren	Aug. '62		
Wright, H		May 20, '65	

Roll Company I—2nd Florida Cavalry.

NAMES.	MUSTERED IN.	MUSTERED OUT.	REMARKS.
OFFICERS.			
Captains—			
A. Smith			Resigned.

Roll Company I—2nd Florida Cavalry.
(CONTINUED.)

NAMES.	MUSTERED IN.	MUSTERED OUT.	REMARKS.
S. A. Parramore		April '65	Promoted from Sergeant to Captain.
1st Lieutenant—			
2nd Lieutenant—			
J. N. Horn			
3rd Lieutenant—			
A. A. Griffin			
ENLISTED MEN.			
Albritton, John T	Oct. '63		
Adams, Dennis		April '65	
Adams, R. W		April '65	
Allen, Henry	Mch. '62	April '65	
Bannum, W. B		April '65	
Bishop, Joseph	April 9, '62	April '65	Transferred from A to F.
Blanton, David F		April '65	
Bunling, A. B	Dec. '64	April '65	
Calvin, Davis		April '65	
Carlton, I. P		April '65	
Carlton, Thomas A		April '65	
Carter, J		April '65	
Carter, J. W		April '65	
Caraway, William H	April '61	April '65	
Caraway, W. P	'62	April '65	
Cave, I. W		April '65	
Coker, B		April '65	
Coker, T. J		April '65	
Collins, F. M		April '65	
Collins, George C		April '65	
Collins, J. H		April '65	
Cone, W. R		April '65	
Dean, J. W		April '65	
Drew, W. B		April '65	
Earnest, E		April '65	
Earnest, N. W		April '65	
Ellison, T. T		April '65	
Ezell, J. W		April '65	
Farnell, C. P	'63	May 20, '65	
Ferrell, E. J	'62	April '65	Transferred to Houston's Artillery in '63.
Fields, A. T		April '65	Promoted Bugler.
Finnegan, J. R		April '65	Promoted Sergeant.
Flowers, J. W		April '65	
Forward, William F	Jan. '65	April '65	
Griffin, W. D		April '65	
Grubbs, W. H	April 15, '62	April '65	
Hampton, G. W		April '65	Promoted Sergeant.
Hamilton, I. A		April '65	
Hampton, J. J		April '65	
Hampton, J. L		April '65	Promoted Corporal.
Hampton, I. W		April '65	
Hulett, W		April '65	Wounded at Natural Bridge.
Hendry, J. W		April '65	
Hendry, Robert W	'62	April '65	
Henderson, Edward H		April '65	
Henderson, Jasper M	'62	April '65	
Hines, H. B		April '65	
Howard, W. F		April '65	
Jelks, N. P			Wounded at Natural Bridge.
Jenkins, R. D		April '65	
Johnson, I. B		April '65	Sergeant.
Johnson, T. A		April '65	
Johnson, W. P		April '65	
Jones, O. D			Wounded at Natural Bridge.
Lipscomb, John		April '65	
Lipscomb, William C	Feb. 1, '64		Shot at Natural Bridge, Fla., March 6, '65.
Loper, Curtis A	Mch. 8, '62	April '65	Transferred to Company F, 5th Battallion Cavalry.
Lundy, James T		April '65	
McCall, J. H		April '65	
McCall, M. P	Mch. 5, '62	April '65	
McMullen, David	'62	April '65	
McMullen, E. H	'62	April '65	
McMullen, Thomas J	Feb. 15, '62		Transferred to Company K, 10th Regiment, June 10, '63; lost right arm at Petersburg, Va., '64.
McPherson, J. J		April '65	
Mathis, John H		April '65	
Mathis, J. W	'62	April '65	
Mayd, I. W		April '65	
Mays, R. J	'62	April '65	
Morse, John R	Mch. '62	April '65	
Oneal, C. C		April '65	
Oneal, John W		April '65	
O'Quinn, A. M		April '65	
Overstreet, G. W		April '65	
Paulling, F. F		April '65	
Pierce, S		April '65	
Poppell, Brinkley	Aug. 21, '63	April '65	

Roll Company I—2nd Florida Cavalry.
(CONTINUED.)

NAMES.	MUSTERED IN.	MUSTERED OUT.	REMARKS.
Randell, Theodore		April '65	
Robinson, J. B.		April '65	
Roebuck, J. H.	'62	April '65	Lost several fingers at Natural Bridge, Fla.
Roulhoc, Jas. Blount G.		April '65	
Rowell, John.		April '65	
Shaw, J. A.		April '65	Sergeant.
Shaw, J. T.		April '65	
Sheffield, I. B.		April '65	
Shiver, Isaac.	Jan. '63	April '65	
Slaughter, Moses W.	April '62	April '65	
Slaughter, U. W.		April '65	
Smith, D. R.		April '65	
Smith, L. D.			Wounded at Natural Bridge.
Smith, W. J.		April '65	
Spradley, Richard		April '65	
Strickland, M. F.		April '65	
Strickland, W. W.		April '65	
Sutten, J. T.		April '65	
Talbert, D. M.		April '65	Corporal.
Tatem, J. F.		April '65	
Thigpen, W.		April '65	
Thomaston, John C.		April '65	
Tillis, Richard		April '65	
Tillman, J.			Corporal.
Tucker, Jordan	April '62	April '65	
Vickers, E.		April '65	
Wadsworth, B. D.		April '65	
Wallace, F. M.		April '65	Corporal.
Ward, Council.		April '65	
Ward, Evan W.	Oct. '61	April '65	
Ward, Isaiah.		April '65	
Ward, John.		April '65	
Ward, William H.		April '65	
Whitlock, W. W.		April '65	Promoted Sergeant.
Wilder, William W		April '65	
Witt, W. W.		April 65	
Wordsworth, D. D.		April '65	
Worrell, George.		April '65	

Roll Company K—2nd Florida Cavalry.

NAMES.	MUSTERED IN.	MUSTERED OUT.	REMARKS.
OFFICERS.			
Captains—			
Robert Harrison			Promoted Major.
F. J. Clarke			Promoted Captain; resigned July 30, '63.
Jesse N. Jones		April 17, '65	Promoted from 2nd Lieutenant to Captain.
1st Lieutenant—			
John D. Jones			2nd Lieutenant; promoted 1st Lieutenant
2nd Lieutenant—			
W. T. Sorley			Resigned November 28, '63.
3rd Lieutenant—			
Peter Cone	May 16, '62		Promoted Lieutenant; wounded at Olustee November, '64.
ENLISTED MEN.			
Adams, William		April '65	
Bacon, R. S.		April '65	Sergeant.
Beaty, D. P.		April '65	
Beem, D. E.		April '65	
Bradley, J. H.		April '65	
Butler, S. H.		April '65	
Campbell, R.		April '65	Sergeant.
Caraway, W.		April '65	
Chalker, A. S.		April '65	
Chalker, James D.		April '65	
Cone, J. B.		April '65	Sergeant.
Crosby, Andrew	May 17, '62	April '65	
Dial, John		April '65	
Dyas, William		April '65	
Dowling, Isaac	Feb. 20, '64	April '65	
Futch, C. B.		April '65	
Gardner, J		April '65	
Geiger, J. W.		April '65	
Geiger, N. H.		April '65	
Gilchrist.		April '65	
Goodbread, Philip	May 16, '62	April '65	
Green, W. G.	May 10, '62	April '65	

Roll Company K—2nd Florida Cavalry.

(CONTINUED.)

NAMES.	MUSTERED IN.	MUSTERED OUT.	REMARKS.
Gwynn, W. W.	Sept. '63		Captured; imprisoned at Fort Delaware, Md., and there died late in '64 or '65.
Harrison, James E.	May 17, '62	April '65	
Harrison, James O.	May '63	April '65	
Hawkins, M. B.			Wounded at Natural Bridge.
Hicks, N. A.		April '65	
Higginbotham, Alex J.	May '62	May 15, '65	
Higginbotham, G. A.		May '65	
Higginbothem, James Harvey	Oct. 22, '62		Died in hospital at Madison of pneumonia February 6, '64.
Higginbothem, John H.		April '65	
Johnson, Phineas		April '65	
Jones, Archibald	May 17, '62		Killed by deserters while in line of duty at Lake City, Fla. January 6 '65.
Jones, J. H.		April '65	
Jones, S. D.		April '65	
Jones, W.		April '65	
Jones, W. L.	May '62	May 17, '65	
Kite, B.		April '65	
Leggett, J. B.		April '65	
Lewis, I. L.		April 17, '65	
Little, Charles		April '65	
Little, I. G.		April '65	Corporal.
Little, J. B.		April '65	
McCleany, C. B.		April '65	
McIntosh, J. A.		April '65	
Masters, R. T.		April '65	
May, T. J.		April '65	
Morgan, E. O.		April '65	
Morgan, L. M.		April '65	
Morgan, M. M.		April '65	
Morgan, T. S.		April '65	
Oglesby, C.		April '65	
Pelot, John C.		April '65	Sergeant.
Pendarvis, G. A.		April '65	
Pickett, G. W.		April '65	
Price, D. W.		April '65	
Pringle, William		April '65	
Reddick, Jackson		April '65	
Roberts, N. E.		April '65	
Rowe, R. L.		April '65	
Rouse, W. N.		April '65	
Roux, L. F.		April '65	Sergeant.
Roux, T. S.		April '65	
Sanders, F.		April '65	
Sauls, Allen	'62	April '65	
Sauls, Emethy	Aug. 10, '63	April '65	
Sheffield, S. F.		April '65	
Shuttleworth, J.		April '65	
Silcox, D. J.		April '65	
Simmons, Henry K.			Killed, Natural Bridge March 4, '64.
Smith, D. M.		April '65	
Smith, Hutchinson	May 16, '62	April 17, '65	
Smith, Jerry			Drowned at Rocky Bluff, Fla., June, '63.
Soutton, M.		April '65	Corporal.
Stewart, D. C.		April '65	Corporal.
Tanner, A. C.		April '65	
Thigpen, O. A.	Jan. '63	May '65	
Tison, J. E.		April '65	
Turkett, J. S.	Sept. 1, '63	April '65	
Turknett, L.	Sept. 1, '63		Paroled from Fort Delaware prison.
Turner, A. W.		April '65	
Turner, B. H.		April '65	
Turner, E.		April '65	
Turner, W. W.		April '65	
Vanzant, D. J.		April '65	
Vanzant, William M.		April '65	
Warren, J. J.		April '65	
Wells, E.		April '65	
Wells, J.		April '65	
West, M. C.		April '65	
Wilson, D.		April '65	
Wilson, John C.	Feb. '63	April 17, '65	Was ruptured at Natural Bridge fight.
Wilson, Z. C.		April '65	
Wingate, J.		April '65	
Wingate, Joel B.		May 18, '65	
Wingate, T. J.		April '65	
Wingus, J. B.	'63	April 17, 65	
Yulee, C. M.		April '65	

Roll, Field and Staff—15th Confederate Cavalry.

NAMES.	MUSTERED IN.	MUSTERED OUT.	REMARKS.
Colonel—			
Harry Maury			
Lieutenant-Colonel—			
Major—			
B. H. Partridge			Captain; promoted Major.
Surgeon—			
Assistant-Surgeon—			
Adjutant—			
Sergeant-Major—			
Quartermaster—			
Commissary—			
Quartermaster-Sergeant—			
Commissary-Sergeant—			
Chaplain—			
Daniel H. Bryan			
Hospital Steward—			

Roll Company A (Magnolia Dragoons)—15th Confederate Cavalry.

NAMES.	MUSTERED IN.	MUSTERED OUT	REMARKS.
OFFICERS.			
Captains—			
R. H. Partridge			Promoted Major.
John Ulmer		May '65	2nd Lieutenant; promoted 1st Lieutenant, then Captain.
1st Lieutenant—			
T. H. Triplett	April 30, '62		
2nd Lieutenant—			
F. B. Taylor	April 30, '62	May '65	Promoted from Sergeant to 2nd Lieutenant.
3rd Lieutenants—			
J. R. Tucker	April 30, '62		
J. P. Grantham			
ENLISTED MEN.			
Allen, David	April 30, '62		
Anderson, A	April 30, '62		
Barrington, Edward P	April 30, '62		
Baldy, J. H	April 30, '62		
Barnes, M. C	April 30, '62		
Barclay, E. D	April 30, '62		Corporal.
Bayenwood, C. H	April 30, '62		
Beazley, William			
Bell, W. R	April 30, '62		
Bentley, B. M	April 30, '62		
Blackbourne, W. A	April 30, '62		
Bozeman, C. H			
Brooks, James A	April 30, '62		Sergeant.
Brooks, John F	April 30, '62	May '65	
Brown, J. O	April 30, '62		
Bryan, D. H	April 30, '62	May '65	Sergeant; promoted Chaplain.
Burns, Michael C	May '62		
Busba, B. S	April 30, '62		
Carman, Willis	April 30, '62		
Cason, John	April 30, '62		
Clark, D. C	April 30, '62		
Clark, W. C	April 30, '62		
Cobb, I. V. W	April 30, '62		Corporal; promoted Sergeant.
Cone, A	April 30, '62		
Cooksey, J. A	April 30, '62		
Crowell, D. I	April 30, '62		
Davis, W. L	April 30, '62		
Dawkins, G. W	April 30, '62		
Dawkins, W. H	April 30, '62		
DeCaussey, C. B	April 30, '62		
DeCaussey, Marion	April 30, '62		
Drake, E	April 30, '62		
Dunkins, W. H	April 30, '62		
Ellenwood, Stephen	April 30, '62		
Freeman, J	April 30, '62		

Roll Company A (Magnolia Dragoons)—15th Confederate Cavalry.

(Continued.)

NAMES.	MUSTERED IN	MUSTERED OUT.	REMARKS.
Frisbee, David	April 30, '62		
Gamble, J.	April 30, '62		
Gelzer, William	April 30, '62	May '65	Corporal.
Gillett, M. P.	April 30, '62		
Graham, D. S.	April 30, '62		
Grantham, Q. P.	April 30, '62		Sergeant.
Hallman, J. A.	April 30, '62		
Hardee, T.	April 30, '62		
Hardee, William B.	April 30, '62		Sergeant.
Harris, G. W.	April 30, '62		
Hart, David	April 30, '62		
Hightower, Z. H.	April 30, '62		
Hines, D. W.			
Holmes, E. J.	April 30, '62	May '65	
Houston, S. J.			
James, William	April 30, '62		
Jeffcoat, M. A.	April 30, '62		
Kilpatrick, J. M.	April 30, '62		Transferred to Florida Light Artillery.
Knighton, A.	April 30, '62		
Knighton, Alexander R.	Mch. '62		
LaFitte, P. M.	April 30, '62		
Lord, W. R.	April 30, '62		
McClellan, Charles E.	April 30, '62		
McReney, George	April 30, '62		
McVoy, William	Oct. '62	May '65	
Manning, A. M.	April 30, '62		
Mason, Frank	April 30, '62		
Mathews, S. N.	April 30, '62		
Mikell F. A.	April 30, '62		
Miller, W. R.	April 30, '62		
Moore, James	April 30, '62		
Monroe, F.	April 30, '62		
Monroe, J. I.	April 30, '62		
Moss, Z. A.	April 30, '62		
Mott, J. R.	April 30, '62		
Neely, S. W.	April 30, '62		
Nichols, J. S.	April 30, '62		
Nobles, William Dennis	'62	May '65	Wounded at Mt. Pleasant, Ala., '63.
Oder, J. O.	April 30, '62		
Oder, Thomas	April 30, '62		
Partridge, B. M.	April 30, '62		
Partridge, Ben W.	April 30, '62	May '65	Captured at Gonzalez, Fla., October, '62: imprisoned at Fort Pickens.
Peeler, Webber	April 30, '62		
Porter, C. I.	April 30, '62		
Renfroe, J. C.	April 30, '62		
Roney, G. W.	April 30, '62		
Redd, J. G	April 30, '62		
Russell, Benjamin	April 30, '62		
Russell, F.	April 30, '62		
Scruggs, Richard		April 30, '62	Corporal.
Shackelford, A. W.	Feb. 15. '63	May '65	Run over by mule; captured May 15, '65.
Sheppard, Benjamin	April 30, '62	May '65	
Sheppard, Berry	April 30, '62		
Simpkins, Thompson	April 30, '62		
Slaughter, Henry T.	April 30, '62		Sergeant.
Slaughter, J. H.	April 30, '62		
Sloan, James	April 30, '62		
Spratt, J. L.	April 30, '62		
Spratt, L. M.	April 30, '62		
Surls, Calvin	April 30, '62		
Taylor, W. R.	April 30, '62		
Taylor, W. T.	April 30, '62		
Tucker, Joel H.	April 30, '62	May '65	
Turner, J. D.	April 30, '62		
Walker, W. S.	April 30, '62		
Walters, A.	April 30, '62		
Wilford, John	April 30, '62		
Williams, W. J.		May '65	
Wooton, Lafayette	April 30, '62		

Roll Company B—15th Confederate Cavalry.

NAMES.	MUSTERED IN.	MUSTERED OUT.	REMARKS.
OFFICERS.			
Captain—			
Richard L. Smith	Mch. 14, '62		

Roll Company B—15th Confederate Cavalry.

(CONTINUED.)

NAMES.	MUSTERED IN.	MUSTERED OUT.	REMARKS.
1st Lieutenant—			
Joseph B. Roulhack	Mch. 14, '62		
2nd Lieutenant—			
John T. Davis, Sr	Mch. 14, '62		
3rd Lieutenant—			
Charles W. Davis	Mch. 14, '62		
ENLISTED MEN.			
Alderman, A. F.			
Askew, Charles A	Mch. 16, '62		
Baker, Beverly	May 3, '62		
Baker, Lawrence	May 3, '62		
Baltzell, George A	May 3, '62	May '65	
Bellamy, Benjamin A	May 3, '62	May '65	
Bone, William J	May 3, '62		
Boone, Daniel A	Mch. 14, '62		Sergeant.
Boone, Robert C	Mch. 16, '62		
Brunson, William	April 1, '62		...
Bullock, C.	Mch. 14, '62		
Calloway, John H	Mch. 14, '62		
Campton, Richard H	Mch. 14, '62		
Cook, John W	Mch. 14, '62		
Cox, Aurelius P	Mch. 14, '62		
Daniel, Lauson	Mch. 14, '62		
Daniel, W. J.			
Davis, Walter	Mch. 20, '62		
Derring, John D			
Dickson, T. G.			
Dudley, James B	Mch. 20, '62		
Dykes, George R	Mch. 20, '62		
Dykes, Jacob I	Mch. 14, '62		
Dykes, William H	Mch. 20, '62		
Edwards, John W	Mch. 14, '62		Corporal.
Faulk, George W	April 25, '62		
Findley, Benjamin L	Mch. 20, '62		
Finlayson, John L	Mch. 20, '62		
Gilbert, John B	Mch. 20, '62	May '65	
Grant, Stephen C	Mch. 14, '62		Corporal.
Haley, Michael	Mch. 14, '62		
Harvey, James H	Mch. 14, '62		
Harvey, John H	Mch. 3, '62		
Herring, John D	Mch. 3, '62		
Hewward, Joseph P	Mch. 3, '62		
Hinson, William H	Mch. 20, '62		
Hunter, Joseph T	Mch. 14, '62		Sergeant.
Irwin, Joseph	Mch. 14, '62		
King, Isaac P	Mch. 14, '62		
Kirkland, Green B	Mch. 14, '62		
Land, Benjamin F	Mch. 14, '62		
Land, Henry G	Mch. 3, '62	May '65	
Land, Jas. C.		May '65	
Land, Jehu R	Mch. 14, '62		Corporal.
Land, Stephen W	Mch. 14, '62		
Lewis, William A	Mch. 14, '62		Musician.
Lindsey, Elishu F	Mch. 25, '62		
Long, Edwin D	Mch. 14, '62		
McGriff, Richard	Mch. 14, '62		
McLeroy, Robert T	Mch. 14, '62		
Martin, William	Mch. 14, '62		
Mathews, John	Mch. 14, '62		
Myrich, Littleton	Mch. 3, '62		
Newsom, Lewis L	Mch. 14, '62		Sergeant.
Nobles, W. H.		May '65	
Oswald, Marion	Mch. 14, '62		Captured by enemy and paroled March 20, '65
Pelt, John J.			
Pittman, Hulan R	Mch. 14, '62		Died at Mobile, Ala., of disease January 4, '65.
Pitman, Robert J	Mch. 14, '62		Sergeant.
Register, Ezekiel A	Mch. 20, '62		
Roberts, James	'64		
Robinson, W. L.		May '65	
Roebuck, James	Mch. 20, '62		
Rooks, John J	Mch. 14, '62		
Staley, John F	Mch. 14, '62		
Stephen, Jacob H	Mch. 14, '62		
Sykes, W. H.		May '65	
Thomas, John C	Mch. 14, '62		
Widgeon, George	Mch. 14, '62		Sergeant.
Widgeon, John	Mch. 14, '62		
Wynn, Colbert	Mch. 16, '62		Musician.
Witherspoon, James	Mch. 16, '62		Corporal.
White, Thomas M	April 20, '62		
Wymes, C. B.		May '65	
Yarborough, George S	April 7, '62		Wounded at Clairborn, Ala.
Yarborough, John H	May 3, '62		
Yarborough, William H	April 7, '62		

Roll Company C—15th Confederate Cavalry.

NAMES.	MUSTERED IN.	MUSTERED OUT	REMARKS
OFFICERS.			
Captain—			
W. B. Amos			
1st Lieutenant—			
E. S. Carter			
2nd Lieutenant—			
W. W. Green			
3rd Lieutenant—			
P. M. Gordon			
ENLISTED MEN.			
Allen, W. W			
Amos, H. C			
Amos, J. W			
Baker, George			Corporal.
Baker, M			
Barton, N			
Black, Henry	'61		Wounded near Mobile, Ala., July '63.
Blake, S. H		May '65	
Campbell, Allen			
Cherry, A. J			
Clary, J. B			
Clary, R. M			Sergeant.
Cobb, James			
Cobb, R			
Cobb, William			Corporal.
Conly, G. M			
Cotton, A. B			
Crawford, J			
Crawford, W			
Crowder, William			Corporal.
Cutts, S			Sergeant.
Cutts, Z			
Ellard, F			
Ellis, J. G			
Elliott, William			
Emmons, George W			
Faulk, James			
Fields, W. H			
Gaskins, S. J			
Goodwin, J			
Gipson, J. G			
Hall, William			
Hart, A			
Hart, J			
Hart, R			
Hassell, F. M			
Hemphill, S. L			
Henderson, John G			
Howard, J. C			
Infinger, C			
Jones, J. C			
Jordan, A. J			
Kennedy, J			
Kennedy, William			
Landley, A. B			
Lasiter, A			
Lasiter, J			
Livingston, G. J			
Livingston, S. J			
Lundy, W. G			
Lunsford, J. P			
Lunsford, W			
McCaskill, W. C			Sergeant.
Miller, H			
Miller, R			
Miller, J. B			
Milton, J. B			
Moore, S. P			
Morrison, A			
Morrison, F			
Morrison, M			
Pate, J			
Pate, N			
Pipken, N			Sergeant.
Reddick, C			
Robinson, D. L			
Roberson, G. F			
Roberson, S. B			
Sanks, G. M			
Sanks, G. W			
Senterfit, M. P			Corporal.
Stayner, D. H			
Stayner, John			
Strickley, H			

Roll Company C—15th Confederate Cavalry.
(CONTINUED.)

NAMES.	MUSTERED IN.	MUSTERED OUT.	REMARKS.
Trull, C. P.			
Weekley, Thomas			
Wilkerson, W.			
Wilson, A. H.			
Wilson, J.			
Wise, H.			

Roll Company D—15th Confederate Cavalry.

NAMES.	MUSTERED IN.	MUSTERED OUT.	REMARKS.
OFFICERS.			
Captain—			
J. B. Vaughn		April '65	
1st Lieutenant—			
John Garner			
2nd Lieutenants—			
W. A. Morgan			
W. P. Rice			
3rd Lieutenant—			
Walker A. Morgan		April '65	Promoted Lieutenant.
ENLISTED MEN.			
Allen, David			
Allen, W			
Barrow, Charles			
Barrow, J. V.			
Bartow, N.			
Bowen, Joshua			
Cameron, Archibald			
Cameron, Daniel			
Campbell, Charles			
Cobb, A. J.			
Cobb, B. W. F.	May 2, '62	April '65	
Cobb, F. H.	May 2, '62		
Cobb, J. W.			
Cobb, S. T.			
Cooper, H. S.			
Cooper, J. B.			Sergeant.
Cooper, M. P.			
Croin, L.			
Daily, Mark			
Dennich, R. H.			
Diamond, John C.	April 18, '63	April '65	
Diamond, William			
Durden, J. F.			
Ellis, Green	Sept. '62		
Enterkin, William			
Garner, W. J.			Corporal.
Glaze, E. H.			
Grimes, J. J.			
Grubbs, Emanuel			
Hall, George			Corporal.
Hamilton, Edwin			
Harrison, William			
Henderson, William			
Henderson, Robert			
Hobls, B. T.			
Holman, J. D.			
Horton, Neil H.			
Houseman, G. O.			
Huggins, Burt			
Huggins, Jesse			
Jarragan, Columbus			
Jarragan, Edward			
Jarragan, W. V.			
Johnson, Caleb A			
Johnson, F. C.			
Johnson, H. N.			
Jones, James L.			Corporal.
Jones, John			
Jones, Josiah			
Jones, L. A.			1st Sergeant.
Jones, Lewis			
Knight, Benjamin			
Lemens, N.			
Levins, J. L.			
Lewis, James			

Roll Company D—15th Confederate Cavalry.
(CONTINUED.)

NAMES.	MUSTERED IN.	MUSTERED OUT.	REMARKS.
McDavid, James E.			
McDavid, Joel E.			
McDavid, W. H.		May '65	
McDavid, R. M.		May '65	
McCardy, F. M.			
McCardy, G. W.			
McLeod, Roderick.			
McLeod, T. H.			
Maxwell, W. D.			
Milstenn, J. E.		May '65	
Morgan, Samuel.			
Neely, James.			
Ray, S. F.			
Rener, R. P.			Corporal.
Riera, Antony.		May '65	
Robinson, Alexander.			
Sheppard, E. R.			Sergeant.
Studivant, Mathew.	May '62	May '65	
Tourart, William.	'61	May '65	
Turner, R. H.		May '65	Promoted Lieutenant Co. C.
Vickery, J. W.			
Waters, J. L.			
Waters, Travis.			
Waters, W. H.			Sergeant.
Watson, Henry.			
White, Drue.			
White, Joseph.	May 1, '62	April '65	
Williams, E. B.			
Wilson, Charles.			
Wilkerson, Daniel.			Sergeant.

Roll Company E—15th Confederate Cavalry.

NAMES.	MUSTERED IN.	MUSTERED OUT	REMARKS.
OFFICERS.			
Captain—			
N. R. Leigh.			
1st Lieutenant—			
A. P. Feagin.			
2nd Lieutenants—			
G. F. Perrinot.			
W. Townsend.			
3rd Lieutenant—			
ENLISTED MEN.			
Allen, William W.			
Amos, J. W.			Sergeant.
Balland, J. H.			
Black, Henry.			
Blake, S. H.			
Brown, John.			
Butler, A. H.			
Campbell, C. E.			
Campbell, D. A.			
Campbell, J. D.			
Campbell, Malcolm.			
Campbell, W. P.			
Clements, J. M.			Corporal.
Cobb, Francis M.	May 10, '62	April '65	
Conklin, J. L.			Corporal.
Crain, Lewis.	Nov. 1, '62	April '65	
Dean, Richard.			
Dixon, C. H.			
Dixon, Francis.			
Dixon, H. H.	Sept. 17, '61		
Dixon, W. J.			
Drury, John.			
Duncan, Peter.			
Ethridge, M. W.			
Feagin, H. J.			
Fincher, James.			
Finley, William.			
Fleming, J. E.			
Fleming, Robert P.			
Frater, John W.			Corporal; acting Battalion Quartermaster; captured, Pine Barren Bridge, September, '64; imprisoned on Ship Island; paroled at Vicksburg, '65.
Fuqua, James.			

Roll Company E—15th Confederate Cavalry.
(CONTINUED.)

NAMES.	MUSTERED IN.	MUSTERED OUT.	REMARKS.
Green, J. H.			Sergeant.
Henderson, J. G.			
Hendley, J. D.			
Hickman, Berry			
Jarvis, H. B.			
Jernigan, F.			
Jernigan, J. E.			
Jernigan, J. S.			Bugler.
Jernigan, Mark	Aug. '61		
Jernigan, N. B.			
Johnson, B. M.			
Johnson, J. A.			
Johnson, W. J.			
Jones, M. B.			
Jones, S. C.			
Kelly, J. T.			
Kenedy, H. T.			
Lewis, Frank			
Leonard, W. A.			
Lewis, W. H.			
McArthur, J. C.			
McMillan, D.			Elected to the Legislature, '64, and honorably discharged.
McRae, L.			1st Sergeant.
Malone, Ephriam	Sept. '62	April '65	
Mann, J. W.			
Marshall, Benjamin			
Mask, J. J.			Sergeant.
Mason, N. M.			
Mayo, Fred B.			
Mayo, Mark		April '65	
Miller, T. R.			
Mims, David			
Mints, J. J.			
Murphy, J. B.			
Nixon, Henry			
Odum, A. J.			
Parker, Elisha			
Parker, H. T.			
Parker, J. T.			
Parker, Noah, Sr.			
Parker, Noah, Jr.			
Parker, P. T.			
Parker, Samuel			
Parker, W. H.			
Parker, W. M.			
Peary, Jason			
Peary, W. A.			
Pitts, T. J.			
Rayburn, G. P.			
Rogers, J. F.			
Rugley, R. D.			
Simmons, J. H.	Sept. '62	April '65	
Simmons, Leroy			
Skinner, H. S.			Corporal.
Sowell, A. J.			
Spier, W. T.			
Stewart, John			
Stewart, Samuel			
Stenson, S. R.			
Sunday, J. G.			
Sunday, J. W.			
Thompson, Jeff.			
White, Andrew			
White, L.		April '65	
Whitmore, William A.			
Wiggins, George			

Roll, Field and Staff—5th Florida Battalion Cavalry.

NAMES.	MUSTERED IN.	MUSTERED OUT.	REMARKS.
Colonel—			
Lieutenant-Colonel—			
George W. Scott	'62	'65	
Major—			
William H. Milton	'62	'65	

Roll, Field and Staff—5th Florida Battalion Cavalry.
(CONTINUED.)

NAMES.	MUSTERED IN.	MUSTERED OUT.	REMARKS.
Surgeon—			
▶ William J. Carroll.........	....	....	
Assistant-Surgeon—			
Adjutant—			
W. P. Pillans.............	....	....	
Sergeant-Major—			
Quartermaster—			
Commissary—			
Quartermaster-Sergeant—			
Commissary-Sergeant—			
Chaplain—			
Hospital Steward—			

Roll Company A (Booth's Company)—5th Florida Battalion Cavalry.

NAMES.	MUSTERED IN.	MUSTERED OUT.	REMARKS.
OFFICERS.			
Captain—			
J. C. Booth..................	Aug. 5, '62	May 19, '65	Promoted Captain to rank as such from July 20, '64; order of Gen. S. Jones.
1st Lieutenant—			
J. B. Barnes..................	Aug. 15, '62	May 19, '65	Promoted 1st Lieutenant, to rank as such from July 20, '64; order Gen. S. Jones.
2nd Lieutenant-Sr—			
W. McPherson..........	May 12, '63	May 19, '65	On scout May 2, '64, order Captain McElvy; promoted Sr. 2nd Lieutenant July 20, '64, order of General Jones.
2nd Lieutenant-Jr—			
H. L. Johnson.............	Mch. 29, '64	May 19, '65	Promoted 2nd Leutenant Jr, by election February 1, '65.
ENLISTED MEN.			
Baker, Rube V. M.............	Mch. 31, '64	May 19, '65	
Barkley, Edgar R.............	Mch. 22, '65	May 19, '65	
Barnes, Benjamin F...........	Aug. 29, '62	May 19, '65	
Bazmore, G. F................	Nov. 1, '63	May 19, '65	Post courier January 14, '64, order Colonel Montgomery.
Bell, George S...............	Mch. 6, '64	May 19, '65	In hospital at Marianna since March 27, '65, by order S. Crews, Assistant-Surgeon, P. A. C. S.
Bell, Stephen B—...........	Aug. 26, '62		3rd Sergeant; sick furlough 30 days April 17, '64, order General Jones.
Bevis, Andrew J.............	July 25, '63	May 19, '65	
Buie, James A...............	Aug. 5, '62	May 19, '65	
Buie, Daniel C..............	Aug. 2, '64	May 19, '65	Detailed in artillery November 16, '64, order Captain W. H. Milton
Bond, Thomas R.............	Aug. 27, '62	May 19, '65	2nd Sergeant.
Bodiford, Wesly H...........	Nov. 1, '63	May 19, '65	On scout May 2, '65, order Captain McElvy.
Burns, Thomas..............	May 15, '63	May 19, '65	
Bush, Henry................	Mch. 29, '64	May 19, '65	
Butler, E. A...............	April 25, '64	May 19, '65	
Byrd, John A..............	Nov. 1, '63	May 19, '65	Captured by enemy December 1, '65 (?4).
Boles, J. B. R............	Mch. 21, '65	May 19, '65	
Collins, Albert D..........	June 11, '63	May 19, '65	In Quartermaster's department April 18, '65 for 90 days, order General Jones.
Collins, Thomas............	June 24, '63		Sick furlough 60 days, March 17, '65. order General Jones.
Colson, James A...........	Dec. 21, '63	May 19, '65	
Chambliss, J. H...........	Dec. 7, '63	May 19, '65	In Quartermaster's department March 13, '65, by order Captain McElvy.
Dickson, E. H.............	April 25, '64	May 19, '65	
Dickson, Marmaduke.........	Dec. 1, '63	May 19, '65	On scout May 2, '65, order Captain McElvy.
Dickson, William F........	Mch. 3, '64	May 19, '65	
Deakle, E. N..............	Nov. 22,	May 19, '65	
Donalson, John E..........	April 22, '64	May 19, '65	Corporal.
Deason, Abram.............	June 26, '63		Absent without leave since May 2, '65.
Donaldson, W. O..........	Mch. 27, '65	May 19, '65	Courier to Quincy, Fla., May 20, '65, order Captain McElvey.
Edwards, Augustus........	Aug. 5, '62		
Edwards, Thomas J........	Aug. 5, '62	May 19, '65	
Edwards, Charles.........	April 22, '64	May 19, '65	
Goodson, Rufus..........	May 8, '62	May 19, '65	Absent without leave since May 3, '65.
Glen. Owen S...........	Aug. 5, '62	May 19, '65	Farrier.
Goodson, Ishmeal.......	Feb. 26, '63	May 19, '65	In hospital since July 16, '64, order L. Crews, Assistant-Surgeon P. A. C. S.
Gray, William V........	April 27, '64	May 19, '65	
Green, John W.........	April 20, '65	May 19, '65	
Gammon. W. P.........	Nov. 27, '63	May 19, '65	

Roll Company A (Booth's Company)—5th Florida Battalion Cavalry.

(CONTINUED.)

NAMES.	MUSTERED IN.	MUSTERED OUT.	REMARKS.
Goodson, Madison	May 8, '62	May 19, '65	Detailed in artillery November 16, '65, order Captain Milton.
Goodson, Labon	May 8, '62	May 19, '65	Post courier July 31, '63, order Colonel Montgomery.
Harper, John	Aug. 7, '62		Sergeant.
Hollis, Isaac	July 25, '63		Captured by the enemy March 20, '65, and since paroled.
Horn, Augustus B	Nov. 23, '63	May 19, '65	Detailed in artillery November 16, '65, order Captain Milton.
Hudspeth, Joel A	Jan. 1, '64	May 19, '65	
Hawkins, Charles E	Mch. 17, '64		Post Clerk May 15,'64, order Colonel Montgomery.
Hearn, James E	Feb. 28, '64	May 19, '65	In Quartermaster's department 60 days March 26, '65, order Gen. Sam Jones.
Hearn, Robert A	July 25, '63	May 19, '65	
Hollis, Charles	July 25, '63		Captured by enemy March 20, '65; since paroled.
Hartsfield, H. M	Nov. 24, '64	May 19, '65	
Johnson, Green B	May 18, '63		Corporal; captured by enemy March 20, '65; since paroled.
Johnson, H. L	Mch. 29, '64		Promoted 2nd Lieutenant, Jr., by election. February 1, '65.
Knapp, W. Henry	Feb. 24, '64	May 19, '65	Captured by enemy March 20, '65; since paroled.
Long, R. Cicero	April 22, '64		In hospital at Marianna since May 3, '65. order L. Crews, P. A. C. S.
Logan, William H	Nov. 1, '63	May 19, '65	
McGee, Moses	Nov. 1, '63	May 19, '65	In hospital October 22, '63, order Assistant-Surgeon L. Crews.
McKay, J. F. E	May 18, '63		Sergeant; in hospital at Marianna April 22, '64, order L. Crews, Assistant-Surgeon, P. A. C. S.
McKenzie, J. C	Sept. 4, '63	May 19, '65	
Mercer, James W	Aug. 28, '63	May 10, '65	
Mathews, Moses G	July 30, '63	May 10, '65	Captured by enemy March 20, '65; since paroled.
McLeroy, J. E	April 27, '64	May 10, '65	
Peacock, James K	May 17, '63	May 10 '65	
Peacock, S. F	Nov. 1, '63	May 10, '65	
Pearre, E. E	Oct. 23, '63	May 10, '65	On scout May 3, '65, order Captain McElvey.
Pearre, John D	Oct. 23, '63	May 10, '65	On scout May 3, '65, order Captain McElvey.
Pender, Robert R	April 27, '64	May 10, '65	
Pittman, Jones M	Nov. 1, '63		Captured by enemy March 20, '65; since paroled.
Parks, John	June 25, '64	May 10 '65	
Parker, Moses	Nov. 6, '63		Detail of five days May 2, '65, by order Captain McElvey.
Rodgers, W. A	Nov. 18, '64	May 10 '65	
Stapleton, Thomas L	Nov. 1, '63	May 10, '65	
Stephens, John M	Oct. 5, '63		In hospital December 19, '64, order L. Crews, Assistant-Surgeon, P. A. C. S.
Strickand, W. G	Aug. 5, '62	May 10, '65	Detail of five days May 1, '65, by order Captain McElvey.
Strickland, B. F	Aug. 5, '62		
Strickland, H. H	July 3, '63		Absent without leave since March 15, '65.
Sullivan, S. N	Mch. 16, '62	May 10, '65	
Skiper, Arthur M	Nov. 1, '63		Captured by enemy March 20, '65; since paroled.
Smith, J. R	Nov. 1, '63		Corporal.
Thomas, Louis S	Dec. 7, '63	May 10, '65	Sick furlough 60 days, April 25, '65, order Gen. Sam Jones.
Taylor, Jesse W	Mch. 26, '64	May 10, '65	
Ward, John J	Sept. 10, '63		Absent without leave since April 28, '65.
West, Isaac W	Nov. 1, '63	May 10, '65	Detailed in hospital April 4, '65 90 days, order Gen. Sam Jones.
West, Joseph M	Feb. 15, '63	May 10, '65	In Quartermaster's department June 13, '63, order Colonel Montgomery.
Whitington, J. W	Sept. 8, '63	May 10, '65	
Whitington, L. D	Sept. 8, '63		Detailed to civil authority September 18, '64, order Colonel Montgomery.
Wood, Almerine J	Mch. 15, '63	May 10, '65	Corporal.
Whitehead, Amos G	Mch. 18, '64		Detailed in Medical Department 90 days September 19, '64, order General Jackson.
Williams, Berry	Sept. 17, '63	May 10, '65	In Quartermaster's Department 60 days March 25, '65, order General Jones.
Williams, W. M. A	Jan. 3, '65	May 10, '65	Detailed courier to Chattahoochee May 3, '65, by order Captain McElvey.
Wood, Jesse C	Oct. 19, '64	May 10, '65	
DIED.			
Deese, Jackson	Nov. 1, '63		Died in hospital at Marianna, Fla., February 18. '65.
Pickle, John D	May 24, '63		Died December 26, '64.
Stovall, Frank M	Jan. 25, '64		Killed by enemy March 23, '65.
DESERTED.			
Burkett, John	Nov. 1, '63		Deserted January 14, '65.
Dell, Maxey M	Nov. 1, '63		Deserted February 15, '65.
Fleming, William W	Sept. 8, '63		Deserted May 2, '65.
Hare, Litttleberry	Aug. 5, '63		Deserted January 7, '65.
Hutcherron, D. L	Aug. 9, '63		Deserted May 2, '65.
Kingery, Bryan M	Nov 1, '63		Deserted March 8, '65.
Land, John R	Sept. 10, '62		Deserted March 15, '65.
Mathews, E. T	Dec. 13, '63		Deserted January 4, '65.

This company was paroled at Marianna, Florida, May 10, '65, by W. H. Milton, commanding the battalion.

Roll Company B—5th Florida Battalion Cavalry.

NAMES.	MUSTERED IN.	MUSTERED OUT.	REMARKS.
OFFICERS.			
Captain—			
A. C. Smith	Mch. 7, '63		
1st Lieutenant—			
A. W. Smith	Mch. 7, '63		
2nd Lieutenant—			
H. H. Love			Assigned to duty by order of Maj.-Gen. Sam Jones April 17, '65.
ENLISTED MEN.			
Alderman, Asa	Mch. 5, '62		Ordered to Quincy hospital about January 12, '65.
Armstrong, J	Oct. 30, '63		
Byrd, A	Aug. 4, '63		Absent without leave since February 12, '65.
Barber, William			
Blount, J. R	Sept. 30, '63		Ordered to Tallahassee hospital April 30, '65.
Bryan, J. L	Aug. 15, '63		Absent without leave since some time in September, '65
Cowin, J. A	Mch. 7, '63		
Collins, T. H	April 8, '65		Corporal; absent with sick leave.
Clark, A. E	Mch. 7, '63		Absent without leave since April 15, '65.
Clark, J. J	April 1, '64		Absent without leave since April 15, '65.
Cox, W. E	Mch. 7, '63		
Chason, J	July 10, '63		
Crockett, James	July 13, '63		Sergeant; furloughed for 30 days from April 28, '65.
Chason, T. J	Mch. 19, '63		Furlough five days from April 28, '65.
Campbell, W. M	Aug. 10, '63		Absent without leave since April 25, '65.
Campbell, G. D	May 15, '63		
Chester, F. J			
Collins. G. R	Sept. 20, '64		Ordered to Quincy hospital some time in December, '64.
Conner, James	Mch. 7, '63		Furloughed for ten days from April 28, '65.
Dagger, J. F			
Elkins, H	Mch. 7, '63		Absent since January 21, '65.
Edwards, G. W	Mch. 7, '63		Absent since March 8, '65.
Edwards, H	Mch. 7, '63		
Edwards, H. G	Mch. 7, '63		Ordered before a Medical Examining Board for a discharge.
Edwards, C	May 8, '64		Absent without leave since December 23, '64.
Freeman, R. L	Oct. 10, '63		
Folks, W. S			
Forehand, L	April 4, '63		Absent without leave since March 5, '65.
Faircloth, D	July 8, '63		Absent without leave since March 5, '65.
Gatlins. William			
Gottin, W. B	July 27, '63		
Gregory, E. H	June 5, '63		Sergeant.
Hardin, A	Mch. 7, '65		Ordered to Quincy hospital November 28, '64.
Hardin, J. F	July 6, '63		Absent on sick furlough 15 days from May 1, '65.
Harrison, B	July 14, '63		Absent without leave since April 29 '65.
Hare, J	July 13, '63		
Hare, W	June 22, '63		Absent without leave since December 24, '64.
Hendry, R. W			
Hentz William			
Hubbard, H	Mch. 7, '63		
Ingram, W. I	Mch. 7, '63		Ordered to Tallahassee hospital.
Inman, J. E	Mch. 7, '63		
Johnson, G. F	Mch. 7, '65		
Johnson, A. J	May 8, '64		Absent without leave since December 23, '64.
Johnson, Neal	Mch. 7, '63		Absent without leave since December 26, '64.
Lang, W. R			
Logan, D	June 10, '63		
Langston, J. B	July 15, '63		
Linear, A. B	Mch. 25, '63		Absent without leave since January 21, '65.
Lockey, Joseph B			
Mercer, George F			
Messer, B	Mch. 7, '63		
Messer, F	July 9, '63		
Messer, Z. T	Dec. 20, '64		Absent without leave since May 2, '65.
Michaux, J. T. S			
Miller, J. W	Mch. 7, '63		Absent without leave since April 16, '65.
Miller, A. J	Mch. 7, '63		Absent without leave since April 29, '65.
Miller, J. M	Mch. 7, '63		Absent without leave since January 14, '65.
McDonald, A. D	Mch. 10, '63		Ordered to Quincy hospital March 15, '65.
McPhaul, Alexander	Mch. 7, '63		Sergeant.
McClellan, G	Aug. 6, '63		Absent without leave since December 22, '64.
McKown, J. F	Jan. 6, '65		
McCall, James W	Mch. 7, '63		Sergeant.
McElroy, A. B			
McDonald, I. A	June 30, '63		Corporal.
Nixon, J. M	Aug. 20, '63		Captured by the enemy at Rice's Bluff January 26, '65.
Owens, M. B			
Peacock, Frank			
Peebles, W. T	Mch. 7, '63		Detailed in Quartermaster's Department at Quincy, Fla.
Pearson, J. W	Mch. 19, '63		
Pittman, O. W			
Pitts, D	Mch. 7, '63		
Poppell, J. W	Mch. 7, '63		Ordered to Tallahassee hospital April 30, '65.
Pyle, E. H			

Roll Company B)—5th Florida Battalion Cavalry.
(Continued.)

NAMES.	MUSTERED IN.	MUSTERED OUT.	REMARKS.
Reichert, Christopher..........			
Renew, J..........	April 15, '63		Absent without leave since January 14, '65.
Rogers, Henry..........	April 1, '62		Absent without leave since April 29, '65.
Silas, J..........	Mch. 7, '63		Absent without leave since April 9, '65.
Shephard..........	May 1, '63		Corporal.
Shuler, T. P..........	Oct. 10, '63		Corporal.
Shuler, W. E.			
Smith, H. B..........	Mch. 7, '63		Ordered to Quincy hospital March 2, '65.
Smith, Mut..........	April 1, '62		Absent without leave since December 25, '64.
Smith, J. P..........	April 1, '62		Absent without leave since December 25, '64.
Sweet, B. S..........	Mch. 7, '63		Detailed in Assistant-Quartermaster's Depart-
Swiley, S..........	Mch. 7, '63		Detailed to make (Slaies) at Quincy. ment at Chattahoochee, Fla.
Stokes, J. M..........	Mch. 7, '63		Absent without leave since March 1, '65.
Stokes, H..........	Mch. 7, '63		Absent without leave since October 11, '64.
Swicord, M..........	Sept. 5, '64		Ordered to Tallahassee hospital April 28, '65.
Tharp, J. A..........	Mch. 7, '63		Absent without leave since May 3, '65.
Turner, A..........	July 10, '63		Ordered to Tallahassee hospital April 23, '65.
Ventry, C. H..........	Mch. 7, '63		
Weeks, J..........	Mch. 7, '63		Absent without leave since January 1, '65.
Williams, J......	Mch. 7, '63		
Watson, B. F..........	Mch. 7, '63		1st Lieutenant; dropped from the roll by order of the Military Examining Board January 18, '65.
Scott, Leonadis..........	Mch. 7, '63		2nd Lieutenant; dropped from the roll by order of the Military Examining Board January 18, '65.

Roll Company C—5th Florida Battalion Cavalry.

NAMES.	MUSTERED IN.	MUSTERED OUT.	REMARKS.
OFFICERS.			
Captain—			
D. W. Gwynn..........	Mch. 5, '62		
1st Lieutenant—			
E. A. Hart..........	Mch. 5, '62		
2nd Lieutenants—			
R. E. Lester..........	Mch. 5, '62		
E. W. Burroughs..........	Jan. 21, '63		
ENLISTED MEN.			
Allen, William H..........		April '65	
Anders, J. A..........	Mch. 5, '62		Sergeant.
Bradford, W. M..........	Mch. 5, '62		
Bond, W. L..........	Jan. 18, '64		
Bond, E..........	Mch. 5, '62		
Billingsley, A. S.			
Billingsley, J. S..........	Mch. 17, '62		
Burns, M..........	April 19, '63		
Blalock, W. H..........	Mch. 8, '62		
Braswell, J. W..........	June 16, '64		
Croom, G. A..........	Oct. 13, '63		
Croom, A. C..........	Mch. 5, '62		
Coleman, W. K..........		April 12, '62	
Crowder, A. H..........	Mch. 5, '62		
Crowder, R. H..........	April 12, '62		
Cam, J..........	Feb. 3, '64		
Chairs, Benjamin..........	Feb. 19, '65		
Daniell, Robert..........			
Dennis, G. E..........	Feb. 9, '64		
Denham, W..........	Oct. 1, '62		Sergeant.
Denham, James S..........	June 19, '63		Sergeant.
Dugger, J. L.			
Dykes, H. K..........	Dec. 1, '63		
Ellis, W..........	Nov 11, '62		
Edwards, C. G..........	Oct 9, '64		
Fletcher, J. M..........	Mch. 5, '62		
Fletcher, M. N..........	Mch. 5, '62		
Fletcher, Richard..........			
Finklen, A. J..........	Mch. 5, '62		
Gregory, H. C..........	Mch. 5, '62		
Green, F. T..........	Aug. 1, '63		
Gray, J..........	Aug. 1, '63		
Humphries, J. H..........	Mch. 5, '62		
Hart, B. F..........	June 24, '62		
Hines, W. W..........			
Hunt, E..........	Aug. 25, '63		

Roll Company C—5th Florida Battalion Cavalry.
(CONTINUED.)

NAMES.	MUSTERED IN.	MUSTERED OUT.	REMARKS.
Harris, W.	April 9, '62		
Harris, W. W.	May 30, '63		
Hall, T. T.	July 14, '64		
Horn, C. J.	Mch. 25, '65		
Joyner, B. H.	Mch. 5, '62		
Johnson, B. W.	Aug. 7, '63		Corporal.
Kindon, G. A.	Mch. 5, '62		
Koker, T. J.			
Laing, W. E.	Mch. 5, '62		
Laing, T. J.	Mch. 5, '62		
Lash, C.	Jan. 19, '64		
Lester, S. F.	Mch. 5, '62		
Long, R. C.	May 23, '63		
Murray, W. A.	Jan. 23, '64		Bugler.
McCook, P. H.	Sept. 1, '62		Wounded at Natural Bridge.
Mash, H. T.	Mch. 5, '64		
Mash, J. J.	Mch. 5, '64		
Mash, M. M.	Jan. 20, '65		
Mathews, S.	April 9, '62		
Matheson, J. L.	Mch. 29, '62		
McIntosh, Bert	May 3, '62		
Owens, T. W.	Mch. 5, '62		
Paramore, R. W.	Mch. 5, '62		
Russell, J. B.	Aug. 19, '63		
Raker, Thomas	Feb. 27, '64		
Raysor, George	Jan. 29, '64		Corporal.
Raker, M.	July 1, '63		
Rhodes, E.	April 16, '63		
Raysor, A.	Aug. 30, '64		
Raines, R.	April 26, '64		
Shelfer, George	Mch. 5, '62		Sergeant.
Shelfer, Henry M.			
Stroman, J. L.	April 19, '62		
Shelfer, Joseph J.	July 15, '62		
Shelfer, W. H.	Mch. 5, '62		
Spears, W. E.	April 12, '62		
Saunders, W. T.	Aug. 1, '63		
Swearingen, T. F.	Jan. 30, '64		
Stony, I.	Jan. 31, '64		
Sturgess, D.	Aug. 18, '63		Corporal.
Simkins, T. B.	Oct. 13, '63		
Sills, John C.	Feb. 14, '64		
Sills, W.	June 8, '64		
Smallwood, F.	Feb. 10, '65		
Sylvester, R. H.			
Turnbull, Theo	Jan. 30, '64		
Tatum, T. P.	April 19, '62		
Watson J. H.	Mch. 5, '62		
Watkins, J. J.	Aug. 19, '63		Corporal.
Watson, J. J.	April 19, '62		
Woodward, W. W.	April 19, '62		
Woodward, A. L.	Mch. 5, '62		
Wilson, B. D.	Dec. 8, '62		
Whitley, J.	June 15, '63		
Whitfield, R. B.	Jan. 28, '64		
Whitfield, R. A.	Aug. 1, '63		
Wethington, J. Q.	Sept. 16, '63		
Wyche, Thomas	July 25, '64		
Whitehurst J. J.	Nov. 25, '64		

Roll Company D—5th Florida Battalion Cavalry.

NAMES.	MUSTERED IN.	MUSTERED OUT.	REMARKS.
OFFICERS			
Captain—			
L. G. McElvy			
1st Lieutenant—			
Leegar			
2nd Lieutenant—			
Donald W. Nicholson		May '65	Promoted Lieutenant.
3rd Lieutenants—			
G. B. Mills		May '65	Promoted Lieutenant; resigned.
J. C. Walker			
ENLISTED MEN.			
Ball, Green			
Burns, Thomas L.	Aug. 15, '64		

Roll Company D—5th Florida Battalion Cavalry.
(CONTINUED.)

NAMES.	MUSTERED IN.	MUSTERED OUT.	REMARKS.
Chester, F. J.	Aug. 15, '63	May 12, '65	
Chester, G. L.			
Dykes, J. T.			
Ferrell, D. G.	Aug. 1, '63		
Laing, Earley E.			
Lang, Elbert H.	Aug. 22, '63		
McElroy, A. B.		May 12, '65	
Munroe, Thomas F.			
Mills, J. M.			
Owens, J. M.			
Sealey, H. C.	Jan. '65	May 15, '65	
Sealey, J. E.		May 15, '65	
Sealey, J. J.		May 15, '65	
Sealey, Stephen E.			Promoted Corporal; died at Lake City January, '64 from disease.
Shaw, A. W.			
Shaw, J. K.		May 15, '65	
Shelfer, H. M.		May '65	
Stokes, Joshua		May '65	
Vanlandingham, James E.	Sept. '63	May 12, '65	
Wilder, E. H.	Mch. '62	May '65	Wounded in left leg.

Roll Company E (William A. Jeter's Company)—5th Florida Battalion Cavalry.

NAMES.	MUSTERED IN.	MUSTERED OUT.	REMARKS.
OFFICERS.			
Captain—			
William A. Jeter	Sept. 15, '63	May 10, '65	February 7, '65, detached duty order of Captain McElvey.
1st Lieutenant—			
Reuben L. Harrison		May 10, '65	Captured by United States forces January 17, '65.
2nd Lieutenant—			
Hiram W. Pickett	April 1, '62	May 10, '65	Senior Lieutenant.
3rd Lieutenants—			
R. E. Lester			
John H. Glenn	Mch. 10, '62	May 10, '65	
ENLISTED MEN.			
Baker, Robert G.	Mch. 10, '62		Sergeant.
Baker, Andrew J.	Aug. 5, '62		May 3, '65, absent without leave.
Baker, Morgan B.	Jan. 1, '63		January 17, '65, captured by United States forces.
Barber, Columbus C.	Mch. 24, '64		January 17, '65, captured by United States forces.
Barnes, Newton R.	April 26, '64		November 16, '64, detached duty order of Captain Milton.
Bolin, William	April 10, '62		November 30, '65. captured by U. S. forces.
Bracken, Simeon	Sept. 14, '64		February 19, '65, absent without leave.
Brookins, J. L.			
Brown, Joseph	Dec. 7, '64		January 17, '65, captured by United States forces.
Bruner, Joshua	Feb. 15, '65		
Burke, John			
Burnett, Z.	Feb 11, '65		February 11, '65, detached duty order of Captain McElvey.
Coston, James M.	Nov. 18, '64		February 7, '65. detached duty order of Captain McElvey.
Chambliss, Ira P.	Jan. 20, '65		May 3, '65, absent without leave.
Chambliss, George W.	Mch. 26, '65		
Corbitt, Thomas Nichols			
Corbin, Samuel	April 29, '65		May 4, '65, absent without leave.
Courtney, William			
Davidson, Columbus H.	July 1, '63		May 1, '65, absent without leave.
Dennis, John W.	Mch. 4, '63		Corporal.
Durdin, John.	Jan. 1, '63	May 19, '65	Farier.
Durdin John Jr.	Sept. 8, '62	May 19, '65	May 3. '65, absent without leave.
Durdin, Wiley	Sept. 8, '62	May 19, '65	
Deal, Wiley B	Aug. 15, '63	May 19, '65	November 16,'64, detached duty order of Captain Milton.
Daughtrey, Robert M	Oct. 12, '64		April 17. '65, absent without leave.
Edenfield, B. F.	Sept. 8, '62		February 7, '65, detached duty order of Captain McElvey.
Edenfield, W. M.	Aug. 11, '62	May 19 '65	May 5, '65, absent without leanve.
Fowler, Lawson H.	Oct. 1, '62		January 17, '65, captured by United States forces.
Forrester, Joseph D	Nov. 8, '63		February 12, '65, absent wthout leave.
Gilbert, Thomas G	April 24, '64	May 19, '65	November 16, '64, detached duty order of Captain Milton.
Horne, Lewis	Aug. 5, '62	May 19, '65	
Heath, Madison T	Feb. 1, '64	May 19, '65	April 21. '65. on 15 days furlough order of General Sam Jones.
Howard, A. J.	May 1 '63		January 17, '65.captured by United States forces,

Roll Company E (William A. Jeter's Company)—5th Florida Battalion Cavalry.

(CONTINUED.)

NAMES.	MUSTERED IN.	MUSTERED OUT.	REMARKS.
Howard, Joshua	Oct. 1, '63		July 9, '64, detailed in Sub Department order of the Secretary of War.
Hudson, Herbert	Mch. 10, '62		January 17, '65, captured by UnitedStates forces.
Humphries, John W	Sept. 6, '62		April 10, '65, absent without leave.
Hentz, William	April 10, '62	May 19, '65	November 5, '64, on detached duty order of Captain Milton. (Sergeant).
Horne, Chalmers D	Aug. 1, '64	May 19, '65	Corporal.
Humphries, Joel C	Sept. 6, '62		April 20, '65, absent without leave.
Hamick, W. L	Sept 25, '64		
Hamick, C. C	May 1, '65		
Hinson, B. A	Aug. 11, '62		May 3, '65, absent without leave.
Hathcock, Daniel	Dec. 7, '64		January 17, '64, captured by United States forces.
Jordan, James O	Mch. 10, '62	May 19, '65	
Johnson, L. C	Aug. 25, '64		May 3, '65, absent without leave.
Jenkins, Robert N	June 11, '64		May 3, '65, absent without leave.
Jones, B. E	Sept. 15, '64	May 19, '65	
Jones, Amos L	Jan. 15, '65		February 7 '65, detached duty order of Captain McElvey.
Kirkland, Art	Jan. 4, '64		February 7, '65, detached duty order of Captain McElvey.
Kent, Alexander	April 20, '64	May 19, '65	February 7, '65 detached duty order of Captain McElvey.
Kent, Burris	Jan. 1, '63	May 19, '65	February 7, '65, detached duty order of Captain McElvey.
Kinney, S	Oct. 15, '64		January 17, captured by United States forces.
Lawrence, Joseph	Mch. 10, '62		January 17, captured by United States forces.
Lawrence, Joseph Jr	April 21, '63		January 17, '65, captured by United States forces.
Lander, Charles D	Aug. 8, '63	May 19, '65	May 5, '65, absent without leave.
Lipford, John H	May 9, '64		November 16, '64, detached duty order of Captain Milton.
Littlefield, John E	May 1, '63		May 1, '65, absent without leave.
McCleland, John L. M	Oct. 1, '62		Sergeant; captured January 17, '65, by United States forces.
McCleland, James M	May 1, '63		February 25, '65, absent; sick.
Mixon, Aris	Sept. 1, '64		November 16, '64 detached duty order Captain Milton.
Mercer, James W			
Mercer, Asa	Oct. 1, '63		February 7, '65, detached duty order of Captain McElvey.
Moore, Charles E	June 1, '64		
Moore, Daniel T			
Neel, W. H			
Perkins. William B	July 1, '63	May 19, '65	May 2, '65, absent without leave.
Patton, George A	Mch. 10, '62		Corporal.
Perkins, Isaac	Mch. 16, '64	May 10, '65	November 16, '64, detached duty order of Captain Milton.
Perkins, J. S			
Petry, William	Feb. 15, '65	May 10, '65	February 15, '65, detached duty order of Captain McElvey.
Rhaimes, Nathan	Apr 10, '62		January 17, 65, captured by United States forces.
Richards, George W	Mch. 1, '63		March 4, '65, absent without leave.
Roche, Joel			
Roche, N. B			
Skelton, William			
Sketo, William			
Skipper, Edward B	Aug. 15, '63	May 10, 65	
Silas, Thomas A	Mch. 10, '62		January 17, '65 captured by United States forces.
Scoorlock, Walter L	Jan. 8, '64		May 3, '65, absent without leave (Sergeant).
Sexton Friley B	May 1, '63	May 10, '65	May 3, '65, absent without leave; Corporal.
Smith James M	April 1, '62		February 7, '65. detached duty order of Captain McElvey.
Smith, John L	Aug. 11, '64		February 7, '65, detached duty order of Captain McElvey.
Smith, Robert R	Mch. 10, '62		April 20, '65 detached order of Captain McElvey.
Shelfer Levi	May 26, '63		January 17, '65, detached duty order of Captain Milton.
Scurlock, Henry F	Feb. 20, '64		February 7, '65, detached duty order of Captain McElvey.
Spikes, Hez	Aug. 25, '64		February 4, '65, absent without leave.
Striplin, Elisha	Feb. 1, '64		May 3, '65, absent without leave.
Searsay, W A	Nov. 25, '64		May 1, '65, absent without leave.
Tindel, Green	Sept. 15, '64	May 10, '65	
Traylor, Moses	May 2, '63	May 10, '65	May 2, '65, absent without leave.
Taylor, Robert J	Aug. 2, '62		Blacksmith.
Tomberlin James	Aug. 5, '62		May 1, '65, detached duty order Captain McElvey; Corporal.
Traylor, John M	May 8, '64	May 10, '65	February 7, '65, detached duty order of Captain McElvey.
Traylor, Champion, T	Aug. 18, '64	May 10, '65	May 3, '65, absent without leave.
Trotter, W. W	Nov. 10, '63		July 9, '64, detailed in Subsistence Department, order Secretary of War.
Thompson, Nelson	June 1, '64		March 7, '65, absent without leave.
Taylor, James	Nov. 10, '64		March 23, '65, absent without leave.
Williams, James	Aug. 8, '63		July 17, '64, captured by United States forces.

Roll Company E (William A. Jeter's Company)—5th Florida Battalion Cavalry.
(CONTINUED.)

NAMES.	MUSTERED IN.	MUSTERED OUT.	REMARKS.
Whiddon, Alexander	Jan. 5, '64		
Witherington, F. M.	Oct. 1, '62		April 15, '65, absent without leave.
White, Marion J.	Feb. 1, '64		February 7, '65, detailed duty order of Captain McElvey.
White, Lewis	Sept. 4, '64		February 7, '65, detached duty order of Captain McElvey.
Watford, John W.	Feb. 7, '64		May 8, '65, absent without leave.
Watford, Perry S.	July 29, '64		April 15, '65, absent without leave.
Watson, B. F.	Feb. 2, '65		March 25, '65, detached duty order of Captain McElvey.
Woods, A. J.	Feb. 2, '65		This company was paroled at Marianna, Florida, May 10, '65, by Maj. W. H. Milton, commanding the battalion.

Roll Company F (A. J. Dozier's Company)—5th Florida Battalion Cavalry.

NAMES.	MUSTERED IN.	MUSTERED OUT.	REMARKS.
OFFICERS.			
Captain—			
A. J. Dozier	May 15, '62		
1st Lieutenant—			
R. J. Mays	Aug. 20, '63		
2nd Lieutenants—			
E. E. Whitner	May 17, '63		
H. C. Croom	Feb. '62		
ENLISTED MEN			
Barclay, Thad	Mch. 22, '62		
Barineau, J. C.			
Barwick, J. W.	Aug. 4, '63		
Bennett, W. H.	Nov. 19, '63		
Bishop, Joseph	April 9, '62		
Blanton, D. F.	May 6, '62		
Boon, Joel	June 26, '64		
Boyd, R. A.	Feb. 21, '65		
Bryant, A. D.	Nov. 19, '63		
Carlton, J. P.	April 28, '62		
Carlton, Thomas T.	June 26, '62		Promoted Captain.
Cameron, W. J.	Aug. 14, '63		Corporal.
Carlton, T. L.	Nov. 4, '63		
Cone, W. R.			
Daniel, B. F.			
Dial, W. A.	Mch. 5, '63		
Elliott, R. K.	Mch. 13, '63		
Espy, Joseph	Aug. 20, '63		
Florrid, Lewis			
Fountain, W. E.			Died at home in Taylor county, November 4, '64.
Geiger, Allen	April 12, '64		
Geiger, Noah	April 12, '04		
Grimmer, D.	Mch. 1, '62		
Griffin, W. D.	Mch. 1, '62		Sergeant.
Grubbs, W. H.	April 29, '62		
Hamilton, T. A.	Sept. 26, '62		
Hamilton, J.	Oct. 7, '64		
Hendry, R. W.	April 29, '62		
Holton, Christopher	Nov. 7, '63		His back injured by being thrown from a horse.
Lamb, Q. N.	Aug. 16, '63		
Lamb, Thomas	Nov. 16, '63		
Loper, Curtis	Mch. 8, '62		
Lundy, Thad	April 29, '62		
Lewis, Thomas	Nov. 9, '63		
Mays, J. S.	Jan. 27, '65		
Mays, S. P.	Feb. 6, '65		Sergeant.
Morse, John R.	Mch. 12, '62		Corporal.
McCullers, M. R.	Sept. 21, '64		
O'Quinn, A. M.	April 29, '62		
O'Neal, John W.	April 10, '62		Sergeant.
Perry, Porter	Aug. 14, '63		
Reichert, C. F.	Nov. 9, '63		
Register, G. F.	July 31, '63		
Sapp, John			Died at home in Wakulla county, October 25, '64.
Saxon, H. O.			
Shepard, R. G.			
Spradley, Richard	Mch. 19, '62		
Starr, Thomas	Aug. 14, '63		

Roll Company F (A. J. Dozier's Company)—5th Florida Battalion Cavalry.
(CONTINUED.)

NAMES.	MUSTERED IN.	MUSTERED OUT.	REMARKS.
Tabb, W. A.	Mch. 12, '62	April '65	Corporal; transferred in '63 to Co. F, 5th Battalion
Tatem, J. D.	Mch. 29, '64		Cavalry; died October 10, '76.
Triplett, Eli.			Wounded, Natural Bridge.
Wallace, T. M.	Mch. 1, '62		
Wamsley, T. M.	June 7, '64		
Wilder, H. H.	Mch. 12, '62		
Wilder, John M.	Mch. 1, '62		

Roll Company G—5th Florida Battalion Cavalry.

NAMES.	MUSTERED IN.	MUSTERED OUT.	REMARKS.
OFFICERS.			
Captain—			
William H. Milton			Promoted Major 5th Florida Battalion.
1st Lieutenant—			
Henry K. Simmons			Killed at Natural Bridge March 4, '65.
2nd Lieutenants—			
William D. Barnes			
Jesse C. Booth			
Sol Warren			Promoted 2nd Lieutenant.
3rd Lieutenant—			
ENLISTED MEN.			
Anderson, Angus	Oct. 15, '62		
Barber, Andrew			
Barber, John			
Barnes, B. H.			
Barnes, J. B.			
Barrington, John C.	Aug. '62	May '65	
Beatley, Hugh W			
Bell, George S.			
Bell, Stephen B			
Bevill, John R.			
Bevis, J. A.			
Bevis, Thomas L	April	May '65	
Blount, Archibald.			
Bond, Thomas R.			
Bowen, George M.			
Buford, J. C.			
Buie, D. C.			
Bush, Henry	Feb. '64	May '65	
Cathon, S. A.			1st Sergeant.
Carpenter, Henry.			
Carmichael, J. W.			
Clark, William.		May '65	
Council, John G.			
Craig, John A.			
Crawford, John		May '65	Transferrred to 2nd Florida Cavalry.
Deckle, E. N.			
Dickson, Duke			
Dickson, W. F.			
Durden, John	Mch. 15, '62	April 5, '65	
Dyass, W. R.			
Edenfield, Richard F.	Aug. '62	April 5, '65	
Edgerton, W. C.			
Edwards, Able H.			
Edwards, Augustus.			
Edwards, Charles B.			
Edwards, Cullen			
Edwards, Hiram			
Edwards, Jefferson.			
Edwards, John.			
Edwards, Thomas J.	Aug. '62	April '65	
Farnell, J. P.			
Farr, William.			
French, Robert.			
Gay, James J			
Gaylord, N. R.	July 12, '63	April 9, '65	
Geiger, James W	May '63	April 9, '65	
Glenn, Owen S.	June '62	April 9, '65	Corporal.
Goodbread, J. Lex.	Nov. 12, '62	April 9, '65	
Granger, James I.	Feb. '63	April 9, '65	
Granger, J. K.			
Granger, J. R.			
Granger, J. W.			
Griffin, William E.			

Roll Company G—5th Florida Battalion Cavalry.
(Continued.)

NAMES.	MUSTERED IN.	MUSTERED OUT.	REMARKS.
Hamilton, E. S.			
Hamilton, Joseph R.			
Hancock, G. W.			
Harper, John	Sept. '63	May 15, '65	
Haw, Littleberry			
Hawkins, R. R.			
Hawkins, William R.			
Holland, Hayward			
Horne, Lewis			
Howard, Hardy			
Howard			
Hunt, Thomas	Aug. '63		
Jackson, Martin			
Jeffcoat, R. W.			Sergeant.
Jernigan, W. H.	Jan. 1, '63	April 9, '65	
Johnson, James			
Johnson, W. M.			Bugler.
Judoh, E. J.			Sergeant.
King, Henry			
King Jacob H.			
Land, S. W.			
Lanier, Thomas			Corporal.
Lee, H. M.			
Love, James E.			
Lowe, Philip E.			
McAlpine, Augustus			
McInnis, Samuel		April 9, '65	
McKnight, Adam C.	April	April 9, '65	Wounded at Natural Bridge, Fla.
McMillan, John			
Martin, Robert C.		April 9, '65	
Mercer, James W.	Aug. 28, '63	April 9, '65	Thrown from horse and hip dislocated June 10, '64
Miller, John W.			
Milton, H. R.	July 12, '63	April 9, '65	
Mims, Larkin			
Norwood, Jesse			
Oswald, H.		April 9, '65	
Packard, D. C.			
Packard, D. M.			Sergeant.
Parker, H. C.		April 9, '65	
Peacato, J. C.		April 9, '65	
Posey, Alfred			
Rainey, Alison		April 9, '65	
Raker, Jacob	Feb. '64	April 9, '65	.
Ramsey			
Revill, J. R.			
Roach, Joseph			
Roach, N. B.			
Roberts, James			
Sanford, M. J.	Sept. 62	May '65	
Seiger, Marshall		April '65	
Shepherd, M. D. C.			
Smith, F. M.			
Smith, J. T.		April '65	
Smith, N.	June 10, '63	April '65	Wounded during the war.
Smith, T. Y.		April '65	
Spooner, Caleb		May '65	
Stansel, Jesse P.		May '65	
Stansel, Jesse T.		April 9, '65	
Stanaland, G. N.		April 9, '65	
Stephens, Jacob	'61	April 9, '65	
Stephens, Benjamin A.			
Strickland, A. M.	Aug. '62	April 9, '65	Captured at Ocklockonee Bay, Fla., November '64, and paroled at Vicksburg, Miss., May, '65.
Strickland, R. F.			....Corporal.
Strickland, W. G.			
Sullivan, S. N.		April 9, '65	
Taurakers, Nathan		April 9, '65	
Taylor, R. J.		April 9, '65	
Thompson, John E.		April 9, '65	
Todd, McDaniel L.			
Tomberton, James			
Waldron, K. S.		April 9, '65	
Whaley Thos. E.			
Weeks, J. H.	Aug, '63	April 9, '65	
Weeks, W. T.		April 9, '65	Promoted 2nd Lieutenant of Co. F, 2nd Cavalry.
Wheldon, M. J.		April 9, '65	
White, C. J.			Sergeant.
Whitley, Samuel S.			
Whittington, James	Aug. '62	April 9, '65	
Whiley, Alexander			
Williams, Ben N.		April 9, '65	
Wimberley, Tarrant			

Roll· Company G—5th Florida Battalion Cavalry.
(CONTINUED.)

NAMES.	MUSTERED IN.	MUSTERED OUT.	REMARKS.
Winburn, C.	Feb. 15. '63	May 18, '65	Captured November 17, '64, and confined at Ship Island, Miss.
Woodward, Little H.			
Zent, Richard A.			
Zent, Robert F.			

Roll Company I (Capt. A. F. Perry's Company)—5th Florida Battalion Cavalry.
(CONTINUED.)

NAMES.	MUSTERED IN.	MUSTERED OUT.	REMARKS.
OFFICERS.			
Captains—			
Robert Chisholm			Died.
A. F. Perry		May 10, '65	
1st Lieutenant—			
W. C. Wilson		May 10, '65	
2nd Lieutenant—			
W. A. Rutherford		May 10, '65	
2nd Lieutenant-Jr—			
R. A. Solomon		May 10, '65	
ENLISTED MEN.			
Anderson, John	Jan. 9, '64	May 10, '65	
Adams, E. W. J.	July 28, '64		
Alford, A. M. K.	Jan. 14, '65		
Belser, Lit.	Jan. 9, '64		
Brown, John T.	Jan. 9, '64		
Bowden, W. L.	July 9, '64	May 10, '65	
Baies, M.	Mch. 8, '64	May 10, '65	
Barnes, J. H.	June 12, '64	May 10, '65	
Brett, J. W.	Jan. 19, '64		Captured by enemy September 23, '64.
Boon, Robert	April 5, '64		
Beauchamp, David	Jan. 25, '64	May 10, '65	
Bishop, William	Mch. 17, '65		
Bowden, Samuel	Jan. 9, '64	May 10, '65	1st Sergeant.
Chambers, J. W.	Jan. 9, '64	May 10, '65	
Chambers, J. B.	Jan. 9, '64	May 10, '65	
Callaway, J. W.	Mch. 15, '64	May 10, '65	
Callaway, R. H.	May 15, '64	May 10, '65	
Carter, J. W.	April 10, '64	May 10, '65	
Cowart, A. J.	Jan. 9, '64		
Culbirth, David		Jan. 9, '64	
Carlisle, William	Feb. 10, '64	May 10, '65	
Clark, T. B.	Jan. 9, '64	May 10, '65	2nd Sergeant.
Cargile, Frank	May 30, '64		
Cassady, F. H.	July 27, '64	May 10, '65	
Cawthon, S. S.	Jan. 9, '64	May 10, '65	
Connely, C. P.	Mch. 17, '65	May 10, '65	
Cassady, H. S.	Mch. 17, '65	May 10, '65	
Connely, J. Z. S.	Mch. 17, '65	May 10, '65	3rd Corporal.
Dansey, S. E.	Feb. 1, 64		
Dansey, G. M.	Oct. 31, '64		
Daniel, S. E.	Oct. 31, '64	May 10, '65	3rd Sergeant.
Davis, A.			
Dawkins, R. H.	Feb. 1, '64		Captured by enemy February 19, '65.
Durham, H. C.	Jan. 9, '64	May 10, '65	
Dubose John P.	Jan. 16. '65		
Everitt, B. F.	April 18, '64	May 10, '65	
Everitt, E. F.		May 10, '65	
Edwards, F. J.	Oct. 31, '64		
Fewell, R. A.	Jan. 9, '64		
Fennell, Perry	Jan. 9, '64		
Fullerton, A.	Jan. 9, '64	May 10, '65	2nd Corporal.
Fordham, B. J.	April 10. '64		
Grimesley, H. H.	Feb. 2, '64		
Holmes, L. H.	Feb. 1, '64		
Hatten, W. L.	April 9, '64		Died (?) in enemy's hands January 6, '64.
Holmes, John J.	May 7, '64	May 10, '65	
Hardy, John G.	Jan. 9, '64		
Hall, Allen	Feb. 27, '64	May 10, '65	
Hall, John	Aug. 17, '64	May 10, '65	
Hall, J. T.	Jan. 28, '65		
Hall, J. W.	Jan. 28, '65		
Hall, W. W.	Mch. 29, '65		
Harrison, John	Jan. 9, '64		
Huff, J. F.	Oct. 31, '64		
Hudgins, A. M.	Feb. 1, '65		
Johns, C. P.	Aug. 29, '64		

Roll Company I (Capt. A. F. Perry's Company)—5th Florida Battalion Cavalry.
(Continued.)

NAMES.	MUSTERED IN.	MUSTERED OUT.	REMARKS.
Jones, J. G.	April 3, '65		
Jackson, B. H.	Jan. 28, '65		
King, Franklin E.	May 2, '64	May 10, '65	
Lee, J. D.	Mch. 22, '64	May 10, '65	
Lee, J. G. B.	Aug. 10, '64	May 10, '65	
Lewis, Arthur	April 10, '64		
Lucas, J. W.	Sept. 24, '64		
Loman, A. W.	Jan. 19, '65		
Montgomery. R, W.	Jan. 9, '64		
Martin, A. D.	Jan. 9, '64	May 10, '65	
Mags, T, W.			
Miller, W. J.	Mch. 17, '65		5th Sergeant.
Merriwether, Charles H.	Aug. 10, '64	May 10, '65	
Monday, James	Jan. 9, '64	May 10,	
Mercer, A. J.	Jan. 25, '64	May 10, '65	
McDaniel, John W.	Mch. 16, '64	May 10, '65	
McDonald, J. B.	Jan. 9, '64	May 10, '65	
McDaniel, William R.	Feb. 10, '64	May 10, '65	
McSwain, Angus	Oct. 31, '64		1st Corporal.
McRae, C. C.	Jan. 19, '65		
McLeod, William	Mch. 27, '65		
Owens, W. D.	Feb. 20, '64	May 10, '65	
Page, J. H.	Mch. 5, '64	May 10, '65	
Parker, C. H.	Jan. 9, '64		Captured by enemy September 23, '64.
Pittman, Hutin R.	Jan. 9, '64		Died in Elmira, N. Y., December 21, '64.
Pitts, Jackson	Sept. 10, '64		
Pitts, Ira.	April 28, '64		
Register, J. S.	Jan. 9, '64	May 10, '65	
Register, M. G.	Feb. 20, '64	May 10, '65	
Robinson, J. H.	Jan. 30, '64	May 10, '65	
Russ, John G.	Feb. 25, '64	May 10, '65	
Richards, R. J.	Aug. 3, '64		
Ray, B. H.	Jan. 9, '64	May 10, '65	
Renfroe, N. E.	Jan. 25, '65		
Renfroe, M. L. F.	Jan. 25, '65		
Renfroe, N.		Jan. 25, '65	
Sanders, B.	Jan. 9, '64		
Singletary, John	Jan. 9, '64		
Spence, A. T.	Feb. 11, '64		
Strickland, Ithial H.	July 9, '64		
Sims, Ashley	April 28, 64		
Solomon, F. W.	May 10, '64	May 10, '65	
Solomon, F. Wiley	April 28, '64	May 10, '65	
Stanford, W. J.	Feb. 18, '65	May 10, '65	
Stanford, A. G.	Oct. 28, '64	May 10, '65	
Stanford, Monroe	Jan. 9, '64		4th Sergeant.
Stanford, S. M.		May 10, '65	
Sheats, C. N.	Feb. 1, '64		
Tennille, William	April 8,		
Thomas, J. C.	Feb. 10, '64		
Wooten, A. J.	Jan. 9, '64	May 10, '65	
Wilson, T. S.	Jan. 1, '65		
Wester, D. C.	Mch. 4, '64	May 10, '65	
Watson, J. M.	Jan. 9, '64		
Watson, M. M.	Jan. 16, '65		
Wise, L. L.	Jan. 16, '65		
Wise, J. E.	Jan. 16, '65		This company was paroled at Marianna, Florida, May 10, '65, by Maj. W. H. Milton, commanding the battalion.

Roll Capt. Charles E. E. Dyke's Light Artillery.

NAMES.	MUSTERED IN.	MUSTERED OUT.	REMARKS.
OFFICERS.			
Captain—			
Charles E. Dyke			1st Lieutenant; promoted Captain of battery.
Surgeon—			
W. F. Robertson		May '65	Promoted Surgeon.
1st Lieutenant—			
Joe N. Whitner			3rd Lieutenant; promoted 1st Lieutenant.
2nd Lieutenant—			
E. W. Gamble			
3rd Lieutenant—			
Frank B. Fox	Aug. 11, '62	June 15, '65	Promoted 3rd Lieutenant; captured, imprisoned at Camp Chase, O., April 13, '65.

Roll Capt. Charles E. E. Dyke's Light Artillery.
(CONTINUED.)

NAMES.	MUSTERED IN.		MUSTERED OUT.		REMARKS.
ENLISTED MEN.					
Adams, Thomas					
Alston, James A					
Atkinson, Craven					Killed at Olustee, Feb. 20, '64.
Austen, M. D.					
Baker, Jacob A					Died February 24, '64 at Lake City, Fla.
Barron, Reuben T					
Barrow, Joseph F	Sept.	61	June 15,	'65	Wounded at Olustee, '64.
Barrow, J. R.					
Bernreuter, Charles J					Musician.
Bernreuter, Henry			June	'65	
Billingsly, G. W					
Bishop, B. L	Feb. 1	'62	May	'65	Slightly wounded at Olustee, Feb. 29, '64.
Bishop, Wm					Slightly wounded at Olustee, Feb. 20, '64.
Boyde, Thomas					
Bramlet, W. L.					
Brickie.					
Bunker, E. H.			May	'65	
Carn, David W	April	'62	May	'65	
Chestnut, A. D.					
Chestnut, John.					
Clem, Thomas V					
Combs, A. R.	April	'62			Promoted Sergeant.
Cone, A. D.					
Douglass, A. F.					
Eakin, George W	April 15,	'62			
Edmonson, Joseph A					
Edwards, O. C.	April	'62	May	'65	
English, J. C.					
English, Joseph H					
Floyd, W. H.	April	'62	May	'65	
Freeman, John W			May	'65	
Garwood, Charles					
Gilbert, A.					
Grambling, D. E.					
Grambling, M. A.					Artificer.
Hamrick, D. J.			May	'65	
Hancock, Josiah.					
Hinton, James H					Captured in N. C., sent to Camp Chase April 13, '65 and from there was paroled June 15, '65.
Hinton, S. S.	Sept.	'63			Discharged from Captain Lash's Company at Murfreesborough on account of disability; re-enlisted in Gamble's Artillery.
Hobby, Barney		'64	May	'65	
Hudnall, T. L.					
Johnson, Frank.					
Joiner, S. T.					
Jones, Alfred		'62	May	'65	
Lee, James.					
Martin, James P			May	'65	
Martin, Joseph.					
Mason, Adam W					
Mathis, Thomas Sr	April 15,	'62	May	'65	
Mathews, William.					Sergeant.
Montford, Joshua	April	'62	May	'65	
Myers, E. H.	April	'64	May	'65	
Nealy, Samuel W					
Neary, Thomas.					Wounded at Olustee.
Newman, J. J.					
McCants A. C.					Wounded at Olustee, Feb. 20, '64.
O'Conner, Dennis					
Odom, M. S.					
O'Neal, J. W.					
Pappy, Francisco B			May	'65	Promoted Sergeant.
Paterson, Hugh	Mch. 3,	'64	May	'65	
Paul, G. W.					
Purdy, J. E.					Artificer.
Renew, Moses G			May	'65	
Rhodes, J. J.					
Sauls, James D	Feb. 1,	'64	May	'65	Thrown from horse, in battle of Olustee, February 20, '64; left hip dislocated.
Sessions, L. M. C.					
Shepard, R. G.					Corporal.
Shilling, John.					
Simmons, William A. W			May	'65	
Skipper, J. G.					
Skipper, J. W.					
Smith, E. C.			May	'65	
Smith, M. B.					Killed at Olustee, Feb. 20, '64.
Smith, W. J.					
Taylor, J. L.			May	'65	
Stephens, Richard.					
Tounsend, C. L.					
Townsend, F. M.			May	'65	
Townsend, John A.					
Townsend, William H			May	'65	

Roll Capt. Charles E. E. Dyke's Light Artillery.

(CONTINUED.)

NAMES.	MUSTERED IN.	MUSTERED OUT.	REMARKS.
Van Brunt, J. C.			
Ward, Harvey			
Ward, Thomas			
Whitaker, John H.		May '65	
Wilson, Frank			
Wood, G. P.		May '65	

GAMBLE'S ARTILLERY.

Gamble's Artillery was organized in the spring of 1862. In November following the Battery was divided into two companies. Kilcreas was elected Captain of the second company with Patrick Houston as 1st Lieutenant. The Battery served at Johns Island, near Charleston, at Natural Bridge and various other places in Florida.

Roll Capt. R. H. Gamble's Light Artillery.

NAMES.	MUSTERED IN.	MUSTERED OUT.	REMARKS.
OFFICERS.			
Captains—			
Robert H. Gamble			Retired, '63.
F. L. Villepigue			1st Lieutenant; promoted Captain, when Gamble's Battalion was divided; resigned January 12, '65.
Patrick Houston			Sergeant; promoted 1st Lieutenant of Kilcrease's Artillery and on resignation of Villepigue, promoted Captain.
1st Lieutenant—			
John Williford			
2nd Lieutenant—			
——May			
3rd Lieutenant—			
——Forrest			
ENLISTED MEN.			
Albritton, J. T.			
Anderson, C. C.			
Anderson, Robert			
Atkinson, J. B.			
Babbitt, F. L.			
Ball, Willis			
Baldy, W. C.			
Barrington, Wilson			
Bennett, Reuben	June '63	May '65	
Bennett, T. R.			
Bennett, W. L.			
Berry, H. H.		May '65	
Berry, K. L.			
Blake, Charles F.			
Blanton, J. Elles		May '65	
Blanton, S. L.			
Boatwright, John B.			
Boyde, Thomas A.			
Braden, H. B.			
Branning, D. L.			
Britton, Jonathan W.			Transferred, Houston.
Brooks, B. F.			
Budd, J. T.			
Burton, C. M.			Corporal.
Butler, J. W.			
Byrd, B. F.			
Campbell, W. C.			
Carrell, W. C.			
Carpenter, E.			
Cardy, John			Sergeant.
Cavilley, Joseph			Artificer.
Chaires, Furman			Sergeant.
Chaires, S. P.			
Chaires, T. B.			
Chambers, Patrick B.	Mch. 23, '61	Mch. 20, '65	Wounded in Mississippi by Artillery wagon running over foot.
Clayton, A. B.	April '62	April '65	

Roll Capt. R. H. Gamble's Lignt Artillary.
(CONTINUED.)

NAMES.	MUSTERED IN	MUSTERED OUT.	REMARKS.
Clayton, W. J.			
Coles, John P.			Commissary Sergeant.
Collier, James S.	Mch. '65	April 20, '65	
Cox, John T.	Mch. 15,	April '65	
Dale, William O.			
Davenport, William			
Dawkins, Willis	Nov. '62	April '65	
Dearborn, Jackson			
Demilly, John F.			
Dudley, Spencer			
Duval, Philip S.			
Ecles, James			Deserted.
Edmondson, G. W.			
Edwards, James T.	May '62	May 15, '65	
Edwards, Samuel			
Ennis, William	Sept. '63	May '65	
Evans, Nathan P.			
Farrell, Norman			
Fenns, Josiah			
Findison, Charles A.			Musician.
Fisher, George H.			
Fisher, J. H.			
Fisher, William			...1st Sergeant.
Gamble, Albert M.			
Garrett, George W.			
Geriell, G. E.			Died of consumption March, '66.
Gwaltney, James H.	May '61	May '65	Transferred to Villepigue, then Houston's Co.
Hamilton, Hampton P.			
Hamilton, T. D.			
Hamilton, Thomas P.	April '62	May '65	
Hammond, S. T.			
Hampton, W. A.			
Haven, G. B.			
Harris, J. A.			
Hockett, John			Artificer.
Hogue, John H.			
Hopkins, Charles F.			Transferred to Infantry.
Horne, Henry M.	Mch. '63	May '65	
Horne, J. W.			
Horton, Levi			
Hutton, T. J.			
Jones, George L.			
Jones, Joseph			
Jones, William N.	Sept. 1, '62		
Kersey, E. J.			
Kilpatrick, J. W.			Transferred from Co. A, 15th Con. to Gamble's
Kindon, W. H.			Artillery.
Kirkpatrick, T. W.		April '65	
Lambert, Anthony			
LaTrobe, C. H.			
Laurence, Thomas W.			
Leonhard, H.			
Lewis, Jesse	Oct. '64		Corporal.
Lewis, P. R.			
Lynn, J. B.			Slightly wounded at O.ustee, Feb. 20, '64.
McLaughlin, E. B.			Artificer.
Mabry, W. M.			
Mabry, William W.	April 29, '62	April '65	
Markey, Thomas J.	May '64	April '65	
May, Alfred M.			
May, George A.		April '65	
May, J. C.			
May, William N.			
Meyer, John			
Miller, W. H.		April '65	
Moodie, E. J.	Feb. 16, '63	April '65	
Morris, James A.	Jan. 1, '62	April 65	Transferred,'64 to Kilcrease Battery.
Nally, Thomas H. C.			Died of disease October 20, '63.
Narzworth, J. Y.		April '65	
Nevin, John			
Nicholson, M. J.			
Norris, E. A.		April '65	
Owens, Edward		April '65	
Perry, W. H.		April '65	
Perry, J. W.		April '65	
Philips, R. F.			Sergeant.
Puller, Joseph			
Putnam, John			Wounded, Natural Bridge.
Randolph, T. P.			Corporal.
Richards, Jacob D.		April '65	
Richardson, Daniel		'62 April '65	
Richardson, David	May '62	April '65	
Rooney, J. A. J.			
Rye, Hosea F.	Mch. 2, '63	April '65	

Roll Captain R. H. Gamble's Light Artillery.
(CONTINUED.)

NAMES.	MUSTERED IN.	MUSTERED OUT.	REMARKS.
Saunders, J. R.			
Scurry, Grant			
Sellier, Charles F.			
Shaffer, Fred P.		April '65	
Simmons, William J.	May '62	April '65	
Slusser, Levi			
Smith, John J.			
Smith, S. N.	'62	May '65	
Stafford, J. J.			
Stafford, R. F.			
Stanaland, G. N.		May '65	
Strickland, E. C.			
Sutley, Absalom R.			Died March 30, '65.
Taylor, James H.			
Vann, James E.	Jan. '63		
Walker, D. S.			
Walker, J. J.			
Walker, P. J.			
Wheeler, J. H.		May '65	
Whistler, W. S.			
White, Littleton M.			
Williams, Mack	'62	May '65	
Williams, Robert M.		May '65	
Williams, Thomas F.			
Williford, John		May '65	
Wilson, R. D.		May '65	
Wolf, William W.			Corporal.
Womack, H. M.		May '65	

MARION LIGHT ARTILLERY.

Marion Light Artillery was organized May, 1861, and saw its first service on Amelia Island. In June, 1862, they were ordered to Dalton, Ga., and from there to East Tennessee, where they became a part of the Army of Gen. E. Kirby Smith. At the battle of Richmond, Ky. August 30, 1862, the Marion Light Artillery was the only Florida command present, where both officers and men were complimented for gallantry. On its return to Tennessee the battery was on post duty in East Tennessee, participating in only an occassional skirmish until September, 1863, when they joined the Army of General Bragg in North Georgia and took part in that campaign. They were engaged in the battles of Chickamauga and Missionary Ridge, and in 1864 went through the Atlanta and Nashville campaigns as a part of Col. Melancthon Smith's Artillery Battalion, attached to the Division of Gen. B. F. Cheathem. After the retreat from Tennessee the battery was stationed near Mobile, where it was engaged during the Federal advance in 1865. After the fall of Mobile the Battery was transferred to Gen. Richard Taylor's department, and surrendered at Meridian, Miss., in May, 1865.

Roll Marion Light Artillery.

NAMES.	MUSTERED IN.	MUSTERED OUT.	REMARKS.
OFFICERS			
Captains—			
John M. Martin	June '61		Resigned, '62, after he was wounded in Kentucky; then elected to Congress; then promoted Colonel of the 9th Infantry.
Robert P. McCants	June '61		2nd Lieutenant; promoted Captain; resigned, '63.
Thomas J. Parry	June '61	May 10, '65	Promoted Captain; shot at Dalton, Ga., in battle.

Roll Marion Light Artillery.
(CONTINUED.)

NAMES.	MUSTERED IN.	MUSTERED OUT.	REMARKS.
1st Lieutenants—			
J. J. Dickinson	June '61		Resigned May, '62.
A. J. Neal	June '61		3rd Lieutenant; Promoted 2nd Lieutenant, '62; then 1st Lieutenant, '63; killed '64,.
———— Davis	June '61	May 10, '65	3rd Lieutenant; promoted 2nd, then 1st Lieutenant.
2nd Lieutenant—			
William Tidwell	June '61		Promoted 2nd Lieutenant; killed at Richmond Ky.
3rd Lieutenants—			
———— Curry			Died, '62.
G. K. Broome	June '61	May 10, '65	Promoted 3rd Lieutenant.
ENLISTED MEN.			
Barrington, A. F.			
Bethel, John A			
Bennett, Richard G			
Blair, Richard			
Bostwick, James H	July '61		
Borring, John W			
Bradham, Henry			Transferred from Roland Thomas' Co., 7th Regiment; died of disease at Knoxville, Tenn., December 1, '62.
Brinson, James J	Dec. 15, '61		Shot at Dalton, Ga., May 9, '64.
Broadwater, Jonah S			
Brooker, Silas E	Sept. 10, '61	May 12, '65	
Broward, Pulaski			
Buford, Joseph C	Dec. 12, '61	May 10, '65	Wounded at Kennesaw Mountain, Ga., June 18, '64.
Cain, William D			
Carlton, Robert A			
Carman, Cornelius			
Coker, Wesley A			
Cook, Zedeceah			
Cooper, Andrew			
Cribb, Robert H	Nov. '61	May 10, '65	Wounded at Richmond, Ky., August, '62.
Crosby, Thomas W			
Curry, Edward			
Dozier, Leonard		May 10, '65	Promoted 2nd Sergeant.
Drew, L			
Driggers, Jasper J			
Driggers, John			
Dryden, W. T	May 10, '62	May 10, '65	Discharged August 20, '63, for disability; re-enlisted, '64, in A. A. Stewart's Co.
Dupree, Erastus D			
Dupree. Lucian D	Sept. '61		Corporal.
Dye, William T			
Fife, R. M.	Dec. 20, '61		
Geiger, John S	Dec. 12, '61	May 18, '65	
Goin, James M			
Going, Aaron S			
Gordon, Thomas W			1st Sergeant.
Graydon, Benjamin F			
Haddock, D. T.			
Haggaon, Thomas N	Jan. 1, '62		
Hammond, T. N			
Hammond, Samuel N			
Hartley, Joseph A	May 12, '62	May '65	Transferred, October, '62, to Captain Westcott's Co., Brevard's Co. Battalion.
Higgenbotham, S	Sept. '61	May '65	Wounded at Chickamauga, Ga.
Hilton, James M			
Holmes, Henry M			Sergeant.
Holshouser, William W			Corporal; promoted Sergeant; killed, '64.
Hogan, Daniel N	April 25, '62		Wounded at Nashville, Tenn., December 15, '64.
Hogans, Reuben			
Hogans, William J			
Hull, Benjamin A			
Hull, R. A	Oct. '61		
Ivey, Michael J			
Jenkins, Samuel T			
Johnston, Daniel J			
Johnston, Franklin A			
Johnson, James I			
Jones, Ormond			Sergeant.
Jordan, William E			
King, John			
King, William W			
Lane, Edmund B	Nov. 16, '61	May 16, '65	
Leitner, J. D			Sergeant.
Leitner, Willis F			
McBride, James		May '65	
McNabb, James W			
McNabb, Joshua N. G	July '61	May 10, '65	Sergeant.
McRory, Charles F		May '65	
Mabry, W. W		May '65	
Marlowe, T. C	Dec. '61	May '65	
Masters, Ben		May '65	
Mathews, John W			

Roll Marion Light Artillery.
(CONTINUED.)

NAMES.	MUSTERED IN.		MUSTERED OUT.		REMARKS.
Meadows, Jacob G.					
Mills, Samuel P.					
Minton, H. S.	May	'62	May	'65	
Minton, John S.					
Minton, J. T.			May	'65	
Mirandu, Thomas E.			May	'65	Wounded at Nashville December 15, '64.
Morrison, C. J.			May	'65	
Morrison, Daniel.					
Morrison, Hug A.	Dec. 12,	'61	May	'65	
Morrison, John B.					
Morrison, William J.					
Nobles, Edward.			May	'65	
Nobles, Nathaniel.					
Norton, N. B.			May	'65	
Norton, W. R.			May	'65	
Otes, D. Dunlap.					
Pasteur, George.					
Perry, Alexander H.					
Peters, Harris H.	June 15,	'61	May	'65	Wounded at Kennesaw Mountain, Ga.
Peterson, Henry.					
Riles, John.	April	'61	May	'65	
Plunkett, Elijah.					
Robertson, John N.					
Robertson, Jalez.					
Russell, R. R.			May	'65	
Saunders, Benjamin.	Jan. 15,	'62	May	'65	Wounded at Lovejoy, Ga., August 10, '64.
Seigler, John M.					
Simmons, W. A. W.			May	'65	
Smith, John H.	Mch.	'62			Killed near Marietta, Ga., August 18, '64.
Smith, Thomas J. H.					
Sparkman, Isaac.	April	'61	May 3,	'65	
Stevens, William C.			May	'65	
Strickland, John C.			April	'65	
Strickland, M. C.					Corporal.
Sturdevant, Joseph J.					
Swearengen, Samuel.			May	'65	
Taratus, M. H.	May 12,	'62	April 9,	'65	Wounded at Lovejoy, Ga.
Tillman, John E.			May	'65	
Timmons, S. E.	Oct. 17,	'61	May	'65	
Tracy, L. P.			May	'65	Corporal.
Wall, H. D.	April 15,	'62	May	'65	
Webb Franklin.	April 23,	'61	May	'65	
Willis, Joseph J.					
Zeigler, Joseph J.					

MORTON CONFEDERATES—CAPT. C. C. HENDERSON.

This c mpany was organized at Milton, Florida, in the spring of 1861. They were ordered to report at Memph's Tennessee, and were there mustered in as Co. C, of the 40th Tennessee Regiment, a regiment made up of four companies f om Arkansas, four from Alabama, one from Kentucky and Henderson's company from Florida, under command of Col. L. M. Walker. The Regiment later became the 5th Confederate Infantry. Co. C was stationed for some months at Fort Pillow, on the M ssissippi River; from there they were ordered to New Madrid, Mo., where they did garrison duty in the latter part of February, 1862, in anticipation of the Federal advance. After being under fire at New Madrid for some time, operations at the same time going on against Island No. 10, they were compelled to withdraw to the east side of the river, where the Confederate forces surrendered April 8, 1862. Captain Henderson, Lieutenant McMillan and five of his men succeeded in making their escape into the river swamps and eventually reached Fort Pillow. The rest of the command was imprisoned at Camp Butler, Ill., until September, 1862, when they were exchanged at Vicksburg, Miss. The company never reorganized, its term of enlistment having expired, the men jo ning other commands.

Roll Capt. C. C. Henderson's Company C—1st Mixed Regular Infantry.

NAMES.	MUSTERED IN.	MUSTERED OUT.	REMARKS.
OFFICERS.			
Captain—			
C. C. Henderson	'61		
1st Lieutenant—			
D. McMillan	'61		
2nd Lieutenants—			
Isaiah Cobb	'61		
George W. Harvey			
3rd Lieutenant—			
ENLISTED MEN.			
Bradley, W. W.			
Browning, C.			
Brooke, B.			
Brown, H. H.			
Brown, Jesse			
Brown, W. E.			
Bryant, James	'61		
Capers, G.			
Chance, H.			
Chance, J. H.			Sergeant.
Cobb, O.			
Cobb, S. R.			Sergeant.
Crawford, William	'61		
Cushing, J. P.	'61		
Cushing, W. B.	'61		
Dixon, C.	'61		
Dixon, W.	'61		
Fletcher, John	'61		
Foster, H.	'61		
Frater, H. F.	'61		
Grant, John	'61		
Grant, W. J.	'61		
Grimes, H. J.	'61		
Hall, Henry	'61		
Hall, James	'61		
Hardy, W. S.	'61		Sergeant.
Hasey, Isaac	'61		
Higgins, H.	'61		
Jones, Thomas	'61		
Jordan, E.	'61		Corporal.
Keer, John	'61		
McCauley, P.	'61		
McDuffie, J. A.	'61		
Miller, A. J.	'61		
Miller, E.	'61		
Miller, H.	'61		
Miller, H. H.	'61		
Morgan, John	'61		
Odum, J. A.	'61		
Parker, J. S. H.	'61		Corporal.
Peacock, E.	'61		
Pendleton, J.	'61		Corporal.
Pilcher, S. C.	'61		
Piner, G. W.	'61		
Riley, William	'61		
Sanders, N.	'61		
Shorter, Eli	'61		Corporal.
Smith, J. R.	'61		
Smith, S. H.	'61		
Sparrow, P. S.			Sergeant.
Strickland, J. L.	'61		
Strickland, R. S.	'61		
Strickland, S.	'61		
Villar, H.	'61		

MILTON ARTILLERY.

The Milton Light Artillery was raised in Apalachicola· in 1861 by J. L. Dunham with Lieutenants Abell senior 1st, Bull junior 1st, Stephens senior 2nd and Rambo junior 2nd; with ix guns, three 12 lb. brass rifle pieces and two 12 lb. Howitzers. In the spring of 1862 the Battery was ordered to

East Florida and camped near the Three Mile Branch, Jacksonville (Camp Finnegan). The company took part in the fight at St. Johns Bluff and the several engagements around Jacksonville. In the summer of 1863 the Milton Light Artillery was divided. Captain Dunham kept four of the guns, Abell was made Captain and was given the other two guns and two more were furnished him, making another four gun battery. Captain Dunham retained two of the Lieutenants, Bull and Rambo. Mortimer Bates was elected junior 2nd Lieutenant. Only a few months passed when Lieutenant Bull was killed by one Pickett in Lake City; Bates then came in command of the left section of one Battery. George Hines succeeded to the position of junior 2nd Lieutenant The section Bates commanded took part in the fight at Darby's Hill (McClenney). A part of the company took part in the battle of Olustee, Natural Bridge, and Bates' section did effective service on the St. Johns, aiding in capturing the Columbine and doing much damage to the Ottawa and another steamer at Horse Landing on the St. Johns. The Battery was a fine one and had it been in Virginia or in the Western Army would have made a name that the State would have been proud of; as it was both companies, A and B of the Milton Artillery, did splendid service and are entitled to as much credit as their more fortunate comrades who won honors at the battle front in the great contests of the war.

Roll Battery A—J. L. Dunham's Light Artillery.

NAMES.	MUSTERED IN.	MUSTERED OUT.	REMARKS.
OFFICERS.			
Captain—			
Joseph L. Dunham			
1st Lieutenants—			
Henry F. Abel			When Dunham's Battery was divided Abel was made Captain of the 2nd division
Mortimer W. Bates			Promoted 2nd Lieutenant, then 1st Lieutenant.
2nd Lieutenant—			
Drury Rambo			
3rd Lieutenants—			
Simon K. Bull			Murdered near Jacksonville, '02.
Charles F. Stevens			Succeeded Bull.
ENLISTED MEN.			
Adams, Thomas H			Corporal.
Aiken, James A			
Allen, J. C			Guidon.
Amerson, Ferinand			Artificer.
Andrews, Joel R			
Armestead, George			
Armstrong, George M			
Atkins, James A			
Bailey, John V			Corporal.
Barman, John			
Barman, Oliver F			
Bender, William			
Benton, Alexander			
Benton, John W			
Benteza, Waukeen			
Bishop, Benjamin F			
Blanket, Joseph			
Blocker, R. C	Sept. '63	April '65	
Branch, Henry B			
Brown, James			
Burnes, Mathew			
Butler, Job			
Butler, John			

Roll Battery A---J. L. Dunham's Light Artillery.
(CONTINUED,)

NAMES.	MUSTERED IN	MUSTERED OUT.	REMARKS.
Carson, L. D. Dr			
Carraway, Taylor			
Carter, James			Corporal.
Chance, Stephen			Sergeant.
Costa, Thomas			
Couchman, John W			
Croghan, John			
Davis, John W			
Dermont, Nicholas		April '65	Transferred to Navy.
Dubber, Cornelius			
Duffin, Philip D			Corporal.
Dykes, Jacob. Jr			
Edge, John B			
Edwards, John G			
Flanders, Robert H			Sergeant.
Floyde, Gabriel J			
Ganus, William			
Goodman, Marion			
Glover, William H			
Grady, Cornelius			
Grierson, William A			1st Sergeant.
Gump, Gustavo			
Hare, Harrison			Corporal.
Hays, Samuel N			
Hill, R. J	May 20, '64	April '65	
Holts, Russell			
Jackson, Jerry H			
Jackson, S. O			
Johnson, Daniel R			
Johnson, George B			Corporal.
Johnson, James M			
Johnson, John W			
Jones, Evan			
Justice, John D. K			
Justice, John W			
Justice, William B			
Keenan, James			
Keen, James			
Keen, Thomas	Feb. '62	April '65	Lost right arm by Railroad April, '02.
Keen, William R			
Kirkland, Guilford	May '62		
Lovett, Patrick		April '65	Corporal.
Lovett, Peter		April '65	
Long, David N			
Lore, Jefferson			
Luchandi, Manuel			
McArdle, Augustus			
McDaniel, J. M			Artificer.
McDonough, Roger			
McDonough, Michael J			
Maloy, James E			
Marshall, George			
Massena, Antone		April '65	
Massina, D		April '65	
Massina, Frank			
Massina, John			
Messer, Joel			
Mercer, Julius C			
Miller, Asbury W			
Miller, Henry C			
Miller, John			
Miller, Mason C			
Mulard, Gaspar			
Murat, Antone J		April '61	Corporal.
Murphy, Alexander N			
Nidley, James			
Oaks, Napolean B			
O'Brien, Gabriel F			Sergeant.
O'Neal, James E			
O'Neal, Samuel G			Corporal.
Pagan, Joseph			
Palingguist, Francis P			
Penn, James P			
Perry, Henry B			
Powell, Benjamin F			Sergeant.
Powell, James		April 26 '65	Shot in chin in Georgia, '63.
Powel, John	61	April 26, '65	
Powell, W. P	'61	April 26, '65	
Provansana, Mario			Wounded at Fisher and disabled; transferred to Navy.
Quincis, Salvador		April 26, '65	
Raickmeyr Robert		April 26, '65	
Richards. Raleigh			
Roan Joseph			

Roll Battery A—J. L. Dunham's Light Artillery.
(CONTINUED.)

NAMES.	MUSTERED IN.	MUSTERED OUT.	REMARKS.
Robinson, John M			Artificer.
Rogers, Eugene W			
Rogers, John		April 26, '65	
Rowlett, Daniel			
Rudd, Jeffry			
Ryan, William R			Sergeant.
Sangregonia, Veto		April 26 '65	
Schollio, Philip		April 26, '65	
Schwartz, Jacob			Corporal.
Sia, Joseph			
Simpson, John			
Smith, Charles W			
Smith, John H			
Stanfield, Jasper			
Stephens, William			
Summers, Daniel J			
Ulrich, John			
Warrick, Gustav			
Whigham, Joseph M			
Whigham, Madison W			
Whiddon, Bennett S	Oct. 6, '62	April '65	
Whiddon, William E			
Wilbur, Charles H			Corporal.
Wilkes, Thomas J			Corporal.
Williams, Antone			
Witherspoon, T. J	Sept. '61	April '65	
Wood, J. S		April '65	
Wooten, Josiah			Sergeant.
Yates, James			
Yates, James M		April '65	

Roll H. F. Abell's Light Artillery.

NAMES.	MUSTERED IN.	MUSTERED OUT.	REMARKS.
OFFICERS.			
Captain—			
Henry F. Abell			
1st Lieut'enant—			
Joseph W. Allen	April 15, '63		Promoted 1st Lieutenant from 2nd Lieutenant.
2nd Lieutenant—			
3rd Lieutenant—			
Josephus Averitt			
ENLISTED MEN.			
Barrentine, Stephen			
Beach, Charles L			Artificer.
Binton, Alexander			
Bowles, William H			
Bradley, George K	Aug. '63	April '65	
Brown, Absolam			
Bruce, Donald			Corporal.
Clark, William			
Collins, J. H			Promoted 1st Sergeant.
Cox, William L			
Craven, James			
Crawford, Richard H. W			Corporal.
Crawford, William H			Corporal.
Gashan, Anthony			
Gill, William H	April 1, '63	April 26, '65	
Griffin, George D			Wounded at Natural Bridge.
Harrison, Francis			Bugler.
Humor, William			
Humphrey, John			
Johnson, Emory			Bugler.
Kenton, James M			
Kirkland, Guilford			
McLane, William			
Malphurs, Joseph W		April 26, '65	Lost great toe by railroad accident.
Mann, Robert D			
Minton, William R	'62	April 26, '64	Wounded at Natural Bridge, Fla., March 6, '65
Murat, A. J		April 26, '65	
O'Brien, Gabrie			Deserted; took oath of allegience.
O'Neal, Henry E			
Perry, Elijah J	July 28 '63	April 26, '65	Shot at Olustee, Fla., February 1, '64.
Pewitt, Josiah L			
Powell, Edward		April 26, '65	

Roll H. F. Abell's Light Artillery.
(CONTINUED.)

NAMES.	MUSTERED IN.	MUSTERED OUT.	REMARKS.
Powell, James			
Powell, John			
Powell, William			
Simmons, Elijah	'63	April 26, '65	
Stanley, Ned J.			Died in prison.
Strange, Shackelford			
Stofe·, Alonzo F.			Sergeant.
Swain, Henry C.			Artificer.
Thomas, Mathew	Aug. 1, '63	April 26, '65	Hearing injured at Olustee, Fla.. February 20, '64.
Trimmer, W. H.		Apri 26, '65	Discharged from Fort Delaware.
Warren, Marshall			
Whidden, Bennett S.			
Whidden, Daniel B.			

Roll, Field and Staff—1st Florida Reserves.

NAMES.	MUSTERED IN.	MUSTERED OUT.	REMARKS.
Colonel—			
J. Jacqueline Daniels			
Lieutenant-Colonel—			
William D. Barnes			
Major—			
William H. Dial			
Surgeons—			
Assistant Surgeons—			
Adjutants—			
F. F. L'Engle, Lt. and Adj			
J. B. Blackwell			
Sergeant Major—			
Quartermaster—			
Commissary—			
Chaplains—			
Quartermaster-Sergeants—			
Commissary-Sergeants—			
Hospital Steward—			

Roll Company A—1st Florida Reserves.

NAMES.	MUSTERED IN.	MUSTERED OUT.	REMARKS.
OFFICERS.			
Captain—			
Isaac B. Nichols			
1st Lieutenant—			
2nd Lieutenant—			
3rd Lieutenant—			
ENLISTED MEN.			
Bauknight, A. B.	May '64		
Blackwell Jesse G.	Mch. 31, '64		Promoted Adjutant of Regiment; wounded while chasing deserters between Live Oak and Jasper.
Cassels, Samuel V.	Mch. '64		
Chesser, G. D.			
Haddock, Z. T.	April 1, '64	April 9, '65	
Harvall, D. G.			
Harvard, D. G.			
Johnson, D. W.			
McPhifer, D.		April 9, '65	
Mixon, Charles B.	April 30, '64	April 9, '65	With Company H, 2nd Cavalry.

Roll Company A—1st Florida Reserves.
(CONTINUED.)

NAMES.	MUSTERED IN.	MUSTERED OUT.	REMARKS.
Mixon, W. H.		April 9, '65	
Patterson, W. R.			
Peacock, Willis		April 9, '65	
Reddick, J. P.		April 9, '65	
Russell David Y.	May 12, '63	April 9, '65	
Tillman, William D.	May '64		Discharged December, '64, at Lake City.

Roll Company B—1st Florida Reserves.

NAMES.	MUSTERED IN.	MUSTERED OUT.	REMARKS.
OFFICERS.			
Captain—			
J. B. Spencer			Served to close of the war.
1st Lieutenant—			
J. G. Blackwell			1st Lieutenant and Adjutant.
ENLISTED MEN.			
Averett, B. F.			
Averett, J. E.			
Barker, W. H.			
Barrington, Hezekiah E.			
Blair, Henry A.		May '65	
Bland, James			
Brock, James A.	Jan. '64	May '65	
Bryan, Milton J.			
Cason, W. C.			
Cheshire, M. T.			
Creekmore, A. R.	Mch. '64	May '65	
Delough, Edward	April '64		
Dempsey, Mathew W.	June 20, '63		
Dorman, B. B.	Mch. 15, '64		Discharged March 15, '65,;for disability.
Dupree, George W.	May '64	May '65	
Ellis, J. B.			Wounded, Natural Bridge.
Frier, Joshua			
Gardner, William T.	April 64		
Gibbs, James	Mch. '64	May '65	
Gibbs, Shaderick	April 1, '64		
Green, S. A.			
Hall, Nehemiah			
Harrel, John J.			
Helvington, James H.			
Hunt, John W.		May '65	
Johns, Henry			
Jones, C.			
Jones, S. M.		May '65	
Leigh, Phileman			
Meeks, Green A.		May '65	
Meeks, H. C.		May '65	
Polhill, T. A.		May '65	
Reeves, Jonathan		May '65	
Shiver, James A.		May '65	
Stendwell, C. H.		May '65	
Walston, W. F.			
White, George C.	'64	May '65	
White, James L.		May '65	Accidentally shot in left arm June, '64.
Willis, J. J.			
Willis, J. W.		May '65	
Wilson, Alex.		May '65	
Wilson, Alfred	'64	May '65	
Wilson, J. J.		May '65	
Wilson, R. W.		May '65	

Roll Company C—1st Florida Reserves.

NAMES.	MUSTERED IN.	MUSTERED OUT.	REMARKS.
OFFICERS.			
Captain—			
W. W. Poe.			
1st Lieutenant—			

Roll Company C—1st Florida Reserves.
(CONTINUED.)

NAMES.	MUSTERED IN.	MUSTERED OUT.	REMARKS.
2nd Lieutenant—			
3rd Lieutenant—			
ENLISTED MEN.			
Anderson, John L.	May '64		Wounded at Natural Bridge; discharged from pri-
Bates, James M.			son at Elmira, N. Y., March, '65.
Belser, Stephen T.			
Bevis, William	May 12, '64	May '65	
Bevis, Win.			
Carroll, John S.			
Floyd, B. S.			
Ford, W. J.			
Johnson, James D.	May 12, '64	May '65	
Johnson, J. I.			
Lanier, G. A.			
Lanier, John.	May '64	May 20, '65	
McDonald, W. L.		May '65	
Maer, William E	April '64	May 20, '65	
Neel, Henry C.		May '65	
Nichols, Alfred	Aug. 15, '64	May '65	
Oswald, R. E.		May '65	
Parish, J. H.		May '65	
Tidwell, W. J.	May 12, '64	May '65	Discharged October 1, '64 for disability.

Roll Company D—1st Florida Reserves.

NAMES.	MUSTERED IN.	MUSTERED OUT.	REMARKS.
OFFICERS.			
Captain—			
John H. Bryant			
1st Lieutenant—			
2nd Lieutenant—			
Thomas T. McDaniel	May '64		Promoted 2nd Lieutenant.
3rd Lieutenant—			
ENLISTED MEN.			
Acree, Samuel	June 1, '64		
Barrington, Hezekiah E.	April 15, '64		Promoted Corporal.
Bell, George W.			
Bryant, T. J.			
Burnett, James.			
Burnett, Richard.			
Caruth, William			
Cornett, William M.			
Cottingham, Elkanah.			
Deas, Bryant M.	'62		
Deas, Joseph.	'62		
Drew, M. C.			
Fletcher, Napoleon B.	July '64		
Fletcher, Reuben.			Accused of desertion.
Gaston, Alex.	May 15, '64		Died at Lake City, Fla., September 30, '64 from disease.
Ginn, Charles W.			Mortally wounded at Olustee February 20, '64 and died in two weeks at Lake City, Fla.
Gramling, A. Walker.			
Gramling, William A.	May '64		
Grinstead, Duncan E.			
Henderson, H. B.	April '64		Discharged November 12, '64 for disability.
Hickey, Jefferson C.	June 15, '64		
Hunt, Josiah H.			
James, Reuben.			
Jackson, Golden.	'63		
Knowles, R. A.			
Land, G. W.	July 18, '64		
Land, H.			
Land, Henry W.			
Land, W.			
Lewis, James J.	May '63		Promoted Lieutenant, Co. A; discharged February 28, '65, for consumption.
Loper, A. J.			
McAlpin, D. M.	April 15, '64	May 15, '65	
McCollough, John F.		May 15, '65	
McKinney, Madison.	April '64	April 10, '65	
Owens, Joseph P.		April 10, 65	
Page, S. H.	June '64	April 10, '65	
Peek, O. F.		April 10, '65	
Pert, J. J.		April 10, '65	

Roll Company D—1st Florida Reserves.
(CONTINUED.)

NAMES.	MUSTERED IN.	MUSTERED OUT.	REMARKS.
Peterson, Timothy,		April 10, '65	
Pridgehan, John E.		April 10, '65	
Sullivan, J.		April 10, '65	
Webb, J. P.		April 10, '65	
Webb, L.		April 10, '65	
Willis, J. D.	May '64	April 10, '65	

Roll Company E—1st Florida Reserves.

NAMES.	MUSTERED IN.	MUSTERED OUT.	REMARKS.
OFFICERS.			
Captain—			
Wilson D. Tuberville	May 15, '63	April '65	Promoted Captain.
1st Lieutenant—			
2nd Lieutenant—			
3rd Lieutenant—			
ENLISTED MEN.			
Alford, E. H.			
Alligood, William	May '62		
Anderson, M. B.			
Boyd, W. H.	April '64		
Bradshaw, W. J.			
Core, G. W.			
Crump, John R.	Aug. '64		Discharged '64 for disability.
Demilly, W. A.			
Edwards, H. K.			
Felkel, H. T.			
Ferrell, W. B.			
Forbes, R. B.	'64		
Gwaltney, J. H.			
Hamlin, Wells	'62	May '65	Reenlisted in Captain Tuberville's Co.
Hinson, John J.	'64	May 15, '65	
Hodge, B. B.	May '64		
Horn, John Thomas	Mch. '64	May 15, '65	Wounded at Natural Bridge by explosion of bomb.
Hulberson, M. B.			
Joyner, W. B.			
Linzey, Moses	Mch. 15, '65		Discharged April 1, '65, for disability.
Pelt, Durant		May 15, '65	
Pigott, S. T.		May 15, '65	
Priest, C. C.		May 15, '65	
Reynolds, John I.	'64	May 15, '65	
Roach, Charles W.		May 15, '65	
Roberts, Leonidas	May 1, '64	May 15, '65	
Roddenbery, Sampson		May 15, '65	
Skipper, C. H.		May 15, '65	
Stafford, S. T.		May 15, '65	

Roll Company F—1st Florida Reserves.

NAMES.	MUSTERED IN.	MUSTERED OUT.	REMARKS.
OFFICERS.			
Captain—			
Wiley A. Barwick			
1st Lieutenant—			
2nd Lieutenant—			
3rd Lieutenant—			
ENLISTED MEN.			
Bishop, James L.	Mch. '64		
Bishop, J. N.			
Bishop, Martin			
Bozeman, Elishua W.			Died at home while on furlough November 24, '64.
Grubbs, John			Killed at Natural Bridge, Fla., March, '65.
Hamrick, J. M.	Mch. 5, 64		

Roll Company F—1st Florida Reserves.
(CONTINUED.)

NAMES.	MUSTERED IN.	MUSTERED OUT	REMARKS.
Hartsfield, Jake F.	June '64		
Henry, C. W.			
Hodges, J. R.	'64	May '65	
Huggins, J. T.			
Kinney, Russell.	Mch. '64		
Lee, J. S.			
Letchworth, Thomas G.	May '64		Wounded at Natural Bridge March, '65.
Lightsey, Henry.			
Martin, Samuel.	'62	May 20, '65	
May, M. S.		May 20, '65	
Odom, Samuel.			Wounded at Natural Bridge.
Patterson, William R.	June '62	June '65	
Porter, Joseph C.		June 20, '65	
Standley, W. E.	May '62	June 20, '65	Wounded on way to Natural Bridge by falling from a car.
Thomas, W. C.		June 20, '65	
Tindale, Jeremiah.			Discharged for disability.
Woods, W. H. A.		June 20, '65	

Roll Company G—1st Florida Reserves.

NAMES.	MUSTERED IN.	MUSTERED OUT.	REMARKS.
OFFICERS.			
Captain—			
—— Hawkins			
1st Lieutenant—			
2nd Lieutenant—			
3rd Lieutenant—			
ENLISTED MEN.			
Arnold, Daniel J.	May 1, '63	May 10, '65	
Bell, Benjamin.	May 10, '64		Lost hearing from explosion of a bomb at Natural Bridge.
Dortch, David J.	Mch. '64		
Harvey, Jesse W.			
Hodges, H. J.	July '64	May 10, '65	
Hoover, W. T.			
Jones, Calhoun.			
Lock, David.	Jan. '64	May '65	
Motes, David.	'64	May '65	
Roberts, John F.	July 1, 64	April 26, 65	
Thomas, W. C.		April 26, '65	

Roll Company I—1st Florida Reserves.

NAMES.	MUSTERED IN.	MUSTERED OUT.	REMARKS.
OFFICERS.			
Captain—			
Green B. Hodges.			
1st Lieutenant—			
2nd Lieutenant—			
Joshua A. Jones.	April '64	May '65	Promoted 2nd Lieutenant; shot at No. 4, near Cedar Keys, Fla., July, '64.
3rd Lieutenant—			
ENLISTED MEN.			
Adkins, E. N.	May 8, '64	May '65	
Alderman, Daniel A.	May '64	June 3, '65	
Alvarez, Drew.			
Alvarez, O. M.			
Alvarez, Roman.			
Baker, E. C.	May '64		
Brown, Isham.			
Conner, William.	May '64	June 3, '65	Lost left leg from fall through tressel near St. Marks, August 10, '64.
Douglas, F. H.			
Dukes, M. W.	Mch. 20, '64		
Durrance, Nathan B.			
Hodges, E. D.			
Hutchinson, Joseph F.	'64	May '65	

Roll Company I—1st Florida Reserves.
(CONTINUED.)

NAMES.	MUSTERED IN.	MUSTERED OUT.	REMARKS.
Kelley, Samuel B.			
Parish, H. M.		May '65	
Reddick, Drew	April 18, '64		Died April 20, '65.
Reeves, J. W.	June '64	May '65	
Rimes, J. M.		May '65	
Sheffield, James K.	April '64	May 18, '65	
Simmons, Charles T.	May '64	May '65	
Simmons, John F.			Wounded at Natural Bridge March, '65.
Walker, E.		April 9, '65	

Roll Company K—1st Florida Reserves.

NAMES.	MUSTERED IN.	MUSTERED OUT.	REMARKS.
OFFICERS.			
Captain—			
Joshua L. McGahagin	May '64	April '65	
1st Lieutenant—			
John W. Jeffords	May '64		
2nd Lieutenant—			
John M. Graham		April '65	
3rd Lieutenant—			
James Gore	May '64		
ENLISTED MEN.			
Adams, James	May '64		Died in hospital.
Agnew, Enoch W	May '64	April '65	2nd Corporal.
Beal, Moses	May '64		
Beal, Toss	May '64	April '65	
Blair, William	May '64	April '65	
Brantley, William	May '64	April '65	
Brinson, James S	May '64	April '65	
Brooks, Frederick			
Buckston, Littleton	May '64	April '65	
Caldwell, F. E.	May '64		
Carroll, Benjamin	May '64		
Caruthers, Wiley	May '64	April '65	
Caruthers, Reuben	May '65	April '65	
Colding, George W	May '64		Sergeant.
Colding, William	May '64	April '65	
Ellis, Isham	May '64		Deserted.
Ellis, John	May '64		Deserted.
Fort, Isaiah J	May '64		
Gaskins, William	May '64	April '65	
Gerald, Henry	May '64	April '65	
Granger, Hugh	May '64	April '65	
Holley, Alexander	May '64	April '65	1st Corporal.
Hall, William	May '64	April '65	
Harvey, Jasper	May '64	April '65	
Hill, John	May '64	April '65	
Hull, Benjamin J	May '64	April '65	Sergeant.
Hull, James E. B	May 28, '64	April '65	
Johnson, Frank C	May '64	April '65	
Leitner, Pierce B	May '64	April '65	
Luker, Alfred	May '64	April '65	
McGahagin, William E	May '64	April '65	2nd Sergeant.
Ma.., Elbert	May '64	April '65	
Manning, John	May '64		Deserted.
Manning, Johnathan	May '64		
Marsh, Henry	May '64	April '65	
Marsh, Joseph	May '64	April '65	
Morrison, Daniel W	May '64		Died in hospital.
Perry, Joshua	May '64	April '65	
Perry, Preston	May '64		
Perry, William	May '64		
Rainer, Hardy	May '64	April '65	
Roach, John	May '64		Corporal.
Ross, George J	May '64	April '65	
Russell, Ichabod	May '64	April '65	
Saddler, William	May '64	April '65	
Scott, J. Warren	May '64	April '65	1st Sergeant.
Smith, Marshall	May '64	April '65	
Smith, Rufus H	May '64	April '65	
Turner, William	May '64	April '65	
Turner, William C., Jr	May '64	April '65	
Weaver, Bryant	May '64	April '65	
Weaver, Jackson	May '64	April '65	
Williams, John D	May '64	April '65	Sergeant.
Williamson, Paul	May '64		Died in hospital.
Williamson, Thomas	May '64	April '65	
Worey, Jacob	May '64	April '65	

Roll Company L—1st Florida Reserves.

NAMES.	MUSTERED IN.	MUSTERED OUT.	REMARKS.
OFFICERS.			
Captain—			
S. S. Gilchrist	.... '64	....	
1st Lieutenant—			
2nd Lieutenant—			
3rd Lieutenant—			
ENLISTED MEN.			
Causseaux, W. W.	June '64	May 15, '65	
Dunaway Samuel H.			
Edwards, W. W.	May '64	May 15, '65	
Floyd, Theophilus	Mch. 15, '64	April 15, '65	
Gatlin, R. D.			
Green, Thomas	Jan. '65		
Gunn, William	June 3, '64		Promoted Corporal.
Haygood, Richard R.	June '64	May '65	
Hinson, D M			
Johnson, A. J.			
Kemp, J. B.			
McDougal, Archibald N	June '64	May 15, '65	
McIntosh Augustus L.	April 1, '64	May 15, '65	
McPhail, J. D.		May 15, '65	
Martin, M. L.		May '65	
Mitchell, Thomas		May '65	
Rudd, Elias J.	April '64	May 15, '65	
Shaw, L. W.		May '65	
Strange, S. S.		May '65	
Todd, William	June 8, '64	May '65	
Waldon, Orvin		May '65	

Roll Company . .—1st Florida Reserves.

NAMES.	MUSTERED IN.	MUSTERED OUT.	REMARKS.
OFFICERS.			
Captain—			
James W. Faulkner	....	....	
1st Lieutenant—			
2nd Lieutenant—			
3rd Lieutenant—			
ENLISTED MEN.			
Adams, F. M.			
Faulkner, A. J.	May '64		Served 12 months in 1st Fla. Regiment at Pensa-
Gunter, Thomas L.	April '64		cola and reenlisted in this Co.
Henderson, William C.	'64	April '65	
Hodges, Ezekiel			
Mathis, M. C.	June 15, '64	May 20, '65	
Parker, Miles W		April '65	
Smith, S. N.	April '64	April 20, '65	
Wilder, J. M.		April 20, '65	

Roll Company . .—1st Florida Reserves.

NAMES.	MUSTERED IN.	MUSTERED OUT.	REMARKS.
OFFICERS.			
Captain—			
Sim Manning			
1st Lieutenant—			
J. L. Brooks			Promoted 1st Lieutenant.
2nd Lieutenant—			
3rd Lieutenant—			
ENLISTED MEN.			
Hartsfield, William			

Roll Company .. —1st Florida Reserves.
(CONTINUED.)

NAMES.	MUSTERED IN.	MUSTERED OUT.	REMARKS.
High, J. P.	Aug. '63	April 9, '65	
McClellan, J. L.		April 9, '65	
Palmer, J. Dabney	'62	April 9, '65	
Townsend, Charles	May 8, '64	April 9, '65	
Walker, J. E.		April 9, '65	
Woods, W. H. A.			

Roll Company .. —2nd Florida Reserves.

NAMES.	MUSTERED IN.	MUSTERED OUT.	REMARKS.
OFFICERS.			
Captain—			
Samuel Agnew			
1st Lieutenant—			
ENLISTED MEN.			
Agnew, E. W.			
Brooks, Thomas			
Godwin, J. J.	Sept. '63		
Harvey, William J.	'64	May '65	
Johns, James W.			
Johnson, Ezekiel			
Johnson, Mikel L.	July '63		Wounded at Cedar Keys, Fla.
Mundon, Isaac		May '65	
Pasteur, John		May '65	
Pedrick, Thomas		May '65	Wounded by explosion of shell at Chattanooga,
Peterson, Charles		May '65	Tenn., '64.

Roll Company A—Florida Militia.

NAMES.	MUSTERED IN.	MUSTERED OUT	REMARKS
OFFICERS.			
Captain—			
L. M. Gamble			
1st Lieutenant—			
2nd Lieutenant—			
3rd Lieutenant—			
ENLISTED MEN.			
Barineau, B. M.	'64	May '65	
Collins, Jeremiah	Oct. 7, '62		
Condry, W. G.			
Farrier, John L.	Oct. '63	May 20, '65	
Owens, R. W.		May '65	

Roll Company B—1st Confederate Battalion.

NAMES.	MUSTERED IN.	MUSTERED OUT.	REMARKS.
OFFICERS.			
Captain—			
J. M. Johnson			Died at Mobile, Ala, May, '81.
1st Lieutenant—			
Joseph Moore			Died during the war at Fort Pillow, Tenn.
2nd Lieutenant—			
3rd Lieutenant—			
ENLISTED MEN.			
Davis, Thomas	Oct. 10, '61		Wounded at Corinth, Miss., '62.
Delmar, Eugene	'61		Wounded at Fort Pillow, Tenn., August, '62 from explosion of shell, captured and paroled from prison at close of war.
Hugon, Benjamin J.	Sept. '61		Wounded at the Wilderness May 6, '64.

Roll Company B—1st Confederate Battalion.
(CONTINUED.)

NAMES.	MUSTERED IN.	MUSTERED OUT.	REMARKS.
Moore, W. H.			Shot at Petersburg October 1, '64; paroled at close of the war.
Capers, G. C.			
Capers, J. O.			
Delacy, Andrew	May '64		
Johnson, J. E.			
Joseph, Antonio	'61	May '65	
Mouley, W. H.		May '65	

Roll Capt. John T. Leslie's Company—Munnerlyn's Battalion.

NAMES.	MUSTERED IN.	MUSTERED OUT.	REMARKS.
OFFICERS.			
Captain—			
John T. Leslie			
1st Lieutenant—			
2nd Lieutenant—			
3rd Lieutenant—			
ENLISTED MEN.			
Casey, Joseph	June '63		
Collins, John			
Davis, Irvin	May '63	May '65	
Hawkins, John W			
Henderson, W. B.			
Hopson, Allen J.	Sept. '62		Ran over by government wagon and ruptured.
Jones, Mitchell	June '64	May '65	Transferred to Captain John Parson's Co.
Jones, Redding B.	April '62	May '65	
Jordan, Henry	'63	May '65	
Lanier, J. H.			
McClelland, J. L.			Discharged, under age; reenlisted, Captain Hendry's Co.
Mooney, John		May '65	
Platt, William	'63	July '65	
Prine, James E.	June '63	July '65	Discharged for disability.
Sloan, Daniel		July '65	
Wells, G. W.		July '65	
Wilson, R. M.		July '65	

NAMES.	MUSTERED IN.	MUSTERED OUT.	REMARKS.
Captain—			
W. W. Wall			
ENLISTED MEN.			
Darby, John W			
Hope, W. M.			

NAMES.	MUSTERED IN.	MUSTERED OUT.	REMARKS.
Captain—			
C. F. Stubbs			
ENLISTED MEN.			
Blount, William			
Blount, William O. I.			
Blount, W. S. T.			
Burnett, J. H.			
Rogers R. F.			Mustered out at close of war.

NAMES.	MUSTERED IN.	MUSTERED OUT.	REMARKS.
Captain—			
W. B. Watson			
ENLISTED MEN.			
Blitch, F. W	'63		Paroled at close of war.
Britch, J. G.			
McMullen, David		April '65	

Roll Capt. E. J. Lutterloh's Company—Independent Cavalry.

NAMES.	MUSTERED IN.	MUSTERED OUT.	REMARKS.
OFFICERS.			
Captain—			
E. J. Lutterloh			
1st Lieutenant—			
2nd Lieutenant—			
James A. Brock	April 15, '61		
3rd Lieutenant—			
ENLISTED MEN.			
Beach, John L			
Bush, Jeptha	April 15, '61		
Cannon, Madison			
Dotson, W. J			
Faircloth, Daniel D			
Hardee, J. S			
Hatcher, Isham	'62	April '65	
Hines, Isaac			
Holder, William D			
Hogans, Daniel B	'63		Discharged in '64, for disability.
Hudson, S. W			
Leavett, George S			
Osteen, Solomon	Aug. 1, '64	April '65	
Philpot, Thomas W	July '64	April '65	Shot at No. 4, near Cedar Keys.
Rucker, B. F		April '65	
Sheppard, Simeon A		April '65	
Slaughter, C. L		April '65	
Turner, J. S		April '65	
Townsend, John H	July 15, '64	April '65	
Watson, W. J	Sept. '63	April '65	
Wood, J. W	Aug. 1, '64		

Roll Capt. E. A. Fernandez' Company—Detached Cavalry.

NAMES.	MUSTERED IN.	MUSTERED OUT.	REMARKS.
OFFICERS.			
Captain—			
E. A. Fernandez			
1st Lieutenant—			
2nd Lieutenant—			
3rd Lieutenant—			
ENLISTED MEN.			
Campbell, J. W	Sept. 1, '64	May '65	
Cook, Bryant	Jan. 1, '63	May '65	
Harrell, H. S			
Harris, P. M			
Johnson, Green	Feb. '65		Wounded accidentally at New Troy, Fla., March 15, '65.
Ogden, W. H		May '65	
Price, G. W		May '65	
Smith, E		May '65	

Roll Capt. F. A. Hendry's Company—Independent Cavalry.

NAMES.	MUSTERED IN.	MUSTERED OUT.	REMARKS.
OFFICERS.			
Captain—			
F. A. Hendry			
1st Lieutenant—			
2nd Lieutenant—			
3rd Lieutenant—			
ENLISTED MEN.			
Blount, Benjamin F			
Blount, J. J			
Brooker, E			
Durrance, John R	April 1, '63	April '65	
Flint, William R	'64	April '65	Shot accidentally by comrade of same Co.
Green, James	'64		
Hendry, W. M			
Keen, E. B	July 13, '64	April '65	
Pearce, P. S		April '65	

Roll Capt. F. A. Hendry's Company---Independent Cavalry.
(CONTINUED.)

NAMES.	MUSTERED IN.	MUSTERED OUT	REMARKS.
Rainey, Joseph	'63	April '65	
Sapp, John	May '64	May '65	
Summerlin, Jasper		April '65	
Wiggins, R. C.	June 15, '64	April '65	Wounded while guarding a vessel at Bay Port, Fla

THE NAVY IN FLORIDA.

A steamer named the Spray was fitted up as a war vessel and did very efficient service along the Gulf coast. On May 10, 1861, the Spray attacked the United States schooner William C. Atwate, manned with 31 men, off Cedar Keys. The Atwater was taken into Appalachicola and converted into a blockade runner. It was captured in January, 1862, by he United States steamer Itasca. In June, 1861, the privateer "Jefferson Davis," a small brig with letters of marque from the Confederate Government, sailed out of Charleston harbor under command of Capt. L. M. Coxetter. The crew of this vessel was composed largely of Floridians; among them William Baya, afterward Lieutenant-Colonel of the 8th Florida Regiment, was Lieutenant of Marines. In a cruise of three months on the Atlantic coast this vessel captured eleven prizes. Being chased by United States war vessel in August she attempted to run into St. Augustine but was wrecked on the bar.

On June 25, 1861, a levy of 20 men from the companies of Captains Williams and More, afterward Cos. B and C, from the 2nd Regiment, then stationed at Cedar Keys, went in the steamer Madison on which a six-pounder was mounted, and recaptured four schooners, which had been taken by the United States steamer Massachusetts, a few days before, and sent them, with Leuitenant Seldon, U. S. N., and 19 marines, the prize crew, into Cedar Keys.

Roll Confederate Navy of Florida.

NAMES.	MUSTERED IN.	MUSTERED OUT.	REMARKS.
Bazzell, C. E.			Under Capt. C. R. Jones; Steamer "Chattahoochee."
Castello, George			Under Captain George Hays.
Cattenetti, Domings			Under Captain Lewis.
Chase, J. H.	Dec. '62		Under Captain McLaughlin; (Naval Batt).
Comforter, Nicholas			Under Captain Lewis.
Coonrod, Lorenzo D.			Under Captain C. R. Jones "Chattachoochee"; transferred to Gun Boat "Savannah," N. C.,'63.
Cone, Fountain H.	'63		Under Captain Lewis; Gun Boat "Spray."
Cone, William H.	April 11, '64		Gun Boat "Spray."
Dykes, John			
Harmon, T. H.	'64		Under Captain Jones; "Chattachoochee,"
Garo, Abram	Mch. '62		Under Captain McGary; Gun Boat "Spray."
Johnston, Edward			Confederate Ram, Savannah; engineer, captured, '63 and died in prison at Fort Warren October 13, '63.
Moore, James W.			Under Captain Lewis; Gun Boat "Spray."
Philips, James M.	Nov. '61		Under Capt. Geo. Hays.
Taylor, G. T.	'62		Under Captain Jones; "Chattachoochee."
Theobald, John	'62	May '65	Under Captain Lewis; Gun Boat "Spray."
Shiple, J. H.		May '65	Under Captain Lewis; Gun Boat "Spray."
Syfrette, F. M. E.	Sept. '62	May '65	Under Captain Jones; "Chattachoochee."

Roll Conscript Camp at Marianna, Fla., in Charge of Maj. J. E. Galliger.

NAMES.	MUSTERED IN.	MUSTERED OUT.	REMARKS.
OFFICERS.			
Major—			
J. E. Galliger...............			
ENLISTED MEN.			
Anderson, Danile L...........			
McCallam, R. L..............		April '65	
McRae, Charles.............	June 1, '64	April '65	
McSwain, A................		April '65	
Sconiers, William F.........	June 1, '64	April '65	
Snell, William.............	June 11, '64	April '65	

Roll of Volunteer Conscripts; Baneau's Battalion; Anderson's Brigade.

NAMES.	MUSTERED IN.	MUSTERED OUT.	REMARKS.
ENLISTED MEN.			
Broome, Thomas H............			Lieutenant; commanding.
Dirmany, J. T...............	Sept. '62		Lost right eye at Olustee, Fla., February 20, '64.

Roll of Conscript Camp at Madison, in Charge of Colonel J. J. Daniels.

NAMES.	MUSTERED IN.	MUSTERED OUT.	REMARKS.
ENLISTED MEN.			
Bellamay, W. D.............			Promoted Sergeant.
Clements, J. G.............			
Shaw, W. W................	'64	April '65	

Roll Camp of Instruction at Madison, Fla., in Charge of Colonel Rogers.

NAMES.	MUSTERED IN.	MUSTERED OUT.	REMARKS.
ENLISTED MEN.			
Allen, J. J................			
Blount, W. S. I............			
Fraser, C. C...............			
Harrell, H. S..............	Mch. '64		Discharged November, '64 for disability.
Jenkins, Chesley J.........	Feb. 1, '63		Injured accidentally by himself with a hatchet, and disabled, '63.
Jenkins, F. J..............			
Johns, A. J................			
Philips, James.............	Mch. 15, '62		Discharged January 6, '64 for disability.
Thornton, John.............			
Thornton, William..........	'62		Paroled at close of war.

Roll Soldiers of Florida, Miscellaneous.

NAMES.	MUSTERED IN.	MUSTERED OUT.	REMARKS.
Alexander, C. R............	'61		Under Captain A. Godwin; Home Guards.
Ball, J. W................			Was in battle of Natural Bridge.
Barrineau, John C.........			Under Capt. M. M. Johnson.
Bell, V. T................			Under Captain Robinson; Home Guards; participated in fight at Marianna September 27, '64.
Bevis, A..................			
Conner, William...........			In Hutchinson's detachment at Natural Bridge.
Dixon, A. B...............	Dec. '62		Captain of Home Guards; wounded at Bluff Spring, Fla., December, '64.
Downing, John T...........	'62		Under Capt. Thomas H. Broome, attached to Bannon's Battalion of of Ga., Anderson's Brigade.
Dyneu, Jerry..............	May '64		Under Captain John Parsons; Independent Co.
Folsom, J. Y..............			Under Captain Robinson; Home Guards.

Roll Soldiers o fFlorida, Miscellaneous.

(CONTINUED.)

NAMES.	MUSTERED IN.		MUSTERED OUT.		REMARKS.
Gwyn, B. G.		'64	May	'65	Under Captain Lou Williams; Reserves.
Hall, Rolin			May	'65	Under Captain Phil Dell; 1st Reserves.
Hattiwanger, Levi	Feb. 28,	'64	May	'65	Under Captain Hawkins B, 2nd Reserves; promoted 1st Sergeant Co. B, 2nd Regiment.
Haynes, Milton	Sept.	'63	May	'65	Under Captain Stark; 2nd Battalion, Co. H; promoted Captain Co.–5th Battalion.
Hodge, Sam S.		'64		'65	Under Captain Richardson; Home Guards.
Horn, E. F.					Under Captain James Hunt; Co. F.
Jones, C.					Under Captain Hawkins; Co. B, 2nd Reserves.
Jones, J. A.					Under Captain James Hunt; Co. F.
Jones, S. D.					Under Captain J. N. Jones and Colonel McCormick.
Lewis, Arthur					Under Captain Jesse J. Norwood;wounded September 27, at Marianna, Fla., and died two days afterwards.
McNealy, Adam					
Mathews, William	Sept. 27, '64				Under Captain Robinson; Home Guards, captured and died in prison at N. Y.
Merrett, A.			May	'65	Under Captain Jesse J. Norwood.
Nettles, William W.			May	'65	Under Captain Daniel Sloan.
Nims, J. R.			May	'65	Under Captain Jesse Pritchett; promoted 2nd Lieutenant of Home Guards.
Peary. T, J.	Mch. 5, '62			'64	From Gadsden County, Fla., enlisted in 29th Ga, Regiment; lost finger at Kennesaw Mt., lost arm aad disabled at Jonesborough, Ga.
Raker, Leonidas		'64	May	'65	Under Captain Richardson; Home Guards.
Sylvester, J. P.			May	'65	Under Capt. W. B. Henderson.
Timmons, Timothy G.	June	'62	April	'64	Under Captain King of 1st Reserves.
Wofford, J. I.				'64	Under Captain Starke.
Belcher, W. A.					Corporal.
Bell, J. W.					
Black, George E.		'61			Under Capt. J. F. P. Johnson; Hollands Batt.
Bryant, J. W.	Mch.	'61			Under Captain Pyles; transferred to , '62 Captain Moore, Ind.; wounded in R. R. accident, Gainesville.
Butler, Lee					Captain; wounded, Natural Bridge March, '65.
Collins, John Marion					
Denham, James					Sergeant; wounded, Natural Bridge March 4, '65.
Farrier, James M.					
Frink, J. W.					Under Capt. J. C. Wilcox; Independent.
Hart, Oscar					Wounded, Natural Bridge March 4, '65.
Mathis, Joshua		'64			Under Captain James King; Independent.
Morgan, T. F.					Wounded, Natural Bridge March 4, '65.
Robinson, J. L.					Under Captain Richardson; Home Guards.
Spivey, J. E.					
Summerall, David					
Taylor, John D.					
Tharp, Samuel					
Walker, E. G.					Died March 11, '97.
Wallace, Thomas J.					
Waters, John W.					
White, John B.					
Whitton, Elias					Died September 13, '99.
Wilder, E. H.					
Williams, J. J.					Wounded, March, '65 Natural Bridge.
Williams, Jeptha V.					Died June 3, '01.
Wingate, Jerry					
Wyche,					Wounded, Natural Bridge March 4, '65.

Roll, Field and Staff—Florida Brigade, Army of Northern Virginia.

NAMES.	MUSTERED IN.		MUSTERED OUT.	REMARKS.
Brigadier-Generals—				
Edward A. Perry	Mch.	'91		Captain of Co. A, 2nd Infantry, promoted Colonel; May 10, '62, Brigadier-General, August, '62; wounded at Frazier's Farm June 30, '62; at the Wilderness May 5, '64, and disabled.
Joseph Finnegan		'61		Resigned, '64.
Theodore Brevard		'61		Captain of Co. D, 2nd Regiment, Major of Cavalry in '62-'63; Colonel, 11th Florida Regiment, '64; promoted Brigadier-General,'65.
David Lang				Captain Co. C, 8th Regiment, Colonel September 17, '62; commanded Fla. Brigade at the battle of Gettysburg, '63, commanded Fla. Brigade from May 5, '64 until relieved by General Brevard; commanded Fla. Brigade at surrender.

Roll, Field and Staff—Florida Brigade, Army of Northern Virginia.
(CONTINUED.)

NAMES.	MUSTERED IN.	MUSTERED OUT.	REMARKS.
Adjutant-General— B. F. Simmons, 1st Lt. & A......			1st Lieutenant and A. A. G.; surrendered at Appomattox.
Brigade Quartermaster— D. W. Hinkle..............			Major; surrendered at Appomattox.
Assist. Brigade Quartermaster— Louis Hyer....................			Captain; surrendered at Appomatox.
J. H. Johnson................			Captain; surrendered at Appomatox.
Brigade Commissary— Thomas C. Elder.............			Major; surrendered at Appomatox.
Assist Brigade Commissary— R. W. Reid.................			Captain; surrendered at Appomatox.
Ordnance— W. H. Clark...............			1st Lieutenant; surrendered at Appomatox.

MEDICAL OFFICERS.

Return of medical officers of the Army, Volunteer Corps and Militia, including physicians employed under contract, together with detail physicians of the Confederate States, serving in the State of Florida March 1865.

NAME.	RANK.	DATE COM.	POST OR STATION.	WHERE SERVED.	REMARKS.
John S. Bond............	Surgeon.	'61	Staff	Bragg's Army	Died in Jacksonville, Fla., '83.
A. S. Baldwin............	Surgeon		Lake City		Died in Jacksonville, Fla.,
Henry A. Bacon........	Surgeon	'63	Field		Died, hospital at Fernandina, '67.
L. W. Chamberlain....	Asst. Surg.	July 19, '62	Camp Jackson	Bat. Inf.	
W. D. Colmer............	Asst. Surg.	Feb. 13, '63	Lake City	Hospital	Detail by General Finnegan at request of Major Baldwin.
D. Carn...................	Surgeon	'63	Field	3rd Florida Inf.	
J. E. A. Davidson......	Surgeon	'62	Quincy		Medical purveyor.
R. P. Daniel.............	Surgeon	'61	Virginia	8th Florida Inf.	
J. W. Eppes..............	Surgeon	'62	Field	2nd Florida Cav.	Trans. Georgetown Hospital.
B. C. Fishburn..........	Surgeon	Jan. 1, '62	Field	Detached Cav.	
C. Gamble...............	Surgeon	'61	Field	Army of Tenn.	
J. D. Godfrey............	Surgeon	'62	Field	5th Florida Inf.	
Thomas P. Gary.......	Surgeon	'64	Field	7th Florida Inf.	Died in Ocala, '91.
Horatio Hallifield......	Surgeon	Aug., '62	Field	5th Florida Bat.	
H. M. Holmes...........	Asst. Surg.	'63	Army, Tenn.	Marion Artillery	
D. Hutchingson........	Asst. Surg.	'62	Lake City	Hospital	
J. S. Hackney..........	A. A. Surg.	'64	Fort Reed	Watson's Co.	Died, Tampa '88.
Du P. Hooper...........	Asst. Surg.	'62	Virginia	8th Florida Inf.	Died December 12, '63, on duty at Fredericksburg, Va.
P. W. B. Hodges.......	Surgeon		Field	1st Florida Inf.	
G. E. Hawes............	Surgeon		Virginia	2nd Florida Inf.	
G. L. Key................	A. A. Surg.	'64	Fort Meade	F. A. Henry's Co.	
W. A. Lively.............	A. A. Surg.	'64	Cook	J. T. Leslie's Co.	
J. E. LeEngle...........	A. A. Surg.	'64	Lake City	Hospital	
J. L. Mapp..............	A. A. Surg.	May 25, '63	5th Fla. Bat.		
E. P. Paschar..........	A. A. Surg.	Mch. 15, '64	Live Oak	Eng. Corps	Detail Co. K, 2nd Florida.
Henry Pope............	A. A. Surg.				
Thomas M. Palmer....	Surgeon	'61	Richmond, Va.	Florida hospital	Jacksonville, Address.
Hy. H. Robinson......	Surgeon		Marianna	Hospital	
S. Stringer.............	Surgeon	July 13, '62	Staff	Sub. District Fla.	Died Brooksville, April 6, '01.
W. J. Scull.............	A. A. Surg.	'62	Field	Dunham's Art.	Dead.
A. P. Smith.............	Asst. Surg.	Mch., '63	Field	2nd Florida Cav.	Dead.
E. T. Sabal.............	Surgeon		Richmond, Va.	Hospital	
S. M. E. Todd..........	Surgeon		Field	Camp Instruction	Dead.
J. P. Wall...............	Asst. Surg.	Oct., '61	Hospital	Richmond, Va.	Dead.
J. A. Williams..........	Asst. Surg.		Field	Co. H, Florida Cav	
W. M. Wilson...........	Asst. Surg.		Field	Villepigue's Bat.	Captured at Darby's still July 25, '64.
H. M. Wheeden........	Surgeon	'62	Field	4th Florida Reg.	
Theodore West........	Asst. Surg.		Field	8th Florida Reg.	Marianna, Fla.
J. Turnbull.............	A. A. Surg.	Oct. 28, '64	Field	Abel's Battery	
A. M. Cox...............	A. A. Surg.	Aug., '63	Field	Impress Labor	
W. E. Collier...........	A. A. Surg.		Field	Ryn's Co.	Dead.
G. M. L. Simmons.....	A. A. Surg.		Bear Landing	Agnew's Co.	
J. M. Jackson..........	A. A. Surg.	Nov. 14, '64	Clay Landing	Lutteloh's Co.	
A. P. Linford...........	A. A. Surg.	Nov. 27, '63	Field	2nd Florida Cav.	Dead
D. H. Hudson..........	A. A. Surg.	Jan. 25, '65	Field		Detail from Campbell's Art'y.
J. McCall...............	A. A. Surg.		Field	2nd Florida Cav.	
J. H. Randolph........	Surgeon		Tallahassee	Sub. District Fla.	Dead.

N. B. The above report was made from official documents in the possession of S. Stringer, Surgeon, P. A. C. S.

Brigade Band.

NAMES.	MUSTERED IN.	MUSTERED OUT.	REMARKS.
John M. Reddick		April 9, '65	Chief Musician; surrendered at Appomatox.
John R. Harris			Musician; surrendered at Appomatox.
John Stewart			Musician surrendered at Appomatox.
William R. King			Musician; surrendered at Appomatox.
Owen B. Cribbs			Musician; surrendered at Appomatox.
James A. Newland			Musician; surrendered at Appomatox.
Thomas Andrew			Musician; surrendered at Appomatox.
R. G. Hunter			Musician; surrendered at Appomatox.
Lawson Snead			Musician; surrendered at Appomatox.
Levi Johnson			Musician; surrendered at Appomatox.
W. H. Younger			Musician; surrendered at Appomatox.
John Barrineau			Musician; surrendered at Appomatox.
David W. Core			Drum Major; surrendered at Appomatox.
Gordan Cribbs			Kettle Drum.
Mighael Winn			Bass Drum.
Alonzo Hernandez			2 B. Flat.
John Thompkins			2 B. Flat.
Charles Davis			Cymbal.

Civil War Biographies.

These Biographies are added as suggestion of what the revised and completed work should contain. The story of the officer is most often the condensed story of the Company, Regiment, Brigade or Division.

General Edmond Kirby Smith.

Appointed Major of Cavalry May, 1861; promoted Lieutenant-Colonel May, 1861; Brigadier-General June, 1861; Major-General 1863; General August, 1863.

Gen. Edmond Kirby Smith was born in St. Augustine, Fla., on May 16, 1824; died at Sewannee, Tenn., March 28, 1893. His father was Joseph L. Smith, the first presiding judge of the United States Superior Court for the Eastern District of Florida. General Smith was appointed and admitted to West Point July 1, 1841; graduated July 1, 1845, standing twenty-fifth in his class; appointed brevet 2nd Lieutenant in the 5th Infantry July 1, 1845; 2nd Lieutenant in the 7th Infantry August 26, 1846; 1st Lieutenant March 9, 1851; Captain of 2nd Cavalry March 3, 1855; Major January 31, 1861. He was breveted 1st Lieutenant April 18, 1847, for gallant and meritorious conduct in the battle of Cerro Gordo, and Captain August 20, 1847, in the battle of Contreras and Cherubusco, Mexico; resigned April 26, 1861. After the close of the Mexican War Lieutenant Smith was assigned to West Point, where he remained for three years as assistant instructor in mathematics; later he served under Major Emory, on the boundary commission to locate the line between Mexico and the United States. Upon the organization of the cavalry regiments in 1855, he was assigned to the 2nd Regiment as Captain and ordered to Texas, where he was engaged against the Comanche Indians. Upon the secession of Florida in April, 1861, he resigned his commission in the United States Army and tendered his services to the Confederate States.

His value was fully appreciated by the Confederate officials and he was given the position of Major of Cavalry, and almost immediately promoted Lieutenant-Colonel under Van Dorn; before he could join his command he was set to work at Lynchburg to organize the troops gathered there. There Gen. Joseph E. Johnston found him, made him his Adjutant-General and took him to Harper's Ferry. While acting as Adjutant-General he was promoted to Brigadier-General and assigned to a brigade in Johnston's army. When the battle of Manassas was fought he marched thirty miles to join the movement and arrived at such an opportune time that, with Kershaw, he succeeded in changing impending defeat into a brilliant Confederate victory. In this battle he was severely wounded, which disabled him for several months.

Upon his recovery he was sent to East Tennessee, where he took command of the detached right wing of Bragg's army. In 1863 he was promoted to Major-General, and, by order of President Davis, assumed command of the trans-Mississippi department.   After Grant's capture of Vicksburg and the effectual cutting of the Confederacy in two, communications with General Smith's headquarters were so irregular, that the Confederate Government found it advisable to endow General Smith with greater powers and a higher rank.   He was made full General, becoming the sixth officer of the Confederacy to hold that rank; the others being Cooper, Lee, "Joe" Johnston, Beauregard, and Bragg, in the order named.   After the close of the war he became president of the Atlantic & Pacific Telegraph Co., which position he resigned to accept the presidency of the University of Nashville, which he held until 1875. He was then made professor of mathematics in the University of the South, at Sewannee, which position he held at the time of his death.

Major-General William H. Chase.

General Chase, for many years the leading citizen of Pensacola, was a native of Massachusetts.   Appointed cadet in the military academy at West Point and graduated thirtieth in his class;   appointed brevet 2nd Lieutenant of Engineers March 4, 1815; 2nd Lieutenant April 15, 1815; 1st Lieutenant March 31, 1818; Captain January 1, 1825; Major July 7, 1838; resigned October 30, 1856; appointed Colonel Florida State troops 1861; promoted Major-General Florida State troops 1861.

During his career in the United States Army he filled many an important position in the Engineer service, superintending the construction of Forts Pike and Jackson on the Mississippi River, the defences of Pensacola harbor, Fort Taylor and many other works, as well as river and harbor improvements.   He was active in promotion of internal improvements, and after his resignation was president of the Alabama & Florida Railroad Company.   At the beginning of the year 1861, when the first organization of troops was made in Florida, Colonel Chase was appointed Major-General of State troops.   In this capacity he was in command at Pensacola, seized the public works on the mainland and summoned Fort Pickens to surrender.   He was in command at Pensacola until Gen. Braxton Bragg was assigned to duty there in March, 1861.   On account of his advanced age General Chase did not participate in later military operations   He died at Pensacola February 8, 1870, at the age o 72.

Major-General William Wing Loring.

Appointed Brigadier-General May 20, 1861;   promoted Major-General February 15, 1862.

Maj.-Gen. William Wing Lor'ng was a soldier from his boyhood. He was born in Wilmington, N. C., December 4, 1818; in early chi dhood became a resident of Florida, and when only 14 years of age was in the ranks of the volunteers, fighting Indians in the swamps and everglades. He did not have a West Point training, but he was educated in the true school of the so'dier— active campaign life. On June 16, 1837, he was appointed a 2nd Lieutenant. After that he went to school at Alexandria, Va., and Georgetown, D. C. He afterward studied law and was admitted in 1842 to practice. He then went back to Florida and before long was elected to the State legislature, of which he remained a member for three years. In the Seminole War of 1836-38 he was appointed senior Captain of a regiment of mounted riflemen, and in the following year he was made Major commanding. He served under General Scott in all the battles of the Mexican War, from Vera Cruz to the City of Mexico Mexico, and for gallant conduct was breveted Lieutenant-Colonel. While entering the City of Mexico at the head of his regiment he lost his left arm. After the war the citizens of Apalachicola, Fla., presented him with a sword. In 1849, during the gold fever in California, Colonel Loring was ordered to take his regiment across the continent and take command of the Department of Oregon. On this occasion he marched his command a distance of 2,500 miles, taking with him a train of 600 mule teams. He held the command of the Department of Oregon until 1851. For five years he was in command on the frontier and fought many combats with the Indians. Then by permission, he visited Europe and studied the military systems of the various nations. On his return he was placed in command of the Department of New Mexico; but during that very year the long sectional quarrel between the North and South changed from a war of words to open hostilities. Loring naturally sided with the South. The Confederate Government was glad to accept his services, and on May 20, 1861, commissioned him as Brigadier-General. After the defeat and death of Gen. Robert Garnett, in western Virginia, General Loring was sent to take charge of the Confederate forces in that quarter. He commanded one wing of the army under Lee, n the Cheat Mountain campaign, where the soldiers had little fighting but abundance of hardship. In December, 1861, Loring's command united with Stonewall Jackson at Winchester, and in January was engaged in the winter expedition to Bath, Hancock and Romney. Through General Loring's solicitations to the War Department at Richmond his division, which had been left at Romney, was ordered back to Winchester, This interference on the part of the government at Richmond came near causing the resignation of General Ja kson. On February 15, 1862, General Loring was commissioned Major-General and assigned to the command of the army of Southwest Virginia. Nothing of any great importance occurred in that region, the soldiers being for the most part occupied in picket duty and occasional skirmishes with the enemy. In December, 1862, Loring was sent to take command of the 1st corps of the Army of Mississippi. He had charge for a while at Fort Pemberton, which was designed to defend Vicksburg from any expedition sent by way of Yazoo Pass. It was a cotton-bale fortification, constructed by Captain Robinson of the Confederate Engineers, and situated on the over-flow bottom lands of the Tallahatchie and Yallabusha Rivers, near their junction. Here General Loring, with three cannon and 1,500 men, defeated a fleet and land force. In the hottest of the fight Loring stood upon the cotton-bale parapet and shouted to his men: 'G ve them blizzards, boys! Give them blizzards!" From this time his men nicknamed him "Old Blizzards." At the disastrous battle of Baker's Creek Loring was cut off from the rest of the army. Finding there was no chance to unite with the main body he marched his division eastward and joined General Johnston at Jackson. He and his troops were thus fortunately saved from being shut up and captured at Vicksburg. He was subsequently under the command of Johnston and then Polk n North Mississippi. At the opening of the campaign of 1864

Polk hastened to Georgia to make a junction with the army under Joseph E. Johnston. During the Atlanta campaign General Loring commanded a division in Polk's corps and, after the death of Polk, the corps itself until the appointment of Gen. A. P. Stewart. Loring continued to command his division 'n Stewarts'corps until the surrender of the army of Tennessee in North Carolina. After the war he went abroad and, in 1869, with other Confederate officers entered the service of the Khedive of Egypt, and was appointed Inspector-General. In 1870 he was made Commandant of Alexandria and given charge of the coast defences of Egypt. In 1875-76, during the Abyssinian War, General Loring commanded the Egyptian Army. He was raised to the dignity of pasha for his services. In 1879 he and the other American officers in the service of the Khedive were mustered out and returned to the United States; after which he resided in Florida for a while and then made his home in New York, where he wrote his book entitled 'A Confederate Soldier in Egypt." He died in New York December 30, 1886.

Major-General Martin L. Smith.

Appointed Major of Engineers April 1, 1861; promoted Brigadier-Genera April 11, 1862; Major-Genera Nov. 4, 1862.

Maj.-Gen. Martin L. Smith was another of the many gentlemen of Northern birth who, residing in the South, adopted the sentiments of the people among whom they lived, and with zeal and loyalty supported the Confederate cause. State sovereignty was the political doctrine of the majority of the founders of the Republic, and at times has been asserted by leading men of every political party. Hence it is not surprising that Northern men living in the South were just as prompt to resent any infringement of the rights of their adopted States as were the native-born citizens. It is a well-known fact that many people l ving in the North believed in the justice of the Southern cause and sympathized with the Southern people in their desperate struggle against overwhelming odds. General Smith was born in New York City in 1819. He entered the mliitary academy in 1838 and was graduated in 1842 as brevet 2nd Lieutenant, Topographical Engineers. He became full 2nd Lieutenant in 1843; served during the Mexican War as Lieutenant of Topographical Engineers, and was brevetted 1st Lieutenant May 30, 1848, for meritorious conduct while making surveys in the enemy's country He was also employed by the Government in making surveys for the improvement of Savannah River and for a ship canal across the Florida peninsula. In July, 1856, he was commissioned Captain for 14 years' continuous service. During this time he had also been engaged in surveys in the Department of Texas. From 1856 to 1861 he was chief engineer of the Fernandina & Cedar Keys Railroad in Florida.

Spending most of his mature life among the people of the South, Captain Smith, from his observation and experience of Southern affairs, became fully convinced of the justice of the position taken by the Southern people, and when it became evident that war would soon begin he resigned his commiss on April 1, 1861, and offered his services to the Confederate States. He was at once commissioned as Major in the corps of Engineers May, 16, 1861, and accredited to Florida. In this position his services were so well approved that on April 11, 1862, he was made a Brigadier-General. He was at first assigned to the Army of Northern Virginia as Chief of Engineers, but was soon after sent to the West. He performed important duties at New Orleans, and on June 26, 1862, was put in charge of the 3rd district of South Mississippi and East Louisiana. At the head of the engineer corps he planned and constructed the defences of Vicksburg, where he resisted the naval attack of the summer of 1862; was in chief command in December, 1862, and repu'sed the attack of General Sherman; and during the campaign of May, 1863, and the siege of Vicksburg, commanded with great distinction a division composed of the brigades of Shoup, Baldwin and Vaughn. More than any other Confederate General he was identified with the romantic story of the famous stronghold of the great river, the loss of which doomed the cause for which he fought. On November 4 1862, he had been promoted to Major-General. After his exchange he continued to serve the Confederacy as chief of engineers until the close of the war, his last service being at Mobile, Ala. He did not long survive the war, dying at Savannah, Ga., July 29, 1866.

Major-General James Patton Anderson.

Captain Co. I Florida Infantry, March, 1861; promoted Colonel 1st Florida Infantry April 6, 1861; Brigadier-General February, 1862; Major-General 1862.

Maj -Gen. James Patton Anderson was born in Tennessee about 1820. Like other enterprising Americans he lived in so many different sections of the Union that it is difficult to decide to which State he really should be ass'gned in this record of Confederate Generals. At the opening of the Mexican War he was living in Mississippi and became Lieutenant-Colonel of Mississippi volunteers Although he had not had the advantages of an education at the United States military academy, the Mexican conflict proved a good school for him in the m'litary art. The good use he made of his opportunities in that practical military training school was afterward evidenced by the skill with which he managed troops upon the great arena of war from 1861 to 1865. The man who obtained a good reputation on that great theater of action had to keep abreast of many illustrious men of the same rank with himself, and that is what General Anderson did. After the close of the Mexican War General Anderson lived for a time in Olympia, in what was then Washington Territory and served as territorial delegate to the national House of Representatives in 1855. Before the opening of the Confederate War he was a member of the secession convention. Feeling, as did most Southern men, that the South was right, he entered heart and soul into the struggle to maintain Southern rights and honor As early as December, 1860, before the e had been any secession, but when everybody felt certain that such action would be taken, military companies were being formed and drilled. Anderson was Captain of such a company—the Jefferson Rifles. In April, 1861, he was Colonel of the 1st Florida Regiment of Infantry, ready to go wherever the Confederate President might order. Stationed for some time at Pensacola, he was in command of one of the Confederate columns in the fight on Santa

Rosa Island October, 1861. Early in 1862 he was promoted to Brigadier-General, his command having been transferred to Corinth, Miss. At the battle of Shiloh his brigade was composed of the 17th Louisiana, the Louisiana Guard Response Battalion, the Florida Battalion (1st Regiment) under Maj. T. A. McDonell, 9th Texas, 20th Louisiana and a company of the Washington Artillery. Of his service General Bragg said: "Brig.-Gen. Patton Anderson was among the foremost where the fighting was hardest and never failed to overcome whatever resistance was opposed to him. With a brigade composed almost entirely of raw troops his personal gallantry and soldierly bear'ng supplied the place of instruction and discipl'ne." At Perryville he commanded a division of Hardee's corps, and was in charge of the extreme right. At Murfreesborough he commanded Walthall's brigade of Withers' division, Polk's corps. His participation in the magnificent right wheel of the army was inferior o that of none of the general officers who won fame on that day. It was his brigade which was ordered to take three batteries "at any cost," and succeeded under the lead of "its cool, steadfast and skillful commander." Subsequently he commanded Chalmer's brigade and, during September 18 and 19, was in command of Hindman's division, in the Chickamauga campaign. He was mentioned by General Longstreet as distinguished for conduct and ability. He commanded the same division at Missionary Ridge. On February 17, 1864, he was promoted to Major-General and was assigned to command of the district of Florida. After serving five months in that capacity he was ordered to report to General Hood at Atlanta, Ga., in July, 1864, and on his arrival was assigned to his old division, which he commanded in the battle of Ezra Church, during the siege and until wounded in the battle of Jonesboro, which compelled him to leave the field, resulting in his absence from the army until March, 1865. Then, much against the advice and judgment of his physicians, he returned to the army in North Carolina and was assigned to command of Taliafero's division, Rhett's and Elliott's brigades from Charleston, and was with it when it surrendered at Greensboro, N. C. After the close of hostilities he returned to Tennessee and died at Memphis in 1873.

Brigadier-General James McQueen McIntosh.

Appointed Colonel 1861; promoted Brigadier-General 1861.

James McQueen McIntosh, appointed cadet at large from Florida to West Point, July 1, 1845, graduated forty-third in his class July 1, 1849, and appointed brevet 2nd Lieutenant of the 1st Infantry; transferred to the 8th Infantry February 11, 1851; promoted to 2nd Lieutenant May 15, 1851; promoted 1st Lieutenant to 1st Cavalry March 3, 1855; promoted Captain January, 1857; resigned May 7, 1861, and offered his services to the Confederate Army, 1861, and was killed at Pea Ridge, Arkansas, March 7, 1862.

Brigadier-General Joseph Finnegan.

Appointed Brigadier-General April 5, 1862.

Brig.-Gen. Joseph Finnegan, a prominent lawyer and statesman in Florida before the war, was early in 1861 placed by Governor Milton at the head of military affairs in the State He was commissioned Brigadier-General on April 5, 1861, and from the 8th of that month until the battle of Olustee commanded the Department or District of Middle and East Florida: The coast of Florida was, from the beginning of the war, at the mercy of the Federal fleet, and within the limits of the State were only a few scattered Confederate troops. Early in 1864, when it had been found that Charleston was too strong for the Federal army and fleet combined, General Gilmore, who commanded the Department of the South, decided to make an effort to overrun Florida and annex it to the Union. It was considered desirable by the United States authorities that some of the Southern States should be brought so completely under the control of the Union Army as to enable such of the inhabitants, white and black as might desire to do so, to form what they called "loyal" State governments and be readmitted to the Union. Florida seemed to offer good prospect of success in such an undertaking. An army under Gen. Truman Seymour and the fleet of Admiral Dahlgren attempted the task of subduing Florida, and General Finnegan found himself in a dangerous po i-tion, demanding skillful generalship and courageous firmness. So well did he perform his part that a signal victory was obtained at Olustee and the Federal enterprise entirely defeated. He was soon succeeded by General Gardner as commander of the district of Middle and Western Florida, and was sent to Virginia in May at the head of a Florida brigade, with which Perry's old brigade was consolidated. At the second battle of Cold Harbor General Finnegan and his Florida brigade had a good opportunity for distinction, and made memorable use of the occasion to the credit of themselves and their State. This was the memorable June 3, when Grant's charging columns broke through a weak point in Breckinridge's line. Immediately Finnegan's brigade rushed into the breach and in a desperate fight drove back the assailants with heavy loss to Hancock's troops. General Finnegan served from that time with the Army of Northern Virginia until March 20, 1856, when he was again assigned to duty in Florida. After the war he returned to the profession of law. On October 29, 1885, he died at Sanford, Fla.

Brigadier-General Edward Aylesworth Perry.

Captain Co. A, 2nd Florida Infantry, April, 1861; promoted Colonel 2nd Florida Infantry May 10, 1862; Brigadier-General August 28, 1862.

Brig.-Gen. Edward Aylesworth Perry was born in Richmond, Berkshire county, Mass., March 15, 1833. He entered Yale college, but before the completion of his course, removed to Alabama where he studied law. After admission to the bar, in 1857 he moved to Pensacola, Fla., where he began the practice of his chosen profession. He fully shared the sentiments of the people of his adopted State, and when the Civil War commenced he raised a company, of which he was elected Captain. His command became a part of the 2nd Florida Regiment, of which Captain Perry became Colonel in May, 1862. The Regiment was sent to Virginia and was attached to the division of Gen. James Longstreet. Colonel Perry commanded the regiment at Seven Pines and in the Seven Days' battles around Richmond, and from the first the regiment and its commander were conspicuous for valor and efficiency. At Frazier's Farm he was severely wounded. Gen. Longstreet mentions h m among others as distinguished for gallantry and skill. He was commissioned Brigadier-General on August 28, 1862, and upon his recovery put in command of the newly organized Florida brigade, which he led at Chancellorsville. In the battle of Gettysburg Perry's brigade, commanded by Col. David Lang,(General Perry was in the hospital severely ill with typhoid fever), with Wright's and Wilcox's, pressed close up to the Federal lines and at one time broke through; but for lack of support had to be withdrawn from the advanced position. It is claimed by Perry's brigade that its losses at Gettysburg were heavier than those of any other brigade of the Confederate Army. In the battle of the Wilderness General Perry was a second time severely wounded. After the close of the war he returned to the practice of law in the city of Pensacola. During the gloomy period of reconstruction he remained true to the interests of the people of Florida. The result of the war had not changed his views of the constitutional rights of the States, and not even by silence did he give seeming approval to the corrupt methods of usurpations of that epoch. He took an active interest in political affairs, and in 1884 he was elected Governor of Florida on the Democratic ticket. This office he had held for four years, and within a year after the expiration of his term he died, October 15, 1889.

Brigadier-General William S. Walker.

Appointed Captain 1861; Colonel 1862; promoted Brigadier General October 30, 1862.

Brig-Gen. William Stephen Walker, born in Pennsylvania, was appointed First Lieutenant of Infantry U. S. A. Feb. 27. 1847, from Mississippi, April 9, 1807; he was transferred to the Voltigeurs Regiment of which he became Adjutant. The regiment was disbanded Aug. 31, 1848, and he left the service a Brevet Captain for gallant and meritorias service at Chapultepce in the war with Mexico. On March 31, 1855 he was appointed from the District of Columbia, a Captain in the famous 1st U. S. Cavalry from which he resigned May 1, 1861 and entered the Confederate service as a Captain of Infantry. In 1862 he was commissioned Colonel, and on October 22, in command at Pocotaligo, S. C., he defeated a Union force that attempted to seize the Charleston and Savannah railroad. Eight days later he was promoted to Brigadier-General, and during the balance of the year he was in command of the 3rd military district of South Carolina from sudden incursions of the enemy. As the spring of 1864 opened, all the troops that could possibly be spared from the Department of South Carolina, Georgia and Florida were sent to the armies in Virginia and Georgia. On April 29, 1864, General Walker was ordered to Kinston, N, C.. to take command of that post, and soon afterward he was called by Beauregard to assist in the defense of Petersburg, at that time seriously threatened by Butler's advance. General Walker reached the army concentrated by Beauregard in time to share in the attack upon Butler. During a fight on May 20 he accidentally rode into the enemy's lines and when called upon to surrender refused and was fired upon. His horse was killed and he himself so severely wounded in the foot that amputation became necessary. He remained a prisoner of war until exchanged in the fall, when on October 29 he was placed in command at Weldon. He was commanding in

North Carolina when the war ended   General Walker removed to Georgia after the war and in 1898 was a citizen of Atlanta.

Brigadier-General William G. M. Davis.

Colonel 1st Florida Cavalry March, 1861; promoted Brigadier-General November 4, 1862.

Brig.-Gen. W. G. M. Davis was before the war a lawyer in Florida, widely known as a gentleman of great legal ability and high rank in his profession. Forsaking his practice in 1861, he raised a regiment and was on January 1, 1862, commissioned Colonel of the 1st Florida Cavalry and put in command of the provisional forces of East Florida.   The Federals had already seized Fernandina, Jacksonville and other places along the coast.   The chief business of Colonel Davis' regiment was to watch the movements of the enemy carefully, and as far as possible to prevent raiding or scouting parties of the Federals from penetrating into the interior.   Gov. John Milton was very much opposed to the raising of cavalry commands for the defense of Florida, insisting that nothing but artillery and infantry were needed for the defense of the State.   The executive council of the State passed a resolution requesting the Governor to correspond with the President as to the necessity of the regiment being converted into an infantry regiment and being kept in the State for its defense.   On March 25, 1862, Colonel Davis and his regiment were ordered to report to Gen. Albert Sidney Johnson and were assigned to East Tennessee, where they were kept busy watching the movements of the enemy, scouting and overawing the disaffected in that part of the Confederacy.   On November 4, 1862, he was commissioned Brigadier-General and was placed in command of the Department of East Tennessee.   His brigade embraced the 1st Florida Cavalry, the 6th and 7th Florida Infantry and Martin's Light Battery.   His scene of operation was a wild and difficult mountain region throughout which were people disaffected toward the Confederacy   It was necessary to control and at the same time to use much discretion in dealing with them.   So the task of a department commander in that section was a very difficult one.   During the time in which he exercised command his department was quite free from the presence of Federal troops.   On May 5, 1862, he resigned his commission and retired from the military service of the Confederate States.

Brigadier-General Francis A. Shoup.

Appointed Lieutenant of artillery; promoted Major of artillery October 1861; promoted Brigadier-General September 12, 1862.

Brig.-Gen. Francis A. Shoup was born at Laurel, Franklin county, Ind., March 22, 1864. He was appointed a cadet at West Point from Indiana, and was graduated in 1855 as brevet 2nd Lieutenant of artillery.   He served in garrison at Key West and Fort Moultrie; was commissioned 2nd Lieutenant December 6, 1855, and served against the Seminoles in Florida from 1856 to 1858.   He resigned in 1860 and beginning the study of law was admitted to the bar at St. Augustine, Fla., early in 1861.   In the war of 1861-65 he espoused heartily the cause of the South and, early in the struggle under the order of the Governor of Florida, he erected a battery at Fernandina. He was appointed a Lieutenant of artillery in the Confederate Army and was ordered to report to General Hardee in the trans-Mississippi Department. In October, 1861, he was commissioned Major of artillery and was in command of a battalion of 12 guns with the Arkansas troops in Kentucky. General Hardee, in assuming command of the Army of Central Kentucky, made him chief of artillery, in which capacity he served at the battle of Shiloh. He it was who massed the artillery against the position occupied by the command of Prentiss on the memorable first day at Shiloh, thus becoming an important factor in the capture of that fine body of Union troops. Under Beauregard he held the important post of inspector of artillery. He was sent with Hindman to Arkansas; was his chief of artillery and as such participated in the battle of Prairie Grove. On September 12, 1862, he was promoted to Brigadier-General; and in April, 1863, he was ordered to Mobile, Ala., as chief of artillery for General Buckner. At Vicksburg he commanded a Louisiana brigade and was captured upon the fall of that city. After being exchanged he served as chief of artillery to Joseph E. Johnston and gained the hearty commendation of his commander and the esteem of the soldiers. It was in a great measure due to his skillful management of the artillery that not a gun was lost n the several retreats of the Army of Tennessee from Dalton to Atlanta in 1864. The works at the Chattahoochee, which Sherman declared were the best he had ever seen, were constructed under his supervision. Upon the removal of Johnston, Gen. Hood made Shoup his chief of staff After the fall of Atlanta he was relieved at his own request. He was the author of a pamphlet urging the enlistment of negro troops, which was submitted to the Confederate Congress. The year after the close of the war he was elected to the chair of applied mathematics in the University of Mississippi. Here he studied for the ministry and was admitted to orders in the Episcopal church, of which he had become a member while the Confederate Army was in camp at Dalton April, 1864. He officiated as rector at Waterford. N, Y., Nashville, Tenn., and New Orleans, La.; also filled the chair of metaphysics in the University of the South, at Sewannee, Tenn He is author of a work on " Infantry Tactics "; while in Atlanta, in 1864, prepared a text-book on ' Artillery Division Drill," and in 1874 he published the " Elements of Algebra."

Brigadier-General Jesse Johnson Finley.

Captain Co. D, 6th Florida Infantry March, 1862; promoted Colonel, April 14, 1862; Brigadier-General November 16, 1863.

Brig.-Gen. Jesse Johnson Finley was born in Wilson county, Tenn., on November 18, 1812. He was educated at Lebanon and began the study of law. But about that time the Seminole War was begun and young Finley, having recruited a company of mounted volunteers, served in the army as Captain. Returning home in 1838 he was admitted to the bar. In 1840 he moved to Mississippi county, Ark. The young lawyer, who seems to have been a born leader of men, at once rose to prominence and was elected to the State Senate in 1841. The following year he resigned this position and, going to Memphis, Tenn., began the practice of law. He was elected Mayor of that city in 1845. In 1846 he removed to Marianna, Fla. Here he soon became prominent and, in 1850, was elected to the State Senate. In 1852 he was a presidential elector on the Whig ticket, and in 1861 he was made judge of the Confederate court. In March, 1862, he resigned this post of honor and entered the army as a private; was soon promoted to a captaincy, and on April 14, 1862, was commissioned as Colonel of the 6th Florida Regiment. He was on duty in East Tennessee in Davis' brigade, Heth's division, Kirby Smith's department; took part in the Kentucky campaign and, after the return to Knoxville, served as president of the court-martial for the department until ordered to Tullahoma. He commanded h s regiment in the battle of Chickamauga with distinction. On November 16, 1863, he was commissioned Brigadier-General and assigned to command of he Florida Infantry in the Army of Tennessee, united in a brigade of Bate's division, Hardee's corps. He commanded this gallant brigade at Missionary Ridge, and rendered distinguished service with the rear guard under General Bate. In the May campaign of 1864 he took part until at the battle of Resaca he was severely wounded, causing his disability until after Johnston's army had reached Atlanta. At Jonesboro, November 15, 1864, in an assualt upon the enemy's lines he was again seriously wounded by a fragment of shell, which also killed his horse. He declined to be sent to the rear to take the train until all his wounded men were embarked and narrowly escaped capture, being saved through the faithfulness of a driver who took him in a commissary wagon after the last train had left He was unfit for duty during the subsequent campaign of General Hood. Soon after the army was ordered to North Carolina, his wound being partially healed, he started to rejoin his brigade; but his progress being interfered with by the Federal movements, he reported to General Cobb at Columbus, and was assigned to duty When Wilson's Federal troops entered Columbus he made his escape with General Toombs to Eufaula, and soon afterward hostilities ceased. General Finley then returned to Florida and lived for a time in Lake City. In 1875 he removed to Jacksonville. He served in Congress from 1875 to 1879. In 1879 he was again elected but the seat was contested and given to his opponent. In 1887 he was appointed by Governor Perry to fill a vacancy in the United States Senate until an election could be held. Since the expiration of that service he has lived quietly at his Florida home.

Brigadier-General William Miller.

Major 1862; promoted Colonel 1st Florida Infant y July, 1862; Brigadier-General August 2, 1864.

Brig.-Gen. William Miller—Before and after the secession of Florida there was great mustering of the State troops and busy preparations were everywhere made for the coming struggle, wh ch all feared might come, though many hoped that it would be avoided Among those who forsook the occupations of peace to take part in defense of State sovereignty was Wm. Miller, one of the most gallant of Florida's soldiers. He was in command of a battalion, which was consolidated with McDonell's battalion of the 1st Regiment in the operations culminating in the battle of Perryville, Ky. In the Kenucky campaign the 1st Regiment from Florida was in the brigade of Gen. John C. Brown and the division of Gen. J. Patton Anderson.   In the battle of Perryville General Brown was wounded and Colonel Miller led the brigade through the rest of the fight.   At Murfreesborough this regiment was in the brigade of Gen. William Preston and the division of Gen. John C. Brecken-ridge.   In the magnificent but disastrous charge of that division on January 2, 1863, the gallant Miller, commanding the 1st and 3rd Florida consolidated, was wounded.   General Preston in his report says: "Colonel Miller, of the 1st and 3rd Florida, was wounded on Friday while bravely leading his regi-ment, which he withdrew, retaining the command notwithstanding his wounds."   While being healed of his injury Colonel Miller was placed in charge of the Confederate conscript bureau in Southern Florida and Alabama.   On August 2, 1864, he was commissioned Brigadier-General, and on September 8 was ordered to take immediate command of the reserve forces of the State of Florida, to complete their organization and place them at once in service. On September 29, in addition to his other duties, General Miller was assigned to the command of the District of Florida, where he took an active part in the events of that period and until the close of the war.

Brigadier-General Robert Bullock.

Captain Co. G, 7th Florida Infantry, March, 1862; promoted Lieutenant-Colonel April 11, 1862; Colonel June 2, 1863; Brigadier-General 1865.

Gen Robert Bullock was one of the influential men of Florida before the war.   When his State seceded he gave his hearty support to her decision; organized a company in Marion county and, when the 7th Florida was organ-ized, he was made Lieutenant-Colonel.   In 1862 this regiment served in East Tennessee in the brigade of Gen. W. D. M. Davis   The department at that time was commanded by Gen. E. Kirby Smith.   At the time of the battle of Murfreesboro this brigade was still in Smith's department, and on June 2 Lieutenant-Colonel Bullock was commissioned Colonel.   When all available Confederate commands were being concentratad by Bragg to meet the ad-vancing army of Rosecrans, the 7th Florida was one of the regiments assigned to Trigg's brigade of the division at Chickamauga and bear strong testimony to the desperate nature of the fighting there.   At the battle of Missionary Ridge the 7th Florida fought in the brigade of General Finley and the divis-ion of General Bate.   In this brigade and division it continued to serve throughout the Atlanta campaign, under Colonel Bullock, who had already distinguished himself as a cool and gallant commander.   Some of the hardest fighting of the Atlanta campaign was done by this divisihn, and the 7th Florida acted a gallant part in all.   During the campaign into Tennessee Colonel Bul-lock led Finley's brigade and was one of the gallant participants in the terrible battle of Franklin.

Maj.-Gen. William Bate, in his official report of the Tennessee campaign, pays a high compliment to Colonel Bullock.   He says: "T. B. Smith, com-manding Tyler's brigade, and Col. Robert Bullock, commanding Finley's, bore themselves with heroic courage both through good and evil fortune, al-ways executing orders with zeal and alacrity and bearing themselves in the face of the enemy as became reputations which each had theretofore bravely won. The latter was severely wounded near Murfreesboro, and was succeeded by Major Lash, whose coolness and gallantry were marked." Colonel Bullock came out of the Tennessee campaign with the temporary rank of Brigadier-General; he was afterward confirmed and commissioned as Brigadier-General.

Brigadier-General Theodore W. Brevard.

Captain Co. D, 2nd Florida Infantry; appointed Major 1862; promoted Lieutenant-Colonel, 1st Florida Battalion, December, 1863; Colonel 11th Florida Regiment, June, 1864; Brigadier-General March 22, 1865.

After the organization, May 10, 1862 Captain Brevard returned to Florida, served for a time as inspector and mustering officer, but was shortly appointed Major and commissioned to raise a battalion   This was first a cavalry command, known as Brevard's Partisans Rangers, and consisted of four companies.   With this command Major Brevard served in Florida until May, 1864.   In the skirmish that occurred in the suburbs of Jacksonville, 1863, Major Brevard was commended for gallant conduct by General Finley.   In December, 1863, the 1st battallion, Major Brevard, was increased to five companies and Major Brevard promoted to Lieutenant-Colonel.   On February 20, 1864, the battalion took part in the battle of Olustee, doing gallant ervice. In obedience to orders from the War Department at Richmond Finnegan's b igade, of which the 1st battallion formed a part, left for Virginia May 17, arriving at Richmond on May 25, 1864.   On May 28 they were joined by the remnant of Perry's brigade and, under the command of General Finnegan, took part in the second battle of Cold Harbor.   On June 8 the several battalions were formed into regiments and in August, 1864, Lieutenant-Colonel Brevard was promoted Colonel of the 11th Florida, which regiment he commanded until the battle of Sailor's Creek, April 6, 1865, where he and his entire command were captured.   On March 22, 1865, Colonel Brevard was commissioned Brigadier-General, but General Lee's army surrendered and the war ended before his commission could reach him.   After the close of the war Colonel Brevard returned to Tallahassee, where he resumed the practice of his profession.   General Brevard died in Tallahassee.

Colonel David Lang.

Captain Co. C, 8th Florida Infantry, May 15, 1862; promoted Colonel September 17 1862.

Col. David Lang, of the 8th Florida Infantry, was born in Camden county, Ga., in 1838, and educated at the Georgia Military Institute, at Marietta, where he graduated in 1857. As a young man he gave much attention to civil engineering and, soon after his graduation, came to Florida and was elected surveyor of Suwannee county.   When the organization of troops for the Confederate States service began he enlisted as a private in Co. H, 1st Florida Infantry, and was appointed 1st Sergeant. With the 1st Regiment he served one year at Pensacola, under Col. Patton Anderson, and at the expiration of his enlistment was mustered out at Montgomery, Ala., April 3, 1862.   Returning to Florida Sergeant Lang raised a company, of which he was elected Captain; this company was mustered into the Confederate service May 15, 1862, as Co. C, 8th Florida Regiment Infantry. Upon the completion of the organization of the regiment it was ordered to Virginia, and reached Richmond early in July. At the second battle of Manassas, August 29, 1862, Captain Lang found opportunity for distinction; on September 17, 1862, he was engaged in the battle of Sharpsburg. In this fight he was severely wounded in the shoulder, but was on duty again before the battle of Fredericksburg, December 11 to 15, 1862, in which he commanded his regiment, attracting general and favorable comment by the gallantry with which he and his men held at bay the enemy in their attempt to cross the Rappahannock River. His position was exposed to a terrific fire of artillery and musketry, and he was again wounded. Captain Lang was promoted Colonel, to date from the battle of Sharpsburg, September 17, 1862. He commanded the regiment at Chancellorsville and then, on account of the illness of General Perry, took command of the Florida brigade and led it with marked ability and bravery through the Pennsylvania campaign, the great battle of Gettysburg and the retreat to Virginia; continuing in command until the Bristow campaign, October 22, 1863, when General Perry was again on duty. In the battle of the Wilderness May 6, 1864, General Perry was wounded and disabled, and Colonel Lang resumed command of the brigade and it was under his orders during the tremendous conflicts that followed at Spottsylvania Court House, South Anna River and until a few days before the second Cold Harbor. On May 28, 1864, Perry's brigade was attached to General Finnegan's brigade, with Gen Joseph Finnegan in command, and Colonel Lang again took command of his regiment, which he held during the seige of Petersburg and until March 20, 1865, when General Finnegan was transferred to Florida, and General Lang resumed the command of the Florida brigade, to hold it until the surrender at Appomattox. After his return to Florida Colonel Lang resided successively in Suwannee county, Madison county and at Cedar Keys until 1885, when he was appointed Adjutant-General of the State, which position he held until 1893. From 1893 till 1901 he was Private Secretary under Governors Mitchell and Bloxham.

John Day Perkins.

John Day Perkins was born in Tallahassee, Florida, November 15, 1843, his parents being Thomas J. and Amelia M. Perkins. At the outbreak of the Civil War, in 1861, when a mere boy, he ran away from home in order to join a company then being organized in Pensacola; but his father, on account of his extreme youth, brought him back home.

In August of 1861 the Howel Guards, named in honor of Miss Howell, a sister of Mrs. Jefferson Davis, was organized in Leon county, Florida. John Day Perkins was then not 18 years of age; his father, impressed by his strong determinat on to enlist in active service, consented to his joining this company It was composed of 115 men, and left Tallahassee August 27, 1861, as an independent volunteer company, going by rail to Monticello, marching from there to Boston, Ga., and from thence by rail to Richmond, where they went into camp for two or three months.

G. W. Parkhill was Captain; John Eppes, 1st Lieutenant, but he resigned in a few months and R. C. Parkhill was elected to his place; E. L. Hampton, 2nd Lieutenant; Amos Whitehead, 3rd Lieutenant, but he resigned; and John Day Perkins, Corporal. There were other officers also. At the battle of Gaines' Mill G. W. Parkhill was killed and R. C. Parkhill promoted to Captain. Hampton became 1st Lieutenant. And at Winchester, Va., in 1863, John Day Perkins was elected as 2nd Lieutenant.

After having remained in camp at Richmond for three months the company went to Evansport on the Potomac and took charge of a siege gun, or ship point battery, remaining there until May, 1862. John Day Perkins was made Gunner of one of the heavy guns and did all of the shooting with it. Leaving Evansport, they were ordered to Richmond. Upon reaching Frederick City they were attached to the 5th Alabama battalion, under command of Roger A. Pryor; here they encountered the enemy, had several engagements. after which they proceeded to Richmond, where they were mustered into the 2nd Florida Regiment as Co. M, Col. E. A. Perry's brigade, Anderson's division, Hill's corps.

R. C. Parkhill was wounded at Frazier s Farm and later resigned. Hampton was made Captain and John Day Perkins, 1st Lieutenant.

At Gettysburg Hampton was killed and Lieutenant Perkins was made Captain, having command of the company during the battle. On the second day's fight at Gettysburg, July 2, Captain Perkins, while leading in a charge, was wounded, losing his left leg and thumb; he fell on the battle field, remaining there through the entire battle, beneath the heaviest fire of both the enemy and his own men; he was left on the field for two days without food or water, exposed to the burning rays of the July sun, being compelled to bandage his shattered limb with mud and muck to avoid bleeding to death; he was then taken prisoner and removed to the Federal prison at Fort McHenry, where he was confined for nine months and then allowed to return home, being unexchanged. The Federal physicians, after amputating his leg, told him he could not live; shortly thereafter, while laying on his cot, he heard several Northern ladies visiting through the Fort ask, "Where is that little Jonnie Reb Captain?" Somewhat indignant, but aroused by pride and love for his cause, he raised himself up and said—"Here he is." Approaching his bed from curiosity but seeing a boy of but 20, they were touched with sympathy and said, "Oh—he is nothing but a boy. Poor boy, so far from home," and then turned away.

After his return home he made application for field service but was rejected because of the loss of his leg; but was assigned as Enrolling Officer in Conscript Camp at Quincy, Florida, June 14, 1864. He was then ordered to Tallahassee March 2, 1865, being made Post Commander by the Secretary of War, to relieve Captain Blocher, in which capacity he remained until he close of the war in 1865.

He was engaged in the battles of Fredericksburg, Frazier's Farm, Chancellorsville, Mannassas, all of the seven days' fighting around Richmond. Gettysburg and other hard fought battles.

It has been said by his associates in service and comrades in battle that no truer patriot, more gallant Southerner or braver soldier ever lived than John Day Perkins.

Captain Augustus O. MacDonell.

Captain Augustus O. MacDonell, a prominent railroad official of Jacksonville, is a veteran of the 1st Florida Infantry and of the Army of Tennessee. He was born at Savannah, Ga., April 10, 1839, and was reared in Early county of that State. AtGainesville, Fla., in 1860 he became a member of the Gainesville Minute Men, a volunteer company, with which he entered the Confederate service in April 1861, as Company B, 1st Regiment Florida Infantry. This was the first company organized for the Confederate service in Florida. Mr. MacDonell served as a private for one year at Pensacola, and re-enlisting in the spring of 1862, was elected 2nd Lieutenan of Company K. of the 1st Florida Battallion, organized from those of the 1st Regiment who remained in the service. In this rank he served at the battle of Shiloh, April 6-7, 1862, and subsequently was promoted to 1st Lieutenant, and in the spring of 1863 was advanced to the rank of Captain of his Company. Among the battles and campaigns in which he participated after Shiloh, were the siege of Corinth, battle of Farmington, Miss., the transfer to Chattanooga, the march into Kentucky,and battle of Perryville, October 8, 1862, where he was severely wounded, causing his disability for two months. So many men were lost by the 1st and 3rd Florida that they were thereafter consolidated as one regimental command. Lieutenant MacDonell was fit for duty again in time for the battle of Murfreesboro, December 31, 1862, and January 2, 1863, and in this battle he narrowly escaped serious injury, his sword being shattered by a fragment of shell. In the spring of 1863 he was detached from his command for special service in the Southeast, returning to his company just after the battle of Chickamauga and Missionary Ridge; he was immediately placed on the firing line and was actively engaged in the February campaign about Dalton, and the Atlanta campaign, with its numerous skirmishes on battles of Resaca, Dallas, Kennesaw Mountain, Peachtree Creek, and July 22 and 28. Capt. MacDonell commanded his company with credit through this great campaign, one of the most remarkable in the history f warfare, until he was captured by the enemy in the hand-to-hand fight along the entrenched lines southwest of Atlanta, August 7, 1864. This ended his military record, so far as effective service is concerned. He was a prisoner of war at Johnson's Island, Lake Erie, through the winter of 1864-65, suffering much from cold and insufficient food, and was held there unti' July 1865.

Capt. MacDonell has been a resident of Florida since the war, and began his career as a railroad man in 1871. He is now Assistant General Passenger Agent of the Seaboard Air Line Railroad.

PART III
Florida
in the
Spanish-American War.
1898-1899

Company C—3rd United States Volunteer Infantry.

NAMES.	MUSTERED IN.	MUSTERED OUT.	REMARKS.
OFFICERS.			
Captains—			
William H. Cobb	June 17, '98		Resigned.
John A. Condon	June 17, '98	May 2, '99	
1st Lieutenants—			
Albert W. Gilchrist	June 17, '98	May '2, '99	Detailed as Post Adjutant; promoted Captain and
I. Brooks Clark	June 17, '89	May 2, '99	assigned to command of Co. B.
2nd Lieutenants—			
Martin L. Williams	June 17, '98		Promoted 1st Lieutenant and assigned to Co. B.
Alton A. Clark	June 17, '98	May 2, '99	
ENLISTED MEN.			
Alderman, Junius G	June 17, '98	May 2, '99	
Alderman, William P	June 17, '98	May 2, '99	Artificer.
Alford, John H	June 17, '98		Discharged.
Allen, Hiram	June 17, '98	May 2, '99	
Arnett, James N	June 17, '98	May 2, '99	
Arnold, Addison	June 17, '98	May 2, '99	
Asbell, John	June 17, '98	May 2, '99	
Best, James H	June 17, '98	May 2, '99	
Bingham, L. H	June 17, '98	May 2, '99	
Blount, Hugh G	June 17, '98		1st Corporal; promoted Sergeant-Major; died at Guantanamo.
Bond, Walter	June 17, '98	May 2, '99	
Boynton, William H	June 17, '98	May 2, '99	
Brantley, John	June 17, '98	May 2, '99	
Britt, Benjamin H	June 17, '98	May 2, '99	7th Corporal
Brooker, George P	June 17, '98	May 2, '99	
Brown, John W	June 17, '98	May 2, '99	
Buchanan, Emory B	June 17, '98	May 2, '99	
Carter, Sterling L	June 17, '98	May 2, '99	
Carleton, C. L	June 17, '98	May 2, '99	
Carney, Charles W	June 17, '98		8th Corporal; discharged.
Childs, Benjamin F	June 17, '98	Kay 2, '99	
Clark, Robert E	June 17, '98	May 2, '99	
Cochran, Alfred S	June 17, '98	May 2, '99	
Cochran, Calhoun A	June 17, '98	May 2, '99	
Davis, Charles M	June 17, '.8	May 2, '99	
Day, James D	June 17, '98	May 2, '99	Corporal; promoted 4th Sergeant.
Dean, Thadeus R., Jr	June 17, '98	May 2, '99	
Dill, James D	June 17, '98	May 2, '99	
Drawdy, James W	June 17, '98	May 2, '99	
Ferrill, James C	June 17, '98	May 2, '00	
Gay, Mathew C	June 17, '98		Promoted Quartermaster-Sergeant of the Regiment; honorably discharged.
Gilmore, John L	June 17, '98	May 2, '99	3rd Sergeant.
Gocio, Harry C	June 17, '98	May 2, '99	2nd Corporal.
Green, Herbert	June 17, '98		Discharged.
Hamilton, John	June 17, '98	May 2, '99	
Hampton, Archie	June 17, '98	May 2, '99	4th Corporal
Hancock, Thomas L	June 17, '98	May 2, '99	Trumpeter.
Hansen, Newton	June 17, '98	May 2, '99	
Harris, Henry T	June 17, '98	May 2, '99	
Harward, Samuel	June 17, '98	May 2, '99	5th Corporal.
Hayman, Nathan L	June 17, '98	May 2, '99	
Hayman, Jerry J	June 17, '98		Discharged.
Hays, Frank	June 17, '98		Honorable discharge.
Henderson, Fred Pope	June 17, '98	May 2, '99	6th Corporal; promoted 1st Sergeant Co. L.
Henderson, Henry D	June 17, '98	May 2, '99	2nd Corporal; promoted Color Sergeant.
Heinisch, Arthur	June 17, '98	May 2, '99	
Hendry, Francis F	June 17, '98	May 2, '99	
Herndon, Ned C	June 17, '98	May 2, '99	
Herndon, Thomas J	June 17, '98	May 2, '99	3rd Sergeant; promoted Quartermaster-Sergeant.
Hickey, James G	June 17, '98	May 2, '99	
Hicks, Wanton J	June 17, '98	May 2, '99	
Higley, Charles P	June 17, '98	May 2, '99	
Hiag, Jonathan, Jr	June 17, '98	May 2, '99	
Hodge, Green W	June 17, '98		Discharged.
Hodge, William B	June 17, '98	May 2, '99	
Isaacs, George W	June 17, '98	May 2, '99	
James, William D	June 17, '98	May 2, '99	
Jenkins, Julian H	June 17, '96	May 2, '99	3rd Corporal; promoted Quartermaster-Sergeant
Johnson, Luther C	June 17, '98	May 2, '99	1st Corporal.
Johnson, Samuel J	June 17, '98	May 2, '99	
Jones, W. O.	June 17, '98	May 2, '99	Wagoner.
Kanne, Walter R	June 17, '98	May 2, '99	
Kennedy, John W	June 17, '98	May 2, '99	
Langford, Curtis R	June 17, '98	May 2, '99	
Lovett, William J	June 17, '98	May 2, '99	
Maddox, Bryon	June 17, '98	May 2, '99	
Montgomery, John D	June 17, '98	May 2, '99	
Murrell, Edward W., Jr	June 17, '98	May 2, '99	
Mutch, George	June 17, '98	May 2, '99	
Padgett, Jerome W	June 17, '98	May 2, '99	
Page, Jacob T	June 17, '98	May 2, '99	Trumpeter.
Parker, John N	June 17, '98	May 2, '99	
Read, Peyton R	June 17, '98		Discharged.

Company C—3rd United States Volunteer Infantry.
(CONTINUED.)

NAMES.	MUSTERED IN.	MUSTERED OUT.	REMARKS.
Richards, Maxwell M	June 17, '98	May 2, '99	
Sauls, Joseph L	June 17, '98	May 2, '99	4th Sergeant; promoted Color Sergeant of the Regiment and assigned to Co. L.
Scott, Jesse H	June 17, '98	May 2, '99	6th Corporal.
Sellers, Alonzo D	June 17, '98	May 2, '99	
Sheridan, Dennis P	June 17, '98	May 2, '99	
Sillito, Lewis A	June 17, '98		Discharged.
Smith, Drew E	June 17, '98	May 2, '99	
Stanley, Caleb	June 17, '98	May 2, '99	Cook.
Stephens, Coleman	June 17, '98	May 2, '99	
Stewart, William A	June 17, '98	May 2, '99	
Stroup, Larken M	June 17, '98	May 2, '99	
Swearingen, John J	June 17, '98		Discharged.
Tippins, Edward D	June 17, '98	May 2, '99	
Thomas, Barney A	June 17, '98	May 2, '99	
Vischer, George G	June 17, '98	May 2, '99	3rd Corporal.
Wadsworth, Samuel T	June 17, '98	May 2, '99	
Wadsworth, William J	June 17, '98	May 2, '99	
Watkins, Richard E	June 17, '98	May 2, '99	5th Corporal; promoted Sergeant-Major.
Watson, Benjamin W	June 17, '98	May 2, '99	
Webb, William H	June 17, '98		Discharged.
Whidden, James I	June 17, '98	May 2, '99	
Whitesides, Claude L	June 17, '98	May 2, '99	
Wilson, M. A	June 17, '98	May 2, '99	1st Sergeant; honorably discharged.
Wirt, Earl L	June 17, '98	May 2, '99	Promoted 1st Sergeant.
Wirt, Thereon E	June 17, '98	May 2, '99	7th Corporal; 4th Sergeant.

3d Battalion—1st Florida Regiment.

This Battalion was organized at Tampa, Florida, May 23, 1898, as part of the 1st Regiment, Florida Volunteer Infantry. On May 27, in obedience to verbal orders of Major General commanding 5th A. C., it marched from Fort Brooke Reservation to Palmetto Beach, a distance of about 2 miles. On July 25, in compliance with orders Commanding General 1st Brigade, 3rd Division, 4th Army Corps, camp was broken at Tampa and the cars taken for Fernandina, a distance of 241 miles. On August 23 camp was broken at Fernandina in compliance with orders commanding General, 4th Army Corps, and the cars taken for Huntsville, Ala., a distance of 700 miles. On October 8th the 1st and 2nd Battalion were ordered mustered out of the service and proceeded to Tallahassee, Florida, leaving the Battalion as at present composed. On January 4, 1899, orders were received for its muster out, which was accomplished on January 27, 1899.

Roll Field, Staff and Band—1st Florida Infantry.

NAMES.	MUSTERED IN.	MUSTERED OUT.	REMARKS.
Colonels—			
William. F. Williams	May 24, '98		Resigned June 24, '98.
Charles P. Lovel	May 24, '98	Dec. 3, '98	Major; promoted Colonel.
Lieutenant-Colonel—			
Irvin E. Webster	May 27, '98		
Majors—			
Robert E. Davidson	May 25, '98		
John W. Sackett	May 27, '98		Transferred to command of Battalion Provisional Engineers; ordered to Porto Rico; returned to United States September 16, '98; rejoined Regiment October 1, '98; Major of 3rd Battalion.
Adjutant—			
Frank A. Ross	May 23, '98		Regimental Adjutant (1st Lieutenant; trans- was ferred as Adjutant to the 3rd Battalion October 8, '98.
Surgeon—			
Dr. R. P. Isler	April 5, '98		Major and Regimental Surgeon.

Roll, Field, Staff and Band—1st Florida Infantry.
(Continued.)

AMES	MUSTERED IN.	MUSTERED OUT.	REMARKS.
Assistant-Surgeons—			
Charles A. Dunham	April 25, '98		Assistant-Surgeon; rank of 1st Lieutenant.
Charles B. McKinnon	May 1, '98		Assistant-Surgeon; rank of 1st Lieutenant.
Quartermasters—			
Andrew J. Harris	May 18, '98		1st Lieutenant; Regimental Quartermaster; resigned June 27, '98.
Frank X. Shuler			Appointed 1st Lieutenant and Regimental Quartermaster June 28, '98; Captain and Regimental Quartermaster September 20, '98.
Sergeant-Major—			
Charles S. Fleming	April 23, '98		
Quartermaster-Sergeants—			
Whiting Hyer	May 1, '98		Discharged September 10, '98.
Amory B. Amsden	April 25, '98		
Battalion Adjutants—			
Albert Wright	April 25, '98		1st Lieutenant.
Charles H. Chestnut	April 23, '98		1st Lieutenant; transferred to Co. F.
Henry W. Fowler	April 22, '98		1st Lieutenant.
Chaplain—			
William. W. Eleway	July 28, '98		Chaplain with rank of Major.
Hospital Stewards—			
James G. DeVaux	April 23, '98		Discharged August 6, '98.
James B. Carlisle	June 16, '98		Transferred to 1st Florida Battalion October 7, '98.
BAND.			
William D. Hallowell	July 5, '98		Chief Musician; transferred to Co. G.
Felipe Vasquez	July 5, '98		Principal Musician; reduced to the ranks.
Edward J. Lynch	July 5, '98		Principal Musician; transferred to Co.
Leon A. Blake	July 5, '98		Private Musician.
Antonio Cubello	July 5, '98		Private.
Arthur Fitzgerald	July 5, '98		Private; transferred to Co.
Henry W. Sherman	July 5, '98		Private.
J. W. Bracken	July 5, '98		Band Sergeant; transferred to Co.
William. H. Barr	July 15, '98		Transferred fom Co. H.
George E. Dillon	April 25, '98		Transferred from Co. M.
Eugene B. Mooney	April 25, '98		Transferred from Co. I.
Alego Monters	April 25, '98		Transferred from Co. I.
Jose Santiso	April 25, '98		Transferred from Co. I.
Artero Vasquez	April 25, '98		Transferred from Co. M.
John J. VanPelt	April 25, '98		Transferred from Co. I.
Oscar K. Cansford	April 25, '98		Transferred from Co.
Elmer E. Cain	April 25, '98		Transferred from Co.
Lewis J. Hardwick	April 25, '98		Transferred from Co.
Charles Medury	April 25, '98		Transferred from Co.
Patrick H. Malone	April 25, '98		Transferred from Co.
Anthony Malone	April 25, '98		Transferred from Co.

Company A—1st Florida Regiment.

This company was organized at Ocala, Florida, May 24, 1884, under the name of Ocala Rifles; it was afterward known as Co. A, 2nd Battalion Florida State Troops. When the United States called for troops to serve in the Spanish-American War this company was accepted by the Governor for service in the United States Volunteers. On April 25, 1898, they left Ocala by rail for Tampa, Fla., arrived there the same day and went into camp at Fort Brooke, at which place the company was mustered in May 20, 1898. Broke camp May 27, 1898, and marched to Camp DeSoto, Tampa, Fla., where it went into camp. June 30, 1898, broke camp and marched to Tampa Heights, going on duty with the United States Siege Artillery commanded by Major Wills. Left Tampa by rail July 21, 1898, for Fernandina, arriving at camp July 22, 1898; remained there until August 1, 1898, then left by rail for Huntsville, Ala.; arrived there August 25, 1898; left Huntsville October 9, 1898, arrived at Tallahassee October 11, 1898, to which place the company had been ordered for the purpose of being mustered out of service. The company was furloughed October 16, 1898, for thirty days; company mustered out December 3, 1898.

Roll Company A—1st Florida Infantry.

NAMES.	MUSTERED IN.	MUSTERED OUT.	REMARKS.
OFFICERS.			
Captain.—			
Robert E. Davidson	April 25, '98	Dec. 3, '98	Promoted Major; June 30, '98.
Samuel R. Birdsey Jr	April 25, '98	Dec. 3, '98	1st Lieutenant; promoted Captain July, '98, vice Davidson promotion.
1st Lieutenant—			
Cevie V. Roberts	April 25, '98	Dec. 3, '98	2nd Lieutenant promoted 1st Lieutenant; July 1, '98.
2nd Lieutenant—			
Charles M. Hilliard	April 25, '98	Dec. 3, '98	Transferred from Co. D to Co. A June, '98.
ENLISTED MEN.			
Abshier, William F.	April 25, '98	Dec. 3, '98	
Agnew, Samuel A	April 25, '98	Dec. 3, '98	Deserted August, 8 '98 at Fernandina, Fla.
Allen, John W	April 25, '98	Dec. 3, '98	
Atkinson, S. D.	June 2, '98	Dec. 3, '98	
Ayers, Lewis B	April 25, '98	Dec. 3, '98	
Bangs, William N	April 25, '98	Dec. 3, '98	Sergeant.
Beasley, Harry L	April 25, '98	Dec. 3, '98	Corporal; appointed August 1, '98.
Ballard, Leander F	April 25, '98	Dec. 3, '98	Artificer.
Birdsey, Ralph T	April 25, '98	Dec. 3, '98	Q. M. Sergeant.
Bishoff, Frank J	April 25, '98	Dec. 3, '98	
Brier, DeWitt	June 27, '98	Dec. 3, '98	Musician.
Boulware, James H	July 20, '98	Dec. 3, '98	
Brown, Alfred L	April 25, '98	Dec. 3, '98	Died at Fernandina August 22, '98.
Brunson, James O	April 25, '98	Dec. 3, '98	Discharged August 7, '98, for disability.
Calhoon, Walter D	June 10, '98	Dec. 3, '98	
Calhoon, William B	April 25, '98	Dec. 3, '98	
Carter, George R	April 25, '98	Dec. 3, '98	
Clark, Henry M	April 25, '98	Dec. 3, '98	
Clay, Jackson W	April 25, '98	Dec. 3, '98	
Clements, Charles B	April 25, '98	Dec. 3, '98	Corporal.
Cockrave, Thomas J	July 2, '98	Dec. 3, '98	
Coon, Holmes L	April 25, '98	Dec. 3, '98	Deserted August 8, '98 at Fernandina.
Cress, Charles	April 25, '98	Dec. 3, '98	Corporal; August1, '98.
Cresson, Henry C	April 25, '98	Dec. 3, '98	
Croft, John W	April 25, '98	Dec. 3, '98	
Crosette, Edgar L	April 25, '98	Dec. 3, '98	1st Sergeant.
Curry, Hudson	April 25, '98	Dec. 3, '98	
Ditto, Frank W	April 25, '98	Dec. 3, '98	Corporal; appointed August 1, '98.
Ditton, Samuel L	April 25, '98	Dec. 3, '98	Corporal; appointed Sergeant.
Dunn, William C	July 9, '98	Dec. 3, '98	
Edwards, William P	April 25, '98	Dec. 3, '98	Corporal; appointed June 1, '98.
Finch, Chester O	June 20, '98	Dec. 3, '98	
Flood, Harry T	April 25, '98	Dec. 3, '98	Transferred to Co. B, October 4, '98.
Fort, Leroy	July 20, '98	Dec. 3, '98	
Frink Samuel L	June 10, '98	Dec. 3, '98	
Frank Henry	June 10, '98	Dec. 3, '98	
Gary, William T	April 25, '98	Dec. 3, '98	Corporal; appointed color Sergeant September 26, '98.
Galipau, J. J	June 25, '98	Dec. 3, '98	
Gaskill, William H	April 25, '98	Dec. 3, '98	
Gaskill, Asa J	April 25, '98	Dec. 3, '98	
Geiger, Joshua C	April 25, '98	Dec. 3, '98	
Giddens, Clayton E	April 25, '98	Dec. 3, '98	
Giddens, Alfred D	June 11, '98	Dec. 3, '98	
Graham, John M	April 25, '98	Dec. 3, '98	
Halsell, Austen B	April 25, '98	Dec. 3, '98	
Hamilton, Benjamin E	April 25, '98	Dec. 3, '98	
Harrell, Arthur C	April 25, '98	Dec. 3, '98	
Harrell, John D	April 25, '98	Dec. 3, '98	
Harris, C. A	June 22, '98	Dec. 3, '98	
Harris, Thomas H	April 25, '98	Dec. 3, '98	
Harvey, Fred	April 25, '98	Dec. 3, '98	
Herlong, H. W	July 7, '98	Dec. 3, '98	
Hiers, Bryant D	April 23, '98	Dec. 3, '98	Corporal; appointed May 20, '98.
Hightower, Percy	July 16, '98	Dec. 3, '98	
Hines, Richard	May 12, '98	Dec. 3, '98	
Hinson, George	April 23, '98	Dec. 3, '98	Deserted August 7, '98 at Fernandina, Fla.
House, Claude P	April 23, '98	Dec. 3, '98	
Ingram, Archie F	April 23, '98	Dec. 3, '98	
Ives, Washington M. Jr	April 23, '98	Dec. 3, '98	Corporal; transferred to hospital corps, '98.
Jarrett, Charles H	April 23, '98	Dec. 3, '98	
King, John H	April 23, '98	Dec. 3, '98	
Lancaster, George E	April 23, '98	Dec. 3, '98	
Lancaster, John W	July 8, '98	Dec. 3, '98	Sergeant; promoted 2nd Lieutenant, transferred as 2nd Lieutenant to Co. D October 16, '98.
Lapham, H. H	June 27, '98	Dec. 3, '98	
Laurence, P. B	May 10, '98	Dec. 3, '98	
Lloyd, Charles H	April 23, '98	Dec. 3, '98	
Livingston, Thomas M	April 23, '98	Dec. 3, '98	Corporal; Adj. 1, '98.
McIntosh, Edward L	April 23, '98	Dec. 3, '98	Sergeant.
McClendon, F. M.	June 23, '98	Dec. 3, '98	
McDavid, James S	April 25, '98	Dec. 3, '98	
McCowan, H. L	Aug. 22, '98	Dec. 3, '98	Corporal; appointed August 1, '98.
Mark, Victor E	April 25, '98	Dec. 3, '98	
Marsh, James M	April 25, '98	Dec. 3, '98	

Roll Company A—1st Florida Infantry.

NAMES.	MUSTERED IN.	MUSTERED OUT.	REMARKS.
Mathews, John H	April 25, '98	Dec. 3, '98	Corporal; appointed July 1, '98.
Maloney, Alvin F	May 27, '98		Discharged September 8, '98, for disability.
Martin, Lewis	April 25, '98	Dec. 3, '98	
Messing, Sig	April 25, '98		Discharged September 8, '98.
Mead, W. S	July 30, '98	Dec. 3, '98	
Moody, John P	April 25, '98	Dec. 3, '98	Corporal.
Moody, Solomon W	April 25, '98	Dec. 3, '98	
O'Hanlon, Doyle	April 25, '98	Dec. 3, '98	
Payne, Richard W	April 25, '98	Dec. 3, '98	
Pillsbury, William	June 7, '98	Dec. 3, '98	
Pyles, Thomas N	June 25, '98	Dec. 3, '98	
Perry, Alfred T	April 25, '98	Dec. 3, '98	
Posten, Samuel P	April 25, '98	Dec. 3, '98	
Rawles, E. C	June 27, '98	Dec. 3, '98	
Rawls, M. H	June 27, '98	Dec. 3, '98	
Rearden, John L	June 27, '98		Discharged September 28, '98, for disability.
Rickards, Paul C	April 25, '98	Dec. 3, '98	Musician.
Shortridge, Lewis H	April 25, '98	Dec. 3, '98	
Skipper, Rederick M	June 28, '98	Dec. 3, '98	
Smith, Elevyn L	April 25, '98	Dec. 3, '98	
Sparr, Ernest L	April 25, '98	Dec. 3, '98	Sergeant.
Sowden, Charles T Jr	April 23, '98	Dec. 3, '98	
Stanley, Fred W	April 23, '98	Dec. 3, '98	
Stewart, Charles J	April 23, '98	Dec. 3, '98	
Strobar, William P	April 23, '98	Dec. 3, '98	
Thomas, Otho W	June 28, '98	Dec. 3, '98	
Thower, Benjamin K. J	June 28, '98	Dec. 3, '98	
Turner, Frank S	April 23, '98	Dec. 3, '98	
Triplet, Wade H	April 23, '98	Dec. 3, '98	
Tireman, Claude	April 23, '98	Dec. 3, '98	Transferred to Co. F October 9, '98.
Vanness, Ralph E	April 23, '98	Dec. 3, '98	
Walker, Charles B	July 16, '98	Dec. 3, '98	Discharged September 10, '98.
White, William B. M	April 23, '98	Dec. 3, '98	
Williams, James	April 23, '98	Dec. 3, '98	
Williamson, Frank	April 23, '98	Dec. 3, '98	
Yandle, Charles B	April 23, '98	Dec. 3, '98	
Yonge, Chandler B	April 23, '98	Dec. 3, '98	
Zimmerman, Karl H	April 23, '98	Dec. 3, '98	
Buchan, Isaac N	April 23, '98	Dec. 3, '98	Corporal; appointed August 1, '98.
Ludwig, John W	June 1, '98	Dec. 3, '98	Transferred to hospital corps June 7, '98.
McCant, S. D	May 22, '98		Transferred to Co. F October 9, '98.

Company B—1st Florida Regiment.

This company left Leesburg, Fla., May 14, 1898, by order of Adjutant-General Houston, of the State of Florida, for Tampa, to be mustered into the service of the United States. They arrived in Tampa the same date, camping at Fort Brooke; mustered into service of United States May 20, 1898. On May 27 broke camp, marched a distance of two miles to DeSoto Park and pitched camp; left DeSoto Park for Fernandina, Fla., by rail July 21, 1898; arrived in Fernandina July 22; marched one mile and pitched camp; left Fernandina, Fla., August 22 1898, for Huntsville, Ala.; camped that night in streets of Fernandina; left August 23 for Huntsville; arrived there August 25. marched one and one-half miles; pitched temporary camp in shelter tents; on August 26 marched one mile to permanent camp. This company transferred to the 3rd Battalion to be retained in service September 29, 1898; mustered out of service January 27, 1899.

Roll Company B (Capt. George E. Lovell)—1st Florida Infantry.

NAMES	MUSTERED IN.	MUSTERED OUT.	REMARKS.
OFFICERS.			
Captain—			
George E. Lovell	April 23, '98	Jan. 27, '99	Promoted to Colonel of the Regiment July 20, '98.

Roll Company B (Capt. George E. Lovell)—1st Florida Infantry.
(CONTINUED.)

NAMES.	MUSTERED IN.	MUSTERED OUT.	REMARKS.
1st Lieutenants—			
Joseph C. West	April 23, '98		
Augustus C. Hart	April 23, '98	Jan. 27, '99	Transferred from Co. C October 9. '98,
2nd Lieutenant—			
Joseph R. Cunningham	April 23, '98		
ENLISTED MEN.			
Barker, James H.	July 9, '98		
Benton, Samuel A.	April 23, '98	Jan. 27, '99	
Barnett, Jeremiah I.	April 23, '98	Jan. 27, '99	
Bozeman, Daniel T.	April 23, '98	Jan. 27, '99	
Bosanquet, C. A.	June 22, '98	Jan. , '99	
Branch, Benjamin S.	April 23, '98	Jan. 27, '99	Transferred to Co. E October 9, '98,
Brown, Charles U.	April 23, '98	Jan. 27, '99	Corporal; appointed July 22, '98.
Bridger, George F	Jan. 9, '98	Jan. 27, '99	Sergeant.
Corley, Bartley	April 23, '98	Jan. 27, '99	
Corman, Alex B.	April 23, '98	Jan. 27, '99	
Cureton, Clarence	April 23, '98	Jan. 27, '99	
Cureton, George B.	April 23, '98	Jan. 27, '99	
Coughlin, John	April 23, '98	Jan. 27, '99	
Chamberlin, Garrett V.	April 23, '98	Jan. 27, '99	
Collens, Jesse S.	June 25, '98	Jan. 27, '98	Corporal; appointed November 1, '98.
Crenshaw, Charles E.	July 25, '98	Jan. 27, '99	Discharged, disabled August 29, '98.
Dixon, John H.	May 10, '98	Jan. 27, '99	
Dixon, Samuel W.	May 10, '98		Discharged, disabled August 11, '98.
DeWitt, John W.	May 10, '98	Jan. 27, '99	
Diehl, Walter	May 10, '98	Jan. 27, '99	
Froscher, Elbert A.	May 10, '98	Jan. 27, '99	Corporal; appointed November 1, '98.
Fink, William H.	April 23, '98	Jan. 27, '99	
Flynn, Paul J.	July 22, '98	Jan. 27, '99	
Fails, Ralph C.	April 23, '98	Jan. 27, '99	
Gordon, Thomas H.	April 23, '98	Jan. 27, '99	Sergeant.
Green, Willie A.	April 25, '98	Jan. 27, '99	
Gruver, John A.	July 2, '98	Jan. 27, '99	Transferred to United States Signal Corps.
Griffith, Eugene O.	April 25, '98	Jan. 27, '99	
Hardman, Herbert W.	April 25, '98		Deserted November 18, '98 at Huntsville, Ala.
Havens, James D.	April 25, '98	Jan. 27, '99	Transferred from Co. L.
Harmond, Robert S.	April 25, '98	Jan. 27, '99	
Harrison, William C.	April 25, '98	Jan. 27, '99	
Hackney, Robert L.	July 19, '98	Jan. 27, '99	
Hennis, John.	July 21, '98	Jan. 27, '99	
Jackson, Joseph	July 25, '98	Jan. 27, '98	
Jackson, James	April 23, '98	Jan. 27, '99	
Jones, Lonnie R.	April 23, '98		Discharged disability September 30. '98.
Jordan, Elias W.	May 10, '98	Jan. 27, '99	
Jordan, Joel A.	May 10, '98	Jan. 27, '99	
Jones, Oliver	April 25, '98	Jan. 27, '99	
Kininger, Joseph I.	April 25, '98	Jan. 27, '99	Sergeant.
Kramer, Frederick S.	May 10, '98	Jan. 27, '99	Artificer, appointed June 1, '98.
Lovelace, Henry	April 23, '98	Jan. 27, '99	Corporal; July 22, '98 transferred to Co. M Oct. 8 '98.
Lamoreaux, Cleo C.	April 23, '98	Jan. 27, '99	Transferred to Co. A October 8, '98.
Laurence, Percy B.	April 23, '98	Jan. 27, '99	
Martin, Joseph B.	April 23, '98	Jan. 27, '99	
Martin, John F.	April 27, '98	Jan. 27, '99	
Magill, Thomas A.	April 27, '98	Jan. 27, '99	
McCully, Andrew P.		Jan. 27, '99	Corporal; appointed.
McClendon, Jesse	April 25, '98	Jan. 27, '99	Corporal.
McClendon, Richison	April 27, '98	Jan. 27, '99	Discharged, disability August 11, '98.
Mixon, James D.	May 10, '98		Corporal; appointed November 1, '98.
Mehaffy, James M.	May 10, '98	Jan. 27, '99	
Mattox, Herschel B.	May 10, '98	Jan. 27, '99	
Milholin, Thomas J.	July 22, '98	Jan. 27, '99	
Nelson, William E.	April 23, '98		Deserted August 11, at Fernandina.
Otto, George	July 9, '65		1st Sergeant.
Noble, Adam	April 23, '98	Jan. 27, '99	Q. M. Sergeant.
Noble, Charles S.	April 23, '98	Jan. 27, '99	Corporal.
Noble, Mason J.	April 23, '98	Jan. 27, '99	
Owens, Zackary	July 6, '98	Jan. 27, '99	
Pearce, Preston P.	April 23, '98	Jan. 27, '99	
Pepper, Sydney D.	April 23, '98	Jan. 27, '99	Transferred to hospital corps June 22, '98.
Peter, Emmett B.	April 23, '9—	Jan. 27, '99	
Purdy, Albert M.	April 23, '98	Jan. 27, '99	
Puckett, Thomas R.	April 23, '98	Jan. 27, '99	Transferred to Co. M October 8, '98.
Register, James T.	April 23, '98	Jan. 27, '99	
Rizer, Harry W.	April 23, '98	Jan. 27, '99	
Roe, Charles E.	July 19, '98	Jan. 27, '99	
Ross, William	April 23, '98	Jan. 27, '99	Corporal.
Sims, Joseph L.	April 23, '98	Jan. 27, '99	Sergeant; traansferred to Co. C October 8, '98.
Stephens, Albert R.	May 6, '98	Jan. 27, '99	Corporal.
Sparkman, Hugh C.	April 23, '98		Died at Fernandina. Fla., August 28, '98.
Stone, John F.	April 23, '98	Jan. 27, '99	
Smith, Harry B.	July 13, '98	Jan. 27, '99	
Smith, Villen C.	Jan. 15, '98	Jan. 27, '99	Bugler.
Stivinder, Calvin L.			

Roll Company B (Capt. George E. Lovell)—1st Florida Infantry.
(CONTINUED.)

NAMES.	MUSTERED IN.	MUSTERED OUT.	REMARKS.
Slouterman, William T.	April 23, '98		Discharged, disabled August 11, '98.
Smith, Thomas W.	April 23, '98	Jan. 27, '99	
Sessions, Percy W.	April 23, '98	Jan. 27, '99	
Slater, George.	April 23, '98	Jan. 27, '99	
Seclore, Walter M.	April 23, '98	Jan. 27, '99	
Tommey, Joel C.	April 23, '98	Jan. 27, '99	
Wilkinson, Mack J.	May 10, '98	Jan. 27, '99	
Wicks, Sanford W.	May 10, '98	Jan. 27, '99	
Williams, Charles T.	May 10, '98		Discharged, disability August 11, '98.
Whiting, Francis.	May 10, '98	Jan. 27, '99	
Williams, Charles E.	May 10, '98	Jan. 27, '99	Transferred to Co. M October 8, '98.
Watson, Orrin W.	May 10, '98	Jan. 27, '99	
Wilson, George S.	May 10, '98	Jan. 27, '99	Corporal.
Yates, Harry M.	May 10, '98	Jan. 27, '99	
Yates, Gettis W.	May 10, '98	Jan. 27, '99	
Young, Eugene B.	May 10, '98	Jan. 27, '99	
Stith, Jack.	May 10, '98	Jan. 27, '99	
Von Kopperlow, Max L.	July 12, '98	Jan. 27, '99	Bugler; appointed July 15, '98.
Banks, Edward P.	April 25, '98	Jan. 27, '99	Transferred from Co. C.
Bryson, William K.	May 24, '98	Jan. 27, '99	Transferred from Co. M.
Budd, Isaac M.	Aug. 26, '98	Jan. 27, '99	Transferred from Co. M.
Craft, Robert W.	June 22, '98	Jan. 27, '99	
Castelberry, Locke.	April 27, '98	Jan. 27, '99	Transferred from Co. M.
Cain, Elmer C.	April 28, '98	Jan. 27, '99	Transferred from Regimental Band October 5, '98
Flynn, Paul J.	July 22, '98	Jan. 27, '99	
Flood, Harry F.	May 20, '98	Jan. 27, '99	Transferred from Co. A October 8, '98.
Gray, William H.	June 14, '98	Jan. 27, '99	
Hodge, George D.	June 7, '98	Jan. 27, '99	
Helveston, Joseph L.	April 25, '98	Jan. 27, '99	Transferred from Co. L October 8, '98.
Hennes, Joseph.	April 25, '98	Jan. 27, '99	
Kaner, Sam.	June 20, '98	Jan. 27, '99	
Mobley, James.	April 25, '98	Jan. 27, '99	Corporal; reduced to rank.
Markham, Millard L.	June 20, '98	Jan. 27, '99	
Mattair, William E.	June 28, '98	Jan. 27, '99	
Malene, Nnthony.	April 25, '98	Jan. 27, '99	Transferred to Co. B from Regimental Band.
Malene, Patrick H.	April 25, '98	Jan. 27, '99	Transferred to Co. B from Regimental Band.
Mulhattan, Thomas J.	July 22, '98	Jan. 27, '99	Transferred to Co. L October 8, '98.
Pillsbury, Charles C.	Aug. 3, '98	Jan. 27, '99	Transferred from Co. E October 8, '98.
Smith, Villers C.	July 13, '98	Jan. 27, '99	
Smoak, John T.	June 29, '98	Jan. 27, '99	
Tayler, Robert.	June 2, '98	Jan. 27, '99	Transferred from Co. C October 8, '98.
Wellons, Nixon N.	May 10, '98	Jan. 27, '99	Transferred from Co. D June 1, '98.
Wilson, William J.	July 22, '98	Jan. 27, '99	
Adams, Sidney F.	June 22, '98	Jan. 27, '99	Appointed Corporal; July 22,; discharged for disability August 11, '98.
Brown, Charles W.	July 22, '98	Jan. 27, '99	Transferred to Co. L October 8, '98.
Griffith, Eugene O.	June 22, '98	Jan. 27, '99	Transferred to United States Signal Corps July 2, '98.
Wilson, David C.	June 11, '98	Jan. 27, '99	Transferred to Co. C October 8, '98.
Denham, George L.	July 6, '98	Jan. 27, '99	Transferred from Co. L October 8, '98; deserted November 25, '98.

Company C—1st Florida Regiment.

This company was organized in Orlando, Florida, and left there by rail May 14, 1898, for Tampa, a distance of 92 miles; arrived there May 14, and pitched camp at Fort Brooke, Tampa, Fla. Was mustered in there May 20, 1898, broke camp and marched to DeSoto Park and pitched camp May 27; moved with Regiment on July 21 from Tampa to Fernandina, Fla., by rail, a distance of a least 250 miles Arrived at Fernandina July 22, pitched camp there same date; broke camp with Regiment about noon of August 22 and marched into town, a distance of one mile, about 6 p. m. same date, and bivouacked in streets until noon of August 23, when they left by rail for Huntsville, Ala., which latter place was reached about 11 a. m. August 25; distance traveled about six hundred miles, via. Callahan, Fla., Waycross, Macon and Atlanta Ga., and Chattanooga, Tenn.; pitched temporary camp August 25. On August 26 marched about one mile and pitched permanent camp, distance about one mile and a half from town. Broke camp at Huntsville October 9 and departed from there at 8.45 p. m. same date by rail via Chattanooga, Tenn., Atlanta, Macon, Albany and Thomasville, Ga., and Monticello, Fla., for Tallahassee, a distance of about five hundred miles; which latter place was reached about 9 a. m. October 11, 1898, and pitched camp in Houston's Green, distant about one mile from town.

Roll Company C (Capt. John N. Bradshaw)—1st Florida Infantry.

NAMES.	MUSTERED IN.	MUSTERED OUT.	REMARKS.
OFFICERS.			
Captain—			
John N. Bradshaw	April 25, '98	Dec. 3, '98	
1st Lieutenants—			
Augustus C. Hart	April 25, '98		Transferred as 1st Lieutenant to Co. B; special Order No. 136.
Joseph C. West	April 25, '98	Dec. 3, '98	Transferred from Co. B as 1st Lieutenant October 16, '99; Special Order No. 130.
2nd Lieutenants—			
Frank X. Schuller	April 25, '98	Dec. 3, '98	Appointed 1st Lieutenant and Regimental Quartermaster June 2, '98; appointed Captain and Regimental Quartermaster September 10, '98.
Charles E. McDowell	April 25, '98	Dec. 3, '98	1st Sergeant; appointed 2nd Lieutenant July 1, '98.
ENLISTED MEN.			
Allen, Clifford	April 25, '98	Dec. 3, '98	
Allen, John E.	April 25, '98	Dec. 3, '98	
Anderson, John A.	April 25, '98		Died at Fort McPherson, Ga., August 15, '98.
Amsden, Amory O.	April 25, '98	Dec. 3, '98	Corporal; appointed Regimental Quartermaster-Sergeant September 10, '98.
Arnold, Roland	April 25, '98	Dec. 3, '98	Bugler.
Bartlett, Clifford T.	April 25, '98	Dec. 3, '98	
Banks, Edward	April 25, '98	Dec. 3, '98	Corporal; transferred to Co. B; R. G. O. 42, October 9, '98.
Baker, Walter	July 23, '98		
Barker, George A.	April 25, '98	Dec. 3, '98	
Barksdale, Edward H.	April 25, '98	Dec. 3, '98	
Bartlett, Percy G.	April 25, '98	Dec. 3, '98	Promoted Corporal July 9, '98.
Barrow, R. E.	July 3, '98		
Brunson, Laurence E.	April 23, '98	Dec. 3, '98	
Bowman, B. T.	July 17, '98		
Browne, Horace	April 23, '98	Dec. 3, '98	
Bumby, Jesse	April 23, '98	Dec. 3, '98	
Butt, Arthur T.	April 23, '98	Dec. 3, '98	Musician.
Bruton, James H.	April 23, '98	Dec. 3, '98	
Bates, Walter	April 26, '98	Dec. 3, '98	Transferred to Hospital Corps, U. S. A.; Special Order 126.
Bryant, Guy A.	July 17, '98		
Cisco, Victor W.	April 23, '98	Dec. 3, '98	
Campbell, William B.	April 23, '98	Dec. 3, '98	Corporal.
Carter, John C.	May 9, '98	Dec. 3, '98	Artificer.
Clayton, Benjamin W.	April 25, '98	Dec. 3, '98	
Crews, Joseph L.	April 25, '98	Dec. 3, '98	
Cooper, Vanden W.	April 25, '98	Dec. 3, '98	
Combs, Walter H.	April 25, '98	Dec. 3, '98	Transferred to Regimental hospital service June '98.
Curdollo, Frank	April 25, '98	Dec. 3, '98	
Cary, Geoffry Elwes	May 18, '98	Dec. 3, '98	Corporal; discharged September 28, '98; Special Order 118.
Decker, Thomas M.	May 18, '98	Dec. 3, '98	Promoted Quartermaster-Sergeant July 1, '98.
Darling, Thomas J.	April 23, '98	Dec. 3, '98	
Donnehy, Patrick	April 23, '98	Dec. 3, '98	
DeCantillon, William	July 3, '98		Deserted August 28, '98.
Edwards, Marvel	April 23, '98	Dec. 3, '98	
Evans, Frank	April 23, '98	Dec. 3, '98	
Frierson, Thomas M.	July		
Forsythe, James	April 23, '98	Dec. 3, '98	Corporal.
Fulford, John W.	April 23, '98	Dec. 3, '98	
Gainer, Frank E.	April 23, '98	Dec. 3, '98	
Gates, William S.	July 27, '98		
Golladay, William G.	April 23, '98	Dec. 3, '98	
Gleach, Frank M.	April 23, '98	Dec. 3, '98	Promoted Corporal August 1, '98.
Hall, W. R.	July 3, '98		
Hartley, C. E.	July 16, '98		
Hawes, Oscar S.	April 23, '98	Dec. 3, '98	
Hansen, Peter	April 23, '98	Dec. 3, '98	
Holley, Edmund R.	April 23, '98	Dec. 3, '98	
Hurlbut, D. E.	July 17, '98		
Hurlbut, Van D. R.	July 17, '98		
Jackson, Edwin L.	April 23, '98	Dec. 3, '98	
Jaudon, Paul B., Jr.	April 23, '98	Dec. 3, '98	
Kenny, Frank P.	April 23, '98	Dec. 3, '98	Sergeant.
King, Roswell	April 23, '98	Dec. 3, '98	Corporal.
Kettel, Daniel	April 23, '98	Dec. 3, '98	
Lake, Harrold	April 23, '98	Dec. 3, '98	
Lanier, Louis M.	April 23, '98	Dec. 3, '98	
Landis, Arthur C.	April 23, '98	Dec. 3, '98	

Roll Company C (Capt. John N. Bradshaw)—1st Florida Infantry.

(CONTINUED.)

NAMES.	MUSTERED IN.	MUSTERED OUT.	REMARKS.
Lee, Eugene E.	April 23, '98		Deserted October 8, '98.
Lord, Charles R.	July 17, '98		
Lyons, John F.	April 23, '98	Dec. 3, '98	
Lynch, Walter	April 23, '98	Dec. 3, '98	
McConnell, Adolph M.	April 23, '98	Dec. 3, '98	
McGuire, James T.	July 14, '98	Dec. 3, '98	
McLarty, Charles E.	April 23, '98	Dec. 3, '98	
McLarty, W.	June 4, '98	Dec. 3, '98	
McNeil, W. William	April 23, '98	Dec. 3, '98	
Mitchell, C. W.	July 29, '98		
Morey, Eugene B.	April 23, '98	Dec. 3, '98	Sergeant; transferred to Regimental Band July 13, '98.
Norton, Taylor Seymour	April 23, 98	Dec. 3, '98	
Norton-Taylor, Bracy	April 23, '98	Dec. 3, '98	
Nix, Ralph E.	April 23, '98	Dec. 3, '98	
Pennell, Elon G.	July 13, '98	Dec. 3, '98	
Propst, Jacob D.	April 23, '98	Dec. 3, '98	
Partin, John E.	April 23, '98	Dec. 3, '98	
Perkins, Samuel	April 23, '98	Dec. 3, '98	Corporal.
Piatt, A. S.	July 22, '98	Dec. 3, '98	
Piatt, Charles B.	April 23, '98	Dec. 3, '98	
Piatt, Edward H.	April 23, '98	Dec. 3, '98	
Roberson, Edward	April 23, '98	Dec. 3, '98	Sergeant.
Reed, Fonda	July 14, '98	Dec. 3, '98	
Robertson, J. W.	July 22, '98	Dec. 3, '98	Transferred to Co. D October 9, '98.
Robertson, H. C.	July 22, '98	Dec. 3, '98	
Rogers, James	April 23, '98	Dec. 3, '98	Corporal.
Rouke, William	July 10, '98	Dec. 3, '98	
Sacher, Adolph	April 23, '98	Dec. 3, '98	
Sraman, Louis	April 23, '98	Dec. 3, '98	
Scott, Thomas M.	April 25, '98	Dec. 3, '98	
Smith, Thomas F.	April 25, '98	Dec. 3, '98	Transferred to Hospital Corps, U. S. A., June 7 '98.
Smith, Charles S.	April 25, '98	Dec. 3, '98	
Schmidt, Frank	April 25, '98	Dec. 3, '98	
Stafford, Robert F.	April 25, '98	Dec. 3, '98	
Strand, Clarence E.	April 25, '98	Dec. 3, '98	
Shaw, William J.	April 25, '98	Dec. 3, '98	
Taylor, George A.	April 25, '98	Dec. 3, '98	Transferred Co. B October 9, '98.
Taylor, Robert	July 3, '98	Dec. 3, '98	
White, Gabe H.	April 23, '98	Dec. 3, '98	Promoted Corporal August 1. '98.
Walker, Luther	April 23, '98	Dec. 3, '98	
Webb, William T.	April 23, '98	Dec. 3, '98	
White, James M.	April 23, '98	Dec. 3, '98	
White, William W.	April 23, '98	Dec. 3, '98	
Wilson, John R.	April 23, '98	Dec. 3, '98	Quartermaster-Sergeant; promoted 1st Sergeant July 1, '98.
Welch, Charles H.	April 23, '98	Dec. 3, '98	Sergeant.
Roberson, Edward	April 23, '98	Dec. 3, '98	Sergeant.
Forsyth, James	April 23, '98	Dec. 3, '98	Promoted Sergeant July 9, '98.
Bowman, Bert T.	July 15, '98	Dec. 3, '98	
Boone, William B.	July 15, '98	Dec. 3, '98	
Cox, Emory E.	July 19, '98	Dec. 3, '98	
Carlten, Norman J.	June 9, '98	Dec. 3, '98	
Christopher, Rufus S. E.	Aug. 22, '98	Dec. 3, '98	
Garner, Charles E.	June 7, '98	Dec. 3, '98	
Jones, Leroy	April 25, '98	Dec. 3, '98	Transferred from Co. D October 9, '98.
Libby, Fdwin R.			
Miller, Charles F.	Jan. 1, '98	Dec. 3, '98	
Martin, Robert N.	June 22, '98	Dec. 3, '98	
McGuire, James F.	July 12, '98	Dec. 3, '98	
McDonald, Charles L.	Aug. 3, '98	Dec. 3, '98	
Pennell, Elton G.	Aug. 3, '98	Dec. 3, '98	
Reans, Weather H.	June 22, '98	Dec. 3, '98	
Stephens, Albert R.	April 25, '98		Transferred from Co. B October.
Whitehurst, Elbert L.	June 10, '98	Dec. 3, '98	
Wall, William C.	May 11, '98	Dec. 3, '98	
Wilson, Daniel C.	June 11, '98	Dec. 3, '98	
Dumsuer, Hugh W.	June 6, '98		Dropped from roll July 18, '98; deserter United States Signal Corps.
Frierson, Thomas M.	July 23, '98		Discharged September, '98, for disability.
Hartley, Charles E.	July 15, '98		Discharged April 5 for disability.
Lord, Charles R.	July 15, '98		Transferred to Co. F October 9.

Company D—1st Florida Regiment.

This company was organized at Palatka, Fla., by 1st Lieut. D. W. Ramsaur. The company proceeded to Tampa May 12, 1898, a distance of one hundred and ninety miles, per order of Governor Bloxham. Went into camp of instruction on Fort Brooke Reservation May 13. Mustered into the service of the United States May 20; broke camp May 27, and marched to DeSoto Park, a distance of about three miles, with Regiment, per order of Major-General Shafter. In Camp of Instruction at DeSoto Park from May 27 to July 21; broke camp at DeSoto Park and proceded to Fernandina with Regiment by rail July 22, per order of Secretary of War. In camp with Regiment at Fernandina from July 23 to August 22; broke camp at Fernandina August 23 and proceded to Huntsville, Ala., with Regiment by rail, a disance of about seven hundred miles. Arrived in Huntsville Augus. 25, and went into temporary camp in city of Huntsville until August 26, thence into permanent camp about two m les from the city, where the company remained until mustered out of the service of the United States January 27, 1899.

Roll Company D (Capt. William M. Husson)—1st Florida Infantry.

NAMES.	MUSTERED IN.	MUSTERED OUT.	REMARKS.
OFFICERS.			
Captain—			
William M. Husson	April 23, '98	Jan. 27, '99	
1st Lieutenant—			
David W. Ramsaur	April 23, '98	Jan. 27, '99	
2nd Lieutenants—			
John W. Lancaster	April 23, '98	Jan. .27, '99	Transferred from Co. A October 28, '98.
Charles M. Hilliard	April 23, '98		Transferred to Co. A, 1st Florida Volunteer Infantry October 10, '98.
ENLISTED MEN.			
Anderson, G. H.	July 29, '98	Jan. 27, '99	
Bard, Harvey H.	April 23, '98	Jan. 27, '99	
Barclay, Fred A.	July 29, '98	Jan. 27, '99	
Bard, James M.	April 23, '98	Jan. 27, '99	
Branam, James	July 11, '98	Jan. 27, '99	
Bryce, George T.	April 23, '98	Jan. 27, '99	
Beal, Thomas T.	July 11, '98	Jan. 27. '99	
Benbow, David	April 23, '98	Jan. 27. '99	Promoted Corporal.
Boyd, N. M.	July 29, '98		
Brentley, W.	July 29, '98		
Burt, James L.	June 29, '98		Transferred to Hospital Corps June 1, '98.
Bukey, Jesse D.	April 23, '98		Promoted Corporal December 8, '98; discharged December 12, '98, per Special Order No. 302, A. G. O. at Huntsville, Ala.
Beach, Griffin C.	May 1, '98		
Beale, George F.	April 25, '98		
Cary, J. L.	July 29, '98		
Cochrane, P. J.	July 29, '98		
Congers, J.	July 29, '98		
Cowart, Henry E.	April 23, '98		Transferred to Hospital Corps June 22, '98.
Courer, Augustus	July 11, '98		
Corbett, Hugh McL.	May 1, '98		Discharged December 22, '98, per order Secretary of War.
Chancy, Silas L.	May 1, '98		
Crutchfield, James E.	May 1, '98		Promoted Corporal September 8, '98.
Crews, John E.	May 1, '98		Died at Fernandina September 12, '98.
Cross, Ralph A.	May 1, '98		
Culberson, John H.	May 12, '98		
Curtis, Luther B.	April 25, '98		
Cox, William A.	April 25, '98		
Caswell, Carl G.	May 5, '98		Transferred to Co. I, 1st Florida Volunteer Infantry, October 9, '98.
Cox, Darden T.	May 5, '98		
DuMaurier, Don F.	May 5, '98		Artificer; died at Fernandina August 6, '98.
Driggers, James O.	May 1, '98		
Dunn, Stephen C.	April 25, '98		
Gay, Eugene F.	April 25, '98		Promoted Corporal July 16, '98; Sergeant, August 13, '98; discharged September 9, '98, per Special Order No. 218.
Gautier, Redmond B.	April 25, '98		Discharged December 19, '98, per telegraphic order Secretary of War.
Gale, George O.	April 25, '98		
Glisson, A. E.	July 29, '98		
Gomes, Arthur	May 1, '98		
Grover, William H.	May 12, '98		
Hester, H. C.	July 6, '98		
Hill, Charles E.	April 23, '98		
Hoyt, William L.	April 23, '98		
Irving, Frederick	May 12, '98		Promoted Corporal December 8, '98.
Jones, Leroy D.	May 12, '98		Discharged August 29, '98, for disability.
Jones, T. J.	July 29, '98		
Johns, Harland D.	April 25, '98		
Kirby, Elijah L.	April 25, '98		
Line, James E.	April 25, '98		Promoted Corporal.
Lee, H.	July 29, '98		
Lewis, James E.	April 23, '98		
Liles, John T.	May 19, '98		Transferred to Co. M June 1, '98.

Roll Company D (Capt. William M. Husson)—1st Florida Infantry.

(CONTINUED.)

NAMES.	MUSTERED IN.	MUSTERED OUT.	REMARKS.
Livingston Tully R	April 23, '98		Promoted Corporal.
Lipsey, Mills J	April 23, '98		
Livingston, John D	April 23, '98		
Mills, James A	May 12, '98		
McGrau, Patrick	April 23, '98		
McIver, Alexander M	April 23, '98		3rd Sergeant; discharged December 9, '98, per order Secretary of War.
McLendon, J. T	July 12, '98		
Martin, Howard C	April 23, '98		
Madarasz, Louis E	April 23, '98		
Merrill, Joseph H	April 23, '98		Corporal; discharged November 9, '98, per Special Order No. 288.
Nelson, J. E	July 29, '98		
O'Cain, William E	May 12, '98		
Parker, A. K	July 12, '98		
Pinner, Erastus	May 1, '98		
Powell, Lawrence B	May 1, '98		Transferred to Co. M, 1st Florida Infantry, June 1, '98.
Powell, Tate, Jr	May 12, '98		Transferred to Co. M, 1st Florida Infantry, June 1, '98.
Rawlison, Lea M	April 25, '98		
Ray, James C	April 25, '98		Sergeant.
Register, Thomas J	May 1, '98		
Register, John W	April 25, '98		Promoted Corporal December 8, '98.
Rendrel, John	April 23, '98		Enlisted as Quartermaster-Sergeant; reduced to Corporal; discharged December 2, '98, for disability.
Reimer, Frederick C. R	May 12, '98		
Rich, S. K	July 29, '98		
Richardson, John W	April 23, '98		Sergeant; discharged December 13, '98, per Special Order No. 302.
Roberts, Alfred	May 1, '98		
Roberts, George W	July 12, '98		
Ryan, Albert J	April 23, '98		
Ringham, John D	April 23, '98		
Russell, C. A	July 29, '98		
Salls, John A	April 23, '98		
Scott, Fred L	April 23, '98		
Shelley, Andrew J	April 23, '98		Corporal.
Shelley, Carleton Edward	April 23, '98		Corporal; promoted Sergeant September 12, '98; discharged November 18, '98, per Special Order No. 291.
Smailes, Edward M	May 7, '98	Jan. 27, '99	
Sullivan, Vollie T	May 7, '98	Jan. 27, '99	Died at Huntsville, Ala., September 16, '98.
Smith, John	July 29, '98	Jan. 27, '98	
Smith, Rutledge	April 23, '98	Jan. 27, '99	Promoted July 16, '98; discharged November 18 '98, per Special Order No. 291.
Thomas, T. H. S	July 1, '98	Jan. 27, '99	
Tison, John H	April 23, '98	Jan. 27, '99	
Truman, J. W	July 29, '98	Jan. 27, '99	
Vary, Foster V. B	April 23, '98	Jan. 27, '99	1st Sergeant.
Usina, John	July 29, '98	Jan. 27, '99	
Wall, William C	May 5, '98	Jan. 27, '99	Transferred to Co. C October 9, '98.
Watson, S. W	July 29, '98	Jan. 27, '99	Artificer.
Weaver, Arthur H	April 23, '98	Jan. 27, '99	
Wigg, Thomas H	April 23, '98	Jan. 27, '99	Promoted Corporal.
Wigg, St. John	April 23, '98	Jan. 27, '99	Corporal.
Weiss, Charles L	April 23, '98	Jan. 27, '99	Corporal; promoted Sergeant.
Wellose, Nixon N	May 19, '98	Jan. 27, '99	Transferred to Co. B June 1, '98.
White, Kirk M	April 23, '98	Jan. 27, '99	Sergeant.
Vassie, Harry A	April 23, '98	Jan. 27, '99	Musician.
Yates, Moses	July 29, '98	Jan. 27, '99	
Young, James W	April 25, '98	Jan. 27, '99	Wagoner.
Wilder, Hezekiah H		Jan. 27, '99	Transferred from Co. M June 1, '98; promoted September 12, '98.
Crary, John D	June 29, '98	Jan. 27, '99	Promoted Corporal December 8, '98.
Volly, Walter H	June 23, '98	Jan. 27, '99	Promoted Corporal December 8, '98.
Barrow, Robert E	July 1, '96	Jan. 27, '99	
Bracken, John W		Jan. 27, '98	Transferred from Co. G.
Brown, William	Aug. 17, '98	Jan. 27, '99	Transferred from Co. I, Oct. 9, '98.
Groson, Walter R	May 12, '98	Jan. 27, '99	Transferred from Co. M.
Edwards, James H	June 22, '98	Jan. 27, '99	
Fitzgerald, Arthur N	April 25, '98	Jan. 27, '99	Transferred from Co. G.
Jones, Reuben T	May 20, '98	Jan. 27, '99	Transferred from Co. M.
Lee, Henry	June 29, '98	Jan. 27, '99	
Roberts, Hugh	June 29, '98	Jan. 27, '99	
Robertson, James W	June 21, '98	Jan. 27, '99	
Scammell, Roy M	July 6, '98	Jan. 27, '99	
Points, John D	April 25, '98		Corporal; discharged November 18, '98, per Special Order No. 291.
Jones, Leroy D	April 25, '98		Transferred to Co. C, 1st Florida Volunteer Infantry, October 9, '98.
Wilder, Thomas J	May 12, '98		Transferred to Co. D June 1, '98; retransferred to Co. M October 9, '98.

Company E—1st Florida Regiment.

This company was organized in Jacksonville, Fla., and left there by rail May 12, 1898, for Tampa, a distance of 212 miles; arrived there May 13, and pitched camp at Fort Brooke, Tampa, Fla, and was mustered in there May 23, broke camp and marched to DeSoto Camp, Fla., where they pitched camp on May 27 moved with Regiment on July 21 from Tampa to Fernandina by rail, a distance of about 250 miles; arrived at Fernandina July 22 and pitched camp there same date; broke camp with Regiment at Fernandina about noon of August 22 and marched into town, a distance of one mile, about 6 p. m. same date and bivouacked in streets until noon of August 23, when they left by rail for Huntsville, which latter place was reached about 2 a. m. August 25; distance travelled about 600 miles, via Callahan, Fla., Waycross, Macon and Atlanta, Ga., and Chattanooga, Tenn., and pitched temporary camp August 25. On August 26 marched about one mile and pitched permanent camp, distance about one mile and a half from town. On September 5 broke camp about 7 a. m. and marched into Huntsville, distance of about one and one-half miles and pitched camp in a locality known as Calhoun Grove, relieving Co. D, 5th Maryland Volunteer Infantry as provost guard; broke camp October 5 and returned to Regiment Broke camp at Huntsville October and departed from there at 8.45 p. m. same date by rail, via Chattanooga, Tenn., Atlanta, Macon, Albany and Thomasville, Ga., and Monticello, Fla., for Tallahassee, a distance of about 500 miles, which latter place was reached at 9.30 a. m. on October 11, 1898, and pitched camp in Houston's Grove, distant about one mile from town.

Roll Company E (Capt. John S. Maxwell)—1st Florida Infantry.

NAMES.	MUSTERED IN.	MUSTERED OUT.	REMARKS.
OFFICERS.			
Captain—			
John S. Maxwell	April 23, '98	Dec. 3, '98	
1st Lieutenant—			
Braxton B. McDonnell	April 23, '98		
2nd Lieutenant—			
George R. Weldon	April 23, '98		
ENLISTED MEN.			
Allen, Luie D	May 11, '98		Transferred to Co. G October 8, '98.
Avery, Horace C	May 11, '98		Corporal; discharged September 8, '98 for disability by order of Assistant Adjutant General.
Ball, Thomas P	May 11, '98		
Barker, Harry T	May 11, '98		Sergeant.
Beam, William H	May 10, '98		
Bernreuter, David W	July 7, '98		
Bowden, Richard D	May 6, '98		Discharged June 8, '98, for disability.
Bowen, Fred H	April 23, '98		
Brannen, Herbert G	April 23, '98		Promoted Corporal; September 1, '98.
Brown, Vivian R	May 5, '98		Transferred to Co. G October 8, '98.
Candlish, Herbert S	May 5, '98		Discharged September 8, '98; in compliance with orders from Assistant Adjutant-General.
Cassidey, Herbert J	April 23, '98		Corporal; discharged September 10, '98 for disability, by order of Assistant Adjutant-Gen.
Challen, Louis B	April 23, '98		
Christie, George T	May 10, '98		Promoted Corporal; July 30, '98.
Coburn, Sparkman C	April 23, '98		Musician; transferred to Co. G.
Combs, Bert A	May 5, '98		
Cooper, Clyde T	May 3, '98		Appointed Musician; July 1, '98.
Crolly, William C	May 11, '98		
Curren, Denis	May 5, '98		
Curtiss, Harry B	May 11, '98		Promoted Corporal; July 30, '98.
DeVeaux, James G	May 2, '98		Transferred to Regimental hospital corps May 31, '98; by order of B. F. Pope, Lieutenant-Col.
Drew, Horace R	April 23, '98		Sergeant.
Drysdale, Richard P	April 23, '98		

Roll Company E (Capt. John S. Maxwell)—1st Florida Infantry.
(CONTINUED.)

NAMES	MUSTERED IN.	MUSTERED OUT.	REMARKS.
Dyess, Samuel E.	April 23, '98		Transferred to Co. F October 8, '98.
Ellis, Roy N. Jr.	April 23, '98		Q. M. Sergeant.
Emery, Edward H.	May 10, '98		
Fleming, Charles S.	April 23, '98		Transferred to Regimental Staff as Sergeant-Major; May 25, '98.
Ford, Joseph S.	May 5, '98		
Grant, Isaiah S.	May 5, '98		
Hopkins, Joseph L.	May 5, '98		Corporal; promoted Sergeant, September 1, '98.
Humphreys, Allison B.	May 5, '98		Corporal.
Johnson, Eden P.	May 10, '98	Dec. 3, '98	
Jones, William B.	May 12, '98		
Jordan, Tristran I.	May 11, '98		Appointed Artificer Sept. 12, '98.
Lang, Joseph A.	May 7, '98		
Livingston, Woodward C.	May 7, '98		
Long, Marvin W.	May 10, '98		
Lonney, Thomas J.	May 11, '98		Transferred to Co. F October 8, '98.
McGary, James.	May 5, '98		Transferred to Co. F October 8, '98.
McKenzie, Henry W.	May 5, '98		Promoted Corporal; July 30, '98.
MacDonnell, Alexander H.	May 3, '98		Discharged August 30, '98, for disability, by order of Assistant Adjutant-General.
McCabe, Charles C.	May 10, '98		Musician.
McCracken, Victor.	May 21, '98		Wagoner.
MacDonell, Augustus O. Jr.	April 23, '98		Corporal; promoted Sergeant; discharged August 30, '98, for disability..
MacDonnell, Lee.	April 23, '98		Sergeant.
Markwood, Henry E.	May 5, '98		Promoted Corporal; September 12, '98.
Mitchell, Lee Augustus.	April 23, '98		
Mott, Elisha M.	May 11, '98		Artificer.
Muller, Bernhard.	May 5, '98		
Munroe, Edward L.	April 23, '98		
Murtagh, John S.	April 23, '98		
Nelson, William D.	May 12, '98		Promoted Corporal, September 12, '98.
Page, James W.	April 23, '98		
Pasco, Samuel N.	May 12, '98		
Payne, Harvey R.	April 23, '98		
Putman, James L.	May 11, '98		
Raley, Henry.	May 11, '98		
Reddick, Walter N.	April 23, '98		
Reed, Joseph L.	April 23, '98		
Reese, Joseph D.	May 10, '98		Promoted Corporal, July 30, '98.
Reneau, James S.	May 10, '98		
Roberts, Lonney H.	May 12, '98		
Rockwell, Stoddard W.	April 23, 98		
Rouse, Roscoe.	May 10, '98		
Skipper, Thomas W.	April 23, '98		
Smedley, William G.	May 5, '98		
Snowball, Joseph E.	May 11, '98		
Thompson, Lawrence H.	April 23, '98	Dec. 3, '98	Corporal.
Tucker, Charles W.	April 23, '98		1st Sergeant.
Thames, George W. Jr.	April 23, '98		Corporal; discharged September 10, '98 for disability.
Warrock, Arthur R.	April 23, '98	Dec. 3, '98	
Washington, Fred L.	May 7, '98	Dec. 3, '98	Corporal; promoted September 9, '98.
Watson, Talbot D.	May 11, '98	Dec. 3, '98	
Wilder, Edgar L.	April 23, '98	Dec. 3, '98	
Willard, Frank B.	April 23, '98		Died at Huntsville, Ala., September 29, '98.
Wilson, Henry.	May 6, '98		
Williams, Carl H.	May 3, '98		Discharged September 15, '98 by order of War Department. for disability.
Winterhalter, George.	May 11, '98		
Bassett, Buten.	July 30, '98		
Belisano Ben H.	June 28, '98		
Bernrenter, David W.	July 7, '98		
Bonham, Theo. L.	July 30, '98		
Campbell, James S.	July 5, '98		
Cody, Charles J.	July 5, '98		
Colton, Benjamin W.	July 6, '98		
Daman, William T.	July 15, '98		
Denham, William D.	July 15, '98		
Edmonson, George D.	May 10, '98		
Gary, Fred.	July 26, '98		
Henry, John B.	July 30, '98		
Johnson, Henry.	July 22, '98		Discharged September 23, '98 for disability by order of Assistant Adjutant-General.
Maxwell, James R.	July 9, '98		
Pitts, Jesse A.	July 15, '98		
Rawls, Samuel A.	July 26, '98		
Roberts, Samuel I.	July 9, '98		Promoted Corporal, September 1, '98.
Shadham, William A.	July 5, '98		
Tarner, Elmore A.	June 28, '98		Transferred to Company F October 8, '98.
Ward, William H.	July 5, '98		Transferred to Co. F October 8, '98.
Wells, H. T.	July 19, '98		
Barritt, Frank E.	April 23, '98	Dec. 3, '98	Transferred from Co. F October 8, '98.
Berlack, Abram S.	April 23, '98	Dec. 3, '98	Transferred from Co. F October 8, '98.
Branch, Benjamin S.	April 25, '98	Dec. 3, '98	Transferred from Co. B October 8, '98.
Brown, William F.	April 23, '98	Dec. 3, '98	Transferred from Co. G October 8, '98.
Carroll, Horace C.	July 31, '98	Dec. 3, '98	
Dixon, Reddon W.	Aug. 2, '98	Dec. 3, '98	

Roll Company E (Capt. John S. Maxwell)—1st Florida Infantry.
(CONTINUED.)

NAMES.	MUSTERED IN.	MUSTERED OUT.	REMARKS.
Gates, Edward C.	May 21, '98	Dec. 3, '98	
Hampton, James F.	Aug. 2, '98	Dec. 3, '98	Transferred to 3rd division hospital corps August 18, '98.
Hitchcock, William S.	April 23, '98	Dec. 3, '98	Transferred from Co. F, 1st Fla. Infantry October 8, '98.
Lynch, Harley T.	Aug. 1, '98	Dec. 3, '98	
McRae, Calvin.	Aug. 13, '98	Dec. 3, '98	
Parkin, Harry A.	June 28, '98	Dec. 3, '98	
Parker, Arthur H.	Aug. 13, '98	Dec. 3, '98	
Philips, Davis.	Aug. 13 98	Dec. 3, '98	
Scott, James F.	June 28, '98	Dec. 3, '98	Transferred from Co. F October 8, '98.
Sheppard, Thomas W.	May 11, '98	Dec. 3, '98	
Smith, Joseph F.	May 12, '98	Dec. 3, '98	Transferred from Co. F October 8, '98.
Snow, George W.	April 23, '98	Dec. 3, '98	Transferred from Co. F October 8, '98.
Steadham, William A.	Dec. 3, '98	July 5, '98	
Stevens, James E.	Aug. 13, '98	Dec. 3, '98	
Acosta, George A.	April 23, '98		Discharged September 12, '98 for disability, by order of Assistant Adjutant-General.
Pillsbury, Charles C.	Aug, 1, '98		Transferred to Co. B October 8, '98.

Company F—1st Florida Regiment.

This company was organized at Jacksonville, Fla.; left there at 9 o'clock p. m. May 12, 1898, travelling thence by rail to Tampa, Fla., a distance of about 212 miles; reached destination at 7 o'clock a. m. May 13; went into camp at Fort Brooke, at which place it was mustered into the service of the United States on May 23 by Captain Woodruff, mustering officer. Broke camp May 27 and marched to Palmetto Beach, a distance of two miles, where it went into camp; broke camp at Palmetto Beach at 3 o'clock p. m. July 21 and travelled thence by rail to Fernandina, a distance of 240 miles, arriving at their destination at 7.30 o'clock a. m. July 22; broke camp at Fernandina on the afternoon of August 22 and camped in streets that night; took cars for Huntsville, Ala., at noon August 23; arrived at destination, a distance of about 560 miles, at 2 o'clock p. m on August 25, going into temporary camp on the evening of same date and marching to permanent camp on the morning of August 26, a distance of one mile. Mustered out of service at Huntsville, Ala., January 24, 1899.

Roll Company F (Capt. James Y. Wilson)—1st Florida Infantry.

NAMES.	MUSTERED IN.	MUSTERED OUT.	REMARKS.
OFFICERS.			
Captain—			
James Y. Wilson	April 25, '98	Jan. 27, '99	
1st Lieutenants—			
Charles H. Chestnut	April 25, '98		Transferred to Co. F, October 13, '98; detailed as Battalion Adjutant November 17, '98.
John H. Stephens	April 25, '98		Transferred from Brigade Headquarters to Adjutant's October 13, '98; died at Savannah October 27, '98.
2nd Lieutenant—			
Thomas C. Watts	April 25, '98	Jan. 27, '99	Sergeant; promoted 2nd Lieutenant.
ENLISTED MEN.			
Armington, Fred E.	April 25, '98	Jan. 27, '99	
Adams, Emarcus S.	April 25, '98		
Batton, Charles A.	April 25, '98		Transferred to Co. I October 9, '98.
Baker, William A.	April 25, '98	Jan. 27, '99	Corporal.
Berlack, Abraham S	April 25, '98		Transferred to Co. E October 9, '98.
Barrett, Frank E.	April 25, '98		Transferred to Co. E October 9, '98.
Ball, Herbert.	April 25, '98		Transferred to Hospital Corps.
Beatty, William Y.	April 25, '98	Jan. 27, '99	
Boyde, Walter E.	April 25, '98		Honorably discharged December 22, '98.
Birks, Theodore H.	April 25, '98	Jan. 27, '99	

Roll Company F (Capt. James Y. Wilson)—1st Florida Infantry.
(CONTINUED.)

NAMES.	MUSTERED IN.		MUSTERED OUT.		REMARKS.
Bowden, Halstead E	April 25,	'98			Transferred to Co. I October 9, '99.
Black, James C	April 25,	'98	Jan. 27,	'99	Appointed Corporal December 1, '98.
Blinn, Edwin H	April 25,	'98	Jan. 27,	'99	1st Sergeant.
Byrd, Obe D	April 25,	'98	Jan. 27,	'99	
Byrne, Martin A	April 25,	'98	Jan. 27,	'99	Quartermaster-Sergeant; returned to ranks at his
Bigelow, Robert C	April 25,	'98	Jan. 27,	'99	own request September 1, '98.
Boyer, Alfred Z	April 25,	'98	Jan. 27,	'99	
Brennan, Martin	April 25,	'98	Jun. 27,	'99	
Curry, George A	April 25,	'98	Jan. 27,	'99	Appointed Corporal September 1, '98; detailed
					Company Clerk October 19, '98.
Crews, Thomas D	April 25,	'98			Transferred to Volunteer Signal Corps June 30
					'98.
Cancio, Charles A	April 25,	'98			Transferred to Signal Corps; also Co. I, October
					8, '98.
Conners, John	April 25,	'98			Transferred to Co. M October 9, '98.
Dancy, George L	April 25,	'98			Sergeant; honorably discharged October 8, '98.
Doyle, William H	April 25,	'98	Jan. 27,	'99	
Dingee, Charles H	April 25,	'98	Jan. 27,	'99	Corporal; Sergeant October 9, '98.
Dorman, William A	April 25,	'98	Jan. 27,	'98	
Eager, Francis L	May 5,	'98	Jan. 27,	'99	
Fremont, Thomas	May 13,	'98	Jan. 27,	'99	
Fuller, William	April 25,	'98	Jan. 27,	'99	
Gibson, Edward F	April 25,	'98			Discharged November 17, '98, for disability.
Hall, Samuel T	April 25,	'98	Jan. 27,	'99	Sergeant; reduced to ranks December 1, '98.
Hitchcock, William S	April 25,	'98			Transferred to Co. E October 9, '98.
Hardee, John A	April 25,	'98			Discharged December 24, '98 by order Secretary
Herbert, John	April 25,	'98	Jan. 27,	'99	of War.
Hermandez, Charles A	April 25,	'98	Jan. 27,	'99	
Hoyle, Louis C	April 25,	'98			Corporal; transferred to Co. M October 9, '98.
Hulbert, Benjamin F	May 5,	'98	Jan. 27,	'99	
Hamilton, Luther M	April 25,	'98			Discharged, Special Order No. 155 July 8, '98.
Hines, Richard	April 25,	'98			Transferred to Co. A October 9, '98.
Hedrick, Isaac G	April 25,	'98	Jan. 27,	'99	Appointed Corporal September 1, '98.
Jones, John S	May 5,	'98	Jan. 27,	'99	
Lopez, Edward St. B	April 25,	'98	Jan. 27,	'99	
Leach, Samuel W	April 25,	'98			Quartermaster; transferred to Hospital Corps June
					22, '98.
Livingston, James F	April 25,	'98			Appointed Musician September 1, '98.
Lorrimer, Joseph M	April 25,	'98			Corporal.
Maxwell, William T	April 25.	'98			Corporal; returned to ranks at his own request
					December 8, '98.
Mead, Louis V	April 25,	'98			Sergeant.
Muse, William F	April 25,	'98			Transferred to Co. I October 9, '98.
Morris, Edward	April 25,	'98	Jan. 27,	'99	
MacPhail, Alexander	April 25,	'98			Promoted Corporal September 1, '98; reduced to
Nuttal, Charles	April 25,	'98	Jan. 27,	'99	the ranks January 10, '99.
Nil, John W	April 25,	'98	Jan. 27,	'99	Artificer.
Onderdonk, Charles B	April 25.	'98			Corporal; transferred to Regimental Hospital June
					9, '98; discharged January 2, '99, for disability.
Powers, William H	April 25,	'98			Transferred to Hospital Corps.
Peters, Perry	April 25,	'98	Jan. 27,	'99	Wagoner.
Parker, Egbert J	April 25,	'98	Jan. 27,	'99	
Perry, William G	April 25,	'98	Jan. 27,	'99	
Reynolds, Guy B	April 25,	'98	Jan. 27,	'99	
Race, Austin T	April 25,	'98	Jan. 27,	'99	
Ramos, Emanuel	April 25,	'98	Jan. 27,	'99	
Robinson, Fred S	April 25,	'98	Jan. 27,	'99	
Sargent, Harry B	April 25,	'98			Corporal; discharged September 14, '98.
Spencer, George E	April 25,	'98	Jan. 27,	'99	
Soler, Joseph A	April 25,	'98	Jan. 27,	'99	
Snyder, George H	April 25,	'98	Jan. 27,	'99	Transferred to Co. K October 9, '98.
Smith, Stephens A	April 25,	'98	Jan. 27,	'99	Appointed Corporal December 1, '98.
Smith, Richard M	April 25,	'98	Jan. 27,	'99	
Sterrett, Arthur L	April 25,	'98			Corporal; discharged September 14, '98.
Tipping, Joseph P	April 25,	'98	Jan. 27,	'99	Appointed Corporal September 1, '98.
Travis, William J	April 25,	'98	Jan. 27,	'99	
Taylor, Starke	April 25,	'98	Jan. 27,	'99	
Taylor, Carroll H	April 25,	'98	Jan. 27,	'99	Sergeant.
Taylor, Fred	Aug. 17,	'98	Jan. 27,	'99	
Varnum, Henry	April 25,	'98	Jan. 27,	'99	Transferred to Co. M October 9, '98.
West, Thomas W	April 25,	'98	Jan. 27,	'99	
Williams, Frank J	April 25,	'98			Discharged September 11, '98.
Wheeler, Charles A	April 25,	'98	Jan. 27,	'99	Appointed Corporal September 1, '98.
Walker, Frank	April 25,	'98	Jan. 27,	'99	
Hamilton, Luther M			Jan. 27,	'99	
Hobirk, Arthur C	June 28,	'98	Jan. 27,	'99	
LaRue, Robert E. L	June 28,	'98	Jan. 27,	'99	
O'Berry, Johnson	June 28,	'98	Jan. 27,	'99	
Scott, James T	June 28,	'98	Jan. 27,	'99	Transferred to Co. E October 9, '98.
Yates, Fred G	April 25,	'98	Jan. 27,	'99	Sergeant.
Minsky, Franz M. S. A	May 1,	'98	Jan. 27,	'99	Appointed Corporal January 12, '99.
Middaugh, Frank	Aug. 4,	'98	Jan. 27,	'99	Appointed Corporal January 11, '99.
Conter, August	May 11,	'98	Jan. 27,	'99	Musician; transferred from Co. A October 9, '98.
Blinn, Theodore A	Aug. 5,	'98	Jan. 27,	'99	

Roll Company F (Capt. James Y. Wilson)—1st Florida Infantry.

(CONTINUED.)

NAMES.	MUSTERED IN.	MUSTERED OUT.	REMARKS.
Clausen, Thorvall	Aug. 13, '98	Jan. 27, '99	
Cox, Thomas W	Aug. 4, '98	Jan. 27, '99	
Crickmay, Charles T	Aug. 10, '98	Jan. 27, '99	Transferred from Co. I October 9, '98.
Dyess, Samuel E		Jan. 27, '99	Transferred from Co. E October 9, '98.
Fenn, Charles B	July 15, '98	Jan. 27, '99	Transferred from Co. H October 9, '99.
Fremstead, Martin	April 25, '98	Jan. 27, '99	Transferred from 1st Florida Volunteer Band December 5, '98.
Harwick, Louis J	April 25, '98	Jan. 27, '99	Transferred from 1st Florida Volunteer Infantry Band, December 5, '98.
Harris, John A	May 9, '98	Jan. 27, '99	Transferred from Co. M October 9, '98.
Henson, James G., Jr	Aug. 3, '98	Jan. 27, '99	
Hires, Walter H	Aug. 12, '98	Jan. 27, '99	
Hough, Willis	May 10, '98	Jan. 27, '99	Transferred from Co. I October 9, '98.
Huggins, Lacy	Aug. 5, '98	Jan. 27, '99	
Jansen, Frederick	Aug. 17, '98	Jan. 27, '99	Transferred from Co. I October 9, '98.
Lonney, Thomas J	May 11, '98	Jan. 27, '99	Transferred from Co. E October 9, '98
Lord, Charles R	July 15, '98	Jan. 27, '99	Transferred from Co. C October 9, '98.
Masser, Alonzo B	Aug. 4, '98	Jan. 27, '99	
Middough, Walter	Aug. 4, '98	Jan. 27, '99	
Moseley, John	Aug. 11, '98	Jan. 27, '99	
McCart, Stephen D	Aug. 22, '98	Jan. 27, '99	Transferred from Co. A October 9, '98.
McDonald, Taylor D	Aug. 6, '98	Jan. 27, '99	
Owens, Owen	April 25, '98	Jan. 27, '99	Transferred from Co. M October 9, '98.
Pacetty, Charles	Aug. 5, '98	Jan. 27, '99	
Ridez, Victor	July 27, '98	Jan. 27, '99	
Reuns, Levin	Aug. 29, '98	Jan. 27, '99	
Ross, Carl L	July 30, '98	Jan. 27, '99	
Sharp, Charles C	May 10, '98	Jan. 27, '99	Transferred from Co. L October 9, '98.
Sherwood, Dennis B	Aug. 4, '98	Jan. 27, '99	
Sherwood, Henry G	Aug. 3, '98	Jan. 27, '99	
Turner, Elmore A	June 28, '98	Jan. 27, '99	Transferred from Co. E October 9, '98.
Turner, Joseph B	July 29, '98	Jan. 27, '99	Transferred from Co. I October 9, '98.
Ward, William A	July 5, '98	Jan. 27, '99	Transferred from Co. E October 7, '98.
Williams, William A	Aug. 4, '98	Jan. 27, '99	
Wilson, Thomas S	Aug. 22, '98	Jan. 27, '99	Transferred from Co. M October 9, '98.
Yelvington, Charles H	Aug. 12, '98	Jan. 27, '99	
Cade, Levi W	July 30, '98		Transferred to Co. H October 9, '98.
Coxetter, Louis M	July 31, '98		Transferred to Co. I October 9, '98.
Foote, Lee Roy	July 30, '98		Transferred to Co. I October 9, '98.
McDonald, William	July 3, '98		Transferred to Co. M October 9, '98.
McDonald, Charles L	July 3, '98		Transferred to Co. C October 9, '98.
Pitts, Joseph P	July 30, '98		Transferred to Co. L October 9, '98.
Smith, Joseph F	April 25, '98		Musician; returned to ranks September 1, '98; transferred to Co. E October 9, '98.
Etheredge, Hugh	Aug. 17, '98		Died September 22, '98, of pneumonia and measles.
Philips, James H	Aug. 17, '98		Transferred from Co. M October 9, '98; deserted November 27, '98.

Company G—1st Florida Regiment.

This company was organized at St. Augustine, Fla., and left there by rail May 12, 1898, for Tampa, a distance of 249 miles; arrived there May 13 and pitched camp at Fort Brooke at Tampa, Fla.; the company was mustered in there May 23, 1898; broke camp and marched to DeSoto Park, Tampa, where they pitched camp May 27. Moved with Regiment July 21 from Tampa to Fernandina by rail, a distance of 250 miles and arrived at Fernandina uly 22; pitched camp there the same day. Moved with Regiment August 23, by rail, to Huntsville, Ala. which place was reached August 25, distance traveled about 600 miles; pitched temporary camp August 25 in suburbs of Huntsville August 6; marched about one mile and pitched permanent camp, one and one-half miles from town, where the company was mustered out.

Roll Company G (Capt. Frank J. Howatt)—1st Florida Infantry.

NAMES.	MUSTERED IN.	MUSTERED OUT.	REMARKS.
OFFICERS.			
Captain—			
Frank J. Howatt	April 25, '98	Jan. 27, '99	Enlisted as 1st Lieutenant; appointed Captain

Roll Company G (Capt. Frank J. Howatt)—1st Florida Infantry.

(CONTINUED.)

NAMES.	MUSTERED IN.	MUSTERED OUT.	REMARKS.
1st Lieutenant—			May 18, '98.
J. Clifford R. Foster	April 25, '98	Jan. 27, '99	2nd Sergeant; appointed 1st Lieutenant May 18 '98; Quartermaster of 3rd Battalion, 1st Florida Volunteer Infantry October 10, '98, per Special Order No. 3.
2nd Lieutenant—			
Ernest M. Howatt		Jan. 27, '99	1st Sergeant; appointed 2nd Lieutenant May 18 '98.
ENLISTED MEN.			
Allen, Lene D.	May 11, '98	Jan. 27, '99	Transferred from Co. E October 8, '98.
Arondo, Gonzalez	April 25, '98		
Arnold, Elliot W.	April 25, '98		Corporal; transferred to Co. M.
Baxley, H. D.			Discharged September 4, '98.
Button, Albert B.	April 25, '98		Died at Fort McPherson September 1, '98.
Brown, Wyatt L.	April 25, '98	Jan. 27, '99	
Brown, Burton L.	April 25, '98	Jan. 27, '99	Promoted Corporal.
Brown, Andrew J.	April 25, '98	Jan. 27, '99	
Brown, William F.	April 25, '98		Corporal; transferred to Co. E.
Blackstocks, Levi C.	April 25, '98	Jan. 27, '99	
Blackwilder, George R.	April 25, '98		Promoted Corporal and Sergeant; discharged November 15, '98.
Blanchard, William R.	April 25, '98	Jan. 27, '99	Promoted Corporal January 1, '99.
Burton, Norris L.	April 25, '98	Jan. 27, '99	Promoted Corporal.
Canfield, Roy	April 25, '98		Promoted Corporal; discharged December 1, '98.
Coxetter, James G.	April 25, '98		Transferred to Co. M.
Coxetter, Durham	April 25, '98		Transferred to Co. M.
Clark, Harry F.	April 25, '98	Jan. 27, '99	
Cowan, William D.	April 25, '98	Jan. 27, '99	
Colclough, John N.	April 25, '98	Jan. 27, '99	Promoted Corporal October 11, '98.
Davis, Harry P.	April 25, '98	Jan. 27, '99	Promoted Corporal January 1, '99.
Davis, Charles O.	April 25, '98	Jan. 27, '99	Corporal.
Dardis, Thomas	April 25, '98	Jan. 27, '99	Wagoner.
Einig, Alfred	April 25, '98	Jan. 27, '99	
Farrell, Albert M.	April 25, '98		Deserted September 25, '98, at Huntsville, Ala.
Forrey, Melville E.	April 25, '98	Jan. 27, '99	
Fleming, William B.	April 25, '98	Jan. 27, '99	Promoted Corporal October 11, '98.
Goode, J. Guerry	April 25, '98	Jan. 27, '99	
Gaillard, Charles R.	April 25, '98		Promoted Corporal; transferred to Co. M.
Gallaway, John N.	April 25, '98	Jan. 27, '99	
Geiger, William A.	April 25, '98	Jan. 27, '99	
Genovar, Stanley	April 25, '98		Promoted Corporal and Sergeant; discharged December 19, '98.
Gibbs, R. Kingsley	April 25, '98	Jan. 27, '99	Sergeant; transferred to Co. M.
Gibbs, G. Couper	April 25, '98		Corporal; discharged October 8, '98.
Harper, Thomas J.	April 25, '98	Jan. 27, '99	
Hampton, Samuel A.	April 25, '98	Jan. 27, '99	
Hay, William H.	April 25, '98	Jan. 27, '99	
Hay, Clayton A.	April 25, '98	Jan. 27, '99	
Heslington, Claude A.	April 25, '98	Jan. 27, '99	
Jaughins, Wallace A.	April 25, '98	Jan. 27, '99	
Jibb, William F. L.	April 25, '98	Jan. 27, '99	Promoted Corporal June 23, '98; Sergeant, October 11, '98.
King, Joseph L.	April 25, '98	Jan. 27, '99	
Kellar, Whitfield L.	April 25, '98		Promoted Corporal; discharged December 13, '98.
Leonardy, Wallace T.	April 25, '98		Promoted Corporal; died November 14, '98, at Huntsville, Ala.
Lee, Garron	May 20, '98		Deserted June 3, '98, at Tampa, Fla.
Lindberg, Robert F.	May 20, '98	Jan. 27, '99	
Miller, John T.	May 12, '98	Jan. 27, '99	
Mabbitt, Cecil M.	April 25, '98	Jan. 27, '99	Promoted Corporal and Sergeant.
Meyers, Edward	April 25, '98	Jan. 27, '99	Artificer.
McGuire, A. Frank	April 25, '98	Jan. 27, '99	
MacGonigle, J. Gilchrist	April 25, '98		Corporal; promoted Sergeant; discharged November 15, '98.
McGriff, Robinson C.	April 25, '98	Jan. 27, '99	
Margar, Joseph P.	May 12, '98	Jan. 27, '99	
Nolan, Charles R.	May 20, '98		Deserted September 18, '98, at Huntsville, Ala.
Pitchford, Walter D.	April 25, '98		Promoted Corporal; transferred to Co. M.
Paffe, Anthony J.	April 25, '98	Jan. 27, '99	
Proctor, Troy A.	April 25, '98	Jan. 27, '99	
Porter, Joseph F.	April 25, '98	Jan. 27, '99	
Padgett, Noble	April 25, '98		Transferred to Hospital Corps, U. S. A., June 22, '98.
Palmar, Frank D.	April 25, '98	Jan. 27, '99	Promoted Corporal.
Palmer, Frank W.	April 25, '98	Jan. 27, '99	
Philips, George M.	May 12, '98	Jan. 27, '99	
Proetz, Oscar C.	May 12, '98	Jan. 27, '99	
Reddington, R. George	April 25, '98	Jan. 27, '99	Sergeant.
Ricks, Clarence E.	April 25, '98	Jan. 27, '99	
Sanchez, Eugene M.	April 25, '98	Jan. 27, '99	Corporal; transferred to Co. M.
Smallgrove, George H.	April 25, '98	Jan. 27, '99	Corporal; transferred to Hospital Corps, U. S. A.
Snow, George W.	April 25, '98		Sergeant; transferred to Co. E October 8, '98.
Snow, Henry M., Jr.	April 25, '98	Jan. 27, '99	Promoted 1st Sergeant May 18, '98.
Tasker, Allen T.	April 25, '98	Jan. 27, '99	
Taylor, Westley M.	April 25, '98	Jan. 27, '99	
VanDorn, Charles	April 25, '98	Jan. 27, '99	
Walker, Ralph C.	April 25, '98	Jan. 27, '99	
Weeks, Curtis M.	April 25, '98	Jan. 27, '99	Quartermaster Sergeant.

Roll Company G (Capt. Frank J. Howatt)—1st Florida Infantry.

(CONTINUED.)

NAMES.	MUSTERED IN.	MUSTERED OUT.	REMARKS.
Wyllie, Alfred S.	April 25, '98	Jan. 27, '99	Musician.
Willis, Alvin M.	April 25, '98		Died at Fernandina at Brigade Hospital August 19 of pneumonia.
Wilson, Charles H.	April 25, '98		Discharged December 14, '98.
Waters, Frank K.	April 25, '98	Jan. 27, '99	
Wittich, Edwin R.	April 25, '98		Transferred to Hospital Corps, U. S. A.
Wheeler. William D.	May 20, '98		Discharged September 10, '98, for disability.
Woodward, William.	April 25, '98	Jan. 27, '99	Promoted Corporal.
Yarborough, Howard B.	April 25, '98	Jan. 27, '99	Promoted Corporal October 11, '98.
Bingham, Henry B.	April 25, '98		Discharged September 4, '98 by oder of War Department.
Beverly, George W.	July 28, '98		Died December 11, '98, at Huntsville, Ala.
Beverly, J. Leroy.	July 13, '98	Jan. 27, '99	
Brown, Vivian R.	May 5, '98	Jan. 27, '99	Transferred from Co. E.
Coburn, Charles S.	May 5, '98	Jan. 27, '99	Transferred from Co. E and promoted Corporal.
Brockany, Russell B.	May 5, '98	Jan. 27, '99	
Bell, James J.	May 5, '98	Jan. 27, '99	Transferred from Co. M October 8, '98.
Baxley, Henry D.	May 5, '98		Discharged September 19, '98.
Brockaway, Russell B.	Aug. 17, '98	Jan. 27, '99	
Colligan, James H.	July 13, '98	Jan. 27, '99	
Crawford, Oscar K.	July 13, '98	Jan. 27, '99	Transferred from the Regimental Band December 3, '98.
Copo, William C.	July 28, '98	Jan. 27, '99	
Davis, James W.	Aug. 8, '98	Jan. 27, '99	
Gibson, Charles C.	July 13, '98	Jan. 27, '99	
Hunter, Freeman J.	Aug. 17, '98	Jan. 27, '99	
Hanks, James E. W.	May 24, '98	Jan. 27, '99	Transferred from Co. M October 8, '98.
Henderson, James A.	May 24, '98	Jan. 27, '99	Transferred from Co. M October 8, '98.
Howell, Thomas S.	July 18, '98	Jan. 27, '99	Transferred from Co. M October 8, '98.
Johnson, Frederick H.	Aug. 23, '98	Jan. 27, '99	
Lafever, Granville.	Aug. 23, '98	Jan. 27, '99	
Lynch, Edward J.	Aug. 23, '98	Jan. 27, '99	Transferred from Regimental Band.
Lewis, William J.	July 6, '98		Deserted September 18, '98, at Huntsville, Ala.
Medary, Charles.	April 25, '98	Jan. 27, '99	Transferred from Regimental Band.
Mickler, Walter J.	July 9, '98	Jan. 7, '99	
Malcolm, Alexander.	April 25, '98	Jan. 27, '99	Transferred from Co. M October 8, '98.
Noda, Antonio.	Aug. 10, '98	Jan. 27, '99	
Orsen, Samuel D.	July 12, '98	Jan. 27, '99	
Neligan, Harold F.	Aug. 10, '98		Musician; died December 11, '98, at Huntsville Ala.
Owin, Edward J.	June 22, '98		Died July 12, '98, at Tampa, Fla.
Pomar, Edgar F.	July 28, '98	Jan. 27, '99	
Pomar, Peter P.	July 13, '98		Transferred to Co. M.
Priest, Clarence C.	Aug. 6, '98	Jan. 27, '99	
Pagan, Gill E.	Aug. 8, '98		Transferred to Signal Corps.
Ross, H. H.	Aug. 8, '98	Jan. 27, '99	Transferred from Co. M.
Sharpe, Frank P.	Aug. 6, '98	Jan. 27, '99	
Scott, Henry.	Aug. 10, '98	Jan. 27, '99	
Taylor, Lacy W.	Aug. 10, '98	Jan. 27, '99	Transferred from Co. M.
Thompson, George H.	July 15, '98	Jan. 27, '99	
Wilkinson, Richard S.	June 24, '98	Jan. 27, '99	Transferred from Co. M.
Willax, Harry P.	July 28, '98	Jan. 27, '99	
Wehner, Bruno H.	Aug. 6, '98	Jan. 27, '99	

Company H—1st Florida Regiment.

This company was originally organized as the Escambia Rifles in 1873, and was afterward known as Co. A, 3d Battalion, Florida State Troops. It was called by the Governor of Florida into the service of the United States Volunteer Army May, 1898. Ordered to rendezvous at Tampa, Fla. Left Pensacola on May 13, 1898, arrived May 14 and went into camp at Fort Brooke. Mustered into service of the United States Volunteers May 23, 1898. Broke camp May 27, proceeded to Pa'metto Beach; broke camp there on July 21, going to Fernandina, arriving there July 22; then on August 23 going to Huntsville, Ala., arriving there on August 25; broke camp October 9, proceeding to Ta!lahassee, Fla; arrived there on October 11, where all the men were granted 30 days furlough preparatory to mustering out.

Roll Company H—1st Florida Infantry.

NAMES.	MUSTERED IN.	MUSTERED OUT.	REMARKS.
OFFICERS.			
Captains—			
Richard M. Bushnell	May 1, '98		Resigned.
Robert W. Cobb	May 1, '98	Dec. 3, '98	1st Lieutenant; appointed Captain, October 6,,'98.
1st Lieutenant—			
John Whiting Hyer	May 1, '98	Dec. 3, '98	2nd Lieutenant; appointed 1st Lieutenant, October 26, '98.
2nd Lieutenant—			
Hargis, Robert B	May 1, '98	Dec. 3, '98	Sergeant; appointed 2nd Lieutenant, November 23, '98.
ENLISTED MEN.			
Abt, Peter	May 1, '98	Dec. 3, '98	
Avery, Charles	May 5, '98	Dec. 3, '98	
Alsabrook, William H	May 1, '98		Deserted July 30, '98 at Fernandina, Fla.
Barrow, Robert E	May 5, '98	Dec. 3, '98	
Barry, Joseph P	May 1, '98	Dec. 3, '98	Corporal.
Bell, Benjamin L	May 5, '98	Dec. 3, '98	
Bonifay, Edgall	May 1, '98	Dec. 3, '98	Corporal.
Bonifay, Henry R	May 5, '98	Dec. 3, '98	
Brash, Mannie	May 20, '98	Dec. 3, '98	
Brooks, Leslie E	May 1, '98		Discharged September 8, '98.
Brosnaham, George O. Jr	May 1, '98		Corporal; discharged September 8, '98.
Brown, Henry W	May 5, '98	Dec. 3, '98	
Bryant, Richard H	May 5, '98	Dec. 3, '98	
Chestnut, Curb	May 5, '98	Dec. 3, '98	
Cooley, Samuel R	May 1, '98	Dec. 3, '98	
Cumberworth, Thomas A. E	May 20, '98	Dec. 3, '98	
D'Almberte, Henry T	May 1, '98	Dec. 3, '98	
Daley, Michael J	May 5, '98	Dec. 3, '98	
Dykeman, Harry J	May 20, '98	Dec. 3, '98	Promoted Corporal; September 19, '98.
Daugherty, Jared W	May 20, '98	Dec. 3, '98	Q. M. Sergeant.
Fannin, Ernest A	May 20, '98	Dec. 3, '98	Transferred to hospital corps June 28, '98.
Farley, William A	May 20, '98	Dec. 3, '98	Promoted Corporal; then Sergeant.
Farris, Hugh H	May 5, '98	Dec. 3, '98	
Floyd, Charles H. B	May 20, '98	Dec. 3, '98	
Goodger, Frank	May 5, '98	Dec. 3, '98	
Hahn, William L	May 1, '98		Sergeant; discharged November 23, '98.
Hargis, Robert B	May 1, '98	Dec. 3, '98	
Hurst, John T	May 5, '98		Sergeant; discharged September 6, '98; per Special Order No. 204.
Himberg, Max J	May 1, '98		
Holt, William H	May 5, '98	Dec. 3, '98	
Hoppe, Otto O	May 20, '98	Dec. 3, '98	
Huckabay, George F	May 20, '98	Dec. 3, '98	
Hutchins, Charles M	May 5, '98	Dec. 3, '98	Musician.
Hutchinson, William J	May 1, '98	Dec. 3, '98	Promoted Corporal; September 19, '98.
Knickmeyer, Arthur	May 20, '98	Dec. 3, '98	
Lanier, Floyd	May 5, '98	Dec. 3, '98	
Lee, Stephen	May 10, '98	Dec. 3, '98	Corporal.
Lovelace, Archie	May 5, '98	Dec. 3, '98	
Lovelace, John	May 5, '98	Dec. 3, '98	
Lowery, Joel	May 5, '98	Dec. 3, '98	
Lynch, George A	May 5, '98	Dec. 3, '98	
McGrimis, Charles	May 5, '98	Dec. 3, '98	Artificer.
McLean, James W	May 5, '98	Dec. 3, '98	
Martin, Frank	May 5, '98	Dec. 3, '98	
Martinez, Joseph R	May 5, '98	Dec. 3, '98	Corporal.
Maxon, James T	May 1, '98	Dec. 3, '98	Sergeant.
Menck, John	May 5, '98	Dec. 3, '98	
Mitchell, Benjamin L	May 5, '98	Dec. 3, '98	
Mitchell, Robert J	May 5, '98	Dec. 3 '98	
Mitchell, Solon F	May 5, '98	Dec. 3, '98	
Moreno, Estevan A	May 5, '98	Dec. 3, '98	Q. M. Sergeant.
Nash, John F	May 1, '98	Dec. 3, '98	
Nelson, Oscar	May 5, '98	Dec. 3, '98	
Nyman, Gosslief	May 5, '98	Dec. 3, '98	
Owens, Ernest	May 5, '98	Dec. 3, '98	
Peck, George	May 20, '98	Dec. 3, '98	1st Musician.
Perkins, Henry M	May 5, '98	Dec. 3, '98	Transferred to Hospital Corps June 23, '98.
Peters, Owen D	May 5, '98	Dec. 3, '98	
Peterson, Theodore C	May 5, '98	Dec. 3, '98	
Pierce, Albert	May 20, '98	Dec. 3, '98	
Powers, John A	May 20, '98	Dec. 3, '98	
Price, Hampton M	May 5, '98	Dec. 3, '98	Transferred to Hospital Corps June 7, '98.
Quina, Robert S	May 1, '98		Discharged September 7, '98 per Special Order 205.
Rice, Stephen E. Jr	May 20, '98	Dec. 3, '98	
Riera, Halcott	May 5, '98	Dec. 3, '98	
Richburg, Jefferson D	May 5, '98	Dec. 3, '98	
Sawyer, William	May 20, '98	Dec. 3, '98	
Shakleford, Ernest	May 1, '98	Dec. 3, '98	
Sheppard, Daniel	May 5, '98	Dec. 3, '98	
Shuttleworth, David D. Jr	May 1, '98	Dec. 3, '98	
Sincock, Frank L	May 5, '98	Dec. 3, '98	
Tolman, Thomas B	May 5, '98	Dec. 3, '98	
VanDamm, Joseph V	May 20, '98	Dec. 3, '98	Transferred to Hospital Corps June 22, '98.
Way, Edson	May 5, '98	Dec. 3, '98	Wagoner.

Roll Company H—1st Florida Infantry.
(CONTINUED.)

NAMES.	MUSTERED IN.	MUSTERED OUT.	REMARKS.
Whiting, Frank M	May 1, '98		Sergeant; discharged September 10, '98.
Whiting, Henry H	May 1, '98	Dec. 3, '98	Corporal; transferred to Non-Commissioned Staff
Widmeyer, Christian	May 3, '98	Dec. 3, '98	May 23, '98.
Williams. Wyatt K	May 5, '98	Dec. 3, '98	
Wood, James W	May 5, '98	Dec. 3, '98	
Wood, Thomas M	May 5, '98	Dec. 3, '98	
Baggett. Samuel M	July 8, '98	Dec. 3, '98	
Bradford, Reuben P	July 14, '98	Dec. 3, '98	
DeVeaux, Gordon	July 8, '98	Dec. 3, '98	
Dortch, Joseph W	July 13, '98	Dec. 3, '98	
Fenn, Charles B	July 15, '98	Dec. 3, '98	Transferred to Co. F October 9, '98.
Ferguson, James E	July 14, '98	Dec. 3, '98	
Foster, Edward	July 8, '98	Dec. 3, '98	
Highman, Charles F	July 8, '98	Dec. 3, '98	
Erwin, John J	July 8, '98	Dec. 3, '98	
Jones, Frank	July 8, '98	Dec. 3, '98	
Littlefield. William H	July 8, '98		Discharged August 15, '98, for disability.
Mann, J. W	July 8, '98	Dec. 3, '98	
Miller, Charles	July 14, '98	Dec. 3, '98	
Miller, M. N	July 15, '98	Dec. 3, '98	
Morris, George B.—	July 8, '98	Dec. 3, '98	
Spencer. Clarence A	July 8, '98	Dec. 3, '98	
Steele, James A	July 8, '98	Dec. 8, '98	
Campbell, Raphæl	June 23, '98	Dec. 3, '98	
Cade, Levy W	July 30, '98	Dec. 3, '98	Transferred from Co. F.
Carpenter, John H	Aug. 15, '98	Dec. 3, '98	
Goodman, John H	Aug. 15, '98	Dec. 3, '98	
Hare, John W	Aug. 15, '98	Dec. 3, '98	
Hardwick, Linies	Aug. 15, '98	Dec. 3, '98	
Hardwick, William A	Aug. 15, '98	Dec. 3, '98	
Hartsfield, John P	Aug. 15, '98	Dec. 3, '98	
McMullen, C	Aug. 15, '98	Dec. 3, '98	
Martinez, Charles C	June 23, '98	Dec. 3, '98	
Newell, Bryant	June 23, '98	Dec. 3, '98	
Owen, John E	Aug. 15, '98	Dec. 3, '98	
Pearl, William E	Aug. 15, 98	Dec. 3, '98	
Pope, Henry J	Aug. 15, '98	Dec. 3, '98	
Show, Henry Jr	Aug. 5, '98	Dec. 3, '98	
Webb, Mitchell J	Aug. 4, '98	Dec. 3, '98	
Wilson, Arthur C	Aug. 7, '98	Dec. 3, '98	
Barr, William H	July 13, '98	Dec. 3, '98	Transferred to Regimental Band July 13, '98; per Special Order No. 8.

Company I—1st Florida Regiment.

This company was organized at Pensacola, Fla., August, 1888, under the name of the Chipley Light Infantry, afterward known as Co. B, 3d Battalion, Florida State Troops. It was accepted by the Governor for service in the United States Volunteers on May 1, 1898. Left Pensacola May 13, 1898 by rail for Tampa; arrived there May 14 and went into camp at Fort Brooke, at which place the company was mustered in May 23. Broke camp May 27 and marched to DeSoto Park, Tampa, Fla., where it went into camp June 29; broke camp and marched to Tampa Heights, going on duty with United States Siege Artillery train under Colonel Mills, U. S. A. Left Tampa by rail July 21 for Fernandina; arrived in camp July 22 and remained until August 23, when the company left by rail for Huntsville, Ala.; arrived in camp at that place August 25. Left Huntsville October 9 for Tallahassee, Fla., preparatory to being mustered out; arrived at that place October 11, 1898. October 16 the company was furloughed for 30 days, leaving a detachment in camp guarding government property. Returned to Tallahassee November 15 for the final examination and muster out.

Roll Company I (Capt. Richard M. Cary)—1st Florida Infantry,
(CONTINUED.)

NAMES.	MUSTERED IN.			MUSTERED OUT.			REMARKS.
OFFICERS.							
Captain—							
Richard M. Cary Jr	May	1,	'98	Dec.	3,	'98	
1st Lieutenant—							
Edmund Fox	May	1,	'98	Dec.	3,	'98	
2nd Lieutenant—							
Benjamin W. Robinson	May	1,	'98	Dec.	3,	'98	
ENLISTED MEN.							
Anderson, Yon A	May	10,	'98				Died at Fort McPherson, August 15, '98.
Akers, William	May	18,	'98	Dec.	3,	'98	
Briggs, Frank M	May	1,	'98	Dec.	3,	'98	Appointed Corporal; June 8, '98.
Bailey, Orin A	May	1,	'98	Dec.	3,	'98	
Britton, Thomas E	May	9,	'98	Dec.	3,	'98	
Beardsley, Oscar	May	1,	'98	Dec.	3,	'98	
Bovis, John	May	8,	'98	Dec.	3,	'98	
Broger, John H	May	13,	'98				Discharged without honor July 14, '98.
Barnes, Lee	May	7,	'98	Dec.	3,	'98	
Bracken, John W	April	25,	'98	Dec.	3,	'98	Transferred to Regimental Band June 17, '98.
Briggs, Thomas	May	1,	'98	Dec.	3,	'98	
Crona, Benjamin M	May	1,	'98	Dec.	3,	'98	
Cooey, Daniel P. M	May	19,	'98	Dec.	3,	'98	
Dawson, James	May	18,	'98				Deserted June 7,-'98 at Tampa.
Dole, Thomas A	May	1,	'98	Dec.	3,	'98	
Daniell, William W	May	1,	'93	Dec.	3,	'98	
Dickson, Joseph A	May	13,	'98	Dec.	3,	'98	
Dolive, Adrian M	May	1,	'93	Dec.	3,	'98	Artificer.
Eckel, Jacob	May	18,	'98	Dec.	3,	'98	
Ewald, William F	May	12,	'98	Dec.	3,	'98	Sergeant.
Folkman, James M	May	11,	'98	Dec.	3,	'98	
Friar, Fred A	May	11,	'98	Dec.	3,	'98	
Ferrell, Stephen L	May	18,	'98	Dec.	3,	'98	
Ganze, Thomas A. Jr	May	9,	'98	Dec.	3,	'98	
Gunning, John B	May	10,	'98	Dec.	3,	'98	
Gonzalez, Joseph	May	1,	'93	Dec.	3,	'98	Corporal.
Griffin, Mart	May	1,	'98	Dec.	3,	'98	Q. M. Sergeant.
Knight, Willis	May	01,	'98	Dec.	3,	'98	
Harris, Allie A	May	10,	'98				Died in Fernandina August 19, '98.
Hill, Charles W	May	18,	'93				Deserted July 21, '98 at tTampa.
Hudgens, David	May	18,	'93	Dec.	3,	'98	
Harwick, Louis J	April	25,	'08	Dec.	3,	'98	Transferred to Regimental Band June 17, '98.
Inge, Zebulen M. J	May	10,	'98	Dec.	3,	'98	Transferred to Hospital Corps May 31, '98; by General Order No. 6.
Johnson, Charles	May	2,	'98	Dec.	3,	'98	
Johnson, Frank	May	6,	'98	Dec.	3,	'98	
Jockusen, John	May	17,	'98	Dec.	3,	'98	
Jackson, James O	May	17,	'98	Dec.	3,	'98	
Ketchum, John	May	17,	'98	Dec.	3,	'93	Q. M. Sergeant.
Jones, Clarence J	May	1,	'98	Dec.	3,	'98	Corporal.
Larsen, Adolph	May	16,	'98	Dec.	3,	'98	
Lee, Joseph	May	1,	'93	Dec.	3,	'98	Corporal.
Lewis, Oscar	May	10,	'98	Dec.	3,	'98	
Larcom, Livingston O	May	1,	'93	Dec.	3,	'98	
Landmesser, Philip	May	13,	'98	Dec.	3,	'98	Corporal; died at Fernandina August 15, '98.
Massey, John	May	1,	'98				
Miller, Theodore	May	1,	'98	Dec.	3,	'98	
Minskey, Franz M. S. A	May	1,	'98	Dec.	3,	'98	Appointed Corporal; August 4, '98; transferred to Co. F.
McGuire, Henry	May	17,	'98	Dec.	17,	'98	Corporal.
Mathews, Thomas F	May	19,	'98	Dec.	3,	'93	
Mays, William P	May	18,	'98	Dec.	3,	'93	
McLaughlin, Thomas	May	1,	'98				Corporal; died at Fort Thomas, Ky. September 11, '98.
Montero, Alejo G	April	25,	'98	Dec.	3,	'98	Transferred to Regimental Band, June 11, '98.
Nevel, Earl	May	8,	'98	Dec.	3,	'98	
Nichelsen, Reuben L	May	1,	'98	Dec.	3,	'93	Sergeant.
Nork, Robert	May	1,	'98	Dec.	3,	'98	
Paul, James R	May	19,	'98	Dec.	3,	'98	
Pearl, William E	May	1,	'98	Dec.	3,	'98	Transferred to Co. H June 14, '98.
Pickens, William E	May	1,	'98	Dec.	3,	'98	
Pine, John H	May	7,	'98	Dec.	3,	'98	Musician.
Palmerlee, Herbert S	May	9,	'98	Dec.	3,	'98	
Powell, Samuel U	May	18,	'98	Dec.	3,	'98	
Parsons, John B	May	20,	'98	Dec.	3,	'93	Transferred to Hospital Corps June 20, '98; by General Order No. 26.
Robinson, Louis D	May	1,	'98	Dec.	3,	'98	Musician.
Stewart, James A	May	1,	'98	Dec.	3,	'93	1st Sergeant.
Suarez, Morrill A	May	7,	'98	Dec.	3,	'98	
Smith, Clyde L	May	1,	'98	Dec.	3,	'98	
Shuttleworth, John G	May	1,	'98	Dec.	3,	'98	Artificer.
Stevens, Thomas A	May	18,	'98	Dec.	3,	'93	
Sullivan, John W	May	1,	'98	Dec.	3,	'98	Sergeant.
Santiso, Jose	April	25,	'98	Dec.	3,	'98	Transferred to Regimental Band June 17, '98.
Thompson, Leonard G	May	13,	'98	Dec.	3,	'98	
Thompson, John T	May	18,	'98	Dec.	3,	'98	
Thompson, John W	May	18,	'98	Dec.	3,	'98	

Roll Company I (Capt. Richard M. Cary)—1st Florida Infantry.

(CONTINUED.)

NAMES.	MUSTERED IN.	MUSTERED OUT.	REMARKS.
Van Pelt, John G	April 25, '98		Transferred to Regimental Band June 17, '98.
Walton, William J	May 10, '98		Died at Fort Barrancas, Fla., September 29, '98.
Walker, Jeff M	May 13, '98	Dec. 3, '98	
Whitney, Frank D	May 18, '98	Dec. 3, '98	
Watts, Charles H	May 14, '98	Dec. 3, '98	Wagoner.
Zediker, Zellon D	May 23, '98		Traansferred to Co. F, 2nd Nebraska, V. I., July 15
Barclay, John C	July 31, '98	Dec. 3, '98	'98.
Brown, Lucius C	Aug. 13, '98	Dec. 3, '98	
Brown, Nathan	July 4, '98	Dec. 3, '98	
Burnham, Rufus E	Aug. 13, '98	Dec. 3, '98	
Cawthorn, Hawley	July 29, '98	Dec. 3, '98	
Cockroft, John B	July 29, '98	Dec. 3, '98	
Cawthorn, Allen C	July 29, '98	Dec. 3, '98	
Cawthorn, Harley	July 29, '98	Dec. 3, '98	
Hall, Charles W	July 21, '98	Dec. 3, '98	
Turner, Joseph B	July 29, '98		Transferred to Co. F October 8, '98.
Stubbs, Jesse B	July 28, '98	Dec. 3, '98	
Stubbs, Russell A	June 28, '98	Dec. 3, '98	
Marshall, Lewis	Aug. 10, '98	Dec. 3, '98	Appointed Corporal; September 8, '98.
Lavoine, Charles A	Aug. 20, '98	Dec. 23, '98	Cook.
Batton, Charles A	April 23, '98	Dec. 3, '98	Joined Co. October 9, '98; transferred from Co. F.
Bowden, Halstead E	April 26, '98	Dec. 3, '98	Transferred from Co. F October 9, '98.
Caswell, Carl G	May 12, '98	Dec. 3, '98	Transferred from Co. D October 9, '98.
Caucio, Charles A	April 23, '98	Dec. 3, '98	Transferred from Co. F October 9, '98.
Coxetter, Louis M	July 31, '98	Dec. 3, '98	Transferred from Co. F October 9, '98.
Duff, James	June 11, '98	Dec. 3, '98	
Flannery, Franken	July 30, '98	Dec. 3, '98	
Haddon, Chalmers	Aug. 20, '98	Dec. 3, '98	
Hewett, James B	Aug. 13, '98	Dec. 3, '98	
King, Hugh H	Aug. 20, '98	Dec. 3, '98	
Innabinet, Ovel E	Aug. 3, '98	Dec. 3, '98	
Lindsey, Benjamin F	Aug. 20, '98	Dec. 3, '98	
Lindsey, John J	Aug. 20, '98	Dec. 3, '98	
Mallon, John A	Aug. 20, '98	Dec. 3, '98	
Morrison, William	Aug. 1, '98	Dec. 3, '98	
Muse, William F	May 8, '98	Dec. 3, '98	Transferred from Co. F October 9, '98.
Osborne, Ralph T	Aug. 10, '98	Dec. 3, '98	
Pierce, James B	Aug. 3, '98	Dec. 3, '98	
Ryals, Benjamin	Aug. 20, '98	Dec. 3, '98	
Standley, Walter R	Aug. 13, '98	Dec. 3, '98	
Sellers, John A	Aug. 1, '98	Dec. 3, '98	
Shehan, Harry	Aug. 13, '98	Dec. 3, '98	
Brown, William	Aug. 17, '98		Transferred to Co. D October 9, '98.
Yansen, Frederic	Aug. 17, '98		Transferred to Co. F October 9, '98.
Cricknav, Charles T	Aug. 10, '98		Transferred to Co. F October 9, '98.
Hough, Willis	May 10, '98		Transferred to Co. F

Company K—1st Florida Regiment.

This company was enrolled at Quincy, Fla., by Captain Williamson, April 29, 1898; was ordered to rendezvous at Tampa, Fla., by Governor Bloxham. Left Quincy by rail May 13 for Tampa, arrived there May 14, distance traveled being about 400 miles; went into camp and mustered into the service of the United States May 23, 1898, by Captain Thomas M. Woodruff, U. S. A. Moved camp to Palmetto Beach May 27 distance marched about two miles; the company was attached to the Provisional Battalion and ordered to join Brigadier-General Rodgers, Chief of Artillery, as support to Light Artillery; broke camp June 30 and marched a distance of two miles to Camp Rodgers, where camp was pitched; ordered to rejoin 1st Regiment of Florida Volunteer Infantry; moved camp from Camp Rodgers, Ybor City, to Camp Davidson, Ybor City, July 14, distance marched being one-third of a mile; changed station from Camp Davidson, Ybor City, to Camp Amelia, Fernandina, Fla., July 22, distance traveled about 230 miles; broke camp at Fernandina night of August 22. Bivouacked in streets of Fernandina until 3.30 p. m. August 23, when boarded the train for Huntsville, Ala.; arrived in Huntsville August 25 at 3:30 p. m. Bivouacked on common night of August 25; pitched camp in the morning at Camp Wheeler, Ala. Left Huntsville October 9 for Talla-hassee, Fla., for the purpose of being mustered ont of service. Company fur-loughed October 15, 1898, for 30 days.

Roll Company K (Capt. Samuel T. Williamson)—1st Florida Infantry.

NAMES.	MUSTERED IN.	MUSTERED OUT.	REMARKS.
OFFICERS.			
Captain—			
Samuel T. Williamson	April 29, '98	Dec. 3, '98	
1st Lieutenant—			
James G. Sharon	April 29, '98	Dec. 3, '98	
2nd Lieutenants—			
Harry McFarlin	April 29, '98		Resigned August 1, '98.
Madison H. Wilson	April 29, '98	Dec. 3, '98	1st Sergeant; appointed 2nd Lieutenant August 2, '98.
ENLISTED MEN.			
Ashley, Council C	May 13, '98	Dec. 3, '98	
Alley, Wilbur F	May 11, '98		Transferred to Hospital Corps June 22, '98.
Brooks, J. Marion	May 11, '98	Dec. 3, '98	
Barker, Robert L	May 11, '98	Dec. 3, '98	
Brock, James M	May 11, '98	Dec. 3, '98	
Brock, Doc B	May 11, '98	Dec. 3, '98	
Bonham, Auiel	May 11, '98	Dec. 3, '98	
Bunting, Charles A	May 11, '98	Dec. 3, '98	
Criswell, Charles E	May 13, '98	Dec. 3, '98	
Chester, Robert J	April 29, '98		Died in Fernandina.
Conter, August	April 29, '98		Musician; transferred to Co. F October 9, '98.
Duboise, Marion F	May 11, '98		Died at Fernandina August 17, '98.
Breward, Richard C	May 16, '98	Dec. 3, '98	
Dawdy, Arthur	May 23, '98	Dec. 3, '98	
Farrior, Thomas W	May 11, '98	Dec. 3, '98	
Foster, David F	May 2, '98	Dec. 3, '98	
Fox, Lonnie	May 16, '98	Dec. 3, '98	
Fox, Barney	May 16, '98	Dec. 3, '98	
Griffin, Hugh M	May 11, '98	Dec. 3, '98	
Griffin, Sevier	May 2, '98	Dec. 3, '98	Appointed Corporal September 15, '98.
Gregory, Frank S	April 29, '98	Dec. 3, '98	Appointed Corporal August 1, '98.
Gilbert, Leslie W	May 11, '98	Dec. 3, '98	
Gearing, Oliver	May 23, '98	Dec. 3, '98	
Hozeboom, J. Edwin	May 11, '98	Dec. 3, '98	
Harrell, Robert G	May 2, '98		Transferred to Hospital Corps June 22, '98.
Hubbard, Joseph B	May 29, '98	Dec. 3, '98	Appointed Corporal May 28, '98; Sergeant, September 15, '98.
Harkness, James J	May 11, '98	Dec. 3, '98	
Halbert, James B	May 16, '98	Dec. 3, '98	
Higgins, Oscar L	May 23, '98	Dec. 3, '98	
Hart, James W	May 23, '98		Discharged September 15, '98, for disability.
Harp, John A	May 23, '98	Dec. 3, '98	
Howard, Robert F	April 29, '98		Sergeant; discharged September 7, '98.
Kilpatrick, Robert H	April 16, '98	Dec. 3, '98	
Inabnitt, Henry P	April 23, '98	Dec. 3, '98	
Ivens, Willis H	April 11, '98	Dec. 3, '98	
Lumpkins, Reuben P	April 25, '98	Dec. 3, '98	
Morrow, Claude L	May 2, '98	Dec. 3, '98	Musician.
Massey, George B	April 29, '98		1st Sergeant; discharged September 7, '98.
Morrow, John A	April 11, '98		Discharged August 19, '98, for disability.
May, William A	April 11, '98		Transferred to Hospital Corps June 27, '98.
McMillan, J. D	May 11, '98		Appointed Corporal September 15, '98.
McMillan, D. A	May 11, '98	Dec. 3, '98	
McClellan, Irvin	May 11, '98	Dec. 3, '98	
Merriman, Charles J	May 11, '98	Dec. 3, '98	
Munroe, Thomas F	April 29, '98		Sergeant; died at Quincy August 28, '98.
Owens, Gus B	May 11, '98		Appointed Corporal August 1; Sergeant September 1, '98.
Obert, August	May 11, '98	Dec. 3, '98	
Ostinger, Samuel M	April 29, '98	Dec. 3, '98	
Pitts, Josh D	May 11, '98	Dec. 3, '98	
Patterson, Russell A	May 11, '98	Dec. 3, '98	
Patrick, William D	April 29, '98	Dec. 3, '98	
Puleston, John A	May 11, '98	Dec. 3, '98	
Parramore, William F	May 2, '98	Dec. 3, '98	Appointed Corporal August 1, '98.
Patterson, W. A	May 2, '98	Dec. 3, '98	
Powell, H. Leo	May 15, '98	Dec. 3, '98	
Ripley, Joseph M	May 11, '98	Dec. 3, '98	Promoted 1st Sergeant September 8, '98.
Sanford, Raymond C	April 29, '98	Dec. 3, '98	Corporal; appointed Sergeant September 15, '98.
Snow, W. A	May 2, '98	Dec. 3, '98	Appointed Corporal May 28, '98.
Stephens, Charles E	April 25, '98		Transferred to Hospital Corps June 7, '98.
Stephens, Robert D	May 3, '98		Corporal; discharged September 7, '98.
Stokes, Eugene A	May 3, '98		Died in Fort Thomas, Ky., July 25, '98.
Shackleford, Robert H	May 11, '98	Dec. 3, '98	
Sharon, Hayras F	April 29, '98		Sergeant; discharged September 16, '98 for disability.
Swanson, Joseph G	April 11, '98		Discharged August 8, '98, for disability.
Smith, Charles L	April 11, '98	Dec. 3, '98	
Scarlett, Richard F	May 11, '98		Discharged September 11, '98.
Smith, George W	May 11, '98	Dec. 3, '98	

Roll Company K (Capt. Samuel T. Williamson)—1st Florida Infantry.
(CONTINUED.)

NAMES.	MUSTERED IN.	MUSTERED OUT.	REMARKS.
Smith, Benjamin F.	April 29, '98	Dec. 3, '98	Appointed Corporal September 15, '98.
Turner, Francis M.	May 11, '98	Dec. 3, '98	
Taylor. Leslie A.	May 11, '98	Dec. 3, '98	
VonWeller, George.	May 11, '98	Dec. 3, '98	
Walker, Joseph H.	May 2, '98	Dec. 3, '98	
Wilson, Maetesch.	May 2, '98	Dec. 3, '98	Sergeant.
Wilson, Richard W.	May 12, '98	Dec. 3, '98	Appointed Corporal May 28; Sergeant September 15, '98.
Waller, F. Earl.	May 11, '98	Dec. 3, '98	
Crowell, George.	May 23, '98	Dec. 3, '98	
Rogers, William.	May 23, '98	Dec. 3, '98	
Sims, Thomas T.	May 30, '98	Dec. 3, '98	Appointed Corporal August 1, '98.
Allen, Thomas J.	July 20, '98	Dec. 3, '98	
Allen, William J.	July 20, '98	Dec. 3, '98	
Farrior, Robert L.	May 11, '98	Dec. 3, '98	
Gainey, Benjamin.	July 20, '98	Dec. 3, '98	
Hartsfield, Jesse S.	July 19, '98	Dec. 3, '98	
Lang, Paul A.	June 12, '98	Dec. 3, '98	Appointed Corporal July 1, '98; Sergeant September 15, '98.
Lumpkin, Joseph W.	July 20, '98	Dec. 3, '98	
Potts, V. B.	July 20, '98	Dec. 3, '98	Appointed Artificer August 1, '98.
Rogers, Charles W.	July 19, '98	Dec. 3, '98	
Snyder, George H.	April 29, '98		Transferred from Co. F October 9, '98.
Barrow, John.	Aug. 19, '98	Dec. 3, '98	
Hinson, Volmer F.	Aug. 19, '98	Dec. 3, '98	
Rogers, William A.	May 20, '98	Dec. 3, '98	
Swain, Chalfont L.	Aug. 19, '98	Dec. 3, '98	
Teter, Ira E.	July 10, '98	Dec. 3, '98	
Bell, Archie.			Discharged by Special Order No. 204 August 30, '98.
Kirkpatrick, Charles B.	May 11, '98		Died at Huntsville, Ala., September 14, '98.

Company L—1st Florida Regiment.

This company was organized in 1891 at Live Oak, Fla., as the Suwannee Rifles and at the time of mustering into the United States service was known in the Florida State Troops as Co. A, 4th Battalion. It was accepted by the Governor of the State for United States service in the Spanish-American War on April 23, 1898.

The company left Live Oak for Tampa, Fla., May 12, 1898, arrived there May 13 and went in camp on the old Government reservation known as the "Garrison," at which place it was mustered into the United States service on May 23, 1898. Broke camp at the "Garrison" May 27 and moved into camp at DeSoto Park, Tampa, Fla., on same day. June 29 the company was detached from the Regiment at Fort Brooke Camp and marched to Tampa Heights, going into the service in the United States Siege Artillery train, under Colonel Mills, U. S. A. In July it was again attached to the Regiment; broke camp at Tampa Heights July 21 and left Tampa by rail for Fernandina; arrived and went into camp at Fernandina July 22; broke camp at Fernandina August 22, and left by rail for Huntsville, Ala., August 23; arrived and went into camp at that place August 25, where it remained until October 9, when it moved to Tallahassee preparatory to being mustered out of the service; arrived October 11. October 14 the company was given furlough for 30 days, except detachment left to guard property; returned to Tallahassee November 15, 1898, for the purpose of being regularly mustered out.

Roll Company L (Capt. Willie L. Tedder)--1st Florida Infantry.

NAMES.	MUSTERED IN.	MUSTERED OUT.	REMARKS.
OFFICERS.			
Captain--			
Willie L. Tedder	April 23, '98	Dec. 3, '98	
1st Lieutenant--			
L. K. Kernmenlin	April 23, '98	Dec. 3, '98	Resigned August 29, '98.
Willie H. Lyle	April 23, '98		2nd Lieutenant; appointed 1st Lieutenant September 2, '98.
2nd Lieutenant--			
Archer B. Hays	April 23, '98	Dec. 3, '98	Appointed Sergeant; May 24, elected 2nd Lieutenant September 3, '98.
ENLISTED MEN.			
Burns, George W	April 23, '98	Dec. 3, '98	Appointed Corporal; May 24, '98.
Bynum, Edward	July 4, '98		Discharged by Special Order No. 154.
Brewer, Thomas W	April 23, '98	Dec. 3, '98	Appointed Corporal; September 12, '98.
Bridges, John A	May 9, '98	Dec. 3, '98	
Bryant, Hunter G	May 9, '98	Dec. 3, '98	
Bird, George T	April 23, '98	Dec. 3, '98	Appointed Corporal Sept. 12, '98.
Bethea, Robert H	May 9, '98	Dec. 3, '98	
Bardin, Benjamin T	May 9, '98	Dec. 3, '98	
Crawford, Osco K	May 9, '98	Dec. 3, '98	Transferred to 1st Fla. Band June 28, '98.
Curl, Benjamin M	May 9, '98	Dec. 3, '98	
Corbett, James A	May 9, '98	Dec. 3, '98	
Cobb, Arch B	May 9, '98	Dec. 3, '98	
Cline, Frank E	May 9, '98	Dec. 3, '98	
Cato, Robert P	May 10, '98		Discharged August 2, '98. for disability.
Chalker, Marvin P.	May 9, '98	Dec. 3, '98	
Curran, Edward D	April 23, '98	Dec. 3, '98	
Dutton, Joseph L	April 23, '98	Dec. 3, '98	
Doyle, John P	April 23, '93	Dec. 3, '98	Appointed Sergeant September 12, '98.
Davis, Capus C. C	May 10, '98		Discharged September 28, '98, for disability.
Evans, Lorenzo D	May 9, '93	Dec. 3, '93	
Foster, Thomas J	April 23, '98	Dec. 3, '98	
Frier, Jesse G	May 9, '98	Dec. 3, '98	
Faircloth, William J	May 10, '93		Discharged August 29, '98, for disability.
Fletcher, Benjamin F	May 9, '98	Dec. 3, '98	
Ferriter, John H	April 23, '93	Dec. 3, '98	
Fielding, Hunter	May 9, '93	Dec. 3, '98	
Gamble, Andrew M	May 9, '93	Dec. 3, '98	
Gardner, E. D	April 23, '93	Dec. 3, '98	Appointed Corporal September 12, '98.
Gillstrap, Charles F	April 23, '93	Dec. 3, '98	
Garrett, William J	May 9, '93	Dec. 3, '93	Appointed Corporal May 24, Sergeant.
Hawkins, J. M	April 23, '93	Dec. 3, '93	Appointed Corporal May 24, '98.
Hemming, J. D	May 9, '98	Dec. 3, '98	
Hill, Robert M	May 9, '98	Dec. 3, '98	
Griffin, W. W	May 9, '98	Dec. 3, '93	
Hodge, Harrell	May 9, '93	Dec. 3, '93	
Helvenston, Joseph T	April 23, '93	Dec. 3, '98	Transferred to Co. B October 9, '98.
Harby, Charlie S. Jr	May 9, '93	Dec. 3, '98	Transferred to Hospital Corps June 1, '98.
Hicks, H. M	May 10, '98		Sergeant; deserted July 16, '98.
Hunter, Bloomer O	May 9, '93	Dec. 3, '98	Musician.
Ingalls, Ollie H	April 23, '98	Dec. 3, '96	
Johnson, J. B	April 23, '98	Dec. 3, '98	1st Sergeant.
Jordan, Clifford R	April 23, '98	Dec. 3, '98	
Knowles, John C	April 23, '98	Dec. 3, '98	
Lamb, Joseph P	April 23, '98	Dec. 3, '98	
Lelson, Benjamin	April 23, '98	Dec. 3, '98	
Long, Eustice	April 23, '98	Dec. 3, '98	Corporal; discharged August 27, '98, for disability.
McCullers, David M	April 23, '98	Dec. 3, '93	
Macon, Pickens B	May 9, '98	Dec. 3, '93	
Moore, Willie P.	May 9, '98	Dec. 3, '98	
McLeod, Joseph A	May 9, '98	Dec. 3, '98	
McDaniel, John	April 23, '98	Dec. 3, '98	
Miller, Marvin P	April 23, '98	Dec. 3, '98	
McCarthe, Walter L	May 10, '98		Discharged September 27, '98, for disability.
Nicholas, Willie H	April 23, '98	Dec. 3, '98	
Norton, Charles	April 23, '98	Dec. 3, '98	
Onanstein, Philip	April 23, '98	Dec. 3, '98	
Parnell, John W	April 23, '98	Dec. 3, '98	Wagoner.
Prester, John A	May 9, '98	Dec. 3, '98	Appointed Q. M. Sergeant August 5, '98.
Perry, Roy L	May 9, '93	Dec. 3, '98	
Redding, W. H	April 23, '93	Dec. 3, '98	Sergeant.
Sharpe, Charles C	May 10, '93	Dec. 3, '98	Transferred to Co. F October 9, '98.
Sessions, Rally	May 9, '93	Dec. 3, '98	
Suggs, Presley P.	May 10, '98	Dec. 3, '98	
Small, Rosco W	April 23, '93	Dec. 3, '98	
Smith, W. N	April 23, '93	Dec. 3, '98	Appointed Corporal May 1, '98.
Stevens, Theodore A	April 23, '93	Dec. 3, '98	
Summers, Murrin P	May 10, '93	Dec. 3, '98	
Summers, Percy C	May 10, '93	Dec. 3, '98	
Tyler, Percy H	May 10, '93	Dec. 3, '98	
Williams, Owen J	April 23, '98	Dec. 3, '98	Artificer.
Witt, Barney L	May 9, '93	Dec. 3, '93	
Whatley, William D	May 13, '93	Dec. 3, '98	
White, J. F	May 13, '93	Dec. 3, '93	Sergeant.

Roll Company L (Capt. Willie L. Tedder)—1st Florida Infantry.
(CONTINUED.)

NAMES.	MUSTERED IN.	MUSTERED OUT.	REMARKS.
Wood, Joseph W.	May 9, '98	Dec. 3, '98	Appointed Corporal September 12, '98.
Williams, Fred.	May 10, '98		Discharged June 28, '98 by Special Order No. 176.
Yonge, Chandler R.	May 23, '98		Transferred to Co. A October 9, '98.
Medary, Charles.	May 23, '98	Dec. 3, '98	Transferred to 1st Fla. Band June 17, '98.
Bass, Arlie M.	May 12, '98	Dec. 3, '98	Musician.
Benning, H. P.	July 5, '98	Dec. 3, '98	
Beckman, David M.	May 9, '98	Dec. 3, '98	
Brown, Charles W.	July 22, '98	Dec. 3, '98	
Carlisle, T. J.	July 6, '98	Dec. 3, '98	
Cross, William H.	April 23, '98	Dec. 3. '98	
Dunham, George L.	July 7, '98		Transferred to Co. B October 9, '98.
Gainey, W. A.	July 7, '98	Dec. 3, '98	
Hackett, J. F.	July 24, '98	Dec. 3, '98	
Hurst, John W.	July 29, '98	Dec. 3, '98	
Ives, Norman P.	May 10, '98		Discharged August 25, '98, per Special Order No. 200.
Jernigan, J. T.	May 7, '98	Dec. 3, '98	
Johnson, A. S.	May 7, '98	Dec. 3, '98	
Lewis, W. F.	May 10, '98	Dec. 3, '98	
McCullers, Robert.	May 11, '98	Dec. 3, '98	
Moore, T. J. No. 2.	May 1, '98	Dec. 3, '98	
Moody, Joseph F.	Aug. 20, '98	Dec. 3, '98	
Newlan, G. F.	July 24, '98	Dec. 3, '98	
Pennington, L. F.	July 24, '98	Dec. 3, '98	
Pitts, Joseph P.	July 30, '98	Dec. 3, '98	
Puckett, H. D.	July 24, '98		Deserted August 4, '98.
Putnam, Edward A.	July 15, '98	Dec. 3, '98	
Reynolds, George T.	June 11, '98	Dec. 3, '98	
Riley, Philip.	July 24, '98	Dec. 3. '98	
Silas, William D.	July 29, '98		Discharged September 4, '98, for disability.
Walker, C. L.	July 18, '98	Dec. 3, '98	
Walker, N. C.	July 24, '98	Dec. 3, '98	
Wis, Martise E.	June 11, '98	Dec. 3, '98	
Ward, A. B.	July 24, '98	Dec. 3, '98	
Chevalier, Harroll F.	June 23, '98	Dec. 3, '98	
Milhollin, Thomas J.	July 22, '98	Dec. 3, '98	
Cline, Robert L.	May 13, '98		Discharged August 13, '98; Special Order No. 195.

Company M—1st Florida Regiment.

This company was organized at Starke, Florida, June 17, 1889, and was known as the Bradford County Guards. It was admitted into the Florida State Troops as Co. B, 1st Battalion, April 16, 1890; later transferred to the 4th Battalion, Florida State Troops. Volunteered its services and was accepted by Gov. William D. Bloxham April 23, 1898. Moved from Starke to Tampa, Fla., 167 miles distant, where it arrived via the Florida Central & Peninsular Railroad on May 13; pitched camp on the "Garrison" reservation in the city of Tampa, where it was mustered into the service of the United States on May 24, 1898, by Maj. Thomas M. Woodruff, U, S, A, Broke camp 7 a. m. May 27 and marched to Palmetto Beach, two miles east of Tampa, where it pitched camp and remained until July 22; broke camp August 22 and moved to Fernandina, Fla., where it arrived July 23 at 9 a. m. and pitched camp one mile east of the city. Broke camp August 22 at 2 p. m; marched to city at 7 p. m., where it bivouacked in the streets until noon August 23, when it departed by rail for Huntsville, Ala., where it arrived at 2 a. m. August 25; pitched camp one mile east of the city, remaining there till 9 a. m. August 26, when it moved to a permanent camp one and one-half miles north-east of the city; broke camp at noon October 9 and moved to Tallahassee, Fla., where it arrived at 9 a. m. October 11, 1898, and where it was camped in Houston Grove until mustered out of service.

Roll Company M (Capt. Eugene S. Matthews)—1st Florida Infantry.

NAMES.	MUSTERED IN.	MUSTERED OUT.	REMARKS.
OFFICERS.			
Captain—			
Eugene S. Matthews	April 23, '98	Dec. 3, '98	
1st Lieutenant—			
Augustine V. Long	April 23, '98	Dec. 3, '98	
2nd Lieutenant—			
George C. Livingston	April 23, '98	Dec. 3, '98	
ENLISTED MEN.			
Adams, Julius T.	April 23, '98	Dec. 3, '98	1st Sergeant.
Adams, Robert S.	April 23, '98	Dec. 3, '98	
Austin, Hansford	May 9, '98	Dec. 3, '98	
Benton, Osburn J.	May 8, '98	Dec. 3, '98	
Burnsed, Frank W.	May 8, '98	Dec. 3, '98	
Bell, James G.	April 23, '98	Dec. 3, '98	Transferred to Co. G October 9, '98.
Beville, Edward M.	April 23, '98	Dec. 3, '98	
Bryson, William K.	May 24, '98	Dec. 3, '98	Transferred to Co. B October 9, '98.
Castlebury, Locke	April 23, '98	Dec. 3, '98	Corporal; transferred to Co. B October 9, '98.
Cain, Elmer E.	April 23, '98	Dec. 3, '98	Transferred to Regimental Band June 11, '98.
Chandler, Mark	May 9, '98	Dec. 3, '98	
Carter, John C.	May 8, '98	Dec. 3, '98	
Cullion, Stephen B	May 8, '98	Dec. 3, '98	Appointed Corporal August 22 '98.
Carter, Charles C.	May 12, '98	Dec. 3, '98	
Clark, Arthur M.	May 24, '98	Dec. 3, '98	
Crowson, Walter R.	May 24, '98	Dec. 3, '98	Transferred to Co. D June 1, '98.
Davis, Jesse F.	May 9, '98	Dec. 3, '98	
Dennis, Ralph P.	May 9, '98	Dec. 3, '98	Sergeant.
Dobbs, James C.	May 24, '98	Dec. 3, '98	Artificer.
Dunkley, Hilton J.	May 23, '98	Dec. 3, '98	Corporal.
Dillon, George E.	April 25, '98	Dec. 3, '98	Transferred to Regimental Band June 17, '98.
Freeman, John W	April 13, '98	Dec. 3, '98	
Fremmstead, Martin	April 25, '98	Dec. 3, '98	Transferred to Regimental Band-June 17, '98.
Harris, John A.	May 9, '98	Dec. 3, '98	Transferred to Co. F October 9, '98.
Hedges, Simon B.	May 9, '98	Dec. 3, '98	
Hall, James S.	May 9, '98	Dec. 8, '98	
Henderson, James M.	May 24, '98	Dec. 5, '98	Q. M. Sergeant; transferred to Co. G October 9, '98.
Herrington, Seaborn A.	May 9, '98	Dec. 3, '98	
Hanks, James E. W.	May 24, '98	Dec. 3, '98	Transferred to Co. G October 9, '98.
Johns, Archibald H.	May 24, '98	Dec. 3, '98	Sergeant.
Jones, LeRoy	May 24, '98	Dec. 3, '98	Appointed Corporal August 22, '98.
Jones, Noah	Apri, 23, '98	Dec. 3, '98	
Jones, John M.	April 23, '98	Dec. 3, '98	
Johns, Jefferson	April 23, '98	Dec. 3, '98	
Jones, Reuben T.	May 24, '98	Dec. 3, '98	Transferred to Co. D October 9, '98.
Joughin, William L.	May 24, '98		Discharged without honor November 22, '98.
Kelsey, Daniel B.	May 10, '98	Dec. 3, '98	
Kite, Perry	May 10, '98	Dec. 3, '98	Corporal.
Lemon, George L.	May 10, '98	Dec. 3, '98	
LaFontisee, John O.	May 24, '98		Discharged September 14, '98.
Lippwood, Albert T.	May 24, '98		Deserted September 2, '98.
Malone, Anthony	April 25, '98	Dec. 3, '98	Transferred to Regimental Band June 17, '98.
Malcolm, Alexander	April 23, '98	Dec. 3, '98	Transferred to Co. G October 9, '98.
Moore, Frank A.	April 23, '98	Dec. 3, '98	Sergeant.
Moore, Thomas J.	May 8, '98	Dec. 3, '98	
Martindale, Charles H.	April 23, '98	Dec. 3, '98	
Martin, Oscar H.	May 8, '98	Dec. 3, '98	
Miller, James A.	April 25, '98	Dec. 3, '98	Transferred to Regimental Hospital Corps June 5, '98.
Owens, Owen	April 23, '98	Dec. 3, '98	Corporal; transferred to Co. F October 9, '98.
Prescott, John M.	May 10, '98	Dec. 3, '98	
Ross, Herbert H.	May 10, '98	Dec. 3, '98	
Roberts, Henry M.	May 10, '98	Dec. 3, '98	
Rice, Joab G. Jr.	April 23, '98	Dec. 3, '98	
Reaves, Rollins G.	May 8, '98	Dec. 3, '98	
Smith, Luther J.	May 8, '98	Dec. 3, '98	Appointed Corporal July 17, '98.
Singletary, George C.	May 9, '98	Dec. 3, '98	
Smoak, Julius H.	May 9, '98	Dec. 3, '98	
Smith, Alexander T.	May 7, '98	Dec. 3, '98	
Smith, William M.	May 9, '98	Dec. 3, '98	
Stokes, Arthur A.	May 9, '98	Dec. 3, '98	
Trowbridge, Claude C.	May 9, '98	Dec. 3, '98	Appointed Musician May 24, '98.
Taylor, Frank W.	Aug. 12, '98	Dec. 3, '98	
Taylor, Lacy W.	April 23, '98	Dec. 3, '98	
Timberlake, Henry C.	May 7, '98	Dec. 3, '98	
Varnum, Henry	April 23, '98	Dec. 3, '98	Transferred from Co. F October 9, '98.
Welsh, James E.	May 22, '98	Dec. 3, '98	Wagoner.
Wynn, Isaiah D.	April 23, '98	Dec. 3, '98	
Wilkinson, Richard S.	June 28, '98	Dec. 3, '98	Transferred from Co. G October 9, '98.
Williams, Alta J.	May 8, '98	Dec. 3, '98	
Wimberly, Thomas	May 7, '98		Died at Fernandina August 10, '98.
Wilkes, John	May 7, '98		
Wilson, Isaac N.	May 7, '98		Killed accidentally near Alachua, Fla., October. 22, '98.
Wilson, Thomas S.	Aug. 22, '98	Dec. 3, '98	Transferred to Co. G October 8, '98.
Ward, John J.	May 8, '98		Died November 8, '98, at Brooker, Fla.

Roll Company M (Capt. Eugene S. Matthew)—1st Fforiya Infantry.

NAMES.	MUSTERED IN.	MUSTERED OUT.	REMARKS.
Wilder, Thomas J.	May 24, '98	Dec. 3, '98	Transferred from Co. D October 8, '98.
Wilder, Hezekiah H.	May 24, '98	Dec. 3, '98	
Witkorski, Felix D.	May 24, '98	Dec. 3, '98	Sergeant.
Witkorski, Leo.	May 24, '98	Dec. 3, '98	Corporal.
Williams, Charles E.	April 25, '98	Dec. 3, '98	Transferred from Co. B October 8, '98.
Vazquez, Arthur D.	April 25, '98	Dec. 3, '98	
Beville, J. W.	July 19, '98	Dec. 3, '98	
Brasel, J. L.	July 27, '98	Dec. 3, '98	
Budd, Isaac M.	Aug. 26, '98	Dec. 3, '98	Transferred to Co. B October 9, '98.
Haffner, W. B.	July 9, '98	Dec. 3, '98	
Hemmingway, W. H.	July 9, '98	Dec. 3, '98	
Howell, T. S.	July 9, '98	Dec. 3, '98	Transferred to Co. G October 9, '98.
McDonald, William C.	Aug. 3, '98	Dec. 3, '98	
McLendon, G. B.	July 27, '98	Dec. 3, '98	
Moore, John J.	June 24, '98	Dec. 3, '98	
Moore, L. R.	June 9, '98	Dec. 3, '98	
Powell, Tate	April 23, '98	Dec. 3, '98	Transferred from Co. D; promoted Corporal June 1, '98.
Liles, John T.	April 23, '98	Dec. 3, '98	Transferred from Co. D promoted Corporal; July 19, '98.
Aiken, William T.	Aug. 22, '98	Dec. 3, '98	
Powell, Lawrence B.	April 23, '98	Dec. 3, '98	Transferred from Co. D, promoted musician July 19, '98.
Aiken, Francis J.	Aug. 22, '98	Dec. 3, '98	
Anderson, Joseph W.	Aug. 22, '98	Dec. 3, '98	
Arnold, Eliot.	April 23, '98	Dec. 3, '98	Transferred from Co. G October 9, '98.
Benning, Henry F.	July 5, '98	Dec. 3, '98	
Coxetter, Dunham	April 23, '98	Dec. 3, '98	Transferred from Co. G October 9, '98.
Coxetter, James G.	April 23, '98	Dec. 3, '98	Transferred from Co. G October 9, '98.
Conners, John.	April 23, '98	Dec. 3, '98	Transferred from Co. F October 9, '98.
Davis, Samuel J. T.	Aug. 26, '98	Dec. 3, '98	
Deaner, William F.	Aug. 3, '98	Dec. 3, '98	
Gaillard, Charles R.	April 23, '98	Dec. 3, '98	Transferred from Co. G October 9, '98.
Gibbs, R. Kingsley	April 23, '98	Dec. 3, '98	Transferred from Co. G October 9, '98.
Henley, James H.	Aug. 26, '98	Dec. 3, '98	
Hodge, John T.	Aug. 13, '98	Dec. 3, '98	
Hunter, Irving.	Aug. 17, '98	Dec. 3, '98	
Hinson, E. M.	Aug. 17, '98	Dec. 3, '98	
Hoyle, Louis C.	April 23, '98	Dec. 3, '98	Transferred from Co. F October 9, '98.
Jamerson, William E.	Aug. 18, '98	Dec. 3, '98	
Lamaroux, Elis C.	April 25, '98	Dec. 3, '98	Transferred from Co. B October 9, '98.
Moore, Thomas J. No. 2.	July 1, '98	Dec. 3, '98	
McCorkle, Arthur L.	Aug. 17, '98	Dec. 3, '98	
Newsome, John W.	June 28, '98	Dec. 3, '98	
Pitchford, Walker D.	April 23, '98	Dec. 3, '98	Transferred from Co. G October 9, '98.
Richard, Osceola G.	June 28, '98	Dec. 3, '98	
Robinson, Elmer R.	June 24, '98	Dec. 3, '98	
Register, James G.	April 25, '98	Dec. 3, '98	Transferred from Co. B October 9, '98.
Smith, Franklyn.	Aug. 26, '98	Dec. 3, '98	Transferred from Co. G October 9, '98.
Sanchez, Eugene M.	April 23, '98		Died at Huntsville, Ala., October 23, '98.
Tanner, John S.	Aug. 17, '98	Dec. 3, '98	Transferred from Co. G October 9, '98.
Pomar, Peter.	July 13, '98	Dec. 3, '98	Transferred from Regimental Band June 17, '98.
Malone, Patrick H.	April 25, '98	Dec. 3, '98	Transferred from Co. F October 9, '98.
Philips, James H.	Aug. 17, '98	Dec. 3, '98	

APPENDIX MEXICAN WAR.

During the Mexican War the State of Florida did not have population enough to form a regiment, but two companies were organized. One known as the Independent Company of Florida Volunteers, with the following officers: Captain, William W. I. Kelly; 1st Lieutenant, Hopwell Dorsey; 2nd Lieutenants, A. H. Bright and John Parkhill (Parkhill was killed at Palm Hammock and Bright afterward commanded Co. K, 1st Florida Regiment, C. S. A). The additional company of volunteers which assembled at Tallahassee in 1847, was first commanded by Capt. George Holmes; afterward by Capt. R. G. Livingston. who died in Guadaloupe February, 1848; the 1st Lieutenants were D. M. Stewart, who died at Vera Cruz, and Roman Sanchez; the 2nd Lieutenants William L Scott and Joseph Woodruff.